INSPIRE / PLAN / DISCOVER / EXPERIENCE

EUROPE

EUROPE

CONTENTS

DISCOVER 6

EXPERIENCE 88

Left: The Erechtheion at the Acropolis in Athens
Previous page: The coast of Greece's Máni Peninsula
Cover: The Bavarian Alps near Fussen, Germany

DISCOVER

Aerial view of St. Mark's Square, Venice

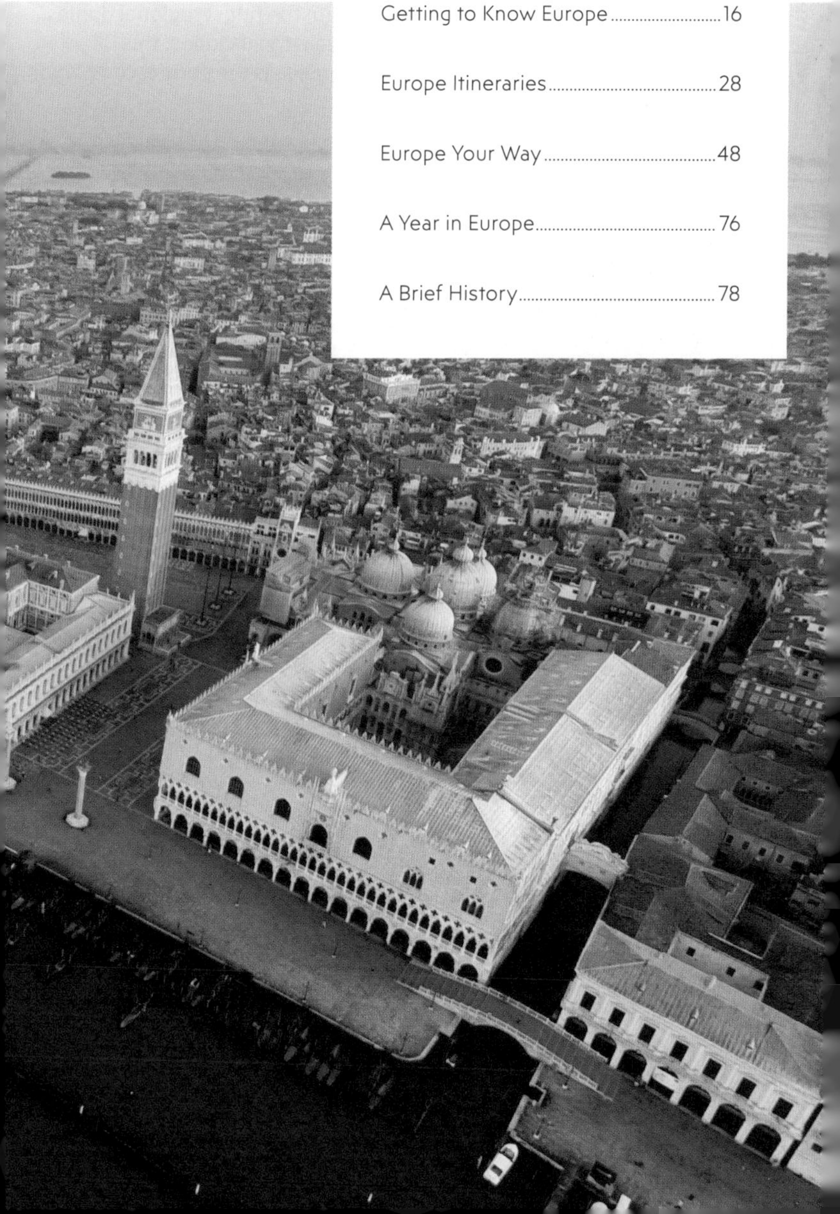

WELCOME TO
EUROPE

Culture-filled days in world-class museums and lively nights out in buzzing bars. Energetic adventures in epic countryside and lazy breaks next to turquoise seas. Fabulous feasts of local produce, paired with the finest regional tipples. Whatever your dream trip includes, this DK Eyewitness travel guide is the perfect companion.

1 Elegant canalside houses in Amsterdam.

2 A display of tempting pastries for sale in Paris.

3 A square in Dubrovnik's charming Old Town.

4 Looking over the Duomo and rooftops of Florence.

With dozens of countries offering a seemingly limitless array of attractions, it's little wonder that a grand tour of Europe features high on many travelers' wish lists. The continent's capitals are havens of culture, from the world-famous art galleries of Paris and Amsterdam to the romantic ruins of Rome and Athens. Even beyond the big cities lie a wealth of treasures, including fairy-tale castles in Germany, Viking longboats in Denmark, and mysterious mega-lithic monuments in Ireland and Great Britain.

And that's not to mention the food and drink. Each country and region has its own special-ties, meaning that wherever you go, there's always something new to try. Savor exquisite cakes in Vienna, sample pizza in its birthplace of Naples, sip the local beer in Brussels, and toast your arrival in Warsaw with a shot of vodka.

Providing the backdrop to all these urban delights is a diverse landscape of spectacular scenery, ever-changing with the seasons in a kaleidoscope of colors. Whether you're basking on the sun-soaked beaches of Portugal and Spain, scaling the Alps in Switzerland, or cruising through Norway's dramatic fjords, Europe's natural wonders are truly mesmerizing.

From the Arctic reaches of Scandinavia to the balmy Mediterranean, we've broken the continent down into easily navigable chapters, with detailed itineraries, expert local know-ledge and colorful, comprehensive maps to help you plan the perfect visit. Whether you're touring for a week, a month, or longer, this DK Eyewitness guide will ensure that you see the very best the continent has to offer. Enjoy the book, and enjoy Europe.

REASONS TO LOVE
EUROPE

Ever-changing landscapes and mouth-watering food and drink. Vibrant cities home to awe-inspiring architecture and non-stop nightlife. There are many reasons to love Europe; here are our favorites.

1 CAPTIVATING CAPITALS

Europe's capital cities are the crown jewels of the continent's urban treasure chest. Each has a personality that's entirely unique – uncover them all, from Amsterdam to Zagreb.

WORLD-CLASS MUSEUMS *2*

Whatever the topic, somewhere in Europe there's a museum dedicated to it. For vast, all-encompassing collections try London's British Museum *(p102)* or the Louvre in Paris *(p188)*.

3 SPECTACULAR SCENERY

Ranging from the jagged, snow-dusted peaks of the Alps to the golden beaches and balmy turquoise sea of the Mediterranean, Europe's landscape is truly breathtaking.

DRAMATIC HISTORY 4

Trace the rise and fall of empires and dynasties, from the birth of democracy in ancient Athens to the landmark establishment of the European Parliament in Brussels.

AMAZING ART 5

The continent's art scene has something for everyone, whether it's perusing the Old Masters at Florence's Uffizi *(p408)* or touring the graffiti art on the Berlin Wall *(p485)*.

MOUTHWATERING CUISINE 6

Europe is a paradise for foodies, with a wealth of local specialties to savor wherever you go – don't miss New Nordic in Scandinavia and the decadent desserts of Central Europe.

ICONIC ARCHITECTURE 7

The Colosseum *(p389)*, the Eiffel Tower *(p194)* – the names of Europe's architectural icons read like a shortlist of the world's best buildings. See how many you can tick off your bucket list.

QUIRKY CUSTOMS 8

Europeans take pride in their traditions, with lively events throughout the year. Among the more unusual are Portugal's Festa dos Tabuleiros *(p362)* and Switzerland's Onion Fair *(p77)*.

9 CAFÉ CULTURE

Hotbeds of intellectual debate and idle gossip, cafés are a European institution. Pull up a chair at an outdoor table and immerse yourself in the bustle of local life.

10 GREEN TRAVEL

With a cross-continental rail network, it's easy to be green when traveling long distances. Most urban centers can be explored on foot, and many are ideal for touring by bicycle.

BUZZING NIGHTLIFE 11

Who needs sleep? From the legendary clubs of Berlin to the hidden ruin pubs of Budapest, you'll find no shortage of hip bars and eclectic music venues to keep you going all night.

LOCAL TIPPLES 12

You're spoilt for choice when it comes to wine, beer, and spirits, with each country offering its own local brews. Sip pilsner in Prague, champagne in Reims, and herby *rakija* in Croatia.

EXPLORE
EUROPE

This guide divides Europe into 20 color-coded sightseeing areas, as shown on the map below. Find out more about each area on the following pages.

Norwegian Sea

Shetland Islands

Orkney Islands

Bergen

Stavanger

Inverness

Glasgow Edinburgh

North Sea

Belfast

Dublin

GREAT BRITAIN
p90

THE NETHERLAND
p260

IRELAND
p150

Birmingham

Cardiff

Amsterdam

London

Brussels

BELGIUM AN LUXEMBOUR
p236

Atlantic Ocean

Paris

Dijon

Tours

FRANCE
p178

Genev

Bay of Biscay

Bordeaux

A Coruña

Toulouse

Bilbao

Marseille

Porto

SPAIN
p286

Barcelona

PORTUGAL
p348

Madrid

Menor

Palma

Mallorca

Lisbon

Valencia

Ibiza

Faro

Seville

Alicante

Mediterranea

Málaga

GETTING TO KNOW
EUROPE

Covering a total surface area of 4 million sq miles (10 million sq km), Europe stretches from the Atlantic Ocean in the west to the Ural Mountains in the east of Russia. This guide focuses on the western half of the continent, from Scandinavia in the north to the Mediterranean coast in the south.

PAGE 90

GREAT BRITAIN

Separated from mainland Europe by the merest sliver of sea, Great Britain stretches from the jagged peaks of the Scottish Highlands down to the quaint seaside villages of Devon and Cornwall. Beyond the pomp and politics, London remains an unparalleled melting pot of global cultures, while Edinburgh and Cardiff showcase Scottish and Welsh culture with style. Step into the past in the picturesque towns of York and Bath, adorned with historic buildings, or stride into the future in Liverpool and Glasgow, where former industrial wastelands have been transformed by exciting regeneration projects.

Best for
World-class museums, pomp and ceremony, sumptuous stately homes

Experience
Browsing some of the world's greatest treasures at the British Museum

Capital city
London

IRELAND

Ireland is a small island, but a spectacular one. Divided since 1921 into Northern Ireland and the Republic of Ireland, it has dazzling locations aplenty across both countries. Dublin is steeped in the legacy of its famous literary sons, while vibrant Galway has a festival for every occasion and Cork city charms visitors with its picturesque waterways and the legend of the nearby Blarney stone. Once battle-scarred, Belfast today is a rejuvenated place, with a fast developing foodie scene, an impressive array of quirky bars, and a thriving nightlife.

Best for
Wild coastlines, ancient castles, Celtic heritage

Experience
An evening of traditional music in Dublin's lively Temple Bar

Capital cities
Dublin (Republic of Ireland), Belfast (Northern Ireland)

FRANCE

Synonymous with romance, fine dining, and inimitable style, France has been immortalized in countless artworks – many of which can be found in Paris's superb galleries and museums. Away from the capital, you'll find one of the world's hottest foodie scenes in Lyon, verdant vineyards in Bordeaux, and glitz and glamour in the sun-kissed south. Scattered in between are a plethora of prehistoric monuments, Roman ruins, magnificent châteaux, and atmospheric abbeys and cathedrals, providing awe-inspiring reminders of the country's long and thrilling history.

Best for
Classic French cuisine, world-class art, wine tasting

Experience
A romantic stroll across Paris's Pont des Arts at sunset

Capital city
Paris

$\rightarrow$

PAGE 236

BELGIUM AND LUXEMBOURG

Famed for its Flemish art and Gothic architecture, Belgium, like neighboring Luxembourg, is a melting pot of Dutch, French, and German influences. Understated Brussels thrums with energy as the administrative capital of Europe, picturesque Bruges charms with its enchanting backwaters, and lively Antwerp oozes cool with its dynamic nightlife. Across the border, Luxembourg City surprises as one of Europe's most scenic capitals, surrounded by the forests and castles of the Ardennes.

Best for
Art and architecture, politics, historic towns

Experience
Watching the world go by in Brussels' stunning Grand Place

Capital cities
Brussels (Belgium), Luxembourg City (Luxembourg)

THE NETHERLANDS

Largely composed of land reclaimed from the sea, the Netherlands is a beguiling blend of past and present. There's no better example of this than Amsterdam, where majestic 17th-century mansions and the Old Masters of the Rijksmuseum coexist with cutting-edge cultural complexes and hedonistic nightlife. Beyond the capital, postcard-pretty villages, windswept beaches, windmill-dotted meadows, and striped bulb-fields punctuate the landscape, interspersed with an assortment of appealing cities, including ultra-modern Rotterdam, historic Haarlem, stately Den Haag, and laid-back Leiden.

Best for
Fields of flowers, art galleries and museums, cycling

Experience
A ride along the Amsterdam's picturesque canals aboard a pedal-driven "canal bike"

Capital city
Amsterdam

SPAIN

Bounded to the east by the turquoise Mediterranean and to the west by the wild Atlantic, Spain is the largest country in southern Europe. Madrid fizzes as the nation's capital, kept on its toes by cultural rival Barcelona. Beneath the towering peaks of the Pyrenees in the north you'll find foodie haven San Sebástian and artistic trail-blazer Bilbao, while historic Toledo is the jewel of the sun-baked central plains. Beaches are the draw in the east, and in the south, a trio of cities – Seville, Cordoba, and Granada – entice with their romantic Moorish architecture.

Best for
Beautiful beaches, tapas bars, late nights

Experience
Panoramic views of Barcelona from Gaudí's colorful Park Güell

Capital city
Madrid

→

PAGE 348

PORTUGAL

For a small country, Portugal is immensely varied. The mountainous Minho and Trás-os-Montes regions in the north preserve a rural way of life, while the southerly Algarve has been transformed into a holiday playground. In between these two extremes, urban Portugal is a tale of two cities. With cutting-edge art galleries, ornate Manueline monasteries, and creamy custard tarts, Lisbon is a firm favorite with visitors. But Porto is a serious rival to the capital – adorned with pretty *azulejo* tiles and tattooed with gritty street art, it's both charmingly historic and modishly cool.

Best for
Festivals, port tasting, azulejo *tiles*

Experience
A pastel de nata *fresh out of the oven at the original Belém bakery in Lisbon*

Capital city
Lisbon

PAGE 374

ITALY

With its magnificent piazzas, rolling hills, and sublime art and architecture, Italy has been luring visitors in search of culture and romance for centuries. The country's cities need little introduction: Rome is an exuberant metropolis, where layers of history form an extraordinary stage for everyday life; Venice is an improbable canal city of lacy Gothic palaces; and Florence is an exquisite monument to the Renaissance. In the countryside, Tuscany offers picturesque medieval towns and vine-grooved hills, while the Italian lakes are a haven of pretty villages and magnificent villas.

Best for
Renaissance art and architecture, pizza and pasta, lively piazzas

Experience
Savoring the original pizza Margherita in Naples

Capital city
Rome

PAGE 442

GREECE

Renowned for its beautiful beaches and awe-inspiring archaeological sites, Greece offers an irresistible combination of natural beauty and engaging culture. The nation's greatest ancient monuments can be found amid the bustling urban sprawl of Athens, but you'll encounter relics of the Mycenaean, Minoan, Classical, and Byzantine civilizations all over the scenic countryside. Sunseekers flock to the crystal-clear seas and characterful villages of islands such as Corfu, Rhodes, and Crete, where the relaxed pace of life is just one of many tempting reasons to linger for an extended stay.

Best for
Ancient ruins, seafood restaurants, picture-perfect beaches

Experience
A summer concert at the Odeon of Herodes Atticus on the Acropolis in Athens

Capital city
Athens

$\rightarrow$

PAGE 478

GERMANY

Winding rivers, mythical forests, and the mighty peaks of the Bavarian Alps, with a generous sprinkling of romantic castles and medieval churches: rural Germany is the stuff of fairy-tales. The country's urban centers are equally appealing, from the world-class galleries and museums of über-cool Berlin to the convivial beer halls of Munich. Almost everywhere you go you'll find traces of the country's extraordinary and often turbulent past, particularly in smaller, historic towns such as Nürnberg, Dresden, and Leipzig, with their delightful regional architecture.

Best for
Fairy-tale castles, musical heritage, beer and wine

Experience
Sampling the local brews in the traditional beer halls of Munich's Englischer Garten

Capital city
Berlin

PAGE 528

AUSTRIA

Situated at the heart of Europe, Austria exudes grandeur – whether it's the magnificent mountain scenery of the Alps or the majestic architectural legacy of the powerful Habsburg Empire. Elegant Vienna waltzes to the tunes of its celebrated classical musicians, fueled by the mouth-wateringly decadent chocolate cake served up at the city's iconic coffee houses. In the Alpine west, outdoor adventure is the order of the day, with charming towns such as Innsbruck and Salzburg providing excellent bases for walking, cycling, and skiing.

Best for
Coffee houses, classical music and opera, Baroque palaces

Experience
The joy of whiling away hours in a classic Viennese coffee house

Capital city
Vienna

PAGE 550

SWITZERLAND

Once a group of independent cantons, the Swiss Confederation has come a long way since its foundation in 1291. Today's federal state is an intriguing blend of different customs, languages, and dialects, lending the country a rich cultural heritage. As much as it is rooted in the past, Switzerland looks to the future, with cutting-edge nightlife in Zürich, world-class art galleries in Basel, and superb fine dining across the country. Away from its cities, this is a land of the great outdoors – in a single day, you can encounter high-altitude lakes, iconic mountains, and awesome glaciers.

Best for
Scenic rail journeys, lakeside cities, hiking

Experience
Taking a tram to Geneva's lovely Italianate district of Carouge, with its independent shops and Saturday market

Capital city
Bern

$\rightarrow$

PAGE 568

SWEDEN

A land of short, crisp winter days and long, balmy summer nights, Sweden is a haven of clean living, sleek design, and rustic cuisine. Most visits here are bookended by stops in the country's two most accessible entry points, Stockholm and Gothenburg – both great bases for uncovering rich history and enjoying *fika*, the Swedish ritual of meeting for coffee and cake. Farther afield you'll find the castles of Lake Mälaren, the thriving university town of Uppsala, and the attractive city of Malmö, nestled amid a soul-stirring wilderness of lakes and forests.

Best for
Midnight sun, eco-friendly lifestyle,
Midsummer festivals

Experience
Singing along with holograms of the band
at the ABBA Museum in Stockholm

Capital city
Stockholm

PAGE 586

NORWAY

From the magical fjords of the south to the frozen wilds of the Arctic north, Norway's landscape beguiles with the promise of adventure. Ultra-cool Oslo is home to fabulous museums, celebrated restaurants, and groundbreaking architecture, while Bergen's attractive waterfront warehouses buzz with bars and eateries. To the north, Trondheim counts picturesque waterways and an impressive cathedral among its attractions, and Tromsø offers the tantalizing prospect of glimpsing the mysterious Northern Lights from inside the Arctic Circle.

Best for
New Nordic cuisine, fjords,
Viking heritage

Experience
Dining on boundary-pushing New
Nordic cuisine in Oslo

Capital city
Oslo

PAGE 602

DENMARK

Denmark has moved on from the days of its fearsome Viking empire, and is today regarded as a benchmark for sustainability, design, and lifestyle – best embodied in the art of *hygge*. Effortlessly cool Copenhagen is the main attraction, packed with world-class restaurants, striking architecture, and Instagram-worthy canals. Outside the capital, you'll discover the formidable castle that inspired *Hamlet* in Helsingør, dynamite dining and innovative art installations in creative Aarhus, and the storybook town of Odense, birthplace of Hans Christian Andersen.

Best for
Danish design, the magic of Hans Christian Andersen, hygge

Experience
The magic of Copenhagen's Tivoli Gardens, illuminated with fairy lights at night

Capital city
Copenhagen

PAGE 618

FINLAND

Often overshadowed by its Nordic neighbors, Finland is the perfect place to get a taste of Scandinavia off the beaten track. With a beautiful unspoiled landscape of forest, lakes, coast, and islands, the country's natural attractions more than hold their own. As do the cities – Helsinki dazzles with eye-catching architecture both old and new, while historic Turku charms with its medieval cobbled streets. This is also a great jumping-off point for a quick trip to St. Petersburg, lying just across the Gulf of Finland and easily accessible from Helsinki.

Best for
Pristine wilderness, impressive architecture, long summer evenings by the waterfront

Experience
Relaxing in a traditional Finnish sauna

Capital city
Helsinki

→

PAGE 632

CZECH REPUBLIC

Remaining largely unchanged for centuries, the Czech Republic offers a fascinating glimpse into Europe's medieval past. Prague is one of the continent's most engaging cities, bewitching visitors with its spires, cobbles, and tiny lanes. The country has more castles than any other, and the magnificent Karlštejn is an easy day trip from the capital. For a bit of R&R, head west to the spa towns of Karlovy Vary and Mariánské Lázne, both of which offer superb facilities and numerous possibilities for hiking in Bohemia's forests.

Best for
Medieval architecture, beer, Art Nouveau

Experience
A tour of Prague's unforgettable Old Jewish Cemetery

Capital city
Prague

PAGE 652

HUNGARY

Sitting at a crossroads between Central and Eastern Europe, Hungary has a rich folk culture that's as distinct as its language. Bestriding the gentle waters of the Danube, the country's capital is not one city but two: stately Buda on the western bank, and bustling Pest on the eastern. Elsewhere, you can peruse religious treasures in Szentendre and Esztergom, explore the natural playground of Lake Balaton, uncover fascinating history at Pécs, and sample the delicious wines of the vineyards at Eger and Tokaj.

Best for
Thermal baths, religious buildings, the Danube

Experience
Enjoying a thermal soak at the world-famous Gellért Baths in Budapest

Capital city
Budapest

PAGE 666

CROATIA

History and ancient mythology permeate Croatia, and nowhere more so than along Dalmatia's spectacular coastline. Traverse the medieval walls of magnificent Dubrovnik, today recognizable from their starring role in *Game of Thrones*; make like an emperor and explore the Palace of Diocletian in ancient Split; or follow in the footsteps of Roman gladiators at Pula's amphitheater. Inland, ultra-cool Zagreb offers an appealing array of cafés and unique museums, while photogenic Plitvice Lakes National Park is a testament to the power and beauty of Mother Nature.

Best for
Café-cruising, beaches, nightlife

Experience
Watching the sunset from Mount Srđ in Dubrovnik

Capital city
Zagreb

PAGE 682

POLAND

One of Europe's biggest countries, Poland has had a stormy history due to its strategic location between Russia and Germany. Today, however, the country is firmly future-facing, with an infectious energy infusing its resurgent cities. Edgy Warsaw is vibrant, dynamic, and eclectic, with the restored architecture of its historic Old Town offset by high-tech museums and trendy cafés. Kraków, meanwhile, enchants with its largely pedestrianized center, whose cobbled streets and laid-back bars invite hours of leisurely exploration.

Best for
Jewish history, vodka, nightlife

Experience
Summer nights on the Vistula riverfront in Warsaw, with its open-air bars and clubs

Capital city
Warsaw

←

 The Shard and the River Thames at night.

 The memorial to Dugald Stewart on Calton Hill.

 A traditional Irish Music session at The Cobblestone.

 Statue of Charles Darwin in the Natural History Museum.

Europe brims with travel possibilities, from short city-hopping tours to epic cross-continent odysseys. These suggested itineraries pick out some of the highlights of each region, providing inspiration to help you plan the perfect trip.

5 DAYS

in Britain and Ireland

Day 1

Start your tour at London's Tate Britain (p98) for a who's who of the nation's most beloved artists. The gallery is on the river and is good spot from which to catch a boat to Greenwich (p118), cruising past many of the city's iconic sights en route. On arrival, grab lunch at the market (p119), then wander up to Greenwich Observatory to take in the view. After admiring the city from afar, catch a Tube to London Bridge for a closer look at the grand old buildings and sleek skyscrapers that line the river. As night falls, ascend to the top of the Shard (p111) to watch the twinkling city lights.

Day 2

Wake up with a refreshing stroll around Hyde Park (p105) before paying a visit to one of South Kensington's world-class museums: the Science Museum (p106), the Natural History Museum (p108), or the Victoria and Albert Museum (p106). Next stop after lunch is Westminster, home to the iconic Houses of Parliament (p94) and Westminster Abbey (p96). From there, wind your way to the West End to take advantage of a cheap pre-theater menu and maybe catch a show, before heading to Euston to board the sleeper train to Scotland.

Day 3

After your early arrival in Edinburgh, get your bearings by walking up Calton Hill (p143) to survey the city. Nearby Holyroodhouse (p143) marks the start of the Royal Mile (p142) to Edinburgh Castle (p140); a stroll along this historic thoroughfare provides a fascinating glimpse into the city's medieval past. Enjoy lunch with a view in one of the cafés on Princes Street, then spend the afternoon exploring the beautiful Georgian architecture of the New Town (p140). Finish up the day with a wee dram of Scottish whisky after dinner.

Day 4

Take advantage of the morning calm to wander the atmospheric streets of the Old Town, stopping off at the historic Greyfriars Kirk (p143) and the fascinating National Museum of Scotland (p141). After a final British lunch, make your way to the airport for the short hop across the Irish Sea to Dublin. Dive straight in to the local culture on arrival, by spending an evening on the Dublin Literary Pub Crawl (p62).

Day 5

Devote today to exploring Dublin's history. Start with a visit to Trinity College (p154), home to the priceless Book of Kells, then make your way to Dublin Castle (p158) for a tour of its stately rooms. From there, a pleasant walk takes you along the banks of the Liffey (p161), over O'Connell Bridge, and up to the historic buildings of Parnell Square (p162) in the north of the city. Finish your tour at The Cobblestone pub (p163) for an evening of traditional Irish music.

1 One of Amsterdam's picturesque canals.

2 Rembrandt's *The Night Watch* in the Rijksmuseum.

3 Belgian chocolates.

4 Arc de Triomphe, Paris.

10 DAYS
in Benelux and France

Day 1

Start in Amsterdam at the Rijksmuseum (p272), for a tour of Dutch art through the centuries – Rembrandt's *The Night Watch* is one of many 17th-century highlights. Nearby is the equally outstanding Van Gogh Museum (p276), dedicated to the Netherlands' other most-famous painter. Once you've had your fill of artworks, zigzag north through the narrow streets and gridded canals of trendy Jordaan to learn the heartbreaking story of teenage Jewish diarist Anne Frank, at the house where she and her family hid from the Nazis (p269). In the evening, check out the city's famed nightlife – top clubbing spots include Paradiso (www.paradiso.nl) and LGBT+ venue Club NYX (www.clubnyx.nl).

Day 2

Spend the morning on a breezy canal tour of Amsterdam's lesser-known water-ways. On the way, the boat will cruise past gable-ended houses, high bridges, tulip-trimmed houseboats, and richly decorated mansions. Disembark around De Wallen, the city's most historic district, and hire a bike to rattle around the inner city as the locals do. The area is packed with time-stopped brown cafés (traditional Dutch pubs), so pop into a couple for beer and *bitterballen* (deep-fried meatballs): Café De Dokter (www.cafe-de-dokter.nl) and Cafe De Pels (www.cafedepels.nl) are two unbeatable favorites.

Day 3

Hop on a train to Brussels, arriving in time for a late-morning moment savoring the architectural jewels of the city's Grand Place (p240). From here, the alleyways fan out to heavenly chocolate shops and charming cafés, meandering to the land-mark Manneken Pis statue (p244). Don't linger too long, as there's more to see: become a big kid for the afternoon while learning about Hergé's Tintin and the Smurfs at the Belgian Comic Strip Center (p244), then bump into building-sized comic strip heroes on a walk of the city's larger-than-life murals. *Moules frites* are on every menu: as night falls, sample them on Rue Des Bouchers.

Day 4

Carry on south from Brussels via train to Paris, starting your tour of the City of Lights at its ultimate beacon on the Champ de Mars: the Eiffel Tower (p194). Detour northwest to Place Charles de Gaulle to see Paris's other iconic national monument, the Arc de Triomphe (p199), before taking the metro to Montmartre (p202), with its art galleries, bistros, and boutiques. While there, huff and puff up the stone stairway to the dazzling Sacré-Coeur Basilica for the most memorable view in Paris. If you've still got energy to burn come nightfall, take in a late cabaret show at the legendary Moulin Rouge dance hall (www.moulinrouge.fr).

Day 5

Decide on an art-filled day at the Louvre (p188), in the company of the *Mona Lisa* and *Venus de Milo*, or rise early to avoid the crowds on a full-day trip to the spectacular Palace of Versailles (p204) on Paris's outskirts. Both venues have more than enough attractions to reward a whole day of exploration, so take your time to uncover their treasures – there are cafés and restaurants on site when you need a break. Later, settle for dinner in the laid-back Latin Quarter on the Seine's Left Bank, finishing with a stroll across the bridge to Île de la Cité (p182), for a thought-provoking view of the fire-damaged Notre-Dame cathedral (p183).

Day 6

Catch a train to the riverside university city of Tours (p216), and use it as a gateway for a tour of the Loire Valley's architectural heritage – there are numerous companies with which you can pre-arrange trips. Highlights in the area include Château de Chambord (p217), a vast Renaissance palace; Château de Chenonceau (p214), with its jaw-dropping tapestries and collection of Old Masters; and Château de Villandry, home to a fairytale maze and once-upon-a-time turrets. Return to Tours by twilight for dinner in the city's medieval Old Town, amid the atmospheric shadows of the monumental Cathédrale St-Gatien.

Day 7

Today starts with another train journey, this time past sprawling vineyards to Bordeaux (p224). Disembark by lunchtime and begin your immersive wine education at the Cité du Vin, an eye-catching cultural center uncorked on the banks of the Garonne river – a tasting tour takes you through 2,000 years of Bordeaux winemaking. Afterward, hop on the riverside tram back into the city's 18th-century center and wander the lamp-lit streets to discover the Grand Théâtre, situated across from the equally ravishing Grand Hotel. A night of fine food and wine in the vicinity of the elegant Place de la Bourse is the perfect way to round off the day.

1 Paris's Latin Quarter.

2 The gardens of Château de Villandry.

3 The wine shop at La Cité du Vin, Bordeaux.

4 Sunset over the vineyards of Bordeaux.

5 Cycling past Avignon's Pont St-Bénézet.

6 Interior of the Basilique St-Nazaire, Carcassonne.

Day 8

Prepare to loosen your belt. Ahead is an organized day tour, sampling local produce and drinking plummy reds amid farms, orchards, and award-winning vineyards. With 300,000 acres (120,000 ha) of vine fruit and 8,000 estates to explore – not to mention the delightful stone village of St-Émilion and the picture-perfect châteaux of Médoc and Margaux – you might be tempted to linger in the region for longer. If you've still got room on your return to Bordeaux, drop in for last orders at Le Bar à Vin *(www.baravin.bordeaux. com)*, a cosy nook run by the École du Vin de Bordeaux in the heart of the city's beautiful UNESCO World Heritage core.

Day 9

Shake-off the cobwebs with coffee and croissants on the morning train to Carcassonne *(p226)*. The fortified hilltop town has an evocative citadel to explore, and winding stone alleys that lead to a higgedly-piggedly marriage of exquisite restaurants and fashionable boutiques. The Porte Narbonnaise is the textbook

medieval gate tower, and the imposing Château Comtal and the Gothic Basilica of St. Nazarius complete the city's must-do greatest hits.

Day 10

One last train – this time through the scenic lavender fields of Provence to ancient Avignon *(p230)*. The former seat of Catholic popes, the city brims with papal tombs, cathedrals, and Renaissance masterpieces. Start by exploring the 14th-century Palais des Papes, before leaving the vast Gothic palace for the Petit Palais across the square. Stumble upon courtyards of private mansions refreshed with renovated facades, then climb the bastions for knockout views of the immense plains of the Rhône river. It's the perfect final memory with which to end your grand tour.

←

1 Antoni Gaudí's colorful Park Güell, Barcelona.

2 Pavement cafés in Madrid's Plaza Mayor.

3 Looking out over Lisbon.

4 *Pasteis de Belém* custard tarts, Lisbon.

5 DAYS
in the Iberian Peninsula

Day 1

Start in Barcelona, spending your first morning exploring the city's historic Gothic Quarter. Highlights to look out for include the cathedral *(p318)* and the fascinating Museu d'Història de Barcelona *(p318)*, with its underground Roman ruins. After lunch at Mercat de Santa Caterina *(Av Francesc Cambó 16)*, wind your way south to the portside cafés and beaches of Barceloneta – maybe with a stop at the Museu Picasso *(p319)* along the way. Finish the day with a night tour of Gaudí's Casa Milà *(p321)*, accompanied by live jazz on the roof.

Day 2

Pick up where you left off last night with a morning spent visiting some of Gaudí's other architectural treasures. Take a jaunt to La Sagrada Família *(p322)* to marvel at his fanciful basilica, then head northwest to explore the fabulously imaginative Park Güell *(p325)*. Make sure you're back in the center of town by early evening, as you've got a train to Madrid to catch – you should reach the capital in time for a late dinner.

Day 3

Spend this morning meandering through Madrid's cobbled Old Town, dipping into the Gothic-revival Catedral Almudena and the splendid Palacio Real *(p293)*. Savor a lunch of local produce at the Mercado de San Miguel *(p299)*, then drift your way through Plaza Mayor *(p290)* and Puerta del Sol *(p290)*. From here, it's an easy metro ride to the Centro de Arte Reina Sofía *(p298)*, home to Picasso's iconic *Guernica*. End the day with dinner and a nightcap in the lively Huertas district.

Day 4

Dive deeper into Madrid's artistic side at the Museo del Prado *(p294)*, packed with Spanish masterpieces. Nearby is the leafy Parque del Retiro *(p299)*, which makes a lovely spot for a stroll when you're ready to move on. Cool off with a drink at the long-standing Gran Café Gijón *(www.cafe gijon.com)*, then spend the rest of the day browsing the hip streets of the Chueca neighborhood. As evening falls, collect your bags and head to Atocha station to catch the overnight train to Lisbon.

Day 5

Spend the morning exploring Lisbon's Belém district *(p358)*, brimming with jaw-dropping monuments; be sure to make time for a break to sample the area's famed *pasteis de Belém*. When your tummy starts to rumble again, head to LXFactory *(www. lxfactory.com)* for lunch and to peruse the trendy galleries and stores. From there, make your way to the charming Alfama neighborhood *(p354)* to soak up the stunning views from Castelo de São Jorge *(p354)*. Celebrate your last night with an evening in lively Bairro Alto *(p356)*, being serenaded by local *fado* music.

1 Odeon of Herodes Atticus, on the Acropolis, Athens.

2 Fontana dei Quattro Fiumi in Piazza Navona, Rome.

3 The famous flea market on Athens' Platía Monastirakiou.

4 Mosaic in the Baptistry of Florence's Duomo.

2 WEEKS

in the Mediterranean

Day 1

Begin your tour of Europe's sunny south in Athens, diving straight into the city's Classical sights. Start at the ruins of the Ancient Agora *(p452)*, then climb up to the Acropolis *(p448)* for an awe-inspiring encounter with the Parthenon and its neighboring temples. Descend toward bustling Plaka *(p446)* for a late lunch before browsing the area's quirky crafts and antiques stores. As evening starts to fall, head over to the Temple of Olympian Zeus *(p452)* for dramatic sunset views of the Acropolis.

Day 2

Devote the morning to exploring Monastiráki *(p446)*, making sure to call at the amazing flea market. Pick up a selection of savories from one of the bakeries here, to enjoy as part of a picnic lunch in the National Gardens. After soaking up some sun (or shade), make your way to the Byzantine and Christian Museum *(p453)* to marvel at the rare icons, before moving on to the Museum of Cycladic Art *(p455)*, with its exquisite ancient works. End the day in style with a performance amid the spectacular surroundings of the Odeon of Herodes Atticus *(p451)*.

Day 3

Next stop: Rome. Getting there from Athens on public transport takes over 24 hours (via a combination of bus, ferry, and train), so it's quickest to catch a plane for this leg of the trip – be sure to book a seat well in advance. Celebrate your arrival in the Eternal City with a leisurely evening among the cafés and Baroque fountains of Piazza Navona *(p385)*.

Day 4

It's back to the ancient world today, with a wander through the evocative ruins of the Roman Forum *(p386)* and a visit to the legendary Colosseum *(p389)*. Take some time to ascend the Palatine *(p388)*, the leafy hill on which Rome's emperors once lived. You've earned a rest by now, so relax for a while at a café on Piazza di Spagna, before scaling the famous Spanish Steps *(p390)*. End the evening by casting a coin into the Trevi Fountain *(p388)*, to ensure your future return to the city.

Day 5

Dedicate this morning to the Vatican, where you can admire Michelangelo's astounding Sistine Chapel and works by other masters at the Vatican Museums *(p382)*. The lofty interior of St. Peter's basilica *(p380)* is equally impressive, as are the city views from the top of its dome. When you're ready to move on, cross the Tiber toward the Roman-era Pantheon *(p384)* before spending a final atmospheric evening in Rome's Centro Storico.

Day 6

Treat yourself to a leisurely breakfast before taking one of the frequent express trains from Rome to Florence; you'll be there in a little over an hour. On arrival, make a beeline for Piazza del Duomo and its sumptuous cathedral *(p404)*: don't miss the stunning 13th-century mosaics in the Baptistry. From there, enjoy an evocative stroll through the city's medieval streets, ending up at the Galleria dell'Accademia *(p400)*, home of Michelangelo's iconic *David*. The nearby Mercato Centrale *(www. mercatocentrale.it)* is a great place to try some local dishes for dinner.

Day 7

Florence was home to many Renaissance artists, so delving into the city's artistic legacy is a must: the intoxicating collection at the Uffizi Gallery *(p408)* provides the perfect introduction. Soak up the ambience of the adjacent Piazza della Signoria *(p406)*, then cross the river to Oltrarno via the ancient Ponte Vecchio *(p410)*, to gorge yourself on more fine art at the Palazzo Pitti *(p411)*. Refresh with the horticultural splendors of the Boboli Gardens *(p410)*, then pass the evening in Oltrarno's bars and traditional trattorias.

Day 8

Board a mid-morning train from Florence to Venice, arriving by lunchtime. The best way to begin your tour of the city is with a *vaporetto* (water bus) ride along the Grand Canal *(p426)* to Piazza San Marco and the ravishing St. Mark's cathedral *(p424)* – take the lift to the top of the campanile for a view stretching all the way to the Alps. Lose yourself for the rest of the day amid the city's labyrinthine streets and charming squares.

Day 9

After a leisurely start to the day, head back to the Grand Canal, this time to the bustling Rialto Bridge area – you can stock up on lunch supplies at the busy market nearby. In the afternoon, venture out to the island of Murano *(p431)* and its splendid glass museum. There's a chance to watch the glassblowers at work and pick up some quality souvenirs at the factories that still function here. Back in Venice, toast your last night in the city with an Aperol spritz and *cicchetti* (snacks) in the bars of the Campo San Giacomo area.

Day 10

Make an early start to catch the bus from Venice to Zagreb, getting to the Croatian capital by mid-afternoon. Once there, head for Zagreb's main square area and dive straight in to its bustling café life. Be sure to also take a look at the spellbinding Croatian National Theatre building *(p671)*, just around the corner. For the evening, cute Tkalčićeva street *(p670)* offers an abundance of restaurants and bars.

1 The Uffizi, Florence.
2 A glassworker in action at a Murano glass factory.
3 Venice's Grand Canal.
4 Outdoor cafés in Zagreb.
5 Dubrovnik's coastline.

Day 11

Begin with the trademark twin towers of the Cathedral of the Assumption (p670) before joining the throng at Dolac market (p670). A short stroll leads to the Upper Town (p670), a tranquil Baroque quarter that is home to the thought-provoking Museum of Broken Relationships. Next, meet the Egyptian mummies at the Archeological Museum (p671) before taking a breather in the nearby park. Summer food festivals are often held here; otherwise, Teslina and Masarykova streets are full of dining opportunities.

Day 12

It's a long road journey from Zagreb to Dubrovnik (8–9 hours by car; 11–12 hours by bus) and you might prefer to fly in order to save time. The road journey, however, is spectacular, taking in the mountain-fringed wilderness areas of inland Croatia before winding along the spellbinding coast. On arrival, stride down Dubrovnik's majestic Stradun (p672), before delving into the restaurant- and bar-packed alleyways on either side.

Day 13

Walk along Dubrovnik's medieval walls (p672) as early as you can; they can get very crowded later in the day. Once you've finished, make your way to the Rector's Palace (p674) – packed with sumptuous artworks, it's the best of the city's museums. Behind the nearby cathedral (p674) lies a maze of evocative alleyways, perfect for leisurely ambling. After lunch, spend time in the soothing cloister of the Dominican Monastery (p674), before scaling the steps to the imperious Lovrijenac Fortress (p675). In the evening, ascend to the top of Mount Srđ (p674) by cable car for stunning sunset views.

Day 14

Spend your final day relaxing beside the dreamy turquoise waters of the Adriatic sea. The gorgeous island of Lokrum is a great place to chill out, and is only a 15-minute ferry ride away. A forested nature reserve, Lokrum is home to some beautiful historic buildings, as well as botanical gardens and countless idyllic coves – perfect for a cooling dip.

1 The sumptuous Residenz palace in Munich.

2 The center of Innsbruck, overlooked by the Alps.

3 Zurich's Kunsthaus.

4 The historic clock tower in Bern's Old Town.

5 DAYS

around the Alps

Day 1

Begin in Munich, starting with a visit to the glittering state rooms of the Residenz palace (p506), built to show off the power and wealth of five centuries of Bavarian rulers. Finish in time to catch the midday chimes of the Glockenspiel in the Neues Rathaus, on nearby Marienplatz (p504); Café Glockenspiel (www.cafe-glockenspiel. de) here makes a good spot for lunch, or alternatively you can grab a picnic from the Viktualienmarkt a few streets away. Laze the rest of the day away by the river and beer halls of the Englischer Garten (p511), returning to town for an evening of opera at the Nationaltheater (www.staatsoper.de).

Day 2

Spend an artistic morning in Barerstrasse (best reached by tram), admiring art treasures from the Middle Ages to the present day at the Alte Pinakothek (p508) and Pinakothek der Moderne (p509). When you're ready for lunch, head to a beer hall such as Wirtshaus in der Au (p511) – no trip to Munich is complete without experiencing this local ritual. Afterward, explore the exhibits in the Deutsches Museum (p510), Germany's most-visited science and technology museum, then catch a late-afternoon train to Innsbruck (p546), arriving in the Austrian city in time for dinner.

Day 3

Wake early to beat the crowds at the Hofburg imperial palace, then spend the rest of the morning mingling with locals in the surrounding streets of the charming Old Town. After a late lunch, catch the afternoon train to Zürich (p560), soaking up the beautiful Tirol scenery from the window. You'll arrive in Switzerland by early evening, giving you enough time for a sunset lake cruise on the Zürichersee.

Day 4

Get an overview of Zürich by ascending the Grossmunster cathedral tower for a panorama of the city and its alpine back-drop. From there, cross over the river to admire the Fraumünster's stained-glass windows by Marc Chagall, before heading to Confiserie Sprüngli (www.spruengli.ch) for an early lunch – check out the glittering window displays along Bahnhofstrasse en route. Devote the rest of the day to Swiss culture, brushing up on history at the National Museum and art at the Kunsthaus. Pass the evening in the buzzing bars and restaurants of the Niederdorf district.

Day 5

Set off early to catch the 90-minute train to Bern (p556). There, it's just a few minutes' walk from the station to the Old Town, with its arcaded, cobbled streets and fountain-splashed squares. Take in the cathedral and the clock tower, before sauntering down to the river to meet the residents of Bern's Bear Park. After lunch, acquaint yourself with the work of Bern's most renowned local artist at the wave-like Zentrum Paul Klee. Toast the end of your tour with a local brew from the Café Einstein au Jardin (www.einstein-jardin.ch), admiring the views from its garden terrace.

1 Brandenburg Gate, Berlin.

2 Charles Bridge, leading into Prague's Malá Strana district.

3 Interior of the glass dome atop Berlin's Reichstag.

4 Colorful houses lining Golden Lane, Prague.

10 DAYS
in Central Europe

Day 1

Start in Berlin by visiting the icons of a unified Germany: climb up inside the glass dome of the Reichstag (p483), then circuit the mighty Brandenburg Gate (p482). From here, make your way along Unter den Linden (p483), a leafy promenade that reveals the swagger of 19th-century Prussia; there are plenty of places where you can pause for lunch. The handsome Schlossbrücke bridge at the end of the street hints at the cultural feast on Museuminsel; the Pergamonmuseum (p487), with its remarkable collection of antiquities, is a particular highlight. Round off the day with a quiet evening stroll in the picturesque Nikolaiviertel (p490) to get a sense of Berlin's medieval roots.

Day 2

Explore Berlin's more recent past by heading to Checkpoint Charlie (p490), the East–West crossing point immortalized in many a Cold War thriller. Nearby, the history of one of Berlin's most important communities is revealed in the Jüdisches Museum (p490); further north, the wave-like Holocaust Denkmal (p484) represents the scale of Nazi crimes in stark sculptural form. Take a break from history with a relaxing stroll in the Tiergarten (p484), enjoying lunch at one of the cafés there. Afterward, pore over the Old Masters in the Gemäldegalerie at the Kulturforum (p484), then admire the mosaics in the Kaiser-Wilhelm-Gedächtniskirche (p491), the symbol of West Berlin. Finish with a stroll down Kurfürstendamm (p491), lined with stylish boutiques and restaurants.

Day 3

Take a morning train from Berlin to Prague, soaking up views of the scenic Elbe valley from the window and making use of the dining car for an early lunch. Once in Prague, make tracks for the famously photogenic Old Town Square (p642) – try to arrange to be below the Town Hall Clock on the hour, when its chimes are accompanied by a parade of mechanical figures. On the east side of the square, in the shadow of the spire-topped Týn church, you'll find the pretty Kinský Palace, housing ancient art. From there, head north into Josefov, the former Jewish quarter, and take an evocative stroll through the Old Jewish Cemetery (p643). Spend the evening sampling the excellent local beer in one of the city's numerous pubs.

Day 4

Begin the day on busy Wenceslas Square (p647), a vast public space that has witnessed many dramatic events in Czech history. Explore the collections of the National Museum (p647), before strolling along Národní Třída to the opulent National Theater (p646). From there, take tram 22 across the river to the historic Malá Strana quarter, and make your way up picturesque Nerudova Street (p641) to Hradčany Hill. There's plenty to explore here, including St. Vitus's Cathedral (p636), the Old Royal Palace (p636), and the supremely photogenic Golden Lane (p639). Wind your way back to the Old Town for dinner, via the romantic, statue-encrusted Charles Bridge (p642).

Day 5

Get up early to catch a morning express train from Prague to Vienna, speeding through the green and rolling countryside of Bohemia and Moravia. Arriving in the Austrian capital around lunchtime, start your afternoon in Vienna at the landmark Stephansdom cathedral (p532), followed by a wander through the pedestrianized streets of the historic city center. Make sure to include a stroll along elegant Kärntnerstrasse, before making your way to the Hofburg (p534), the imperial palace of the Habsburgs. After admiring the elegant buildings in this opulent complex, take a ride on Vienna's swift and efficient metro to the Prater (p542), to take in the evening air and go for a spin on the park's famous giant Ferris wheel.

Day 6

Start the day at Museums-Quartier Wien (p538), beginning with the Leopold Museum and its unmissable collection of works by Klimt and Schiele. Continue the art appreciation next door at the Kunsthistorisches Museum (p539), which

has hall after hall of Old Masters to admire. In the afternoon, hop on the Ring Tram for a ride around the Ringstrasse, Vienna's grandest boulevard, then make your way to the Belvedere (p543) for some more fine Austrian art and a stroll in the attractive gardens. Head back into the center for an evening listening to Vienna's world-famous classical musicians performing at the Staatsoper (p533).

Day 7

The train from Vienna to Budapest takes under three hours, allowing you well over half a day's sightseeing time in Hungary's majestic capital. Start at the café-filled Vigadó Square, before window-shopping on Váci utca, central Pest's most famous promenading street. Walk along Múzeum Körút to get a flavor of 19th-century Pest, visiting the Hungarian National Museum (p659) for a run-down of Hungarian culture. Afterward, cross over the river to Buda to reinvigorate yourself with a dip at the famed Gellért Baths (p656), before embarking on a night out at one of the city's atmospheric ruin pubs.

1. Hofburg complex, Vienna.
2. Prater park, Vienna.
3. Gellért Baths, Budapest.
4. The bastions of Buda Castle, Budapest.
5. Łazienki Park, Warsaw.

Day 8

Take the Sikló funicular to the hilltop settlement of Buda, packed with historic buildings and evocative Baroque-era streets. Admire the decorative interior of Mátyás church (p656), before checking out the sweeping views of Pest from the nearby bastions. From here, it's a short stroll to the former Royal Palace (p658), with its elegant courtyards and gardens. Inside the palace, the Hungarian National Gallery contains a stunning collection of artworks, from medieval to modern. Wander back into town in time to catch the evening sleeper train to Warsaw.

Day 9

Get to grips with Polish history with a tour of the Royal Castle (p687) and its sumptuous state rooms. St. John's Cathedral (p686) stands next door, so pop inside for a quick look before continuing to the beautifully restored Old Town Market Square (p686). Linger over lunch at one of the Old Town's many restaurant terraces. Resume with a stroll along the Royal Route (p688), the set-piece boulevard lined with fine churches and palaces. From here it's a short walk to the gargantuan Palace of Culture and Science (p690), a defining relic of the Stalinist 1950s. As the day draws to a close, make a beeline for the elegant street of Nowy Świat, lined with bustling cafés and bistros.

Day 10

Start your day at the POLIN Museum of the History of Polish Jews (p689), an absorbing introduction to Poland's Jewish history; the humbling Monument to the Ghetto Heroes (p689) is found next door. After lunch, spend a relaxed afternoon roaming the paths of Łazienki Park (p690), Warsaw's largest green space. Take a boat ride on the peaceful lake, then pay your respects to Poland's most famous composer at the Chopin Monument. As evening falls, meander along the Vistula riverside path, lined with food trucks and open-air bars – ideal for relaxing on the final evening of your action-packed tour.

7 DAYS
in Scandinavia

Day 1

Start on the Oslo waterfront at Akershus castle *(p590)* for a trip back in time to Norway's medieval era. From there, head north to Stortinget, the Norwegian Parliament, for a walk along Karl Johans Gate to Kongelige Slottet, the Royal Palace *(p592)*. When you've had your fill of regal grandeur, catch a tram to Vigelandsparken *(p593)* to marvel at the mind-bending sculptures of Gustav Vigeland, before backtracking to the Munchmuseet *(p592)* to pay tribute to celebrated painter Edvard Munch. Come evening, check out the hip restaurants and bars of Grünerløkka – candlelit Fru Hagen *(www.fruhagen.no)* is a great place to start.

Day 2

Catch a train across the Swedish border to Gothenburg *(p580)* for maritime history, sailing tradition, and stunning seafood. Arriving in the early afternoon, jump into the deep end with a boat tour of the city's Inner Harbor, from where you can spy the angular Opera House; Barken Viking, a beautifully preserved four-masted boat; and the Maritiman, the world's largest

floating ship museum. Later, feast on just-landed North Sea crayfish at Feskekörka *(www.lolaakinmade.com)*, a seafood market turned "fish church."

Day 3

Set out early for Copenhagen, traveling south via train along the beautifully fragmented Götaland coast to what many claim is the world's happiest city. Reserve the afternoon for postcard moments in front of the pastel-colored houses of Nyhavn *(p609)* and the statue of Hans Christian Andersen's *Little Mermaid* *(p610)*, found farther north, near Kastellet. Take a boat back into the center for a night of old-fashioned entertainment amid the twinkling fairy lights at Tivoli Gardens' venerable amusement park *(p606)*.

Day 4

The Danish capital is best explored by bicycle, so hit the cycle expressways on a morning ride from Christiansborg Palace *(p608)* to 17th-century Rosenborg Slot *(p611)*. In between, stop at Torvehallerne

① Oslo Harbor at night.

② Interior of Rosenborg Slot, Copenhagen.

③ Stortorget, Stockholm's main square.

④ Copenhagen's waterfront.

⑤ Helsinki Cathedral.

market (p609) for street food and some of the world's best coffee. Carry on to free-wheeling Christiania (p610) for a glimpse of hippie heaven, before circling back to Nørrebro for a night of craft beer and food at Mikkeller & Friends (www.mikkeller.dk).

Day 5

Rise early to get a train across the country-spanning Øresund Bridge, accelerating north to the Swedish capital in time for early afternoon. All the most memorable Stockholm visits incorporate the old town area of Gamla Stan, so spend the rest of the day discovering the Royal Palace (p573) and Storkyrkan (p572), the city's 700-year-old church. Make sure to fit in a stop for *fika* (a coffee and cake break) with cream-filled *selmor* buns at the basement cafés on Stortorget. In the evening, enjoy dinner and cocktails in Sodermalm.

Day 6

Fuel-up on coffee and take an early tram to Djurgården to get ahead of the crowds at the ABBA Museum (p575). Dedicated to

one of Sweden's greatest-ever exports, this pop history museum features a run-through of memorabilia and interactive exhibits. Afterward, wander to the Vasamuseet (p576), a maritime museum featuring a 17th-century warship, or jump on a bus for a glimpse of the Sweden of the past at Skansen, an open-air living history museum (p576). Keep an eye on the clock: you need to be at the ferry terminal by late after-noon to catch an overnight boat to Finland.

Day 7

Arrive in Helsinki mid-morning for a pastry-loaded brunch at Cafe Ekberg (www.ekberg. fi), a bakery that's wowed locals since the 1850s. Afterward, take a leisurely stroll to Kiasma, Museum of Contemporary Art (p624), enjoying the city's seamless union of Scandi- and Russian-influenced archi-tecture along the way. Spend the afternoon lingering in the boutiques around Market Square (p622), then finish with a steam and soak at a traditional sauna. Yrjönkatu Swimming Hall (www.hel.fi) is the oldest in the city and the perfect place to say farewell to Scandinavia.

Big Ben

Proudly standing sentinel over London's Houses of Parliament *(p94)*, Big Ben has kept exact time for the British nation more or less continuously since it was first set in motion in 1859. Impress your travel companions with the knowledge that Big Ben is not actually the name of the four-faced clock, but of the tower's 15.1-ton bell.

A view of Big Ben and the Houses of Parliament from Westminster Bridge

EUROPE'S
BIG HITTERS

Europe is packed with spectacular sights, a select few of which have achieved near-mythical status, becoming enduring symbols of the cities in which they stand. They may be clichés, but who cares: here are our top five icons that should be on every Europhile's bucket list.

Colosseum

Let your imagination run riot as you explore the mighty shell of Rome's Colosseum *(p389)*, once the scene of dramatic gladiator battles and wild animal fights. Its tiers of arches each represent one of the Classical orders – unadorned Doric on the first level, scrolled Ionic on the second, and acanthus-leaf Corinthian on the top – and have inspired facades throughout the world.

→

The Colosseum in Rome, with its three tiers of arcades

Acropolis

The crown jewel of Greece, the Acropolis *(p448)* is home to some of the most influential buildings in the history of Western architecture. Its breathtaking marble temples were built to honor Athena, the patron goddess of Athens, and are still remarkable for their proportion and scale – marvel at the visual trickery employed by the sculptors of the Parthenon, which was ingeniously designed to counteract the laws of perspective in order to appear completely symmetrical. It's best to visit first thing in the morning or at sunset, to avoid the crowds and the midday heat.

→

Aerial view over the Acropolis and the city of Athens

Sagrada Família

Architect Antoni Gaudí left an indelible mark on Barcelona, with his fantastical buildings bearing roofs modeled on scaly dragons and facades that look like whipped cream. His greatest masterpiece of all is the Sagrada Família *(p322)*: you can't miss this unconventional church's bulbous, multicolored spires, which are visible from almost every corner of the city.

←

The magnificent interior of the Sagrada Família, adorned with natural motifs

Eiffel Tower

Gracefully rising from the heart of the city, the Eiffel Tower *(p194)* is the most recognizable structure in Paris. Some people scale its full height while others view it from afar, but one way or another you're bound to experience this rite of passage – you'll never forget your first encounter with the Iron Lady.

→

The wrought-iron Eiffel Tower, soaring above the center Paris

▷ **Curry Craving**
Ever since medieval merchants first brought exotic spices to British shores, Britons have absorbed culinary influences from across the globe. Curry first became popular in the 18th century, during the rise of the British Empire, and today there are reputedly more Indian restaurants in Greater London than in Mumbai and Delhi combined. Famously, chicken tikka masala eclipsed fish and chips as Britain's favorite dish some years ago; head to London's Brick Lane – the "curry capital of Europe" – to sample the classic version, or visit one of the branches of Dishoom *(www.dishoom. com)* for delicious Bombay café-style food.

EUROPE FOR
FOODIES

Take your tastebuds on a voyage of discovery through an entire continent of flavor. Whether you're after Michelin-starred fine dining or a simple snack, you'll find a huge range of options featuring fresh local produce as the star ingredient. Here are a few of our favorite specialties to whet your appetite.

◁ **Tapas vs Pintxos**
The bar counters of Spain's Basque Lands are heaped with *pintxos* - slices of bread, covered with anything from *tortilla* (potato omelet) to foie gras. *Pintxos* are the Basque answer to tapas - small plates of *croquetas* (croquettes), *patatas bravas* (spicy fried potatoes), and more. Sample both to decide which comes out on top.

▷ Sweet Treats

You can't visit Austria without trying the cake, and with no end of cafés and bakeries, there are plenty of temptations. Indulge your sweet tooth at Hotel Sacher *(www.sacher.com)* with a slice of the eponymous chocolate cake, or at chic Café Landtman *(www.landtmann.at)*, where you'll find perfect *apfelstrudel*.

◁ A Dish for Every Region

Everywhere you go in France you'll find distinctive local cuisines. In Normandy, fresh seafood dishes – such as *moules marinière* (mussels in white wine) – are *de rigueur*, while in the east, *tarte flambée* is found in every tavern. In the Alps, carbs rule: join locals in a warming *pot-au-feu*, a delicious hearty stew.

▷ The Art of New Nordic

New Nordic cuisine combines age-old methods of cooking with new techniques, plus fresh, seasonal ingredients from Scandinavia's countryside. You're spoiled for New Nordic options in Copenhagen, home to legendary noma *(www.noma.dk)*, but there are plenty of other enticing offerings, including Maaemo *(p593)* in Oslo, Gastrologik *(www.gastrologik.se)* in Stockholm, and Spis *(www.spis.fi)* in Helsinki.

◁ Beyond Pizza and Pasta

The gastronomic traditions of Italy are a vibrant mosaic, with specialties differing from one town to the next. Rome's food has its origins in working-class areas and is based on cheap cuts of meat and offal, while Florence's dishes are famously hearty, including Fiorentina (t-bone) steaks, *panzanella* (tomato, onion, and dry bread salad), and *crostini*. For a uniquely Venetian experience, make your way to a local *bacari* (bar) for plates of *chicchetti* (tapas-like bites) washed down with an *aperitivo*.

Puppet Performance

Puppet shows have been entertaining Czech audiences for centuries. Prague has several puppet theaters, the best of which are the Marionette Kingdom (Říše loutek), Spejbl and Hurvínek Theater, and Puppet Theater Jiskra. Tickets are cheap and although the shows are in Czech, kids don't seem to mind - and may even pick up a few words.

→

Traditional puppets on display in a shop in central Prague

EUROPE FOR
FAMILIES

Europe has countless museums and zoos to keep kids entertained, and there's an abundance of outdoor spaces and theme parks where they can blow off steam. With plenty of traditional activities to choose from, here's a selection of the more unusual family experiences that the continent offers.

KINDERCAFES IN BERLIN

Berlin's *kindercafes* (children's cafés) – mostly situated in inner-city areas such as Friedrichshain, Prenzlauer Berg, and Kreuzberg, that are popular with young families - are unique spaces that cater to both children and parents. The former get dedicated play areas, which often include indoor sandpits, ball pools, mazes, and the like, while the whole family can tuck into a decent array of drinks and snacks. Many also have info boards with details on local events, and some sell diapers and even second-hand toys and kids' clothing.

Offbeat Accommodations

Nighttime can be as exciting as daytime in Great Britain, thanks to a host of quirky places to stay. Sleep in a treehouse in the heart of the Cornish countryside *(www.luxurylodges.com/clowance)*, cozy down for the night in a gypsy wagon in the Lake District *(www.wanderlusts.co.uk)*, or stay in a mock-medieval wooden cottage at Warwick Castle *(www.warwick-castle.com)*, near Stratford-upon-Avon.

Visitors exploring the grounds of Warwick Castle ↑

Here Be Monsters

Liven up a trip to Rome by delving into the city's dark side for some spine-tingling thrills. Gasp at the bone sculptures in the creepy Capuchin Crypt *(Via Vittorio Veneto 27)*, and test the family's honesty at the Mouth of Truth in Santa Maria in Cosmedin church *(Piazza della Bocca della Verità 18)* – legend tells that the formidable jaws of this ancient carving will bite off the hands of liars. An easy day trip from Rome is the Bomarzo Monster Park in Lazio *(www.sacrobosco.it)*, scattered with grotesque statues, including a huge screaming face and a giant ripping a man in two.

→
Statue of Orcus, god of the underworld, at the Bomarzo Monster Park

On the Tracks

If your kids are obsessed with trains, then make a beeline for Budapest. A ride through the forested Buda Hills on the Children's Railway – run almost completely by children aged between 10 and 14 – is guaranteed to delight, as is a trip on the historic funicular that travels up from the Chain Bridge to the Royal Palace.

←
Youthful attendants on Budapest's Children's Railway

Water Biking

Cycling isn't restricted to the streets in Amsterdam – pedal-powered "canal bikes" are a fun way to explore the city's canals. As well as being eco-friendly, they also offer the chance to discover smaller waterways that the big canal cruisers can't reach. Stromma *(www.stromma.com)* hires out pedal boats by the hour.

→
A family enjoying a four-seater pedal boat on Amsterdam's canal ring

Moorish Marvels

Characterized by horseshoe arches, elaborate stuccowork, and ornamental calligraphy, Spain's Moorish architecture transports you to the Islamic world. Marvel at the richly tiled Real Alcázar in Seville *(p342)*, walk under the striped arches of Cordoba's Mezquita *(p340)*, or explore the sumptuous interior of the Alhambra *(p336)*. For a truly special experience, take a night tour of the Alhambra to see the moon reflected in the patios' pools.

→

The horseshoe arches in the Mezquita, Córdoba's Great Mosque

EUROPE FOR
ARCHITECTURE

There's no shortage of dazzling structures across Europe, with buildings old and new designed by some of the world's most famous names. A handful of architectural icons tend to hog the headlines, but there are countless treasures to be discovered in their shadows.

Communist Constructions

Come face to face with the ambiguities of Communist rule with a visit to the monumental Palace of Culture and Science in Warsaw *(p690)*, built in the early 1950s when Poland was in the grip of Stalinism. The nearby MDM district, with Neo-Renaissance blocks adorned with Socialist Realist reliefs, is another piece of treasured socialist utopia.

←

The Palace of Culture and Science in Warsaw, a city landmark

Prayers in Stone

From the hulking Romanesque creations of the early Normans to modern masterpieces, Britain's grandiose cathedrals represent its architectural apotheosis. The statistics alone are staggering: Winchester has the longest medieval nave in Europe *(p122)*; York Minster's majestic East Window is the largest expanse of medieval stained glass in the world *(p138)*, and the 72,000-ton dome at Wren's magnificent St. Paul's still dwarfs almost all others *(p109)*.

→

The elegant dome of St. Paul's, viewed from the Millennium Bridge

Neo-Classical Gems

A reaction against the Baroque style, Neo-Classicism became a trend in Germany in the late 18th century. Inspired by the Classical architecture of antiquity, it is most closely associated with Karl Friedrich Schinkel in Berlin and Leo von Klenze in Munich. While in Berlin, admire Schinkel's Neue Wache and Carl Gotthard Langhans' Brandenburg Gate *(p482)*; in Munich, don't miss Klenze's Glyptothek *(p509)*.

←

Schinkel's glorious Neue Wache, a Neo-Classical guardhouse in Berlin

STYLISTIC TERMS

Romanesque
An early medieval style that adapted Roman techniques such as the rounded arch.

Gothic
Characterized by the use of the pointed arch, Gothic architecture sought to build taller, airier buildings.

Baroque
This ornate, theatrical style featured curves and rich decoration.

Neo-Classical
Inspired by the Classical architectural ideals of buildings in ancient Greece and Rome.

↑ Visitors exploring the spectacular MuCEM in Marseille

Extraordinary Exhibition Spaces

Many of France's museums and galleries are works of art in their own right. Highlights include the stunning MuCEM museum in Marseille *(p231)*, encased in a filigree skin that filters gorgeous light into the galleries, and Paris's Fondation Louis Vuitton *(p207)*, in an undulating glass-and-titanium edifice by Frank Gehry.

Vincent van Gogh

Vincent van Gogh (1853–90) began his painting career in the Netherlands, but his most famous works were inspired by the south of France. The sun-soaked colors of Provence can be seen in the works on display in Amsterdam's Van Gogh Museum (p276). Follow in his footsteps and head to Arles (p228) to see the scenes that inspired him for yourself.

→
Vincent's Bedroom in Arles (1888), at the Van Gogh Museum

EUROPE FOR
ART LOVERS

Europe's world-class museums and galleries exhibit an astonishing array of visual art, from ancient antiquities and medieval religious pieces to dazzling 19th- and 20th-century masterpieces. Here's the lowdown on where to see works by some of the continent's most celebrated artists.

TOP 3 ART MUSEUMS

Musée du Louvre
This Parisian landmark is the world's most-visited museum and home of the *Mona Lisa* (p188).

Tate Modern
Housed in a former London power station, it holds one of the world's top collections of contemporary art (p110).

Vatican Museums
Accumulated by a series of popes, this vast art collection includes the remarkable Sistine Chapel ceiling (p382).

Edvard Munch

A pioneer of Expressionism, Edvard Munch (1863–1944) painted intense and timeless artworks inspired by landscapes in and around Oslo. The best known of these is *The Scream*, versions of which are held in the city's Nasjonalmuseet (p593) and Munchmuseet (p592). The painting was prompted by a walk in Oslo's Ekebergparken, and today you can paint your own version at the park's "Munch Spot."

→
The Munchmuseet, a striking building on Oslo's waterfront

Pablo Picasso

Born in Spain, Picasso (1881-1973) spent much of his life in France; today, both countries showcase his work. In Spain, the superb Picasso Museum sits near the artist's birth-place in Málaga *(p333)*, and his iconic *Guernica* takes center stage at the Reina Sofía in Madrid *(p298)*. In France, you can explore 5,000 of the artist's works at the Musée Picasso in Paris *(p184)*, or visit his former home and studio in Antibes *(p233)*.

→

Admiring the artworks on display at the Museo Picasso Málaga

Michelangelo

Considered the best artist of his age, Michelangelo (1475-1564) was a major figure in the Italian Renaissance. Admire his colossal *David* - perhaps the most famous sculpture in the world - at Florence's Galleria dell'Accademia *(p400)* and marvel at his incredible frescoes on the ceiling of the Sistine Chapel in the Vatican *(p382)*, depicting 366 figures from the Bible.

←

Michelangelo's *David* (1501-4) at the Galleria dell'Accademia in Florence

Rembrandt van Rijn

Born in Leiden, Dutch artist Rembrandt Harmenszoon van Rijn (1606- 69) moved to Amsterdam in 1631, where he found many wealthy patrons. *The Night Watch* (1642) is his most venerated work and you can admire it - and many of his other paintings - in Amsterdam's Rijksmuseum *(p272)*. For an insight into the artist's life, head to the city's Museum Het Rembrandthuis *(p266)*.

→

The Night Watch, in pride of place in the Rijksmuseum

Dramatic Coastlines

Ireland's edges offer some of its most spectacular scenery. The Giant's Causeway *(p175)* is truly one of the most unique landscapes in the world, and the Cliffs of Moher are a breathtaking demonstration of the power of nature. Across the Irish Sea, you can walk the full length of Wales along the country's pioneering Coast Path *(www.walescoastpath.gov.uk)*.

↑ Waves crashing against the stone columns of the Giant's Causeway

EUROPE FOR
NATURAL BEAUTY

Scenery is one of the continent's greatest attractions, with the sheer variety almost as impressive as the vistas themselves. Ranging from idyllic beaches to towering mountains, with everything else in between, there's no end of natural wonders for visitors to explore.

Beautiful Beaches

With twinkling turquoise seas, pristine sand, dramatic cliffs, and golden sun, the beaches of the Mediterranean are picture-perfect. Greece's islands are home to some of the prettiest, including Shipwreck Bay on Zákynthos *(p469)*, the small cove of Kyrá Panagiá on Kárpathos *(p473)*, and the black sands at Eríssa on Santoríni *(p470)*.

↑ The idyllica beach at Kyrá Panagiá on the Greek island of Kárpathos

Norwegian Fjords

It can be hard to know where to begin with Norway's 1,000 fjords. For sheer size, your best bet is Sognefjord *(p597)* – the "King of the Fjords" – but many of its arms are arguably even more high impact: the most scenic picks include Aurlandsfjord, Lustrafjord, and Nærøyfjord.

→

Sky reflected in the water of Lustrafjord, an arm of Sognefjord

Monumental Mountains

Stretching across eight countries, the Alps form Europe's most extensive mountain range. Iconic peaks include Mont Blanc in France and the Matterhorn *(p559)* in Switzerland; both are challenging climbs, best admired from afar. Hiking is the most immersive way to enjoy the Alps' majesty - try Germany's 75-mile (120-km) King Ludwig Path for epic scenery and views of the fairy-tale Schloss Neuschwanstein *(p513)*.

←

Two hikers walking over an icy path, with the Matterhorn in the distance

Rural Idylls

Carpeted with a patchwork of verdant, vine-covered hills, wine regions such as Bordeaux *(p224)* and the Mosel Valley *(p516)* are unfailingly picturesque. The most beautiful of all is Val d'Orcia, near Siena *(p396)*: its cypress-clad hills are the epitome of the Tuscan countryside.

←

The undulating hills of Val d'Orcia, situated in the heart of Tuscany

◁ Varied Vodka

Vodka has long been a key part of social rituals in Poland, where the spirit comes in many forms - dabble with Żubrówka, flavored with bison grass; sample ruby-red Wiśniówka, made with cherries; or sip on herb-infused Żołądkowa Gorzka.

▷ Refreshing Rakija

Something of a social tradition across all of Croatia, *rakija* - a potent spirit steeped with local fruit and herbs - is consumed as both an aperitif and a digestif. Similar to brandy, it is commonly made with fruits such as grapes, pears, and plums, but more unusual flavors include *travarica* (fennel, sage, and juniper), *medovača* (honey), and *biska* (mistletoe). Look out for *maraschino*, made from marasca cherries, in and around Zadar *(p678)*.

EUROPE
RAISE A GLASS

Wine and beer have been part of European culture for millennia, and there's no doubt that the continent is home to some of the world's best producers of both. Alongside these staples, you'll also find an intriguing array of local spirits, leaving you spoilt for choice when it comes to ordering at the bar.

◁ Sumptuous Champagne

Bubbly is central to the heritage of the Champagne region, and the best way to get to know both is to visit the cellars where the good stuff is aged. Reims *(p209)* is the epicenter of champagne houses, home to world-famous producers such as Moët et Chandon and Taittinger.

◁ Aromatic Gin

Once known as "mother's ruin," British gin has undergone a renaissance to emerge as one of the nation's favorite tipples. Traditionally, it divides into two types: citrussy, juniper-led London Dry gin, and the slightly sweeter, earthier Plymouth style. If you can't choose a favorite, mix your own at the City of London Distillery's gin lab *(www.city oflondondistillery.com)*.

▷ Lovely Lambic

In the valley of the River Senne in Belgium, there is a natural airborne yeast called Brettanomyces. For centuries, brewers have used it to create a distinctive beer, with a slightly winey edge, called *lambic* – the quintessential beer of Brussels. When fermented a second time it becomes *gueuze*, which is fizzy like champagne, or you can try it flavored with cherries as *kriek*.

◁ Eat, Drink, and Be Sherry

There's nothing quite like a glass of ice-cold sherry on a sultry summer evening. The name of the fortified wine comes from the English pronunciation of Jerez, and the city of Jerez de la Frontera *(p339)* is home to Spain's oldest sherry producer – Bodegas Fundador *(www. grupoemperadorspain.com)* – which has a vast store that houses more than 40,000 barrels. Book a tour and tasting to learn about the production process, or treat yourself to a paired lunch, where every dish is comple-mented by a different sherry.

Pages and Pints

Ireland's pubs are at the heart of the country's social life, so it's little wonder that local writers have drawn inspiration from them. The award-winning Dublin Literary Pub Crawl *(www.dublinpubcrawl. com)* follows the footsteps of authors through the pubs they frequented, with actors performing the works of Beckett, Joyce, and others over a hugely entertaining couple of hours.

←

A statue of James Joyce in a Dublin pub, by local sculptor Ian Pollock

EUROPE FOR
BOOKWORMS

Home to countless beloved fictional characters and celebrated authors, Europe beckons bibliophiles from far and wide. Bring the scenes of your imagination to life with visits to the captivating locations that have inspired some of the world's most popular works.

SHOP

Shakespeare and Company
A Left Bank literary institution that has been a mecca for writers and readers since 1951.

⌂ Paris, France
🅦 shakespeareand company.com

Livraria Lello
This fabulous Art Deco store is said to have been J. K. Rowling's inspiration for *Harry Potter and the Philosopher's Stone.*

⌂ Porto, Portugal
🅦 livrarialello.pt

Fabulous Fairy-tales

The fairy-tales of Hans Christian Andersen have become the stuff of legend. See his former homes along Copenhagen's Nyhavn *(p609)* and follow a trail of sculptures inspired by his stories in his birthplace of Odense *(p615).*

→

An open-air performance of one of Andersen's fairy-tales in Odense

Magic Words

No sign of that letter from Hogwarts? Not to worry: there's plenty of opportunity in Great Britain to unleash your inner Harry Potter. Board the train at Platform 9¾ at Kings Cross Station in London, take a scenic train ride via Scotland's Glenfinnan Viaduct along the route of the Hogwarts Express, or master the art of broomstick flying at Alnwick Castle *(www.alnwickcastle.com)*. Fans of the movies can also make a day trip from London to the Warner Bros. Studio Tour – The Making of Harry Potter *(www.wbstudiotour.co.uk)*.

→

Platform 9¾ at King's Cross train station in London

Detective Drama

One of the best-selling crime writers of the modern age, Norwegian Jo Nesbø has sold over 36 million books worldwide. You can follow in the footsteps of tormented police detective Harry Hole, the protagonist of Nesbø's dark Oslo crime series, on a tour of the Norwegian capital. Head to Hole's favorite bar, Schrøder's *(Waldemar Thranes Gate 8)*, and check out his address at Sofies Gate 5; his name is by the buzzer.

←

Fictional Harry Hole's apartment buzzer, Oslo

Gothic Horror

While staying on Lake Geneva in 1816, Mary Shelley was challenged to write a ghost story; the result was the horror classic *Frankenstein*. Visit Plainpalais in Geneva to see a statue of the monster; the grounds of Villa Diodati, where Shelley had the idea; and the *Frankenstein* exhibit at the Bodmer Foundation *(www.fondationbodmer.ch)*.

→

The grizzly iron statue of Frankenstein's monster in Geneva

▷ Tudor Legacy

Genius or madman? Shrewd leader or tyrannical despot? Few historical figures keep as firm a grip on the public imagination as Britain's King Henry VIII, even 500 years on from his death. Wander the poignant skeletal remains of Fountains Abbey and Tintern Abbey, or piece together the tragic story of Anne Boleyn at Hever Castle and the Tower of London (p112), and it's hard not to feel a tinge of fear at the destructive instincts of this formidable monarch. Yet in the magnificent Hampton Court (p119), Henry created one of the most exquisite palaces in England. Follow in his (sizeable) footsteps and you'll be enthralled.

EUROPE FOR
HISTORY BUFFS

Beginning at the dawn of humanity, Europe's history has been an often turbulent tale of repeating cycles of greatness, decline, and rebirth. Traces of influential societies and events can be found across the continent, offering an instructive insight into the formation of the Europe that we know today.

△ Ancient Legends

Undertake your own odyssey on a tour of Greece's legendary ancient sites. Wander in the footsteps of the Minotaur at the Palace of Knossos on Crete (p475), consult the Oracle at Delphi for the advice of the gods (p457), or test your sporting prowess in the grounds of Ancient Olympia (p466).

▷ Viking Adventures

"Viking" comes from the Old Norse for "to travel," so it's not surprising that their ships were models of art and science. Three of the world's best-preserved vessels rest in Norway at the Vikingskipshuset in Oslo *(p594)*, while at the Danish Vikingeskibsmuseet in Roskilde *(p612)* you can try sailing in a replica boat.

◁ Neolithic Marvel

Built over 5,200 years ago, Newgrange in Ireland *(p166)* is remarkable; the only building materials and tools available then were made of stone. A Neolithic passage tomb, it also acts as an ancient solar observatory; every year on December 21 the sun aligns perfectly with the structure, illuminating a deep inner chamber.

▷ Napoleonic Warpath

French revolutionary superstar turned despot Napoleon Bonaparte escaped forced exile in 1815 and returned to Paris before being defeated at Waterloo. Load up the car and trace his journey along the Route Napoléon, a 202-mile (325-km) stretch of road that winds from the Côte d'Azur *(p233)* through the mountains of Provence to Grenoble *(p224)*, where the general gathered his armies.

◁ Holocaust Memorial

The Nazi extermination camp at Auschwitz-Birkenau in Poland *(p697)* is a unique and harrowing symbol of the horrors of the years around World War II. It accounted for more victims than any other single site: an estimated 1.1 million people lost their lives here; of these, a staggering 90 per cent were Jewish. The bleak remains of the camp and the mountain of survivor testimony at the museum reveal the atrocities that were inflicted upon the prisoners interned here and stand as both a memorial and a record of the Holocaust.

Burning of the Böögg

A tradition since the 16th century, the Sechseläuten occurs in Zürich *(p566)* on the third Monday in April and heralds the start of spring. Its centerpiece is the burning of the Böögg, a snowman effigy packed with firecrackers, put atop a bonfire, and set alight at 6pm. Supposedly, the quicker the Böögg's head explodes, the nicer the summer will be. Afterward, festival-goers stay to barbecue sausages in the bonfire's embers.

→

The Sechseläuten festival in Zürich, with the flaming Böögg as the centerpiece

EUROPE FOR
FESTIVALS

The continent's festival calendar is packed with food, film, and cultural events, meaning that whenever you visit there's always a celebration to join. Many of the big-ticket galas are familiar names around the world, so here are a few lesser-known gems to get you in the festive spirit.

Midnight Sun

The magic of Midsummer is marked across Scandinavia in June, with the biggest events in Sweden and Finland. Participants don wreaths of flowers – an old symbol of fertility and rebirth - and drink and sing until the early hours. Head to the Swedish town of Dalarna *(p580)* or the Finnish island of Seurasaari for full immersion in the Midsummer madness.

←

Participants in the Midsummer celebrations in Gothenburg, Sweden

Looking for Love

Lonely hearts have headed to the small Irish spa town of Lisdoonvarna for over 150 years, in the hope of finding love at Europe's biggest singles' festival. Originally launched to find wives for farmers, it is now a global, LGBT+-friendly event. Willie Daly, Ireland's most famous matchmaker, is on hand to help – but you don't have to be looking for a soulmate to join in, with live music, dancing, and events at every pub in town during September.

$\rightarrow$

Couples dancing at the annual Lisdoonvarna matchmaking festival

Fine Wine

On the third Thursday of November each year, Place St-Jean in Lyon, France *(p223)*, turns itself over to the Beaujol'en Scène committee, in a brief but glorious festival that celebrates Beaujolais Nouveau (the new season's wine). Roll up to watch torch-lit processions and marching bands, then take part in tapping the barrels to discover the Beaujolais' *terroir*. Don't be late – everything is recorded by midnight on the dot.

$\leftarrow$

Beaujolais Nouveau barrels being rolled into the center of Lyon by the winegrowers

TOP 3 MUSIC FESTIVALS

Fête de la Musique
Bands take over streets and squares throughout France for 24 hours on June 21.

Rock am Ring and Rock im Park
Held simultaneously in the German city of Nürnberg *(p502)*, together these rock festivals comprise one of the largest music events in the world.

Prague Spring Music Festival
A three-week international classical music event held in Prague *(p636)*, starting in May.

$\uparrow$ Street festivities during Porto's Festa de São João

It's Hammer Time

June is a time of summer carnivals in Portugal, with none more riotous than the Festa de São João in Porto *(p368)*. The whole city decamps to traditional neighborhoods for a night of drinking, dancing, and hitting each other with plastic hammers – a custom with pagan origins, and that used to be carried out with leeks.

Wild Blooms

Almost as colorful as Greek village life is the variety of wildflowers that bloom in spring, especially the ubiquitous yellow broom. The island of Crete *(p474)* is a true botanist's dream, with no fewer than 1,700 species, including 60 different types of orchid. Go on a guided tour with Pure Crete to see the best of the blooms *(www.purecrete.com)*.

$\rightarrow$

Passing beautiful blooms while walking in Crete

EUROPE
IN BLOOM

As soon as the weather starts to warm, a rainbow-colored wave of flowers cascades across the continent. You'll find blossoming green spaces in most places during spring and summer, from inner-city parks to the wilds of the countryside. Here's a selection of the most photogenic highlights.

TOP 4 GARDENS TO VISIT

Kew Gardens
A World Heritage Site in London, displaying an astonishing 30,000 plants *(p119)*.

Gardens of Versailles
Spectacular formal gardens and pristine parkland at a lavish French palace *(p204)*.

Generalife
An elegant Moorish garden providing a tranquil haven next to the Alhambra in Granada *(p335)*.

Boboli Gardens
A perfectly manicured Renaissance garden situated in the heart of Florence *(p410)*.

Lavender Fields

Come summer in France, the rolling fields of Provence transform into a bee-buzzing purple haze of blossoming lavender, the "blue gold" that makes its way into soaps, honey, and sorbets. The village of Sault is the epicenter of lavender production, but you can find picture-perfect fields throughout the countryside, surrounding rocky hills like Grignan and medieval villages such as Gordes.

$\rightarrow$

Walking through the fragant lavender fields of Provence

Beautiful Bulbfields

From January to May, the bulb-fields in the Netherlands' Bloembollenstreek *(p279)* erupt in wondrous strips of color, attracting visitors from around the world. Tulips are the most famous flowers associated with the region, but you'll also find numerous other species including lilies, daffodils, and crocuses. For the best views of the spectacle, hire a bike and take a gentle ride from Haarlem to Leiden alongside the flower-laden fields – they're at their peak in March or April, which is also when the gardens at Keukenhof, a large flower park in Lisse, are at their best.

$\rightarrow$

A dazzling display of colorful tulips in Keukenhof park

Poignant Poppies

Crimson poppies carpet Belgium's former battlefields *(p256)* in a bittersweet blaze of color from June to August. Immortalized in John McCrae's poem "In Flanders Fields," the flowers ironically flourished under the violent conditions of World War I; today they grow in smaller numbers, but remain a moving symbol of those who lost their lives.

$\leftarrow$

Wild poppies growing in a meadow in the Flanders region of Belgium

Charming Cherry Blossom

Walk the streets of the Altstadt district of Bonn *(p518)* in April and you might think you've been transported to Tokyo: pastel-pink cherry blossoms line the avenues, forming delicate tunnels of flowers. The spectacle is fleeting, however, lasting for just a couple of weeks.

$\rightarrow$

Strolling through a cherry blossom-lined street in Bonn

Fantasy World

Finding the scenery in Dubrovnik familiar? That might be because the historic walled city *(p672)* played a starring role as King's Landing in the blockbuster TV series *Game of Thrones* (2011–19). Countless other European locations were also used for the show, including the Real Alcázar in Seville *(p342)*, which doubled as the seat of House Martell in Dorne, and the Dark Hedges in Northern Ireland, an extraordinary tree-lined avenue near the Giant's Causeway *(p175)* that appeared as the King's Road.

$\rightarrow$

The Old Town of Dubrovnik, a key location in *Game of Thrones*

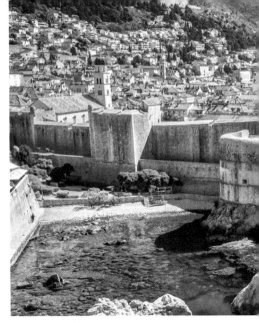

EUROPE
ON SCREEN

With its awe-inspiring landscapes and exhilarating cities, it's little wonder that Europe has captured the imagination of so many great television- and film-makers. Follow in the footsteps of your favorite stars to see the sights behind the sets.

Spain's Wild West

Embrace your inner Clint Eastwood in the arid wilderness of Andalusia's Tabernas Desert - the surprising location for scores of spaghetti Westerns, including *A Fistful of Dollars* (1964) and *The Good, The Bad, and The Ugly* (1966). Their sets are now incorporated into two theme parks - Fort Bravo *(www.fortbravo.es)* and Oasys - Parque Temático del Desierto de Tabernas *(www.oasysparquetematico.com)* - where you can re-enact scenes or watch stuntmen performing brawls.

$\leftarrow$

A Western set at Oasys – Parque Temático de Desierto de Tabernas

Here We Go Again

The scenery on the Greek islands of Skiáthos and Skópelos is enough to make anyone burst into song - so, naturally, they were the perfect location for the 2008 smash hit musical *Mamma Mia!* Most familiar of the locations is the church of Agios Ioannis on Skópelos, in which the film's climax takes place. It requires a steep hike, but offers spectacular views.

Meryl Streep and Pierce Brosnan as Donna and Sam in *Mamma Mia!*

Mystery and Murder

Post-World War II Vienna was the memorable setting for the classic film noir *The Third Man*, starring Orson Welles at his most malevolent. Devotees can reenact the final scene in the grimy sewers of the city on the Third Man Tour (*www.drittemann tour.at*) or pay their respects to the film's most iconic sequence by riding the Prater's Ferris wheel (*p542*).

↑ The moody streets of Vienna in Carol Reed's *The Third Man*

▷ Nocturnal Scuba-Diving

The Greek seas are a radically different and busy world after sunset, with octopus, acrobatic squid, ghostly cuttlefish, colorful nudibranchs, and spotted moray eels on the prowl amid the many shipwrecks. Most of the Greek Islands' numerous scuba-outfitters offer night dives for experienced divers. Some of the best experiences are found in the Cyclades, on Mýkonos *(p470)* and Santoríni *(p470)*.

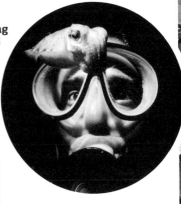

◁ Go Flamenco

More than just a dance, flamenco is an expression of the joys and sorrows of life. Finding authentic flamenco in Spain can be surprisingly difficult and some *tablaos* (flamenco venues) lack *duende* (spirit). Avoid the tourist traps and head for Casa Patas in Madrid *(www.casapatas.com)*, Tablao Cordobés in Barcelona *(www. tablaocordobes.es)*, and El Arenal *(www. tablaoelarenal.com)* in Seville.

EUROPE
AFTER DARK

Life in Europe continues at full speed in the evenings, particularly in summer when the sun sets late. An enticing cocktail of clubs, concerts, and cultural events offers an ever-changing supply of entertainment, so each night brims with possibility. The question is, where to begin?

◁ The Passeggiata

In every town, village, and city in Italy, locals put on their finery and head out for an evening stroll. They might do a little window shopping or stop for an *aperitivo*, but the main purpose of the *passeggiata* is to see and be seen. In Rome, the most fashionable spot is the Via del Corso, while in Florence the focus is on Via dei Calzaiuoli.

△ Ruin Pubs

Hidden within unassuming and dilapidated buildings in Budapest are super-cool ruin pubs *(romkocsma)*, decorated inside with graffiti-covered walls, kitsch bric-a-brac, and mismatched furniture. Make for the narrow Kazinczy utca – the birthplace of this quirky phenomenon – to spend an evening in the legendary Szimpla *(www.en.szimpla.hu)*.

▷ Club Culture

Ever since the fall of the Berlin Wall coincided with the rise of techno, Germany has been the unofficial king of the clubbing scene. Berlin is still the go-to for a serious night out – try Berghain *(www.berghain.de)* and Tresor *(www.tresor berlin. com)* – but top-quality DJs play across the country. Major techno festivals include Time Warp, Toxicator, and Nation of Gondwana.

△ Concert Capital

Once home to fine classical composers, Vienna's music scene is world famous. The Vienna Philharmonic Orchestra has performed since 1870 at the Musikverein, renowned for its impeccable acoustics, while the opulent Staatsoper *(p533)* stages nearly 300 performances a year.

▽ Above their Station

People generally just pass through railroad stations, but some of Portugal's transportation hubs are destinations in themselves. Porto's São Bento station is home to some 20,000 *azulejos* (ceramic tiles), and Lisbon's metro stops are adorned with many of the city's best contemporary *azulejo* artworks – keep an eye out for Modernist artist Maria Keil's geometric designs at Parque and Restauradores stations.

EUROPE
OFF THE
BEATEN TRACK

Europe is home to an impressive array of world-famous sights, and in peak season the crowds can sometimes feel overwhelming. But even in the heart of the continent's ever-popular capital cities, there are plenty of quieter spots where you can escape the tourist hordes.

◁ Secluded Suburbs

The suburbs of Žižkov and Vinohrady border Prague's New Town but receive a fraction of its tourists. The top attraction of Vinohrady, a trendy neighborhood of Art Nouveau tenements, is the weird and wonderful Church of the Most Sacred Heart of Our Lord. Žižkov – named after a Hussite warlord – is traditionally a working-class neighborhood, but has a similarly hip vibe to Vinohrady. Žižkov Hill has views over the New Town and contains little-visited sights such as the National Monument, which has a fascinating exhibit on 20th-century Czech history.

▷ Open House

If Buckingham Palace doesn't appeal, try visiting one of London's more unusual residences. The enchanting Dennis Severs' House *(www.denissevershouse.co.uk)* dodges everything modern, with candlelit rooms decked out in high Georgian style, while the idiosyncratic Sir John Soane's Museum *(www. soane.org)* holds an Egyptian sarcophagus.

◁ Take a Tour

For an unconventional view of Vienna, join one of the guided walking tours offered by Space and Place *(www.spaceandplace.at)*. Their Vienna Ugly Tour flies in the face of the city's reputation for imperial splendor and takes you instead to 19 of its least attractive buildings, including the Federal Ministry and the Hungarian Cultural Center.

▷ A Unique Museum

Blink and you'll miss Berlin's Museum of Things *(www.museumderdinge.org)*, tucked away on the third floor of a factory in the city's Kreuzberg district. Centered around the work of the Deutscher Werkbund (German Association of Craftsmen), it showcases a dizzying range of everyday items designed as a marriage of form and function, from toys to furniture and appliances.

◁ Roman Art Nouveau

To see a side of Rome that few people imagine, head to the cluster of streets between Piazza Buenos Aires and Via Tagliamento, and discover an Art Nouveau quarter of fantastic villas and fairy-tale palaces created by architect Gino Coppodè.

A YEAR IN
EUROPE

JANUARY

△ **New Year Celebration Concerts** *(Jan 1)*. These musical celebrations in Vienna are an institution.
La Befana *(Jan 6)*. Children in Italy receive gifts from La Befana, the Christmas witch.
Festival of Northern Lights *(second half of Jan)*. A heady combination of an aurora borealis light show and live music in Tromsø.

FEBRUARY

△ **Feast of St. Blaise** *(Feb 3)*. Dubrovnik honors its patron saint with processions and fairs.
Six Nations Rugby *(early Feb–late Mar)*. A keenly fought rugby contest involving England, France, Ireland, Italy, Scotland, and Wales.
Carnival *(Feb/Mar)*. Feasts and processions are held across the continent, in a final hurrah before Lent.

MAY

World Village Festival *(May)*. A free festival in Helsinki, showcasing art and culture from around the world.
△ **Cannes Film Festival** *(mid–late May)*. The world's premier movie industry event, held on the glamorous French Riviera.
Science Picnic, Warsaw *(May or Jun)*. Europe's largest outdoor science festival.

JUNE

△ **Pride** *(Jun–Aug)*. Parades and parties take place across the continent to celebrate the LGBT+ community.
Venice Art Biennale *(Jun–Sep)*. Held in odd-numbered years, this is the world's biggest exhibition of contemporary art.
Donauinselfest *(late Jun)*. This open-air rock and pop festival is a huge free event in Vienna.

SEPTEMBER

Regata Storica *(first Sun)*. A procession of historic boats and a colorful gondola race in Venice.
△ **Oktoberfest** *(last two weeks in Sep)*. Munich's world-famous beer festival is held over 16 days, and opens with a parade.
Galway International Oyster and Seafood Festival *(last weekend)*. This Irish festival offers a tempting array of tastings, entertainment, parades, food trails, and champagne.

OCTOBER

Tag der Deutschen Einheit *(Oct 3)*. Concerts and parades in honor of German reunification.
CAFe Budapest Contemporary Arts Festival *(early Oct)*. One of Europe's leading celebrations of contemporary arts.
△ **Día de la Hispanidad** *(Oct 12)*. Spain's national holiday marks Columbus's "discovery" of America in 1492.

MARCH

Matějská Fair *(late Feb–mid-Apr)*. This huge annual fair in Prague draws thousands from across the Czech Republic with its traditional attractions and rides.

△ **Las Fallas** *(Mar 15–19)*. Huge papier-mâché figures and scenes are paraded through the city of Valencia in Spain, before being set alight on massive pyres.

St. Patrick's Day *(Mar 17)*. Ireland's patron saint is celebrated with five days of parades, concerts, *céili* dances, and fireworks in Dublin.

APRIL

Peixe em Lisboa *(early–mid-Apr)*. This fish festival in Lisbon features tastings at restaurants and demonstrations by chefs.

△ **Koningsdag** *(Apr 27)*. The Netherlands celebrates the king's birthday, with Amsterdam becoming one big street – and boat – party.

Easter Week *(Apr/May)*. Celebrated throughout Europe, this is a particularly important event in Greece, where it far outweighs Christmas on the Orthodox calendar.

AUGUST

△ **Swiss National Day** *(Aug 1)*. A parade is held in Zurich, with bonfires and fireworks elsewhere.

Edinburgh International Festival and Edinburgh Festival Fringe *(Aug)*. Great Britain's greatest celebration of arts and culture.

Hans Christian Andersen Festival *(mid–late Aug)*. The Norwegian city of Odense is populated with characters from Andersen's fairy-tales.

JULY

△ **Tour de France** *(late Jun–late Jul)*. Millions of spectators line the roads of France to cheer on cyclists chasing the yellow jersey.

Ommegang *(first Tue & Thu in Jul)*. Some 2,000 participants in traditional costumes perform an *ommegang* (tour) in Brussels' Grand Place.

The Proms *(mid-July–mid-Sep)*. An eight-week festival of classical music in London.

DECEMBER

△ **Christmas Markets** *(throughout Dec)*. Open-air markets appear across Europe, selling local crafts and warming winter food and drink.

Lucia Celebrations *(Dec 13)*. Candelit processions are held throughout Sweden in honor of Lucia, a mythical figure and the bearer of light.

New Year's Eve *(Dec 31)*. Midnight pyrotechnics and street parties herald the start of the New Year in Europe's major cities.

NOVEMBER

△ **All Saints' Day** *(Nov 1)*. Throughout Europe, families visit the graves of their loved ones.

Les Trois Glorieuses *(3rd Sun)*. The "Three Glorious Days" in Burgundy include tastings of new wine vintages, processions, and an auction.

Onion Fair *(late Nov)*. People flock to Bern from across Switzerland to ring in the onion harvest.

A BRIEF
HISTORY

Europe's beautiful architecture, diverse societies, and delicious cuisines are the result of thousands of years of trade and industry, war and revolution. From the great civilizations of the Greeks and Romans to the chilly politics of the Cold War, the history of this continent is complex and fascinating.

Prehistoric Europe and the First Civilizations

Modern humans arrived in Europe over 40,000 years ago, shifting from a hunter-gatherer to an agricultural lifestyle around 7000 BC. Metal tools evolved around 3200 BC, starting the Bronze Age, and 500 years later the Minoan civilization – possibly Europe's first literate civilization – appeared on Crete. As the Iron Age emerged, the use of steel enabled more complex societies to develop – but this was not the case everywhere. The Iron Age ended gradually: in Great Britain it lasted until the Roman invasion in AD 43, but in Greece it ended sooner, with the rise of Ancient Greek culture.

1 A map of the Roman Empire in the 3rd century AD.

2 Prehistoric cave art, Lascaux, France.

3 Soliders paying tribute to Alexander the Great.

4 Remains of the Roman city of Pompeii.

Timeline of events

c. 40,000 BC

The first early modern humans migrate into Europe from the Middle East and Central Asia.

c. 3200 BC

Start of the Bronze Age in Europe.

c. 2700 BC

Minoan civilization develops on Crete and spreads to mainland Europe.

c. 7000 BC

Start of the Neolithic period in Europe.

c. 1190 BC

Start of the Iron Age in Europe.

The Classical Age

Ancient Greek civilization began in the 9th century BC, reaching its zenith in the Classical period, which started around 500 BC and ended after the death of Alexander the Great in 323 BC. Many influential elements of Greek culture were formed during this time, including various moral philosophies and principles of architecture.

In 146 BC, Greece was annexed by the Roman Republic, which by 27 BC had become the Roman Empire. In AD 79, Mount Vesuvius erupted and buried the city of Pompeii in around 16 ft (5 m) of ash. When later rediscovered, the city gave archeologists a snapshot of Roman life: it had sewage and sanitation; mosaics and murals were common; and the populace had access to everything from public baths to an amphitheater.

At its peak in AD 117, the Roman Empire contained around 20 per cent of the world's population, but by the 4th century it had begun to fracture, splitting into the Western and Eastern (or Byzantine) Roman Empires around 395. The Western Roman Empire collapsed in 476, resulting in the division of its territory into small kingdoms and signaling the start of the Middle Ages.

↑ A ceramic vase created by the Bronze Age Minoan civilization

447 BC

Work begins on the Parthenon, the great temple on the Acropolis in Athens.

AD 117

The Roman Empire reaches its greatest extent under the rule of Emperor Trajan.

313

Constantine becomes the first Roman emperor to convert to Christianity.

27 BC

The Roman Empire is established, with Augustus named as the first emperor.

476

The Western Roman Empire collapses, signaling the end of Roman dominance in Europe.

The Dark Ages

The Middle Ages (or Dark Ages) are mostly remembered for unrest, war, and disease – especially the Black Death, which claimed up to one-third of Europe's population. This period also saw the rise of the Vikings, who carried out a wave of invasions that spread as far as North America. They were not the only ones with their sights set on expansion: in 711 the Islamic conquest of Iberia began, leading to the foundation of al-Andalus. This period of Moorish rule sparked fears among Christian rulers that Islam would spread, inciting the First Crusade in 1095.

The Renaissance

The end of the Middle Ages was marked by the invention of movable type in 1439, with 20 million books printed in the 50 years after Gutenberg's first press. The Renaissance followed, when ancient Greek and Roman philosophies were revived by polymath "Renaissance Men" like Michelangelo and Leonardo da Vinci, and the world opened up in the Age of Exploration. Alongside this flowering of art and logic, however, as many as 60,000 people were executed in witch trials from 1560 to 1800.

AND YET IT MOVES

In 1633, Pisan-born scientist Galileo Galilei was accused of heresy by the Catholic Church for saying that the Earth moves around the Sun, not the other way around. He was forced to recant to avoid torture and execution, and spent the rest of his life under house arrest. It was not until 1992 that the Church publicly acknowledged it had been wrong.

Timeline of events

711
The Moorish invasion of Spain leads to the founding of al-Andalus.

793
The start of the Viking Age.

1347–51
The Black Death ravages Europe, killing up to one-third of the population.

1337–1453
The Hundred Years' War between England and France.

1440s
Gutenberg's press revolutionizes printing in Europe.

The Age of Exploration also led to the worldwide slave trade, and the explorers' plundered riches caused rampant inflation. This, combined with the brutal Thirty Years' War (1618–48) in Central Europe, and the famine and unrest caused by the harsh winters of the Little Ice Age (1300–1850), meant that the Renaissance era was just as unstable as the Middle Ages.

Revolution and Rising Powers

By the 18th century, the German kingdom of Prussia was one of the major powers in Northern Europe under Frederick the Great. His successes in battle established Prussia as a powerful military and economic force, while his focus on education, the arts, and freedom of the press made it a cosmopolitan place to live. In Western Europe, instability and inequality were increasing in France, culminating in 1789 in the French Revolution. The monarchy was deposed as part of a far-reaching restructuring of political and social systems, leading to the end of feudalism and the establishment of individual rights for all men. The French First Republic, established in 1792, lasted until Napoleon Bonaparte declared the First Empire in 1804.

1 A depiction of victims of the Black Death.

2 The first proof sheet from Gutenberg's press.

3 The Battle of Lützen in the Thirty Years' War.

4 Frederick the Great, king of Prussia.

Did You Know?

The University of Bologna is the oldest in Europe; it was founded in 1088 and has existed ever since.

1453
The Fall of Constantinople to the Ottomans marks the end of the Byzantine Empire.

1492
Columbus's first voyage to America, at the height of the Age of Exploration.

1517
Martin Luther sparks the Reformation with his 95 Theses; Protestantism sweeps across much of Northern Europe.

1649–58
Under Oliver Cromwell, England is run as a republic, then as a protectorate; in 1660 the monarchy is restored.

1789
The French Revolution begins, leading to the execution of Louis XVI and Marie Antoinette.

Empire and Industry

Napoleon sought to expand French territory in the Napoleonic Wars of 1803–15; he was ultimately unsuccessful, and instead Britain emerged as Europe's key military and naval power. During Queen Victoria's reign (1837–1901) the British Empire became the largest in history, its dramatic expansion underpinned by the innovative technologies of the Industrial Revolution. But the generally higher quality of life in this period did not extend to everyone: British growth came at the expense of the indigenous communities in its colonies, and during 1845–9, the Great Famine in Ireland caused the deaths of around 1 million people.

Fighting for Rights

In 1848, Europe experienced the Year of Revolution. In France, the reinstated monarchy was overthrown once again; Denmark introduced representative democracy; the Netherlands abolished absolute monarchy; and the Hungarian Revolution ended serfdom in Hungary and the Austrian Empire.

More social change was to follow. The slave trade was steadily abolished across the continent (Denmark had been the first

1 An early steam railroad in Great Britain.

2 An Irish family during the Great Famine.

3 Women's suffrage protestors in Britain.

4 French soldiers in the trenches in World War I.

Did You Know?

Tanks were first used in war in September 1916, during the Battle of the Somme.

Timeline of events

1803
Denmark becomes the first European country to end the slave trade.

1813
The Netherlands gains independence from France.

1831
Creation of the kingdom of Belgium.

1830–40
The Industrial Revolution reaches its peak; George Stephenson's *Rocket* becomes the steam locomotive prototype.

1838–1901
The Reign of Queen Victoria, and the height of the British Empire.

European nation to declare the slave trade illegal in 1803), and the women's suffrage movement began gaining momentum. Finland extended the vote to women in 1906 – the first state in Europe to do so – but most other countries only made this change during or after World War I.

Death in the Trenches

World War I began as a conflict between Austria-Hungary and Serbia, sparked by the 1914 assassination of Archduke Franz Ferdinand, heir to the Austro-Hungarian Empire. It soon grew to involve most countries in Europe, and many beyond. Rapid advancements in artillery, plus the use of military aircraft and chemical warfare, made this a very different experience to the wars of the 19th century, resulting in over 16 million deaths. It was also one of the first conflicts to be widely filmed and photographed, which both enabled more effective propaganda and brought the horrors of trench warfare to the home front.

After peace was declared in 1918, Europe faced another tragedy: a pandemic of Spanish Flu, which killed over 50 million people, including many young adults who had made up the front lines.

↑ Archduke Franz Ferdinand, heir to the Austro-Hungarian throne

1839

Luxembourg is recognized as a sovereign nation.

1861

The kingdom of Italy is proclaimed, bringing most of Italy under Piedmontese rule; full unification follows in 1870.

1870

German victory in the Franco-Prussian War leads to the unification of Germany.

1914–18

World War I leads to the death of millions and the redrawing of state lines in Europe.

1918–20

The Spanish Flu kills up to 100 million people worldwide.

Redrawing the Lines

The 1919 Treaty of Versailles was perhaps the most significant of the treaties that brokered peace in Europe. Importantly, its terms required Germany to take responsibility for "all loss and damage" during the war, and to pay heavy reparations and relinquish 25,000 sq miles (64,750 sq km) of territory – restrictions that helped to sow the seeds of World War II.

In Russia, meanwhile, tensions had boiled over during World War I into the Russian Revolution of 1917. By 1918, the monarchy had been overthrown and a new Communist government set up, and in 1922 the USSR (Union of Soviet Socialist Republics) was established, incorporating several newly independent states such as Ukraine and Georgia.

Revolutionary events also occured in Ireland during this period. Irish Nationalists had been seeking independence from the UK for decades, resulting in the Easter Rising of 1916. The situation developed into the War of Independence (1919–21), and Ireland finally seceded from Great Britain in 1922, with the northern portion of the island remaining as part of the United Kingdom of Great Britain and Northern Ireland.

LGBT+ BERLIN

Before becoming the target of the Nazi Party in the early 1930s, the LGBT+ community in Berlin was well established and pioneering. The world's first gay magazine began publication there in 1896, the district of Schönberg had famous gay-friendly clubs, and the Scientific-Humanitarian Committee was lobbying for LGBT+ rights as early as 1897.

Timeline of events

1919

The Treaty of Versailles creates new states, including Poland, Finland, Czechoslovakia, and Hungary; the War Guilt clause places full blame for World War I on Germany.

1921

The Anglo-Irish treaty is signed, guaranteeing independence for much of Ireland.

1921–2

The Russian Famine causes the deaths of an estimated 5 million people.

1922

The Soviet Union is established; the Fascist Mussolini becomes prime minister of Italy.

2

3

Civil War and Total War

After the formation of the Spanish Second Republic in 1931, the Great Depression and the rise of Fascism led to civil war in Spain in 1936. This war continued until 1939, ending with the triumph of Franco and the Nationalists. Meanwhile, Fascism was growing in other parts of Europe. Mussolini had been prime minister of Italy since 1922, but with the rise of Hitler – who became Führer of Germany in 1934 – Europe began sliding toward another conflict. After the Nazi invasion of Poland in 1939, Britain declared war against Germany, launching the start of World War II.

A state of "total war" emerged, where the lines between military and civilian targets were blurred. This, combined with atrocities like the Holocaust, made it the deadliest conflict in history, with over 70 million people killed – 20 million of them civilians. Poland suffered the worst losses, with the deaths of around 17 per cent of its population. The end of the war led to a global shift in power, effectively ending most of the European empires and inspiring the establishment of the UN in hopes of preventing future conflicts on this scale. It was this new political order that set the stage for the following 50 years of Cold War.

1 National leaders signing the Treaty of Versailles in 1919.

2 Bomb damage in London from air raids during World War II.

3 The signing of the Charter of the United Nations in 1945.

1934

Hitler is named Führer of Germany, a role that gives him supreme power.

1936–9

Spanish Civil War; the Nationalists win, and General Franco remains in power until his death in 1975.

1945

Germany is partitioned as part of the postwar settlement.

1939

World War II begins when Germany invades Poland, causing Britain to declare war.

1941

Germany invades the USSR, bringing Soviet Russia into World War II on the side of the Allied Powers.

The Cold War and the Collapse of the USSR

The Cold War saw much of the world split into the Eastern Bloc (the USSR and its allies) and the Western Bloc (the USA and its allies). The atmosphere was tense, with the proliferation of nuclear weapons raising the stakes. Most of Central and Eastern Europe was under Soviet control, and opposition was brutally crushed. The 1956 Hungarian Revolution was quelled with the use of tanks, while 20,000 USSR troops entered Czechoslovakia to suppress the 1968 Prague Spring. There were also protests in Western Europe. In 1968, student protests in Paris grew into a national strike; Spain saw pro-democracy demonstrations; and a Northern Irish civil rights march resulted in riots. In 1974, Portugal's Carnation Revolution ended 48 years of authoritarian rule.

In the 1980s the Cold War started to thaw. Gorbachev became leader of the USSR in 1985 and moved towards liberalization. When some states sought to leave the Union, Gorbachev decided against intervening with the military, notably during the fall of the Berlin Wall in 1989, which led to Germany's subsequent reunification in 1990. In 1991, the USSR was dissolved, and all Soviet republics were granted independence.

PAX EUROPAEA

The EU was awarded the Nobel Peace Prize in 2012 in recognition of its role in the Pax Europaea (European Peace), during which no EU member states have been at war with each other (although there have been some conflicts in the wider continent). This period of relative peace began in the wake of World War II, and stands in stark contrast to the previous centuries.

Timeline of events

1957
The Treaty of Rome lays the foundations for the European Union.

1968
Protests in France and other parts of Europe.

1974
The Carnation Revolution in Portugal leads to the end of a 48-year period of authoritarian rule.

1980
A strike at Gdańsk's Lenin Shipyard leads to protests across Poland.

1989
Collapse of the USSR in Eastern Europe.

From a Unified Europe to the Great Recession

Moving into the 21st century, Europe was in a period of relative calm. The EU helped maintain peace, while the 1998 Good Friday Agreement helped to end the Troubles in Northern Ireland. However, the 2007–8 financial crash led to the Great Recession, resulting in a shift to economic austerity and more conservative politics. Greece suffered a massive recession, and in 2012 the country underwent the biggest debt restructuring in history. In 2015, the continent experienced the largest refugee crisis since the 1940s, with people displaced by war, climate change, and economic hardship seeking refuge in Europe. These issues all contributed to a shift toward populism and right-wing politics in many European countries.

Europe Today

Although Europe faces many challenges, the continent is more peaceful, prosperous, and diverse than ever before. Despite the UK voting to leave the EU in a 2016 referendum, Europe as a whole remains committed to political engagement, with the highest voter turnout for 20 years at the 2019 EU elections.

⬆ ① Police in Paris during the 1968 riots.

② The fall of the Berlin Wall in 1989.

③ The signing of the Good Friday Agreement.

④ Polish citizens voting in the 2019 EU elections.

1993

The Maastricht Treaty comes into effect on November 1, formally establishing the EU.

1993
Czechoslovakia is peacefully divided into the Czech Republic and Slovakia; the European Economic Community (EEC) evolves into the European Union (EU).

1998
The Good Friday Agreement is signed, largely ending the Troubles in Ireland.

2001
The Netherlands becomes the first country to legalize same-sex marriage.

2002
The euro is introduced as the official currency in 12 countries of the EU.

2016
In a referendum, the UK narrowly votes to leave the EU.

EXPERIENCE

Saint-Cirq-Lapopie in the French Pyrenees

Hot-air balloons over Bristol's Clifton Suspension Bridge

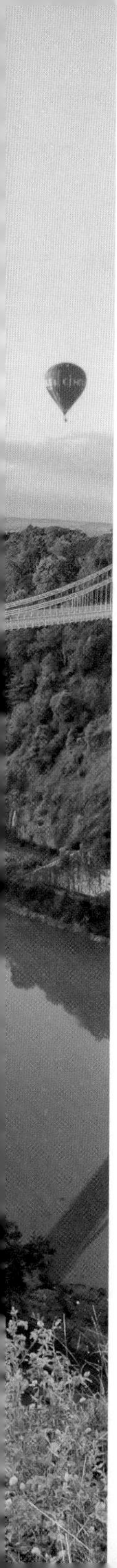

GREAT BRITAIN

Separated from the rest of Europe by the English Channel, Britain has been intrinsically shaped by its geographical position as an island. In the 1st millennium AD, it was invaded in turn by the Romans, the Saxons and Angles of Germany, and the Vikings, but the Battle of Hastings in 1066, in which England was conquered by the Normans of France, marked the final successful invasion of Britain by a foreign power. Wales was conquered by England in 1282, and by 1296 control was also gained over Scotland – though the Scots won back their independence in 1314. Between 1485 and 1603 the Tudor dynasty consolidated England's strength and laid the foundations for Britain's future commercial success, with the defeat of the Spanish Armada in 1588 confirming the nation's position as a major maritime power. Subsequent internal struggles led to the Civil War in 1642, but by the time of the Act of Union with Scotland in 1707, the whole island was united. Internal security and maritime strength allowed Britain to seek wealth overseas, and success in the Napoleonic Wars in 1815 established Britain's pre-eminence in Europe. Capitalizing on the opportunities offered by industrialization and the exploitation of its ever-expanding empire, Britain became the most powerful nation in the world. This was not to last: drained by its role in two world wars, Britain's influence waned after 1945, and by the 1970s, most of its former colonies had become independent. The 21st century has seen two contentious referendums in the country – one on Scottish independence, which failed, the other on Great Britain leaving the EU, with leave winning by a narrow majority.

GREAT BRITAIN

1 London
2 Windsor Castle
3 Canterbury
4 Winchester
5 Salisbury
6 Brighton
7 Bath
8 Stonehenge
9 Bristol
10 Devon and Cornwall
11 Snowdonia
12 Caernarfon
13 Cardiff
14 Oxford
15 Stratford-upon-Avon
16 Blenheim Palace
17 Cambridge
18 Liverpool
19 Chester
20 Manchester
21 Durham
22 Lake District
23 York
24 Edinburgh
25 Stirling
26 Glasgow
27 St. Andrews
28 Aberdeen
29 Inverness
30 Isle of Skye
31 Cairngorms

GREAT BRITAIN

Atlantic Ocean

Celtic Sea

0 kilometers 100
0 miles 100

N

Hebrides
Lewis
Stornoway
Harris
Tarbert
Ullapool
Lochmaddy
North Uist
Uig
Wester Ross
South Uist
ISLE OF SKYE 30
Kyle of Lochalsh
Lochboisdale
Mallaig
Borra
Hebrides
Fort William
Tobermory
Craignure
Mull
Oban
Jura
Islay
Lon
A83 Greer
Port Ellen
Kintyre
Campbeltown
Arran

Londonderry (Derry)
Ballycastle
Larne
Stranraer
Donegal
NORTHERN IRELAND
Belfast
Enniskillen
Newry
Newcastle
Is
Cavan
Dundalk
IRELAND
Irish Sea
Athlone
Dublin
Angl
Holyhea
Roscrea
IRELAND
p150
Limerick
L Penins
Waterford
Wexford
Rosslare
Killarney
Dungarvan
Cardigan
Cork
St. Davids
Pembroke
Clov
CORNW
10
Newquay
St. Ives
Truro
Penzance
Scilly Isles

❶
LONDON

✕ 🅰 🚃 *i* www.visitlondon.com

Built on pomp and ceremony, London has become a cosmopolitan capital. This diverse city has it all: amazing art and ground-breaking music, royal palaces and historic pubs, futuristic skyscrapers and picturesque parks.

① ⊘ ⊘ 🏛

Houses of Parliament

🅰 SW1 🚇 Westminster
🚌 3, 11, 12, 24, 53, 88, 148, 159, 211, 453 🕐 For details of tours and to buy tickets, check website
🌐 parliament.uk

Since the 16th century, this site has been the seat of the two Houses of Parliament: the House of Commons, made up of elected Members of Parliament (MPs), and the upper house, the House of Lords. Formerly filled with hereditary peers, bishops, and life peers, the latter was reformed in 2000.

The present Neo-Gothic building replaced the original palace, which was destroyed by fire in 1834.

To hear debates in either of the houses from the visitors' galleries, join the queue outside the Cromwell Green visitor entrance. To attend Prime Minister's Questions (held every Wednesday at noon), apply for tickets to your local MP – visitors are unlikely to gain entrance on the day as there is often a long queue. Various guided tours of the building are held on Saturdays throughout the year, as well as weekdays when Parliament is not in session.

Central London, seen from a capsule at the top of the London Eye

London Eye

🏛 South Bank SE1
🚇 Waterloo, Westminster
🚌 RV1, 77, 381 🕐 Daily; check website for hours
🚫 Dec 25, Jan 5–16
🌐 londoneye.com

Reaching to a height of 443 ft (135 m) above the Thames river, this was the world's tallest Ferris wheel when it opened in 2000 as part of London's millennium celebrations. Its capsules offer a gentle 30-minute ride over a full turn, with breathtaking views over the city and for up to 26 miles (42 km) beyond. "Flights" are on the hour or half-hour and must be booked in advance; collect tickets at County Hall, next to the Eye, at least 30 minutes before your flight time.

INSIDER TIP
Getting Around

London's subway system – the "tube" or "underground" – runs from about 5:30am until just after midnight. (Some lines operate a 24-hour service on Fridays and Saturdays.) London buses are frequent and plentiful, and helpful for visiting areas without a tube station, and overground rail services are useful for trips farther afield. It's not convenient to drive in London; congestion and emission zone charges make it very expensive. The well-known black cabs are a safe and convenient way to travel.

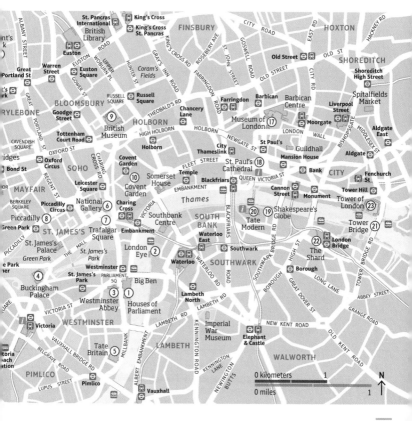

③ ⌀ ⌀ ⌑ ⌖

WESTMINSTER ABBEY

The West Towers were designed by Nicholas Hawksmoor.

🏛 Broad Sanctuary SW1 🚇 St James's Park, Westminster
🚌 11, 24, 148, 211 ⛴ Westminster Pier ⏰ Check website
for specific parts of the church 🌐 westminster-abbey.org

The final resting place of 17 of Britain's monarchs and numerous political and cultural icons, the glorious Gothic Westminster Abbey is the stunning setting for coronations, royal marriages, and Christian worship.

Within the abbey walls are some of the best examples of medieval architecture in London and one of the most impressive collections of tombs and monuments in the world. The first abbey church was established in the 10th century by St. Dunstan and a group of Benedictine monks. The present structure dates largely from the 13th century; the new French-influenced design was begun in 1245 at the behest of Henry VII. It survived Henry VIII's dissolution of the monasteries in the 16th century due to its unique role as the royal coronation church. The interior presents a diverse array of architectural and sculptural styles, from the austere French Gothic of the nave, through Henry VII's stunning Tudor chapel, to the riotous 18th-century monuments. One of the latest additions is the 2018 Weston Tower housing the Queen's Diamond Jubilee Galleries, full of historical treasures.

← The ornate stalls of the quire, where daily choral services are held

Timeline

1050
△ New Benedictine abbey church begun by Edward the Confessor

1245
New church begun to the designs of Henry of Reyns

1269
△ Body of Edward the Confessor is moved to a new shrine in the abbey

1540
△ Monastery dissolved on the orders of King Henry VIII

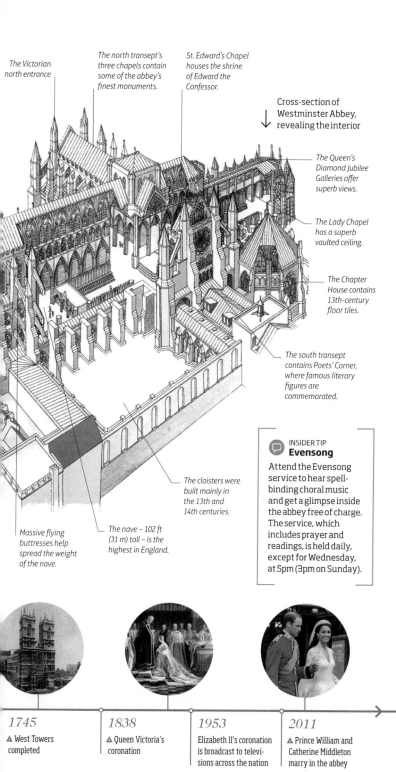

The Victorian north entrance

The north transept's three chapels contain some of the abbey's finest monuments.

St. Edward's Chapel houses the shrine of Edward the Confessor.

Cross-section of Westminster Abbey, revealing the interior

The Queen's Diamond Jubilee Galleries offer superb views.

The Lady Chapel has a superb vaulted ceiling.

The Chapter House contains 13th-century floor tiles.

The south transept contains Poets' Corner, where famous literary figures are commemorated.

The cloisters were built mainly in the 13th and 14th centuries.

Massive flying buttresses help spread the weight of the nave.

The nave – 102 ft (31 m) tall – is the highest in England.

> 💬 **INSIDER TIP**
> **Evensong**
> Attend the Evensong service to hear spell-binding choral music and get a glimpse inside the abbey free of charge. The service, which includes prayer and readings, is held daily, except for Wednesday, at 5pm (3pm on Sunday).

1745
△ West Towers completed

1838
△ Queen Victoria's coronation

1953
Elizabeth II's coronation is broadcast to televisions across the nation

2011
△ Prince William and Catherine Middleton marry in the abbey

④

Buckingham Palace

⌂ SW1 ⊖ St James's Park, Victoria, Green Park ⊞ C1, C10, 11, 16, 36, 38, 52, 73, 211 ◷ State Rooms: end Jul-Aug: 9:30am-7:30pm daily; Sep: 9:30am-6:30pm daily; Changing of the Guard: 10am on alternate days (subject to change)
⊛ royalcollection.org.uk

Conversion of the 18th-century Buckingham House was begun for George IV in 1826, but the first monarch to occupy the palace was Queen Victoria, in 1837. Today, it is the official London home of Queen Elizabeth II – when the monarch is in residence, the Royal Standard flag is flown.

The palace tour takes visitors up the grand staircase and through the splendor of the State Rooms. The Queen carries out many formal ceremonies in the richly gilded Throne Room, and the Ballroom is used for state banquets and investitures. Valuable works of art, such as *The Music Lesson* (c. 1660) by Dutch master Jan Vermeer, are on display in the Picture Gallery. Another selection of works from the monarch's art collection is displayed in the Queen's Gallery, a small building to one side of the palace.

The famous Changing of the Guard takes place on the palace forecourt. Here, crowds gather to watch the colorful half-hour parade of guards, dressed in red jackets and tall, furry hats called bearskins, exchanging the palace keys.

Overlooking the forecourt, the East Wing facade of the palace was redesigned by Aston Webb in 1913. He also created the spacious, tree-lined avenue known as the Mall, which leads from the palace to Trafalgar Square. Used for royal processions on special occasions, the Mall is closed to traffic on Sundays. The national flags of foreign heads of state fly from its flagpoles during official visits.

The avenue follows the edge of St. James's Park, a reserve for wildfowl and popular picnic spot in the heart of the city. In summer, concerts are held on the park bandstand.

Did You Know?

Secret tunnels connect Buckingham Palace to Clarence House and the Houses of Parliament.

⑤

Tate Britain

⌂ Millbank SW1 ⊖ Pimlico ⊞ C10, 77a, 88, 507 ⛴ Between Tate Britain and Tate Modern ◷ 10am-6pm daily ⊗ Dec 24-26 ⊛ tate.org.uk

Founded in 1897, the Tate Gallery – now called Tate Britain – shows the world's largest display of British art. Housed in a fabulous Neo-Classical building facing the river, the gallery was founded on the private collection of

Dusk at Buckingham Palace and *(inset)* the Changing of the Guard ceremony passing by

the sugar merchant Henry Tate and works from the older National Gallery. The art on display ranges from Tudor times to the present day, and includes sculpture and modern installation pieces.

One of the most exquisite early works is a portrait of a bejeweled Elizabeth I (c. 1575), by Nicholas Hilliard. Elsewhere, the influence of the 17th-century Flemish artist Sir Anthony van Dyck on English painters can be seen in William Dobson's *Endymion Porter* (1642–5) and the works of Thomas Gainsborough, and there are some fine examples of William Hogarth's sharply satirical pictures.

Tate Britain also holds a large number of paintings by the visionary poet and artist William Blake. His work was imbued with a mystical intensity, a typical example being *Satan Smiting Job with Sore Boils* (c. 1826). Other famous paintings include John Constable's *Flatford Mill* (1816–7), one of his many depictions of the Essex countryside, and a collection of works by M. W. Turner, whose paintings were left to the nation after his death on condition that they were kept together. His watercolor *A City on a River at Sunset* (1832) is a highlight.

The Tate also has many works by the 19th-century Pre-Raphaelites, as well as several modern and contemporary artists.

National Gallery

Trafalgar Sq WC2

Charing Cross, Leicester Sq, Piccadilly Circus

3, 6, 9, 11 & many others

10am-6pm daily (to 9pm Fri) Jan 1, Dec 24-26

nationalgallery.org.uk

London's leading art museum, the National Gallery has more than 2,300 paintings, most in permanent display. The collection was started in 1824

when the House of Commons agreed to purchase 38 major paintings. These became the core of a national collection of European art that now ranges from Giotto in the 13th century to the 19th-century Impressionists. The gallery's particular strengths are in Dutch, Italian Renaissance, and 17th-century Spanish painting.

The paintings are hung in chronological order. In 1991, the modern Sainsbury Wing was added to the main Neo-Classical building (1834–8) to house the impressive Early Renaissance collection (1260–1510), though note that *The Leonardo Cartoon* (c. 1500), a chalk drawing by Leonardo da Vinci of the Virgin and Child, St. Anne, and John the Baptist, is in a more prominent position near the Trafalgar Square entrance. Other Italian painters represented include Masaccio, Piero della Francesca, and Botticelli. Perhaps the most famous of the Northern European works is *The Arnolfini Marriage* by Jan van Eyck (1434).

Most of the gallery's other exhibits are housed on the second floor of the main building. Particularly notable among the 16th-century paintings is *The Adoration of the Kings* (1564) by Flemish artist Pieter Brueghel the Elder. *Christ Mocked* (1490–1500) by Hieronymus Bosch is included in the Netherlandish and

German section, while the superb Dutch collection gives two rooms to Rembrandt. Caravaggio and Annibale Carracci and are strongly represented among the Italian painters. Spanish artist Diego Velázquez's only surviving female nude, *The Rokeby Venus* (1647–51), is one of the most popular and well-known of the 17th-century works of art. The great age of 19th-century landscape painting is perhaps best represented by Constable's masterful *The Hay Wain* (1821).

In the Impressionist section, Renoir's *Boating on the Seine* (1879–80) demonstrates the free, flickering touch used by the movement's artists to capture the fleeting moment. Other 19th-century highlights include Van Gogh's *Sunflowers*, Monet's *Waterlilies*, Rousseau's *Tropical Storm with Tiger*, and Seurat's *Bathers at Asnières*.

Lesser paintings of all periods are on the lower floor of the main building.

↑ Visitors at the National Gallery taking the time to appreciate some of the works on display

> INSIDER TIP
> ### Get a Guide
> If you are short of time in the National Gallery, there is a free one-hour guided tour that runs twice daily, at 11:30am and 2:30pm. It takes in the most iconic works.

⑦
Trafalgar Square

🏛 WC2 ⊖ Charing Cross
🚌 3, 6, 9, 11, 12, 13, 15, 23, 24, 29, 53, 88, 91, 139, 159, 176, 453

London's main venue for rallies and outdoor public meetings, Trafalgar Square was conceived by John Nash and mostly constructed during the 1830s. The 165-ft- (50-m-) tall column commemorates Admiral Lord Nelson, Britain's most famous seafarer, and dates from 1842. Edwin Landseer's four lions were added 25 years later.

Three surrounding plinths support statues of the great and the good; funds ran out before the fourth plinth, on the northwest corner, could be filled. It now hosts one of London's most idiosyncratic art displays, as artworks are commissioned specially for it and change every year or so.

The north side of the square is taken up by the National Gallery (p99), with Canada House on the west side and South Africa House on the east. In the northeast corner stands St. Martin-in-the-Fields, an 18th-century church by James Gibbs that became a model for the Colonial style of church-building in the US.

Adjoining the National Gallery, the **National Portrait Gallery** chronicles Britain's history through portraits, photographs, and sculptures. Subjects range from Elizabeth I to photographs of politicians, actors, and rock stars.

Farther north, Leicester Square is at the heart of the West End's entertainment district, with the city's leading cinemas and lively nightclubs, while London's Chinatown attracts a steady throng of diners and shoppers. It is bordered by Shaftesbury Avenue, the main artery of London's theaterland.

 INSIDER TIP
Lunchtime Learning

The National Portrait Gallery's Lunchtime Lectures (£3 online or in person) take place on Thursdays, are delivered by staff or by visiting speakers, and last about an hour.

National Portrait Gallery
🌐 ♿ 🚻 ⏱ 🏛 2 St. Martin's Place WC2 ⏰ 10am–6pm daily (to 9pm Fri) 🚫 Dec 24–26 🌐 npg.org.uk

⑧
Piccadilly

🏛 W1 ⊖ Piccadilly Circus, Green Park 🚌 9, 14, 19, 22, 3

The thoroughfare called Piccadilly links Hyde Park Corner with Piccadilly Circus,

The view looking across Trafalgar Square toward St. Martin-in-the-Fields

but the name also refers to the surrounding area. Today, Piccadilly has two contrasting faces: a bustling commercial district of shopping arcades, eateries, and cinemas; and St. James's, to the south, which is focused on a wealthier, more glamorous clientele.

Piccadilly Circus, with its dazzling neon lights, is a focal point of the West End. It began as an early 19th-century crossroads between Piccadilly and John Nash's Regent Street. Crowds congregate beneath the delicately poised figure of Eros, the Greek god of love, erected in 1892.

Among the many notable sights along Piccadilly, the **Royal Academy**, founded in 1768, houses a permanent art collection, including a Michelangelo relief of the *Madonna and Child* (1505). Its annual summer exhibition is renowned for its clever juxtaposition of new and established works.

The tranquil St. James's Church was designed by Sir Christopher Wren in 1684, and the 18th-century **Spencer House** contains fine period furniture and paintings. This Palladian palace was built for an ancestor of Princess Diana.

Shopping in and around Piccadilly is very expensive, especially in Bond Street, where many famous designer labels have stores, and in the Burlington Arcade. On Piccadilly itself, Fortnum & Mason *(p105)*, founded in 1707, is one of London's most prestigious food stores, while the grand Ritz hotel is a popular afternoon-tea venue for the suitably dressed *(p111)*. Jermyn Street is renowned for high-quality men's clothing.

South of Piccadilly is St. James's Square, which has long been the most desirable address in London. Pall Mall, named after the 17th-century game of *palle-maille* (a cross between croquet and golf) once played here, is lined with private gentlemen's clubs. It leads to the 16th-century St. James's Palace, built for Henry VIII.

Royal Academy

⊘ ⊘ ⊟ ⊕ 🏛 Burlington House, Piccadilly W1
🕐 10am–6pm daily (to 10pm Fri) 🚫 Good Fri, Dec 24–26
🌐 royalacademy.org.uk

Spencer House

⊘ ⊘ 🏛 27 St. James's Pl SW1
🕐 10am–4:30pm Sun 🚫 Aug
🌐 spencerhouse.co.uk

THE HEART OF SOHO

Adjoining Piccadilly is the district of Soho, centered around Old Compton Street, which is full of restaurants, bars, clubs, and shops. Home for centuries to poets, writers, and musicians, it's now an LGBT+ hub, with the Admiral Duncan pub one of the most popular spots. Head down Frith Street for iconic jazz club Ronnie Scott's and Bar Italia; above the latter, John Logie Baird first demonstrated TV in 1926.

The bustling evening crowds passing through
↓ Piccadilly Circus

(9) 🏍 🍴 🖥 🛍

BRITISH MUSEUM

🏠 Great Russell St WC1 ⊖ Tottenham Court Rd, Holborn, Russell Square
🚌 7, 8, 10, 14, 19, 24, 25, 29, 30, 38, 55, 68, 134, 188 ⏰ 10am–5:30pm daily
(to 8:30pm Fri) 🚫 Jan 1, Dec 24–26 🌐 thebritishmuseum.org

The British Museum holds one of the world's greatest collections of
historical and cultural artifacts. This immense hoard of treasure comprises
more than 8 million objects spanning the entire history of mankind, from
prehistoric times to the present day.

↑ The Enlightenment Gallery, formerly
the library of King George III

The oldest public museum in the world, the
British Museum was established in 1753 to
house the books, antiquities, and plant and
animal specimens of the physician Sir Hans
Sloane. The collection expanded rapidly, and
during the 19th century the museum acquired
a mass of Classical and Middle Eastern antiquities, some of which still make up the top
attractions here, such as the Rosetta Stone
and the Parthenon sculptures (p450). Robert
Smirke designed the main part of the building
(1823–50), but the architectural highlight is the
modern Great Court, with its remarkable roof.
The 94 galleries house items drawn from a dizzying range of cultures and civilizations, from
Stone Age Europe and Ancient Egypt to modern
Japan and contemporary North America. The
museum offers an excellent set of free tours –
check the website for where and when to meet

The Greek Revival-style
↓ main entrance, Great
Russell Street

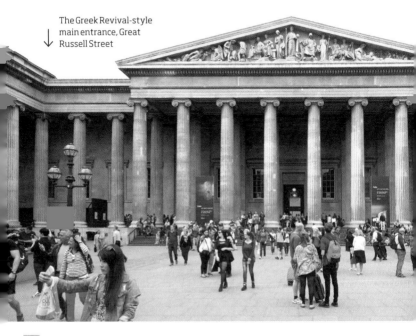

THE GREAT COURT AND THE READING ROOM

Surrounding the 19th-century Reading Room of the former British Library, the Great Court was designed by Sir Norman Foster. It is covered by a light-weight roof, creating London's first indoor public square. From the outside, the Reading Room is now scarcely recognizable as the space that was favored by the likes of Karl Marx, Mahatma Gandhi, and George Bernard Shaw.

Prehistoric and Roman Britain

▶ The most impressive items in this collection include the Mold gold cape made from a sheet of decorated gold; an antlered headdress worn by hunter-gatherers some 9,000 years ago; and "Lindow Man," a 1st-century AD sacrificial victim preserved in a bog until 1984.

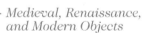

Medieval, Renaissance, and Modern Objects

The spectacular Sutton Hoo ship treasure, the burial hoard of a 7th-century Anglo-Saxon king, is in Room 41. The artifacts include a helmet and shield, Celtic bowls, and gold and garnet jewelry. Adjacent galleries contain a collection of clocks and watches. Exquisite time-pieces include a 400-year-old clock from Prague, designed as a model galleon; in its day, it pitched, played music, and even fired a cannon. The museum's modern includes Wedgwood pottery, glassware, and a series of Russian revolutionary plates.

Middle East

The Middle Eastern collections cover 7,000 years of history, with such items as the 7th-century BC Assyrian reliefs from King Ashurbanipal's palace at Nineveh, two large human-headed bulls from 7th-century BC Khorsabad, and the Black Obelisk of Assyrian King Shalmaneser III. Rooms 51–59, on the upper floor, contain pieces from ancient Sumeria and part of the Oxus Treasure (which lay buried for over 2,000 years).

Ancient Egypt

Egyptian sculptures in Room 4 include a colossal statue of King Ramses II. Also on show is the Rosetta Stone, used by Jean-François Champollion as a primer for deciphering hieroglyphs. An extraordinary array of mummies, jewelry, and Coptic art is in Rooms 61–66 upstairs, including a famous bronze cat with a gold nose ring.

Greece and Rome

◀ The Greek and Roman collections include the controversial Elgin Marbles. These 5th-century BC reliefs once decorated the Parthenon at the Acropolis in Athens. Other highlights include the Nereid Monument, and sculptures and friezes from the Mausoleum at Halicarnassus. The beautiful 1st-century BC cameo-glass Portland Vase is located in the Roman Empire section.

Oriental Art

Fine porcelain and Shang bronzes (c. 1500–1050 BC) are highlights of the Chinese collection. Particularly impressive are the ceremonial ancient Chinese bronze vessels, with their animal-head shapes. The collection of Asian religious sculpture includes sculpted reliefs that recount stories from the life of the Buddha. A Korean section contains some gigantic works of Buddhist art. Islamic art, including a jade terrapin found in a water tank, is in Room 34.

Africa

An interesting collection of African sculptures, textiles, and graphic art can be found in Room 25, located in the basement. Famous bronzes from the Kingdom of Benin stand alongside modern African prints, paintings, and drawings, plus an array of colorful fabrics.

⑩ Covent Garden

 WC2 🚇 Covent Garden
🚌 1, 6, 9, 13, 15, 23, 59, 68, 87, 91, 168, 171, 176

Buzzing open-air cafés, street entertainers, stylish shops, and markets make Covent Garden a magnet for visitors.

At its center is the Piazza, designed by 17th-century architect Inigo Jones as an elegant residential square, after an example from the Tuscan town of Livorno. For a time, houses around the Piazza were highly sought-after, but decline accelerated when a fruit and vegetable market developed. In 1973, the market moved to a new site and Covent Garden was revamped. Today, only St. Paul's Church remains of Inigo Jones's buildings.

📷 PICTURE PERFECT
Neal's Yard

A riot of rainbow-colored walls, window frames, and flower baskets, Neal's Yard - secreted in the triangle between Monmouth Street, Neal Street, and Shorts Gardens - is the perfect spot to brighten any set of photographs.

In the corner of the Piazza is the Royal Opera House – designed in 1858 by E. M. Barry, but totally renovated in 1997–9 – which is home to the Royal Opera and Royal Ballet companies. Many of the world's greatest dance performers have graced its stage.

The site of the Theatre Royal, completed in 1812, has been occupied by a theater since 1663. St. Martin's Theatre is home to the world's longest-running play, *The Mousetrap*.

Other attractions include the **London Transport Museum**, the shops around Neal Street, and the Seven Dials food market.

London Transport Museum

 🄰 Covent Garden WC2 🕙 10am-6pm daily 🚫 Dec 24-26 🌐 ltmuseum.co.uk

---

⑪ Madame Tussauds

🄰 Marylebone Rd NW1 🚇 Baker St 🕙 From 9am daily; closing times vary 🚫 Dec 24 (pm) & Dec 25 🌐 madametussauds.co.uk

Madame Tussaud began her wax-modeling career making death masks of victims of the French Revolution. In 1835,

after moving to England, she set up an exhibition of her work in Baker Street, near the museum's present site.

Traditional techniques are still used to create the figures of royalty, politicians, actors, pop stars, and sports heroes.

In the Chamber of Horrors, some of the original French Revolution death masks are displayed, while the Party area features film stars, royals, and figures from the world of pop music. There is also a *Star Wars* exhibit where iconic scenes from the movie series have been recreated.

In the final section – the Spirit of London – visitors travel in stylized taxi-cabs and participate in momentous events in the city's history, from the Great Fire of 1666 to the Swinging Sixties.

←
People strolling and snacking under the airy roof of Covent Garden's Apple Market

12

Regent's Park

NW1 Regent's Park, Great Portland St, Camden Town From 5am daily; closing times vary royalparks.org.uk

This area of land was enclosed as a park in 1812. Designer John Nash originally envisaged a kind of garden suburb, with 56 villas in Classical styles, but only eight were built (three of which have survived).

The boating lake has many varieties of water birds and is marvellously romantic. Queen Mary's Gardens are a mass of wonderful sights and smells in summer, when visitors can also enjoy performances at the Open Air Theatre nearby.

London Zoo, with its imaginative animal enclosures, borders the park, and is an important center of research and conservation work.

London Zoo
From 10am daily; closing times vary Dec 25 zsl.org/zsl-london-zoo

13

Hyde Park

W2 Hyde Park Corner, Knightsbridge, Lancaster Gate, Marble Arch Dawn-midnight daily royalparks.org.uk

The ancient manor of Hyde was part of the lands of Westminster Abbey seized by Henry VIII at the Dissolution of the Monasteries in 1536. James I opened the park to the public in the early 17th century, and it was soon one of the city's most fashionable public spaces. Consequently, it also became popular with duelists and highwaymen, prompting William III to have 300 lights hung along Rotten Row, making it the first street in England to be lit at night.

In 1730, the Westbourne River was dammed by Queen Caroline to create an artificial lake – the Serpentine. Today, cafés, restaurants, and the Serpentine Gallery of modern art dot the fringes of the lake, which is popular for boating and swimming.

At the southeast corner of the park stands Apsley House, the grand former home of the Duke of Wellington. Now a museum of memorabilia to the great politician and soldier, it features lavish interiors adorned with silk hangings and gilt decoration.

Ever since a law passed in 1872 made it legal to assemble an audience and address it on whatever topic you choose, Speaker's Corner, at the northeast corner of the park, has been the established venue for budding orators. Crowds gather on Sundays to listen to lively speeches.

Adjoining Hyde Park are Kensington Gardens, the former grounds of Kensington Palace, which were opened to the public in 1841. A royal residence for centuries, the palace was Princess Diana's home until her untimely death.

Attractions in the gardens include the bronze statue of J. M. Barrie's fictional Peter Pan (1912), by George Frampton, and the Round Pond where model boats are sailed.

In Hyde Park, the Serpentine lake and *(inset)* Isis sculpture ↓

SHOP

Fortnum & Mason
Fine foods and opulent sales floors are the hallmarks of Fortnum & Mason. Established in 1707, this is one of the city's most renowned and extravagant stores.

181 Piccadilly W1
fortnumandmason.com

Harrods
Once said to be able to supply anything, from a packet of pins to an elephant; it's not quite true today, but Harrods remains as grand as ever.

87-135 Brompton Rd, Knightsbridge SW1
harrods.com

STAY

Artist Residence

Every room is unique in this original boutique hotel with a first-rate bar and restaurant.

🏠 52 Cambridge St SW1
🌐 artistresidence.co.uk

£££

Claridge's

Join celebs and royalty, and stay in one of over 200 luxurious rooms at this historic hotel in an Art Deco building. This London classic has been in business since 1812.

🏠 49 Brook Street W1
🌐 claridges.co.uk

£££

Barclay House

The three luxurious rooms at this classy B&B in an exquisite Victorian property have underfloor heating and rainforest showers.

🏠 21 Barclay Rd SW6
🌐 barclayhouselondon.com

£££

Lime Tree Hotel

Very comfortable, individually decorated rooms make this large boutique hotel a cut above the rest.

🏠 135 Ebury St SW1
🌐 limetreehotel.co.uk

£££

The Main House

A chic guest house with suites combining modern luxuries and antique furniture.

🏠 6 Colville Road W11
🌐 themainhouse.co.uk

£££

Science Museum

🏠 Exhibition Rd SW7
🚇 South Kensington
🚌 C1, 14, 49, 70, 74, 345, 360, 414, 430 ⏰ 10am–6pm daily ⛔ Dec 24–26
🌐 sciencemuseum.org.uk

Centuries of scientific and technological development are illustrated at the Science Museum, which aims to bring entertainment to the process of learning, with interactive displays for children and staff on hand to provide explanations. Of equal importance is the social context of science: how inventions have transformed day-to-day life, and the process of discovery itself.

One of the most popular displays is "Flight," which gives visitors the opportunity to experiment with aeronautical concepts. "Exploring Space" exhibits the scarred Apollo 10 spacecraft which carried three astronauts to the moon and back in May 1969.

The "Making the Modern World" gallery displays objects that have shaped the world as we know it. Among them are Stephenson's *Rocket*, the most advanced steam locomotive of its day, and Crick and Watson's DNA model.

"Power and Land Transport," which displays working steam engines, vintage trains, cars, and motorbikes, is another popular section. "The Secret Life of the Home" explores how science and technology have changed everyday objects over time.

The Wellcome Wing is devoted to contemporary science and technology; the Wellcome Trust also helped fund the Medicine Galleries, which explore over 400 years of medical history. "Tomorrow's World" is a constantly updated exhibition devoted to the latest scientific breakthroughs. Our understanding of human identity is the subject of "Who Am I?," where visitors can learn about genetics and current biomedical discoveries. The wing also contains an IMAX® cinema and a 4D motion-effects theater.

Victoria and Albert Museum

🏠 Cromwell Rd SW7
🚇 South Kensington
🚌 C1, 14, 74 ⏰ 10am–5:45pm daily (to 10pm Fri) ⛔ Dec 24–26 🌐 vam.ac.uk

Originally founded in 1852 as a Museum of Manufacturing – to inspire and raise standards among students of design – the V&A, as it is popularly known, was renamed by

Queen Victoria in 1899, in memory of her late husband. It contains one of the world's richest collections of fine and applied arts.

Housed in a building designed by Sir Aston Webb, the museum has undergone a dramatic restructuring of much of its collection and gallery spaces, alongside a grand development of the central John Madejski Garden.

Donatello's marble relief of *The Ascension* is included in the Sculpture collection, along with sculptures from India, the Middle East, and Asia. Craftsmanship in porcelain, glass, and pottery is displayed on levels 4 and 6, with rare pieces by Picasso and Bernard Leach, intricate Middle Eastern tiles, and a wide selection of Chinese pieces.

The most celebrated item in the vast array of furniture is the *Great Bed of Ware*, made

↑ Large-scale medieval and Renaissance works at the Victoria and Albert Museum

around 1590. The Victorian designers who decorated the plush Morris, Gamble, and Poynter Rooms recreated historic styles with newer industrial materials. The fully furnished interiors offer a vivid picture of social life through their displays of furniture and other domestic objects.

The V&A has a wide collection of metalwork, including a 16th-century salt cellar, the *Burghley Nef*. The Silver Gallery explores the history and techniques of silver making.

Gallery III is devoted to the making of sculpture, ranging from medieval ivories to modern bronzes. The South Asia Gallery includes the automated *Tippoo's Tiger* (c. 1790), which mauls a European soldier when activated. Eight galleries devoted to the arts of East Asia display rare jade and ceramics, a giant Buddha's head from AD 700–900, and a Ming canopied bed. Among exhibits in the China Gallery is a watercolor on silk from the Qing Dynasty (1644–1912). The Toshiba Gallery focuses on Japanese art, including Samurai armor and woodblock prints.

The world-renowned Fashion Court on level 1 spans more than four centuries, from the mid-1500s to the present day, and is the world's most comprehensive collection of clothing. Highlights include rare 17th-century gowns, 1930s eveningwear, and postwar couture, plus several key items from contemporary designers.

The museum also houses valuable illustrated documents in the National Art Library and the Photographs Gallery.

← Children having fun with the hands-on exhibits at the Science Museum

The blue whale skeleton in the Natural History Museum's vast entrance hall

Natural History Museum

🏛 Cromwell Rd SW7
🚇 South Kensington
🚌 C1, 14, 49, 70, 74, 345, 360, 414, 430 ⏰ 10am–5:50pm daily 🚫 Dec 24-26
🌐 nhm.ac.uk

With its impressive sculpted stonework, this vast building designed by Alfred Waterhouse is the most flamboyant of the South Kensington museums. Inside its elegant galleries, issues such as the evolution of the planet, the origin of species, and the development of human beings are explored through a dynamic combination of interactive displays and traditional exhibits.

The museum is divided into four zones: Red, Green, Blue, and Orange (the Darwin Centre). The main entrance hall features a full-size blue whale skeleton suspended from the roof. The Ecology exhibition begins its exploration of the complex web of the natural world, and man's role in it, through a convincing replica of a rain forest. The most popular exhibits in this area are in the Dinosaur section, which has real dinosaur skeletons and life-like animatronics. "Creepy Crawlies," with specimens from the insect and spider world, and the Mammals exhibition, enable visitors to see endangered and dangerous creatures.

In the state-of-the-art Darwin Centre visitors can take an interactive journey inside a vast concrete cocoon that houses millions of specimens. Here, too, is the Attenborough Studio, which features live shows, films, and talks, many of them free.

Museum of London

🏛 150 London Wall EC2
🚇 Barbican, St Paul's
🚌 4, 8, 25, 56, 100, 172, 242, 388, 521 ⏰ 10am–6pm daily 🚫 Dec 24-26
🌐 museumoflondon.org.uk

This fascinating museum traces life in London from prehistoric times to the 20th century, across the course of nine permanent galleries.

TOP 5 **NATURAL HISTORY MUSEUM EXHIBITS**

Triceratops Skull
The gigantic skull of a plant-eating Triceratops dinosaur.

Latrobe Gold Nugget
A rare crystalized gold nugget from Australia weighing 25 oz (717 g).

Butterflies
A tropical butterfly house filled with these beautiful and colorful flying insects.

Archaeopteryx
This valuable fossil of a feathered dinosaur provided the link between birds and dinosaurs.

Earthquake Simulator
Experience the rumblings of an earthquake in this simulation.

THE BARBICAN ESTATE

Housing over 4,000 residents in its Brutalist tower and terrace blocks, this ambitious piece of postwar city planning near the Museum of London was designed by Chamberlin, Powell & Bon and built on a site devastated by World War II bombs. It is a maze of concrete sidewalks, overhead walkways, stone staircases, and looming tower blocks, but it is softened considerably by islands of green - small gardens dotted around the estate - and by an ornamental lake and fountains.

Objects from Roman London include a brightly colored 2nd-century fresco, while from the Tudor city, an example of an early English Delft plate, made in 1602 at Aldgate, bears an inscription praising Elizabeth I.

The 17th-century section contains the shirt Charles I wore at his execution, and an audio-visual display recreating the Great Fire of 1666. A dress in Spitalfields silk, dating from 1753, is among the many fine costumes on display.

One of the most popular exhibits is the lavishly gilded Lord Mayor's State Coach, built in 1757 and still used for the Lord Mayor's Show, held in November each year.

The Victorian Walk takes visitors back to the time of Charles Dickens, vividly recreating the atmosphere of 19th-century London with authentic shop interiors.

---

(18) ⬡ Ⓜ ▭ ⬡

St. Paul's Cathedral

⬡ Ludgate Hill EC4
⬡ City Thameslink
⬡ St Paul's, Mansion House
⬡ 4, 11, 15, 17, 23, 25, 76, 172 ⬡ 8:30am–4:30pm Mon–Sat; for services only Sun, Dec 25 & Good Fri
⬡ stpauls.co.uk

Rebuilt on the site of a medieval cathedral after the Great Fire of 1666, this magnificent Baroque building, designed by Sir Christopher Wren, was completed in 1710.

St. Paul's has been the setting for great ceremonial events, including the funeral of Sir Winston Churchill in 1965 and the 1981 wedding of Prince Charles and Lady Diana.

At 360 ft (110 m) high, the dome is the second largest in the world, after St. Peter's in Rome (p380). Supported by a brick cone, the lantern weighs a massive 850 tons. The dome's gallery provides a splendid view over London.

Modifications to Wren's original plan include the towers of the west front, the double colonnade of the west portico, and the balustrade – added against his wishes in 1718.

Wren created a cool and majestic interior. The nave, transepts, and choir are arranged in the traditional shape of a cross. Its climax is in the great open space of the crossing, below the main dome, which is decorated with monochrome frescoes by Sir James Thornhill, a leading architectural painter of the time. From the south aisle, 259 steps ascend to the circular Whispering Gallery (currently closed), so-called because of the unusual acoustics.

Memorials to famous figures, such as Lawrence of Arabia and Lord Nelson, can be seen in the crypt. The inscription on Wren's tomb is fitting: "Reader, if you seek a monument, look all around you."

↑ A double-decker bus traveling past St. Paul's Cathedral, Sir Christopher Wren's masterpiece

← Shakespeare's Globe, an accurate reproduction of the original theater from 1599

art, featuring paintings and sculptures by some of the most significant artists of the 20th and 21st centuries, including Pablo Picasso, Mark Rothko, and Salvador Dalí.

The focal point of the building is the awesome Turbine Hall, which is often filled by a specially commissioned work. Other exhibition spaces feature collections on a single theme or host hugely popular temporary shows. On Level 10 of the fantastic Blavatnik Building extension, the 360-degree viewing terrace gives spectacular views of London; similar panoramas can also be enjoyed from the restaurant on Level 9.

(19)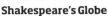

Shakespeare's Globe

214 New Globe Walk SE1
London Bridge, Cannon St, Southwark 11, 15, 17, 23, 26 & others Tours: daily, check website for times; performances: Apr-Oct Dec 24 & 25 shakespearesglobe.com

Built on the south bank of the Thames, Shakespeare's Globe is a fine reconstruction of the Elizabethan theater where many of the famous playwright's works were first performed. Seeing a play here can be a lively experience, with those with standing tickets in front of the stage encouraged to cheer or jeer.

(20)

Tate Modern

Bankside SE1
Waterloo, Southwark, Blackfriars RV1, 45, 63, 100, 381, 344 From Tate Britain 10am-6pm daily (to 10pm Fri & Sat) Dec 24-26 tate.org.uk/modern

Looming over the Thames from its south bank, this gallery in a former power station holds one of the world's premier collections of modern and contemporary art. Opened to coincide with the new millennium, it has a collection of over 70,000 works of

(21)

Tower Bridge

SE1 Tower Hill, London Bridge RV1, 15, 42, 78, 100 towerbridge.org.uk

This flamboyant piece of Victorian engineering, completed in 1894, soon became a symbol of London.

Its two Gothic towers, made of a supporting steel framework clad in stone, contain the mechanism for raising the roadway to permit large ships to pass through. When raised, the roadway creates a space 135 ft (40 m) high and 200 ft (60 m) wide. In its heyday, it was raised and lowered five times a day.

The bridge now houses the **Tower Bridge Exhibition**, with displays which bring its history to life. There are fine river views from the walkways between the towers, and the steam-engine room, which was in use until 1976, can also be visited.

Tower Bridge Exhibition

⊛ 🕒 9:30am–5:30pm daily

🚫 Dec 24–26

The Shard

🏠 London Bridge St, SE1

🚇 London Bridge 🕒 9am–10pm daily, but check in advance 🚫 Dec 25

🌐 theviewfrom theshard.com

Designed by the Italian architect Renzo

↑ The iconic Shard, a pyramid-shaped, glass-clad skyscraper

Piano, The Shard is one of the tallest buildings in Europe, at 1,016 ft (310 m). Its iconic pyramid shape dominates London's skyline, with the color of its angular walls appearing to change with the weather, thanks to the crystalline facade that reflects the sunlight and sky.

The building's 87 floors are variously home to offices, top restaurants and bars, the five-star Shangri-La hotel, and apartments. The main indoor viewing gallery is on floor 69 while floor 72 (the building's last habitable floor) has a partially outdoor observation deck, with unbeatable 360-degree panoramas covering 40 miles (64 km).

EAT

Skylon

A refined restaurant overlooking the river.

🏠 Southbank Centre

🌐 skylonrestaurant. co.uk

€€€

Afternoon Tea at The Ritz

Enjoy sandwiches, scones, cakes, and tea accompanied by a pianist and harpist. No trainers or jeans.

🏠 4150 Piccadilly W1

🌐 theritzlondon.com

€€€

XU

XU recreates the look of a 1930s Taipei social club. The food is a fusion of Taiwanese and Cantonese cuisines.

🏠 30 Rupert St W1

🌐 xulondon.com

€€€

Barrafina

An ultracool Spanish joint with industrial modern decor.

🏠 Dean St W1

🌐 barrafina.co.uk

€€€

Southbank Centre Food Market

Street eats, from pizza to Korean BBQ.

🏠 Rear of the Royal Festival Hall 🕒 Fri–Sun

€€€

←

Tower Bridge, an enduring symbol of London spanning the River Thames

23

TOWER OF LONDON

Tower Hill EC3 · Tower Hill, DLR Tower Gateway · 15, 42, 78, 100 · Tower Pier · 9am-5:30pm Tue-Sat; 10am-5:30pm Sun & Mon (Nov-Feb: to 4:30pm) · hrp.org.uk

Founded in 1066 by William the Conqueror, the Tower of London has served as a former fortress, palace, and prison. Visitors flock here to see the Crown Jewels and hear tales of its dark and intriguing history.

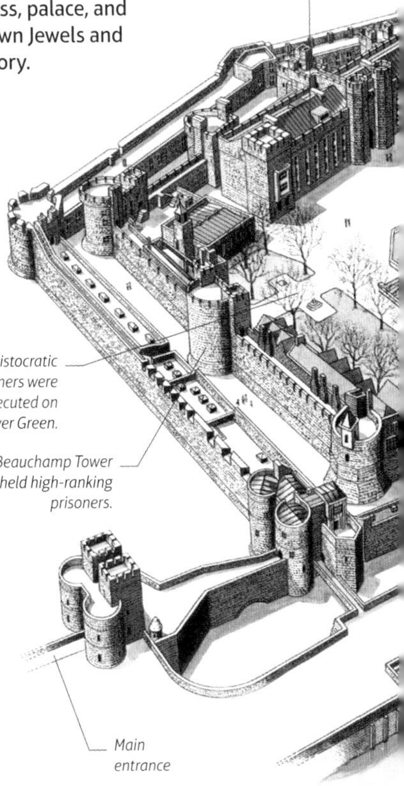
The Crown Jewels are kept in the Jewel House.
Aristocratic prisoners were executed on Tower Green.
Beauchamp Tower held high-ranking prisoners.
Main entrance

The Tower has attracted tourists since the reign of Charles II (1660–85), when both the Crown Jewels and the Line of Kings collection of armor were first shown to the public. The area within the mighty walls houses the remaining parts of the medieval palace built by Henry III, as well as several towers that held prisoners, including Anne Boleyn and Thomas Cromwell. For much of its 900-year history, the Tower was somewhere to be feared. Those who had committed treason or threatened the throne were held within its dank walls – many did not get out alive. High-ranking prisoners could live in some comfort with servants, but the rest suffered hardship and torture before meeting violent deaths on nearby Tower Hill.

The Princes in the Tower

One of the Tower's darkest mysteries concerns two boy princes, sons and heirs of Edward IV. They were put here by their uncle, Richard of Gloucester, when their father died in 1483. Neither was seen again and Richard was crowned later that year. In 1674, the skeletons of two children were found nearby.

INSIDER TIP
Tour with a Beefeater

Join a Yeoman Warder, or Beefeater, on a tour of the Tower. A lively retelling of tales of executions, plots, and prisoners, this is an entertaining way to explore the Tower's history. Tours are included in the admission fee and set off every 30 minutes from near the main entrance, lasting for an hour.

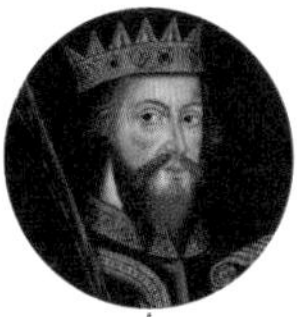

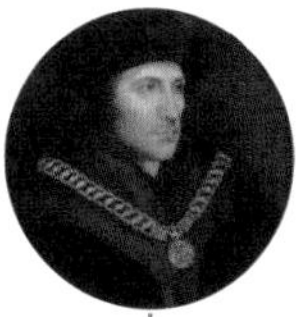

Timeline

1066
▲ William I erects a temporary castle

1534–5
▲ Thomas More imprisoned and executed

The White Tower displays armor worn by Tudor and Stuart kings.

The imposing Norman Tower of London, the setting for key historical events ↑

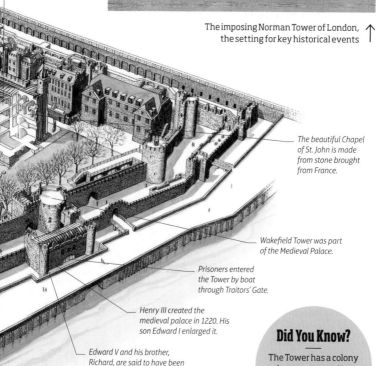

The beautiful Chapel of St. John is made from stone brought from France.

Wakefield Tower was part of the Medieval Palace.

Prisoners entered the Tower by boat through Traitors' Gate.

Henry III created the medieval palace in 1220. His son Edward I enlarged it.

Edward V and his brother, Richard, are said to have been murdered in the Bloody Tower.

↑ The walls enclose towers, residences, and open areas

Did You Know?

The Tower has a colony of ravens. Legend has it that if they leave the complex, the kingdom will fall.

1553–4
△ Lady Jane Grey held and executed

1603–16
△ Walter Raleigh imprisoned in Tower

1671
△ "Colonel Blood" tries to steal Crown Jewels

1941
△ Prominent Nazi Rudolf Hess held in Queen's House

A SHORT WALK
WHITEHALL AND WESTMINSTER

Distance 1.25 miles (2 km) **Nearest tube**
Westminster **Time** 30 minutes

Westminster has been at the center of political and religious power in England since the 11th century, when King Canute built a palace here and Edward the Confessor founded Westminster Abbey. Whitehall is synonymous with the ministries concentrated around it. On weekdays, the streets are crowded with civil servants going about their business, replaced at weekends by a steady flow of tourists.

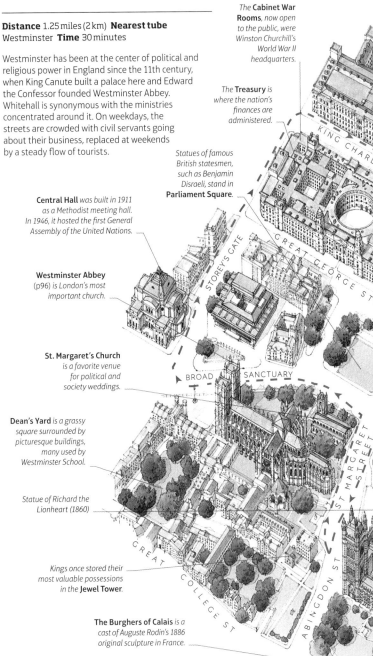

The **Cabinet War Rooms**, now open to the public, were Winston Churchill's World War II headquarters.

The **Treasury** is where the nation's finances are administered.

Statues of famous British statesmen, such as Benjamin Disraeli, stand in **Parliament Square**.

Central Hall was built in 1911 as a Methodist meeting hall. In 1946, it hosted the first General Assembly of the United Nations.

Westminster Abbey (p96) is London's most important church.

St. Margaret's Church is a favorite venue for political and society weddings.

Dean's Yard is a grassy square surrounded by picturesque buildings, many used by Westminster School.

Statue of Richard the Lionheart (1860)

Kings once stored their most valuable possessions in the **Jewel Tower**.

The Burghers of Calais is a cast of Auguste Rodin's 1886 original sculpture in France.

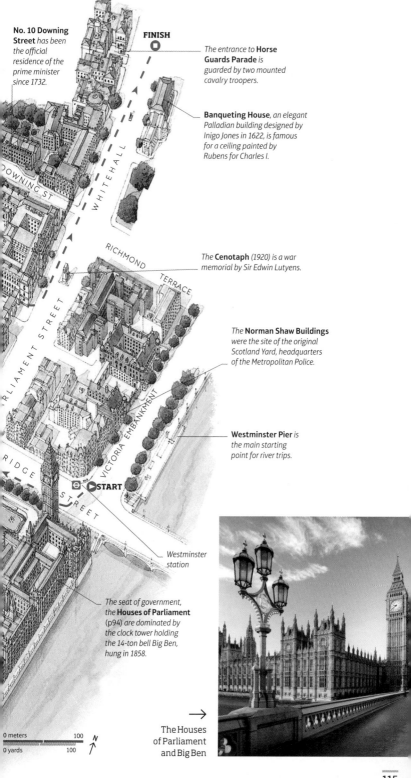

No. 10 Downing Street *has been the official residence of the prime minister since 1732.*

FINISH

The entrance to **Horse Guards Parade** *is guarded by two mounted cavalry troopers.*

Banqueting House, *an elegant Palladian building designed by Inigo Jones in 1622, is famous for a ceiling painted by Rubens for Charles I.*

DOWNING ST

WHITEHALL

RICHMOND TERRACE

The **Cenotaph** *(1920) is a war memorial by Sir Edwin Lutyens.*

PARLIAMENT STREET

The **Norman Shaw Buildings** *were the site of the original Scotland Yard, headquarters of the Metropolitan Police.*

VICTORIA EMBANKMENT

Westminster Pier *is the main starting point for river trips.*

BRIDGE STREET

START

Westminster station

The seat of government, the **Houses of Parliament** *(p94) are dominated by the clock tower holding the 14-ton bell Big Ben, hung in 1858.*

0 meters 100
0 yards 100

N

→ The Houses of Parliament and Big Ben

A SHORT WALK

SOUTH KENSINGTON

Distance 1.5 miles (2 km) **Nearest tube** South Kensington **Time** 30 minutes

The numerous museums and colleges created in the wake of the Great Exhibition of 1851 continue to give this neighborhood its dignified character. Visited as much by Londoners as tourists, the museum area is liveliest at the weekend and on summer evenings during the Royal Albert Hall's famous season of classical "Prom" concerts.

David Hockney and Peter Blake are among the great artists who trained at the **Royal College of Art.**

The former **Royal College of Organists** *was decorated by F. W. Moody in 1876.*

The **Royal Albert Hall**, *opened in 1871, hosts a range of concerts and events.*

The **Royal College of Music**, *founded in 1882, exhibits historic musical instruments from around the world.*

Did You Know?

The Royal Albert Hall was partly funded by selling seats on a 999-year lease.

The **Natural History Museum**'s *facade is decorated with a menagerie of sculptures (p108).*

The **Science Museum** *houses a range of exhibits celebrating the history of science and technology (p106).*

PRINCE

IMPERIAL COLLEGE ROAD

CROMWELL ROAD

EXHI

CROM

START

| 0 meters | 100 |
| 0 yards | 100 |

N

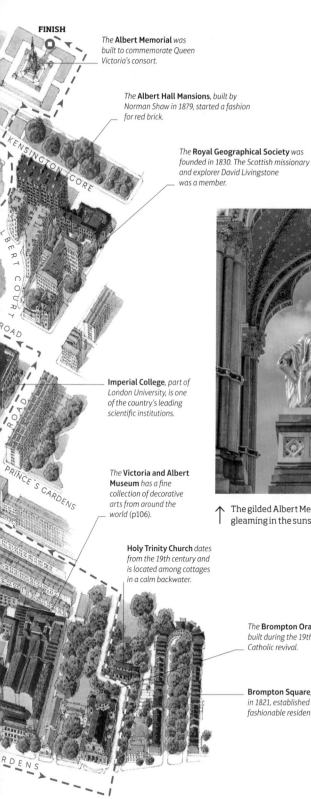

FINISH

The **Albert Memorial** was built to commemorate Queen Victoria's consort.

The **Albert Hall Mansions**, built by Norman Shaw in 1879, started a fashion for red brick.

The **Royal Geographical Society** was founded in 1830. The Scottish missionary and explorer David Livingstone was a member.

KENSINGTON GORE

ALBERT COURT

ROAD

ROAD

PRINCE'S GARDENS

Imperial College, part of London University, is one of the country's leading scientific institutions.

The **Victoria and Albert Museum** has a fine collection of decorative arts from around the world (p106).

Holy Trinity Church dates from the 19th century and is located among cottages in a calm backwater.

R D E N S

↑ The gilded Albert Memorial gleaming in the sunshine

The **Brompton Oratory** was built during the 19th-century Catholic revival.

Brompton Square, begun in 1821, established this as a fashionable residential area.

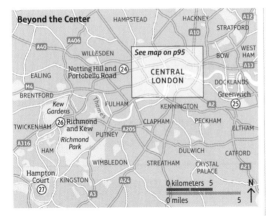

Beyond the Center

See map on p95

CENTRAL LONDON

LONDON: BEYOND THE CENTER

㉔
Notting Hill and Portobello Road

W11 ☐ Notting Hill Gate, Ladbroke Grove

Notting Hill and Portobello Road have been a focus for the Caribbean community since the peak years of immigration in the 1950s and 1960s. Today, this is a trendy and upscale residential district, whose vibrant cosmopolitan spirit was celebrated in the 1999 film starring Julia Roberts and Hugh Grant.

Bustling Portobello Road market has hundreds of stands and shops selling a variety of collectables. The southern end consists almost

---

INSIDER TIP
Notting Hill Carnival

Notting Hill's West Indian flavor is best experienced during this street carnival, Europe's largest. First held in 1966, it takes over the entire area on the August bank holiday weekend, with music and costumed parades.

---

exclusively of stands selling antiques, jewelry, and souvenirs popular with tourists.

㉕
Greenwich

☐ SE10 ☐ Greenwich, Maze Hill, & DLR to Cutty Sark, Greenwich ☐ From Westminster

Best known as the place from which the world's time is measured, Greenwich is steeped in maritime history. The meridian line that divides the earth's eastern and western hemispheres passes through the **Royal Observatory Greenwich**. Designed in the 17th century by Christopher Wren, the building is topped by a ball on a rod, dropped at 1pm every day since 1833 so that ships' chronometers could be set by it. Today, the observatory houses a museum and a planetarium.

The exquisite **Queen's House** at the bottom of the park has been restored to its late-17th-century glory; highlights are the unusually shaped main hall and the spiral "tulip staircase." The adjoining **National Maritime Museum** has exhibits ranging

from Fijian open-ocean canoes through Elizabethan galleons to modern ships. Nearby, the Old Royal Naval College was designed in two halves so the Queen's House could retain its river view. Now home to a univerisity, its chapel and Painted Hall are open to the public. A little farther along the river is the Cutty Sark, the last surviving 19th-century clipper ship.

Royal Observatory Greenwich

☐ Blackheath Ave ☐ 10am-5:30pm daily ☐ Dec 24-26 ☐ rmg.co.uk/royal-observatory

Queen's House and National Maritime Museum

☐ Romney Rd SE10 ☐ 10am-5pm daily ☐ Dec 24-26 ☐ nmm.ac.uk

㉖
Richmond and Kew

☐ SW15 ☐ Kew Gardens, Richmond ☐ To Kew Bridge, Richmond

The attractive village of Richmond took its name from a palace built in 1500 by Henry VII (formerly the Earl of Richmond), the remains of which can be seen off the green. The vast Richmond

The imposing architecture of Hampton Court, seen from the Baroque Privy Garden

Park was once Charles I's royal hunting ground and is today a national nature reserve.

Nearby **Ham House**, built in 1610 for Sir Thomas Vavasour (Knight Marshal to James I), had its heyday later in the 17th century when the aristocratic Lauderdale family moved in. The house was extended and refurbished as a palatial villa, reflecting the Duke of Lauderdale's status as one of Charles II's most powerful ministers. Much of this luxurious interior decor remains. On the opposite side of the Thames stands Marble Hill House, a Palladian villa completed in 1729 for the mistress of George II.

Just north of here is **Kew Gardens**, the most complete botanic gardens in the world. The lush grounds are meticulously maintained, with examples of nearly every plant that can be grown in Britain. Highlights include the Palm House – a jewel of Victorian engineering, housing thousands of exotic tropical blooms – and the delicate plants of the vast Temperate House. The gardens became a UNESCO World Heritage Site in 2003.

Ham House

♨ ⊕ 🖥 🛍 🚇 Ham St, Ham 🚌 65, 371 🕐 Daily; check website for hours 🅧 Dec 24 & 25 🌐 nationaltrust.org

Kew Gardens

♨ 🍴 🖥 🛍 🚇 Kew 🚉 Kew Gardens 🚌 65, 237, 267, 391 🕐 From 10am daily (closing times vary) 🅧 Dec 24 & 25 🌐 kew.org

27 ♨ 🅟 🖥 🛍

Hampton Court

🚇 East Molesey, Surrey 🚉🚌 Hampton Court 🚌 R68, 111, 216, 411, 461, 513 🕐 10am–6pm daily (to 4:30pm in winter) 🅧 Dec 24–26 🌐 hrp.org.uk

Cardinal Wolsey, chief minister to Henry VIII, began building Hampton Court in 1514. A few years later, in the hope of retaining royal favor, he gave it to the king. The palace was extended by Henry, and again at the end of the 17th century by William III and Mary II, with the help of Christopher Wren.

From the outside, the palace is a harmonious blend of Tudor and English Baroque. A remarkable feature is the Astronomical Clock, created for Henry VIII in 1540.

Inside, Wren's Classical royal rooms, such as the King's Apartments, contrast with Tudor architecture, such as the Great Hall. The stained-glass window here shows Henry VIII flanked by the coats of arms of his six wives. Superb woodwork in the Chapel Royal dates from a major refurbishment by Queen Anne (c. 1711). Many of the State Apartments feature furniture, paintings, and tapestries from the Royal Collection. Nine canvases depicting the *Triumph of Julius Caesar* (1490) are housed in the Mantegna Gallery.

The restored Baroque privy garden, originally created for William and Mary, features radiating avenues of majestic limes and formal flowerbeds. The Fountain Garden still has a few yews planted during their reign. Other attractions are the maze and the Great Vine, planted in 1768.

2 ⚡ 🏛 📺 🛍

WINDSOR CASTLE

🏰 Castle Hill 🚉 Windsor & Eton Central, Windsor & Eton Riverside
🕐 Mar–Oct: 9:45am–5:15pm daily; Nov–Feb: 10am–4:15pm daily 🌐 rct.uk

Used for state visits and as a weekend retreat by the Queen, Windsor Castle is the oldest and largest continuously occupied castle in the world. Discover almost 1,000 years of royal history as you explore its impressive towers and battlements.

William the Conqueror established a castle here in the 11th century as the site was on high ground and just a day's journey from his base in the Tower of London. Successive monarchs made alterations to the structure, rendering it a remarkable monument to royalty's changing tastes. Henry II and Edward III were responsible for the bulk of the work until the castle was remodelled by George IV in 1823. George V's affection for it was shown when he chose Windsor for his family surname in 1917.

Pick up an audio guide – the commentary takes you through the highlights of the State Apartments and St. George's Chapel.

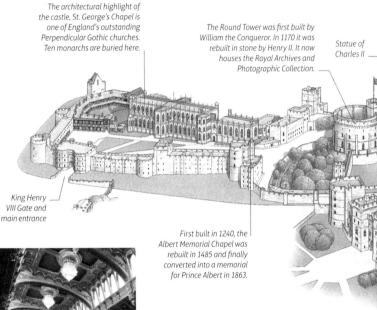

The architectural highlight of the castle, St. George's Chapel is one of England's outstanding Perpendicular Gothic churches. Ten monarchs are buried here.

The Round Tower was first built by William the Conqueror. In 1170 it was rebuilt in stone by Henry II. It now houses the Royal Archives and Photographic Collection.

Statue of Charles II

King Henry VIII Gate and main entrance

First built in 1240, the Albert Memorial Chapel was rebuilt in 1485 and finally converted into a memorial for Prince Albert in 1863.

↑ The banqueting hall in the Waterloo Chamber, adorned in red and gold

WHAT ELSE TO SEE IN WINDSOR

Developed to serve the needs of the enormous castle on the hill above, the town of Windsor is full of quaint Georgian shops, houses, and inns. The most prominent building is the Guildhall, where Prince Charles and Camilla Parker-Bowles were married in 2005. Eton College, one of the most prestigious schools in Britain, lies just a short walk away. Windsor Great Park stretches from the castle 3 miles (5 km) to Snow Hill. Four miles (7 km) to the southeast is the meadow of Runnymede, where King John was forced to sign the Magna Carta in 1215.

INSIDER TIP
Changing the Guard

Time your visit to see the Changing the Guard spectacle. Led by a regimental band, the guards march from the barracks through the town to the Guard Room at the castle. Check the website for timings.

→
The long approach to the castle entrance, framed by manicured lawns

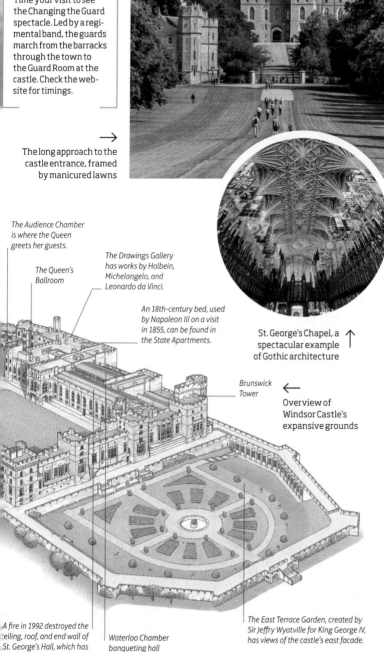

The Audience Chamber is where the Queen greets her guests.

The Queen's Ballroom

The Drawings Gallery has works by Holbein, Michelangelo, and Leonardo da Vinci.

An 18th-century bed, used by Napoleon III on a visit in 1855, can be found in the State Apartments.

St. George's Chapel, a ↑ spectacular example of Gothic architecture

Brunswick Tower ←

Overview of Windsor Castle's expansive grounds

A fire in 1992 destroyed the ceiling, roof, and end wall of St. George's Hall, which has since been rebuilt.

Waterloo Chamber banqueting hall was created in 1823.

The East Terrace Garden, created by Sir Jeffry Wyatville for King George IV, has views of the castle's east facade.

3
Canterbury

⌂ Kent 🚆🚌 𝒊 The Beaney House of Art & Knowledge, 18 High Street; www.canterbury.co.uk

Canterbury was an important Roman town even before St. Augustine arrived in 597, sent by the pope to convert the Anglo-Saxons to Christianity. The town rose in prominence, soon becoming the center of Christianity in England.

Under the Normans, the city maintained its position as the country's leading archbishopric. A new **cathedral** was built on the ruins of the Anglo-Saxon cathedral in 1070. Enlarged and rebuilt many times, it embraces examples of all styles of medieval architecture.

In 1170, Thomas Becket, the Archbishop of Canterbury and enemy of King Henry II, was murdered here. Trinity Chapel was built to house his remains. *The Canterbury Tales* by Geoffrey Chaucer, one of the greatest works of early English literature, tells of a group of pilgrims who are traveling from London to Becket's shrine in 1387.

Adjacent to the ruins of St. Augustine's Abbey is St. Martin's Church, one of the oldest in England. Beneath Canterbury's streets lies the Roman Museum, highlights of which include the foundations of a Roman house.

Cathedral

🏷🏷🖼🖼🖼 ⌂ Christ Church Gate ⏰ Winter: 9am–5pm Mon–Sat, 10am–4:30pm Sun; summer: 9am–5:30pm daily (to 4:30pm Sun) 🚫 During services & concerts, Good Fri, Dec 25 🌐 canterbury-cathedral.org

↑ A charming cobbled lane in Canterbury, with the cathedral at the far end

4
Winchester

⌂ Hampshire 🚆🚌 𝒊 Guildhall, High Street; www.visitwinchester.co.uk

The capital of the ancient kingdom of Wessex, the city of Winchester was also the headquarters of England's Anglo-Saxon kings.

William the Conqueror built one of his first English castles here. The only surviving part is the **Great Hall**, erected in 1235 and now home to the Round Table of King Arthur, said to have been built by the wizard Merlin, but actually made in the 13th century.

Winchester's fine **cathedral** was begun in 1079. Originally a Benedictine monastery, it has preserved much of its Norman architecture despite many alterations. The writer Jane Austen is buried here.

Great Hall

🏷🏷🖼 ⌂ Castle Ave ⏰ 10am–4:30pm daily 🚫 Dec 25 & 26 🌐 hants.gov.uk/greathall

Cathedral

🏷🏷🖼🖼 ⌂ The Close ⏰ 9:30am–5pm Mon–Sat, 12:30–3pm Sun 🌐 winchester-cathedral.org.uk

5
Salisbury

⌂ Wiltshire 🚆🚌 𝒊 Fish Row; www.visitwiltshire.co.uk

Salisbury was founded in 1220, when the Norman hilltop settlement of Old Sarum was abandoned in favor of a site amid lush water meadows where the Nadder, Bourne, Avon, Ebble, and Wylye meet.

The **cathedral** built here in the early 13th century is a fine example of the Early English style of Gothic architecture, typified by tall lancet windows.

In the medieval King's House, the **Salisbury and**

↑ Brighton's Oriental-style Royal Pavilion reflected in a pond

South Wiltshire Museum

has displays on early man, Stonehenge, and Old Sarum.

The busy High Street leads to the 13th-century Church of St. Thomas, which has a lovely carved timber roof (1450).

Cathedral

⊗ ⊗ ☺ ☺ ◩ The Close
🕐 9am–5pm Mon–Sat, noon–4pm Sun ⓦ salisbury cathedral.org.uk

Salisbury and South Wiltshire Museum

⊗ ☺ ☺ ◩ The Close
🕐 10am–5pm Mon–Sat, noon–5pm Sun ⓒ Jan 1, Dec 25 & 26 ⓦ salisbury museum.org.uk

Did You Know?

Salisbury Cathedral's spire is the tallest in England.

⓺

Brighton

🏠 Sussex 🚉🚌 ⓘ Town Hall, Bartholomew Rd; www.visitbrighton.com

London's nearest south-coast resort, Brighton is a haven of buzzing nightlife and independent shops, with a thriving LGBT+ scene.

The Prince Regent (later George IV) resided in the city's magnificent **Royal Pavilion** with the Catholic widow Mrs. Fitzherbert after their secret marriage. In 1815, he employed architect John Nash to transform the house into the fantastic Indo-Gothic palace that we see today.

Traditional seaside fun is focused on Brighton's pebble beach and the late-Victorian Brighton Pier. Also worth visiting is the maze of shops and winding alleys from the original village of Brighthelmstone, called The Lanes.

Royal Pavilion

⊗ ⊗ ☺ ☺ ◩ Old Steine
🕐 Winter: 10am–5:15pm daily; summer: 9:30am–5:45pm daily ⓒ Dec 25 & 26 ⓦ brightonmuseums.org.uk/royalpavilion

EAT

Brighton is home to a thriving food scene; here are our top picks.

Food for Friends

Knockout vegetarian and vegan delights in a light-filled setting.

◩ 17-18 Prince Albert St ⓦ foodforfriends.com

£ £ £

Ginger Pig

This classy pub in neighboring Hove offers delicious British food.

◩ 3 Hove St, Hove ⓦ thegingerpigpub.com

£ £ £

Terre à Terre

Serving world-inspired vegetarian dishes in The Lanes.

◩ 71 East St ⓦ terreaterre.co.uk.

£ £ £

The Roman Baths, built in the 1st century AD around a natural hot spring ↑

❼

BATH

 Avon ✈ Bristol, 20 miles (32 km) W 🚌 ℹ Bridgwater House, 2 Terrace Walk; www.visitbath.co.uk

The beautiful and compact city of Bath is set among the rolling green hills of the Avon Valley. The traffic-free heart of this lively spa resort is filled with interesting museums, charming cafés, and enticing shops, while the city's characteristic honey-colored Georgian houses form an elegant backdrop.

①

Bath Abbey

📍 Abbey Churchyard
🕐 Hours vary, check website 🕐 During services
🌐 bathabbey.org

This splendid abbey was supposedly designed by divine agency. According to legend, Bishop Oliver King dreamed of angels going up and down to heaven, inspiring the ladders carved on the facade of the west front. The bishop began work in 1499, rebuilding a church founded in the 8th century. Memorials cover the walls and the varied Georgian inscriptions make fascinating reading. The fan vaulting of the nave was added by Sir George Gilbert Scott in 1874.

②   🍴 🛍

Roman Baths

📍 Entrance in Abbey Churchyard 🕐 Hours vary, check website 🕐 Dec 25 & 26 🌐 romanbaths.co.uk

According to legend, Bath owes its origin to the Celtic King Bladud who discovered the curative properties of its natural hot springs in 860 BC. Cast out from his kingdom as a leper, Bladud cured himself by imitating his swine and rolling in the hot mud at Bath.

The Romans built baths around the spring in the 1st century AD, but it was when Queen Anne visited in 1702–3 that Bath reached its zenith as a fashionable watering place. The bath complex was rebuilt

---

JANE AUSTEN

The name most synonymous with Bath is Jane Austen, whose six years here informed some of her greatest novels, notably *Persuasion*. Devotees will certainly want to pay a visit to the Jane Austen Centre on 40 Gay Street, where exhibits include the only known waxwork of the author. A plaque outside the door at No. 4 Sydney Place marks Jane Austen's first dwelling in Bath.

in Neo-Classical style to echo its Roman origins; the Great Bath, at the heart of the Roman complex, was only rediscovered in the 1870s. Excavated artifacts and fragments of the original structure are displayed on the lower levels, while the 18th-century Pump Room remains an elegant tearoom.

Assembly Rooms and Fashion Museum

🏛 Bennett St 🕐 Mar–Oct: 10:30am–6pm daily; Nov–Feb: 10:30am–5pm daily 🗓 Dec 25 & 26 🌐 fashion museum.co.uk

The Assembly Rooms were built by Wood the Younger in 1769, as a meeting place for the elite and as a backdrop for glittering balls. Jane Austen's novel *Northanger Abbey* (1818) describes the gossip and flirtation that went on here. In the basement is a collection of costumes from the 1500s to the present day.

No. 1 Royal Crescent

🏛 Royal Crescent 🕐 10am–5pm daily 🗓 Jan 1, Dec 25 & 26 🌐 no1royalcrescent. org.uk

This handsome museum lets you inside the first house of this beautiful Georgian crescent, built between 1767 and 1774. It gives a glimpse of what life was like for 18th-century aristocrats, as well as access to the servants' quarters. Look out for the spit turned by a dog wheel, and Georgian mousetraps.

Thermae Bath Spa

🏛 Hot Bath St 🕐 9am–9:30pm daily 🗓 Jan 1, Dec 25 & 26 🌐 thermae bathspa.com

Tourists have bathed in Bath's mineral-rich waters since Roman times, and the opening of the Thermae Bath Spa in 2006 once again made Bath a popular day-spa destination. There are three pools fed by natural thermal waters: the New Royal Bath has two baths, including an open-air rooftop pool with views over the city; across the road, the oval Cross Bath is a more intimate open-air bath. The spa also offers steam rooms, footbaths and an array of treatments, bookable in advance. The signature therapy is watsu, a water-based version of the shiatsu massage.

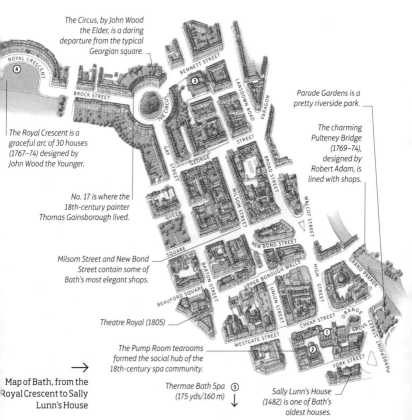

The Circus, by John Wood the Elder, is a daring departure from the typical Georgian square.

Parade Gardens is a pretty riverside park.

The charming Pulteney Bridge (1769–74), designed by Robert Adam, is lined with shops.

The Royal Crescent is a graceful arc of 30 houses (1767–74) designed by John Wood the Younger.

No. 17 is where the 18th-century painter Thomas Gainsborough lived.

Milsom Street and New Bond Street contain some of Bath's most elegant shops.

Theatre Royal (1805)

The Pump Room tearooms formed the social hub of the 18th-century spa community.

Thermae Bath Spa ⑤ (175 yds/160 m)

Sally Lunn's House (1482) is one of Bath's oldest houses.

→ Map of Bath, from the Royal Crescent to Sally Lunn's House

8

Stonehenge

 Off A303, Wiltshire 3 from Salisbury Daily; check website for hours Dec 25 english-heritage.org.uk

Constructed in several stages from about 3000 BC onward, Stonehenge is Europe's most famous prehistoric monument. We can only guess at the reasons as to why it was built, but the alignment of the stones leaves little doubt that the circle reflects the changing trajectory of the sun through the sky, as well as the passing of the seasons.

Stonehenge's monumental scale is all the more impressive given that the only tools available were ones made of stone, wood, and bone. To quarry, transport, and erect the huge stones, its builders must have had the command of immense resources and pools of labor.

Stonehenge was completed in about 1250 BC; despite popular belief, it was not built by the Druids, who flourished in Britain 1,000 years later.

The visitor center, located 1 mile (2 km) from the stones, presents a fascinating history of the site and there is also a museum packed with interesting ancient artifacts.

9

Bristol

Avon E Shed, 1 Canon's Road; www.visitbristol.co.uk

At the mouth of the Avon, the city of Bristol was once the main British port for trans-atlantic trade. The city grew rich on the transportation of wine, tobacco, and, in the 17th and 18th centuries, slaves.

Designed by Isambard Kingdom Brunel, the SS *Great Britain* was the world's first large iron passenger ship. Launched in 1843, it traveled 32 times round the world. The restored ship is now in the dock where it was originally built, and nearby is the Being Brunel museum, exploring the life of the great engineer.

Other museums in the attractive harborside area include M-Shed, which tells the city's history, and We the Curious, a science center with hundreds of exciting interactive exhibits and a planetarium.

Among the city's other landmarks are the magnificent 14th-century St. Mary Redcliffe church, claimed by Queen Elizabeth I to be "the fairest in England," and Brunel's iconic Clifton Suspension Bridge, spanning the dramatic Avon Gorge from Clifton Village to Leigh Woods.

BANSKY

As mysterious as he is prolific, Bristol-born Banksy is the world's best-known graffiti artist. There are excellent tours around the city taking in his works (including "Mild Mild West" and "Masked Gorilla"), along with other excellent street art. Alternatively, visit www.bristol-street-art.co.uk to devise your own itinerary.

10

Devon and Cornwall

Exeter (Devon), Truro (Cornwall) Quay House, Quayside, Exeter; www.visitdevon.co.uk; Boscawen Street, Truro; www.visitcornwall.com

Miles of stunning coastline dominate this delightful part of Britain. Seaside resorts alternate with secluded coves and fishing villages, while inland, lush pastures contrast with stark, treeless moorland.

Near Land's End, mainland Britain's most westerly point, the former Benedictine monastery of St. Michael's

↑ Shoppers and diners soaking up the atmosphere of Exeter Quay, Exeter

Mount rises dramatically from the waters of Mount Bay off Cornwall's southern coast. On the north coast, St. Ives is renowned for its two art museums, the Barbara Hepworth Museum and the Tate St. Ives. The **Eden Project** in St. Austell explores the vital relationship between plants, people, and resources. Two huge geodesic domes, known as biomes, dominate the site, which holds some 4,500 species of plants.

The administrative capital of Cornwall is Truro, a city of gracious Georgian buildings and cobbled streets. Devon's capital is Exeter, a lively city with fine Roman and medieval relics. The mainly 14th-century Cathedral Church of St. Peter is one of Britain's most superbly ornamented cathedrals.

At the heart of Devon's **Dartmoor National Park** is a bleak, windswept landscape, dotted with tors – outcrops of granite rock – and grazed by herds of wild ponies.

Eden Project

⊘ 🍴 😊 ⊕ 🚗 St. Austell 🚉 St. Austell, then bus 🕐 9am–6pm daily (Aug–Sep: to 6:30pm) 🚫 Dec 25 🌐 edenproject.com

Dartmoor National Park

🚗 Devon 🚉🚌 To Exeter, Plymouth or Totnes, then local bus ℹ️ Visitor Centre, Princetown; 01822-890414

EAT

Box-E
This is a fantastic little outfit in an old shipping container with a small but ambitious menu.

🏠 Unit 10, 1 Cargo Wharf, Bristol 🌐 boxebristol.com

£££

Wilsons
Food of great distinction, combined in exciting dishes.

🏠 Chandos St, Bristol 🌐 wilsonsrestaurant. co.uk

£££

Porthmeor Beach Café
While away an hour or two on the breezy terrace perched above the beach, tucking into shared small plates with a cocktail or two.

🏠 Porthmeor Beach, St Ives 🌐 porthmeor-beach.co.uk

£££

← Monumental Stonehenge, arranged according to astronomical calculations

↑ Walking along the Llanberis Path, one of several routes up Snowdon

⓫
Snowdonia

🏛 Gwynedd 🚉 Betws-y-Coed 🚉 Station Road, Barmouth; www.visit snowdonia.info

The scenery of Snowdonia National Park ranges from rugged mountain country to moors and beaches. The area is well known as a destination for hikers, and villages such as Betws-y-Coed and Llanberis are busy hill-walking centers.

The main focus of this vast area is Snowdon, which

ACTIVITIES IN SNOWDONIA NATIONAL PARK

Beyond hiking and cycling, Snowdonia is also popular for rock climbing, especially on the craggy sides of the Llanberis Pass. Go Below (www.go-below. co.uk) arranges zip-lining through caverns and visits to under-ground lakes, while Surf Snowdonia (www. adventureparcsnow donia.com), at Rowen, operates one of the biggest artificial wave machines in the world.

at 3,560 ft (1,085 m) is the highest peak in Wales. Hikers should be wary of sudden weather changes on the mountains. In summer, less-intrepid visitors can take the Snowdon Mountain Railway from Llanberis to the summit.

⓬
Caernarfon

🏛 Gwynedd 🚌 🔋 Castle St; www. visitsnowdonia.info

A famous castle looms over this busy town, built after Edward I's defeat of the last native Welsh prince, Llywelyn ap Gruffydd, in 1283. Modern streets spread beyond the medieval center and open into a market square.

Caernarfon Castle was built as the seat of government for north Wales. A UNESCO World Heritage Site, it contains interesting displays, including an exhibition tracing the history of the Princes of Wales.

On the hill above the town are the ruins of Segontium, a Roman fort built around AD 78.

Caernarfon Castle

♿🕐🅿 🏛 Y Maes 🕐 9:30am–5pm daily (Jul & Aug: to 6pm; winter: reduced hours) 🚫 Jan 1, Dec 24–26 🌐 cadw.gov.wales

⓭
Cardiff

🏛 Glamorgan 🚉🚌 🔋 The Hayes; www. visitcardiff.com

Cardiff was first occupied by the Romans, who built a fort here in AD 75. In the 1830s, the town began to develop as a port, and by 1913 it was the world's leading coal exporter. Confirmed as the Welsh capital in 1955, it is now devoted to commerce and administration and has a thriving student population.

Cardiff Castle was built in the medieval era on the site of the Roman fort. It was reno-vated in the 19th century, creating an ornate mansion rich in romantic detail.

Cardiff's civic center is set around Alexandra Gardens. The Neo-Classical City Hall (1905) is dominated by its huge dome and clock tower. On the first floor, the Marble Hall is adorned with statues of prominent Welsh figures.

To the south of the center, the docklands have been

transformed by the creation of a marina and waterfront. Here, the Pier Head Building, constructed in 1896, is a reminder of the city's heyday.

Established during the 1940s at St. Fagans, on the western edge of the city, the open-air **St. Fagans National History Museum** was one of the first of its kind. Buildings from all over Wales, including workers' terraced cottages, farmhouses, a tollhouse, shops,

a chapel, and a schoolhouse have been painstakingly reconstructed within the 100-acre (40-ha) parklands, along with a recreated Celtic village. Visitors can also explore a Tudor mansion that boasts its own beautiful gardens in the grounds.

Cardiff Castle

🦆 🦆 🦆 🦆 🔲 Castle St
🕐 9am–5pm daily (Mar–Oct: to 6pm) 🚫 Jan 1, Dec 25 & 26
🌐 cardiffcastle.com

St. Fagans National History Museum

🦆 🏛 🔲 St. Fagans
🕐 10am–5pm daily
🌐 museum.wales

Cardiff's lively pedestrian area, lined with shops; *(inset)* imposing Cardiff Castle ↓

> **Christ Church, the largest of the Oxford colleges, dates from 1525, when Cardinal Wolsey founded it as an ecclesiastical college.**

↑ A student on the elegant staircase of Christ Church College, Oxford

The university's library, the Bodleian, was founded in 1320. One of its most famous rooms is the Divinity School (1488), which has a beautiful Gothic vaulted ceiling. The circular Radcliffe Camera (1748) is a reading room (the word camera means room in Latin).

Oxford is more than just a university town and there is a wealth of interesting sights aside from the colleges. One of the best British museums outside London, the **Ashmolean Museum** was opened in 1683. The museum's exceptional art collection includes works by Bellini, Raphael, Turner, Rembrandt, Michelangelo, Picasso, and a large group of Pre-Raphaelites. There is also the Alfred Jewel, an Anglo-Saxon artifact more than 1,000 years old.

Carfax Tower is all that remains of the 14th-century Church of St. Martin, demolished in 1896. Watch the clock strike the quarter hours, and climb to the top for a panoramic view of the city.

The Martyrs' Memorial commemorates the three Protestants burned at the stake on Broad Street – Bishops Latimer and Ridley in 1555, and Archbishop Cranmer in 1556 – during the reign of Catholic Queen Mary.

St. Mary the Virgin Church is the official church of the university, and is said to be the most visited parish church in England.

14
Oxford

🏠 Oxfordshire 🚃🚌
ℹ️ 15–16 Broad St; www.experienceoxfordshire.org

Oxford has long been a strategic point on the western routes into London – its name describes its position as a convenient spot for crossing the river (a ford for oxen).

The university was founded in 1167 by English students expelled from Paris. The development of England's first university created the spectacular skyline of tall towers and "dreaming spires."

Many of the 38 colleges that make up Oxford University were founded between the 13th and 16th centuries and cluster around the city center. The colleges were designed along the lines of monastic buildings, but were surrounded by gardens. Christ Church, the largest of the Oxford colleges, dates from 1525, when Cardinal Wolsey founded it as an ecclesiastical college. It has produced 13 British prime ministers in the last 200 years. Other colleges worth paying a visit to include All Souls, Magdalen, Merton, Lincoln, and Corpus Christi.

> 💬 INSIDER TIP
> **Walking Tours**
>
> Oxford Official Walking Tours *(www.experienceoxfordshire.org)* runs several guided walks, including special-interest tours focusing on themes such as Alice in Wonderland and Harry Potter.

→

An open-air performance at Shakespeare's Birthplace in Stratford-upon-Avon

Two of the most interesting museums in the city adjoin each other. The **University Museum of Natural History** contains fossils of dinosaurs as well as the remains of a dodo. The **Pitt Rivers Museum** has one of the world's most extensive ethnographic collections – including masks and totems from Africa and East Asia – and also features archaeological displays.

Completed in 1669 and designed by Christopher Wren, the Sheldonian Theatre was built as a place to hold university degree ceremonies. The ornate ceiling depicts the triumph of religion, art, and science over envy, hatred, and malice.

Ashmolean Museum

Ⓐ Ⓒ Ⓓ Ⓔ **Ⓐ** Beaumont St
Ⓒ 10am–5pm daily Ⓒ Dec 24–26 Ⓦ ashmolean.org

University Museum of Natural History and Pitt Rivers Museum

Ⓔ Ⓕ **Ⓐ** Parks Rd
Ⓒ University: 10am–5pm daily; Pitt Rivers: noon–4:30pm Mon, 10am–4:30pm Tue–Sun Ⓒ Easter, Dec 24–26 Ⓦ oumnh.ox.ac.uk/prm.ox. ac.uk

---

THE ROYAL SHAKESPEARE COMPANY

The Royal Shakespeare Company (RSC) is renowned for its new interpretations of Shakespeare's work. It was established in the 1960s as a resident company for the 1932 Shakespeare Memorial Theatre, now the Royal Shakespeare Theatre. It has seen the best theatrical talent tread its boards, from Laurence Olivier to Helen Mirren to Kenneth Branagh. The RSC also tours, with seasons in London, Newcastle, and New York. Stratford has two main stages run by the RSC - the Royal Shakespeare Theatre and the Swan Theatre, both on Waterside - as well as the smaller Other Place at 22 Southern Lane.

Stratford-upon-Avon

Ⓐ Warwickshire Ⓡ ⓐ
ⓘ Bridge Foot; www.visit stratforduponavon.co.uk

Stratford-upon-Avon attracts hordes of tourists eager to see buildings connected with William Shakespeare, born here in 1564. The town is also the provincial home of the Royal Shakespeare Company, whose performances are staged at the riverside Royal Shakespeare Theatre.

The High Street turns into Chapel Street, the site of New Place, where Shakespeare died in 1616, and which is now a herb garden. The playwright is buried at Holy Trinity Church.

Bought for the nation in 1847, Shakespeare's Birthplace was restored to its Elizabethan style. Considered a shrine to the writer, who lived here for many years, it offers a fascinating insight into his life.

Another Stratford native, John Harvard, emigrated to America and in 1638 left his estate to a new college, later renamed Harvard University. Harvard House displays family mementos.

No tour of Stratford would be complete without a visit to Anne Hathaway's Cottage. Before her 1582 marriage to Shakespeare, Anne lived here, 1 mile (1.5 km) from the town. Despite fire damage, the cottage is still impressive, with some 16th-century furniture.

16 🛡️ Ⓜ️ 🍴 🖥️ 🛍️

BLENHEIM PALACE

🏠 Woodstock, Oxfordshire 🕐 Palace and gardens: 10am–5:30pm daily; Park: 9am–6pm daily 🗓️ Nov 20 & 21, Dec 25 🚉 Oxford 🚌 53 from Oxford train station 🌐 blenheimpalace.com

Designed by Nicholas Hawksmoor and Sir John Vanbrugh in the early 1700s, Blenheim Palace is a Baroque masterpiece and is the only British historic house to be named a UNESCO World Heritage Site. The vast, splendid gardens and parkland make for glorious walks.

After John Churchill, the 1st Duke of Marlborough, defeated the French at the Battle of Blenheim in 1704, Queen Anne gave him the Manor of Woodstock and had this palatial house built for him. It was later the birthplace of Winston Churchill in 1874, who was a descendant of the dukes of Marlborough, and now houses an exhibition with displays on the life, work, paintings, and writings of the former British prime minister. Today it is home to the 12th duke. Visitors can wander through 300 years of history in splendid rooms full of tapestries, paintings, china, and statues. Renowned landscape architect Lancelot (Capability) Brown designed parts of the beautiful gardens and park, which include a yew maze, lakes, a rose garden, arboretum, and the Grand Bridge designed by Vanbrugh.

The Grand Bridge, begun in 1708, has a 101-ft (31-m) main span and contains rooms within its structure.

The chapel features a marble monument to the 1st Duke of Marlborough and his family.

→ The layout of the magnificent Blenheim Palace

The magnificent water terraces were laid out in the 1920s by French architect Achille Duchêne in 17th-century style.

WOODSTOCK

Located about 8 miles (13 km) northwest of Oxford, the small, quiet town of Woodstock grew up as a coach stop around the royal hunting lodge that later became Blenheim Palace. With its pretty stone houses, antiques shops, traditional pubs, and tearooms, it is a relaxing place to take afternoon tea after a visit to the palace. The Oxfordshire Museum on Park Street has displays on local history, art, and wildlife.

Blenheim Palace with water terraces and a fountain, and *(inset)* the lavish Red Drawing Room

Blenheim Palace: The Untold Story exhibition

The Great Hall has a splendid ceiling by Thornhill (1716).

Grinling Gibbons lions (1709)

Clock tower

East Gate

The Italian Garden contains the Mermaid Fountain (early 1900s) by US sculptor Waldo Story.

The Green Drawing Room has a full-length portrait of the 4th Duke by George Romney (1734–1802).

Third State Room

Great Court

Second State Room

First State Room

Red Drawing Room

Green Writing Room

The Long Library was designed by Vanbrugh as a picture gallery. The portraits include one of Queen Anne by Sir Godfrey Kneller (1646–1723).

The Saloon's walls and ceiling have detailed paintings by French artist Louis Laguerre (1663–1721).

Did You Know?

Other than royal buildings, Blenheim is the only structure in England to have "Palace" in its title.

EAT

The Eagle

Cambridge's most famous pub is a must. See where Crick and Watson announced their discovery of DNA, or view the poignant World War II graffiti in the RAF Bar.

🏠 Benet St, Cambridge
🌐 greeneking-pubs.co.uk

Chez Jules

Despite the half-timbered exterior, this cheerful bistro specializing in classic French brasserie fare is modern and airy inside.

🏠 71 Northgate St, Chester
🌐 chezjules.com

⓱

Cambridge

🏠 Cambridgeshire 🚗🚌
ℹ️ The Guildhall, Peas Hill; www.visitcambridge.org

Cambridge has been an important town since Roman times, being located at the first navigable point on the River Cam. When, in 1209, a group of scholars broke away from Oxford University after academic and religious disputes, they came here.

Cambridge University has 31 colleges, the oldest being Peterhouse (1284) and the newest Robinson (1977). Many of the older colleges have peaceful gardens backing onto the Cam, known as "Backs." An enjoyable way to view these is to rent a punt (a long narrow boat propelled using a pole) from one of the boatyards along the river – with a "chauffeur," if needed.

Henry VI founded King's College in 1441. Work on the college's chapel – one of the most important examples of late-medieval English architecture – began five years later, and took almost 100 years to complete. Henry stipulated that a choir of six lay clerks and 16 boy choristers – educated at the College school – should sing daily at services. This still happens in term time, but today the choir also gives concerts all over the world.

St. John's College spans the Cam and features the beautiful Bridge of Sighs, named after its Venetian counterpart.

The collection at the **Fitzwilliam Museum** includes paintings by Titian and the 17th-century Dutch masters, plus works by the French Impressionists, and most of the important British artists of the past 300 years. **Kettle's Yard** houses modern art with a focus on the British avant-garde of the early 1900s.

Fitzwilliam Museum

♿🚫📷🕐 🏠 Trumpington St
🕐 10am–5pm Tue–Sat, noon–5pm Sun 🚫 Jan 1, Good Fri, Dec 24–26 & 31
🌐 fitzmuseum.cam.ac.uk

Kettle's Yard

🚫📷 🏠 Castle Street
🕐 11am–5pm Tue–Sun
🌐 kettlesyard.co.uk

→ Punting on the River Cam, past university buildings, Cambridge

The warm, light-filled interior of The Walker art gallery in Liverpool

18

Liverpool

🏠 Liverpool ✈️ 🚗 🚌 🚆
ℹ️ Mathew St; www.
visitliverpool.com

Liverpool's history has been shaped by its position on the western seaboard. During the 17th and 18th centuries, the city played a major role in the transatlantic slave trade, then after the first ocean steamer set sail from here in 1840, emigrants to the Americas poured into the city, including a large number of Irish refugees of the potato famine.

Liverpool's waterfront is overlooked by the well-known Royal Liver Building. The 19th-century warehouses around Albert Dock have been redeveloped as museums, galleries, restaurants, and shops. Among these, the Maritime Museum and **Tate Liverpool**, which houses one of the best collections of contemporary art in England outside of London, are well worth visiting.

Albert Dock is also home to The Beatles Story, a walk-through exhibition that charts the rise to fame of the world-renowned Liverpudlian band in the 1960s.

One of the most prestigious art galleries in the city is **The Walker**.

Paintings here range from early Italian and Flemish works to 20th-century art.

Liverpool's Gothic-style Anglican Cathedral, completed in 1978 by Sir Giles Gilbert Scott, is the world's largest. The Roman Catholic Metropolitan Cathedral of Christ the King (1962–7) is a circular building surmounted by a stylized crown of thorns 290 ft (88 m) high.

Tate Liverpool

♿ 😊 🕐 🏠 Albert Dock
🕐 10am–5:50pm daily
🚫 Dec 24–26 🌐 tate.org.uk

The Walker

♿ 😊 🕐 🏠 William Brown St
🕐 10am–5pm daily
🚫 Jan 1, Dec 24–26 & 31
🌐 liverpoolmuseums.org.uk

19

Chester

🏠 Cheshire 🚆 🚌
ℹ️ Town Hall, Northgate St;
www.visitcheshire.com

The main streets of Chester are lined with timber buildings, many dating from the 13th and 14th centuries. Known as the Chester Rows, these feature two tiers of stores and a continuous upper gallery. The Rows are at their most attractive where Eastgate Street meets Bridge Street.

South of the Cross – a reconstruction of a 15th-century stone crucifix – the **Grosvenor Museum** explains Chester's history. To the north is the cathedral. Its choir stalls have splendid misericords and delicate spirelets on the canopies. The cathedral is surrounded on two sides by high city walls, originally Roman, but rebuilt at intervals.

Grosvenor Museum

♿ ♿ 😊 🕐 🏠 Grosvenor St
🕐 10:30am–5pm Mon–Sat,
1–4pm Sun 🚫 Jan 1, Dec 24–
28 🌐 grosvenormuseum.
westcheshiremuseums.
co.uk

THE BEATLES

Liverpool is famous as the home town of The Beatles, and many locations linked to the band are today revered as shrines. Bus and walking tours go past the Salvation Army children's home at Strawberry Fields, Penny Lane, and the boys' old homes. The most visited site is Matthew Street, home of the Cavern Club. The original site is now a shopping arcade, but its bricks were used to build a replica. Nearby are statues of The Beatles and Eleanor Rigby.

20
Manchester

🏛 Manchester ✈🚇🚌
ℹ Piccadilly Plaza, Portland
Street; www.visit
manchester.com

Manchester is famous as
a pioneer of the industrial
age, and today is the north of
England's premier shopping
and media hub.

Among the city's many fine
19th-century buildings are
the Neo-Gothic cathedral;
the Royal Exchange, now a
theater; and the Free Trade
Hall, now a hotel, with only
the original facade remaining.
The Manchester Ship Canal,
opened in 1894, is a magnificent engineering feat.

The Museum of Science
and Industry captures the
city's spirit of industrial might
with an informative display of
working steam engines and
an exhibition on the Liverpool
and Manchester Railway.
Another museum of note is
the **Whitworth Art Gallery**,
with its splendid collection of
contemporary art, textiles,
and prints. Housed in a 19th-
century porticoed building,
the City Art Galleries contain
an excellent selection of
British art, as well as early
Italian, Flemish, and French
paintings and decorative
art objects.

Whitworth Art Gallery
 🏛 University of
Manchester, Oxford Rd
🕐 10am–5pm daily (to 9pm
Thu) 🚫 Jan 1, Dec 24–26
🌐 whitworth.manchester.
ac.uk

21
Durham

🏛 County Durham 🚇🚌
🌐 thisisdurham.com

Durham was built on a rocky
peninsula in 995. The site was
chosen as the last resting place
for the remains of St. Cuthbert.
The relics of the Venerable
Bede were brought here 27
years later, adding to the
town's attraction to pilgrims.

Durham's cathedral, built
between 1093 and 1274, is a
striking Norman structure. The
vast dimensions of the ancient
columns, piers, and vaults,
and the lozenge, chevron, and
dogtooth patterns carved into
them, are its main innovative
features. The exotic Galilee
Chapel, begun in 1170, was
inspired by the mosque at
Córdoba, Spain (p340).

The Norman **castle**, begun in
1072, served as an Episcopal
Palace until 1832, when
Bishop William van Mildert
gave it away to found England's
third university here. In the
castle grounds, Tunstal's
Chapel was built around 1542
and has some fine woodwork,
including a unicorn misericord.
The castle keep, on a mound,
is now part of the university.

Durham Castle
 🕐 Daily for guided tours
only; check website for
timings 🌐 dur.ac.uk/
durham.castle

22
Lake District

🏛 Cumbria 🚉 Kendal,
Windermere 🚌 Kendal,
Keswick, Windermere
ℹ Made in Cumbria, 48a
Branthwaite Brow, Kendal,
; Moot Hall, Market Sq,
Keswick; www.visit
cumbria.com

The Lake District is home to
some of the country's most
spectacular scenery, with
high peaks, lonely fells, and
beautiful lakes. The area

↑ Manchester city center, displaying several
centuries of different architectural styles

↑ Peaceful Derwent Water, near the town of Keswick, in the Lake District

 GREAT VIEW
Wastwater

A silent reflection of stunning surroundings, brooding Wastwater is a soul-stirring lake. There are spectacular viewpoints on the road along the western edge and from paths to the shore at the top of the lake.

constitutes Britain's largest national park and offers a range of outdoor activities, from hill walking to boating.

The market town of Kendal is the southern gateway to the Lake District. Of interest here is the Museum of Lakeland Life and Industry, housed in the stable block of the 18th-century Abbot Hall.

The nearest lake to Kendal is Windermere, which, at more than 10 miles (16 km) long, is England's largest lake. A year-round car ferry connects Windermere's east and west shores, and summer steamers link the main towns on the north-south axis. One of the most popular stops is the pretty town of Bowness on the east shore.

Ambleside, another attractive lakeside town, is a good base for walkers and climbers. Nearby is Hill Top, the 17th-century farmhouse where Beatrix Potter wrote many of her famous children's stories.

The Lake District's most famous son, the Romantic poet William Wordsworth, lived for a while at Grasmere, on the shores of the lake of the same name, north of Ambleside. His home, Dove Cottage, contains a museum dedicated to his life.

To the west of Windermere lie Coniston Water and picturesque Duddon Valley, popular walking country.

In the northern part of the Lake District, Keswick – with its lake, Derwent Water – has been a busy vacation destination since Victorian days. Among the fine exhibits of the Keswick Museum and Art Gallery are original manuscripts of Lakeland writers, such as Robert Southey and Wordsworth. To the east of the town lies the ancient stone circle of Castlerigg. North of Keswick is Skiddaw, England's fourth-highest peak and a straightforward climb for anyone reasonably fit.

㉓

YORK

📍Yorkshire 🚉 ℹ️ Museum St; www.visityork.org

Its multilayered history makes York's compact city center a delight to explore, with evidence of its Roman, Saxon, Viking, and medieval heritage at every turn of its narrow, winding streets – walking into the city's well-preserved core is like entering a living museum. Overlooking all is the magnificent York Minster, dating from the time when this Christian stronghold was England's second city.

①
Jorvik Viking Centre

📍Coppergate Walk
🕐10am-5pm daily (Nov-Mar: to 4pm) 🚫Dec 24-26
🌐jorvikvikingcentre.co.uk

Advance booking is advised for the popular Jorvik Viking Centre, built on the site of the original Viking settlement that archaeologists uncovered at Coppergate. Using new technology and artifacts from the site, a dynamic vision of 10th-century York is recreated, bringing the Viking world to life. A short walk away, in the Church of St. Saviour's, is the center's sister attraction, DIG, where visitors can take part in an archaeological excavation.

②
Merchant Adventurers' Hall

📍The Hall, Fossgate
🕐10am-4:30pm Sun-Fri, 10am-1:30pm Sat
🌐merchantshallyork.org

Much of York's wealth in the late Middle Ages came from the cloth trade. The Merchant Adventurers' Hall, the headquarters of a powerful guild of traders, is a well-preserved timber-framed building that dates from 1357. The Great Hall is probably the best example of its kind in Europe. Below the Great Hall is the hospital, which was used by the guild until 1900, and a private chapel.

③
York Minster

📍Deangate 🕐9am-4:30pm Mon-Sat, 12:30-3pm Sun
🌐yorkminster.org

Between 1100 and 1500, York was England's second city. York Minster, the largest Gothic church in

St. Mary's Abbey

St. Olave's is an 11th-century church founded in memory of St. Olaf, King of Norway.

The Yorkshire Museum contains a fine collection of fossils, discovered at Whitby in the 19th century.

→ York's city center stretching along the River Ouse

The Gothic spires of York Minster, seen from the medieval city walls

Northern Europe, was begun in 1220 and completed 250 years later. It is home to a magnificent collection of medieval stained glass. Some windows were paid for by lay donors who specified a particular subject, others reflect ecclesiastical patronage. The vast Great East Window (1405–8) depicts the Creation. In 1984, a fire in the south transept shattered its magnificent rose window; it has since been restored.

National Railway Museum

🏠 Leeman Rd 🕐 10am–5pm daily (summer: to 6pm) 🚫 Dec 24–26 🌐 railwaymuseum.org.uk

In the 19th century, York's position on the route to Scotland made it a major rail center. Train enthusiasts should head for the National Railway Museum, the largest of its kind in the world, where exhibits include uniforms, rolling stock from 1797 onward, and Queen Victoria's Royal Train carriage, as well as the latest rail innovations.

EAT

Il Paradiso del Cibo
This small Sardinian café-restaurant offers an authentic taste of Italy.

🏠 40 Walmgate 🌐 ilparadisodelcibo york.com

££££

Skosh
Inventive British-international fusion food, served in tapas-sized portions.

🏠 98 Micklegate 🌐 skoshyork.co.uk

££££

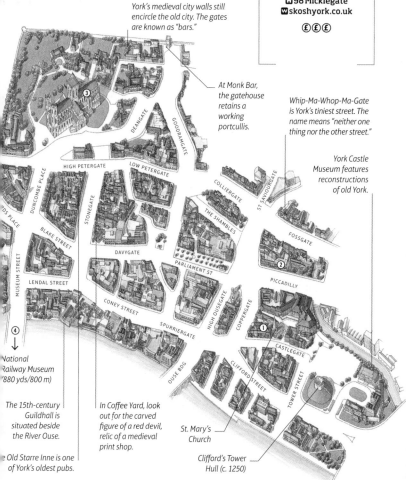

York's medieval city walls still encircle the old city. The gates are known as "bars."

At Monk Bar, the gatehouse retains a working portcullis.

Whip-Ma-Whop-Ma-Gate is York's tiniest street. The name means "neither one thing nor the other street."

York Castle Museum features reconstructions of old York.

National Railway Museum (880 yds/800 m)

The 15th-century Guildhall is situated beside the River Ouse.

In Coffee Yard, look out for the carved figure of a red devil, relic of a medieval print shop.

St. Mary's Church

Old Starre Inne is one of York's oldest pubs.

Clifford's Tower Hull (c. 1250)

 24

EDINBURGH

 249 High Street; www.edinburgh.org

The gateway to Scotland, Edinburgh gained its status as the country's capital during the reign of James IV (1488–1513). With its striking medieval and Georgian districts, replete with sights and cultural treasures, the city is one of Europe's most handsome capitals. Edinburgh also has a reputation for the arts, and every summer it hosts Britain's largest multimedia extravaganza, the Edinburgh Festival.

① Edinburgh Castle

Castle Hill **9:30am–6pm daily (Oct–Mar: to 5pm)** **Dec 25 & 26** **edinburghcastle.gov.uk**

Standing on the basalt core of an extinct volcano, the castle comprises buildings dating from the 12th to the 20th centuries, reflecting its changing role as fortress, military garrison, and state prison. It was a favorite royal residence until the Union of 1603, after which monarchs resided in England.

The castle holds the Stone of Destiny (also known as the Stone of Scone), a relic of ancient Scottish kings seized by the English in 1296, and returned in 1996. Inside the 12th-century St. Margaret's Chapel, a stained-glass window depicts Malcolm III's queen, after whom it is named.

Other important buildings include the 15th-century Great Hall, meeting place of the Scottish parliament until 1639. A 15th-century Burgundian siege gun, known as Mons Meg, is kept in the vaults, where French graffiti recalls the prisoners held here in the 18th- and 19th-century wars. The One o' Clock Gun is still fired at 1pm daily.

② New Town

Stretching to the north of Princes Street, the New Town was developed in the 1700s to relieve the unsanitary conditions of the Old Town. On the north side of elegant

The skyline of Edinburgh at dusk, with the imposing castle in the background

Charlotte Square, the **Georgian House** has been furnished to show the lifestyle of its 18th-century residents.

Later developments include the magnificent Moray Estate, where a linked series of large houses forms a crescent, an oval, and a 12-sided circus.

Georgian House

 7 Charlotte Sq
Late Mar–Oct: 10am–4:15pm daily; Mar, Nov & Dec: see website for details
nts.org.uk

National Museum of Scotland

Chambers St
10am–5pm daily
Dec 25 nms.ac.uk

A great Victorian glass palace, completed in 1888, houses the National Museum of Scotland. It started life as an industrial museum, but over time acquired an eclectic array of more than 20,000 exhibits, ranging from stuffed animals to ethnographic artifacts.

A collection of Scottish antiquities tells the story of the country, starting with its geology and natural history, through to later industrial developments. Among its many stunning exhibits is St. Fillan's Crozier, said to have been carried at the head of the Scottish army at Bannockburn in 1314.

Scottish National Portrait Gallery

1 Queen St 10am–5pm daily Dec 25 & 26
nationalgalleries.org

This gallery, in a red-sandstone Gothic-revival building, owns a wonderful collection of paintings that details the history of 12 generations of Stuarts, from the time of Robert the Bruce to Queen Anne. It also houses portraits of famous Scots, including a depiction of the country's best-loved poet, Robert Burns, by Alexander Nasmyth. Others portrayed include Flora MacDonald, who helped Bonnie Prince Charlie escape after his defeat by the English in 1745, and Ramsay MacDonald, who became Britain's first Labour prime minister in 1924.

The building also holds the Scottish National Photography collection, which contains over 30,000 images from the 1840s to the present day, with particular focus on Scotland.

 INSIDER TIP
Getting Around

Central Edinburgh is compact, so walking or cycling are excellent ways to explore. Other options include trams and buses. Car use is discouraged, because the streets tend to be congested with traffic, and parking is difficult.

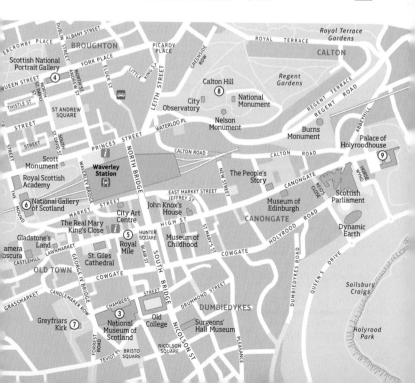

⑤
Royal Mile

Linking the castle to the Palace of Holyroodhouse, the Royal Mile was the main thoroughfare of medieval Edinburgh. Today it goes past many of the city's oldest buildings and several interesting museums.

Near the castle are the Tartan Weaving Mill & Exhibition, the lower floors of which date from the early 1600s and were once the home of the Laird of Cockpen, and the popular 19th-century Camera Obscura and World of Illusions. A little farther on, **Gladstone's Land** is a restored 17th-century merchant's house. Another fine mansion, built in 1622, has been converted into the Writers' Museum, housing memorabilia of Robert Burns, Sir Walter Scott, and Robert Louis Stevenson.

St. Giles Cathedral, properly known as the High Kirk of Edinburgh, was the base from which Protestant minister John Knox led the Scottish Reformation. The cathedral's Thistle Chapel has impressive rib-vaulting and carved heraldic canopies. Just past St. Giles, the Italianate Parliament House, built in the 1630s, has housed the Scottish Courts since the 1707 Act of Union with England and Wales.

Farther east, opposite John Knox's House (1450), is the excellent Museum of Childhood, while The People's Story (1591) tells the social history of Edinburgh.

Gladstone's Land

 ♿🎧 **477B** Lawnmarket **☉** 11am–5pm daily **⛫** nts.org.uk

National Gallery of Scotland

The Mound ☉ 10am–5pm daily (to 7pm Thu) **☒** Dec 25 & 26 **⛫** nationalgalleries.org

Designed by William Henry Playfair, the National Gallery of Scotland opened in 1859. Serried ranks of paintings hang on deep red walls behind a profusion of statues and period furniture. Some of the highlights among the Scottish works are the society portraits by Allan Ramsay and Henry Raeburn, including the latter's famous *Reverend Robert Walker Skating on Duddingston Loch* (c. 1800).

German works include Gerard David's *Three Legends of St. Nicholas*, dating from the early 16th century. Italian paintings include a fine *Madonna* by Raphael, as well as works by Titian and Tintoretto. From Spain there is a delightful genre painting of *An Old Woman Cooking Eggs* by Velázquez (c. 1620).

An entire room is devoted to *The Seven Sacraments* by Nicholas Poussin, dating from around 1640. Dutch and

---

 INSIDER TIP
Gallery Bus

The daily Gallery Bus circuit takes in the Scottish National Gallery, the National Portrait Gallery (drop off only), and the National Gallery of Modern Art, all for a modest £1 donation.

Flemish painters represented include Rembrandt, Van Dyck, and Rubens, while among the British offerings are important works by Reynolds and Gainsborough.

Greyfriars Kirk

🏠 Greyfriars Place 🕐 Apr-Oct: 10:30am-4:30pm Mon-Fri, noon-4pm Sat; Nov-Mar: 10:30am-3:30pm Thu 🌐 greyfriarskirk.com

In 1638, the National Covenant, marking the Protestant stand against Charles I's imposition of an episcopal church, was signed at Greyfriars Kirk. Throughout the wars of the 17th century, the kirkyard was used as a mass grave for executed Covenanters. The Martyrs' Monument is a sobering reminder of the many Scots who lost their lives. Greyfriars is also known for its links with a faithful dog, Bobby, who lived beside his master's grave from 1858 to 1872. Greyfriars Bobby's statue stands outside Greyfriars Kirk.

⑧

Calton Hill

📍 City center east, via Waterloo Pl

Calton Hill, at the east end of Princes Street, is a large open space dotted with Neo-Classical monuments. Among these is one of Edinburgh's more memorable landmarks – a half-finished "Parthenon." Conceived as the National Monument to the dead of the Napoleonic Wars, the structure was started in 1822 but never finished. Nearby, the Nelson Monument commemorates the British victory at Trafalgar.

The Classical theme continues with Duncan's Monument and the old City Observatory, designed by William Playfair in 1818 and based on the Tower of the Winds in Athens. The Astronomical Society of Edinburgh arranges tours and free lectures here.

Palace of Holyroodhouse

🏠 East end of the Royal Mile 🕐 9:30am-6pm daily (Nov-Mar: to 4:30pm) 🔒 Dec 25-26 & when in use by the royal family 🌐 rct.uk

Queen Elizabeth II's official Scottish residence was built by James IV in the grounds of an abbey in 1498, and remodeled for Charles II in the 1670s. The Royal Apartments (including the Throne Room and Royal Dining Room) are used for investitures and banquets. A chamber in the so-called James V tower is said to have been the scene of David Rizzio's murder in 1566. He was the Italian secretary of Mary, Queen of Scots. She witnessed the grisly act, which was authorized by her jealous husband, Lord Darnley. Bonnie Prince Charlie, last of the Stuart pretenders to the English throne, also held

court at Holyrood Palace, in 1745. The Queen's Gallery has an interesting program of art exhibitions.

The adjacent Holyrood Park, a former royal hunting ground, is home to three lochs, wildfowl, and the Salisbury Crags. Its high point is the hill known as Arthur's Seat, an extinct volcano and well-known Edinburgh landmark.

↑ The memorial to Dugald Stewart on Calton Hill, with the city in the background

㉕
Stirling

🏛 Stirlingshire 🚌🚂 ℹ Old Town Jail, St. John St; www. yourstirling.com

Stirling developed around its **castle**, one of the finest examples of Renaissance architecture in Scotland. Dating from the 15th century, it was last defended – against the Jacobites – in 1746, and stands within sight of no fewer than seven battlefields. One of these – Bannockburn – was where Robert the Bruce defeated the English in 1314.

Stirling's Old Town is still protected by the original 16th-century walls, built to keep out Henry VIII. Two buildings stand out among the city's monuments: the medieval Church of the Holy Rude and the ornate Mar's Wark.

Stirling Castle

⊘⊘⊙🅟🛈 🏛 Castle Wynd ⏰ 9:30am–5pm daily (summer: to 6pm) 🚫 Dec 25 & 26 🌐 stirlingcastle.scot

㉖
Glasgow

🏛 Glasgow ✈🚈🚌 ℹ 156a-158 Buchanan St; www. peoplemakeglasgow.com

During the industrial 19th century, coal seams in Lanark-shire fueled Glasgow's cotton mills and ironworks, belying its Celtic name, *Glas cu*, meaning "dear green place." Relics of this manufacturing past contrast starkly with the glossy image of modern Glasgow, renowned for its free galleries and museums, cosmopolitan restaurants and bars, trendy shopping districts, and lively and youthful nightlife.

Glasgow's cathedral was one of the few in Scotland to escape destruction during the Scottish Reformation, and is a rare example of an almost-complete 13th-century church. The crypt holds the tomb of St. Mungo, a 6th-century bishop and the city's patron saint. In the cathedral precinct, the St. Mungo Museum of Religious Life and Art illustrates religious themes with a superb range of artifacts.

Glasgow's most important galleries and museums can be found in the more affluent West End. The **Kelvingrove Art Gallery and Museum**, in a striking red sandstone building dating from 1901, is home to a splendid collection of art, with works by Botticelli, Giorgione, Rembrandt, Degas, Millet, and Monet, while the Scottish Gallery contains the famous *Massacre of Glencoe* by James Hamilton. Other highlights here include

The airy main hall at Kelvingrove Art Gallery and Museum; *(inset)* the gallery exterior

GOLF

Scotland's national game was pioneered on the sandy links around St. Andrews. Mary, Queen of Scots enjoyed the game and was berated in 1568 for playing straight after the murder of her husband. Other world-class golf courses in Scotland include Royal Troon and Gleneagles.

dinosaur skeletons, Egyptian artifacts, and a real spitfire suspended in the main hall.

The **Hunterian Art Gallery** houses Scotland's largest print collection and paintings by major European artists from the 16th century to the present. A display of works by Glasgow's most celebrated designer, Charles Rennie Mackintosh, is supplemented with a reconstruction of No. 6 Florentine Terrace, where he lived from 1906 to 1914. Other sights include Pollok House, a Georgian building housing one of Britain's best

collections of 16th- to 19th-century Spanish art; the Tenement House, a modest apartment in a tenement block preserved from Edwardian times; and Provand's Lordship (1471), the city's oldest-surviving house. The House for an Art Lover is a showcase for the work of Charles Rennie Mackintosh. For a social history of the city from the 12th to the 20th century, visit the People's Palace, a cultural museum in the city's East End.

Kelvingrove Art Gallery and Museum

♿🅿️🄿 🚗 Argyle St, Kelvingrove ⌚10am–5pm Mon–Thu & Sat, 11am–5pm Fri & Sun 🗓️Jan 1 & 2, Dec 25 & 26 🌐glasgowlife.org.uk/museums

Hunterian Art Gallery

♿🅿️🄿 🚗82 Hillhead St ⌚10am–5pm Tue–Sat, 11am–4pm Sun 🗓️Dec 24–Jan 5 & public hols 🌐gla.ac.uk/hunterian

---

St. Andrews

🚗Fife 🚆Leuchars 🚌
ℹ️70 Market St; www.visitstandrews.com

Scotland's oldest university town, St. Andrews is also a shrine for golfers from all over the world. Its main streets and cobbled alleys, lined with university buildings and medieval churches, converge on the ruined 12th-century

cathedral. Once the largest in Scotland, it was later pillaged for stones to build the town.

The Royal and Ancient Golf Club, founded in 1754, has a magnificent links course and is the ruling arbiter of the game. The city has other golf courses, open to the public for a small fee. These include the Old Course, which regularly hosts the British Open. St. Andrews is also home to the **British Golf Museum**.

British Golf Museum

⊗🄿 🚗Bruce Embankment ⌚9:30am–5pm daily (Nov–Mar: 10am–4pm daily) 🌐britishgolfmuseum.co.uk

---

EAT

The Birds and Bees

This family-friendly gastropub serves brasserie favorites.

🚗Easter Cornton Rd, Stirling 🌐thebirdsandthebeesstirling.com

£££

Ubiquitous Chip

At this champion of Scottish produce, the casual vibe belies a fine-dining menu.

🚗12 Ashton Lane, Glasgow 🌐ubiquitouschip.co.uk

£££

Moonfish

Imaginative bites precede delightful British mains at this hideaway restaurant.

🚗9 Connection Wynd, Aberdeen 🌐moonfishcafe.co.uk 🗓️Sun & Mon

£££

↑ Grand granite buildings lining Union Street, Aberdeen's main thoroughfare

Highlands. Dominating the high ground above the town is Inverness Castle, a Victorian building of red sandstone. Below it is the **Inverness Museum and Art Gallery**, where exhibits include a fine collection of Inverness silver. Across the river, the Scottish Kiltmaker Visitor Centre offers an insight into the history and tradition of the kilt.

In summer, **Jacobite Cruises** runs regular boat trips along the Caledonian Canal and on Loch Ness, southwest of Inverness. The loch is 24 miles (39 km) long and up to 1,000 ft (305 m) deep. On the western shore, the ruins of the 16th-century Urquhart Castle can be seen. The Official Loch Ness Exhibition Centre, in nearby Drumnadrochit, provides information about the loch and its mythical monster.

28
Aberdeen

🏠 Grampian 🚆🚌🚍 ℹ️ 23 Union St; www.visit abdn.com

Europe's offshore oil capital, Aberdeen is also one of Britain's most important fishing ports, and hosts Scotland's largest fish market.

Among its fine buildings is the 16th-century home of a former provost (mayor) of the city. Period rooms inside **Provost Skene's House** span 200 years of design and include the 17th-century Great Hall, a Regency Room, and a Georgian Dining Room. The Painted Gallery holds an important cycle of religious art, dating from the 17th century.

Founded in 1495, King's College was the city's first university. The chapel has a distinctive lantern tower and stained-glass windows by Douglas Strachan.

St. Andrew's Cathedral is the Mother Church of the Episcopal Communion in the United States. Coats of arms on the ceiling depict the American states.

Housed in a historic building overlooking the harbor, Aberdeen Maritime Museum traces the city's long seafaring tradition.

Provost Skene's House

🏠 Guestrow ↺ For refurbishment until 2020 🌐 aagm.co.uk

29
Inverness

🏠 Inverness-shire 🚆🚌🚍 ℹ️ 36 High St; www.visit invernesslochness.com

Inverness is the center of communication, commerce, and administration for the

Inverness Museum and Art Gallery

☺️ 🏠 1 Castle Wynd 🕐 Apr-Oct: 10am-5pm Tue-Sat; Nov-Mar: noon-4pm Tue-Thu, 11am-4pm Fri & Sat ↺ Jan 1 & 2, Dec 25 & 26 🌐 highlifehighland.com

Jacobite Cruises

🌐 jacobite.co.uk

→ Boats moored in the still waters of Portree harbor at sunset, Isle of Skye

(a plateau of volcanic towers and spikes in the north) to the Cuillins (one of Britain's most spectacular mountain ranges) is majestic. Bonnie Prince Charlie escaped here from the mainland disguised as a maidservant following the defeat of his army at Culloden.

Skye's main settlement is Portree, with its colorful harbor. Dunvegan Castle, on the island's northwest coast, has been the seat of the Clan MacLeod chiefs for over seven centuries. South of here, the Talisker distillery produces top Highland malts.

↑ Reindeer enjoying the snow in the Cairngorm Reindeer Centre

 30

Isle of Skye

⏻ Inner Hebrides 🚌 From Mallaig or Glenelg 🚌 ℹ Bayfield House, Portree; www.isleofskye.com

Skye, the largest of the Inner Hebrides, can be reached by the bridge linking Kyle of Lochalsh and Kyleakin. The coast is shaped by a series of dramatic sea lochs, while the landscape from the Quiraing

 31

Cairngorms

⏻ The Highlands 🚗🚌 Aviemore ℹ 7 Grampian Rd, Aviemore; www.visitcairngorms.com

Rising to a height of 4,296 ft (1,309 m), the Cairngorm mountains form the highest landmass in Britain.

Cairn Gorm itself is the site of one of Britain's first ski centers, with 28 runs to choose from. The chairlift that climbs Cairn Gorm affords superb views over the Spey

Valley. Rothiemurchus Estate has a visitor center offering guided walks.

There are also plenty of opportunities for wildlife encounters, with walks among Britain's only herd of reindeer at the Cairngorm Reindeer Centre, and the chance to view bison, bears, wolves, and boar in the Kincraig Highland Wildlife Park.

TOP 4 WALKS IN THE CAIRNGORN

Loch Brandy
An easy half-day walk from Clova village to a mirror-like loch.

Glen Doll
A two- to three-hour stroll on a well-surfaced path from Glen Doll to Corrie Fee, a dramatic natural amphitheater.

Lairig Ghru
This age-old mountain trail stretches from Speywaide to Deeside and climbs to 2,740 ft (835 m). A tough but rewarding full-day hike with amazing views.

Jock's Road
This iconic long-distance trail traverses three Munro summits. Allow a full day to complete the walk.

PRACTICAL
INFORMATION

Here you will find all the essential advice and information you will need before and during your stay in Great Britain.

AT A GLANCE

CURRENCY
Pound Sterling
(GBP)

TIME ZONE
GMT/BST. British
Summer Time runs
from the last Sunday
in March to the last
Sunday in October.

LANGUAGE
English

ELECTRICITY SUPPLY
Power sockets are
type G, fitting three-
pronged plugs.
Standard voltage
is 230V.

EMERGENCY NUMBERS

POLICE, AMBULANCE, COASTGUARD,
AND FIRE SERVICES

999

TAP WATER
Unless stated
otherwise, tap
water in Great Britain
is safe to drink.

Getting There

London's Heathrow Airport is served by many airlines, with direct flights from most major cities. Other key international airports include London Gatwick, London Stansted, Manchester, Birmingham, and Edinburgh.

The Channel Tunnel offers a nonstop rail link between Britain and Europe. Eurostar services (for foot passengers) run from St. Pancras station in London to Lille and Paris in France, Brussels in Belgium, and Amsterdam in the Netherlands. The Eurotunnel service transports vehicles between Folkestone and Calais.

Regular car and passenger ferries travel across the Channel and the North and Irish seas, the major ones including DFDS Seaways and P&O Ferries. Brittany Ferries run longer (often overnight) services from Plymouth, Poole, and Portsmouth to the west coast of France, as well as one seasonal 20-hour service between Plymouth and Santander in Spain.

Personal Security

Britain is generally a safe country, but it is always a good idea to take sensible precautions against pickpockets. If you have anything stolen, report the crime as soon as possible to the nearest police station. Get a copy of the crime report in order to claim on your insurance.

Health

You can buy a wide range of medicines from pharmacies, which in Britain are also known as chemists. Emergency medical treatment in a British National Health Service (NHS) emergency room is free, but any kind of additional medical care could prove to be very expensive if you don't have insurance or your country does not have a reciprocal healthcare agreement.

Passports and Visas

A valid passport is needed to enter Britain. Visitors from the EU, the United States, Canada, New Zealand, and Australia do not require a visa

to enter the country. At the time of writing, Britain was in the middle of Brexit negotiations, so check the current visa requirements before visiting if you're an EU citizen.

Travelers with Specific Needs

Most modern buildings and infrastructure have been designed with wheelchairs in mind, while many British trains and buses have been adapted. The best dedicated guide for wheelchair users is Holidays in the British Isles, published by **Disability Rights UK**. Accessibility information for public transport is available from regional public transport websites.
Disability Rights UK
🇼 disabilityrightsuk.org

Money

Major credit, debit, and prepaid currency cards are accepted in most shops and restaurants. However, it is always worth carrying a little cash, as some smaller businesses, markets, and local public transportion may operate a cash-only policy. Though technically having the same value, Scottish banknotes are not always accepted outside Scotland, so it is best to exchange them before leaving.

Cell Phones and Wi-Fi

Free Wi-Fi hotspots are widely available in cities, most forms of accommodation, and on many buses and trains. Cafés and restaurants usually permit the use of their Wi-Fi on the condition that you make a purchase.

Visitors traveling to Great Britain with EU tariffs can use their devices here without being affected by data roaming charges. (This situation may change, however, when the UK leaves the EU.) Visitors from other countries should check their contracts before departure in order to avoid unexpected charges.

Getting Around

Britain's small size means that internal air travel is rarely necessary, but flights are available between major cities.

The railroad system can sometimes be confusing for visitors. Lines are run by several different private companies, but are coordinated by **National Rail**, which runs a joint information service. On-the-day fares can be expensive, so if you are planning to travel long distances then try to book tickets several weeks in advance. The **Interrail** Great Britain Pass offers deals on travel within a one-month period.

Long-distance buses are usually referred to as coaches. Coach services are generally cheaper than rail travel, but slower. Tickets can be purchased online, as well as at coach stations and airports. The largest coach operator is **National Express**, but **Megabus** is sometimes cheaper. **Oxford Tube** runs coaches between London and Oxford, and **Scottish Citylink** has services linking London, the north of England, and Scotland.

Numerous national and international car rental companies operate in Britain, but renting a car can be expensive. Rental cars with automatic transmission are rare, and must be booked in advance. For many foreign travelers, driving in Britain is a challenge simply because you drive on the left. The measurement of distances in miles can add to the confusion, as can narrow roads, the many roundabouts, congestion, and scarce parking in cities. But in rural areas, driving can be the key way to get around.
Interrail
🇼 interrail.eu
Megabus
🇼 uk.megabus.com/
National Express
🇼 nationalexpress.com
National Rail
🇼 nationalrail.co.uk
Oxford Tube
🇼 oxfordtube.com
Scottish Citylink
🇼 citylink.co.uk

Visitor Information

The **British Tourist Authority** (Visit Britain) has offices in a number of major cities worldwide. Tourist information is available in many towns and public places, and at some sites of historical interest. Both the national tourist boards (Visit England, Visit Wales, and Visit Scotland) and their regional counterparts have numerous resources on their excellent websites.
British Tourist Authority
🇼 visitbritain.com

IRELAND

Ireland's history is one of internal strife, invasion, and reconciliation. Until the Viking invasions of the 9th century, the island was relatively peaceful: Christianity was embraced by the Celtic tribes in the 5th century AD, and Irish monks played a role in the early development of European Christianity. The Vikings never succeeded in gaining control of Ireland, but in 1169, the English arrived with greater ambitions. Many Irish chiefs submitted to Henry II of England, whose knights carved out large fiefdoms for themselves. In 1532, when Henry VIII broke with the Catholic church, Ireland became a battleground between Irish Catholics and English armies dispatched to crush resistance. Irish lands were confiscated and granted to Protestants from England and Scotland, and repressive laws denied Irish Catholics basic freedoms. An even bleaker period of Irish history arrived with the Great Famine of 1845–8, during which millions died or were forced to emigrate. A campaign for Home Rule gained strength after this, but it took the Irish War of Independence of 1919–21 to force the issue. The Treaty of 1921 divided the island in two, with the south gaining full independence in 1937. Civil-rights protests in the 1960s initiated decades of unrest in Northern Ireland – known as the "Troubles" – with bombing campaigns by both Loyalist and Republican groups. In 1998, the Good Friday Agreement led to the inauguration of the Northern Ireland Assembly, which has brought with it a sustained era of peace.

IRELAND

Ballycastle

Belmullet

Ballina

Crossmolina

N59

Achill
Island

Mulrany

Foxford

Clare
Island

Westport

N5

Cas

Inishbofin

Clarem

CONNEMARA
14

Clifden

Cashel

N59

Lough
Corrib

Roundstone

Moycullen

Rossaveal

GALW

ARAN ISLANDS **15**

Ballyvaughan

Lisdoonvarna

*Atlantic
Ocean*

N67

E

Kilkee

Kilrush

Tarbert

Listowel

Newcast
Wes

N69

Tralee

Castleisland

*Dingle
Peninsula*

DINGLE **12**

Killorglin

11 KILLAR

Cahersiveen

Valentia Island

Ring of Kerry

Kenmare

Waterville

N71

*The Skellig
Islands*

Glengarriff

Clon

Dufrus

Skibb

*Mizen
Head*

IRELAND

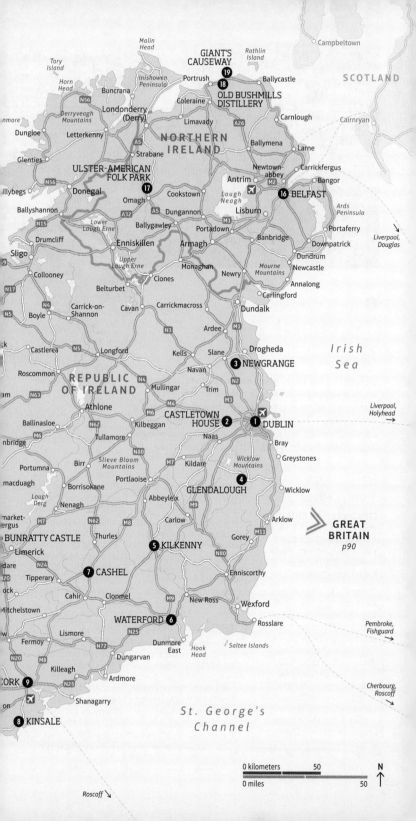

❶

DUBLIN

 🛈 www.visitdublin.com

Bisected by the Liffey River, Ireland's capital is famous for its many pubs and its cultural heritage. The first harbor in Dublin was established in the early 9th century, by the Vikings. The city thereafter suffered centuries of wars and conflict, but in recent decades has established its own identity and is today a thriving destination.

 ①

Trinity College

🏛 College Green 🚉 DART to Pearse 🚌 4, 7, 10, 14, 15, 46, 48, & many others 🕐 Old Library: hours vary, check website 🗓 10 days at Christmas 🌐 tcd.ie

Trinity was founded in 1592 by Elizabeth I on the site of an Augustinian monastery as a bastion of Protestantism. It was not until the 1970s that Catholics started entering the university. Its cobbled quads and lawns still have a monastic feel, providing a pleasant haven in the heart of the city. In front of the main entrance, on College Green, are statues of two of Trinity's most famous 18th-century students, playwright Oliver Goldsmith and political writer Edmund Burke. Literary alumni of later times include the playwrights Oscar Wilde and Samuel Beckett.

The oldest surviving part of the college is the red-brick building (the Rubrics) on the east side of Library Square, built around 1700. The Old Library itself dates from 1732. Its spectacular Long Room measures 210 ft (64 m) in length and houses 200,000 antiquarian texts, as well as marble busts of scholars and the oldest harp in Ireland. Below the library is the Treasury, where the college's most precious volumes – the beautifully illuminated manuscripts produced in Ireland from the 8th to the 10th century – are kept. The most famous, the Book of Kells, may have been created by monks from Iona, who fled to Kells in 806 after a Viking

THE BOOK OF KELLS

The most richly decorated of all the Irish illuminated manuscripts dating from the 8th–10th centuries, the Book of Kells contains the four gospels in Latin, copied onto leaves of high-quality vellum. It is remarkable both for the beauty of the script and for the inspired fantasy of the illumination. There is no record of its existence before the early 11th century, but it was probably created in about 800. It would have taken many years of work by the scriptorium of a monastery. The manuscript was moved to Trinity College in the 17th century for safekeeping.

Aerial view over Dublin; *(inset)* the Long Room in the Old Library at Trinity College

raid. The scribes embellished the text with intricate patterns as well as human figures and animals. Almost as fine is the *Book of Durrow*, which dates from the late 7th century.

Merrion Square

DART to Pearse 🚌 4, 7, 25, 44, 66, & many others

Merrion Square is one of Dublin's largest and grandest Georgian squares. Covering about 12 acres (5 ha), the square was laid out by John Ensor around 1762.

On the west side are the impressive facades of the Natural History Museum, the National Gallery of Ireland, and the front garden of Leinster House, seat of the Dáil and the Seanad (the two houses of the Irish Parliament). The other three sides of this handsome square are lined with lovely Georgian townhouses. Many have brightly painted doors and original features, such as wrought-iron balconies, ornate doorknockers, and fanlights. The oldest and finest residences are on the north side.

Some of the houses – now predominantly used as office space – have plaques detailing famous former occupants, such as Catholic emancipation leader Daniel O'Connell (No. 58) and poet W. B. Yeats (No. 82). Oscar Wilde spent his childhood at No. 1.

The attractive central park has colorful flower and shrub beds. In the 1840s, it served a grim function as a soup kitchen, feeding the hungry during the Great Famine.

> INSIDER TIP
> **Getting Around**
>
> The DART train links Pearse, Connolly, and Tara Street stations in the city center to the coastal suburbs. The Luas Light Rail serves the inland suburbs. Buses run every 15–40 minutes; the Nitelink covers selected routes from midnight to 4am on Friday and Saturday.

National Gallery of Ireland

🏛 Merrion Square West & Clare St 🚆 DART to Pearse 🚌 4, 7, 25, 44, & many others ⏰ 9:15am–5:30pm Tue–Sat (to 8:30pm Thu), 11am–5:30pm Sun & Mon 🚫 Good Fri & Dec 24–26 🌐 nationalgallery.ie

This purpose-built gallery was opened to the public in 1864. It houses more than 15,000 works of art from the 13th century to the present day, with a significant collection of works from the Italian, French, Flemish, and Dutch schools. The fine art collection is made up of celebrated masterpieces by the likes of Rembrandt, Vermeer, Gainsborough, Van Gogh, Renoir, and Picasso.

The gallery also holds the most important collection of Irish painting, dating from the 17th century, plus a section dedicated to the works of Jack B. Yeats.

Running alongside the permanent collection is a program of temporary exhibitions. These range from artists' retrospectives to shows with a focus on a particular thematic subject, like landscapes or interiors.

National Museum of Ireland – Archaeology

🏛 Kildare St 🚆 DART to Pearse 🚋 Luas green line to St Stephen's Green 🚌 15, 25, 38, 140, & many others ⏰ 10am–5pm Tue–Sat, 1–5pm Sun & Mon 🚫 Good Fri & Dec 25 🌐 museum.ie

The National Museum of Ireland – Archaeology was

The National Gallery of Ireland's rich collection, and ↓ (inset) its entrance

built in the 1880s to the plans of Cork architect Sir Thomas Deane. Its splendid domed rotunda, inspired by Palladian design, features marble pillars and an elegant mosaic floor decorated with the signs of the zodiac. The ground floor holds *Ór – Ireland's Gold*, a collection of Bronze Age finds, including many beautiful pieces of jewelry. Objects from the later Iron Age Celtic period are on display in the Treasury. There are also many well-known treasures from the era of Irish Christianity (p167). The first floor houses Viking artifacts and the Ancient Egypt gallery. The Viking exhibition features coins, pottery, and swords excavated in the 1970s from the Viking settlement discovered beside the Liffey at Wood Quay, near Christ Church Cathedral (p160).

The museum has another branch, the National Museum of Ireland – Decorative Arts & History, at Benburb Street, west of the city center. It is housed in the vast Collins Barracks, established in 1700 by William III. The principal exhibits are the museum's

collections of furniture, silver, weaponry, and scientific instruments, as well as an exhibit on the 1916 Easter Rising and events that occurred in the decade 1913–23.

---

⑤ Grafton Street

 14, 15, 46, & many others

The spine of Dublin's most stylish shopping district, Grafton Street runs south from College Green to the glass St. Stephen's Green Shopping Centre. This busy pedestrianized strip, with its energetic buskers and talented street-theater artists, is home to one of Dublin's best department stores, Brown Thomas. There are also many excellent jewelers, plus a number of popular traditional pubs hidden along the surrounding side streets.

At the junction with Nassau Street is a statue by Jean Rynhart of *Molly Malone* (1988), the celebrated "cockles and mussels" street trader of the well-known Irish folk song.

↑ Crowds outside a traditional pub on a cobbled street in the charming Temple Bar area

⑥ Temple Bar

11, 16A, 46A, & many others

The area of cobbled streets between Dame Street and the Liffey are named after Sir William Temple, who acquired the land in the early 1600s. The term "bar" meant a riverside path. In the 1800s, it was home to small businesses, but over the years went into decline. In the early 1960s, the land was bought up with plans for redevelopment. Artists and retailers took short-term leases, but stayed on when the plans were scrapped and Temple Bar prospered. Today, it is a lively place, with restaurants, bars, clubs, shops, and galleries. Organizations based here include the Irish Film Institute, which has three screens, as well as a bookshop and café; **Project Arts Centre**, a contemporary-arts center for theater, dance, film, music, and visual art; and the Gallery of Photography, the only Irish art gallery that is devoted solely to photographs.

Project Arts Centre

39 East Essex St
10am–6pm Mon–Fri, 11am–6pm Sat; closing times are extended when a show is on
projectartscentre.ie

EAT

Bewley's
Dublin's most iconic café, with a range of fresh-baked treats.

 78-79 Grafton St
bewleys.com

€€€

Dolce Sicily
This Georgian café offers a selection of divine Sicilian pastries.

 43 Dawson St
dolcesicily.ie

€€€

Le Petit Parisien
Parisian-style café with delectable patisserie.

 17 Wicklow St
lepetitparisien.ie

€€€

The Rolling Donut
The uniquely flavored doughnuts here include vegan options.

 55 King St South
therollingdonut.ie

€€€

⑦ 🏛 🖼 🖵

DUBLIN CASTLE

🏠 Off Dame St, Dublin 2 🚌 49, 77A, 123 🕐 Castle: 9:45am-5:45pm daily; Chester Beatty Library: 9:45am-5:15pm daily 🚫 Castle: Jan 1, Good Fri, Dec 24-28; Chester Beatty Library: Jan 1, Good Fri, Dec 24-26, public hols 🌐 dublincastle.ie

One of the most important buildings in Irish history, Dublin Castle was erected on the site of a Viking fortress in the 13th century and remained the seat of English rule here for seven centuries.

Constructed in 1204, the original medieval fortress here was almost completely destroyed by fire in 1684 – all that remains is the Record Tower. The castle was rebuilt in the 17th and 18th centuries, with the addition of the luxurious State Apartments – home to the British-appointed Viceroys of Ireland. The castle was handed over to Ireland in 1922, when the Irish Free State was declared, and today it is both a key visitor attraction and a government complex. In the grounds is the Chester Beatty Library, housing numerous artistic and religious treasures.

↑ Bedford Tower, the centerpiece of the Upper Yard

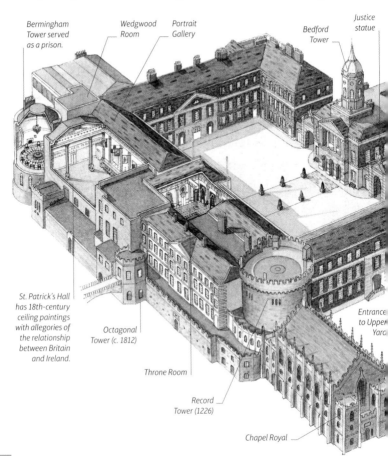

Bermingham Tower served as a prison.

Wedgwood Room

Portrait Gallery

Justice statue

Bedford Tower

St. Patrick's Hall has 18th-century ceiling paintings with allegories of the relationship between Britain and Ireland.

Octagonal Tower (c. 1812)

Throne Room

Record Tower (1226)

Chapel Royal

Entrance to Upper Yard

1 The figure of Justice faces the Upper Yard above the main entrance from Cork Hill. The statue initially aroused much cynicism among Dubliners, who felt she was turning her back on the city.

2 The Chapel Royal was completed in 1814 by Francis Johnston. The 103 heads on the exterior of this Neo-Gothic church were carved by Edward Smyth.

3 The Throne Room, one of the grandest of the State Apartments, contains a throne first installed for the visit of King George IV in 1821.

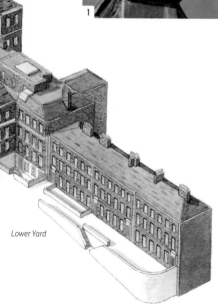

Lower Yard

The castle, with most buildings laid out around the main Upper Yard

ROBERT EMMET

Leader of the abortive Irish Rebellion of 1803, Robert Emmet is remembered as a heroic champion of Irish liberty. His plan was to capture Dublin Castle as a signal for the country to rise up against the Act of Union. However, the plan failed; Emmet was detained in the Kilmainham Gaol and hanged, but the defiant, patriotic speech he made from the dock helped to inspire future generations of Irish freedom fighters.

St. Patrick's Cathedral

🏛 St Patrick's Close 🚌 49, 54A, 56A, 77A, 151 ⏰ Hours vary, check website 🚫 Dec 25 (pm) & 26 🌐 stpatricks cathedral.ie

Ireland's largest church was founded beside a sacred well where St. Patrick is said to have baptized converts around AD 450. It was originally just a wooden chapel, but in 1192, Archbishop John Comyn commissioned a magnificent new stone structure.

The cathedral is 300 ft (91 m) long; at the western end is a 141 ft (43 m) tower, restored by Archbishop Minot in 1370 and now known as the Minot Tower. Much of the present building dates back to work completed between 1254 and 1270.

The interior is dotted with memorials, the most elaborate of which is the one erected in 1632 by Richard Boyle, Earl of Cork, in memory of his second wife Katherine. It is decorated with painted carvings of members of the Boyle family. Others remembered in the church include Douglas Hyde, Ireland's first president.

Many visitors come to see the memorials associated with Jonathan Swift (1667–1745), Dean of St. Patrick's and a scathing satirist best known as the author of *Gulliver's Travels*. In the south aisle is "Swift's Corner," which has memorabilia including an altar table and his death mask. On the southwest side of the nave, two brass plates mark his grave and that of his beloved "Stella," Esther Johnson.

Christ Church Cathedral

🏛 Christchurch Place 🚌 13, 49, 54A, 56A, 77A, 123 ⏰ Hours vary, check website 🚫 Dec 26 & 27 🌐 christchurchdublin.ie

Christ Church Cathedral was commissioned in 1172 by Richard de Clare, known as Strongbow, the Anglo-Norman conqueror of Dublin, and by Archbishop Laurence O'Toole. During the Reformation period, the cathedral passed to the Protestant Church of Ireland. As part of the remodeling by architect George Street in the 1870s, the Old Synod Hall

was built and linked to the cathedral by an attractive covered bridge.

In the atmospheric crypt are fragments removed from the cathedral during the building's restoration, as well as the mummified bodies of a cat and a rat found in an organ pipe in the 1860s. There is also a permanent exhibition of the cathedral's treasures.

The nave has some fine early Gothic arches. At the west end is a memorial known as the Strongbow Monument. The large effigy in chain armor is probably not Strongbow, but the curious half-figure beside it may be part of his original tomb. The Chapel of St. Laud houses a casket containing the heart of St. Laurence O'Toole.

> INSIDER TIP
> **Portobello**
>
> A 15-minute walk south from Christ Church Cathedral is Portobello - a route lined by bars and restaurants. Bastible is a popular bistro; Fallon's Bar has a great buzz; and Leonard's Corner is perfect for a cosy pint.

St. Patrick's Cathedral and its adjoining flower-filled gardens

 10

Dublinia and the Viking World

St Michael's Hill 13, 49, 54A, 123 Mar–Sep: 10am–6:30pm daily; Oct–Feb: 10am–5:30pm daily Dec 24–26 dublinia.ie

This heritage center in the Neo-Gothic Synod Hall covers the period of Dublin's history from the arrival of the Anglo-Normans in 1170 to the closure of the monasteries in the 1540s. It features life-size reconstructions of the medieval city, plus a Viking warship and an interactive archaeology exhibition.

11

The Liffey

25, 25A, 51, 66, 66A, 67, 67A, 68, 69, & many others

Though modest in size, the Liffey river features strongly in Dubliners' everyday lives.

 →

The iconic, cast-iron Ha'penny Bridge, crossing the Liffey river

THE VIKINGS IN DUBLIN

In 841, Viking raiders built a fort where the Poddle river met the Liffey at a black pool (Dubh Linn), now the site of Dublin Castle. Following their defeat at the Battle of Clontarf in 1014, the Vikings integrated with the local Irish, adopting Christian beliefs. After Strongbow's Anglo-Norman invasion in 1169, the Hiberno-Viking trading community declined.

The handiest pedestrian link between Temple Bar (p157) and the north of the city is the attractive Ha'penny Bridge, which opened in 1816. Its official name is the Liffey Bridge; its better-known nickname comes from the halfpenny toll levied on it up until 1919.

The two most impressive buildings on the Liffey are the Custom House and the Four Courts, both of which were designed by James Gandon at the end of the 18th century. In 1921, supporters of Sinn Féin celebrated their election victory by setting light to the Custom House, seen as a symbol of British imperialism. The building was not fully restored until 1991, when it reopened as government offices. A series of 14 magnificent heads by Edward Smyth, personifying Ireland's rivers and the Atlantic Ocean, form the keystones of its arches and entrances.

The Four Courts suffered a similar fate during the Irish Civil War of 1921–2, when it was bombarded by government troops after being seized by anti-Treaty rebels. Here, too, the buildings were restored to their original design. A copper-covered dome rises above a portico crowned with the figures of Moses, Justice, and Mercy.

↑ The vibrant fall colors of a tree-filled landscape in expansive Phoenix Park

building is a sculpture of the mythical Irish hero Cuchulainn, dedicated to those who died.

A walk up the central mall is the best way to inspect the series of sculptures lining the street. At the south end stands a massive memorial to Daniel O'Connell, and at the north end is the monument to Charles Stewart Parnell.

---

⑭
Phoenix Park

🏛 Park Gate, Conyngham Rd, Dublin 8 🚌 25, 66, 67, 68, 69 ⏰ Daily

Ringed by a 7-mile (11-km) wall, this is Europe's largest enclosed city park. It originated in 1662 as a deer park for the Duke of Ormonde, and was opened to the public in 1745. The name "Phoenix" is

⑫
Parnell Square

🚌 3, 11A, 13, 16A, 19A, 38, & many others

Despite looking somewhat neglected, Parnell Square contains a number of noteworthy sights, including the Rotunda Hospital, Europe's first purpose-built maternity hospital, opened in 1757. The hospital's former grand supper room now functions as the Gate Theatre, famous for producing new plays.

On the north side of the square, two 18th-century townhouses have been converted into museums: the **Dublin Writers Museum**, devoted to Irish literature, and the **Dublin City Gallery**, **The Hugh Lane**, housing Impressionist paintings.

Dublin Writers Museum

♲ 🏛 18 Parnell Sq North
⏰ 10am-5pm Mon-Sat, 11am-5pm Sun ⏰ Dec 25 & 26 🌐 writersmuseum.com

Dublin City Gallery, The Hugh Lane

🏛 Charlemont House
⏰ Hours vary, check website
⏰ Dec 24-27 & public hols
🌐 hughlane.ie

⑬
O'Connell Street

🚌 2, 3, 11, 13, 16A, & many others

Dublin's main thoroughfare, formerly called Sackville Street, was renamed in 1922 after Daniel O'Connell, known as the "Liberator" for his tireless campaigns for Catholic rights in the 19th century. The street was laid out in the 1700s as an elegant residential parade, but nowadays little remains of its original grandeur.

A few venerable buildings survive, including the General Post Office, which became a symbol of the 1916 Easter Rising. Members of the Irish Volunteers and Irish Citizen Army seized the building on Easter Monday, and the Proclamation of the Irish Republic was read by Patrick Pearse from its steps. The rebels remained inside for a week, but the British eventually forced them out. Fourteen of the leaders were subsequently caught and shot. Inside the

198

—

Number of calories in a pint of Guinness® – fewer than in a pint of orange juice!

→

Visitors enjoying a guided tour of the Guinness Storehouse®

said to be a corruption of the Gaelic Fionn Uisce, or "clear water;" a statue of the mythical bird sits atop the Phoenix Column at the park's center.

Other monuments include the Wellington Testimonial, a 204 ft (63 m) obelisk with bronze bas-reliefs made from captured French cannons. The 90-ft (27-m) steel Papal Cross marks the spot where the pope said Mass in 1979.

The park is also home to the hugely popular **Dublin Zoo**, as well as the Áras an Uachtaráin, the Irish President's official residence, for which 525 tickets are issued every Saturday for a free guided tour. The 17th-century Ashtown Castle is now the Phoenix Park Visitor Centre, with displays on the park's history.

The best way to take in the entire sprawling site is via bicycle; these can be rented at the Park Gate entrance on Chesterfield Avenue. Adult, child, and tandem bikes are available for hire.

Dublin Zoo

🖼 🍴 🖥 🛍 ⏰ Hours vary, check website 🆆 dublinzoo.ie

Guinness Storehouse®

🏠 St James's Gate, Dublin 8 🚌 51B, 78A, 123 ⏰ 9am–7pm daily 🚫 Jan 1, Good Fri, Dec 24–26 🆆 guinness-storehouse.com

Guinness is a black or "stout" beer with a malty flavor and a smooth creamy head. The St. James's Gate brewery where it is made is the largest in Europe.

Housed in a warehouse formerly used for hop storage, the World of Guinness exhibition chronicles 200 years of brewing at the site. Displays show how production methods have changed since 1759, when Arthur Guinness took over the backstreet brewery. Guinness started brewing ale, but was aware of a black beer called "porter," popular in London's markets. The new recipe he developed was so successful that he made his first export shipment in 1769.

The tour ends with a complimentary pint of Guinness in the Granty Bar, where visitors can also enjoy 360-degree views of the city.

DRINK

The Cobblestone

This is one of Dublin's best pubs for live traditional music – there always seems to be a session on, no matter when you visit. There are also music lessons, regular set dancing, history talks, and more.

🏠 77 King St North, Smithfield 🆆 cobblestonepub.ie

Vintage Cocktail Club

Tucked behind a nondescript door, this is surely the best cocktail bar in the city. It has a chic 1920s decor and an extensive drinks menu.

🏠 15 Crown Alley 🆆 vintagecocktail club.com

A SHORT WALK
SOUTHEAST DUBLIN

Distance 1.5 miles (2 km) **Nearest Luas** Trinity
Time 20 minutes

The area around College Green, dominated by the facades of the Bank of Ireland and Trinity College, is very much the heart of Dublin. The alleys and malls cutting across busy pedestrianized Grafton Street feature many of Dublin's better stores, hotels, and restaurants, while just off Kildare Street are the Irish Parliament, the National Library, and the National Museum of Ireland – Archaeology. To escape the city bustle, many head for sanctuary on St. Stephen's Green.

↑ Families feeding the ducks at the lake in St. Stephen's Green

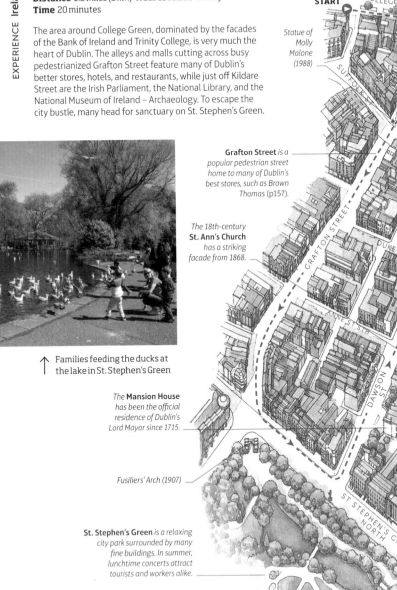

*The **Bank of Ireland** is a grand Georgian edifice, originally built as the Irish Parliament.*

START COLLEGE G

Statue of Molly Malone (1988)

SUFFOLK S

Grafton Street *is a popular pedestrian street home to many of Dublin's best stores, such as Brown Thomas (p157).*

The 18th-century **St. Ann's Church** *has a striking facade from 1868.*

GRAFTON STREET

DUKE ST

ANNE ST TH

DAWSON ST

*The **Mansion House** has been the official residence of Dublin's Lord Mayor since 1715.*

Fusiliers' Arch (1907)

ST STEPHEN'S GREE
NORTH

St. Stephen's Green *is a relaxing city park surrounded by many fine buildings. In summer, lunchtime concerts attract tourists and workers alike.*

0 meters   50   N
0 yards   50   ↑

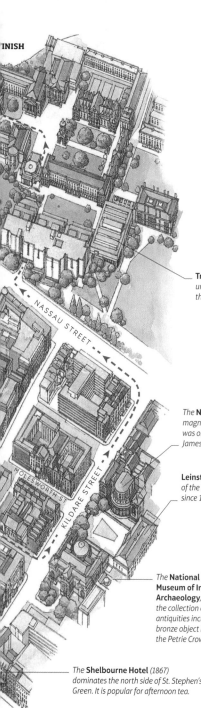

↑ Fusiliers' Arch memorial at the entrance to St. Stephen's Green

Trinity College, *Dublin's premier university, has modern artworks throughout its grounds* (p154).

The **National Library**, *whose magnificent old reading room was once a hangout of novelist James Joyce.*

Leinster House, *seat of the Irish Parliament since 1922.*

The **National Museum of Ireland – Archaeology**, *where the collection of Irish antiquities includes a bronze object known as the Petrie Crown* (p156).

The **Shelbourne Hotel** (1867) *dominates the north side of St. Stephen's Green. It is popular for afternoon tea.*

Did You Know?

Until the 1770s, most of Dublin's public executions took place in St. Stephen's Green.

② Castletown House

🏠 Celbridge, Co. Kildare
🚌 67, 67A from Dublin
🕐 Mid-Mar-Oct: 10am–6pm daily; Nov–mid-Mar: grounds only 🌐 castletown.ie

Built in 1722–32 for William Conolly, Speaker of the Irish Parliament, Castletown was Ireland's first grand Palladian-style country house. Most of the interiors were commissioned by Lady Louisa Lennox, wife of Conolly's great-nephew, Tom, who lived here in the late 18th century. It was she who added the magnificent long gallery at the top of the house, with its Pompeiian-style friezes, cobalt-blue walls, busts, and niches framing Classical statuary.

A portrait of Lady Louisa is incorporated in the Rococo stuccowork by the Francini brothers in the staircase hall. Another reminder of Lady Louisa is the print room, the last surviving, intact example of its kind. In the 18th century, ladies pasted prints directly on to the wall and framed them with elaborate festoons.

↑ Original paintings and furniture in Castletown House

③ Newgrange

🏠 5 miles (8 km) E of Slane, Co. Meath 🚆 To Drogheda
🚌 To visitor center via Drogheda

The origins of Newgrange, one of the most important passage graves in Europe, are steeped in mystery. Built around 3200 BC, it was redis-covered in 1699. When it was later excavated in the 1960s, archaeologists realized that at dawn on the winter solstice (December 21), a beam of sunlight shines through the opening above the entrance to the tomb – a feature that is unique to Newgrange. The light travels along the 62-ft (19-m) passage and hits the central recess in the burial chamber. It is thus the world's oldest solar observatory.

Between 1962 and 1975, the grave and the mound, or cairn, that covers it were restored. The retaining wall at the front of the cairn was rebuilt using white quartz and granite stones found scattered around the site. It is estimated that the original tomb, created by people who had neither the wheel nor metal tools, may have taken up to 70 years to build. About 200,000 tons of loose stones were transported to build the cairn, with larger slabs used to make the circle around the mound and the retaining kerb. Many of the kerbstones and the slabs lining the passage and chamber are decorated with zigzags, spirals, and other geometric motifs.

Each of the three recesses in the central chamber con-tained a chiseled "basin stone" that held funerary offerings and the bones of the dead. The chamber's corbeled ceil-ing has proved completely waterproof for 5,000 years.

Newgrange is very popular, especially in summer, so it is likely that there will be queues and you will have to wait your turn at the **Brú na Bóinne**

Interpretive Centre, which has displays on the area's Stone Age heritage. Tours of Newgrange also include the nearby tomb at Knowth, whose treasures form the greatest concentration of megalithic art in Europe.

Brú na Bóinne Interpretive Centre
  🕐 Hours vary, check website 🌐 newgrange.com

④ Glendalough

🏠 Co. Wicklow 🚌 St. Kevin's Bus from Dublin 🕐 Visitor Centre: 9:30am–5pm daily (mid-Mar–mid-Oct: to 6pm) 🔒 Visitor Centre: Dec 23–28 🌐 glendalough.ie

The steep, wooded slopes of Glendalough, the "valley of the two lakes," harbor one of Ireland's most atmospheric ruined monasteries. Founded by St. Kevin in the 6th century, it functioned as a monastic center until the Dissolution of the Monasteries in 1539.

The age of many of the buildings is uncertain, but most date from the 10th to the 12th century. Many were restored during the 1870s.

←

Kilkenny and the Nore river, with the medieval castle in the background

the main ruins lie near the smaller Lower Lake. You enter the monastery through the double stone arch of the gatehouse, from where a short walk leads to a graveyard with a restored round tower in one corner. Other ruins near here include the roofless cathedral, the tiny Priest's House, and St. Kevin's Cross. Below, nestled in the lush valley, stands a small oratory. It is popularly known as St. Kevin's Kitchen, because its belfry resembles a chimney.

A path along the south bank of the river leads to the Upper Lake and some of the other buildings associated with St. Kevin. Here, the scenery is wilder and the tranquility of Glendalough can be more strongly appreciated.

⑤
Kilkenny

🏰 Co. Kilkenny 🚌🚆
ℹ Shee Alms House, Rose Inn St; www.kilkenny.ie

Kilkenny sits in a lovely setting beside the Nore river, and many of its houses feature the local black limestone, known as Kilkenny marble. A brewery city, filled with atmospheric old pubs, Kilkenny also hosts a major arts festival.

Built in the 12th century, **Kilkenny Castle** was remodeled in Victorian times. It is set in extensive parkland, and was the seat of the Butler family from around 1391 until 1967, when it was presented to the people of Kilkenny. Two wings of the castle have been restored to their 19th-century splendor, and include a library, a drawing room, and the magnificent Long Gallery. The River Wing houses the Butler Gallery of Contemporary Art.

The area once known as Englishtown is home to grand buildings such as Rothe House, a fine Tudor merchant's residence. The area of narrow alleyways, or "slips," meanwhile, is part of Kilkenny's medieval heritage. The Irishtown district is dominated by the 13th-century St. Canice's Cathedral. This Gothic building is flanked by a round tower and features a finely sculpted west door. In the south transept are 16th-century tombs with effigies of the Butler family.

Kilkenny Castle
♿🕑 🏰 The Parade 🕐 Hours vary, check website 🔒 Good Fri, Dec 24-26 🌐 kilkenny castle.ie

Did You Know?

Ireland's first convicted witch, Dame Alice Kyteler, was born in Kilkenny in 1280.

EARLY-CELTIC CHRISTIANITY

Ireland became Christian in the 5th century, after the missions of St. Patrick and others. The Irish church had strong links with the east – decorative motifs in illuminated manuscripts reflect Egyptian Christian imagery, and materials used in making the inks came from the Middle East. Important early Christian sites besides Glendalough include Clonmacnoise, the Rock of Cashel (p168), Clonfert, Kells, and Devenish Island. Though most of the monastic buildings are ruins, many have continued to be used as cemeteries up to modern times. Monasteries were built on the Aran Islands (p173) and even on remote Skellig Michael, off the Kerry Coast.

6

Waterford

Co. Waterford
120 Parade Quay; www.visitwaterford.com

Ireland's oldest city, Waterford was founded by the Vikings in 914, and later extended by the Anglo-Normans. Its commanding position on the estuary of the Suir River made it southeast Ireland's main port. The 18th century saw the establishment of local industries, including the world-famous glassworks.

The remains of the city walls define the area fortified by the Normans. The largest surviving structure from this era is Reginald's Tower, overlooking the river. Despite the city's medieval layout, most of Waterford's finest buildings are Georgian, including Christchurch Cathedral, designed in the 1770s by local architect John Roberts.

The **Waterford Crystal Factory** lies 1.5 miles (2.5 km) south of the center. Here, you can learn about and observe the process of crystal-making, on a tour that covers more than 225 years of history and takes in master craftsmen at work on individual pieces.

Waterford Crystal Factory

Kilbarry Apr-Oct: 9am-4:15pm daily; Nov-Mar: 9:30am-3:15pm Mon-Fri Dec 21-Jan 4 waterfordvisitorcentre.com

7

Cashel

Co. Tipperary
Heritage Centre, Main St; www.cashel.ie

The town's great attraction is the magnificent medieval **Rock of Cashel**. Many people stay overnight to enjoy eerie floodlit views of the rocky stronghold rising dramatically out of the Tipperary plain. The Rock was a symbol of royal and ecclesiastical power for more than a thousand years. From the 5th century AD, it was the seat of the Kings of Munster, rulers of southwest Ireland. In 1101, they handed Cashel over to the Church, and it flourished as a religious center until 1647, when a siege by a Cromwellian army ended in the brutal massacre of its 3,000 occupants. A good proportion of the medieval complex still stands, though the main building, the Gothic cathedral, is roofless. The earlier Cormac's Chapel is an outstanding example of Romanesque architecture; other prominent features include a restored round tower and the weatherbeaten St. Patrick's Cross. The figure that is carved on the east face of the cross is said to be St. Patrick.

SHOP

The Book Centre

Browse the shelves of this unique bookshop, housed in a 1930s Art Deco cinema with the original screen still visible.

25 John Roberts Square, Waterford
thebookcentre.ie

The English Market

A covered fruit and veg market established in 1610, this is one of the oldest municipal markets in the world. Now a bustling hub offering all manner of delectables, it has a wide variety of traders and is a pleasure to explore.

Princes St, Cork
englishmarket.ie

←

Visitors admiring the superb Romanesque carvings in Cormac's Chapel, Cashel

↑ Charming row of colorful houses lining the banks of the Lee river, Cork

Rock of Cashel

⊘⊗ ⏰ Hours vary, check website 🚫 Dec 24-26 🌐 heritageireland.ie

---

 8

Kinsale

🏠 Co. Cork 🚌 ℹ️ Pier Road; www.kinsale.ie

One of the prettiest small towns in Ireland, Kinsale has had a long and checkered history. The defeat of the Irish forces and their Spanish allies at the Battle of Kinsale in 1601, for example, signaled the end of the old Gaelic order.

An important naval base in the 17th and 18th centuries, Kinsale today is a popular yachting center. The town is also famous for the quality of its cuisine and has a popular annual festival of gourmet food and drink.

Charles Fort, a fine star-shaped bastion fort to the east of the town, was built by the English in the 1670s to protect Kinsale against foreign naval forces. To reach it, take the signposted coastal walk from the quayside.

Charles Fort

⊘⊗☺ 🏠 2 miles (3 km) E of Kinsale 📞 021-4772 263 ⏰ 10am-6pm daily Nov-mid-Mar: to 5pm) 🚫 Christmas week

---

9

Cork

🏠 Co. Cork ✈️🚆🚌 ℹ️ Tourist House, Grand Parade; www.purecork.ie

Cork city derives its name from the marshy banks of the Lee River – its Irish name, Corcaigh, means marsh – where St. Finbarr founded a monastery around AD 650. The center of Cork today occupies an island between two arms of the river. Its water-ways, bridges, and narrow alleys, combined with the Georgian architecture of the old Quays, give the city a continental feel. In the 18th century, many of today's streets were in fact water-ways, lined with warehouses and merchants' residences.

Noted for its chic bars, multicultural restaurants, bookstores, and boutiques, Paul Street is the hub of the liveliest district in town. The nearby **Crawford Art Gallery** has some fine 19th and 20th century Irish works of art.

A prominent landmark is the steeple of St. Anne Shandon on a hill in the north of the city. It is topped by a weather vane in the shape of a salmon. Visitors can climb up and ring the bells.

Beautiful countryside surrounds Cork, especially along the valley of the Lee River. Outings include a tour of the whiskey distillery at the **Jameson Experience, Midleton**, and a trip to **Blarney Castle**, where a legendary stone bestows magical eloquence on all who kiss it.

Crawford Art Gallery

⑦☺🏛 🏠 Emmet Place ⏰ 10am-5pm Mon-Sat (to 8pm Thu), 11am-4pm Sun 🚫 Public hols, Jan 1, Dec 25 & 26 🌐 crawfordartgallery.ie

Jameson Experience, Midleton

⊘⊗☺☺ 🏠 Midleton, Co. Cork ⏰ 10am-6pm daily 🚫 Jan 1, Good Fri, Dec 24-27 🌐 jamesonwhiskey.com

Blarney Castle

 🏠 Blarney, Co. Cork ⏰ Hours vary, check website 🚫 Dec 24 & 25 🌐 blarney castle.ie

---

> 💬 INSIDER TIP
> **Irish Dancing**
>
> Dancing plays a key role in Irish trad music, with lively beats compelling listeners to move their feet. To join in with the centuries-old reels and jigs yourself, head to Céilí by the Lee *(10 Phoenix St)*, Cork's best Irish dancing night.

BUNRATTY CASTLE

🏠 Bunratty, Co. Clare 🚌 From Limerick, Ennis & Shannon Airport
🕙 9am–5:30pm daily (Jun–Aug: to 6pm) 🚫 Good Fri, Dec 23–26
🌐 shannonheritage.com

This formidable structure is one of Ireland's major tourist attractions. Combining a restored 15th-century fortress and a 19th-century folk park, with nightly four-course mock-medieval banquets, Bunratty Castle is as close to time-travel as you're likely to get.

The castle was built in the 15th century by the MacNamaras, but its most important residents were the O'Briens, Earls of Thomond, who lived here from 1558 until the 1640s. Abandoned in the 19th century, the castle was derelict when Lord Gort bought it in the 1950s, but it has been restored to look as it did under the so-called "Great Earl," who died in 1624. The adjacent Folk Park recreates life at the end of the 19th century, with a village complete with stores and dwellings.

① The exterior of Bunratty Castle, Ireland's most complete medieval fortress.

② The South Solar, or upper chamber, housed guest apartments and features an elaborately carved ceiling.

③ Bunratty Castle is unusual for the high arches on both sides of the keep. The first-floor entrance – designed to deter invaders – is more typical of castles of the period.

Entrance

The Murder Hole was designed for pouring boiling water or pitch onto the heads of attackers.

The chimney provided a vent for the smoke given off by the Great Hall's fire.

The Great Hall served both as a banqueting hall and audience chamber.

South Solar

← The extensively restored 15th-century castle

The Earl's Robing Room was also used as a private audience chamber.

The Main Guard was where the castle's soldiers ate, slept, and listened to music from the Minstrels' Gallery.

The North Front entrance was raised well above ground level to deter invaders.

BUNRATTY FOLK PARK

A meticulous recreation of rural life in Ireland at the end of the 19th century, Bunratty Folk Park began with the reconstruction of a farmhouse that was saved during the building of nearby Shannon Airport. It now consists of a complete village, incorporating shops and a whole range of domestic architecture, from a laborer's cottage to an elegant Georgian house. Other buildings include a farmhouse typical of the Moher region in the Burren and a working corn mill. During the summer, visitors can meet with various costumed characters from the period. The park also has a gift shop and a café.

⑪ Killarney

🏠 Co. Kerry 🚆🚌 🛈 Beech Road; www.killarney.ie

Although Killarney is often derided as "a tourist town," this does not detract from its cheerful atmosphere. The infectious Kerry humor is personified by the wise-cracking "jarveys," whose families have run jaunting cars (pony-and-trap rides) here for generations. The town does get very crowded in the summer, thanks to the lure of the Lakes of Killarney. The three lakes and many of the heather-covered hills surrounding them lie within Killarney National Park. Although the landscape is dotted with ruined castles and abbeys, the lakes are the focus of attention here: the moody, watery scenery is subject to subtle shifts of light and color. Well-known beauty spots in the area include the Meeting of the Waters, the Ladies' View – so called because it delighted Queen Victoria's ladies-in-waiting in 1861 – and the Gap of Dunloe, a dramatic mountain pass. The largest of the lakes, Lough Leane, is dotted with uninhabited islands. Boat trips across the lake run from Ross Castle on the shore nearest Killarney.

Overlooking the lakes is **Muckross House**, an imposing Elizabethan-style mansion built in 1843, set in beautiful gardens. The house is now home to the Museum of Kerry Folklife, while next door is the Walled Garden Centre, which incorporates the garden, a restaurant, and a craft center.

Killarney is also the starting point for the popular Ring of Kerry circular tour around the Iveragh Peninsula. Allow a day's drive to enjoy its captivating scenery.

Muckross House

 🏠 2 miles (4 km) S of Killarney ⏰ Hours vary, check website 🚫 Jan 1, Dec 24-26 🌐 muckross-house.ie

The Lakes of Killarney, over looked *(inset)* by Muckross House ↓

⑫ Dingle

🏠 Co. Kerry 🚌 🛈 Strand St; www.dingle-peninsula.ie

This once remote Irish-speaking town is today a thriving fishing port and popular tourist center. Brightly painted craft shops and cafés abound, and the quayside is fringed with lively bars offering music and seafood. The harbor is home to Dingle's biggest star, Fungi the dolphin, who has been a permanent resident since 1983 and can be visited by boat or on swimming trips.

Dingle is a good base for exploring the archaeological remains of the Dingle Peninsula. The most fascinating is the Gallarus Oratory, to the northwest. This tiny dry-stone church was built from the 6th to the 9th century. West of Dingle are the Iron Age fort of Dunbeg and Early Christian beehive huts.

Galway

Co. Galway

The Fairgreen, Foster St; 091-537 700

Standing on the banks of the Corrib River, Galway is the center for the Irish-speaking regions in the west of Ireland and a lively university city. In the 15th and 16th centuries, it was a prosperous trading port, controlled by 14 merchant families. Its allegiance to the English Crown cost the city dear when, in 1652, it was sacked by Cromwell's forces. In the 18th century, Galway fell into decline, but in recent years its profile has revived through the growth of high-tech industries here.

Many of the best stores, pubs, theaters, and historic sights are packed into the narrow lanes of the "Latin Quarter" around Quay Street. Nearby is the Collegiate Church of St. Nicholas, founded in 1320 and the city's finest medieval building. To the south of the church stands the 16th-century Spanish Arch, where ships from Spain unloaded their cargoes. Facing the arch, across the Corrib, is the Claddagh. The only remnants of this once close-knit, Gaelic-speaking community are its friendly pubs and Claddagh rings – betrothal rings that are traditionally handed down from mother to daughter.

INSIDER TIP
Galway Festivals

The Galway International Arts Festival (July) is Ireland's biggest arts festival, offering theater, music, comedy and art. In September, Galway hosts the world's longest-running oyster festival - three days of seafood trails, shucking competitions, tastings, and family events.

↑ The craggy cliff faces of Inishmore, the largest of the Aran Islands

Connemara

Co. Galway **To Clifden or Letterfrack** **Mar-Oct: Galway Road, Clifden; 095-21163**

This wild region encompasses bogs, mountains, and rugged coastline. The small town of Clifden is a popular base for exploring, and is also the start of the Sky Road, an 7-mile (11-km) circular route with spectacular ocean views. South of Clifden, the coast road to Roundstone skirts a massive bog, impromptu landing site of the first transatlantic flight made by Alcock and Brown in 1919.

Connemara National Park, near Letterfrack, offers spectacular scenery, dominated by the mountains known as the Twelve Bens. Here, visitors may see red deer and Connemara ponies. Nearby **Kylemore Abbey** is a 19th-century battlemented fantasy, complete with walled garden and nature trails. It became an abbey when Benedictine nuns, fleeing from Belgium during World War I, sought refuge here.

Connemara National Park

Letterfrack **9am-5:30pm daily** **connemara nationalpark.ie**

Kylemore Abbey

 On the N59 **9am-7pm daily** **kylemoreabbey.ie**

Aran Islands

Co. Galway **From Connemara** **From Rossaveal or Doolin (Mar-Oct)** **Kilronan, Inishmore; 099-61263**

Inishmore, Inishmaan, and Inisheer – the Aran Islands – are formed from a limestone ridge. The largest, Inishmore, is 8 miles (13 km) long and 2 miles (3 km) wide. All three feature austere landscapes crisscrossed with dry-stone walls, coastal views, and prehistoric stone forts. Ferries sail at least once a day in winter and several times daily in summer. Cars cannot be taken to the islands.

Christianity was brought to the islands in the 5th century by St. Enda, starting a long monastic tradition. Protected for centuries by their isolated position, the islands today are a bastion of traditional culture. They are famous for their distinctive knitwear and for the traditional costume that was once worn by residents of the islands.

↑ The stunning Titanic Belfast museum, which chronicles the ship's construction and tragic voyage

16
Belfast

 Co. Antrim 🛫🚆🚌
🛈 9 Donegal Square;
www.visit-belfast.com

Belfast was the only city in Ireland to experience the full force of the Industrial Revolution. Its shipbuilding, rope-making, tobacco, and linen industries caused the population to rise to almost 400,000 by the end of World War I. The wealth it enjoyed is still evident in its imposing public buildings. The Troubles (p151) and the decline of traditional industries have damaged its economic life, but Belfast remains a handsome city. The cross-community desire for peace is palpable, with many new restaurants and clubs and a thriving arts scene.

Most of Belfast's main streets (and bus routes) radiate out from Donegall Square. In its center stands the 1906 City Hall, with its huge central copper dome. Statues around the building include Queen Victoria at the front and, on the east side, Sir Edward Harland, founder of the Harland and Wolff shipyard, which built the Titanic. A memorial to those who died when the ship sank in 1912 stands close by. Sights on and around the square include the Linen Hall Library, the Grand Opera House in Great Victoria Street, and the famed Crown Liquor Saloon, which dates back to the 1880s.

Other notable attractions in the city include St. Anne's Cathedral in Donegall Street, and the regenerated Titanic Quarter, home to a film studio and the eye-catching **Titanic Belfast** museum, which tells the story of the famous ship.

Away from the center, Belfast has pleasant suburbs unaffected by the civil strife of the Troubles. The area around Queen's University, toward the south of the city, has two major attractions in the **Ulster Museum** and the Botanic Gardens. The museum covers all aspects of Ulster, from archaeology to technology.

Titanic Belfast
⚓🎢😊🛍 🛈 Queen's Rd
🕐 Hours vary, check website
🚫 Dec 24–26
🖥 titanicbelfast.com

Ulster Museum
🎨😊🛍 🛈 Botanic Gardens
🕐 10am–5pm Tue–Sun
🖥 nmni.com

The Troubles (p151)

17

Ulster-American Folk Park

🛈 Co. Tyrone 🚌 From Omagh
🕐 10am–5pm Tue–Sun (Oct–Feb: to 4pm) 🖥 nmni.com

One of the best open-air museums of its kind, this park grew up around the restored boyhood home of Judge Thomas Mellon (founder of the Pittsburgh banking dynasty). The park's permanent exhibition, called "Emigrants," examines why two million people left Ulster for America during the 18th and 19th centuries. It also shows what became of them, following stories of both fortune and failure.

The park has more than 30 historic buildings – some

EAT

Belfast is packed with great restaurants; here are four favorites.

Graze
🛈 402 Upper Newtownards Rd
🖥 grazebelfast. weebly.com

€€€

Mourne Seafood Bar
🛈 34–36 Bank St
🖥 mournesea food.com/belfast

€€€

OX
🛈 1 Oxford St
🖥 oxbelfast.com

€€€

Deane's EIPIC
🛈 28–40 Howard St
🖥 deaneseipic.com

€€€

original, some replicas – all staffed with costumed interpretative guides. There's also an Ulster streetscape, a reconstructed emigrant ship, and a Pennsylvania farmstead. The six-roomed farmhouse is based on one built by Thomas Mellon and his father in their early years in America.

The Centre for Migration Studies assists the descendants of emigrants in tracing their family roots. Popular American festivals, such as Halloween and Independence Day, are celebrated at the park.

18

Old Bushmills Distillery

Bushmills, Co. Antrim From Giant's Causeway & Coleraine 9:30am-4:45pm Mon-Sat, noon-4:45pm Sun Good Fri pm, Jul 12, 2 weeks at Christmas bushmills.com

Bushmills has an attractive square and an excellent river for fishing, but its main claim to fame is whiskey. The Old Bushmills plant prides itself on being the oldest distillery in the world, its "Grant to Distil" dating from 1608.

In 1974, Bushmills joined the Irish Distillers Group, based at the Midleton plant near Cork (p169), but its brands have retained their distinctive character. "Old Bushmills" is unusual in that it is made from a blend of single malt and a single grain. The tour of the distillery ends with a sampling session in the "1608 Bar," which is housed in the former malt kilns.

19

Giant's Causeway

Co. Antrim To Portrush From Portrush, Bushmills, or Coleraine Visitors' Centre Dawn-dusk daily nationaltrust.org.uk/giants-causeway

The bizarre regularity of the Giant's Causeway's basalt columns has made it the subject of numerous legends. The most popular tells how the giant Finn MacCool laid the causeway to provide a path across the sea to Scotland so that he could do battle with a rival Scottish giant. The geological explanation is that 61 million years ago, in a series of volcanic eruptions, molten lava poured from narrow fissures in the ground, filling in the valleys. The basalt lava cooled rapidly. In the process, it shrank and cracked evenly into polygonal blocks. Towards the end of the Ice Age, erosion by sea ice exposed the rocks and shaped the Causeway. Most of the columns are hexagonal, but some have four, five, eight, or even ten sides. They are generally about 12 in (30 cm) across. There are, in fact, three causeways: the Grand, Middle, and Little. Distinctive features have been given poetic names, such as the "Honeycomb" and the "Wishing Chair."

Busloads of tourists arrive from the visitors' center, but it is easy to escape the crowds by taking one of the coastal paths to the site.

→ The dramatic and unusual rock formations of the Giant's Causeway

PRACTICAL
INFORMATION

Here you will find all the essential advice and information you will need before and during your stay in Ireland.

AT A GLANCE

CURRENCY

Republic of Ireland:
Euro (EUR)

Northern Ireland:
Pound Sterling (GBP)

TIME ZONE
GMT/BST and IST.
British and Irish
Summer Time runs
from the last Sunday
in March to the last
Sunday in October.

LANGUAGE
English and Irish

ELECTRICITY SUPPLY
Power sockets are
type G, fitting three-
pronged plugs.
Standard voltage
is 230V.

EMERGENCY NUMBERS

REPUBLIC OF IRELAND	NORTHERN IRELAND
112	**999**

TAP WATER
Unless stated
otherwise, tap
water in Ireland
is safe to drink.

Getting There

Ireland's four main international airports are Dublin, Shannon, Cork, and Belfast. All are well served by regular bus and rail services.

Ferries from ports in Britain and France are also a popular way of getting to Ireland; there are large seasonal variations in fares, but discounts may be available online. Irish Ferries and Stena Line operate regular crossings from Holyhead, Pembroke, and Fishguard in Wales to Dublin Port, Dun Laoghaire, and Rosslare. There are also Irish Ferries services from Holyhead to Dublin and to Rosslare from Cherbourg and Roscoff. From Scotland, both Stena Line and P&O Ferries have crossings from Cairnryan (Stranraer) to Larne (north of Belfast). You can buy combined coach/ferry and train/ferry tickets from coach and train stations all over Britain.

Personal Security

Ireland is generally a safe country, but it is a good idea to take sensible precautions against pickpockets. If you have anything stolen, report the crime to the nearest police station. Get a copy of the crime report in order to claim on your insurance. Note that travel insurance for the UK will not cover you for the Republic, so make sure you purchase an adequate insurance policy.

In Northern Ireland during July, you may find yourself caught up in slow-moving traffic behind an Orange march. Local tensions can be higher at this time, but the affected areas are easily avoided. If you see a sign while driving that indicates you are approaching a checkpoint, slow down and use dipped headlights

Health

EU citizens with a European Health Insurance Card (EHIC) are entitled to free emergency medical care throughout Ireland. (The situation may change in Northern Ireland once the UK leaves the EU.) However, it is also advisable to take out some form of supplementary health insurance. Visitors from outside the EU must arrange their own private medical insurance.

Passports and Visas

Visitors from EU member states, the US, Canada, Australia, and New Zealand need a valid passport, but not a visa, for entry into the Republic or Northern Ireland. UK nationals do not need a passport to enter the Republic, but may find one useful as proof of identity. For visa information specific to your home country, consult your nearest Irish or British embassy or check online.

LGBT+ Safety

Homosexuality is legal and widely accepted in Ireland. However, smaller towns and rural areas are often more conservative in their views. As such, overt displays of affection may receive a negative response from locals.

Travelers with Specific Needs

Most of Ireland's main sights and public buildings have wheelchair access. Amenities in more rural parts of the country may be more limited, so it is always worth calling ahead. **The Citizens Information Board** provides information for the Republic, publishing county guides to accommodation, transport, restaurants, and amenities. In Northern Ireland, **Disability Action** advises on accessibility, while **ADAPT** provides information on disabled access to over 400 cultural venues.

ADAPT
W adaptni.org
The Citizens Information Board
W citizensinformation.ie
Disability Action
W disabilityaction.org

Money

Major credit and debit cards are accepted in most shops and restaurants, while prepaid currency cards are accepted in some. Contactless payments are becoming more widely accepted in both the Republic and Northern Ireland, although not on public transport.

Language

The Republic of Ireland is officially bilingual. English is the spoken language everywhere, apart from a few parts of the far west.

Cell Phones and Wi-Fi

Free Wi-Fi hotspots are generally available in main towns and cities. Cafés and restaurants usually permit the use of their Wi-Fi on the condition that you make a purchase.

Visitors traveling to Ireland and Northern Ireland with EU tariffs can use their devices without being affected by data roaming charges. (This situation may change in Northern Ireland when the UK leaves the EU.) Visitors from other countries should check their contracts before departure to avoid unexpected charges.

Getting Around

Irish Rail (Iarnród Éireann) operates a service to most large towns. Ireland's only cross-border service is a high-speed service linking Belfast and Dublin.

The Republic's national bus company, **Bus Éireann**, runs routes to all cities and most towns. **Ulsterbus/Translink** runs a service in Northern Ireland, with express links between all major towns. A "Rambler" ticket allows a period of unlimited bus travel in the Republic. In the North, a "Bus Rambler" ticket offers the same benefits.

In both the Republic and Northern Ireland, motorists drive on the left. Car rental – particularly in the Republic – can be expensive. It is advisable to book ahead in summer, when demand can be high. If you intend to cross the border, you must inform the rental company, as there may be an additional insurance premium.

Bus Éireann
W buseireann.ie
Irish Rail
W irishrail.ie
Ulsterbus
W translink.co.uk

Visitor Information

Before leaving for Ireland, you can get information from the **Fáilte Ireland** (Irish Tourist Board) or **Northern Ireland Tourist Board** (NITB) offices. Regional tourist offices provide more detailed information on the ground.

Fáilte Ireland
W failteireland.ie
Northern Ireland Tourist Board
W discovernorthernireland.com

FRANCE

From the arrival of the Celtic Gauls in the 1st millennium BC, France has been a European melting pot. Roman conquest by Julius Caesar had an enduring impact but, from the 4th and 5th centuries AD, Germanic invaders destroyed much of the Roman legacy. The Capetian dynasty gradually pieced France together over the Middle Ages – a period of economic prosperity and cultural vitality despite the Black Death and the Hundred Years' War, and threats to power from the dukes of Burgundy and the English Crown. Things faltered in the 16th century, as King François I's ambition of making France a major power was thwarted by the Habsburg Emperor Charles V and the country was plunged into religious conflict during the Reformation. The 17th century, however, saw France, under Louis XIV, rise to dominate Europe both militarily and intellectually. This success came at a heavy cost, and growing social unrest led to the Revolution of 1789 and the end of the absolute monarchy. Out of this new order came major social and institutional reforms, many of which were endorsed by Napoleon, a young military genius who established a vast empire across Europe between 1804 and 1815. The subequent decades saw much political turmoil, but the country nonetheless retained its reputation as a leading center of art and culture. In the 20th century, France suffered traumatic population losses in World War I, and during 1940–44 the country was occupied by Germany. Its recovery was led by the successful development of new technologies – particularly in aviation – and today France is among the most influential members of the EU.

FRANCE

1. Paris
2. Strasbourg
3. Bayeux
4. Reims
5. Rouen
6. Mont-St-Michel
7. Poitiers
8. Carnac
9. Nantes
10. St-Malo
11. Château de Chenonceau
12. Blois
13. Abbaye Royale de Fontevraud
14. Tours
15. Château de Chambord
16. Orléans
17. Chartres Cathedral
18. Dijon
19. Vézelay
20. Beaune
21. Annecy
22. Lyon
23. Grenoble
24. Bordeaux
25. Lascaux
26. Toulouse
27. Carcassonne
28. Pyrenees
29. Nîmes
30. Arles
31. Avignon
32. Camargue
33. Aix-en-Provence
34. Marseille
35. Cannes
36. Nice
37. Monaco

❶

PARIS

 ℹ www.parisinfo.com

France's economic, political, and artistic hub since Roman times, Paris draws visitors with its chic cafés, gourmet restaurants, and fashionable shops. Elegant avenues and boulevards make the city a delight to stroll around.

①
Île de la Cité

Ⓜ Châtelet, Cité

This boat-shaped island on the Seine is the nucleus of Paris. The capital's name derives from the Parisii, one of the Celtic tribes who lived here in the 3rd century BC. The settlement was later expanded by the Romans, the Franks, and the Capetian kings.

Remains of the earliest buildings can be seen in the Crypte Archéologique, below the square in front of Notre-Dame cathedral, which stands at one end of the island. At the opposite end is another Gothic masterpiece: the Sainte-Chapelle church, surrounded by the huge complex of buildings forming the Palais de Justice. One of these, the sinister-looking **Conciergerie**, was a prison from 1391 until 1914. During the French Revolution, Marie-Antoinette was held in a tiny cell here until her execution in 1793. The Conciergerie has a superb Gothic Hall and a 14th-century clock tower. To the east of the

> 💬 INSIDER TIP
> **Getting Around**
>
> In central Paris, the 16 lines of the metro (subway) overlap the routes of the RER trains, which reach outlying areas. Buses are convenient for short distances, and taxis are handy after the metro shuts down. A self-service bike system, Vélib' Métropole, operates in central Paris.

island, tiny Île St-Louis is a haven of riverside quays and quiet streets lined with fine restaurants and chic shops.

Crossing the western end of the Île de la Cité is the oldest bridge in Paris, the Pont Neuf (New Bridge), which dates back to 1578. The Marché

Looking over the city
from the top of the Arc
de Triomphe

aux Fleurs Reine Elizabeth II
takes place from Monday to
Saturday in Place Louis Lépine
and is the city's most famous
flower market.

Conciergerie

♿ 🕑 🏛 2 Blvd du Palais
🕘 9:30am–6pm daily
🚫 Jan 1, May 1, Dec 25
🌐 paris-conciergerie.fr

---

②

Notre-Dame

🏛 6 Place du Parvis-Notre-
Dame Ⓜ Cité 🚌 21, 38, 47,
85, 96 to Île de la Cité
🚪 Until further notice
🌐 notredamedeparis.fr

No other building embodies
the history of Paris more
than Notre-Dame. It stands
majestically on the Île de
la Cité, cradle of the city.
Built on the site of a Roman
temple, the cathedral was
commissioned by Bishop de
Sully in 1160. The first stone
was laid in 1163, marking
the start of two centuries of
toil by armies of medieval
architects and craftsmen. The
cathedral has been witness
to great events of French
history ever since, including
the coronation of Napoleon
Bonaparte (1804) and the
state funeral of Charles de
Gaulle (1970). During the
Revolution, the building was
desecrated and rechristened
the Temple of Reason. Major
renovations (including the
addition of the spire and
gargoyles) were carried out
in the 19th century by architect Viollet-le-Duc.

↑ The North Window's
13th-century stained
glass, Notre-Dame

In April 2019, a fire destroyed
the spire, much of the oak
frame, and the roof, but the
main structure remained
intact. A new spire and roof
will be rebuilt and are hoped
to be completed by 2024.

**To the east of the island, tiny Île
St-Louis is a haven of riverside quays
and quiet streets lined with fine
restaurants and chic shops.**

③

Sainte-Chapelle

🏛 10 Blvd du Palais Ⓜ Cité
🕐 9am–5pm daily (Apr–Sep: to 7pm) 🚫 Jan 1, May 1, Dec 25 🌐 sainte-chapelle.fr

Sainte-Chapelle was built in 1248 to house sacred relics, including Christ's Crown of Thorns, purchased from the Byzantine emperor at great expense by the devout King Louis IX. Hailed as one of the great architectural master-pieces of the Western world, the church was likened to "a gateway to heaven" in the Middle Ages.

Sainte-Chapelle consists of two chapels. The lower chapel was used by servants and minor officials, while the exquisite upper chapel, reached by means of a narrow, spiral staircase, was reserved for the use of the royal family and courtiers. This chapel is adorned with glorious stained-glass windows, separated by pencil-like columns soaring 50 ft (15 m) to the star-studded roof. More than 1,100 biblical scenes from the Old and New Testaments are depicted – from Genesis right through to

the Crucifxion – as well as the story of how the relics were brought to Sainte-Chapelle. The 86 panels of the circular Rose Window, which are best seen at sunset, tell the story of the Apocalypse.

Badly damaged during the Revolution, and converted into a flour warehouse, the church was renovated a century later by architect Viollet-le-Duc. The spire, erected in 1853, rises 245 ft (75 m) into the air.

④

Place des Vosges

Ⓜ Bastille, St-Paul

This perfectly symmetrical square, laid out in 1605 by Henri IV and known as Place Royale, was once the resi-dence of the aristocracy. The square is surrounded by 36 houses, nine on each side. Built of brick and stone, with dormer windows over arcades, they have survived intact for more than 400 years. Today, the historic houses accom-modate a selection of antique stores, art galleries, and fashionable cafés.

The square has been the scene of many historical events over the centuries, including a three-day tournament in celebration of the marriage of Louis XIII to Anne of Austria in 1615. Among the square's famous former residents are the literary hostess Madame de Sévigné, born here in 1626; Cardinal Richelieu, pillar of the monarchy; and novelist Victor Hugo.

⑤

Musée Picasso

🏛 Hôtel Salé, 5 Rue de Thorigny Ⓜ St-Sébastien Froissart, St-Paul
🕐 10:30am–6pm Tue–Fri, 9:30am–6pm Sat & Sun
🚫 Jan 1, May 1, Dec 25
🌐 museepicassoparis.fr

The Spanish-born artist Pablo Picasso spent most of his life in France. On his death, the French state inherited many of his works in lieu of death duties, opening a museum to display them in 1986. Housed in a 17th-century mansion originally built for a salt-tax

←

Stunning stained-glass windows inside the 13th-century Sainte-Chapelle

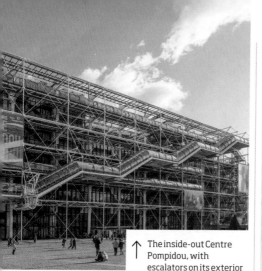

↑ The inside-out Centre Pompidou, with escalators on its exterior

collector, the collection comprises more than 200 paintings, 158 sculptures, 100 ceramic works, and some 3,000 sketches and engravings. The full extent of Picasso's artistic development is presented, from the somber Blue period *Self-Portrait* (1901) to Cubist collages and Neo-Classical works, such as *Pipes of Pan*. Highlights include *The Two Brothers* (1906), *Two Women Running on the Beach* (1922), and *The Kiss* (1969). There is also a sculpture garden.

PICASSO IN FRANCE

Born in Spain, Pablo Picasso first moved to Paris in 1904 as a young artist, drawn by the city's bohemian art scene and raucous nightlife. Later he settled in the south of France. After 1934, Picasso's rejection of Franco's regime meant he would never return to his homeland. Nonetheless, he continued to use Spanish themes in his art, such as the bull (often in the form of a minotaur) and the guitar, which he associated with his Andalusian childhood.

⑥ Centre Pompidou

 Pl G Pompidou Ⓜ Châtelet, Rambuteau, Hôtel de Ville 🚇 Châtelet-Les-Halles 🚌 21, 29, 38, 47, & many others
🆆 centrepompidou.fr

With its skeleton of struts, ducts, and escalators scaling the outside of the building, this famous cultural center has room for the vast **Musée National d'Art Moderne** inside. Among the artists featured in its collection of over 60,000 works are Matisse, Picasso, Miró, and Pollock, representing such schools as Fauvism, Cubism, and Surrealism. Star attractions are *Sorrow of the King* (1952) by Matisse, and Georges Braque's *The Duo* (1937). There are also two floors of temporary exhibitions, plus expansive city views from the sixth floor.

The popular piazza outside the Centre Pompidou is home to the Atelier Brancusi, a reconstruction of the workshop of Romanian-born artist Constantin Brancusi, who lived and worked in Paris.

Musée National d'Art Moderne

⊛⊛ 🕐 11am–9pm Wed–Mon (to 11pm Thu) 🚫 May 1

STAY

Hôtel du Jeu de Paume
Wooden beams and a great location make this 17th-century building a draw.

 54 Rue Saint-Louis-en-l'Île 75004 🆆 jeudepaume hotel.com

€€€

Hôtel Thérèse
A chic boutique hotel with cocooning rooms individually decorated in a soothing palette.

 5 Rue Thérèse 75001 🆆 hoteltherese.fr

€€€

Relais Christine
Guests at this elegant hotel enjoy top-notch service and amenities.

 3 Rue Christine 75006 🆆 relais-christine.com

€€€

Grand Hôtel du Palais Royal
Overlooking the Palais Royal gardens, this luxury hotel has a secluded feel.

 4 Rue de Valois 75001 🆆 grandhoteldu palaisroyal.com

€€€

Paris Perfect Flat Place Dauphine
These apartments with hotel service are ideal for visitors who want to feel like a local.

 25 Place Dauphine 75001 🆆 paris perfect.com

€€€

←
The Panthéon's tall dome, inspired by that of St. Paul's Cathedral in London

⑨
Jardin du Luxembourg

◫ Rue de Médicis / Rue de Vaugirard Ⓜ Odéon
ⓇⒺⓇ Luxembourg

This graceful and historic area offers a peaceful haven in the heart of Paris. The gardens, which cover 60 acres (25 ha), were opened to the public in the 19th century. They are centered on the Luxembourg Palace, which was built for Marie de Médicis, the widow of Henri IV, and is now the home of the French Senate. At the center of the gardens is a lake surrounded by formal terraces, where sunbathers gather on fine summer days.

⑦ 🖼 🖼
Panthéon

◫ Place du Panthéon
Ⓜ Place Monge, Cardinal-Lemoine ⏰ 10am-6pm daily (Apr-Sep: to 6:30pm)
🚫 Jan 1, May 1, Dec 25
🌐 paris-pantheon.fr

The last resting place of some of France's most famous citizens, this magnificent 18th-century church was built to honor Sainte Geneviève, patron saint of Paris. During the Revolution, it was turned into a pantheon to house the tombs of the illustrious.

Based on Rome's pantheon (p384), the temple portico has 22 Corinthian columns, while the tall dome was inspired by that of St. Paul's Cathedral in London (p109). Geneviève's life is celebrated in a series of 19th-century nave murals. Many French notables rest in the crypt, including Voltaire,

Rousseau, and Victor Hugo. The ashes of Pierre and Marie Curie are also held here.

⑧
Place de la Bastille

Ⓜ Bastille

This busy square was the scene of one of the most important events in French history – the storming of the Bastille on July 14, 1789. Little trace of the infamous prison remains, but a row of paving stones from No. 5 to No. 49 Boulevard Henri IV mark the line of former fortifications.

The 170 ft (52 m), hollow bronze Colonne de Juillet stands in the middle of the square to honor the victims of the July Revolution of 1830. On the south side is the 2,700-seat Opéra Bastille, completed in 1989, the bicentennial of the French Revolution.

Musée Rodin

📍 77 Rue de Varenne
Ⓜ Varenne 🚃 Invalides
🚌 69, 82, 87, 92 🕐 10am-6:30pm Tue-Sun 🚫 Jan 1, May 1, Dec 25 🌐 musee-rodin.fr

Artist Auguste Rodin, widely regarded as one of France's greatest sculptors, lived and worked here in the Hôtel Biron, an elegant 18th-century mansion, from 1908 until his death. In return for a state-owned flat and studio, Rodin left his work to the nation, and it is now exhibited here. Some of his most celebrated sculptures are on display in the attractive garden, including *The Burghers of Calais, The Thinker, The Gates of Hell,* and *Balzac.*

The indoor exhibits are arranged in chronological order, spanning the whole of Rodin's career. Major works in the collection include *The Kiss* and *Eve.*

St-Germain-des-Prés

📍 3 Place St-Germain-des-Prés Ⓜ St-Germain-des-Prés 🕐 8am-7:45pm Mon-Sat, 9am-8pm Sun

Originating in 558, this is the oldest church in Paris. St-Germain had become a powerful Benedictine abbey by the Middle Ages, but was largely destroyed by fire in 1794. Major restoration took place in the 19th century. A single tower survives from the original three, housing one of France's most ancient belfries. The 17th-century philosopher René Descartes is one of several notable figures buried here.

After World War II, the area drew many writers and artists, including the leading figure of the Existentialist movement, Jean-Paul Sartre, and writer Simone de Beauvoir. The cafés that were their daily haunts, such as Café de Flore and Les Deux Magots, are now popular with visitors.

TOP 5 PARIS SHOPPING STREETS

Rue Lobineau
Home of the St-Germain covered food market and shopping center.

Rue Bonaparte
Full of swanky shops, including the Pierre Hermé flagship store.

Rue du Bac
Lined with shops selling pastries and other tasty confections.

Rue de Sèvres
The location of Le Bon Marché, the first department store in Paris, which opened in 1852.

Rue de Buci
A former market street that today houses cafés and cute shops.

→ Elegant shops lining leafy Boulevard St-Germain, near St-Germain-des-Prés

The unmistakable glass pyramid of the Louvre in the Cour Napoléon →

⑫ ⚡ Ⓜ 🍴 📷 🛍

MUSÉE DU LOUVRE

🚪Entrance through Pyramid or directly from metro Ⓜ Palais-Royal - Musée du Louvre, Louvre-Rivoli 🚉 Châtelet-Les-Halles 🚌 21, 24, 27, 39, 48, 68, 69, 72, 81, 95 🕐 9am-6pm Wed-Mon (to 9:45pm Wed & Fri, except public hols) 🚫 Jan 1, May 1, Dec 25 🌐 louvre.fr

First opened to the public in 1793 after the Revolution, the Louvre contains one of the most important art collections in the world. Its stunning architecture makes it an icon of Paris.

First built as a fortress in 1190 by King Philippe-Auguste, it lost its imposing keep in the reign of François I, who commissioned a Renaissance-style building. Thereafter, four centuries of kings and emperors improved and enlarged the palace. A glass pyramid designed by I. M. Pei was added to the main courtyard in 1989. The Louvre's treasures can be traced back to the 16th-century collection of François I, who purchased many Italian paintings, including the *Mona Lisa (La Gioconda)*.

GALLERY GUIDE

Eight departments are spread over four floors: Near Eastern antiquities; Egyptian antiquities; Greek, Etruscan and Roman antiquities; Islamic art; sculptures; decorative arts; paintings; and prints and drawings.

① This sculptural spiral staircase forms part of the modern entrance hall designed by Chinese-American architect I. M. Pei.

② The Marly Horses by Guillaume Coustou once stood near the Place de la Concorde.

③ *The Coronation of Napoléon* by Jacques-Louis David is an impressive 20 ft (6 m) high by 32 ft (10 m) wide.

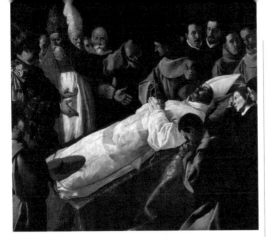

↑ *Lying-in-State of St. Bonaventura* (c. 1629) by the Spanish artist Francisco de Zurbarán

EUROPEAN PAINTING: 1200 TO 1850

Painting from northern Europe is well covered, with works by Flemish, Dutch, German, and English artists including Vermeer, Jan van Eyck, Hans Holbein, and J. M. W. Turner. The Spanish collection tends toward depictions of the more tragic side of life, although several portraits by Goya are in a lighter vein.

The large collection of Italian art covers the period 1200 to 1800. Key figures of the early Renaissance are here, including Giotto and Raphaël, plus Leonardo da Vinci and his celebrated *Mona Lisa* (1504).

The French collection ranges from the 1300s to 1848. There are superb works by Jean Fouquet, George de la Tour and J. A. Watteau, as well as J. H. Fragonard, master of the Rococo.

THE NOTORIOUS MONA LISA

Acquired by King François I, this portrait of a mysterious woman was one of the first paintings displayed in the Louvre when the museum opened. For many years it was simply one Leonardo work among many, but that all changed when the painting was stolen in 1911. The much-publicized theft pushed the artwork into the public eye, with reproductions appearing around the world. Its popularity has not dwindled since.

EUROPEAN SCULPTURE: 1100 TO 1850

Early Flemish and German sculpture in the collection includes a life-size nude figure of the penitent Mary Magdalene by Gregor Erhart (early 16th century). A notable Flemish sculpture is Adrian de Vries's long-limbed *Mercury and Psyche* (1593).

The French section opens with early Romanesque works, including a 12th-century figure of Christ and a head of St. Peter. The works of Pierre Puget have been assembled inside the Cour Puget, while the Cour Marly houses the Marly Horses and other masterpieces of French sculpture, like Jean-Antoine Houdon's busts of Diderot and Voltaire.

The Italian collection includes pre-Renaissance sculptures by Donatello and Duccio, and later masterpieces such as Michelangelo's marble *Slaves* and Cellini's monumental bronze *Nymph of Fontainebleau*.

←

St. Mary Magdalene (c. 1515–20) by the German sculptor Gregor Erhart

DECORATIVE ARTS

Serpentine stone plate (1st century/9th century AD)

This collection features more than 8,000 items, many of which came from the Abbey of St-Denis, where the kings of France were crowned. Treasures on view include a serpentine plate from the 1st century AD with a 9th-century border of gold and precious stones, and a golden scepter made for King Charles V in about 1380. The French crown jewels include swords, scepters, and the splendid coronation crowns of Louis XV and Napoleon. The Regent, one of the purest

The French crown jewels include the Regent, one of the purest diamonds in the world, worn by Louis XV at his coronation in 1722.

diamonds in the world, worn by Louis XV at his coronation in 1722, is also on show. An entire room is taken up with a series of tapestries, the *Hunts of Maximilian*, executed for Emperor Charles V in 1530. The large collection of French furniture ranges from the 16th to the 19th centuries, and includes pieces by the exceptional furniture-maker André Charles Boulle. He is particularly noted for his technique of inlaying copper and tortoiseshell. Among more unusual items is Marie-Antoinette's inlaid steel and bronze writing desk.

The Islamic Art Department, in the Cour Visconti, contains around 18,000 objects covering 3,000 years of history from three continents.

NEAR EASTERN, EGYPTIAN, GREEK, ETRUSCAN, AND ROMAN ANTIQUITIES

The range of antiquities is impressive, featuring objects from the Neolithic period to the fall of the Roman Empire. Among the important works of Mesopotamian art on display is one of the world's oldest documents: a basalt rock bearing a proclamation of laws by Babylonian King Hammurabi, which dates from about 1750 BC.

The warlike Assyrians are represented by delicate carvings, and a fine example of Persian art is the enameled brickwork depicting the king's archers (5th century BC). Egyptian art on display, dating from between 2500 and 1400 BC, and mostly produced for the dead to take to the afterlife, includes lifelike funeral portraits, such as the *Squatting Scribe*, and several sculptures of married couples.

The famous Greek marble statues here, the *Winged Victory of Samothrace* and the *Venus de Milo*, both date from the Hellenistic period (late 3rd to 2nd century BC). A highlight of the Roman section is a 2nd-century AD bronze head of the Emperor Hadrian. Other fine pieces include a bust of Agrippa and a basalt head of Livia. The star of the Etruscan collection is the terra-cotta sarcophagus of a married couple. Among the vast array of earlier fragments, a geometric head from the Cyclades (2700 BC) and a swan-necked bowl hammered out of a gold sheet (2500 BC) are noteworthy.

→

Winged Victory of Samothrace (c. 190 BC)

The immaculately manicured Jardin des Tuileries →

 ⑬

Jardin des Tuileries

Ⓜ Tuileries, Concorde
Ⓒ Apr, May, Sep: 7am-9pm daily; Jun-Aug: 7am-11pm daily; Oct-Mar: 7:30am-7:30pm daily

These magnificent gardens once belonged to the Palais des Tuileries, a palace which was razed to the ground during the time of the Paris Commune in 1871.

The gardens were laid out in the 17th century by André Le Nôtre, royal gardener to Louis XIV. He created a garden in the Neo-Classical style, with a broad central avenue, regularly spaced terraces, and topiary arranged in geometric designs. Ongoing restoration has created a new garden with lime and chestnut trees, and brought the addition of modern sculptures. Also in the gardens is the Jeu de Paume – literally "game of the palm" – built in 1851 to house two royal tennis courts and now a gallery hosting exhibitions of contemporary art.

 ⑭

Musée de l'Orangerie

Ⓐ Jardin des Tuileries, Place de la Concorde
Ⓜ Concorde 🚌 24, 42, 52, 72, 73, 84, 94 Ⓒ 9am-6pm Wed-Mon Ⓒ May 1, Dec 25
🌐 musee-orangerie.fr

This museum first opened to the public in 1927 with an exhibition of Claude Monet's crowning work, his celebrated water-lily series – known as the *Nymphéas* –and they still take pride of place here. Most of the canvases were painted between 1899 and 1921 in the garden at his home in Giverny, Normandy, where Monet lived from 1883 until his death in 1926.

This masterful work is complemented by the Walter Guillaume collection of artists of the École de Paris, from the late Impressionist era to the inter-war period. It features a number of paintings by Cézanne, including still lifes, portraits such as *Madame Cézanne*, and landscapes such as *The Red Rock*. There are also 24 canvases by Renoir, one of the most notable of which is *Les Jeunes Filles au Piano*. Picasso is represented by early works, such as *The Female Bathers*, while Henri Rousseau has nine paintings on show, including *Le Carriole du Père Junier* and *The Wedding*. There are several portraits by Modigliano in the collection, and works by Sisley, Derain, and Utrillo are also featured. All the works are bathed in the natural light that filters through the windows of the airy museum.

Did You Know?

Monet made some 250 paintings of water lilies. About 60 are on view in the Musée de l'Orangerie.

JEU DE PAUME

Nobles used to play a version of handball, *jeu de paume*, in the former royal court that today houses the Galerie Nationale du Jeu de Paume. French players would yell *"tenez"* or "take it" to their opponents. As the game evolved, the word did, too, and the English began to call it tennis, or real tennis, and used rackets instead of their hands. During World War II, the Jeu de Paume became a storehouse where Nazis stashed stolen art. Works deemed offensive - for example, many Picasso and Dali paintings - were burned in front of it in 1942.

---

⑮
Place de la Concorde

Ⓜ Concorde

One of the most magnificent and historic squares in Europe, Place de la Concorde covers more than 20 acres (8 ha). Surprisingly, the land on which it stands was a originally a swamp by the River Seine. It was converted to Place Louis XV in 1763, when royal architect Jacques-Ange Gabriel was asked by the king to design a suitably grand and regal setting for an equestrian statue of himself. Gabriel created an open octagon, with only the north side lined by elegant mansions.

The statue of Louis XV, which lasted here less than 20 years, was replaced by the guillotine (the Black Widow, as it came to be known) during the French Revolution and the square was renamed Place de la Révolution. On January 21, 1793, Louis XVI was beheaded here, followed by more than 1,300 other victims, including Marie Antoinette, Madame du Barry (the last mistress of Louis XV), assassin Charlotte Corday, and high-profile revolutionary leaders Danton and Robespierre. After the Reign of Terror finally came to an end in 1794, the blood-soaked square was optimistically renamed Place de la Concorde in a spirit of reconciliation by chastened Revolutionaries.

The grandeur of the square was enhanced in the 19th century by the arrival of the 3,200-year-old Luxor obelisk, which was presented to King Louis-Philippe as a gift from the viceroy of Egypt (who also donated Cleopatra's Needle in London). Two fountains and eight statues personifying French cities were also installed at this time.

Flanking the Rue Royale on the north side of the square are two of Gabriel's Neo-Classical mansions, the Hôtel de la Marine and the exclusive Hôtel Crillon.

⑯
Musée d'Orsay

📍 Rue de la Légion d'Honneur Ⓜ Solférino 🚇 Musée d'Orsay 🚌 24, 63, 68, 69, 73, 83, 84, 94 🕐 9:30am–6pm Tue–Sun (to 9:45pm Thu) 🚫 Jan 1, May 1, Dec 25 🌐 musee-orsay.fr

Originally built as a railroad terminus in the heart of Paris, Victor Laloux's superb building, completed in 1900, narrowly avoided demolition in the 1970s. It reopened in 1986 as the Musée d'Orsay, with much of the original architecture – including the elegant glass roof – preserved. The majority of the exhibits are paintings and sculptures dating from between 1848 and 1914, but there are also displays of furniture, the decorative arts, and cinema.

Paintings from before 1870 are on the ground floor, presided over by Thomas Couture's massive *Romans in the Age of Decadence* (1847). Neo-Classical masterpieces, such as Ingres' *La Source*, hang near Romantic works

⚠ GREAT VIEW
City Panorama

A great bird's-eye view of the city can be enjoyed from the Musée d'Orsay. Make your way to the building's rear escalator, ride it all the way up, and then head to the small rooftop terrace.

like Delacroix's turbulent *Tiger Hunt* (1854), and canvases by Degas and Manet, including the latter's *Le Déjeuner sur l'Herbe* and *Olympia* (1863).

The museum's central aisle overflows with sculpture, from Daumier's satirical busts of members of parliament to Carpeaux's exuberant *The Dance* (1868). Decorative arts and architecture are on the middle level, where there is also a display of Art Nouveau, including Lalique glassware. Impressionist works on the upper level include Renoir's *Bal du Moulin de la Galette* (1876). Matisse's *Luxe, Calme et Volupté* is a highlight of the post-1900 collection.

↑ The light and spacious entrance hall of the Musée d'Orsay, with its curved glass ceiling

⑰ 🛹 🍽 🖥 🛍

EIFFEL TOWER

⌂ Champ-de-Mars Ⓜ Bir-Hakeim, Trocadéro 🚉 Champ-de-Mars – Tour Eiffel, Trocadéro 🚌 42, 69, 82, 87 ⏰ 9:30am-11:45pm daily 🌐 toureiffel.paris

An impressive feat of engineering and the most distinctive symbol of Paris, the Eiffel Tower (Tour Eiffel) stands 1,063 ft (324 m) tall and offers unrivaled views over the city.

Built for the Universal Exhibition of 1889, and to commemorate the centennial of the French Revolution, the iconic Eiffel Tower was originally intended to be a temporary addition to the Paris skyline. Designed by Gustave Eiffel, it was fiercely decried by 19th-century aesthetes. It was the world's tallest building until 1931, when New York's Empire State Building was completed.

Double-decker elevators take visitors to the top level, which can hold up to 400 people at a time and offers superb views. A number of crazy stunts have been attempted here over the years. In 1989, the French high-wire artist Philippe Petit walked to the second level of the Eiffel Tower from the Trocadéro, across the Seine, on a tightrope.

THE TOWER IN FIGURES

906 ft (276 m): the height of the viewing gallery on the third level.

1,665: the number of steps leading up to the third level.

2.5 million: the number of rivets holding the tower together.

2.5 in (7 cm): the maximum amount the tower ever sways.

11,100 tons: the tower's total weight.

66 tons: the amount of paint needed to decorate the ironwork.

7 in (18 cm): how far the top can move in a curve under the effect of heat.

↑ The view from the tower, ranging up to 45 miles (72 km)

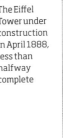

← The Eiffel Tower under construction in April 1888, less than halfway complete

↑ Looking toward the Eiffel Tower from the Jardins du Trocadéro

EAT

Chartier

A budget-friendly favorite for tasty French classics.

 7 Rue du Faubourg Montmartre 75009
 bouillonchartier.com

€€€

Café Christian Constant

This café serves tasty French classics, reasonably priced and near the Eiffel Tower - a rarity.

139 Rue Saint-Dominique 75007
maisonconstant.com

€€€

Pascade

This is the place to discover innovative crêpes, stuffed with gourmet fillings.

14 Rue Daunou 75002
Sun & Mon
pascade.fr

€€€

Pierre Gagnaire

One of Paris's best chefs wows diners with a contemporary menu.

6 Rue Balzac 75008
pierregagnaire.com

€€€

David Toutain

This relaxed Michelin-starred experience is great value. It's worth making reservations - even at lunchtime.

29 Rue Surcouf 75007
Sat & Sun
davidtoutain.com

€€€

Les Invalides

La Tour-Maubourg, Varenne Invalides
28, 63, 69, 80, 82, 83, 87, 92, 93

This sizeable ensemble of monumental buildings is one of the most impressive sights in Paris. The imposing Hôtel des Invalides, from which the area takes its name, was commissioned by Louis XIV in 1671 for his wounded and homeless veterans. Designed by Libéral Bruand, it was completed in 1676 by Jules Hardouin-Mansart. Nearly 6,000 soldiers once resided here; today, there are fewer than 100. Behind the Hôtel's harmonious Classical facade – a masterpiece of French 17th-century architecture – are several museums.

The **Musée de l'Armée** is one of the most comprehensive museums of military history in the world, with exhibits covering all periods from the Stone Age to World War II. Among items on display are François I's ivory hunting horns and a selection of arms from Asia. St-Louis-des-Invalides, the chapel of the Hôtel des Invalides, is also known as the "soldiers' church." It was built between 1679 and 1708 by Jules Hardouin-Mansart, to Bruand's design. The stark,

Classical interior is designed in the shape of a Greek cross and has a fine 17th-century organ by Alexandre Thierry. The Dôme Church, begun in 1676, was reserved for the exclusive use of Louis XIV himself and is one of the greatest examples of *grand siècle* architecture and a monument to Bourbon glory. The crypt houses the tomb of Napoleon, whose body was encased in six coffins in a vast red porphyry sarcophagus.

Also in the complex are the **Musée de l'Ordre de la Libération**, set up to honor feats of heroism during World War II, and the **Musée des Plans-Reliefs**, which has an extensive collection of detailed models of French forts and fortified towns, considered top secret until as late as the 1950s.

Musée de l'Armée

Apr-Oct: 10am-6pm daily; Nov-Mar: 10am-5pm daily musee-armee.f

←
The tomb of Napoleon, in the crypt of the Dôme Church, at Les Invalides

↑ The Palais de Chaillot, with its colonnaded wings, as viewed from the Eiffel Tower

Musée de l'Ordre de la Libération

 Apr-Oct: 10am-6pm daily; Nov-Mar: 10am-5pm daily ordredela liberation.fr

Musée des Plans-Reliefs

Apr-Sep: 10am-6pm daily; Oct-Mar: 10am-5pm daily museedes plansreliefs.culture.fr

(19)

Palais de Chaillot

 Place du Trocadéro 17 Trocadéro Trocadéro 22, 30, 32, 63, 72, 82

With its curved colonnaded wings, each culminating in a vast pavilion, this palace was designed in Neo-Classical style

---

PICTURE PERFECT
Eiffel Tower

The terrace of the Palais de Chaillot affords magnificent views of the Eiffel Tower. Head here to get a panoramic shot of the Iron Lady.

---

for the 1937 Paris Exhibition. It is adorned with sculptures and bas-reliefs, and the pavilion walls are inscribed with words composed by the poet Paul Valéry. The square between the pavilions is decorated with bronze sculptures, ornamental pools, and shooting fountains.

Inside the east wing is the **Cité de l'Architecture et du Patrimoine**, which charts French architecture through the ages, while in the west wing, the **Musée de l'Homme** traces the story of human evolution. Next door is the **Musée National de la Marine** (closed until 2021), devoted to French naval history.

The centerpiece of the lovely Jardins du Trocadéro is a long ornamental pool, bordered by statues. The gardens themselves are perfect for a quiet evening stroll.

Cité de l'Architecture et du Patrimoine

11am-7pm Wed-Sun (to 9pm Thu) 1 Jan, 1 May, 25 Dec citechaillot.fr

Musée de l'Homme

10am-6pm Wed-Mon museedel homme.fr

Musée National de la Marine

Until 2021 for renovations musee-marine.fr

---

(20)

Musée du Quai Branly

37 Quai Branly Alma-Marceau Pont de l'Alma 11am-7pm Tue-Sun (to 9pm Thu-Sat) quai branly.fr

Built to give the arts of Africa, Asia, Oceania, and the Americas a platform as great as that given to Western art in the city, this museum features a collection of more than 3,000 objects. It is particularly strong on African artifacts, with stone, wooden, and ivory masks, as well as ceremonial tools and instruments. The Jean Nouvel-designed building, raised on stilts, is a sight in itself: the ingenious use of glass allows the surrounding greenery to act as a natural backdrop for the collection. The rooftop restaurant offers lovely views over the grounds.

DRINK

Here are five of the best hotel bars where you can enjoy a decadent sundowner (or two) around the spectacular Champs-Élysées.

Le Bar at the Four Seasons Hotel
⌂ 31 Ave George V 75008
🌐 fourseasons.com

Bar de l'Hôtel Belmont
⌂ 30 Rue de Bassano, 75116 🌐 Belmont-parishotel.com

Bar Kléber at The Peninsula
⌂ 19 Ave Kléber 75116
🌐 peninsula.com

Le Bar Botaniste at the Shangri-La
⌂ 10 Ave d'Iéna 75116
🌐 shangri-la.com

Le Bar du Bristol
⌂ 112 Rue du Faubourg-St-Honoré 75008
🌐 oetkercollection.com

→
Looking along the Champs-Élysées, toward the Arc de Triomphe

㉑
Champs-Élysées

Ⓜ Franklin D. Roosevelt, George V, Champs-Élysées-Clemenceau 🚉 Charles de Gaulle-Étoile 🚌 22, 24, 28, 30, 31, 32, 42, 52, & many others

Paris's most famous and popular thoroughfare had its beginnings in about 1667, when landscape gardener André Le Nôtre extended the royal view from the Tuileries by creating a tree-lined avenue. The Champs-Élysées (Elysian Fields) has also been known as the "triumphal way" since the homecoming of Napoleon's body from St. Helena in 1840. With the addition of cafés and restaurants in the late 19th century, it became the most fashionable boulevard in Paris.

The formal gardens that line the Champs-Élysées from Place de la Concorde to the Rond-Point have changed little since they were laid out by architect Jacques Hittorff in 1838, and were used as the setting for the 1855 World's Fair. The Grand Palais and the Petit Palais were also built here for the Universal Exhibition of 1900.

The **Grand Palais** – a huge glass-roofed palace housing the Galeries Nationales – has a fine Classical facade decorated with statuary and Art Nouveau ironwork. Bronze flying horses and chariots stand at the four corners. The Great Hall and the glass cupola can be seen during the palace's exhibitions, and in winter the building's nave turns into the world's biggest indoor ice rink. On the west side of the palace is the **Palais de la Découverte**, a child-oriented science museum with fun workshops and great interactive exhibitions.

Facing the Grand Palais, the **Petit Palais** houses the Musée des Beaux-Arts de la Ville de Paris. Arranged around a semicircular court-yard and garden, the palace is similar in style to the Grand Palais, with Ionic columns, a grand porch, and a dome echoing that of the Invalides across the river. The exhibits are divided into medieval and Renaissance objets d'art, paintings, and drawings; 18th-century furniture and objets d'art; and the City of Paris collection, with works by the French artists Gustave Courbet, Jean Ingres, and Eugène Delacroix.

Grand Palais

🚇 🚊 🚶 ⬛ Porte A, Ave Eisenhower ⬛ From 2020 to 2023 Ⓦ grandpalais.fr

Le Palais de la Découverte

🚇 🚊 🚶 ⬛ From 2020 to 2023 Ⓦ palais-decouverte.fr

Petit Palais

🚇 🚊 🚶 ⬛ Ave Winston Churchill ⏰ 10am–6pm Tue–Sun ⬛ Public hols Ⓦ petitpalais.paris.fr

---

㉒ 🚶 🚊

Arc de Triomphe

⬛ Place Charles de Gaulle
Ⓜ RER Charles de Gaulle-Étoile
🚌 22, 30, 31, 52, 73, 92
⏰ Hours vary, check website
⬛ Jan 1, May 1, May 8 (am), Jul 14 (am), Nov 11 (am), Dec 25
Ⓦ paris-arc-de-triomphe.fr

After his victory at the 1805 Battle of Austerlitz, Napoleon promised his men they would "go home beneath triumphal arches." The first stone of this famous arch was laid the following year. But disruptions to architect Jean Chalgrin's plans – combined with the demise of Napoleonic power – delayed completion until 1836. Standing 164 ft (50 m) high, the Arc is encrusted with flamboyant reliefs, shields, and sculptures depicting military scenes and battles.

On Armistice Day, 1921, the body of the Unknown Soldier was placed beneath the arch to commemorate the dead of World War I. The flame of remembrance which burns above the tomb is rekindled each evening. Today, the Arc de Triomphe is the customary rallying point for many victory celebrations and parades.

The viewing platform on top of the Arc overlooks the length of the Champs-Élysées. Inside the Arc, a museum documents its history and construction.

BARON HAUSSMANN

A lawyer by training and civil servant by profession, Georges-Eugène Haussmann was appointed Prefect of the Seine in 1853 by Napoleon III. For 17 years, Haussmann was responsible for the urban modernization of Paris. With a team of architects and engineers, he demolished the chaotic, insanitary streets of the medieval city and created a well-ventilated capital in a geometrical grid. He also increased the number of streetlights and sidewalks, giving rise to the cafés that enliven modern Parisian street life. The plan involved redesigning the area at one end of the Champs-Élysées and creating a star of 12 avenues centered around the new Arc de Triomphe.

A SHORT WALK
LATIN QUARTER

Distance 1 mile (2 km) **Nearest metro** Cluny -
La Sorbonne **Time** 20 minutes

Since the Middle Ages, this riverside quarter has been
dominated by the Sorbonne – it acquired its name from
early Latin-speaking students. The area is generally
associated with artists, intellectuals, and a bohemian
way of life, and has a history of political unrest. In 1871,
the Place St-Michel became the center of the Paris
Commune, and in May 1968, it was one of the sites of
the student uprisings that briefly engulfed the city.

EXPERIENCE **France**

The northern end of **Boulevard
St-Michel** *is lined with cafés,
bookstores, and boutiques, with
clubs and movie theaters nearby.*

Metro St-Michel

The church of **St-Séverin**, *begun in the
13th century, took three centuries to
build and is a fine example of the
Flamboyant Gothic style.*

Metro Cluny –
La Sorbonne

↑ Davioud's decorative
fountain, standing
in Place St-Michel

START

The **Musée de Cluny**
*holds a fine collection of
medieval art, including
the late-15th-century
series of tapestries The
Lady with the Unicorn.*

Rue du Chat qui Pêche *translates as "street of the fishing cat."*

Little Athens *takes its name from the many Greek restaurants situated in its picturesque streets.*

↑ The iconic Shakespeare and Company bookstore and accompanying café

Shakespeare and Company, *at No. 37 Rue de la Bûcherie, is a delightful, if chaotic, bookshop. Books purchased here are stamped with "Shakespeare & Co. Kilomètre Zéro Paris."*

PETIT PONT

HUCHETTE

QUAI DE MONTEBELLO

PONT AU DOUBLE

RUE GALANDE

RUE LAGRANGE

D ST-GERMAIN

O FINISH

Metro – Maubert Mutualité

Did You Know?

Rue du Chat qui Pêche is the narrowest street in Paris at just 6 ft (1.8 m) wide.

St-Julien-le-Pauvre, *one of the oldest churches in Paris, dates back to the 12th century.*

Rue du Fouarre *used to host lectures in the Middle Ages. The students sat on straw (fouarre) in the street.*

Rue Galande *was home to the rich and the chic in the 17th century, but subsequently became notorious for its taverns.*

0 meters	100
0 yards	100

N ↑

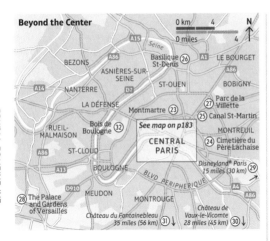

Beyond the Center

of descending terraces. A funicular railway takes visitors up from the bottom of the gardens to the foot of the steps of the basilica.

The famous Moulin Rouge nightclub is also in the vicinity.

Sacré-Coeur

 35 Rue du Chevalier de la Barre ⏰ 6am-10:30pm daily 🌐 sacre-coeur-montmartre.com

PARIS: BEYOND THE CENTER

㉓ Montmartre

Ⓜ Abbesses, Anvers
🚌 30, 31, 54, 80, 85

The steep hill of Montmartre has been associated with artists for 200 years. Théodore Géricault and Camille Corot came here at the start of the 19th century, and in the early 20th century, Maurice Utrillo immortalized the streets in his works. Today, street artists

of varying talents exhibit their work in the Place du Tertre. Exhibitions at the Musée de Montmartre usually feature works of artists associated with the area, while the Musée d'Art Naïf Max Fourny houses almost 600 examples of naive art. Dalí Paris displays over 300 works by the Surrealist artist.

Work on the grandiose **Sacré-Coeur** began in 1876 to Paul Abadie's designs. The basilica, completed in 1914, contains many treasures, including a figure of the *Virgin Mary and Child* (1896) by Brunet. Below the forecourt, Square Willette is laid out on the side of a hill in a series

㉔ Ⓜ Cimetière du Père Lachaise

📍 8 Blvd de Ménilmontant
Ⓜ Père-Lachaise, Philippe Auguste 🚌 26, 54, 60, 61, 64, 69, 76, 102 ⏰ Hours vary, check website
🌐 paris.fr/perelachaise

Paris's most prestigious cemetery is set on a wooded hill overlooking the city. The land was once owned by Père de la Chaise, Louis XIV's confessor, but it was bought by order of Napoleon in 1803 to create a new cemetery. Here lie buried celebrities such as the writer Honoré de Balzac, the famous playwright Molière, the composer Frédéric Chopin, singer Edith

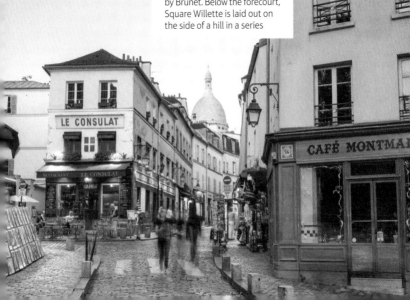

Piaf, and actors Yves Montand and Simone Signoret. Famous foreigners interred in the cemetery include Oscar Wilde and the singer Jim Morrison. The Columbarium, built at the end of the 19th century, houses the ashes of American dancer Isadora Duncan, among others. Striking funerary sculpture and famous graves make this a pleasant place for a leisurely, nostalgic stroll.

↑ One of the many fascinating exhibits at the Cité des Sciences et de l'Industrie, Parc de la Villette

Canal St-Martin

Ⓜ Jaurès, Jacques Bonsergent, Goncourt

A walk along the tree-lined quays of the Canal St-Martin provides a glimpse of Paris at the end of the 19th century. The 3-mile (5-km) canal was opened in 1825 to provide a shortcut for river traffic on the Seine. A few factories and warehouses survive from this time, surrounded today by quirky shops and cafés, iron footbridges, and public gardens. The Canal de l'Ourcq, an offshoot, offers a pleasant stroll to Parc de la Villette.

Basilique St-Denis

Ⓐ 1 Rue de la Légion d'Honneur Ⓜ Basilique de St-Denis 🚉 St-Denis 🚌 153, 239, 253 Ⓞ Hours vary, check website Ⓒ Jan 1, May 1, Dec 25 Ⓦ saint-denis-basilique.fr

Constructed between 1137 and 1281, the basilica is on the site of the tomb of St. Denis, the first bishop of Paris. The basilica was the first church to be built in the Gothic style.

From as early as the 7th century, St-Denis was a burial

A cobbled street in Montmartre, leading to the basilica of Sacré-Coeur

---

place for French rulers, and it was also where the queens of France were crowned. During the Revolution, many tombs were desecrated, but the best were stored, and now form a fine collection of funerary art. Memorials include those of Henri II and Catherine de' Medici, and Louis XVI and Marie-Antoinette.

The mask-like serenity of the medieval effigies, like that of Charles V (1364), contrasts with the realistic portrayal of agony in the Renaissance sculptures of the mausoleum of Louis XII and Anne de Bretagne.

Parc de la Villette

Ⓐ 30 Ave Corentin-Cariou Ⓜ Porte de la Villette 🚉 Pantin 🚌 139, 150, 152

The old slaughterhouses and livestock market of Paris have been transformed into this massive urban park, designed by Bernard Tschumi.

The major attraction here is the **Cité des Sciences et de l'Industrie**, a hugely popular science and technology museum. Architect Adrien Fainsilber has created an imaginative interplay of light, vegetation, and water in the high-tech, five-floor building. At the museum's heart is the Explora exhibit, a guide to the worlds of science and technology. The Géode, a

giant entertainment sphere, houses a hemispherical cinema screen (closed until 2020). Also in the park, the Cité de la Musique is a quirky but elegant complex that holds a music conservatory and a concert hall, while the Zénith Paris theater, built as a venue for pop concerts, seats more than 6,000 spectators. The futuristic **Philharmonie**, by Jean Nouvel, caters mostly to symphonic concerts, but also hosts jazz and world-music performances.

Cité des Sciences et de l'Industrie

⊛ⓉⒽ Ⓞ 10am-6pm Tue-Sat, 10am-7pm Sun Ⓒ Jan 1, May 1, Dec 25 Ⓦ cite-sciences.fr

Philharmonie

⊛⊛ⓉⒽ Ⓐ 221 Ave Jean Jaurès Ⓞ Noon-6pm Tue-Sun (from 10am Sat & Sun) Ⓦ philharmoniedeparis.fr

---

INSIDER TIP
Open-Air Film Festival

Each summer, La Villette hosts the free Festival de Cinéma en Plein Air, screening French and international films in the open air every evening for a month. Deckchairs and blankets can be hired, and many people bring a picnic.

(28) ⚡ Ⓜ 🍴 🖥 🏛

THE PALACE AND GARDENS OF VERSAILLES

🏛 Pl d'Armes, Versailles 🚉 Versailles Chantiers, Versailles Rive Droite 🚈 Versailles Rive Gauche 🚌 171 from Paris 🕐 9am–6:30pm Tue–Sun (winter: to 5:30pm) 🚫 Jan 1, May 1, Dec 25 🌐 chateauversailles.fr

This stunning royal residence is overwhelming in its scale and opulence. The spectacular, lavishly decorated palace and vast gardens, complete with fountains, landscaped topiary, and even a model farm, make Versailles the top day trip from the center of Paris.

Starting in 1668, Louis XIV expanded his father's hunting lodge into the largest palace in Europe, which housed up to 20,000 people at a time. Architects Louis Le Vau and Jules Hardouin-Mansart designed the buildings, which grew as a series of "envelopes" around the lodge. The Opera House was added by Louis XV in 1770.

The sumptuous main apartments are on the first floor of the vast château complex. These were richly decorated by Charles Le Brun with marbles, carvings, murals, and gilded furniture. The climax is the glorious Hall of Mirrors, where 357 great mirrors face 17 tall arched windows.

The grounds of Versailles are just as impressive as the palace. Designed by famed landscaper André Le Nôtre, the formal gardens are a masterpiece: sculptural fountains and secluded groves sit amid geometric flowerbeds and hedges. The 1-mile- (1.7-km-) long Grand Canal leads from the gardens to the enormous park, which features wooded areas and agricultural fields delineated by a network of footpaths. The grounds also encompass the Grand Trianon and Petit Trianon palaces, as well as the Queen's Hamlet – a life-size model village built for Marie Antoinette.

The palace and gardens of Versailles, the epitome of royal grandeur ↓

1 The Marble Courtyard is decorated with marble paving, urns, busts, and a gilded balcony.

2 Mansart's last great work, the two-story Baroque Chapelle Royale was Louis XIV's final addition to Versailles.

3 The formal gardens feature geometric paths leading to groves, lakes, and fountains.

Did You Know?

One third of the estate's budget went to the fountains. Today they are only on during the summer months.

EAT

Ore
This Alain Ducasse dining experience in the Pavillon Dufour is utterly luxurious.

w ducasse-chateau versailles.com

€€€

Angelina
This tea house serving snacks and pastries has two outposts – in the Pavillon d'Orléans and at the Petit Trianon.

w angelina-paris.fr

€€€

(29)

Disneyland® Paris

◪ Marne-la-Vallée, Seine-et-Marne 🚄 TGV to Marne la Vallée/Chessy 🚉 Marne-la-Vallée-Chessy 🚌 ⏱ Hours vary, check website 🌐 disneyland paris.com

Unbeatable for complete escapism, combined with vibrant excitement and sheer energy, Disneyland® Paris offers extreme rides, gentle experiences, and phenomenal visual effects. Situated 20 miles (32 km) east of Paris, the resort is built on a massive scale. The 8.5-sq-mile (22-sq-km) site encompasses two theme parks; seven hotels; a shopping, dining and entertainment village; an ice-skating rink; a lake; two convention centres; and a golf course.

The theme parks are split into Disneyland® Park and the Walt Disney Studios® Park. The former features more than 60 rides and attractions celebrating Hollywood folklore and fantasies, while the latter highlights the ingenuity involved in cinema, animation, and television production through interactive exhibits and live shows.

---

(30)

Château de Vaux-le-Vicomte

◪ Maincy, Seine-et-Marne 🚉 Melun, then taxi or shuttle bus ⏱ Hours vary, check website 🌐 vaux-le-vicomte.com

Located 40 miles (64 km) southeast of Paris, this château enjoys a peaceful setting. Nicolas Fouquet, a powerful court financier to Louis XIV, challenged architect Le Vau and decorator Le Brun to create the most sumptuous palace of the day. The luxury of the resulting château cast the royal palaces into the shade, enraging Louis so much that he confiscated all of Fouquet's estates.

The interior is a gilded banquet of frescoes, stucco, caryatids, and giant busts. The Salon des Muses boasts a frescoed ceiling of dancing nymphs and poetic sphinxes, while La Grande Chambre Carrée is decorated in Louis XIII style, with paneled walls and an impressive triumphal frieze evoking Rome.

Much of Vaux-le-Vicomte's fame is due to landscape gardener André Le Nôtre. Here, he perfected the concept of the *jardin à la française*: avenues framed by statues and box hedges, water gardens with ornate pools, and geometrical parterres "embroidered" with floral motifs.

Disneyland® Paris, home to *(inset)* famous resident ↓ Mickey Mouse

---

TOP 3 RIDES IN DISNEYLAND® PARK

Star Wars Hyperspace Mountain
Formerly known as Space Mountain®, this iconic roller coaster draws big crowds but toward the end of the day you can often walk straight onto the ride.

Big Thunder Mountain
This wild roller-coaster ride on a speeding runaway mine train is a crowd favorite.

Pirates of the Caribbean
A boat ride takes you on a thrilling journey through underground prisons and past dramatic galleon fights.

Château de Fontainebleau

🏠 Seine-et-Marne 🚉
🕐 Hours vary, check
website 🌐 chateau
defontaine bleau.fr

Fontainebleau was a favorite royal residence from the 12th to the mid-19th century. Yet its abiding charm comes not from this grandeur, but from its relative informality and spectacular setting in a forest 40 miles (65 km) south of Paris.

The present château dates back to François I, France's first Renaissance king. Drawn to the area by the local hunting, he created a château modeled on decorative Florentine and Roman styles. Later rulers enlarged and embellished the château, creating a cluster of buildings in various styles from different periods. During the Revolution, the apartments were looted by a mob, and remained bare until the 1800s, when Napoleon refurbished the whole interior.

The impressive Cour du Cheval Blanc, once a simple enclosed courtyard, was transformed by Napoleon into the main approach to the château. Leading up to the house from here is the Escalier du Fer-à-Cheval (1634), an imposing horseshoe-shaped staircase.

The interior suites showcase the château's history as a royal residence. The Galerie François I has a superb collection of Renaissance art. The Salle de Bal, a ballroom designed by Primaticcio (1552), features emblems of Henri II on the walnut-coffered ceiling and reflected in the parquet floor. The apartments of Napoleon I house his grandiose throne, in the former Chambre du Roi. The complex of buildings also contains the Musée Napoléon, in which eight rooms recreate scenes from the emperor's life.

Nearby is the Chapelle de la Sainte Trinité, designed for Henri II in 1550. The chapel acquired its vaulted and frescoed ceiling under Henri IV, and was completed during the reign of Louis XIII.

The gardens are also worth exploring. The Jardin Anglais is a romantic "English" garden planted with cypresses and exotic species, while the Jardin de Diana features a bronze fountain of Diana the Huntress.

↑ Frank Gehry's stunning Fondation Louis Vuitton, in the Bois de Boulogne

㉜

Bois de Boulogne

Ⓜ Porte Maillot 🚉 Neuilly - Porte Maillot 🚌 PC1, 32, 52, 63, 73, 82, 241, 244
🕐 24 hrs daily 🌐 paris.fr

Located between the Seine and the western edges of Paris, this park offers a vast belt of greenery for strolling, cycling, riding, boating, or picnicking. The Bois de Boulogne was once part of the immense Forêt du Rouvre. In the mid-19th century, Napoleon III had the area landscaped by Baron Haussmann along the lines of Hyde Park in London (p105). A number of self-contained parks include the Pré Catelan, which has the widest beech tree in Paris, and the Bagatelle gardens, with an 18th-century villa famous for its rose garden.

Frank Gehry's **Fondation Louis Vuitton**, a dramatic glass structure consisting of 12 glass "sails," contains a gallery of modern art.

After dark the Bois is rather seedy – and best avoided.

Fondation Louis Vuitton
🏠 8 Ave du Mahatma Gandhi Ⓜ Les Sablons 🕐 Hours vary, check website 🚫 1 Jan, 1 May, 25 Dec 🌐 fondation louisvuitton.fr

↑ Traditional half-timbered houses in Strasbourg's scenic Old Town

Did You Know?

Rouget de Lisle wrote the French national anthem "La Marseillaise" in Strasbourg.

2

Strasbourg

🏠 Bas Rhin ✈🚗🚌
🚩 17 Place de la Cathédrale; www.otstrasbourg.fr

Located halfway between Paris and Prague, Strasbourg is often called "the crossroads of Europe." The city wears its cosmopolitanism with ease – after all, it is one of the capitals of the European Union

A boat trip along the waterways that encircle the Old Town gives a good overview of the historic center, taking in the Ponts-Couverts – bridges with medieval watchtowers – and the old tanners' district, dotted with attractive half-timbered houses. Towering over them is the 11th-century Cathédrale Notre-Dame, which offers wonderful views from its roof.

The grand Classical Palais Rohan houses three museums: the Musée des Beaux Arts, the Musée Archéologique, and the Musée des Arts Décoratifs, with one of the finest displays of ceramics in France. Also worth visiting are the Musée d'Art Moderne et Contemporain, Le Vaisseau, a scientific discovery center for children aged 3–15, and the Musée Alsacien, which overflows with exhibits on local traditions, arts, and crafts.

3

Bayeux

🏠 Calvados 🚗🚌 🚩 Pont-St-Jean; www.bayeux-bessin-tourisme.com

The main reason to visit this small town in Normandy is to see the world-renowned Bayeux Tapestry. This incredible work of art depicts William the Conqueror's invasion of England and the 1066 Battle of Hastings from the Norman perspective. The large-scale, 230-ft- (70-m-) long work is displayed in a renovated seminary, the **Bayeux Museum**, which gives a detailed audiovisual account of the events leading up to the battle.

As well as the tapestry, a cluster of 15th–19th-century buildings and the Gothic Cathédrale Notre-Dame are Bayeux's principal attractions.

Bayeux was the first town in Nazi-occupied France to be liberated by the Allies after the D-Day landings in 1944. On the southwest side of the town's ring road, the Musée Mémorial de la Bataille de Normandie traces the events of the Battle of Normandy in World War II.

Bayeux Museum
⊘ 🏠 13 Rue de Nesmond
🕐 Mar-Oct: 9am-6:30 pm daily; Nov-Feb: 9:30am-12pm & 2pm-6pm daily 🕐 Jan
🌐 bayeuxmuseum.com

BAYEUX TAPESTRY

A lively comic strip of the story of the Norman invasion of England from the partisan perspective of the victor, this embroidered hanging is fascinating as a work of art, a portrayal of 11th-century life, a historical document, and an entertaining story.

Reels

** Marne** 🚌🚈
📍 6 Rue Rockefeller;
www.reims-tourism.com

Renowned throughout the world from countless champagne labels, Reims has a rich historical legacy.

The city's most famous monument is the magnificent Gothic **Cathédrale Notre-Dame**, begun in 1211. For several centuries, the cathedral was the setting for the coronation of French kings. Highlights include the 13th-century Great Rose Window and the west facade, decorated with over 2,300 statues.

On the eve of a coronation, the future king spent the night in the Palais du Tau (built in 1690), the archbishop's palace, adjoining the cathedral. Its 15th-century banqueting hall, the Salle du Tau, with its barrel-vaulted ceiling and Arras tapestries, is one of the star attractions.

Among the other fine historic buildings around the city are the 17th-century Ancien Collège des Jésuites, which is now a school, and the Basilique St-Remi, which is the oldest church in Reims.

Relics of the town's Roman past include the Crypto-portique, part of the former forum, and the Porte Mars, a triumphal Augustan arch.

The Musée de la Reddition occupies the building that served as Eisenhower's French headquarters during World War II. It was here, in 1945, that the general received the Germans' surrender, which ended the war.

Cathédrale Notre-Dame
🚫 📍 Place du Cardinal Luçon
🕐 7:30am-7:30pm daily (to 7:15pm Sun & public hols)
🌐 cathedrale-reims.fr

---

⑤
Rouen

📍 Seine Maritime
✈️🚌🚈 **📍 25 Place de la Cathédrale; www.rouentourisme.com**

Formerly a Celtic trading post, Roman garrison, and Viking colony, Rouen became the capital of the Norman Duchy in 911. Today, it is a rich and cultured city that claims a

wealth of splendid historical monuments. Rouen's Gothic cathedral, the Cathédrale Notre-Dame, has a magnificent west facade, made famous by the celebrated Impressionist painter Claude Monet, who made almost 30 paintings of it. A number of these can be seen in the city's excellent **Musée des Beaux Arts**.

From the cathedral, Rue du Gros Horloge leads west, passing under the city's Great Clock, to Place du Vieux Marché, where Joan of Arc *(p217)* was burnt at the stake in 1431.

The Flamboyant Gothic Église St-Maclou and Église St-Ouen are two of Rouen's finest churches. The latter is particularly notable for its restored 14th-century stained-glass windows.

Elsewhere, the Musée de la Céramique displays pieces of Rouen faïence – colorful glazed earthenware – as well as other items of French and foreign china, and the former family home of Gustave Flaubert has been converted into a museum. It houses memorabilia and artifacts from the famous French novelist's life.

Musée des Beaux Arts
🎨 🖼️ 📍 Square Verdrel
🕐 10am-6pm Wed-Mon
🚫 Public hols 🌐 mbarouen.fr

←

The soaring nave of Reims Cathedral, with its exquisite stained glass

MONT-ST-MICHEL

⌂ Manche 🚌 To Pontorson, then bus 🕐 Hours vary, check website ⊘ Jan 1, May 1, Dec 25 🌐 abbaye-mont-saint-michel.fr

Shrouded by mist, the silhouette of Mont-St-Michel is one of the most enchanting sights in France. Now linked to the mainland by a bridge for both shuttles and pedestrians, the island of Mont-Tombe (Tomb on the Hill) stands at the mouth of the Couesnon river, crowned by a fortified abbey that almost doubles its height.

Lying strategically on the frontier between Normandy and Brittany, Mont-St-Michel grew from a humble 8th-century oratory to become a Benedictine monastery that had its greatest influence in the 12th and 13th centuries. Pilgrims known as *miquelots* journeyed from afar to honor the cult of St. Michael, and the monastery was a renowned center of medieval learning. After the French Revolution, the abbey became a prison. It is now a national monument that draws some 3 million visitors a year.

VISITING THE ABBEY

The abbey is built on three levels. Guided tours begin at the West Terrace at the church (highest) level and end on the lowest level in the almonry, where alms were issued to the poor. The monks lived on the highest level; the abbot entertained nobility in the middle; and soldiers and pilgrims farther down the social scale were received at the lowest level.

Four bays of the Romanesque nave in the abbey church survive.

At the top of the Inner Staircase, Gautier's Leap is a terrace named for a prisoner who leaped to his death here.

The small 15th-century St. Aubert's Chapel was built on an outcrop of rock.

Three floors of cannons point in all directions from Gabriel Tower.

The ramparts were built following attacks by the English during the Hundred Years' War.

Entrance

↑ The diminutive island of Mont-St-Michel, topped by a medieval monastery

The abbot's lodgings, where he received visitors, were close to the abbey entrance.

↑ The abbey's 13th-century Anglo-Norman cloisters, with elegant staggered columns

Once the pilgrims' route, the Grand Rue is now crowded with restaurants.

Église St-Pierre dates from the 1400s.

Arcade Tower

← The magnificent abbey of Mont-St-Michel, set atop Mont-Tombe island

STAY

Château du Clos de la Ribaudière

A stately 18th-century mansion that has a heated outdoor pool and alfresco dining on the stone terrace during the summer months.

📍 10 Rue du Champ de Foire, Poitiers
🌐 ribaudiere.com

€€€

Sleep Hotel Tumulus

This friendly hotel offers an outdoor swimming pool and indoor spa area, plus 29 spacious, tastefully decorated rooms.

📍 Chemin du Tumulus, Carnac 🌐 hotel-tumulus.com

€€€

Hôtel de l'Abeille

This grand building offers charming rooms, as well as a relaxing rooftop terrace.

📍 64 Rue Alsace Lorraine, Orléans
🌐 hoteldelabeille.com

€€€

---

❼ Poitiers

📍 Vienne 🚗🚌🚆
ℹ️ 45 Place Charles de Gaulle; www.ot-poitiers.fr

Three of the greatest battles in French history were fought around Poitiers, the most famous in 732 when Charles Martel halted the Arab invasion. Today, the town is a dynamic regional capital with a rich architectural heritage.

Behind the Renaissance facade of the Palais de Justice is the 12th-century great hall of Henry II and Richard the Lionheart. This is thought to have been the scene of Joan of Arc's examination by a council of theologians in 1429.

Notre-Dame-la-Grande, whose west front is covered with 12th-century Poitevin sculpture, stands out among the city's churches, as does the 4th-century Baptistère St-Jean, one of the oldest Christian buildings in France. The Musée Sainte-Croix has archaeological exhibits, paintings, and sculpture.

Just 4.5 miles (7 km) north of Poitiers, **Futuroscope** is a theme park dedicated to visual technology, housing one of the world's largest cinema screens.

Futuroscope

🎟️🎭🎢🎡 📍 Jaunay-Clan ⏰ Hours vary, check website 🚫 Jan–mid-Feb 🌐 futuroscope.com

❽ Carnac

📍 Morbihan 🚌
ℹ️ 74 Ave des Druides; www.ot-carnac.fr

This popular town is probably most famous as one of the world's great prehistoric sites. As long ago as 4000 BC, thousands of ancient granite rocks were arranged in mysterious lines and patterns in the countryside around Carnac by megalithic tribes. Their original purpose is uncertain, though they are thought to have religious significance or to be related to an early astronomical calendar. Celts, Romans, and Christians have since adapted their meaning to tie in with their own beliefs.

You can see some of the menhirs at the Kermario site, on the town's northern outskirts, while in the center, the Musée de Préhistoire gives an interesting insight into the area's ancient history.

←

The awe-inspiring sight of rows of megalithic menhirs near Carnac

↑ The sun setting over the beautiful walled town of St-Malo

9

Nantes

⬛ Loire-Atlantique ✈🚗🚌
📍 9 Rue des Etats; www.
nantes-tourisme.com

The ancient port of Nantes was the ducal capital of Brittany for 600 years, but is now considered a part of the Pays de la Loire. Visually, it is a city of variety, with high-tech towers overlooking the port, canals, and Art Nouveau squares. Chic bars and restaurants cram the medieval nucleus, bounded by Place St-Croix and the château.

The Cathédrale St-Pierre et St-Paul was begun in 1434, but not completed until 1893. It is notable for its sculpted Gothic portals and Renaissance tomb of François II, the last Duke of Brittany.

The impressive Château des Ducs de Bretagne, now with a museum documenting the town's history, was the birthplace of Anne of Brittany, who irrevocably joined her fiercely independent duchy to France with her successive marriages to Charles VIII and Louis XII. A smaller royal lodging lies to the west of it. It was here, in Brittany's Catholic bastion, that Henri IV signed the 1598 Edict of Nantes, which granted freedom of worship to all French Protestants.

The **Musée d'Arts de Nantes** has a splendid array of paintings representing key movements from the 15th to the 20th century.

Packed with mementos, books, and maps, the Musée Jules Verne is dedicated to the life and works of the writer.

Musée d'Arts de Nantes
 🅰 10 Rue Georges Clemenceau ⏱ 11am-7pm Wed-Mon (to 9pm Thu) 🚫 Jan 1 & 5, Nov 1, Dec 25 🌐 museedartsdenantes. nantesmetropole.fr

10

St-Malo

⬛ Ille-et-Vilaine 🚗🚌🚢
📍 Esplanade St-Vincent; www.saint-malo-tourisme. com

Once a fortified island, St-Malo stands in a commanding position at the mouth of the River Rance. In the 16th–19th centuries, the port won prosperity and power through the exploits of its seafaring population. Intra-muros, the old walled city, is encircled by ramparts that provide fine views of St-Malo and its offshore islands. Within the city walls is a web of narrow, cobbled streets with tall 18th-century buildings housing many souvenir stores, seafood restaurants, and crêperies.

St-Malo's castle, the Château de St-Malo, dates from the 14th and 15th centuries. The great keep today houses an interesting museum charting the city's history. In the three-towered fortification known as the Tour Solidor, to the west of St-Malo, is a museum devoted to the ships and sailors that rounded Cape Horn.

HIDDEN GEM
Butterfingers

In St-Malo, stop by the charming La Maison du Beurre Bordier, the last butter-maker in the area to churn by hand. The front of the shop sells a range of flavored butters and cheeses, while at the back is a bijou museum about Breton butter-making *(9 Rue de l'Orme; 02-99 40 88 79)*.

DIANE DE POITIERS

Diane de Poitiers was Henri II's lifelong mistress, holding court as queen of France in all but name. Her beauty inspired many French artists, who frequently depicted her as Diana, the Classical goddess of the hunt. In 1547, Henri offered the Château de Chenonceau to Diane, who created stunning gardens and an arched bridge over the Cher river. After Henri's accidental death in 1559, Diane was forced to leave Chenonceau by his widow, Catherine de' Medici, in exchange for the fortress-like Château de Chaumont. Diane retired to Anet, and remained there until her death in 1566.

→

The Château de Chenonceau reflected in the limpid waters of the Cher river

CHÂTEAU DE CHENONCEAU

Indre-et-Loire **From Tours** **Hours vary, check website** **chenonceau.com**

Chenonceau, stretching romantically across the Cher river, is considered by many to be the loveliest of the Loire châteaux. Surrounded by elegant formal gardens and wooded grounds, this pure Renaissance edifice began life as a modest manor with accompanying water mill.

First built during the Renaissance, Chenonceau was expanded and improved over the centuries by the wives and mistresses of its successive aristocratic owners to become a palace designed solely for romantic pleasure. A magnificent avenue bordered by plane trees leads to symmetrical gardens and the serene vision that Flaubert praised as "floating on air and water." The château's distinctive feature is its Florentine-style 197-ft (60-m) gallery built over a series of arches, its elegant beauty reflected in the languid waters of the Cher. The grandeur continues inside with splendidly furnished rooms, airy bedchambers, and a wonderful collection of fine paintings and tapestries. The main living area was in the square-shaped turreted pavilion built over the foundations of an old water mill in the middle of the river.

INSIDER TIP
Promenades Nocturnes

In July and August the grounds are lit up at night (9–11:30pm), and visitors can take a stroll through the illuminated gardens to the stirring sound of music by great classical composers, from Handel to Corelli.

The grandeur continues inside with splendidly furnished rooms, airy bedchambers, and a wonderful collection of fine paintings and tapestries.

←

The elegant Grande Galerie, where Catherine de' Medici held wild parties and lavish balls

Timeline

1513

▲ Thomas Bohier acquires medieval Chenonceau. His wife, Catherine Briçonnet, undertakes rebuilding it.

1533
Marriage of Catherine de' Medici to Henri II. Chenonceau becomes a royal palace.

1575
Louise de Lorraine marries Henri III, Catherine's third and favorite son.

1730–99
▼ Madame Dupin, the wife of a "farmer-general," makes Chenonceau a salon for artists, writers, and philosophers.

1789
Chenonceau is spared in the bloody French Revolution, thanks to Madame Dupin.

1913
The château is bought by the Menier family, the chocolatiers who still own it today.

1941
Chenonceau chapel is damaged during a bombing raid.

215

A bridge over the River Loire, leading into the Old Town of Blois ↑

Blois

 Loir-et-Cher 🚌🚆
ℹ️ 23 Place du Château; www.bloischambord.co.uk

A powerful feudal stronghold in the 12th century, Blois rose to glory under Louis XII, who established his court here in 1498. The town remained at the center of French royal and political life for much of the next century. Today, Blois is the quintessential Loire town. The partly pedestrianized old quarter is full of romantic courtyards and fine mansions. **Château de Blois**, home to kings Louis XII, François I, and Henri III, has the most sensational history of all the Loire châteaux. It was here, in 1588, that the ambitious Duc de Guise, leader of the Catholic Holy League, was murdered on the orders of Henri III. The building itself juxtaposes four distinct architectural styles, reflecting its varied history.

Included among Blois' most impressive religious monuments are the beautiful three-spired Église St-Nicolas, formerly part of a 12th century Benedictine abbey, and the Cathédrale St-Louis,

which dominates the eastern side of the city. The cathedral is a 17th-century reconstruction of a Gothic church that was almost destroyed in 1678.

Château de Blois

🖼️🕐🏛️ 🏛️ Place du Château
🕐 Hours vary, check website
🚫 Jan 1, Dec 25 🌐 chateau deblois.fr

Abbaye Royale de Fontevraud

🏛️ Maine-et-Loire 🚌
🕐 9:30am–6pm daily (Apr-Sep: to 7pm) 🚫 Dec 25, Jan
🌐 fontevraud.fr

Founded in 1101, this abbey was the largest of its kind in France. It now hosts concerts and exhibitions. The abbey's nuns lived around the Grand Moûtier cloisters, and the leper colony's nurses were housed in the St-Lazare priory, now the abbey's hotel. Little remains of the monastic quarters, but the St-Benoît hospital survives. Most impressive is the octagonal kitchen in the Tour Evraud, a rare example of secular Romanesque architecture.

In the nave of the abbey church, the painted effigy of Henry Plantagenet, Count of Anjou and King of England, lies by those of his wife, Eleanor of Aquitaine, who died here in 1204, and their son, Richard the Lionheart.

Tours

🏛️ Indre-et-Loire ✈️🚆🚌
ℹ️ 78-82 Rue Bernard Palissy; www.tours-tourisme.fr

The pleasant cathedral city of Tours was built on the site of a Roman town, and became an important center of Christianity in the 4th century under St. Martin. In 1461, Louis XI made the city the French capital. However, during Henri IV's reign, the city lost favor with the monarchy and the capital left Tours for Paris.

The medieval old town, Le Vieux Tours, is full of narrow streets lined with beautiful half-timbered houses. St. Martin's tomb lies in the crypt of the New Basilica, built on the site of the medieval Old Basilica. Two towers, the Tour

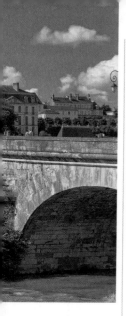

The Château Royal de Tours, a royal residence between the 13th and 15th centuries, houses modern art exhibitions and exhibits that explain the history of Tours.

⑮
Château de Chambord

🏠 Loir-et-Cher 🚌 To Blois, then taxi, shuttle, or bus ⏰ 9am–5pm daily (Mar–Oct: to 6pm) 📅 Jan 1, Dec 25 🌐 chambord.org

The brainchild of François I, the château was originally a hunting lodge in the Forêt de Boulogne. In 1519, the original building was razed and Chambord begun, to a design probably initiated by Leonardo da Vinci. By 1537, the keep, with its towers and terraces, had been completed by 1,800 men and three master masons. The following year, François I began building a private royal pavilion on the northeast corner, with a connecting two-story gallery. His son, Henri II, continued the west wing with the chapel, and Louis XIV completed the 440-roomed edifice in 1685.

The innovative double-helix Grand Staircase is said to have been designed by Da Vinci. The two flights of stairs are cleverly constructed to

Charlemagne and the Tour de l'Horloge, survive from the earlier building.

The foundation stone of the Cathédrale St-Gatien was laid in the early 13th century. Building work continued until the mid-16th century, and the cathedral illustrates how the Gothic style developed over time. The Musée des Beaux Arts, housed in the nearby former archbishop's palace, overlooks beautiful gardens. The collection features works by the likes of Rembrandt, Rubens, and Degas.

💬 INSIDER TIP
Château de Chambord Grounds

Surrounding Chambord are some 19 sq miles (50 sq km) of parkland, heath, and forest, including the largest walled nature reserve in Europe, home to wild boar and deer. Explore the park with a forest guide, or rent a bicycle.

---

ensure that it is impossible for the person going up to meet the person going down.

---

⑯
Orléans

🏠 Loiret 🚌🚆 ℹ️ 2 Place de l'Étape; www.tourisme-orleansmetropole.com

Orléans was the capital of medieval France, and it was here that Joan of Arc battled the English in 1429, during the Hundred Years' War. Later captured by the enemy and accused of witchcraft, she was burned at the stake in Rouen at the age of 19. Since her martyrdom, Joan has become a pervasive presence in Orléans.

A faded grandeur lingers in Vieil Orléans, the old quarter, bounded by the imposing Cathédrale Sainte-Croix, the Loire, and the Place du Martroi. The **Maison de Jeanne d'Arc** was rebuilt in 1961 on the site where Joan lodged in 1429. Inside, audio-visual exhibits and a short film recreate her life.

A selection of European art from the 16th to the early 20th century is on display at the Musée des Beaux-Arts.

Maison de Jeanne d'Arc
🏠 3 Place du Général de Gaulle ⏰ 10am–1pm & 2pm–6pm Tue–Sun (Oct–Mar: pm only) 📅 Public hols 🌐 jeannedarc.com.fr

---

THE HEROINE OF FRANCE

Joan of Arc is the quintessential French national heroine and female martyr. Her divinely led campaign to "drive the English out of France" during the Hundred Years' War has inspired plays, poetry, and films. She became champion of the uncrowned Charles VII but was captured in 1430 and accused of witchcraft. She was burned at the stake in 1431 at the age of 19. In 1920 she was canonized in recognition of her heroism and tragic martyrdom.

17 🅜 🛍

CHARTRES CATHEDRAL

📍 16 Cloister Notre-Dame, Chartres, Eure-et-Loir 🚉 🚌 🕐 8:30am-7:30pm daily
🌐 cathedrale-chartres.org

According to art historian Emile Male, "Chartres is the mind of the Middle Ages manifest." A true masterpiece of Gothic architecture, this monumental, double-spired cathedral towers over the Old Town. Visitors from all over the world come to see its spectacular stained-glass windows and mysterious labyrinth.

Begun in 1020, the original Romanesque cathedral was destroyed by a devastating fire in 1194. Only the north and south towers, south steeple, west portal, and crypt remained. Inside, the sacred *Veil of the Virgin* relic was the sole treasure to survive. Peasant and lord alike labored to rebuild the church in just 25 years. Few alterations were made after 1250, and fortunately Chartres was left unscathed by the Wars of Religion and the French Revolution. The result is an authentic Gothic cathedral. A huge, ongoing program to restore the more than 170 stained-glass windows was launched in the 1970s and may result in partial closures.

The taller of the two spires dates from the start of the 16th century. Flamboyant and Gothic in style, it contrasts sharply with the solemnity and relative simplicity of its Romanesque counterpart.

The vaulted ceiling is supported by a network of ribs.

The stained-glass windows on the west front are 12th-century lancet windows. They are among the oldest of their kind in the world.

The Royal Portal (1145–55) and part of the west front survive from the original Romanesque church.

The elongated statues on the Royal Portal represent Old Testament figures.

Illustration of the magnificent Chartres Cathedral ↑

A Labyrinth is inlaid in the nave floor.

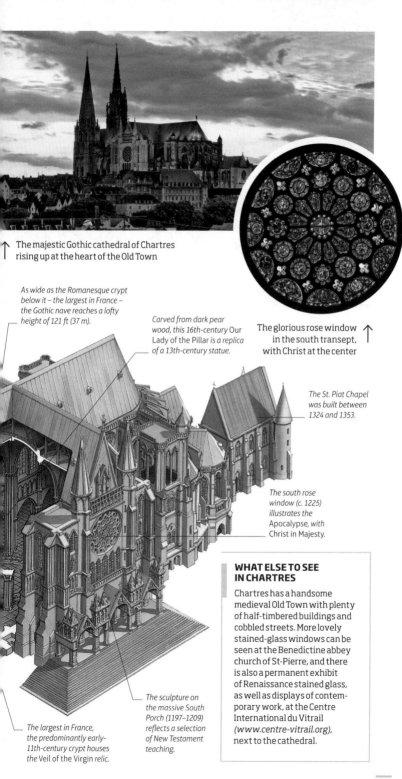

The majestic Gothic cathedral of Chartres rising up at the heart of the Old Town

The glorious rose window in the south transept, with Christ at the center

As wide as the Romanesque crypt below it – the largest in France – the Gothic nave reaches a lofty height of 121 ft (37 m).

Carved from dark pear wood, this 16th-century Our Lady of the Pillar is a replica of a 13th-century statue.

The St. Piat Chapel was built between 1324 and 1353.

The south rose window (c. 1225) illustrates the Apocalypse, with Christ in Majesty.

The sculpture on the massive South Porch (1197–1209) reflects a selection of New Testament teaching.

The largest in France, the predominantly early-11th-century crypt houses the Veil of the Virgin relic.

WHAT ELSE TO SEE IN CHARTRES

Chartres has a handsome medieval Old Town with plenty of half-timbered buildings and cobbled streets. More lovely stained-glass windows can be seen at the Benedictine abbey church of St-Pierre, and there is also a permanent exhibit of Renaissance stained glass, as well as displays of contemporary work, at the Centre International du Vitrail (www.centre-vitrail.org), next to the cathedral.

18

DIJON

 Côte d'Or **11** Rue des Forges;
www.destinationdijon.com

The capital of Burgundy, Dijon has a rich cultural life
and a renowned university. Its center is noted for
its architectural splendor – a legacy of the dukes of
Burgundy. The city is also famous for its mustard
and *pain d'épices* (gingerbread).

①

Musée des Beaux-Arts

🏛 Palais des Etats de
Bourgogne, Cour de Bar
🕐 Oct-May: 9:30am-6pm
Wed-Mon; Jun-Sep: 10am-
6:30pm Wed-Mon 🕐 Public
hols 🌐 beaux-arts.dijon.fr

This prestigious art collection
is housed in the former Palais
des Ducs, set on the magnificent Place de la Libération.
The Salle des Gardes on the
first floor is dominated by
the giant mausoleums of the
dukes, with tombs sculpted
by Claus Sluter. Other exhibits
include two gilded Flemish
retables and a portrait of
Philip the Good by Rogier van

der Weyden. The collection
contains a truly incredible
variety of artworks: paintings by Dutch and Flemish
masters; sculpture by Sluter
and Rude; Swiss and German
primitives; the Donation
Granville of 19th- and 20th-
century French art; 16th- to
18th-century French paintings; and sculptures by
François Pompon. Note the
ducal kitchens with six fire-
places, and the Tour Philippe
le Bon, 150 ft (46 m) tall with
a view of the city's Burgundian
tiled roof tops.
   The museum is currently
undergoing a huge restoration project; during this time
some sections may be closed
(see website for further details).

②

Cathédrale St-Bénigne

🏛 Place St-Bénigne
🕐 8am-8pm daily
🌐 cathedrale-dijon.fr

Very little remains of this
11th-century Benedictine
abbey, though beneath it lies
a Romanesque crypt with a
fine rotunda ringed by three
circles of columns. Note that a
fee applies to enter the crypt.

③

Musée Archéologique

🏛 5 Rue du Docteur
Maret 🕐 9:30am-6pm
Wed-Mon 🕐 Public hols
🌐 archeologie.dijon.fr

This intriguing museum is
housed in the old dormitory
of the Benedictine Abbey of
St. Bénigne. The 11th-century
chapter house, its stocky
columns supporting a barrel-
vaulted roof, houses a fine
collection of Gallo-Roman
sculpture. The ground floor,
with its lovely fan vaulting,
houses the famous *Head of
Christ* by Claus Sluter, originally from the *Well of Moses*.

Dijon's elegant Place de la Libération, beautifully illuminated at sunset

Chartreuse de Champmol

📍 1 Blvd Chanoine Kir
📞 08 92 70 05 58
🕐 10am–6pm daily

Once a Carthusian monastery built by Philip the Bold to service a dynastic burial site, this necropolis was all but destroyed during the Revolution. All that remains is a chapel doorway and the famous *Well of Moses* by Claus Sluter. It is located on the outskirts of the city, now in the grounds of a psychiatric hospital west of Dijon railroad station – it is not very easy to find but worth the effort. The statue, representing Moses and five other prophets, is set on a hexagonal base above a basin. Sluter is renowned for his deeply cut carving and the work here is exquisitely lifelike.

STAY

Vertigo Hotel
A stylish hotel close to the city center, with an excellent spa and a chic bar in which to wind down after sightseeing.

🏠 3 Rue Devosge
🌐 vertigohoteldijon.com

€€€

Hostellerie du Chapeau Rouge
Set in a 19th-century building, this 28-room hotel has a superb two-Michelin-star restaurant run by chef William Frachot. The cuisine celebrates the produce of France's regions.

🏠 5 Rue Michelet
🌐 chapeau-rouge.fr

€€€

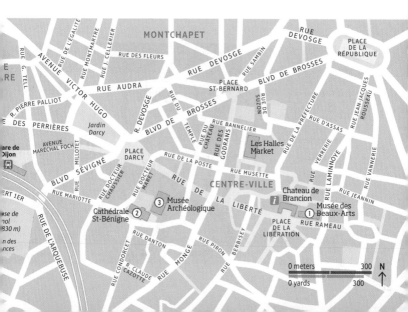

EAT

Lyon has the highest concentration of restaurants in France and is famed for the exceptional quality of its food.

L'Auberge du Pont de Collonges

Legendary chef Paul Bocuse's temple of *haute cuisine* on the banks of the Saône is a gourmet treat for all the senses. An unmissable foodie destination.

40 Rue de la Plage 🌐bocuse.fr

€€€

Têtedoie

Innovative French cuisine is served against panoramic Lyon views, in surprisingly intimate surrounds.

4 Rue Professeur Pierre Marion 🌐tetedoie.com

€€€

Les Halles de Lyon – Paul Bocuse

The city's iconic indoor food market, which houses several bars and restaurants, has won an international reputation for the fine quality of its produce.

102 Cours Lafayette, 69003 🌐halles-de-lyon-paulbocuse.com

€€€

→

The honey-stoned Old Town of Beaune in the golden glow of sunlight

---

Vézelay

🅰Yonne 🚍 ℹ12 Rue St-Étienne; www.vezelay tourisme.com

Visitors come to Vézelay to see the picturesque **Basilique Ste-Madeleine**. In the 12th century, at the height of its glory, the abbey claimed to house the relics of Mary Magdalene, and it was a starting point for the pilgrimage to Santiago de Compostela in Spain *(p312)*.

The star attractions of the Romanesque church are the tympanum sculpture (1120–35) above the central doorway, the exquisitely carved capitals in the nave and narthex, and the immense Gothic choir.

Basilique Ste-Madeleine

🕙 🚉Sermizelles, then bus ⏰8am–8pm daily 🌐basiliquedevezelay.org

---

Beaune

🅰Côte D'Or 🚍 ℹ6 Blvd Pepreuil; www.beaune-tourism.com

The indisputable highlight of the old center of Beaune is the **Hôtel-Dieu**. The hospice was founded in 1443 for the town's inhabitants, many of whom were left poverty-stricken after the Hundred Years' War. Today, it is considered a medieval jewel, with its superb multicolored Burgundian roof tiles. It houses many treasures, including the religious masterpiece the *Last Judgement* polyptych, by Rogier van der Weyden.

The Hôtel des Ducs de Bourgogne, built in the 14th–16th centuries, houses the Musée du Vin de Bourgogne, with displays of traditional winemaking equipment.

Hôtel-Dieu

♿🕙 🅰2 Rue de l'Hôtel-Dieu ⏰Hours vary, check website 🌐hospices-de-beaune.com

---

Annecy

🅰Annecy 🚍🚆 ℹ1 Rue Jean Jaurès; www.lac-annecy.com

Annecy is one of the most beautiful towns in the Alps, set at the northern tip of Lac d'Annecy and surrounded by snowcapped mountains.

A stroll around the town's small medieval quarter, with its canals, flower-covered bridges, and arcaded streets, is one of the main attractions of a stay here. Look out for

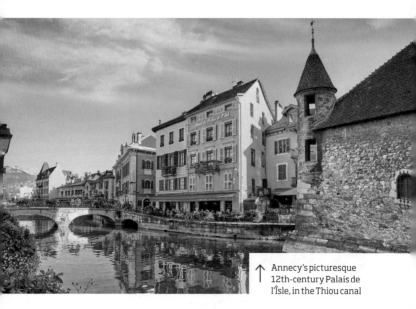

↑ Annecy's picturesque 12th-century Palais de l'Île, in the Thiou canal

 INSIDER TIP
Talloires

A good way to enjoy the spectacular scenery around Annecy is to take a boat to Talloires, a tiny lakeside village noted for its hotels and restaurants.

...he formidable Palais de l'Île, ...12th-century prison in the ...niddle of the Thiou canal.

The turreted Château ...'Annecy, perched high on a ...ill, affords fine panoramic ...ews. The clear waters of the ...ke are perfect for swimming ...nd watersports. Boat trips ...eave from the Quai Thiou.

...yon

...Rhône ✉🚆🚌 ❼ Place
...elle-cour; www.lyon-
...ance.com

...ramatically sited on the banks ...f the Rhône and Saône rivers, ...yon has been a vital gateway ...etween the north and south ...nce ancient times. Vieux Lyon, ...e oldest part of the city, is the site of the Roman settlement of Lugdunum, the commercial and military capital of Gaul, founded by Julius Caesar in 44 BC. Fragments of this prosperous city can be seen in the superb **Musée de la Civilisation Gallo-Romaine**. There are also two excavated Roman amphitheaters: the Grand Théâtre, built in 15 BC to seat 30,000 spectators, and the smaller Odéon.

Other major sights are the 19th-century mock-Byzantine Basilique Notre-Dame de Fourvière, and the Cathédrale St-Jean, begun in the 1100s. Vieux Lyon's fine Renaissance mansions formerly housed bankers and silk merchants.

Housed in the 17th-century Palais St-Pierre, the excellent **Musée des Beaux Arts** show-cases the country's largest and most important collection of fine arts after the Louvre. Modern works, dating from after the mid-20th century, can be admired at the Musée d'Art Contemporain in the north of the city. An exquisite display of silks and tapestries, some dating back to early Christian times, can be seen in the Musée des Tissus. The city's most impressive architectural landmark is the contemporary steel-and-glass science center and natural history museum, the Musée des Confluences.

Musée de la Civilisation Gallo-Romaine
🖈🕐 ⌂17 Rue Cléberg
🕐11am–6pm Tue–Fri, 10am–6pm Sat & Sun 🗙Jan 1, May 1, Dec 25 ⊠lugdunum.grand lyon.com

Musée des Beaux Arts
🖈🕐🕐 ⌂20 Place des Terreaux 🕐10am–6pm Wed–Sun ⊠mba-lyon.fr

↑ *The Gardener* (1837), by Simon Saint-Jean, at Lyon's Musée des Beaux Arts

↑ The pretty city of Grenoble, nestled among the French Alps

23
Grenoble

🏠 Isère 🚈🚍🚆 ℹ️ 14 Rue de la République; www. grenoble-tourisme.com

Ancient capital of Dauphiné, Grenoble is a busy and thriving city, attractively located at the confluence of the Drac and Isère rivers, in the shadow of the mighty Vercors and Chartreuse massifs.

A cable car from the Quai Stéphane-Jay, on the north bank of the Isère, takes you up to the 16th-century Fort de la Bastille, where you are rewarded with magnificent views of the city and surrounding mountains. From here, paths lead down through pretty gardens to the excellent Musée Dauphinois at the foot of the hill. Housed in a 17th-century convent, the museum contains displays on local history, arts, and crafts.

On the other side of the river, the focus of life is the Place Grenette, a lively square lined with sidewalk cafés. Nearby, the Place St-André is the heart of the medieval city, overlooked by Grenoble's oldest buildings, including the 13th-century Église St-André and the 15th-century Palais de Justice.

Also worth visiting is the Musée de Grenoble, the city's principal art museum, which has an especially good collection of modern works.

Musée de Grenoble

🎨🏛️📷🍽️ 🏠 5 Place de Lavalette 🕐 10am-6:30pm Wed-Mon 🚫 Jan 1, May 1, Dec 25 🌐 museedegrenoble.fr

Did You Know?

Free vending machines in Grenoble dispense short stories that take one, three, or five minutes to read.

24
Bordeaux

🏠 Gironde 🚈🚍🚆 ℹ️ 12 Cours du 30 Juillet; www. bordeaux-tourisme.com

Built beside the Garonne river, Bordeaux has been a major port since pre-Roman times and a crossroads of European trade for centuries. The export of wine has always been the basis of the city's prosperity, and today the Bordeaux region produces more than 70 million cases of wine every year.

Along the waterfront, a long sweep of Classical facades is broken by the Esplanade des Quinconces, with its statues and fountains. At one end, the Monument aux Girondins (1804–1902) commemorates the Girondists sent to the guillotine by Robespierre during the Terror (1793–5). The elegant Place de la Bourse is popular for its Mirroir d'Eau water feature. Buildings of architectural interest include the massive Basilique St-Michel, begun in 1350 and completed 200 years later, and the 18th-century Grand Théâtre, a magnificent example of the French Neo-Classical style. The Musée des Beaux Arts holds an excellent collection of paintings, ranging from the Renaissance to our time.

The immersive Cité du Vin museum pays homage to Bordeaux's reputation as a winemaking center, and tours to nearby wine châteaux are organized by the town's tourist office.

The gigantic Cathédrale St-André dates from the 11th century and is a mix of styles.

Musée des Beaux Arts

🎨 🏠 20 Cours d'Albret 🕐 11am-6pm Wed-Mon 🚫 Public hols 🌐 musba-bordeaux.fr

Exploring wall painting in the lit-up Lascaux I cave replic

BORDEAUX WINES

Bordeaux is the world's largest fine wine region and, for its red wines, certainly the most familiar outside France. The great wine-producing areas lie close to the banks of the Gironde, Garonne, and Dordogne rivers. Along with these, the river port of Bordeaux itself has been crucial to the region's wine trade; some of the prettiest châteaux line the river banks, making for easy transportation. Grape varieties used include Cabernet Sauvignon, Merlot, and Petit Verdot (for red wine); and Sémillon and Sauvignon Blanc (for white).

Lascaux

⌂ Montignac **◷ Hours vary, check website** **⊕ lascaux.fr**

Lascaux is the most famous of the prehistoric sites in the Dordogne region. Four young boys and their dog came across the caves and their astounding Palaeolithic paintings in 1940, and the importance of their discovery was swiftly recognized.

Lascaux has been closed to the public since 1963 because of deterioration due to carbon dioxide emitted by breathing. An exact copy, Lascaux II, has been created a few minutes' walk down the hillside, using the same materials. The replica is beautiful and should not be dismissed out of hand.

The newer Lascaux IV, at the Centre International de l'Art Pariétal, provides state-of-the-art replicas of the vivid cave paintings of bulls, high-antlered elk, bison, and horses. It also includes an interactive exhibition that uses digital touchscreens to retrace the history of the discovery of Lascaux, as well as providing a virtual reality tour of the atmospheric caves. The café at Lascaux IV serves excellent regional food.

㉖
Toulouse

⌂ Haute-Garonne
🛈 Donjon du Capitole; www.toulouse-tourisme.com

Toulouse, the most important town in southwest France, is the country's fourth-largest metropolis, and a major industrial and university city.

The area is also famous for its aerospace industry; Concorde, Airbus, and the Ariane space rocket all originated here (advance-booked factory tours are available).

Cité de l'Espace has a planetarium and interactive exhibits on space exploration.

The church known as Les Jacobins was begun in 1229 and took over two centuries to finish. The Gothic masterpiece features a soaring, 22-branched palm tree vault in the apse, and a bell tower (1294) that is much imitated in southwest France. Toulouse was also a noted center of Romanesque art in Europe, due to its position on the pilgrimage route to Santiago de Compostela (p312). The largest Romanesque basilica in Europe, the Basilique de St-Sernin, was built in the 11th–12th centuries to accommodate pilgrims. Sculptures from the period and French, Italian, and Flemish paintings are housed in the **Musée des Augustins**, which incorporates cloisters from a 14th-century Augustinian priory.

The 16th-century palace known as the Hôtel d'Assézat now houses the Fondation Bemberg, named after local art-lover Georges Bemberg, with Renaissance art and 19th- and 20th-century French work.

Musée des Augustins
⑭⑳ **⌂ 21 Rue de Metz**
◷ 10am–6pm Wed–Mon (to 9pm Wed) **◵ Jan 1, May 1, Dec 25** **⊕ augustins.org**

27

Carcassonne

🏛 Aude 🚌🚍🚗 ℹ 28 Rue de Verdun; www.tourisme-carcassonne.fr

The citadel of Carcassonne is a perfectly restored medieval town. It crowns a steep bank above the Aude river, a fairy-tale vision of turrets and ramparts overlooking the Basse Ville (Lower Town) below.

The strategic position of the citadel between the Atlantic and the Mediterranean led to its original settlement, consolidated by the Romans in the 2nd century BC.

At its zenith in the 12th century, the town was ruled by the Trencavels, who built the château and cathedral. The Cathars, a persecuted Christian sect, were given sanctuary here in 1209 but, after a two-week siege, the town fell to the Crusaders sent to eradicate them. The attentions of architectural historian Viollet-le-Duc led to Carcassonne's restoration in the 19th century.

Flanked by sandstone towers, the defenses of the Porte Narbonnaise gate included two portcullises, two iron doors, a moat, and a drawbridge. A fortress within a fortress, the Château Comtal has a surrounding moat and five defensive towers.

Within the Romanesque and Gothic Basilique St-Nazaire is the famous Siege Stone, inscribed with scenes said to depict the siege of 1209.

28

Pyrenees

✈ Pau 🚌🚍 Bayonne & Pau ℹ Place des Basques, Bayonne, www.bayonne-tourisme.com; Place Royale, Pau, www.pau-pyrenees.com

The mountains dominate life in the French Pyrenees. A region in many ways closer to Spain than France, over the centuries its remote terrain and tenacious people have given heretics a hiding place and refugees an escape route.

The Parc National des Pyrénées extends 62 miles (100 km) along the French–Spanish frontier. It has some of the most splendid alpine scenery in Europe, and is rich in flora and fauna. Within the park are 217 miles (350 km) of footpaths.

The region's oldest inhabitants, the Basque people, have maintained their own distinct language and culture. Bayonne, on the Atlantic coast, is the capital of French Basque country, and has been an important town since Roman

→

The Roman amphitheater in Nîmes, used for concerts and bullfights

times. Biarritz, to the west of Bayonne, has two casinos and six good beaches, with the best surfing in Europe. A short distance south, St-Jean-de-Luz is a sleepy fishing village that explodes into life in summer. Its main attraction is the Église St-Jean Baptiste, where Louis XIV married the Infanta Maria Teresa of Spain in 1660.

A lively university town with elegant architecture, Pau is

THE MIRACLE OF LOURDES

In 1858, a 14-year-old girl named Bernadette Soubirous experienced 18 visions of the Virgin at the Grotte Massabielle near the town of Lourdes. Despite being told to keep away from the cave by her mother, she was guided to a spring with miraculous healing powers. The church endorsed the miracles in the 1860s, and since then many people claim to have been cured by the holy water. A huge city of shrines, churches, and hospices has since grown up around the spring.

↑ Hiking in the Pyrenees toward the limestone Cirque du Gavarnie, created by glacial erosion

the most appealing large town in the central Pyrenees. It has long been a favorite resort of affluent foreigners.

Other places of interest include the many mountain ski resorts, the shrine at Lourdes, and the pretty hilltop town of St-Bertrand-de-Comminges.

29

Nîmes

 Gard ✈🚂🚌 🚏 6 Blvd des Arènes; www.nimes-tourisme.com

An important crossroads in the ancient world, Nîmes is well known for its bullfights and Roman antiquities. The city has had a turbulent history, and suffered particularly badly during the 16th-century Wars of Religion, when the Romanesque Cathédrale Notre-Dame et St-Castor was seriously damaged. In the 17th and 18th centuries, however, the town prospered from textile manufacturing, with one of the most enduring products being denim, or *serge de Nîmes*.

All roads in the city lead to the amphitheater, Les Arènes. Built at the end of the 1st century AD, it is still in use today as a venue for concerts, sporting events, and bull-fights, while undergoing continued renovations.

The Maison Carrée is an elegant Roman temple, the pride of Nîmes. Built by Augustus's son-in-law Marcus Agrippa, it is one of the best preserved in the world, with finely fluted Corinthian columns and a sculpted frieze.

Set in the Roman wall is the Porte d'Auguste, a gateway built for travelers on the Domitian Way, which passed through the center of Nîmes. Nearby is the Castellum, a tower used for storing water brought in by aqueduct. The water was distributed around the town by a canal system. Roman artifacts can be seen at the modern **Musée de la Romanité de Nîmes**, located opposite Les Arènes.

Five floors of Nîmes' controversial arts complex, the Carré d'Art, are underground. The complex includes a library, a roof-terrace restaurant set around a glass atrium, and the Musée d'Art Contemporain.

Northeast of the city is the Pont du Gard, a 2,000-year-old aqueduct. The Romans considered this to be the best testimony to the greatness of their empire, and at 160 ft (49 m), it was the highest aqueduct they ever built.

EAT

La Marquiere
A family-run favorite with an Occitan menu.

 13 Rue St-Jean, Carcassonne 🗓 Wed & Thu 🌐 lamarquiere.com

€€€

Auberge du Cheval Blanc
This atmospheric Basque restaurant dates from 1715 and offers traditional dishes, including hake and Bayonne's specialty, cured ham.

 63 Rue Bourgneuf, Bayonne 🌐 cheval-blancbayonne.com

€€€

La Tantina de Burgos
This local favorite serves traditional Basque dishes. Friendly staff bring plates of freshly caught fish and hearty stews.

 2 Place Beau Rivage, Biarritz 📞 05-59 23 24 47

€€€

Chez Simone
A welcoming family restaurant with a lovely terrace overlooking the countryside and a menu of tasty local dishes.

 Le Village, St-Bertrand-de-Comminges 📞 05-61 94 91 05

€€€

Musée de la Romanité de Nîmes

♿👶🎫🕐🎧🛍 🏛 16 Blvd des Arènes 🕐 Apr-Oct: 10am-7pm daily; Nov-Mar: 10am-6pm Wed-Mon 🗓 Jan 1, Dec 25 🌐 museedelaromanite.fr

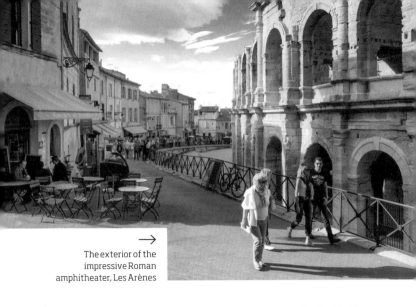

→ The exterior of the impressive Roman amphitheater, Les Arènes

30

ARLES

 Bouches-du-Rhône 🚗🚌 Ave Paulin Talabot
ⓘ Blvd des Lices; www.arlestourisme.com

Like a miniature version of Rome, charming Arles spreads out around a massive arena, and remnants of its Roman heyday are scattered all around its narrow streets. The town is even better known for its connection with Vincent van Gogh, who – inspired by the bright light and rich colors – enjoyed the most creative period of his short life here. Arles is also the gateway to the unique wetlands of the Camargue *(p230)*, thanks to its position on the Rhône.

①
Les Arènes

🏛 Rond-point des Arènes
🕐 9am-6pm daily ⓔ Events
🖥 arenes-arles.com

The largest Roman building in Gaul is as impressive now as when it was built around AD 90. Able to seat 20,000, today it is used for concerts and other spectacles. The top tier of seating provides an excellent panoramic view of Arles. To the southwest is the elegant Théâtre Antique, another beautifully preserved Roman-era stadium with 2,000 tiered seats.

②
Église St-Trophime

🏛 Place de la République
🕐 10am-6pm Wed-Mon
🖥 patrimoine.ville-arles.fr

This is one of Provence's great Romanesque churches. The ornately sculpted portal and beautiful cloisters (for which there is an admission fee) are decorated with biblical scenes. St. Trophime, thought to be the first bishop of Arles in the early 3rd century, appears with St. Peter and St. John on the carved northeast pillar. The nave of the church is hung with Aubusson tapestries.

③
Cryptoportiques

🏛 Hôtel de Ville, Place de la République 🕐 10am-6pm Wed-Mon 🔒 Public holidays 🖥 patrimoine.ville-arles.fr

Beneath the site of the Roman Forum and accessed via the Hôtel de Ville, these huge, horseshoe-shaped underground galleries – up to 33 ft (10 m) wide and ventilated by air shafts – were probably used as granaries or possibly as a barracks for slaves. Constructed in the 1st century AD, then buried beneath later church buildings, these impressive structures were left forgotten and inaccessible until archaeologists began the task of reopening them in 1935.

 PICTURE PERFECT
Following Van Gogh

Visit the atmospheric Place du Forum in the evening for a snap of the Restaurant-Café Van Gogh, still looking just as it did when it inspired his *Café Terrace at Night* (1888).

④
Les Alyscamps

🏛 Ave des Alyscamps
🕐 9am-6pm daily

Christ is claimed to have appeared to early Christians who met in secret at this vast necropolis, which was one of the largest and most famous cemeteries in the Western world. An avenue of marble sarcophagi marks the site where many of the city's dignitaries were buried. Christians were often buried by the tomb of Genesius, a beheaded Christian martyr.

⑤
Luma Foundation

🏛 45 Chemin des Minimes
🕐 11am-6pm Tue-Sun
🌐 luma-arles.org

Soaring above the Old Town like a starship ready for lift-off, architect Frank Gehry's gleaming metallic landmark opened in summer 2018, endowing Arles with a brand-new venue for world-class contemporary art and performance. The Luma Foundation, led by Swiss art collector Maja Hoffmann, forms a 20-acre (8-ha) complex of galleries, theaters, studios, and workshops dedicated to producing new and adventurous work in photography and conceptual art. The collection is split between Gehry's building and six former factory and warehouse spaces.

⑥
Musée Départementale de l'Arles Antique

🏛 Rue du Grand-Prieuré
🕐 10am-6pm Wed-Mon
🌐 patrimoine.ville-arles.fr

A marble statue of the Emperor Augustus, a statue of Venus, and a massive altar dedicated to Apollo are just

↑ Artists painting in the gardens of Fondation Vincent van Gogh

some of the highlights of this museum's collection of Roman sculptures, which date from pre-Christian times to the period that followed Constantine's conversion of the Empire in AD 312. A wing opened in 2013 to house the Arles Rhône 3, a fantastically well-preserved Roman 102-ft- (31-m-) long flat-bottomed wooden river barge that was retrieved from the bed of the Rhône.

⑦
Fondation Vincent van Gogh Arles

🏛 35 Rue du Dr Fanton
🕐 11am-6pm Tue-Sun (Apr-Sep: to 7pm) 🌐 fondation-vincentvangogh-arles.org

Housed in a 15th-century mansion, the Hôtel Léautaud de Donines, this foundation aims to put Van Gogh's work in context and highlights the artist's influence on his contemporaries and successive generations of painters. Artists and students can gain permission to paint on-site.

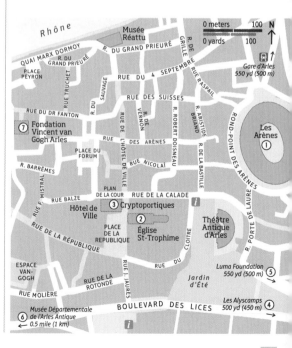

Avignon

Vaucluse ▨▨▨ ▮**41 Cours Jean Jaurès; www. avignon-tourisme.com**

Massive ramparts enclose this fascinating town. The huge **Palais des Papes** – home of the papal court from 1309 to 1377 – is Avignon's dominant feature, but the town contains other riches. To the north of the Palais is the 13th-century Musée du Petit Palais, once the Archbishop of Avignon's residence. It has received such notorious guests as Cesare Borgia and Louis XIV. Now a museum, it displays Romanesque and Gothic sculpture and paintings of the Avignon and Italian schools.

From early July for three weeks, the the Palais des Papes plays host to the Avignon Festival, showcasing ballet, drama, and concerts.

Avignon also boasts some fine churches, such as the 12th-century Cathédrale de Notre-Dame-des-Doms.

The Musée Lapidaire houses statues, mosaics, and carvings from pre-Roman Provence, while the Musée Calvet features a superb array of exhibits, including Roman finds. It also gives an overview of French art during the past 500 years, with works by Rodin, Manet, and Dufy. The Place de l'Horloge is the center of Avignon's social life, with a merry-go-round from 1900 standing under the town hall's Gothic clock tower.

The Pont St-Bénézet, built 1171–85, once had 22 arches, but most were destroyed by floods in 1668. One arch bears the tiny Chapelle St-Nicolas.

Palais des Papes
⊛⊛ **Place du Palais-des-Papes** ⊖**Hours vary, check website** ⊎palais-des-papes.com

Camargue

Bouches-du-Rhône ▨▨ ▮**5 Ave van Gogh, Stes-Maries-de-la-Mer; www. saintesmaries.com**

This flat, sparsely populated land is one of Europe's major wetland regions and natural-history sites. Extensive areas of salt marshes, lakes, pastures, and sand dunes cover a vast 346,000 acres (140,000 ha). The native white horses and black bulls are tended by the region's cowboys, or *gardians*. Numerous seabirds and wild-fowl also occupy the region.

Saintes-Maries-de-la-Mer, the region's main tourist center, has a sandy beach with watersports and boat trips. A few miles inland, the information center at Pont-de-Gau offers wonderful views over the flat lagoon. Photographs and documents

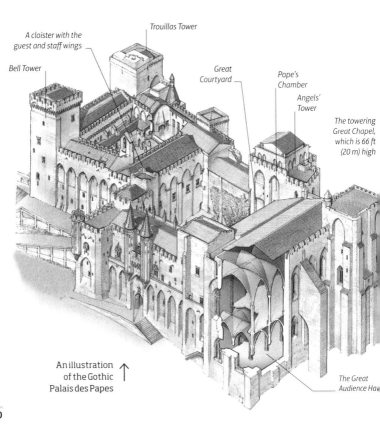

A cloister with the guest and staff wings

Bell Tower

Trouillas Tower

Great Courtyard

Pope's Chamber

Angels' Tower

The towering Great Chapel, which is 66 ft (20 m) high

An illustration of the Gothic Palais des Papes

The Great Audience Hall

chronicle the history of the Camargue. Most of the birds that live in, or migrate within, the region, including thousands of flamingoes that come here to breed, can be seen at the **Parc Ornithologique du Pont-de-Gau.**

In the north of the region, a traditional farmhouse, Mas du Pont de Rousty, has been converted into the **Musée Camarguais**, offering an introduction to the customs and traditions of the area.

Parc Ornithologique du Pont-de-Gau

⊗ 🅰 Pont-de-Gau 🕐 Hours vary, check website 🔒 Dec 25 🌐 parcornithologique.com

Musée Camarguais

⊗ ⓘ 🅰 Parc Naturel Régional de Camargue, Mas du Pont de Rousty 🕐 Hours vary, check website 🔒 Jan 1, May 1, Dec 25 🌐 parc-camargue.fr

---

33

Aix-en-Provence

🅰 Bouches-du-Rhône 🚆🚌 🚉 300 Ave Giuseppe Verdi, Les Allées Provençales; www.aixenprovence tourism.com

Provence's former capital is a student town, with a university that dates back to 1409. Its layout took shape in the 17th century, when ramparts first raised by the Romans were pulled down and the mansion-lined Cours Mirabeau was built.

Aix's old quarter creaks with history, and is home to the Cathédrale St-Sauveur. The town's most famous son is Paul Cézanne, whose studio – designed by the artist himself – is much as he left it when he died in 1906. The main museum is the **Musée Granet**, housing a collection of French, Italian, and Flemish paintings left to Aix by François Granet. Work by Provençal artists, including Cézanne, is also shown. An annex displays further works by master painters and sculptors.

 INSIDER TIP
Going to Market

Aix-en-Provence is famed for its markets. Buy seasonal produce daily at Place Richelme, snack on delectable Provençal cuisine at the Grand Marché, or get literary at the monthly book market.

Musée Granet

⊗ 🅰 Pl St-Jean de Malte 🕐 Hours vary, check website 🔒 Jan 1, May 1, Dec 25 🌐 museegranet-aixen provence.fr

---

34

Marseille

🅰 Bouches-du-Rhône 🚆🚌🚇🚢 🚉 11 La Canebière; www.marseille-tourisme. com

France's most important port and oldest major city centers on the Vieux Port. The Musée des Civilisations de l'Europe et de la Méditerranée (MuCEM) focuses on the history of civilization in Europe, specifically the Mediterranean region.

On the north side of the port are the commercial docks and the Old Town. The Old Town's finest building is the Vieille Charité, a large 17th-century hospice that houses the Musée d'Archéologie Méditerranéenne and the Musée d'Arts Africains, Océaniens, Amérindiens.

The Neo-Byzantine Notre-Dame-de-la-Garde dominates the city, but Marseille's finest piece of religious architecture is the Abbaye de St-Victor, founded in the 5th century, with catacombs, sarcophagi, and the martyr St. Victor's cave.

Inside the Centre Bourse shopping center is the Musée d'Histoire de Marseille. Reconstructions of the city at the height of the Greek period make this a good starting point for a tour.

↑ The colorfully lit apse in the Cathédrale St-Sauveur, Aix-en-Provence

---

 TOP 5 FLAVORS OF THE SOUTH OF FRANCE

Bouillabaisse
This fish soup from Marseille is an assortment of local seafood, flavored with tomatoes, saffron, and olive oil.

Fougasse
Fougasse is a flattish, lattice-like bread studded with black olives, anchovies, onions, and spices.

Aïoli
A sauce made of egg yolk, garlic, and olive oil, aïoli is served with salt cod, boiled eggs, or snails.

Ratatouille
This stew of onions, eggplant, zucchini, tomato, and capsicums is cooked in olive oil and garlic.

Salade Niçoise
Salade Niçoise comes in many versions but must have lettuce, tomatoes, green beans, black olives, eggs, and anchovies.

35

Cannes

🅰 Alpes-Maritimes
🖼🚌 ℹ Palais des
Festivals, 1 Blvd de la
Croisette; www.cannes-
destination.com

The first thing that most people associate with Cannes is its many festivals, especially the Cannes Festival, held each May. The first Cannes Festival took place in 1946 (then called the International Film Festival), and for a while it remained a small and exclusive affair. The mid-1950s marked the change from artistic event to media circus, but Cannes remains a major international marketplace for moviemakers and distributors. The annual festival is held in the huge Palais des Festivals.

There is, however, more to the city than this glittering event. The Old Town is centered in the Le Suquet district, which is dominated by the church of Notre-Dame de l'Espérance, built in the 16th and 17th centuries in the Provençal Gothic style. The famed Boulevard de la Croisette is lined with palm trees, as well as luxury stores and hotels looking out over fine sandy beaches.

36

Nice

🅰 Alpes-Maritimes
🖼🚌 ℹ 5 Promenade
des Anglais; www.nice
tourisme.com

One of the largest resorts on the Mediterranean coast, Nice has the third-busiest airport in France. Its temperate winter climate and verdant subtropical vegetation have long attracted visitors, and today it is also a center for business conferences and package travelers.

There are numerous art museums in Nice, two of which devote themselves to the works of particular artists. The **Musée Matisse**, housed in and below the 17th-century Arena Villa, displays drawings, paintings, bronzes, fabrics, and various artifacts. The **Musée Chagall** holds the largest collection of works by Marc Chagall, with paintings, drawings, sculpture, stained glass, and mosaics.

A strikingly original complex of four marble-faced towers linked by glass passageways houses the Musée d'Art Contemporain. The collection is particularly strong in Neorealism and Pop Art. The Musée des Beaux Arts displays works by the likes of Dufy, Monet, Renoir, and Sisley.

A 19th-century palace, the Palais Masséna is filled with paintings of the Nice school, works by the Impressionists, Provençal ceramics, folk art, and a gold cloak that was once worn by Napoleon's beloved Josephine.

The onion domes of the Cathédrale Orthodoxe Russe St-Nicolas, completed in 1912, make this building Nice's most distinctive landmark.

NICE JAZZ FESTIVAL

Louis Armstrong and His All-Stars headlined at the first Nice Jazz Festival in 1948, as the Riviera emerged from the grim years of World War II and postwar poverty. It was the first big international jazz festival, and more than 70 years on it is still a major event. The Théâtre de Verdure is the main venue, and the six-day event kicks off with a lively carnival parade through the city center.

↓ Summertime strolling along the Boulevard de la Croisette on the Cannes seafront

Across the harbor lies Monaco-Ville, the seat of government. The interior of the 13th-century Palais Princier, with its priceless furniture and magnificent frescoes, is open to the public from April to mid-October.

The aquarium of the Musée Océanographique, which was inaugurated in 1910, holds rare species of marine plants and animals. Marine explorer Jacques Cousteau was director from 1957 to 1988 and established his research center here.

Hotel Negresco overlooking the bay of Nice

Musée Matisse

164 Ave des Arènes de Cimiez ◷ Hours vary, check website ⓦ musee-matisse-nice.org

Musée Chagall

◈◈◈◈◈ 36 Ave du Docteur Ménard ◷ Hours vary, check website ⓧ Jan 1, May 1, Dec 25 ⓦ musees-nationaux-alpesmaritimes.fr

🅟

Monaco

🅐 Monaco ⓧ Nice 🅟
ⓘ 2a Blvd des Moulins; www.visitmonaco.com

Arriving today among the towering skyscrapers of sovereign city-state Monaco, it is hard to envisage the turbulence of its history. At first a Greek settlement, later taken by the Romans, it was bought from the Genoese in 1297 by the Grimaldis who, in spite of bitter family feuds, still rule as the world's oldest monarchy. Monaco covers 0.78 sq miles (2.02 sq km), and although its size has increased by one-third in the form of landfills, it still occupies an area smaller than New York's Central Park.

The best-known section of Monaco is Monte Carlo. People flock to the annual car rally held here in January, but the area owes its renown mainly to its Grand Casino. Source of countless legends, it was instituted by Charles III to save himself from bankruptcy in 1856. So successful was this money-making venture that, by 1870, he was able to abolish taxation for his people. Redesigned in 1878 and set in formal gardens, the casino gives a splendid view over Monaco. Even the most exclusive of the gaming rooms can be visited.

TOP 5 CÔTE D'AZUR RESORTS

St-Tropez
St-Tropez is one of the trendiest resorts; Tahiti-Plage is the coast's showcase for fun, sun, fashion, and glamor.

St-Raphaël
The family resort of St-Raphaël is peaceful, with excellent facilities for tourists.

Juan-les-Pins
At the western edge of the Riviera, Juan-les-Pins is a lively resort. Its all-night bars, nightclubs, and cafés make it popular with teenagers and young adults.

Antibes
Founded by the Greeks, Antibes is one of the oldest towns along this stretch of coast. It is also home to a large museum of Picasso's work, donated by the artist himself.

Menton
At the eastern edge of the Riviera, the beaches of Menton are the warmest along the coast; sunbathers enjoy a beach climate all year round.

PRACTICAL
INFORMATION

Here you will find all the essential advice and information you will need before and during your stay in France.

CURRENCY
Euro (EUR)

TIME ZONE
CET/CEST. Central European Summer Time runs from the last Sunday in March to the last Sunday in October.

LANGUAGE
French

ELECTRICITY SUPPLY
Power sockets are type C and E, fitting C and E plugs with two or three prongs. Standard voltage is 230V.

EMERGENCY NUMBERS

EMERGENCY OPERATOR	POLICE
112	17

AMBULANCE	FIRE SERVICE
18	18

TAP WATER
Unless stated otherwise, tap water in France is safe to drink.

Getting There

Paris is France's main international airline hub. There are also about 40 regional airports, including Nice, Lyon, Marseille, and Toulouse, which handle budget airlines and charters. Some airports by the border in adjacent countries, such as Geneva and Basel, can also be used for destinations in France.

There are many ferry services between Britain and France. P&O Ferries has frequent crossings between Dover and Calais, while Brittany Ferries runs services from Portsmouth to St-Malo, Caen, and Le Havre; from Poole or Portsmouth to Cherbourg; and from Plymouth to Roscoff. DFDS Seaways operates routes between Newhaven and Dieppe, and Dover and Dunkirk.

The Channel Tunnel connects France and Britain by rail, with the Eurostar (for foot passengers) between Lille and Paris and London, and the Eurotunnel, which transports vehicles between Calais and Folkestone. There are also high-speed rail links to numerous other cities throughout mainland Europe.

Long-distance buses generally operate only where there is not a good train service in operation. Eurolines provides services to hundreds of major cities across Europe.

Personal Security

France is generally a safe country, but it is wise to take sensible precautions against pickpockets. If you have anything stolen, report the crime to the nearest police station. Get a copy of the crime report in order to claim on your insurance.

Health

EU citizens with a European Health Insurance Card (EHIC) are entitled to free emergency medical care in France, but it is also advisable to take out some form of supplementary health insurance. Visitors from outside the EU must arrange their own private medical insurance. If you fall sick during your visit, pharmacists are an excellent source of advice – they can diagnose minor ailments and suggest treatment.

Passports and Visas

Currently, there are no visa requirements for EU nationals or visitors from the United States, Canada, Australia, or New Zealand who plan to stay in France for less than three months. Visitors from most other countries require a tourist visa. For visa information specific to your home country, consult your nearest French embassy or check online.

Travelers with Specific Needs

The **Office du Tourisme et des Congrès** has a useful guide that lists easily accessible sights and routes for visitors with mobility issues, while **Jaccede** has details of accessible museums, hotels, bars, restaurants, and cinemas in Paris and other cities. **Vianavigo** provides detailed information on accessible public transport, including a route planner that can be tailored to your individual needs. Rail operator **SNCF** provides information about train travel and a booking service for free assistance on TGVs.

Jaccede
W jaccede.com
Office du Tourisme et des Congrès
W parisinfo.com
SNCF
W accessibilite.sncf.com
Vianavigo
W vianavigo.com

Money

Most establishments accept major credit, debit, and prepaid currency cards, but it's a good idea to carry cash for small purchases. Contactless payments are widely accepted in all major cities.

Cell Phones and Wi-Fi

With a part of its ambitious 5G network already operating, France offers strong mobile signals throughout. Visitors traveling to France with EU tariffs can use their devices without being affected by data roaming charges. Visitors from elsewhere should check their contracts before departure to avoid unexpected charges.

Free Wi-Fi is available in most public places. Hotels, airports, cafés, and restaurants may charge a small fee for usage of their Wi-Fi.

Getting Around

There are a number of domestic airlines in France. However, unless you are eligible for discounts, you may find it cheaper and faster to travel on high-speed trains.

The French state railroad, the Société Nationale des Chemins de Fer **(SNCF)**, has an excellent railroad network that covers nearly all of France. The fastest services are provided by the high-speed TGV (Trains à Grande Vitesse), which link most major cities. Overnight services are popular, and most long-distance trains have *couchettes* (bunks), which you must reserve for a fee. Reservations are also compulsory for all TGV services, trains on public holidays, and for a *siège inclinable* (reclinable seat). It is worth checking to see if you qualify for a discount. Both reservations and tickets must be validated in one of the orange *composteur* machines near the platforms before boarding the train.

All the main international car-rental companies operate in France. The country's motorways allow quick and easy access to all parts of the country, but most of them have a toll system (*autoroutes à péage*), which can be expensive over long distances. A cheaper and more scenic option is to use the toll-free RN (*route nationale*) and D (*départementale*) routes.

SNCF operates some bus routes and issues regional TER (Transports Express Régionaux) timetables and tickets. **Eurolines** also serves a wide range of destinations within France.

Eurolines
W eurolines.eu
SNCF
W sncf.com

Visitor Information

All major cities and large towns have *offices de tourisme*. Small towns and even villages have *syndicats d'initiative*. Both will give you town plans, advice on accommodations, and information on regional recreational and cultural activities. You can also get information before you depart from the **French Government Tourist Office**, or by contacting local tourist offices or the appropriate CRT (Comité Régional de Tourisme).

French Government Tourist Offices
W france.fr

BELGIUM AND LUXEMBOURG

The histories of Belgium and Luxembourg have long been interlinked, with both countries passing through the hands of the same powers. They first rose to prominence at the start of the 12th century, when commerce became the guiding force in Europe, and Belgium's cities became the center of a cloth trade with France, Germany, Italy, and England. Marital alliance brought Belgium and Luxembourg under Burgundian rule in the 14th century, before they were transfered a century later to the Habsburg Empire. By 1555, the two countries were in the hands of the Spanish Habsburgs, whose Catholic repression of Protestants sparked the Dutch Revolt. After the end of the Spanish Habsburg dynasty in 1700, the 1713 Treaty of Utrecht trans-ferred Belgium and Luxembourg to the Austrian Habsburgs. Belgium was again ruled by foreign powers between 1794 and 1830 – first by the French Republicans under Napoleon and then by the Dutch – before independence was finally won, and Leopold I was made king. Nine years later, Luxembourg – a Grand Duchy since 1815 – also gained independence. Both countries' economies flourished in the 19th century, but all was eclipsed with the outbreak of World Wars I and II, and the commandeering of their territories into battle-grounds. Belgium's history in the late 20th century was dominated by the language debate between the Dutch-speaking Flemings and the French-speaking Walloons, which led to the creation of a federal state with three separate regions: Flanders, Wallonia, and Brussels.

North
Sea

Oude-
Tonge

Zierikzee

Middelburg

Goes

Bergen op Ze

Vlissingen

Westerschelde

Terneuzen

Knokke-Heist

Zeebrugge

Blankenberge

Lissewege

A11

ANTWERP 2

Ostend

Maldegem

Zelzate

St-Niklaas

A12

A1

N34

A18

4 BRUGES

A10

Torhout

Aalter

GHENT 3

Lokeren

A14

Willebroek

A12

A1

Veurne

Diksmuide

N50

Deinze

Dendermonde

Mechelen

Ijzer

Roeselare

Leie

A10

Aalst

N8

Ijzer

A17

A14

Scheldt

BRUSSELS 1

Poperinge

Ypres

A19

Kortrijk

Oudenaarde

Ninove

N8

Halle

WATERLOO 5

Mesen

Ronse

Lessines

N42

Armentières

Lille

A8

Ath

Soignies

Nivelle

Leuze-en-
Hainaut

FRANCE

Orchies

Tournai

Beloeil

La Louvière

Bèthune

A16

Charleroi

Douai

Valenciennes

A7

Mons

Binche

Thuin

Hornu

N6

Arras

N40

Bapaume

Cambrai

Maubeuge

Beaumont

Philipp

Caudry

FRANCE
p178

Chimay

Co

BELGIUM AND
LUXEMBOURG

1 Brussels

2 Antwerp

3 Ghent

4 Bruges

5 Waterloo

6 Luxembourg City

7 Echternach

8 Vianden

Hirson

Vervins

0 kilometers   30

0 miles   30

N

BRUSSELS

✈🚆🚌 **ℹ www.visit.brussels**

Brussels is divided into two main areas. Historically a working-class district, the Lower Town is centered on the splendid 17th-century Grand Place, while the Upper Town, traditional home of the aristocracy, is an elegant area that encircles the city's green oasis, the Parc de Bruxelles. As well as cultural gems, you'll find outstanding restaurants, eclectic shops, and vibrant cafés and bars.

①

Grand Place

Ⓜ **Bourse, Gare Centrale**
🚌 **48, 95** 🚊 **3, 4**

The geographical, historical, and commercial heart of the city, the Grand Place is the first port of call for most visitors to Brussels. A market was held on this site as early as the 11th century. During the first half of the 15th century, Brussels' town hall,

the Hôtel de Ville, was built, and city traders began to add individual guildhalls in a medley of styles. In 1695, however, two days of cannon fire by the French destroyed all but the town hall and two facades. Trade guilds were urged to rebuild their halls to designs approved by the town council, resulting in the splendid Baroque ensemble that can be seen today.

Occupying the entire southwest side of the square, the

Gothic Hôtel de Ville *(p243)* is the architectural masterpiece of the Grand Place. Opposite it stands La Maison du Roi (1536). Despite its name, no king ever lived here; rather, the building was used as a

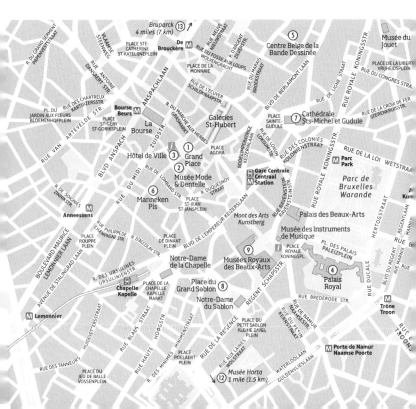

↑ The Grand Place at dusk, its imposing guildhalls lit atmospherically

temporary jail and a tax office. Redesigned in Gothic style in the late 19th century, it is now home to the **Musée de la Ville de Bruxelles**, and contains 16th-century paintings and tapestries, and a

collection of more than 1,000 costumes created for the diminutive Manneken Pis statue (p244).

On the square's eastern flank, the vast Neo-Classical edifice known as La Maison des Ducs de Brabant was designed by Guillaume de Bruyn and consists of six former guildhalls. Facing it are Le Renard, built in the 1690s for the guild of haberdashers, and Le Cornet (1697), the boatmen's guildhall, whose gable resembles a 17th-century frigate's bow. Le Roi d'Espagne building, also known as La Maison des Boulangers, was erected in the late 17th century by the wealthy bakers' guild. The gilt bust over the entrance represents St. Aubert, patron saint of bakers. Today, the building houses one of the Grand Place's best-loved bars – Le Roy d'Espagne – whose first floor offers fine views of the bustling square.

Musée de la Ville de Bruxelles

 🅜 Maison du Roi
🕙 10am-5pm Tue-Sun
🚫 Jan 1, May 1, Nov 1 & 11, Dec 25 🅦 brussels city museum.brussels

②

Musée Mode & Dentelle

🅐 Rue de la Violette 12
🅜 Gare Centrale 🚌 48, 95
🕙 10am-5pm Tue-Sun
🚫 Jan 1, May 1, Nov 1 & 11, Dec 25 🅦 fashionandlace museum.brussels

Located within two 18th-century gabled houses, this museum is dedicated to one of Brussels' most successful exports, Belgian lace, which has been made here since the 12th century. The ground floor has a display of costumes on mannequins showing how lace has adorned fashions of every era. Upstairs is a fine collection of antique lace from France, Flanders, and Italy.

> 💬 INSIDER TIP
> **Getting Around**
>
> Brussels' Lower Town is well served by trams, but the quickest way of getting around is on foot. In the Upper Town, the best option is to take a bus. Brussels' metro is handy for the main sights of interest.

The elegant Hôtel
de Ville, dominating
Brussels' Grand Place ↑

HÔTEL DE VILLE

🏠 Grand Place Ⓜ Bourse, Gare Centrale 🚌 48, 95 🚊 3, 4
🕐 For guided tours; check website for details 🚫 Public hols
& election days 🌐 bruxelles.be

Completed in 1459, Brussels' impressive
Hôtel de Ville quickly emerged as the finest
civic building in the country – a stature it
enjoys to this day.

The idea of erecting a town hall to reflect Brussels'
growth as a major European trading center had been
under consideration since the end of the 13th century,
but it was not until 1401 that the first foundation stone
was laid. Jacques van Thienen was commissioned to
design the east wing, where he used ornate columns,
sculptures, turrets, and arcades. Jan van Ruysbroeck's
elegant spire helped seal the building's reputation
as a masterpiece. Guided tours of the interior, with its
15th-century tapestries and works of art, are available.

↑ Ornate statuary on the exterior
of the Hôtel de Ville

> **INSIDER TIP**
> **Tapis de Fleurs**
>
> For five days in mid-
> August every even-
> numbered year, the
> Grand Place in front of
> the Hôtel de Ville is
> taken over by a massive
> floral display known as
> the Carpet of Flowers.

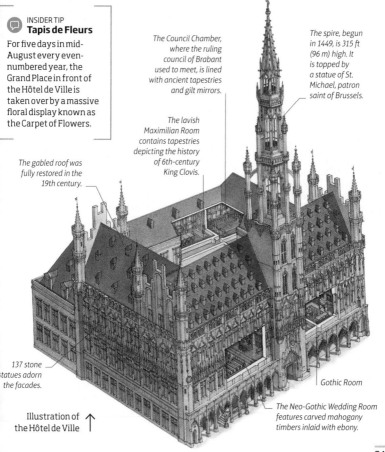

The Council Chamber,
where the ruling
council of Brabant
used to meet, is lined
with ancient tapestries
and gilt mirrors.

The spire, begun
in 1449, is 315 ft
(96 m) high. It
is topped by
a statue of St.
Michael, patron
saint of Brussels.

The lavish
Maximilian Room
contains tapestries
depicting the history
of 6th-century
King Clovis.

The gabled roof was
fully restored in the
19th century.

137 stone
statues adorn
the facades.

Gothic Room

The Neo-Gothic Wedding Room
features carved mahogany
timbers inlaid with ebony.

Illustration of
the Hôtel de Ville ↑

④ 🏛

Palais Royal

📍 Place des Palais
Ⓜ Trône, Parc 🚌 27, 29,
38, 63, 65, 66, 71, 95 🚊 92,
93 🕐 Mid-Jul–mid-Sep:
10:30am–5pm Tue–
Sun 🌐 monarchie.be

The official home of the
Belgian monarchy is one of
the Upper Town's finest 19th-
century buildings. Construction began in the 1820s and
continued under Léopold II
(reigned 1865–1909). The
most lavish state reception
rooms include the Throne
Room, with 28 wall-mounted
chandeliers, and the Hall of
Mirrors, similar to the Hall of
Mirrors at Versailles (p204).

---

⑤

Centre Belge de la Bande Dessinée

📍 20 Rue des Sables
Ⓜ Botanique, Rogier,
Centrale 🚌 29, 38, 63,
66, 71 🚊 25, 55, 92, 93
🕐 10am–6pm daily 🚫 Jan 1,
Dec 25 🌐 comicscenter.net

This museum pays tribute to
the Belgian passion for comic
strips, or bandes dessinées.

A lavish room inside the
Palais Royal, and (inset)
the palace's exterior ↑

One of the exhibitions shows
the great comic-strip heroes,
from Hergé's Tintin – who
made his debut in 1929 – to
the Smurfs and the Flemish
comic-strip characters Suske
and Wiske. Other displays
explain the stages of putting
together a comic strip, and
there is also a series of life-
size cartoon sets, of special
appeal to children. The museum holds 6,000 original
plates, and a valuable archive
of photographs and artifacts.

The collection is housed in
a beautiful building, built in
1903–6 to the design of the
Belgian Art Nouveau architect
Victor Horta.

⑥

Manneken Pis

📍 Rues de l'Etuve & du
Chêne Ⓜ Gare Centrale
🚌 48, 95 🚊 3, 4, 31, 32

This tiny statue of a young
boy relieving himself is one of
Brussels' more unusual sights.
The original bronze statue
by Jérôme Duquesnoy the
Elder was first placed here in
1619. After it was stolen and
damaged in 1817, a replica
was made and returned to its
revered site. The inspiration

TINTIN

The story of Tintin goes back to 1929, when he first
appeared in a children's newspaper supplement, Le Petit
Vingtième. Brussels-born inventor Hergé (Georges Rémi)
evolved the character as he took him through a series of
adventures related to real events, such as the rise of
fascism (King Ottakar's Scepter). The charm of Tintin
is his naive determination, as well as the multitude
of archetypal characters that surround him, including
his faithful dog Snowy and gruff Captain Haddock.

for the statue is unknown, but the mystery only lends itself to rumor and fable and increases the little boy's charm. One theory claims that in the 12th century, the son of a duke was caught urinating against a tree in the midst of a battle, and was thus commemorated in bronze as a symbol of the country's military courage. Visiting heads of state donate miniature versions of their national costume for the boy, and now a collection of over 1,000 outfits, including an Elvis suit, can be seen in the Musée de la Ville (p241).

Cathédrale Sts-Michel et Gudule

 Parvis Ste-Gudule ⓜ Centrale 🚌 29, 38, 63, 65, 66, 71 🚊 92, 93 ⏰ 7am-6pm Mon-Fri, 8am-5pm Sat, 1-6pm Sun 🌐 cathedral isbruxellensis.be

The Cathédrale Sts-Michel et Gudule is Belgium's finest surviving example of Brabant Gothic architecture. There has been a church on this site since at least the 11th century. Work on the Gothic cathedral began in 1226 and continued over a period of 300 years.

The interior is relatively bare, due to Protestant ransacking in 1579 and thefts during the French Revolution. Over the west door, however, is a magnificent 16th-century stained-glass window of the *Last Judgment*. The flamboyantly carved Baroque pulpit is by an Antwerp sculptor, Hendrik Frans Verbruggen.

⑧
Place du Grand Sablon

ⓜ Louise, Parc 🚌 27, 48, 95 🚊 92, 93 🌐 visit.brussels

Located on the slope of the escarpment that divides Brussels in two, the Place du Grand Sablon is like a

stepping stone between the upper and lower towns. Today, this is an area of upscale antiques dealers, fashionable restaurants, and trendy bars, where you can stay out until the early hours of the morning.

At the far end of the square stands the lovely church of Notre-Dame du Sablon, built in the Brabant Gothic style, and featuring some glorious stained-glass windows. On the opposite side of the road to the church is the Place du Petit Sablon. In contrast to the busy café scene of the larger square, these pretty formal gardens are a peaceful spot to stop for a rest. Sit and admire the set of bronze statues by Art Nouveau artist Paul Hankar, each representing a different medieval guild of the city. At the back of the gardens is a fountain, built to commemorate Counts Egmont and Hoorn, the martyrs who led a Dutch uprising against the tyrannical rule of the Spanish under Philip II. On either side of the fountain are 12 further statues of prominent 15th- and 16th-century figures, including Gerhard Mercator, the Flemish geographer and mapmaker.

↑ Relaxing in the Place du Petit Sablon park, near Place du Grand Sablon

Musées Royaux des Beaux-Arts

⌂ Rue du Musée 9 Ⓜ Parc, Centrale 🚌 27, 29, 38, 63, 65, 66, 71, 95 🚊 92, 93 ⊙ 10am–5pm Tue–Fri, 11am–6pm Sat & Sun ⊘ Public hols 🌐 fine-arts-museum.be

Six centuries of art, both Belgian and international, are displayed in the four museums that make up the Musées Royaux des Beaux-Arts: the Musée Oldmasters (15th–18th centuries), the Musée Fin-de-Siècle (1868–1914), the Musée Modern (19th century–present day), and the Musée Magritte.

💬 **INSIDER TIP**
Chocolate Delight

Not far from the Musées Royaux des Beaux-Arts is Wittamer (www.wittamer.com), a world-class chocolatier. It has a seating area, where you can try the wares with a cup of tea or coffee.

The Musée Oldmasters holds one of the world's finest collections of works by the Flemish Primitive School. A work of particular note is *The Annunciation* (c. 1415–25) by the Master of Flémalle. The trademarks of the Flemish Primitives are a lifelike vitality and a clarity of light. The greatest exponent of the style was Rogier van der Weyden, the official city painter of Brussels, who has several splendid works on display at the museum.

Peter Bruegel the Elder, one of the most outstanding Flemish artists, settled in Brussels in 1563. His earthy scenes of peasant life remain his best-known works, and are represented here by paintings such as *The Bird Trap* (1565).

Another highlight of the Musée Oldmasters is the world-famous collection of works by Peter Paul Rubens. *The Assumption of the Virgin* (1626) stands out among his religious canvases. Other notable paintings on display include Van Dyck's *Portrait of Porzia Imperial with her Daughter Maria Francesca* (1620s) and *Three Children with Goatcart* by Frans Hals.

→

The Chamber of the European Parliament, where MEPs sit

The Musée Fin-de-Siècle focuses on the years between 1868 and 1914, when Brussels was the artistic capital of Europe thanks to the efforts of James Ensor, Constantin Meunier, and Victor Horta, among others. In addition to visual arts, the museum explores the literature, poetry,

> The Musée Magritte is devoted to René Magritte, one of Belgium's most famous artists and a major exponent of the Surrealist movement.

and music of the period. A highlight of this collection is a 3-D reconstruction of six Art Nouveau buildings.

Works in the Musée Modern vary greatly in style and subject matter, ranging from Neo-Classicism to Realism, Impressionism, and Symbolism. Jacques-Louis David's dramatic *Death of Marat* (1793) can be seen in the old part of the museum.

The Musée Magritte is devoted to René Magritte, one of Belgium's most famous artists and a major exponent of the Surrealist movement. Spread over five floors, it is the world's largest collection of his work and covers all periods of his life, from the dazzling early Cavernous

period of the late 1920s to the renowned landscape *Domain of Arnheim* (1962).

―――――――――

European Parliament Quarter

Ⓜ Maelbeek, Trône, Schuman 🚌 12, 21, 22, 27, 34, 36, 54, 64, 79, 80
🅦 visit.brussels

This vast steel-and-glass complex is one of three homes of the European Parliament (the others are in Strasbourg, in France, and Luxembourg). This gleaming building has its critics: the huge structure housing the hall that seats the 700-plus MEPs has been dubbed "Les Caprices des Dieux" ("Whims of the Gods"), which refers both to the distinctive shape of the building – similar to a French cheese of the same name – and to its

lofty aspirations. Nearby, Parc Léopold has some Art Nouveau buildings and is a delightful spot for a walk.

The light-filled entrance hall of the Musées Royaux des Beaux-Arts

---

BRUSSELS AND THE EUROPEAN UNION

In 1958, the European Economic Community (EEC), now the European Union (EU), was born and Brussels became its headquarters. Today, the city remains home to numerous EU institutions. The European Commission, the EU body that formulates policies, is based in the Berlaymont building. The city is also one of the seats of the European Parliament, which has over 700 members, known as MEPs (Members of the European Parliament). The most powerful institution is the Council of Ministers (in the Justus Lipsius building), composed of representatives from each member state.

⑪

Parc du Cinquantenaire

🏠 Avenue de Tervuren
Ⓜ Schuman, Mérode 🚌 22, 27, 36, 80 🚋 61, 81, 82

The finest of Léopold II's grand projects, the Parc and Palais du Cinquantenaire were built for the Golden Jubilee celebrations of Belgian independence in 1880. The palace, at the park's entrance, was to comprise a triumphal arch, based on the Arc de Triomphe in Paris (p199), and two large exhibition areas. The arch was completed in 1905. Until 1935, the large halls on either side of the central archway were used to hold trade fairs, before being converted into museums.

The excellent **Musée Art & Histoire** contains a vast array of exhibits. Sections on ancient civilizations cover Egypt, Greece, the Gallo-Roman period, Persia, and the Near East. Other displays feature Byzantium and Islam, China and the Indian subcontinent, and the Pre-Columbian civilizations of the Americas. Decorative arts from all ages include glassware, silverware, porcelain, lace, and tapestries. There are also religious sculptures and stained glass.

The **Musée Royal de l'Armée et d'Histoire Militaire** deals with all aspects of Belgium's military history. There are sections on both world wars, as well as a separate hall containing historic aircraft.

Housed in the south wing of the Cinquantenaire Palace, **Autoworld** has one of the best collections of classic automobiles in the world.

Part formal gardens, part tree-lined walks, the park is popular with Brussels' Eurocrats and families at lunchtimes and weekends.

Musée Art & Histoire

  🖥 Hours vary, check website 🌐 artandhistory.museum

Musée Royal de l'Armée et d'Histoire Militaire

🖥 9am–5pm Tue–Sun 🚫 Jan 1, May 1, Nov 1, Dec 25 🌐 klm-mra.be

Autoworld

🖥 10am–6pm daily (to 5pm in winter) 🚫 Jan 1, Dec 25 🌐 autoworld.be

---

⑫

Musée Horta

🏠 Rue Américaine 25
Ⓜ Albert, Louise 🚌 54
🚋 81, 92, 97 🖥 2–5:30pm Tue–Fri, 11am–5:30pm Sat & Sun 🚫 Public hols
🌐 hortamuseum.be

The architect Victor Horta is considered the father of the Art Nouveau movement,

TOP 3 ART NOUVEAU FACADES

Hôtel Tassel
🏠 Rue Paul-Émile Janson 6
Designed by Horta in 1893–5, this is said to be the first ever Art Nouveau house. The private mansion of a bachelor engineer, it was carefully tailored to his lifestyle.

Hôtel Saint-Cyr
🏠 Square Ambiorix 11
With its loops, curves, and a round window at the top, this house embodies the excess typical of the style. It was designed in 1900 for the painter Saint-Cyr.

La Maison Cauchie
🏠 Rue des Francs 5
Behind a facade of geometric shapes with dreamy murals lies the home of little-known painter Paul Cauchie.

which blossomed at the turn of the 20th century throughout Europe and the US. His impact on Brussels' architectural landscape is unrivaled by any other designer of the time.

The monumental triumphal arch at Brussels' Parc du Cinquantenaire

A museum dedicated to his unique iconic style is today housed in his restored family home, in the city's St. Gilles district. It was Horta himself who designed the house, between 1898 and 1901. The airy interior of the building displays the classic trademarks of the architect's style – including iron, glass, and sinuous curves – in every detail, while retaining a functional approach. The most impressive features are the dining room, with its ornate ceiling featuring scrolled metalwork, and the central staircase. Decorated with curved wrought iron, the stairs are enhanced further by mirrors and glass, bringing plentiful natural light into the house.

(13)

Bruparck

🚇 Boulevard du Centenaire
Ⓜ Heysel 🚌 84, 88 🚊 7, 51
🌐 bruparck.com

Located on the outskirts of the city, this theme park is popular with families. The most visited attraction is **Mini-Europe**, which has over 300 miniature reconstructions (built at a scale of 1:25) of Europe's major sights, from Athens' Acropolis to London's Houses of Parliament.

For movie fans, **Kinepolis** has 25 cinemas, including an IMAX complex. The latest blockbusters are sometimes shown in 3D or even 4DX,

↑ A miniature version of Pisa's Campo dei Miracoli at Mini-Europe, Bruparck

adding special effects like wind, smoke, and smells.

Towering over Bruparck is Brussels most distinctive landmark, the **Atomium**. Designed by Belgian engineer André Waterkeyn for the 1958 World's Fair, and representing an iron crystal magnified 165 billion times, the structure has a viewing platform and restaurant at the top.

Mini-Europe
🎨🍽 🕐 9:30am–8pm daily 🕐 Jan–mid-Mar
🌐 minieurope.com

Kinepolis
🎬 For performances only
🌐 kinepolis.be

Atomium
🎨🍽🏛 🕐 10am–6pm daily (to 10pm in summer)
🌐 atomium.be

STAY

Le Dixseptième
There is no other place quite like this in Brussels: an utterly charming small hotel in the late-17th-century former residence of the Spanish ambassador. It has a number of suites – named after Belgian artists - ingeniously set beneath the roof beams and furnished with a mixture of antique charm and modern flair.

🏠 Rue de la Madeleine 25
🌐 ledixseptieme.be

€€€

Odette en Ville
An intimate eight-room boutique hotel in a 1920s building. Decorated in calming greys and whites, the rooms offer amenities such as underfloor heating. The romantic restaurant has an open fire.

🏠 Rue de Châtelain 25
🌐 odetteenville.be

€€€

↑ The Gothic architecture of the Cathedral of Our Lady, in Antwerp's medieval district

②

Antwerp

⌂ Antwerp ✈🚗🚆
🛈 13 Grote Markt; www.visitantwerpen.be

In the Middle Ages, Antwerp was a hub of the cloth trade, and the principal port of the Duchy of Brabant. Today, it is the main city of Flemish-speaking Belgium, and the center of the international diamond trade.

At the heart of the city's old medieval district is the Grote Markt. The square is overlooked by the ornately gabled Stadhuis (Town Hall), built in 1564, and the Gothic Onze Lieve Vrouwe Kathedraal (Cathedral of Our Lady), which dates back to 1352. Among the paintings found inside the cathedral are two triptychs by Antwerp's most famous son, Peter Paul Rubens.

The narrow, winding streets of the Old Town are lined with fine medieval guildhalls, such as the Vleeshuis, or Meat Hall, once occupied by the Butchers' Guild. Dating from the early 16th century, it is built in alternate stripes of stone and brick, giving it a streaky-bacon-like appearance.

The **Koninklijk Museum voor Schone Kunsten** houses ancient and modern artworks, from 17th-century masterpieces by the "Antwerp Trio"

→ The Graslei and Korenlei quays, seen from the Sint-Michielsbrug bridge, Ghent

of Van Dyck, Jordaens, and Rubens, to works by the Surrealist René Magritte and Rik Wouters.

Rubenshuis was Rubens' home and studio for the last 30 years of his life. You can see his living quarters (featuring period furniture), his studio, and the art gallery where he exhibited both his own and other artists' work.

Koninklijk Museum voor Schone Kunsten

 Leopold de Waelplaats 1–9 ▪22 1, 23 ▪4, 8, 12, 24 🕐 Hours vary, check website ⓦ kmska.be

Rubenshuis

⊘⊘⊘ ▪ Wapper 9–11 ▪22 4, 7, 11 🕐10am–5pm Tue–Sun 🅲 Public hols ⓦ rubenshuis.be

---

③

Ghent

📍 East Flanders 🚃🚌
🛈 Sint-Veerleplein 5; www.visit.gent.be

Ghent's historic center dates from the 13th and 14th centuries, when the city prospered as a result of the cloth trade. The closure of vital canal links in 1648 led to a decline in the town's fortunes, but it flourished again in the 18th and 19th centuries as a major industrial center for textiles.

In the old medieval quarter, the "Castle of the Counts," **Het Gravensteen**, was once the seat of the Counts of Flanders. South from here is Graslei, a charming street that borders the Leie river, lined with well-preserved guildhalls dating from the Middle Ages.

The magnificent St. Baafs-kathedraal has features representing every phase of the Gothic style. In a small side chapel is Jan van Eyck's *Adoration of the Mystic Lamb* (1432). Opposite the cathedral stands the huge 14th-century Belfort (belfry). From here, it is a short walk to the Stadhuis (Town Hall), whose Pacification Hall was the site of the signing of the Pacification of Ghent (a declaration of the Low Countries' repudiation of Spanish rule) in 1576.

Ghent's largest collection of fine art, covering all periods up to the 20th century, is in the **Museum voor Schone Kunsten**, a 20-minute walk southeast of the center. There are works by Rubens and his contemporaries Anthony van Dyck and Jacob Jordaens.

 GREAT VIEW
A View from the Bridge

The Sint-Michielsbrug bridge provides an excellent viewpoint, taking in Ghent's historic Graslei and Korenlei quays and the towers of the Sint-Niklaaskerk, the Belfort, and Sint-Baafskathedraal.

In an 18th-century townhouse, the Design Museum Gent has lavishly furnished period rooms, plus an extension covering modern design, from Art Nouveau to contemporary works.

STAM, Ghent's City Museum, covers the history of the city from prehistoric times to the present day.

Het Gravensteen

⊘ ▪ Sint-Veerleplein 11 🕐10am–6pm daily ⓦ historischehuizen.stad.gent

Museum voor Schone Kunsten

⊘⊘⊘ ▪ Fernand Scribedreef 1, Citadelpark 🕐9:30am–5:30pm Tue–Fri, 10am–6pm Sat & Sun 🅲 Jan 1 & 2, Dec 25 & 26 ⓦ mskgent.be

The Rozenhoedkaai (Quay of the Rosary), on the Dijver Canal ↑

4

BRUGES

⌂ West Flanders 🚂 🚌 ℹ Markt 1 & t' Zand 34, inside Concertgebouw; www.visitbruges.be

One of the most popular tourist destinations in Belgium, this pocket-sized city owes its pre-eminent position to its historic center, where winding lanes and picturesque canals are lined with splendid medieval buildings. In addition to many hotels, restaurants, and bars, Bruges has famous art collections, and is a walk-able city with surprises around every corner.

①
Groeninge Museum

⌂ Dijver 12 🕐 9:30am–5pm Tue–Sun 🚫 Jan 1, Dec 25
🌐 visitbruges.be

Bruges's premier fine-art museum holds a superb collection of early Flemish and Dutch masters. Artists featured include Rogier van der Weyden, Jan van Eyck, Gerard David, and Hans Memling, all of whom were active during the 15th century. Van Eyck's *Virgin and Child with Canon* (1436), a richly detailed painting noted for its realism, and Memling's

Moreel triptych (1484) are among the museum's most outstanding exhibits. Painted in the early 16th century, the dramatic *Last Judgment* triptych is one of a number of works at the museum by Hieronymus Bosch. Peter Brueghel the Younger is also well represented.

Later Belgian works in the collection include *The Thistles* (1885), by the Impressionist artist Emile Claus, portraying a bucolic scene on the banks of the Leie river, and paintings by the Surrealists Paul Delvaux and René Magritte. The museum also hosts temporary exhibitions.

②
Gruuthuse Museum

⌂ Dijver 17 🕐 9:30am–5pm Tue–Sun 🚫 Jan 1, Dec 25
🌐 museabrugge.be

This museum occupies a large medieval mansion close to the Dijver Canal. In the 15th century, it was inhabited by a merchant (the Lord of the Gruuthuse), who had the right to levy a tax on "gruit," an imported mixture of herbs added to barley during the beer-brewing process. The mansion's labyrinthine rooms, with their ancient chimney-pieces and wooden beams, have survived intact, and today contain a collection of fine and applied arts.

 GREAT VIEW
City Panorama

For a breathtaking view over Bruges's medieval streets, climb the 366 steps to the top of the Belfort *(Markt 7)*. Its bells are rung by a mecha-nism, but can also be played from a keyboard on the floor below.

The exhibits range from wood carvings, tapestries, porcelain, and ceramics to medical instruments and weaponry. The authentic kitchen and beautiful oak-paneled chapel (1472) transport visitors back to medieval times.

---

③ Heilig Bloed Basiliek

🏠 Burg 13 📞 050-33 6792 🕐 9:30am-12:30pm & 2-5:30pm daily 🚫 Jan 1

The Basilica of the Holy Blood is Bruges's holiest church, holding one of the most sacred relics in Europe. In the upper chapel, rebuilt after it was destroyed by the French in the 1790s, is a 17th-century tabernacle, which houses a phial said to contain a few drops of blood and water washed from the body of Christ by Joseph of Arimathea.

The church is also associated with the Procession of the Holy Blood, which dates back to the 13th century. This colorful parade winds its way through the streets of the city center on Ascension Day.

---

④ Begijnhof

🏠 Wijngaardplein 1 📞 050-33 0011 🕐 6:30am-6:30pm daily

Béguines were members of a lay sisterhood founded in 1245, who did not take vows but led a devout life. The *begijnhof*, or *béguinage*, is the walled complex in a town that housed the Béguines. In Bruges, this is an area of quiet tree-lined canals edged by white, gabled houses. Visitors can enjoy a stroll here and visit the simple church, built in 1602. One of the houses, now occupied by Benedictine nuns, is open to the public.

---

⑤ Houishbrouwerij de Halve Maan

🏠 Walplein 26 🕐 11am-4pm Sun-Fri, 11am-5pm Sat (Nov-Mar: to 3pm) 🌐 halvemaan.be

At this brewery established in 1856, you can follow the beer-making process, from the first hops to a taste of the finished product in the small bar. There are also good views of Bruges from the oast room.

---

⑥ Volkskundemuseum

🏠 Balstraat 43 🕐 9:30am-5pm Tue-Sun 🚫 Jan 1, Dec 25 🌐 museabrugge.be

This folk museum occupies a row of 17th-century brick alms-houses in the northeast of the town. Each house is dedicated to a different aspect of traditional Flemish life.

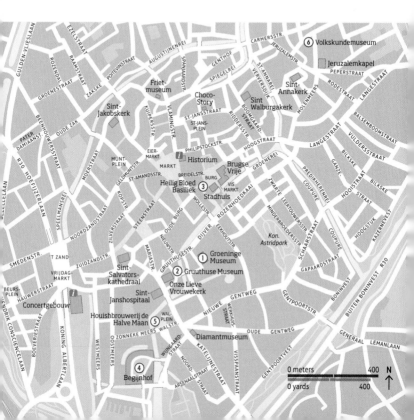

A SHORT WALK
BRUGES

Distance 1 mile (1.5 km) **Nearest bus stop** Brugge Markt **Time** 25 minutes

The beautifully preserved medieval buildings in the center of Bruges are mostly the legacy of the town's heyday as a center of the international cloth trade, which flourished for 200 years from the 13th century. During this golden age, Bruges's merchants lavished their fortunes on fine mansions, churches, and a set of civic buildings of such extravagance that they were the wonder of Northern Europe. Admire their splendor as you stroll through the cobbled streets of the city's historic heart.

↑ Colorful gabled houses and terrace cafés lining the Markt

*The **Markt** is a 13th-century square lined with gabled houses. At the heart of Bruges, the square still holds a market each Saturday.*

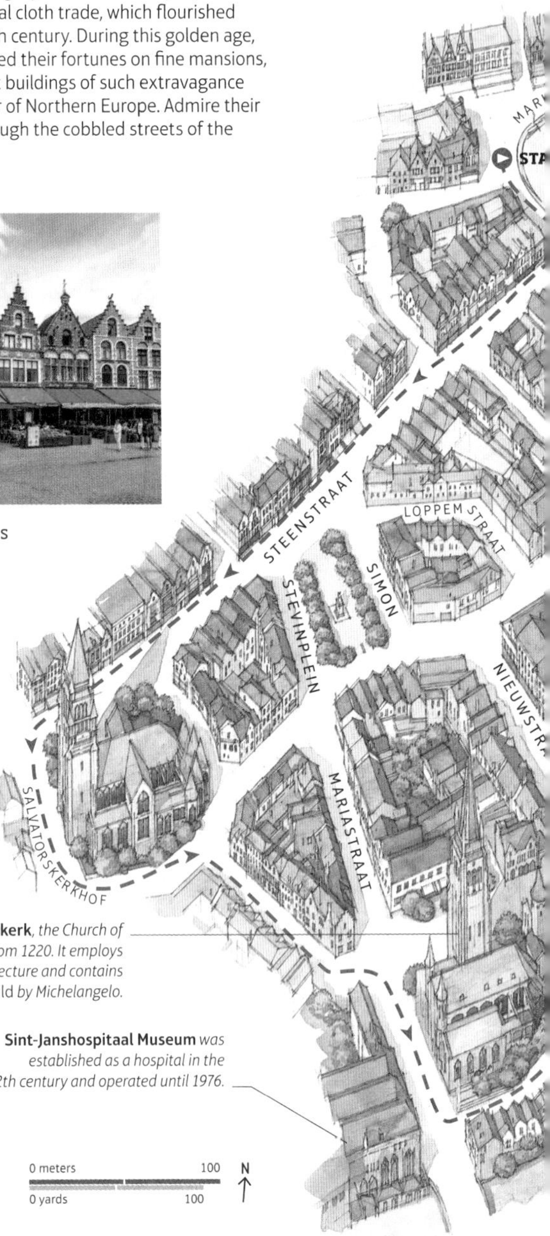

Onze Lieve Vrouwekerk, *the Church of Our Lady, dates from 1220. It employs many styles of architecture and contains a* Madonna and Child *by Michelangelo.*

Sint-Janshospitaal Museum *was established as a hospital in the 12th century and operated until 1976.*

STEENSTRAAT

STEVINPLEIN

SIMON

LOPPEM STRAAT

NIEUWSTR

MARIASTRAAT

SALVATORSKERKHOF

STA

0 meters 100
0 yards 100

N ↑

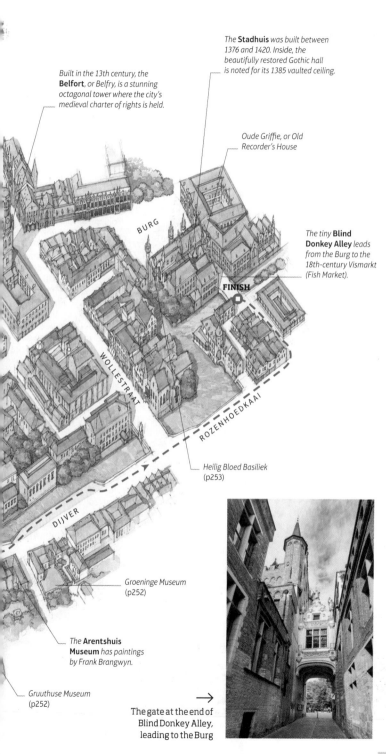

The **Stadhuis** was built between 1376 and 1420. Inside, the beautifully restored Gothic hall is noted for its 1385 vaulted ceiling.

Built in the 13th century, the **Belfort**, or Belfry, is a stunning octagonal tower where the city's medieval charter of rights is held.

Oude Griffie, or Old Recorder's House

The tiny **Blind Donkey Alley** leads from the Burg to the 18th-century Vismarkt (Fish Market).

BURG

FINISH

WOLLESTRAAT

ROZENHOEDKAAI

Heilig Bloed Basiliek (p253)

DIJVER

Groeninge Museum (p252)

The **Arentshuis Museum** has paintings by Frank Brangwyn.

Gruuthuse Museum (p252)

→ The gate at the end of Blind Donkey Alley, leading to the Burg

⑤

Waterloo

🏛 Walloon Brabant
ℹ Chaussée de Bruxelles 218; www.waterloo-tourisme.com

This small town is famous for its association with the Battle of Waterloo, at which Napoleon and his French army were defeated by the Duke of Wellington's British and Allied troops in 1815. The best place to start a visit here is the **Musée Wellington**, in the inn where Wellington stayed the night before the battle. Its rooms are packed with curios, alongside plans and models of the battlefield.

The Église St-Joseph contains dozens of memorial plaques to the British soldiers who died at Waterloo.

For an excellent view over the battlefield, head for the Butte de Lion, a 148-ft- (45-m-) high earthen mound, 2 miles (3 km) out of the town. Next to it is a gallery where Louis Demoulin's fascinating circular painting *Panorama de la Bataille* is displayed.

Musée Wellington

🏛 Chaussée de Bruxelles 147 ⌚ Apr–Sep: 9:30am–6pm daily; Oct–Mar: 10am–5pm daily ⌚ Jan 1, Dec 25 🖥 musee wellington.be

---

THE BATTLEFIELDS OF BELGIUM

Belgium's strategic position between France and Germany has long made it the battleground, or "cockpit," of Europe. Napoleon's defeat at Waterloo was just one of many major conflicts resolved on Belgian soil. In the early 18th century, French expansion under Louis XIV was thwarted here, and in the 20th century, Belgium witnessed some of the bloodiest trench warfare of World War I, including the introduction of poison gas at Ypres (Ieper). Today, there are several vast graveyards, where the tens of thousands of soldiers who died on the Western Front lie buried.

---

⑥

Luxembourg City

🏛 Luxembourg ✈🚆🚌
ℹ 30 Place Guillaume II; www.luxembourg-city.com

The capital of the Grand Duchy of Luxembourg, and a well-known center of international finance, Luxembourg City enjoys a dramatic location, set atop hills and cliffs rising above the Alzette and Pétrusse valleys. The town grew up around a castle built on a rocky promontory, known as the Rocher du Bock, in AD 963. The castle and most of its defenses were demolished in the late 19th century by the city's inhabitants, but some of the fortifications have been preserved, most famously the **Bock Casemates**. This huge network of underground defensive galleries, which dates back to the 17th century, not only provided shelter for thousands of soldiers, but also housed workshops, kitchens, bakeries, and slaughterhouses. The Crypte Archéologique du Bock has displays and an audiovisual presentation on the history of the city's impressive fortifications.

Luxembourg City's Palais Grand Ducal has been the official royal residence since 1890. The oldest parts of the building, which used to be the town hall, date from the latter half of the 16th century. Nearby, the Cathédrale Notre-Dame dates to 1613. Inside is a fine Baroque organ gallery by Daniel Muller.

Among the museums worth visiting are the **Musée National d'Histoire et d'Art**, which has a good archaeological section and a collection of ancient and modern sculpture and paintings, and the **Musée de l'Histoire de la Ville de Luxembourg**, which focuses on the city's history. The angular glass **Musée d'Art Moderne Grand-Duc Jean (MUDAM)** displays contemporary art, design, photography, and fashion.

Bock Casemates

♿🕐 🏛 Montée de Clausen ⌚ Mar–Oct: 10am–5:30pm (summer: to 8:30pm)

←

The distinctive Butte de Lion mound, at the battlefield of Waterloo

↑ Looking over the rooftops of Luxembourg City's hilltop historic center

Musée National d'Histoire et d'Art

◉ 🅰 Place Marché aux Poissons ⏰ 10am-6pm Tue-Sun (to 8pm Thu) 🌐 mnha.lu

Musée de l'Histoire de la Ville de Luxembourg

◉◉ 🅰 14 Rue du Saint-Esprit ⏰ 10am-6pm Tue-Sun (to 8pm Thu) 🌐 citymuseum.lu

Musée d'Art Moderne Grand-Duc Jean (MUDAM)

◉ 🅰 3 Park Dräi Eechelen ⏰ 10am-6pm Wed-Mon (to 9pm Wed) 🌐 mudam.com

---

⑦ Echternach

🅰 Luxembourg 🚌 🛈 9-10 Parvis de la Basilique; www.visitechternach.lu

Located in Petite Suisse (Little Switzerland), a picturesque region of wooded hills north-east of Luxembourg City, Echternach is dotted with fine medieval buildings, including the 15th-century turreted town hall. The star sight, however, is the Benedictine abbey, founded by St. Willibrord in the 7th century. The **Abbey Museum** tells the history of St. Willibrord and displays copies of illuminated manuscripts.

There are good walking and cycle routes in the surrounding countryside.

Abbey Museum

◉◉ 🅰 11 Parvis de la Basilique ⏰ Apr-Oct: 10am-12pm & 2-5pm daily 🌐 museedelabbaye.lu

---

⑧ Vianden

🅰 Luxembourg 🚌 🛈 1a Rue du Vieux Marché; 83 42 57

Surrounded by medieval ramparts, Vianden, in the Luxembourg Ardennes, is a popular tourist destination. The main attraction is the 11th-century **Château de Vianden**. Its rooms feature a range of architectural styles, from the Romanesque to the Renaissance. A cable car takes visitors to the top of a nearby hill, giving superb views of the castle.

Château de Vianden

🅰 Montée du Château ⏰ Apr-Sep: 10am-6pm daily; Oct & Mar: 10am-5pm daily; Nov-Feb: 10am-4pm daily 🚫 Jan 1, Dec 25 🌐 castle-vianden.lu

↑ Collection of ancient armor inside the Château de Vianden

PRACTICAL
INFORMATION

Here you will find all the essential advice and information you will need before and during your stay in Belgium and Luxembourg.

AT A GLANCE

CURRENCY
Euro (EUR)

TIME ZONE
CET/CEST. Central
European Summer
Time runs from the last
Sunday in March to the
last Sunday in October.

LANGUAGE
Belgium: Dutch, French, and German.
Luxembourg: French, German, and
Luxembourgish.

ELECTRICITY SUPPLY
Power sockets are type C
and E, fitting C and E plugs
with two or three prongs.
Standard voltage is 230V.

EMERGENCY NUMBERS

BELGIUM		LUXEMBOURG	
Police	101	Police	113
Ambulance	100	Emergency	112
Fire	100		

TAP WATER
Unless otherwise
stated, tap water
is safe to drink.

Getting There

Belgium's principal airport is Brussels National Airport, known locally as Zaventem. Flights into Luxembourg arrive at Luxembourg Airport, near to Luxembourg City. Most flights from Canada and the US go via another European city.

Belgium can be easily reached by ferry from Britain, with several daily services. DFDS Seaways has a number of daily crossings between Dover and Dunkirk. P&O Ferries also operates regular ferry crossings from Hull to Zeebrugge.

Belgium is at the heart of Europe's high-speed train networks. Eurostar services between Brussels' Gare du Midi and London's St. Pancras station take around 2 hours. The Thalys network links Brussels with Amsterdam, Paris, and Cologne. Luxembourg City is also well connected, with frequent trains to Brussels and Liège in Belgium, Trier in Germany, and Metz in France.

Personal Security

Belgium and Luxembourg are generally a safe countries, but it is a good idea to take sensible precautions against pickpockets. If you have anything stolen, report the crime to the nearest police station. Get a copy of the crime report in order to claim on your insurance. .

Health

EU citizens with a European Health Insurance Card (EHIC) are entitled to free emergency medical care in Belgium and Luxembourg, but it is also advisable to take out some form of supplementary health insurance. Visitors from outside the EU must arrange their own private medical insurance.

If you fall sick during your visit, pharmacists are an excellent source of advice – they can diagnose minor ailments and suggest treatment.

Passports and Visas

Citizens of the EU, US, Australia, New Zealand, and Canada do not require a visa to enter either Belgium or Luxembourg, but must present a

valid passport and hold proof of onward passage (EU citizens need a valid ID document). For visa information specific to your home country, consult your nearest Belgian or Luxembourg embassy or check online. Note that in Belgium it is a legal requirement to carry ID at all times.

Travelers with Specific Needs

Many key sites in historic cities are hard to access for people with limited mobility, due to narrow sidewalks and cobbled streets. Numerous hotels, restaurants, and tourist attractions are adapted to accommodate visitors with specific needs, but it is advisable to call in advance and ask about particular amenities. **Handy.Brussels** has advice for visitors to the capital and **Access Info** has information about visiting Flanders. City tourist offices are another useful source of information, and Belgian Railways has helpful advice pages on its website (see right).

Access Info
W accessinfo.be
Handy.Brussels
W handy.brussels/en

Money

Most establishments accept major credit, debit, and prepaid currency cards, but it's a good idea to carry some cash too. ATMs are widespread.

Language

The two principal languages of Belgium are Dutch, spoken in Flanders in the north, and French, the language of Wallonia in the south. There is also a German-speaking enclave in the far east of the country. Luxembourg has three official languages: French, German, and Luxembourgish. All three are spoken everywhere, to varying extents.

Cell Phones and Wi-Fi

Cell-phone coverage is good, especially in the cities. Visitors traveling to Belgium and Luxembourg with EU tariffs can use their devices without being affected by data roaming charges. Visitors from other countries should check their contracts before departure in order to avoid unexpected charges.

Wi-Fi is available at stations and other public buildings in both Belgium and Luxembourg, as well as at cafés, restaurants, and hotels.

Getting Around

Within Belgium, train services are operated by **Belgian National Railways** (SNCB). The network is modern and efficient, and usually the best way to travel between major cities and towns. Luxembourg's rail system is run by **Chemins de Fer Luxembourgeois** (CFL). In both countries, a variety of train passes are available.

The two main long-distance bus operators in Belgium are **De Lijn**, which covers routes in Flanders, and **TEC**, which provides services in Wallonia. Luxembourg benefits from an extensive bus network, which compensates for the more limited railroad system. One-day passes are available, and can be used on both long-distance and inner-city buses and trains. Eurail Benelux Passes are valid for reduced fares on buses operated by CFL.

The freeways and main roads in Belgium and Luxembourg are well maintained and fast. Variations between the French and Dutch spellings of town names can be confusing; it is advisable to find out both names of your destination before beginning your journey. All the major car-rental firms are represented in Belgium and Luxembourg, but renting a vehicle is fairly expensive.

Belgian National Railways
W belgiantrain.be
Chemins de Fer Luxembourgeois
W cfl.lu
De Lijn
W delijn.be
TEC
W infotec.be

Visitor Information

In Belgium, the **Visit Brussels Information Office** publishes maps and guides, as does **Luxembourg's National Tourist Office** (LNTO). Local tourist information offices can be found in towns and villages throughout both countries.
Luxembourg National Tourist Office
W visitluxembourg.com
Visit Brussels Information Office
W visit.brussels

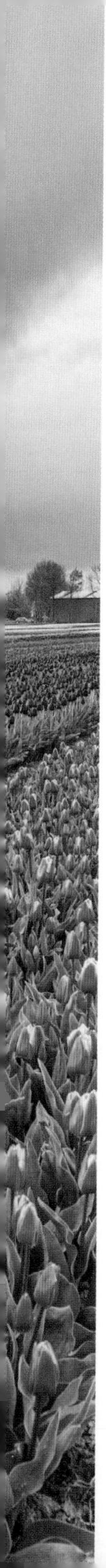

THE NETHERLANDS

Sandwiched between the two great powers of France and Germany, the Netherlands has been shaped by centuries of dynastic warfare. Between the 4th and 8th centuries, following the collapse of the Roman Empire, the area corresponding to present-day Holland was conquered by the Franks. As with all the Low Countries, it was later ruled by the House of Burgundy, before passing into the hands of the Habsburgs. When the Habsburg Empire was divided in 1555, the region came under the control of the Spanish branch of the family, which caused the Dutch Revolt of 1568. The Dutch Republic was finally established in 1579, with the Treaty of Utrecht, but it took until 1648 for the Spanish to officially recognize its sovereignty. The need for wealth to fight Spain's armies stimulated trading success overseas, leading the Dutch to colonize much of Indonesia and establish an empire that profiteered from goods such as spice. Tulip bulbs were imported from Turkey, thus beginning a lucrative flower industry that still flourishes today. However, war with England radically reduced Dutch sea power by the end of the 17th century, and from then on the country's fortunes waned. In 1795, French troops ousted William V of Orange, and in 1813, with the retreat of Napoleon, the Netherlands united with Belgium for 17 years. The Netherlands remained neutral in both world wars, although the Nazi invasion of 1940 left lasting scars on the nation. In the 1960s, the country became a haven for liberal counter-culture, an influence that is still visible today.

THE NETHERLANDS

West Frisi

Vlieland

Texel

Den Burg

Wadden

Den Helder

N9

Schagen   Medemblik

A7

← Newcastle

ALKMAAR 4   H

Egmond   VOLENDAM

A9   Purmerend   2

Heemskerk   MARKEN

Ijmuiden   Zaandam

HAARLEM 5   Alm

Zaandam

AMSTERDA

North Sea

Hoofddorp

Noordwijk   Aalsmeer   Hilversu

LEIDEN 6   A4

Scheveningen   Maarssen

THE HAGUE 8   Zoetermeer   UTRECHT

← Hull, Harwich

DELFT 9   A12   Nieuwegein

Hoek van Holland   Maassluis   A20   Gouda   Culem

Oostvoorne   Nieuwpoort

10 ROTTERDAM   Nieuwpoort

Hellevoetsluis   Dordrecht   A15   Gorinc

N57   Nieuwendijk

Haamstede   Middelharnis   A16   Heusde

N59

Zierikzee   Bruinisse   Willemstad   A59

Domburg   N57   A17   Breda

St Maartensdijk   A58   Tilburg

Middelburg   Goes   Tholen   Roosendaal

Vlissingen   A58   Kruiningen   Zundert

Breskens   Westerschelde   Hoogerheide   Ossendrecht

Sluis   N61   Terneuzen

Oostende   Hulst   **BELGIUM AND LUXEMBOURG** *p236*

Maldegem   Antwerp   Geel

Aalter   Lokeren   Temse   **BELGIUM**

Gent   Mechelen   Aarschot   Di

Aalst

Brussels   Leuven   Sint-Trui

0 kilometers   30

0 miles   30

N ↑

Halle

Herengracht canal, lined with attractive 17th-century buildings ↑

❶

AMSTERDAM

 ✈🚗🚌 ℹ www.iamsterdam.com

Amsterdam was founded in around 1200 as a small fishing village on marshland at the mouth of the Amstel river. Today it is a place where beauty and serenity coexist with a hedonistic side. From the energetic nightclubs to the rich cultural heritage of its 17th-century canal houses and museums, Amsterdam offers an enticing blend of past and present.

① ⊘ ▱
Oude Kerk

🏠 Oudekerksplein 23 🚊 4, 14, 24 🕐 10am-6pm Mon-Sat, 1-5:30pm Sun 🗓 Apr 27, Dec 25 🌐 oudekerk.nl

The origins of the Oude Kerk (Old Church) go back to the early 13th century, when a wooden church dedicated to St. Nicholas, the patron saint of sailors, was built on a burial ground on a sand bank. The present Gothic structure dates from the 14th century, and has grown from a single-aisled church

into a basilica. As it expanded, the building became a gathering place for traders and a refuge for the poor. Though many of the Oude Kerk's paintings and statues were destroyed following the Alteration in 1578, when Amsterdam officially became Protestant, the delicate 15th-century vault paintings on the gilded ceiling escaped damage. In 1755, the paintings were hidden with layers of blue paint and were not revealed until two centuries later, in 1955. The Oude Kerk's stained-glass windows were also undamaged in the ransackings of the late 16th

century; the Lady Chapel contains some of the best examples. The magnificent oak-encased Great Organ, the work of Christian Vater, was added to the church in 1724.

💬 INSIDER TIP
Getting Around

The most useful tram routes are lines 2, 4, 11, 12, 14, and 24, which go to all the main sights. The canalbus service from the Singelgracht to Centraal Station also stops at the major landmarks.

② ⊘ Ⓜ ▱
Museum Ons' Lieve Heer op Solder

🏠 Oudezijds Voorburgwal 38 🚊 4, 14, 24 🕐 10am-6pm Mon-Sat, 1-6pm Sun 🗓 Apr 27 🌐 opsolder.nl

Tucked away on the edge of the Red Light District is a restored 17th-century canal house, with two smaller dwellings to the rear. The combined

↑ Our Lord in the Attic church in the Museum Ons' Lieve Heer op Solder

pper floors conceal a Catholic hurch, known as Ons' Lieve Heer op Solder (Our Lord in he Attic). After the Alteration, many such hidden churches prang up around the city. Built in 1663, the one here erved the Catholic commu-

nity until 1887, when the nearby St. Nicolaaskerk was completed. Above the mock-marble altar is Jacob de Wit's glorious painting *The Baptism of Christ* (1716). The tiny bedroom where the priest slept is hidden off a bend in the stairs.

The building became a museum in 1888, and today contains elegantly refurbished rooms, as well as a first-rate collection of church silver, religious artifacts, and paintings. Restored to its former opulence, the parlor, with its magnificent fireplace, is a splendid example of a living room in the Dutch Classical style of the 17th century. Entry to the museum is through the house next door, where a cloakroom, café, and temporary exhibitions are found.

DRINK

Wynand Fockink
Famous *proeflokaal* (gin bar) with a huge choice of *genevers*, plus beers.

🏠 Pijlsteeg 31
ⓦ wynand-fockink.nl

In de Wildeman
This tavern has at least 18 craft beers on tap and 200 more by the bottle.

🏠 Kolksteeg 3 🕙 Sun
ⓦ indewildeman.nl

RED LIGHT DISTRICT

The city's Red Light District is one of the defining images of Amsterdam. Prostitution in the city dates back to the 13th century and by 1478, the practice had become so widespread, with sea-weary sailors flooding into the city, that attempts were made to contain it. Today, hordes of visitors generate a buzz amid the bars, eateries, and canalside houses.

③

Museum Willet-Holthuysen

⌂ Herengracht 605
🚊 4, 9, 14 ⏰ 10am-5pm
Mon-Fri, 11am-5pm
Sat & Sun 🕔 Public hols
🌐 willetholthuysen.nl

Named after its last residents, the Museum Willet-Holthuysen allows the visitor a glimpse into the lives of the emerging merchant class who lived in luxury along the Grachten-gordel (Canal Ring) in the 17th century.

The house was constructed in 1685 for Jacob Hop, mayor of Amsterdam. It later became the property of coal magnate Pieter Holthuysen in 1855, then passed to his daughter Louisa (and her husband, Abraham Willet, who were both fervent collectors of paintings, glass, silver, and ceramics. When Louisa died childless and a widow in 1895, the house and its many treasures were left to the city on the condition that it became a museum bearing their names. Room by room, the house is being restored and brought back to the time Abraham and Louisa lived here.

At the back is a French-style 18th-century garden, but the most interesting part of the house is arguably below stairs. Special exhibits on the lives of the Willet-Holthuysens' servants are displayed on the lower floor.

Did You Know?

Rembrandt painted himself into many of his works as a spectator.

↑ Admiring Rembrandt's works at the Museum Het Rembrandthuis

④

Museum Het Rembrandthuis

⌂ Jodenbreestraat 4
Ⓜ Nieuwmarkt 🚊 14
⏰ 10am-6pm daily
🕔 Apr 27, Dec 25
🌐 rembrandthuis.nl

Born in Leiden, Rembrandt worked and taught in this house from 1639 until 1656. He lived in the ground-floor rooms with his wife, Saskia, who died here in 1658 leaving Rembrandt with a baby son, Titus. Many of the artist's most famous paintings were created in the first-floor studio, which along with the other rooms in the house has been refurbished and restored to show exactly how it looked in the 17th century.

On display is an excellent selection of Rembrandt's etchings and drawings, including a number of self-portraits showing the artist in a variety of moods and guises. There are also land-scapes, nude studies, and religious pieces, as well as temporary exhibitions of other artists' works.

↑ The elegant 18th-century garden of the Museum Willet-Holthuysen

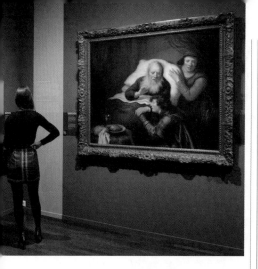

Joods Historisch Museum

🏠 Nieuwe Amstelstraat 1
Ⓜ Waterlooplein 🚊 14
🚋 Nationale Opera & Ballet
🕐 11am–5pm daily
📅 Apr 27, Yom Kippur, Jewish New Year 🌐 jck.nl

Constructed in the 17th and 18th centuries, this complex of four synagogues was built by the Ashkenazi Jews, who arrived in Amsterdam from Eastern Europe in the 1630s. At first restricted to working in certain trades, the Ashkenazi Jews were granted full civil equality in 1796. Their synagogues were central to Jewish life in Amsterdam until the devastation caused by the Nazi occupation of World War II, which left them empty. The buildings were restored in the 1980s and connected by internal walkways, opening in 1987 as a museum dedicated to Jewish culture and the history of Judaism in the Netherlands.

The impressive Grote Synagoge, with its bright and airy interior, was designed by Elias Bouman and first opened in 1671. Next door is the Nieuwe Synagoge (New Synagogue), built in 1752 and dominated by the wooden Holy Ark (1791), which came from a synagogue in the Dutch town of Enkhuizen.

Religious art and artifacts on display include Hanukah lamps, Torah mantles, and scroll finials. The buildings were renovated in 2006; a print room was created in the basement and a children's museum on the upper floor in the former Obbene Shul.

Nieuwe Kerk

🏠 Dam 🚊 2, 4, 11, 12, & many others 🕐 Hours vary, check website 🌐 nieuwekerk.nl

Dating from the late 14th century, Amsterdam's second parish church was built as the population outgrew the Oude Kerk (p264). During its turbulent history, the Nieuwe Kerk (New Church) has been destroyed by fire and rebuilt, as well as stripped of its treasures after the Alteration of 1578, when the Calvinists took civil power.

Albert Vinckenbrinck's flamboyant carved pulpit (1664) is the focal point of the church interior, reflecting the Protestant belief that the sermon is central to worship. Other notable features include Jacob van Campen's ornate Great Organ (1645).

STAY

Grand Hotel Amrath
Located in the grand former Shipping House, rooms here combine Art Deco with 21st-century style.

🏠 Prins Hedrikkade 108 🌐 amrath amsterdam.com

€€€

MISC
A boutique hotel situated in a 17th-century canal house.

🏠 Kloveniersburgwal 20 🌐 misceatdrink sleep.com

€€€

Ambassade Boutique Hotel
Ten canal houses have been merged to create this stunning boutique hotel.

🏠 Herengracht 341 🌐 ambassade-hotel.nl

€€€

Hotel Dwars
This hotel's nine characterful, cozy rooms are decorated with modern and vintage furniture.

🏠 Utrechtsedwarsstraat 🌐 hoteldwars.com

€€€

Hotel Arena
With 139 rooms and suites, decorated in tones of gray and white, this hotel has views over Oosterpark and a pretty courtyard.

🏠 's-Gravesandestraat 🌐 hotelarena.nl

€€€

The marble-floored Citizen's Hall, inside the Koninklijk Paleis

At the core of the collection is a 45-minute historical tour of the city called "Amsterdam DNA." This explores four main local characteristics: spirit of enterprise, freedom of thought, civic virtue, and creativity. Key moments from the city's history are explored chronologically, and there are touch-sensitive multimedia screens showing animations and film footage.

Also contributing to the museum's detailed account of Amsterdam's history are such fascinating items as a globe belonging to the famous cartographer Willem Blaeu and a 1648 model of the Koninklijk Paleis, designed by Jacob van Campen.

Amsterdam's wealth from trade attracted many artists, who chronicled the era in great detail. There are paintings of the city and the port, as well as portraits of both prominent and ordinary citizens, and paintings of anatomy lessons.

One of the museum's most extraordinary exhibits is a 17th-century 17-ft (5.30-m) statue of Goliath (c. 1650).

⑦ 🖼️ 🖼️

Koninklijk Paleis

🏛️ Dam 🚊 2, 4, 11, 12, & many others 🕐 Hours vary, check website 🚫 Public hols and when King is in residence 🌐 paleisamsterdam.nl

The Koninklijk Paleis, still used occasionally by the Dutch royal family for official functions, was built as the Stadhuis (Town Hall). Work began on this vast sandstone edifice in 1648, after the end of the 80 Years' War with Spain. It dominated its surroundings, and more than 13,600 piles were driven into the ground for the foundations. The Classical design by Jacob van Campen reflects the city's mood of confidence after the Dutch victory. Civic pride is also shown in the allegorical sculptures by Artus Quellien that decorate the pediments, and in François Hemony's statues and carillon. Inside, the full magnificence of the palace's architecture is best

appreciated in the huge Burgerzaal (Citizens' Hall). Based on the assembly halls of ancient Rome, this 95-ft-(29-m-) high room runs the length of the building, and has a superb marble floor, as well as epic sculptures by Quellien. Most of the furniture dates from 1808, when Louis Bonaparte took over the building as his royal palace.

---

 ⑧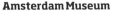

Amsterdam Museum

🏛️ Kalverstraat 92, St Luciensteeg 27 Ⓜ Rokin 🚊 2, 4, 11, 12, & many others 🕐 10am–5pm daily 🚫 Apr 27, Dec 25 🌐 amsterdam museum.nl

The convent of St. Lucien was turned into a civic orphanage in the latter half of the 16th century. The original red-brick convent was enlarged over the years, and in 1975 it opened as the city's historical museum. Today, some of the museum's exhibitions also focus on contemporary Amsterdam.

---

 ⑨

Begijnhof

🏛️ Spui (entrance at Gedempte Begijnensloot) 🚊 2, 4, 11, 12, 14, 24 🕐 9am 5pm daily 🌐 begijnhof amsterdam.nl

The Begijnhof was built in 1346 as a sanctuary for the Begijntjes, a lay Catholic sisterhood who lived like nuns, although they took no monastic vows. In return for lodgings within the complex, these worthy women educated the poor and looked after the sick. Although none of the earliest dwellings survive, the

PICTURE PERFECT
Het Houten Huis

Behind the Begijnhof's Het Houten Huis (No. 34), the oldest house in Amsterdam, is a white wall adorned with biblical plaques. Get the wooden-fronted house - one of just two left in the city - and the plaques in the frame for the perfect shot.

beautiful houses that overlook the Begijnhof's well-kept green include Amsterdam's oldest surviving house, Het Houten Huis, at No. 34. Dating from the second half of the 15th century, it is one of only two wooden-fronted houses in the city, since timber buildings were banned in 1521 after some catastrophic fires.

The southern side of the square is dominated by the Engelse Kerk (English Church), which dates from the 15th century and retains its original medieval tower. The church was confiscated after the Alteration and rented to a group of English and Scottish Presbyterians in 1607. Directly opposite is the Begijnhof Chapel (Nos. 29–30), where the Begijntjes worshipped in secret until religious tolerance was restored in 1795. Tour groups are not permitted in the Begijnhof, and noise should be kept to a minimum.

⑩

Anne Frank House

Wetsermarkt 20
13, 17 Prinsengracht
Hours vary, check website Yom Kippur
annefrank.org

For two years during World War II, the Frank and Van Pels families, both Jewish, hid here until they were betrayed to the Nazis. The 13-year-old Anne began her famous diary in July 1942. First published in 1947 as *Het Achterhuis (The Annex)*, the journal gives a moving account of growing up under persecution and of life in confinement. Anne made her last entry in August 1944, three days before her family was arrested.

Visitors start at the former warehouse on the ground floor, where an introductory video is shown, then proceed to the first-floor offices, where Anne's father worked. On the second floor, behind the revolving bookcase, is the entrance to the annex. The rooms are now empty, except for the posters in Anne's room and Otto Frank's model of the annex as it was during the occupation. The wing on Westermarkt has displays on World War II and anti-Semitism. Book well in advance (online only) for this popular sight.

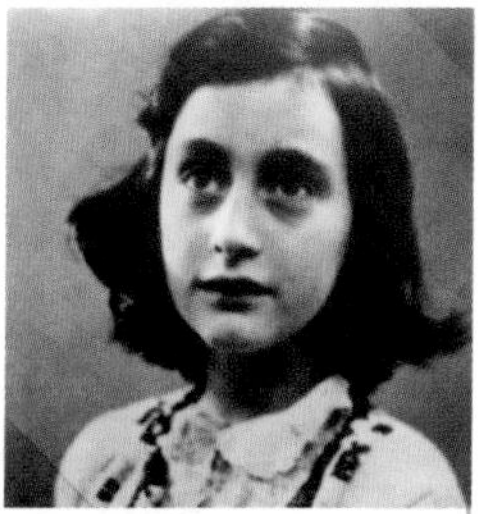

THE DIARY OF ANNE FRANK

Otto Frank returned to Amsterdam in 1945 to discover that his entire family had perished: his wife, Edith, in Auschwitz, and his daughters, Anne and Margot, in Bergen-Belsen. Miep Gies, one of the family's helpers while they were in hiding, had kept Anne's diary. For many, Anne symbolizes the six million Jews murdered by the Nazis in World War II.

A statue of Jesus standing in the middle of Begijnhof's green

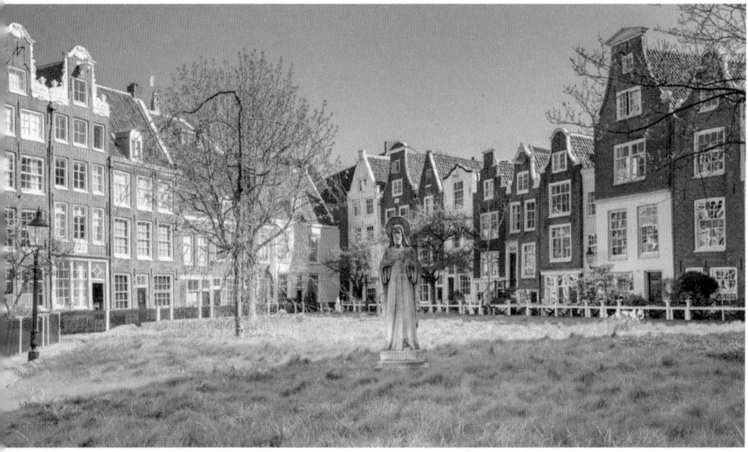

Did You Know?

Canal houses tilt to allow goods to be winched to the attic without crashing into the windows.

 ⑪

Golden Bend

🚊 2, 4, 11, 12, 24

The city's most impressive canalside architecture can be seen along the section of Herengracht between Leidestraat and Vijzelstraat. This stretch of canal is known as the Golden Bend because of the great wealth of the shipbuilders, merchants, and politicians who began building houses here in the 1660s. Most of the opulent mansions have been turned into offices or banks, but their elegance gives an insight into the lifestyle of the earliest residents.

Two of the best-preserved buildings are No. 412, designed by Philips Vingboons in 1664, and No. 475, featuring two sculpted female figures over the front door. Built in 1730, the latter is an example of the Louis XIV style, which became popular in the 18th century. At No. 497 is the **Kattenkabinet** (Cat Museum), one of the few houses on the Golden Bend

accessible to the public. It is worth a visit for its unusual collection of feline artifacts. Also on view here are paintings by Jacob de Wit and an attractive formal garden.

A multimedia exhibition at **Het Grachtenhuis**, a mansion on Herengracht, illustrates Hendrick Staets' plans for the Grachtengordel (Canal Ring).

Kattenkabinet
⊗ ◷ 10am–5pm Mon–Fri; pm Sat & Sun ◷ Public hols
Ⓦ kattenkabinet.nl

Het Grachtenhuis
⊗ ◷ 10am–5pm Tue–Sun
◷ Apr 27, Dec 25 Ⓦ het grachtenhuis.nl

 ⑫

Jordaan

🚊 13, 17 🚌 18, 21, 22

The Jordaan grew up at the same time that Amsterdam's Grachtengordel was being developed in the first half of the 17th century. The marshy area to the west of the more fashionable canals was set aside as an area for workers whose industries were banned from the town center. Its network of narrow streets and waterways followed

the course of old paths and drainage ditches. Immigrants fleeing religious persecution also settled here. It is thought that Huguenot refugees called the district *jardin* (garden), later corrupted to "Jordaan."

Flowing through the heart of the district are the tranquil tree-lined canals known as the Egelantiersgracht and the Bloemgracht. The canalside houses of the former were originally settled by artisans, while the latter was a center for dye and paint manufacture. One of the most charming spots here is St. Andrieshofje, at Nos. 107–114 along the Egelantiersgracht. This *hofje* (almshouse) was built in 1617 and the passage that leads to its courtyard is decorated with splendid blue-and-white tiles.

The 272-ft- (85-m-) high tower of the Westerkerk soars above Jordaan's streets, and gives panoramic views of the city. Begun in 1620, the church has the largest nave of any Dutch Protestant church.

Historically a poor area, Jordaan now has a trendy and laid-back air, with art galleries, quirky stores selling everything from designer clothes to old sinks, and lively brown cafés (pubs) and bars spilling onto the sidewalks during the summer months.

A dusk view of the Golden Bend, with its grand mansions

 ⑬

Het Scheepvaartmuseum

◨ Kattenburgerplein 1
🚌 22, 48 🚊 Oosterdok, Kattenburgergracht
🕐 9am–5pm daily
🚫 Jan 1, Apr 27, Dec 25
🌐 hetscheepvaart museum.nl

Once the arsenal of the Dutch Navy, this vast Classical sandstone edifice was built in 1656. The Navy stayed here until 1973, when the building was converted into the National Maritime Museum, holding the largest collection of boats in the world.

One of the museum's finest exhibits is a 54-ft- (17-m) long gilded barge, made in 1818 for King William I. Another major attraction is a full-size model of a Dutch East Indiaman, the *Amsterdam*. During the 16th century, the Dutch East India Company used such vessels to sail to China, Japan, and Indonesia. The museum courtyard is accessible without a ticket.

⑭

Nemo Science Museum

◨ Oosterdok 2 🚌 22, 48
🕐 10am–5:30pm Tue–Sun (May–Aug: daily) 🚫 Jan 1, Apr 27, Dec 25 🌐 nemo sciencemuseum.nl

In 1997, Holland's national science center moved to this curved building that protrudes 99 ft (30 m) over the water. The center presents technological innovations in a way that allows visitors' creativity full expression. You can interact with virtual reality, operate the latest industrial equipment under supervision, harness science to produce a work of art, participate in countless games, experiments, demonstrations, and workshops, and take in a range of lectures and films.

The Nemo Science Museum, designed by Renzo Piano ↓

EAT

Visrestaurant Lucius
Lobster and crab are specialties at this long-established seafood restaurant with an outstanding set menu.

◨ Spuistraat 247
 lucius.nl

€€€

Restaurant de Waaghals
This organic vegetarian restaurant serves imaginative dishes.

◨ Franshalsstraat 29
🕐 Lunch waaghals.nl

€€€

Vlaardingse Haringhandel
Locals rate the creamy raw herring served here in a bun, with pickles and onions.

◨ Albert Cuypstraat 89
🕐 Sun & dinner

€€€

Brouwerij Het
Cheeses and sausages accompany artisan beers at this brewpub.

◨ AFunenkade 7
 brouwerijhetij.nl

€€€

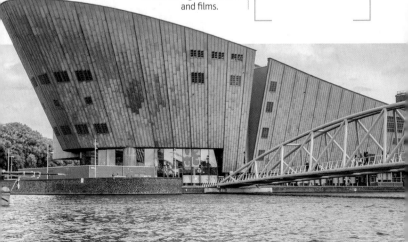

(15) 🛋 🍴 🥤 🛍

RIJKSMUSEUM

🏠 Museumstraat 1 🚊 1, 2, 5, 7, 12, 19 🚏 Stadhouderskade
🕘 9am–5pm daily 🌐 rijksmuseum.nl

The Rijksmuseum is a familiar Amsterdam landmark, with an unrivaled collection of Dutch art that was begun in the early 19th century. The vast exhibition space can seem overwhelming, but with such a wealth of things to see, it's no wonder that it's the city's most-visited museum.

The Rijksmuseum originated as the Nationale Kunstgalerij in The Hague. In 1808, King Louis Napoleon ordered the collection to be moved to Amsterdam, and it briefly occupied the Koninklijk Paleis before it moved to its present location in 1885. The main red-brick building, designed by P. J. H.Cuypers, was initially criticized, most vehemently by Amsterdam's Protestant community for its Catholic Neo-Renaissance style. King William III famously refused to set foot inside.

Nowadays, the building is fondly regarded, and it frequently appears as the background of many of the images taken by novice photographers in the city due to its iconic exterior. Inside, there is an unrivaled collection of about 1 million artworks, several thousand of which are on display in the galleries.

> 💬 INSIDER TIP
> **Beat the Line**
>
> The only way to walk straight inside the museum is to book a guided tour. Otherwise, get there at 9am or 3:30pm, and avoid Fridays and weekends.

↓ The red-brick, Neo-Renaissance façade of the Rijksmuseum

TOP
5 UNMISSABLE EXHIBITS

The Night Watch (1642)
This vast canvas was commissioned by an Amsterdam militia.

The Kitchen Maid (1658)
The stillness and light in this work are typical of Vermeer.

St. Elizabeth's Day Flood (1500)
An unknown artist painted this flood that occurred in 1421.

The Square Man (1951)
This painting is typical of Appel's CoBrA work.

Shiva Nataraja (c. 1100-1200)
This bronze statue shows the Hindu god dancing.

↑ Rembrandt's *The Night Watch* – the museum's most-prized possession and its most-visited piece

← A huge 17th-century model of the *William Rex*, housed in the Rijksmuseum

Exploring the Rijksmuseum

The Rijksmuseum is too vast to be seen in a single visit. If time is limited, start with the incomparable 17th-century Dutch paintings, taking in Rembrandt, Frans Hals, Vermeer, and many other Old Masters. The collection of Asiatic artifacts is equally wonderful, and a tour of the special collections section also provides a rewarding experience. The gardens are well worth a look and are often used as a setting for sculpture exhibitions.

↑ Visitors admiring the art, and taking a break, in one of the galleries

8,000
—
pieces are displayed in the Rijksmuseum's 80 galleries.

The Gallery of Honor, lined with Golden Age masterpieces ↓

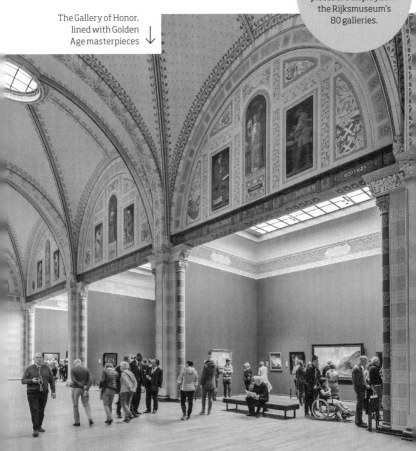

Gallery Guide

GENRE PAINTING

For the contemporaries of Jan Steen, the cosy everyday scene portrayed in *Woman at her Toilet* (c. 1660) was full of symbols that are obscure to the modern viewer. The dog on the pillow may represent fidelity, and the red stockings suggest the woman's sexuality.

1100–1600

Displayed alongside Flemish and Italian art are religious works by Netherlandish painters, such as *The Seven Works of Charity* (1504) by the Master of Alkmaar, Jan van Scorel's *Mary Magdalene* (1528), and Lucas van Leyden's triptych *Adoration of the Golden Calf* (1530).

1650–1700

▷ The 17th century was a golden age for Dutch art. By this time, religious themes in art had been replaced by secular subjects, such as realistic portraiture, landscapes, still lifes, seascapes, domestic interiors, and animal portraits. The most famous artist of this era is Rembrandt, whose works here include *Portrait of Titus in a Monk's Habit* (1660), *Self-Portrait as the Apostle Paul* (1661), and the brilliant *The Night Watch (p273)*. Also not to be missed are Jan Vermeer's serenely light-filled interiors, such as *The Kitchen Maid (right)* and *The Woman Reading a Letter* (1662). Of several portraits by Frans Hals, the best known are *The Wedding Portrait* and *The Merry Drinker* (1630). Other artists whose works contribute to this unforgettable collection include Jacob van Ruisdael, Pieter Saenredam, Jan van de Capelle, and Jan Steen.

1700–1800

Portraiture and still lifes continued to dominate 18th-century Dutch painting. The evocative *Still Life with Flowers and Fruit* by Jan van Huysum stands out among works on display here. Other 18th-century artists represented are Adriaan van der Werff and Cornelis Troost.

1800–1900

The 19th-century collection features works by the Hague School, Dutch artists who came together in around 1870 in The Hague. Their landscape work captures the atmospheric quality of subdued Dutch sunlight. Look out for Anton Mauve's *Morning Ride on the Beach* (1876) and the Polder landscape, *View near the Geestbrug*, by Hendrik Weissenbruch.

1900–Present

Below the rafters is a series of rooms devoted to 20th-century art and design. Highlights include a white version of Gerrit Rietveld's iconic red-and-blue armchair (1923), Karel Appel's imposing oil painting *The Square Man* (1951), and an F.K. 23 Bantam biplane from 1918.

Asiatic Art

Rewards of the Dutch imperial trading past are on show in this section. Some of the earliest artifacts are the most unusual: tiny bronze Tang-dynasty figurines from 7th-century China, and granite rock carvings from Java (c. 8th century). Later exhibits include inlaid Korean boxes and decorative Vietnamese dishes.

Special Collections and Philips Wing

◁ The Special Collections gallery in the basement is a treasure trove of delftware, porcelain, and much more. Temporary exhibitions are held in the Philips Wing.

⑯
Plantage

🚊14

The name Plantage dates from the time when it was an area of green parkland beyond the city wall, where 17th-century Amsterdammers spent their leisure time. Much of the greenery has now gone, but there is still a lot to see and do here.

The area is dominated by **Artis**, a zoo complex with more than 5,000 animal species, a planetarium, and an excellent aquarium. Close by is the **Hortus Botanicus Amsterdam**, which contains one of the world's largest botanical collections.

Plantage has a strong Jewish tradition, and many monuments commemorate Jewish history in Amsterdam. The **Hollandsche Schouwburg**

---

is a somber memorial to the 104,000 Dutch Jewish victims of World War II.

Artis
🦁🦒 🏛Plantage Kerklaan 38-40 🕐Hours vary, check website 🌐artis.nl

Hortus Botanicus Amsterdam
🌿 🏛Plantage Middenlaan 2 🕐10am-5pm daily 🚫Jan 1, Dec 25 🌐dehortus.nl

Hollandsche Schouwburg
🏛Plantage Middenlaan 24 🕐11am-5pm daily 🚫Rosh Hashanah (Jewish New Year), Yom Kippur 🌐jck.nl

---

⑰
Van Gogh Museum

🏛Museumplein 6 🚊2, 3, 5, 12 🕐Hours vary, check website 🚫Jan 1 🌐vangoghmuseum.com

Vincent van Gogh, born in Zundert, began painting in 1880. He worked in the Netherlands for five years, before moving to Paris and then settling at Arles *(p228)* in the south of France in 1888. There he painted more than 200 canvases in 15 months. During his time in France, however, Van Gogh suffered recurrent nervous crises, hallucinations, and severe depression. After a fierce argument with the French artist Gauguin, he cut off part of his own ear and his mental

instability forced him into an asylum. Van Gogh's final years were characterized by tremendous bursts of activity: during the last 70 days of his life he painted 70 canvases. In July 1890 he shot himself and died two days later. He was on the verge of being acclaimed.

Van Gogh's younger brother Theo, an art dealer, amassed a collection of 200 of his paintings and 500 drawings. These, together with around 850 letters written by the artist to Theo, form the core of the museum's collection. Famous works include *The Potato Eaters* (1885), from the artist's Dutch period, and *The Bedroom*

TOP 5 LOCAL DELICACIES

Haring
Smelling of the sea, with a soft texture and crispy exterior, salted raw herring has been a popular Dutch snack since the Middle Ages.

Bitterballen
These deep-fried meatballs are filled with gravy and dipped in a bowl of mustard.

Erwtensoep
Also called *snert*, this is a thick soup of split peas and sausage.

Stamppot
A hearty dish of mashed potatoes, crispy bacon, and winter greens, this is great in cold weather.

Pannenkoeken
When you want a sweet treat, these pancakes are the answer.

↑ The modern extension of the Stedelijk Museum, home to the national museum of modern art

← Visitors passing through the entrance hall of the Van Gogh Museum

(1888), painted to celebrate his achievement of domestic stability in the Yellow House in Arles. One of Van Gogh's last paintings is the dramatic *Wheatfield and Crows* (1890). The menacing crows and violence of the sky show the depth of the artist's mental anguish. In addition to Van Gogh's works, the museum displays paintings by artists such as Gauguin and Toulouse-Lautrec.

---

(18)

Stedelijk Museum

📍 Museumplein 10 🚊 2, 3, 5, 12 🕐 10am–6pm daily (to 10pm Fri) 🌐 stedelijk.nl

The Stedelijk Museum was designed to hold a personal collection bequeathed to the city in 1890 by art connoisseur Sophia de Bruyn. It is housed in a late-19th-century Neo-Classical building, adorned with statues of famous artists and architects. In 1938, the museum became the National Museum of Modern Art, show-casing works by well-known names such as Monet, Picasso, Matisse, and Chagall. Con-stantly changing exhibitions reflect developments not only in painting and sculpture, but also in printing, drawing, photography, and video.

Among the museum's best collections are works by the Dutch painter Mondriaan, one of the founding members of De Stijl (The Style) – an artistic movement which espoused clarity and simplicity.

Other artists represented in the exhibitions include the American photographer Man Ray, the influential Russian Kazimir Malevich – founder of the abstract movement Suprematism – and the Swiss sculptor Jean Tinguely.

---

(19)

Hermitage Amsterdam

📍 Amstel 51 🚇 Waterlooplein 🚊 4, 14 🕐 10am–5pm daily 🗓 Apr 27 🌐 hermitage.nl

This branch of the State Hermitage Museum in St. Petersburg *(p628)* resides in the vast Amstelhof, a for-mer old-people's home. It displays temporary exhi-bitions drawn from the rich St. Petersburg collections and is one of Amsterdam's major museums.

SHOP

De Negen Straatjes
This rectangle of nine small shopping streets (the "Nine Streets") is filled with designer boutiques and vintage stores. Be sure to check out Laura Dols at Wolvenstraat 7, which specializes in the 1950s, and I Love Vintage at Prinsengracht 201.

📍 Amsterdam-Centrum 🌐 de9straatjes.nl

Antiekcentrum Amsterdam
In a labyrinth of rooms, the biggest antiques and curios market in the Netherlands sells everything from glassware to vintage jewelry to dolls.

📍 Elandsgracht 109 🕐 11am–6pm Mon & Wed-Fri, 11am-5pm Sat & Sun 🌐 antiekcentrum amsterdam.nl

② Marken and Volendam

📍 North Holland 🚗🚌🚢
ℹ️ Zeestraat 37; www.vvv-volendam.nl

Located on the shores of the Marker Meer, and less than an hour's drive from Amsterdam, Marken and Volendam are extremely popular with visitors, thanks to their charming old-world character. In spite of the crowds, it is worth spending a few hours exploring their narrow streets and canals, lined with attractive 17th-century gabled timber houses. You may even spot the locals wearing traditional dress.

Places to look out for include the Marker Museum in Marken, which consists of six historical houses. One of the houses is furnished as a traditional fisherman's dwelling. Volendam's

Spaander Hotel, at No. 15 Haven, is also worth a visit. The walls of the hotel's café are covered with works by late 19th-century artists who, came here to paint the town.

③
Paleis Het Loo

📍 Koninklijk Park 1, Apeldoorn 🚂 To Apeldoorn, then bus 10, 16, or 202
🕐 Gardens: Apr–Sep; see website for details
🔒 House: until 2021 for renovations 🌐 paleishetloo.nl

King William III of England, Stadholder of the Netherlands, built Het Loo in 1686 as a royal hunting lodge. Generations of the House of Orange used the lodge as a summer palace, which came to be seen as the "Versailles of the Netherlands." The building's Classical facade belies the opulence of the interior. Among the most lavish apartments are the Royal Bedroom of William III (1713), with its wall coverings and draperies of rich orange

Alkmaar's cheese market, centred on the Waaggebouw *(inset)* ↓

Did You Know?

Around one-third of the Netherlands sits below sea level.

damask and blue silk, and the Old Dining Room (1686). In the latter half of the 20th century, Het Loo's beautiful formal gardens were restored according to old plans.

④ Alkmaar

📍 North Holland 🚂
ℹ️ Waaggebouw, Waagplein 2-3; www.visitalkmaar.com

Alkmaar is one of the few Dutch towns to maintain its traditional cheese market, which has been held here since medieval times. Every Friday morning in summer, local producers lay out Gouda and Edam cheeses in the Waagplein, and from here porters sporting colorful straw hats take them off on sledges for weighing at the Waaggebouw (Weigh

↑ People relaxing at the outdoor cafés of Haarlem's delightful Grote Markt

House). This impressive building, altered in 1582 from a 14th-century chapel, also houses the **Het Hollands Kaasmuseum**, where local cheese-making techniques are explained.

Alkmaar's vast Gothic church, the Grote Kerk, was completed in 1520 and contains the tomb of Floris V, Count of Holland. The nave is dominated by the 17th-century organ, designed by Jacob van Campen and painted by Cesar van Everdingen.

Het Hollands Kaasmuseum

 🏠 Waaggebouw, Waag-plein 2 🕐 Hours vary, check website 🌐 kaasmuseum.nl

---

5

Haarlem

🏠 North Holland 🚉
ℹ️ Grote Markt 2; www. visithaarlem.com

Haarlem is the center of the Dutch printing, pharma-ceutical, and bulb-growing industries. Most of the city's main attractions are within easy walking distance of the Grote Markt, a lively square overlooked by the Gothic Grote Kerk. Also known as Sint Bavo's, this huge church

was built between 1400 and 1550. Its highly decorative organ (1735) has been played by both Handel and Mozart. Also on the Grote Markt is the Stadhuis (Town Hall), which dates from 1250 and displays a mixture of architectural styles. The oldest part of

the building is the beamed medieval banqueting hall.

The Amsterdamse Poort, the medieval gateway that once formed part of the city's defenses, was built in 1355.

Haarlem is well known for its *hofjes* (almshouses), which began to appear in the 16th century. Established in 1610, St. Elisabeth's Gasthuis now houses a historical museum. The **Frans Hals Museum Hof** occupies the almshouse where the artist supposedly lived out his last years. In addition to a superb collection of paintings by Hals himself, there is a selection of Dutch paintings and applied art from the 16th and 17th centuries. Contemporary works are displayed alongside the Old Masters to show interesting points of contrast.

Frans Hals Museum Hof

⊘ ⊘ 🏠 Groot Heiligland 62 🕐 11am–5pm Tue–Sat, noon–5pm Sun 🕐 Jan 1, Dec 25 🌐 franshalsmuseum.nl

---

▌ BULB FIELDS OF THE NETHERLANDS

Bulb species cultivated in the Netherlands include lilies, gladioli, daffodils, hyacinths, irises, crocuses, and dahlias. The most famous bulb of all, however, is the tulip. Originally from Turkey, it was first grown in Dutch soil by Carolus Clusius in 1593. Occupying a 19 mile (30 km) strip between Haarlem and Leiden, the Bloembollenstreek is the most important bulb-growing area in the country. From late January, the area blooms with brightly colored bulbs, building to a climax in mid-April when the tulips flower. For a breathtaking showcase of flowering bulbs, visit the Keukenhof gardens, on the outskirts of Lisse and easily reached by bus from Leiden station or Schiphol Airport (Stationsweg Lisse; www.keukenhof.nl). Avoid the temptation to walk into the fields to take photographs.

One of Leiden's canals, lined with modern and 17th-century buildings

6
Leiden

 South Holland 🚊🚌
ℹ️ Stationsweg 26; www.leiden.nl

Leiden is a prosperous town that dates back to Roman times. Its famous university is the oldest in the Netherlands, founded in 1575 by William of Orange. Created in 1587, the university's botanical garden, the Hortus Botanicus der Rijksuniversiteit Leiden, is still open to the public.

One of Leiden's main attractions is the **Rijksmuseum van Oudheden** (National Museum of Antiquities). Established in 1818, it houses an outstanding collection of Egyptian artifacts, including the 1st-century AD Temple of Taffeh. There are also displays of textiles, musical instruments, Etruscan bronzework, and fragments of Roman mosaics and frescoes.

The magnificent Gothic Pieterskerk was built in the 15th century. It has a splendid organ (1642), enclosed in gilded woodwork.

Dating back to 1640, the old Lakenhal (Cloth Hall) now houses the Stedelijk Museum De Lakenhal, with exhibitions of art and furniture from the 16th century onward. The pride of the collection is Lucas van Leyden's Renaissance triptych, *The Last Judgment* (1526–7). Leiden also has an excellent ethnological museum, the **Museum Volkenkunde**, which contains exhibits from many countries and hosts events on traditions, rituals, and practices of other cultures.

Rijksmuseum van Oudheden

♿🟢🕐 🏛️ Rapenburg 28
🕐 10am–5pm Tue–Sun
🚫 Jan 1, Apr 27, Oct 3, Dec 25
🌐 rmo.nl

Museum Volkenkunde

♿🕐 🏛️ Steenstraat 1
🕐 10am–5pm Tue–Sun
🚫 Jan 1, Apr 27, Oct 3, Dec 25
🌐 mv.nl

7
Utrecht

 Utrecht 🚊🚌 ℹ️ Domplein 9; www.visit-utrecht.com

Utrecht was founded by the Romans in AD 47 to protect a strategic river crossing on the Rhine. The town was one of the first places in the Netherlands to embrace Christianity, and in the Middle Ages, it grew into an important religious center. The city retains many of its medieval churches and monasteries. The Domkerk, Utrecht's cathedral, was begun in 1254. Today, only the north and south transepts, two chapels, and the choir remain, along with the 15th-century cloisters and a chapter house. The Domtoren, which stands apart from the cathedral, is one of the tallest towers in the Netherlands, at 367 ft (112 m).

Among Utrecht's many museums are the **Museum Catharijneconvent**, which deals with the troubled history of religion in the Netherlands and owns an award-winning collection of medieval art, and the Nederlands Spoorwegmuseum, a superb railroad museum, housed in the 19th-century Maliebaan station. At the heart of the collection in the **Centraal Museum** is a series of portraits by artist Jan van Scorel, known as the "Utrecht Caravaggisti." There is also an impressive collection of modern and contemporary art, with works by Van Gogh,

→

The Gothic exterior of the Ridderzaal in The Hague

EAT

Crabbetje

Seafood restaurant serving large portions.

 St. Agatenstraat 5, Leiden dvis restaurantcrabbetje.nl

€€€

Meneer Smakers

Bright and friendly canalside restaurant.

Nobelstraat 143, Utrecht smakers.nl

€€€

Restaurant des Indes

This opulent restaurant serves French-inspired steak and seafood.

Lange Voorhout 54-56, The Hague Sun & Mon desindes.nl

€€€

Courbet, and Damien Hirst, as well as sculpture, costume, and furniture collections.

Museum Catharijneconvent

 Lange Nieuwstraat 38 Hours vary, check website Jan 1 catharijneconvent.nl

Centraal Museum

 Agnietenstraat 1 10am-5pm Tue-Sun Jan 1, Apr 27, Dec 25 centraalmuseum.nl

---

❽

The Hague

South Holland Spui 68; www.den haag.com

The political capital of the Netherlands, The Hague (Den Haag or 's-Gravenhage) is home to prestigious institutions, such as the Dutch parliament and the International Court of Justice.

When The Hague became the seat of government in 1586, it was a small town built around the castle of the Counts of Holland. That castle now stands at the heart of the city and forms part of the Binnenhof, where today's parliament sits. The fairy-tale, Gothic **Ridderzaal** (Hall of the Knights), the 13th-century dining hall of Count Floris V, is open to the public when parliament is not in session.

An outstanding collection of works by Dutch Masters Rembrandt, Jan Vermeer, and Jan Steen is assembled at the Royal Picture Gallery at the

Mauritshuis. More Dutch Golden Age paintings are on view at the Museum Bredius and the **Galerij Prins Willem V**.

The Kunstmuseum Den Haag has an applied arts section that includes the world's largest collection of paintings by Piet Mondrian.

The splendid 17th-century Paleis Noordeinde is the office of King Willem-Alexander.

Ridderzaal

 Binnenhof 8a Guided tours only; book online Public hols prodemos.nl

Mauritshuis

Korte Vijverberg 8 Hours vary, check website Jan 1, Dec 25 mauritshuis.nl

Galerij Prins Willem V

Buitenhof 33 noon-5pm Tue-Sun Jan 1, Dec 25 galerijprinswillemv.nl

---

💬 INSIDER TIP
Scheveningen

Only a 15-minute tram ride from the center of The Hague, Scheveningen has clean, sandy beaches and good seafood restaurants. The resort also has a Sea Life Center, and a museum with exhibits of marine biology and local history.

> Following damage during World War II, Rotterdam's old harbor area and river front have been rebuilt in daring and avant-garde styles.

⑨ Delft

 South Holland 🏠 🚌
ℹ️ Kerkstraat 3; www.delft.com

In the Middle Ages Delft's prosperity was based on weaving and brewing, but today the charming town is most famous for its blue-and-white pottery, known as delftware. De Porceleyne Fles is one of two delftware potteries still in operation, and is open for guided tours.

Delft is also the resting place of William of Orange, who commanded the Dutch Revolt against Spanish rule from his headquarters in the town. His richly decorated tomb lies in the **Nieuwe Kerk**, built between 1383 and 1510, but later restored following damage caused by fire and explosion. The former convent that William used as his military headquarters, and where he was assassinated by order of Philip II of Spain, is today the home of the **Stedelijk Museum Het Prinsenhof**. The museum contains a rare collection of antique delftware, as well as tapestries, silverware, medieval sculpture, and portraits of the Dutch royal family.

Other sites of interest are the **Vermeer Centrum Delft**, which explores the enigmatic life and works of Delft's most famous son, 17th-century artist Jan Vermeer, and the **Oude Kerk**, which dates from the 13th century, with an elegant interior dominated by a carved wooden pulpit with an overhanging canopy. At the east end of the north aisle, a simple stone tablet marks the final resting place of Vermeer.

Nieuwe Kerk
🎫 🏠 Markt ⏰ Hours vary, check website 🌐 oudeen nieuwekerkdelft.nl

Stedelijk Museum Het Prinsenhof
🎫 🛍️ 🏠 St Agathaplein 1 ⏰ Mar–Aug: 11am–5pm daily; Sep–Feb: 11am–5pm Tue–Sun 🚫 Jan 1, Apr 27, Dec 25 🌐 prinsenhof-delft.nl

Vermeer Centrum Delft
🎫 🛍️ 🍽️ 🏠 Voldersgracht 21 ⏰ 10am–5pm daily 🚫 Dec 25 🌐 vermeerdelft.nl

Oude Kerk
🎫 🏠 Heilige Geestkerkhof ⏰ Hours vary, check website 🌐 onkd.nl

⑩ Rotterdam

🏠 South Holland 🚉 🚉 🚌
ℹ️ Coolsingel 114; www.rotterdam.info

Rotterdam is at a strategic position where the Rhine meets the North Sea and has long been a center for trade. Barges from the city transport goods deep into the continent, and ocean-going ships carry exports around the world.

DELFTWARE

Delftware was developed from majolica and introduced to the Netherlands by immigrant Italian potters in the 16th century. Settling around Delft and Haarlem, the potters made wall tiles decorated with Dutch motifs such as animals and flowers. Trade with the east brought samples of delicate Chinese porcelain to the Netherlands, and the market for coarser Dutch majolica crashed. By 1650, local potters had adopted the Chinese model and were designing fine plates, vases, and bowls embellished with Dutch landscapes and biblical scenes.

DELFTWARE
PORCELAIN CLOGS

↑ The tilting yellow cubes of the Kubuswoningen complex in Rotterdam

Following damage during World War II, Rotterdam's old harbor area and river front have been rebuilt in daring and avant-garde styles. Piet Blom's Kubuswoningen (Cube Houses) of 1982 are extraordinary apartments set on concrete stilts. More recent eye-catching examples include Renzo Piano's KPN Telecom head office and De Rotterdam by Rem Koolhaas – three connected tower blocks whose tops are slightly off-kilter.

Museums of note here include the **Wereldmuseum Rotterdam**, with its superb ethnological collection of some 1,800 artifacts, and the **Kunsthal**, hosting exhibitions that alternate between traditional "high art" and pop culture. The **Maritiem Museum Rotterdam**, devoted to the history of shipping, was founded by Prince Hendrik, brother of King William III, in 1873. Its main highlight is an iron-clad warship, De Buffel, built in 1868. The excellent Museum Boijmans-van

Beuningen houses one of the Netherlands' finest art collections, but is closed for renovations until 2026.

For a spectacular view of the city, take the elevator up the 60-ft (185-m) high Euromast. Built in 1960, it is the tallest construction in the country, and has a restaurant and an exhibition area.

Wereldmuseum Rotterdam

⊗⊜⊜ 🖪Willemskade 25
⊙10am–5pm Tue–Sun
🖪Jan 1, Apr 27, Dec 25
⊠wereldmuseum.nl

Kunsthal

⊗⊜⊜ 🖪Westzeedijk 341
⊙10am–5pm Tue–Sat, 11am–5pm Sun & public hols 🖪Jan 1, Apr 27, Dec 25 ⊠kunsthal.nl

Maritiem Museum Rotterdam

⊗⊜⊜⊜ 🖪Leuvehaven 1
⊙10am–5pm Tue–Sat, 11am–5pm Sun & public hols 🖪Jan 1, Apr 27, Dec 25 ⊠maritiem museum.nl

EAT

Huszár
This waterside brasserie occupies a redesigned industrial space. Its menu of no-nonsense Dutch and European dishes uses local organic produce.

🖪Hooikade 13, Delft
⊠huszar.nl

€€€

Restaurant de Jong
Chef Jim de Jong's spectacular six-course menu uses local produce, with vegetables as the focus.

🖪Nobelstraat 143, Rotterdam
⊠restaurantdejong.nl

€€€

PRACTICAL
INFORMATION

Here you will find all the essential advice and information you will need before and during your stay in the Netherlands.

AT A GLANCE

CURRENCY
Euro (EUR)

TIME ZONE
CET/CEST. Central European Summer Time runs from the last Sunday in March to the last Sunday in October.

LANGUAGE
Dutch

ELECTRICITY SUPPLY
Power sockets are type C and F, fitting two-pronged plugs. Standard voltage is 230V.

EMERGENCY NUMBERS

GENERAL EMERGENCY

112

TAP WATER
Unless otherwise stated, tap water in the Netherlands is safe to drink.

Getting There

Amsterdam's Schiphol Airport is a major international transport hub for destinations around the globe. Schiphol is extremely well connected to Amsterdam city center by train, bus, and taxi, and is also connected to other cities in the Netherlands.

Ferry companies offering car and passenger services from the UK to the Netherlands include P&O Ferries, with daily sailings between Hull and Rotterdam, and Stena Line, which sails from Harwich to Hook of Holland. Additionally, DFDS Seaways runs an overnight ferry service from Newcastle to Ijmuiden.

International rail routes provide a fast and efficient link between Amsterdam and many other European cities. High-speed Thalys trains run to Brussels in 2 hours 30 minutes, and to Paris in 4 hours. The Eurostar offers a direct connection between London and Amsterdam, via Rotterdam, while Stena Line offers a train and ferry combination between the two cities.

Long-distance bus travel is an inexpensive, if slow, way to reach the Netherlands. National Express has at least two daily services from the UK to Amsterdam, via the Channel Tunnel.

Personal Security

The Netherlands is generally a safe country, but it is a good idea to take sensible precautions against pickpockets. If you have anything stolen, report the crime as soon as possible to the nearest police station. Get a copy of the crime report in order to claim on your insurance. .

Health

EU citizens with a European Health Insurance Card (EHIC) are entitled to free emergency medical care in the Netherlands, but it is also advisable to take out some form of supplementary health insurance. Visitors from outside the EU must arrange their own private medical insurance to cvoer their trip.

Minor health problems can be dealt with by a chemist (drogist), who stocks non-prescription

drugs. If you need prescription medicines, go to a pharmacy *(apotheek)*. Mosquitoes can be an irritant in Amsterdam, where they are attracted by the canals, so bring plenty of repellent sprays and antihistamine creams with you.

Passports and Visas

Citizens of the EU, Australia, New Zealand, the US, and Canada need only a valid passport to enter the Netherlands. For visa information specific to your home country, consult your nearest Netherlands embassy or check online.

Travelers with Specific Needs

Accessible Travel Netherlands reviews the accessibility and user-friendliness of restaurants, shops, transport, and public buildings in the country. Main train stations have tactile guidance lines and mobile ramps, and a carer or companion can travel for free through the **NS Travel Assistance** service. Many trains have doors with wheelchair access, and most double-decker trains have wheelchair-accessible toilets. All main pedestrian crossings are equipped with sound for the visually impaired.

Accessible Travel Netherlands
w accessibletravelnl.com
NS Travel Assistance
w ns.nl/en/travel-information/traveling-with-a-functional-disability

Money

Most establishments accept major credit, debit, and prepaid currency cards, but it's always a good idea to carry some cash, just in case. Contactless payments are widely accepted.

Cell Phones and Wi-Fi

Many cafés and restaurants offer free Wi-Fi, though some only permit use on the condition that you make a purchase. Free Wi-Fi hotspots are widely available in Amsterdam's city center.

Visitors traveling to the Netherlands with EU tariffs can use their devices abroad without being affected by data roaming charges. Visitors from other countries, should make sure to check their contracts before departure in order to avoid unexpected charges.

Getting Around

The Dutch railroad system, operated by **NS** (Nederlandse Spoorwegen), is one of the most modern and efficient in Europe, with an extensive route network. The NS website offers up-to-date information on train trips for tourists, plus details of special fares.

Buses in the Netherlands are reliable and efficient, and they accept the **OV-chipkaart**, a card that can be loaded with credit (at machines found at bus and train stations, post offices, and supermarkets) and used on all means of public transport. The card is held against a card-reader upon entering and exiting the bus, train, or tram, and the fare is debited depending on the distance traveled.

Major roads (marked N) and highways (labeled A or E) are generally well maintained. When driving in towns and cities, especially in Amsterdam, be careful of cyclists, trams, taxis, and pedestrians. Most of the principal international car-rental firms have offices in Amsterdam and at Schiphol Airport, but local companies are cheaper.

NS
w ns.nl
OV-chipkaart
w ov-chipkaart.nl

Visitor Information

The **NBTC** (Netherlands Board of Tourism and Conventions) has offices in many cities worldwide. Within the Netherlands, the state-run tourist-information organization is the **Vereniging Voor Vreemdelingenverkeer** (VVV). They have around 450 offices throughout the country, which can provide information on sights, transportation, and events, and will also change money and reserve hotel rooms. The **Museum Card** (Museumkaart), available from branches of the VVV and many museums, is valid for a year, and allows free admission to more than 400 museums and galleries. Don't forget to register your card online.

Museum Card
w museumkaart.nl/Registration
NBTC
w holland.com
VVV
w vvv.nl

SPAIN

Spain's past is beleaguered by power struggles. From the 11th century BC, the coastal regions of the Iberian Peninsula were colonized by sophisticated eastern Mediterranean civilizations, including the Phoenicians, Greeks, and Carthaginians. The Romans arrived in 218 BC to take possession of the area's huge mineral wealth, but the fall of the Roman Empire in the 5th century AD left Spain in the hands of the Visigoths, who were subsequently conquered by the Moors around 711. The Moors established al Andalus, Europe's only major Muslim territory, which was largely reconquered in the 11th century by Christian kingdoms of the north. The 1469 marriage of Fernando of Aragón and Isabel of Castile – the "Catholic Monarchs" – led to Spanish unity. They took Granada, the last Moorish stronghold, in 1492. In the same year, Columbus reached the Americas, and the conquistadors began plundering the civilizations of the so-called New World. The 17th century saw a blossoming of artistic and literary output, but it occurred against a backdrop of economic deterioration and ruinous wars. The decline continued in the 19th century, with an invasion by Napoleon's troops and the loss of Spain's American colonies. Political instability led to dictatorship in the 1920s and, a decade later, the Spanish Civil War. The victor, the Nationalist General Franco, ruled by repression until his death in 1975. Since then, Spain has been a democratic state.

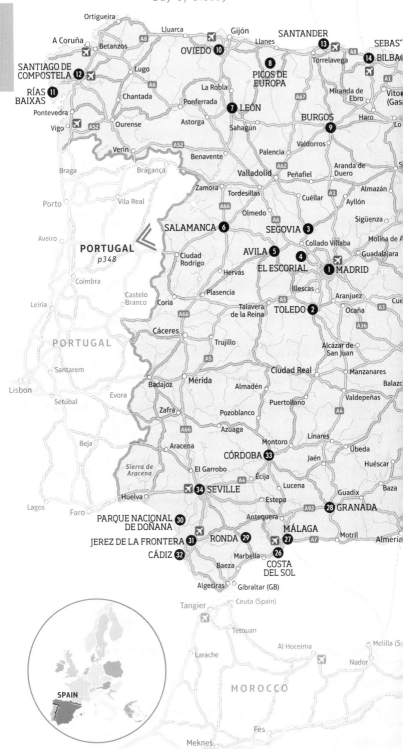

SPAIN

❶
MADRID

✈ ▤ ▦ 🌐 www.esmadrid.com

The origins of Spain's capital date back to AD 852, when the Moors built a fortress near the Manzanares river. It was not until 1561, however, that Madrid became the capital of a newly formed nation-state. The city has a host of glittering attractions, but also feels surprisingly intimate. This is particularly true of its historic heart, where the cobbled streets and tiled taverns have barely changed in centuries. But the capital is far from staid; after dark Madrid really comes to life, with tiny tapas joints, chic cocktail bars, and pulsing clubs.

①
Plaza Mayor

Ⓜ Opera

For hundreds of years, this beautiful 17th-century square was a center of dramatic activity, with bullfights, executions, pageants, and trials by the Inquisition taking place here.

At its center is an equestrian statue of Felipe III, who ordered the square's construction.

Designed by architect Juan Gómez de Mora, the square was started in 1617 and built in just two years. The first major public event was the beatification of the city's patron, St. Isidore, in 1621. Perhaps the greatest occasion, however, was the arrival from Italy of Carlos III (Carlos VII of Naples) in 1760. He became king of Spain after his half-brother, Fernando VI, died without an heir.

The elegant arcades that line the Plaza Mayor are today thronged with cafés and craft stores. One of the more interesting buildings is the Casa de la Panadería, whose facade is decorated with splendid allegorical paintings.

On Sundays, the square is the venue for a collectors' market, with stalls selling items such as coins, stamps, and books.

②
Puerta del Sol

Ⓜ Sol

With its many shops and cafés Puerta del Sol ("Gateway of the Sun") is one of Madrid's liveliest areas. The square marks the site of the original

eastern entrance to the city, once occupied by a gatehouse and a castle.

A statue of Carlos III stands at the center of the square. On its southern edge is the Casa

de Correos, dating from the 1760s. Originally the city's post office, it later became the headquarters of the Ministry of the Interior. During the Franco regime, the police cells below the building were the site of human-rights abuses. In front of the building, a symbol on the ground marks Kilometer Zero, considered the center of Spain's road network.

On the opposite side of the square is a bronze statue of the symbol of Madrid – a bear reaching for the fruit of a *madroño* (strawberry tree).

Puerta del Sol has witnessed many key historical events, such as the 1912 assassination of the liberal prime minister José Canalejas, and the proclamation of the Second Republic in 1931.

El Rastro

🏠 Calle de la Ribera de Curtidores Ⓜ La Latina, Embajadores, Tirso de Molina 🕐 9am–3pm Sun & public hols

Madrid's famous flea market was established in the Middle Ages. It is still popular with

↑ Overlooking Plaza de Cibeles, in Madrid's bustling city center

countless bargain-hunters, who come here to browse around the many stalls selling a huge range of wares – from vintage clothes to furniture. With its central hub in Plaza de Cascorro, the market's main streets are Calle de la Ribera de Curtidores and Calle de Embajadores, the latter of which runs down past the Baroque facade of the Iglesia de San Cayetano.

💬 INSIDER TIP
Getting Around

The metro is the most efficient way of getting around. Lines 1, 2, 3, 5, and 10 serve the main sights; line 8 links Nuevos Ministerios and the airport. Useful buses include the 50, 51, 52, 53, and 150 to the Puerta del Sol, and 2, 9, 14, 15, 27, 74, and 146 to the Plaza de Cibeles. Buses to Barajas Airport depart from the terminal below Plaza de Colón.

Traffic along the Gran Vía, one of Madrid's main thoroughfares ↑

④
Gran Vía

 Plaza de España, Santo Domingo, Callao, Gran Vía

A main traffic artery of the modern city, the Gran Vía was inaugurated in 1910. Lined with movie theaters, souvenir stores, restaurants, and hotels, this grand avenue also has

---

TOP 3 MADRID FIESTAS

San Isidro
Madrid's great party is held around May 15 in honor of St. Isidore, the city's patron saint. The event is marked by art exhibitions, concerts, and fireworks displays.

Dos de Mayo
Exhibitions are held in the Malasaña neighborhood to commemorate the day the people of Madrid rose up against Napoleon's troops on May 2, 1808.

New Year's Eve
The nation focuses on the Puerta del Sol at midnight as crowds gather to swallow a grape on each chime of the clock.

---

many buildings of architectural interest. The most interesting buildings are clustered at the Alcalá end of the street, including the French-inspired Edificio Metrópolis and the Edificio la Estrella (No. 10). The latter is a good example of the eclectic mix of Neo-Classical design and ornamental detail that was fashionable when the street was first developed. Look out for some interesting carved-stone decoration, such as the striking gargoyle-like caryatids at No. 12.

Farther along the Gran Vía, around the Plaza del Callao, are a number of Art Deco buildings, including the well-known Capitol cinema and bingo hall, built in the 1930s.

---

⑤
Monasterio de las Descalzas Reales

 Plaza de las Descalzas 3 **Opera** **10am-2pm & 4-6:30pm Tue-Sat; 10am-3pm Sun & public hols** **Jan 1 & 6, Easter, May 1, Dec 24, 25, & 31** **patrimo nionacional.es**

This religious building is a rare surviving example of 16th-century architecture in Madrid. Around 1560, Felipe II's sister, Doña Juana, decided to convert a medieval palace on this site into a convent.

Doña Juana's rank accounts for the massive store of art amassed by the Descalzas Reales (Royal Barefoot Sisters), which includes a fresco of Felipe IV's family and, above the main staircase, a ceiling by Baroque painter Claudio Coello. The Sala de Tapices contains stunning tapestries, while paintings on display include works by Titian, Murillo, Zurbarán, and Ribera.

---

⑥
Museo Nacional Thyssen-Bornemisza

Paseo del Prado 8 **Banco de España, Sevilla** **1, 2, 5, 9, 14, 15, 20** **Noon-4pm Mon, 10am-7pm Tue-Sun (to 9pm on Sat for temporary exhibitions)** **Jan 1, May 1, Dec 25** **museothyssen.org**

This magnificent museum houses a collection of art assembled by Baron Heinrich Thyssen-Bornemisza and his son, Hans Heinrich. From its beginnings in the 1920s, the collection was intended to illustrate the history of Western art, from the 14th to the 20th century. In 2004, 200 paintings from the Carmen Thyssen-Bornemisza Collection were added. Among the museum's exhibits are masterpieces by Titian, Goya, and Van Gogh.

One of the strongest points of the collection is the series of Dutch and Flemish works. Highlights here include Jan van Eyck's *The Annunciation* (c. 1435–41), Petrus Christus's *Our Lady of the Dry Tree* (c. 1450), and *The Toilet of Venus* (c. 1629), by Peter Paul Rubens.

An extension has created further gallery space to display the museum's collection of Impressionist works, mainly from the 19th century.

Palacio Real

 Calle de Bailén Opera, Plaza de España 3, 25, 39, 148 10am–6pm daily (Apr–Sep: to 8pm) Jan 1 & 6, May 1 & 15, Sep 9, Dec 24, 25, & 31 patrimonio nacional.es

The vast and lavish Palacio Real (Royal Palace) was commissioned by Felipe V after the royal fortress that had occupied the site for centuries was ravaged by fire in 1734. The palace was the home of Spanish royalty until the abdication of Alfonso XIII in 1931. Today it is used by the present king for state occasions only.

The exuberant decor of the interior reflects the tastes of the Bourbon kings Carlos III and Carlos IV. The walls and ceiling of the Porcelain Room, commissioned by the former, are covered in green-and-white royal porcelain, which is embossed with cherubs and wreaths. Named after its Neapolitan designer, the Gasparini Room is equally lavishly decorated. In the adjacent antechamber hangs a portrait of Carlos IV by Goya. Other star attractions are the Dining Room, with its fine ceiling paintings and superb Flemish tapestries, and the 18th-century Throne Room.

Plaza de Toros de las Ventas

 Calle Alcalá 237 Ventas For bullfights & guided visits only las-ventas.com

Whatever your opinion of bullfighting, Las Ventas is undoubtedly one of the most beautiful bullrings in Spain. Built in 1929 in Neo-Mudéjar style, it replaced the city's original bullring, which stood near the Puerta de Alcalá. Outside the bullring are monuments to two renowned Spanish bullfighters: Antonio Bienvenida and José Cubero.

Adjoining the building, the **Museo Taurino** provides a fascinating history of the various rituals associated with bullfighting, and contains memorabilia, such as portraits and sculptures of famous matadors. There is also a display of bullfighting tools, including capes and *banderillas* – sharp darts used to wound the bull.

Museo Taurino
  Calle Alcalá 237 10am–6pm daily (days of bullfights: to 4pm) lasventastour.com

↑ An elegant, lamp-lined staircase inside the 18th-century Palacio Real

⑨ 🛼 🚲 🍴 📷 🛍️

MUSEO DEL PRADO

🏛️ Paseo del Prado Ⓜ Estación del Arte, Banco de España 🚌 9, 10, 14, 19, 27, 34, 37, 45
🕐 10am–8pm daily (to 7pm Sun) 🚫 Jan 1, May 1, Dec 25 🌐 museodelprado.es

A must for any art lover, the Prado Museum houses the world's greatest assembly of Spanish paintings from the 12th to the 19th century, including major works by Velázquez and Goya. It also displays impressive foreign collections, particularly of Italian and Flemish works.

The Neo-Classical main building was designed in 1785 by Juan de Villanueva on the orders of Carlos III to house the Natural History Cabinet. However, it was under his grandson, Charles III, that it opened as the Royal Museum of Paintings and Sculptures in 1819. The collection was initially composed of 311 Spanish paintings, but the current body of more than 20,000 works reflects the historical power of the Spanish Crown. The Low Countries and parts of Italy were under Spanish domination for centuries, and they are well represented in the collection, while the 18th century was an era of French influence, following the Bourbon accession to the Spanish throne.

Upon the deposition of Isabella II in 1868, the museum was nationalized, and the collection grew beyond its original home. The first expansion took place in 1918, and buildings have been added at intervals ever since. In 2007, the Spanish architect Rafael Moneo constructed a new gallery in the cloisters of San Jerónimo's church, where temporary exhibitions are located. Norman Foster and Carlos Rubio Carvajal's redesign of the former army museum (Salón de Reinos) was chosen in 2016 as the museum's next expansion. The Prado is worthy of repeated visits, but if you go only once, be sure to see the Spanish works of the 17th century.

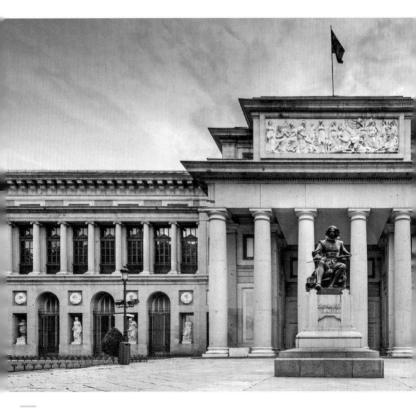

INSIDER TIP
Be Late

If you're on a budget, head to the museum two hours before it closes, when admission is free. You'll have a lot to cover in a short time, but it's the perfect way to get an arty fix.

↑ The large interior of one of the Prado's popular galleries

← Admiring the museum's collection of sculptures of the Greek Muses

ART AT WAR

As tensions peaked and the Spanish Civil War commenced, the League of Nations recommended the removal of some of the Museo del Prado's most precious treasures. Museum staff sent 353 paintings, 168 drawings, and the Dauphin's Treasure first to Valencia, then on to Girona, before they finally arrived safely in Geneva. Although the Spanish Civil War ended in 1939, the advent of World War II meant that the art had to travel back to the Prado – across French territory – under the cover of darkness.

←

The museum's imposing Goya Square entrance as the sun begins to set

↑ Visitors in front of *The Clothed Maja,* an early-19th-century work by Goya

Exploring the Collection

The museum's extensive permanent collection is arranged chronologically over three main floors. Classical sculpture is on the ground floor, the works of Velázquez on the first floor, and the extensive Goya collection across the Murillo side of all three floors. The permanent collection is accessed via the Velázquez and Goya entrances. Visitors to the temporary exhibitions should use the Jerónimos entrance.

Did You Know?

During the 1734 Palacio Real fire, *Las Meninas* was hurled from a bedroom window.

Art enthusiasts viewing paintings in one of the Prado's light-filled galleries ↓

The Collection

Spanish Painting

Right up to the 19th century, Spanish painting focused on religious and royal themes. Examples of Spain's early-medieval art in the Prado include the anonymous mural paintings from the Holy Cross hermitage in Maderuelo. Spanish Gothic art can be seen in the works of Bartolomé Bermejo and Fernando Gallego, while Renaissance features began to emerge in the paintings of Pedro de Berruguete and Fernando Yáñez de la Almedina. Among examples of 16th-century Mannerism are works by Pedro Machuca and Luis de Morales "the Divine." One of the great masters of this period was the Cretan-born artist El Greco, who made his home in Toledo. The distortion of the human figure, typical of the Mannerist style, is carried to an extreme in his painting *The Adoration of the Shepherds* (1612-14). The Golden Age of the 17th century is best represented by Diego Velázquez, Spain's leading court painter. Examples of his royal portraits and religious and mythological paintings are displayed, including his masterpiece, *Las Meninas* (1656). Another great Spanish painter, Francisco de Goya, revived Spanish art in the 18th century. His later work embraces the horrors of war, as seen in *The 3rd of May* (1814), and the series known as The Black Paintings.

Flemish and Dutch Painting

▷ Exceptional Flemish works of art include Rogier van der Weyden's masterpiece, *The Deposition* (c. 1430), and some of Hieronymus Bosch's major paintings, such as the *Temptation of St. Anthony* (c. 1500). Among the 16th-century paintings is the superb *Triumph of Death* (1562) by Brueghel the Elder. There are nearly 100 canvases by the 17th-century Flemish painter Peter Paul Rubens, of which the greatest is *The Adoration of the Magi (right)*. The two most notable Dutch paintings on display are both by Rembrandt: *Artemisia* (c. 1500) and a fine self-portrait.

Italian Painting

◁ The most remarkable Italian paintings are Botticelli's wooden panels depicting *The Story of Nastagio degli Onesti*, Raphael's *The Holy Family with a Lamb* (1507; left), and *Christ Washing the Disciples' Feet* (c. 1547), by Tintoretto. Venetian masters Titian - Charles V's court painter - and Veronese are equally well represented. Also on display are works by Giordano, Fra Angelico, Caravaggio and Tiepolo.

French and German Painting

▷ This section contains works by Poussin, Claude Lorrain, and Antoine Watteau. German art is represented by Albrecht Dürer's lively *Self-Portrait* (1498) and his classical depictions of Adam and Eve *(right)*., as well as by the works of Lucas Cranach and Anton Raphael Mengs.

Casón del Buen Retiro

The Casón is a study center, housing restoration studios, a specialist school, and an art library (special permission required). On weekends, there are guided visits of the dome painted by Luca Giordano (c. 1697).

Centro de Arte Reina Sofía

🏛 Calle Santa Isabel 52
Ⓜ Estación del Arte 🚍 6, 8, 10, 14, 19, 27, 45, 55, 60, 78
🕐 10am-9pm Mon & Wed-Sat, 10am-7pm Sun (to 7:30pm for temporary exhibitions) 🔒 Main public hols 🌐 museoreinasofia.es

Housed in an 18th-century former general hospital, with three additional modern glass buildings, this superb museum traces art through the 20th century. It houses major works by such influential artists as Pablo Picasso, Salvador Dalí, Joan Miró, and Eduardo Chillida. There is also space dedicated to

 INSIDER TIP
Free Time

Entry to the Centro de Arte Reina Sofía is always free after 7pm. However, for a free visit without time constraints, visit after 1:30pm on Sunday, when you'll be able to wander at a more leisurely pace.

post-World War II movements, including Abstract, Pop, and Minimal Art.

The main highlight of the collection is Picasso's *Guernica* (1937). This Civil War protest painting was inspired by the mass air attack in 1937 on the Basque village of Gernika-Lumo by German pilots flying for the Nationalist air force.

Museo Arqueológico Nacional

🏛 Calle Serrano 13
Ⓜ Serrano, Retiro 🚍 1, 9, 19, 51, 74 🕐 9:30am-8pm Tue-Sat, 9:30am-3pm Sun & public hols 🔒 Jan 1 & 6, May 1, Nov 9, Dec 24, 25, & 31 🌐 man.es

Founded by Isabel II in 1867, Madrid's National Archaeological Museum has hundreds of fascinating exhibits, which range from the prehistoric era to the 19th century.

One of the highlights of the prehistoric section is the exhibition on the ancient civilization of El Argar (1800–1100 BC) – an advanced agrarian society that flourished in southeast Spain. There is also a display of jewelry uncovered

at the Roman settlement of Numantia, near Soria, and a 5th-century BC bust, *La Dama de Elche*.

The museum's ground floor is largely devoted to the period between Roman and Mudéjar Spain, and contains some impressive Roman mosaics.

Outstanding pieces from the Visigothic period include a collection of 7th-century gold votive crowns from Toledo province, known as the Treasure of Guarrazar. Also on show are examples of Andalusian pottery from the Islamic era and various Romanesque exhibits, among them an ivory crucifix carved in 1063 for King Fernando I. Steps outside the museum's entrance lead underground to an exact replica of the Altamira caves in Cantabria – complete with their Paleolithic paintings. The earliest engravings and drawings at the site date back to around 18,000 BC, while the boldly colored bison paintings date from around 13,000 BC.

→

The 19th-century Palacio de Cristal, across a peaceful lake in the Parque del Retiro

The airy courtyard of the Centro de Arte Reina Sofía, designed by Jean Nouvel

Museo de América

🏛 Avenida de los Reyes Católicos 6 Ⓜ Moncloa 🕐 9:30am-3pm Tue-Sat (to 7pm Thu), 10am-3pm Sun & public hols 📅 Jan 1 & 6, May 1, Dec 24, 25 & 31 🌐 mecd.gob.es/museo deamerica

This fine museum houses a collection of artifacts relating to Spain's colonization of the Americas. Many of the exhibits, which date back to prehistoric times, were brought to Europe by the early explorers of the New World. The collection is arranged thematically, with individual rooms dedicated to subjects such as society, religion, and communication. One of the undoubted highlights of the museum is the fascinating Mayan *Códice Tro-cortesiano* (AD 1250–1500) from Mexico – a hieroglyphic parchment illustrated with scenes of everyday life. Other interesting items include the Treasure of the Quimbayas, pre-Columbian gold and silver items dating from

AD 500–1000, and the display of contemporary folk art from some of Spain's former American colonies.

Parque del Retiro

Ⓜ Retiro, Ibiza, Estación del Arte 🕐 6am-10pm daily (Apr-Sep: to midnight) 🌐 parquedelretiro.es

The Retiro Park formed part of Felipe IV's royal-palace complex. All that remains of the palace is the Casón del Buen Retiro (now part of the Prado museum) and the Salón de Reinos (the former army museum, also soon to be part of the Prado).

First fully opened to the public in 1869, the Retiro remains a popular place for relaxing in Madrid. The park has a pleasure lake, where rowing boats can be hired. On one side of the lake is a half-moon colonnade, in front of which stands an equestrian statue of King Alfonso XII.

To the south of the lake are two attractive palaces. The Neo-Classical Palacio de Velázquez and the Palacio de Cristal (Crystal Palace) were built by Velázquez Bosco in the late 19th century and hold contemporary art exhibitions.

Botín

The world's oldest restaurant, set in rustic dining rooms, is justly lauded for its excellent *cochinillo* (roast suckling pig).

🏛 Calle Cuchilleros 17 🌐 botin.es

€€€

Mercado de San Miguel

An elegant century-old glass-and-iron construction houses this gastro food court.

🏛 Plaza de San Miguel 🌐 mercadode sanmiguel.es

€€€

Casa Ciriaco

A Madrid institution serving traditional dishes. It was once a meeting place for the literary set.

🏛 Calle Mayor 84 🌐 casaciriaco.es

€€€

TriCiclo

Superb modern Spanish dishes come in three different sizes to fit every budget.

🏛 Calle Santa María 28 🌐 eltriciclo.es

€€€

Casa Alberto

This *taberna* serves Madrilenian dishes in a wood-paneled room decorated with pictures of bullfighters.

🏛 Calle de las Huertas 18 🕐 Sun dinner, Mon 🌐 casaalberto.es

€€€

A SHORT WALK
PASEO DEL PRADO

Distance 1.5 miles (2.5 km) **Nearest metro** Banco de España **Time** 30 minutes

The Paseo del Prado was laid out in the late 18th century – before the museums and lavish hotels of east Madrid took shape – and it soon became a fashionable spot for a stroll. Today, the Paseo's main attraction lies in its museums and art galleries. Most notable are the Museo del Prado (just south of the Plaza Cánovas del Castillo) and the Museo Nacional Thyssen-Bornemisza, both displaying world-famous collections of paintings. Among the monuments built under Carlos III are the Puerta de Alcalá, the Fuente de Neptuno, and the Fuente de Cibeles, which stand in the middle of busy roundabouts.

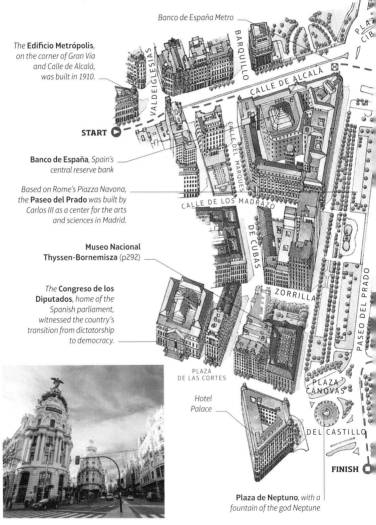

Banco de España Metro

The **Edificio Metrópolis**, on the corner of Gran Vía and Calle de Alcalá, was built in 1910.

BARQUILLO

VALDEIGLESIAS

CALLE DE ALCALÁ

START ▶

Banco de España, Spain's central reserve bank

CALLE DEL MARQUES

Based on Rome's Piazza Navona, the **Paseo del Prado** was built by Carlos III as a center for the arts and sciences in Madrid.

CALLE DE LOS MADRAZO

Museo Nacional Thyssen-Bornemisza (p292)

DE CUBAS

The **Congreso de los Diputados**, home of the Spanish parliament, witnessed the country's transition from dictatorship to democracy.

ZORRILLA

PASEO DEL PRADO

PLAZA DE LAS CORTES

PLAZA CÁNOVAS

Hotel Palace

DEL CASTILLO

FINISH ▶

Plaza de Neptuno, with a fountain of the god Neptune

↑ The Parisian facade of the Edificio Metrópolis, on the Gran Vía

The Monumento del Dos de Mayo

The **Plaza de Cibeles** features a fountain with a statue of the Roman goddess Cybele.

The 19th-century **Palacio de Linares** houses the Casa de América.

Palacio de Comunicaciones

PLAZA DE LA INDEPENDENCIA

CALLE DE ALCALÁ

ALFONSO XII

CALLE DE MONTALBAN

CALLE DE

CALLE DE ALFONSO XII

CALLE ANTONIO MAURA

LA LEALTAD

LLE FELIPE IV

MORETO

↑ Statue of the Roman goddess Cybele in Plaza de Cibeles

Sculpted from granite, the **Puerta de Alcalá**, *a former gateway into the city, is especially beautiful when floodlit at night.*

The **Museo Nacional de Artes Decorativas** was founded in 1912 as a showcase for Spanish ceramics and interior design.

The **Salón de Reinos**, now part of the Prado Museum, has some halls decorated by Velázquez.

Casón del Buen Retiro

The **Hotel Ritz**, with its belle-epoque interior, is one of the most elegant hotels in the whole of Spain.

| 0 meters | 100 | N |
| 0 yards | 100 | ↑ |

2

TOLEDO

 Castilla-La Mancha 🚗🚌 🗺 Plaza del Consistorio 1; www.toledo-turismo.com

Picturesquely sited on a hill above the River Tagus, is the richly historic center of Toledo. The Romans built a fortress on the site of the present-day Alcázar, while in the Middle Ages, Toledo was a melting pot of Christian, Muslim, and Jewish cultures. It was during this period that the city's most outstanding monument – its cathedral – was built. The painter El Greco came to live here in the 16th century, and today the city is home to many of his works.

Did You Know?

Toledo is famous for its marzipan, said to have originated in the 13th century at the convent of San Clemente.

Alcázar

📍 Calle Unión s/n
📞 925 23 88 00
🕐 11am–5pm Tue–Sun

Charles V's fortified palace stands on the site of former Roman, Visigothic, and Muslim fortresses. In 1936, during the Spanish Civil War, it was almost completely destroyed during a 70-day siege by the Republicans. Now restored, the Alcázar houses the Museo del Ejército (National Army Museum), and the siege headquarters have been preserved as a monument to Nationalist heroism. It is also home to the

Borbón-Lorenzana Library (open to the public), which contains 100,000 books and manuscripts from the 16th to the 19th century.

Puerta Antigua de Bisagra

When Alfonso VI of Castile conquered Toledo in 1085, he entered it through this gateway – the only one in the city to have kept its original 10th-century military architecture. The towers feature horseshoe arches and are topped by a 12th-century Arab gatehouse.

Monasterio de San Juan de los Reyes (600 yds/550 m) ⑦

Sinagoga de Santa María la Blanca (550 yds/500 m) ⑩

⑤

Sinagoga del Tránsito (550 yds/500 m) ⑥

⑨

Casa-Museo de El Greco (500 yds/450 m)

INSIDER TIP
Stay Overnight

Toledo is easily reached from Madrid by rail, bus, or car, and is then best explored on foot. To visit all the main sights you need at least two days. Avoid the crowds by going midweek – and stay for a night to experience the city at its most atmospheric.

←

Toledo's historic center, with the illuminated Alcázar high on a hill

↑ Iglesia de Santiago del Arrabal (330 yds/300 m)

Puerta Antigua de Bisagra (330 yds/300 m) ②

Puerta Cristo de la Luz

The Mezquita del Cristo de la Luz, one of the city's two remaining Muslim

The Plaza de Zocodover is the city's main square, with many cafés and shops.

CALLE DE LOS ALFILERITOS

ARDENAL LORENZANA

CALLE DE ALFONSO X

ROMÁN

PLAZA DE ZOCODOVER

CUESTA DE CARLOS V

④

①

ALFONSO XII

CALLE DE LA TRINIDAD

PLAZA MAYOR

③

CALLE DEL CARDENAL CISNEROS

The Archbishop's Palace is a 16th-century building with an austere Renaissance design.

↑ The interior of the Iglesia de Santo Tomé, thought to date back to the 12th century

③
Cathedral

🏛 Calle del Cardenal Cisneros 1 🕐 10am-6pm Mon-Sat, 2-6pm Sun 🌐 catedralprimada.es

The splendor of Toledo's cathedral reflects its history as the spiritual heart of the Spanish church and the seat of the Primate of all Spain. Work began in 1226 on the site of a 7th-century church, but the last vaults were not completed until 1493. This long period of construction explains the cathedral's mixture of styles: the exterior is pure French Gothic, while inside, Spanish decorative

styles, such as Mudéjar – a hybrid Christian-Islamic style – and Plateresque, are used.

Among the cathedral's most outstanding features are the polychrome reredos of the high altar (1504) and the choir. In the treasury is a 16th-century Gothic silver monstrance, over 10 ft (3 m) high. Standing out from the mainly Gothic interior, the Transparente is a stunning Baroque altarpiece of marble, jasper, and bronze, sculpted by Narciso Tomé.

④
Museo de Santa Cruz

🏛 Calle Cervantes 3 🕐 9:30am-6:30pm Mon-Sat, 10am-2pm Sun 🚫 Jan 1, May 1, Dec 25 🌐 patrimonio historicoclm.es

This museum of fine arts has a superb collection of medieval and Renaissance tapestries, paintings, and sculptures. There are also works by the Cretan artist El Greco, as well as examples of two typical Toledan crafts: armor and damascened swords, the latter made by inlaying blackened steel with gold wire. The museum is housed in a fine renovated Renaissance building and has an elegant courtyard.

⑤
Iglesia de Santo Tomé

🏛 Plaza del Conde 4 🕐 10am-5:45pm daily (Mar-mid-Oct: to 6:45pm) 🌐 santotome.org

Visitors come to this church mainly to admire El Greco's masterpiece *The Burial of the Count of Orgaz*. Santo Tomé's tower is one of the best examples of Mudéjar architecture in Toledo.

⑥
Sinagoga del Tránsito, Museo Sefardí

🏛 Calle Samuel Leví 🕐 9:30am-6pm Tue-Sat (Apr-Oct: to 7:30pm), 10am-3pm Sun 🚫 Public hols 🌐 museosefardi.mcu.es

The Sinagoga del Tránsito, a 14th-century former synagogue, is the setting for this museum dedicated to the Sephardic (Spanish Jewish) culture. A wonderfully elaborate and well-preserved Mudéjar interior is hidden behind the synagogue's humble facade.

Monasterio de San Juan de los Reyes

📍 Calle de los Reyes Católicos 17 🕐 10am-5:45pm daily (Mar-mid-Oct: to 6:45pm) 🚫 Jan 1, Dec 25 🌐 sanjuandelosreyes.org

This ornate monastery was commissioned by the Catholic Monarchs in honor of their victory at the battle of Toro in 1476. Largely the work of Juan Guas, the church's main Isabelline structure was completed in 1496. The Gothic cloister (1510) has a multicolored Mudéjar ceiling.

Iglesia de Santiago del Arrabal

📍 Calle Real del Arrabal 📞 925-22 06 36 🕐 For Mass

One of Toledo's most beautiful Mudéjar monuments, this church can be identified by its tower, which dates from the 12th century. The church itself, built slightly later, has a beautiful woodwork ceiling and an ornate Mudéjar pulpit.

EL GRECO

Born in Crete in 1541, El Greco ("the Greek") came to Toledo in 1577 to paint the altarpiece in the convent of Santo Domingo el Antiguo. Enchanted by the city, he stayed here, painting religious portraits and altarpieces. He came to be closely identified with Toledo and died in the city in 1614.

Casa-Museo de El Greco

📍 Paseo del Tránsito 🕐 9:30am-6pm Tue-Sat (May-Oct: to 7:30pm), 10am-3pm Sun 🌐 museodelgreco.mcu.es

It is uncertain whether El Greco actually lived in or simply near to this house, now a museum containing a collection of his works. Canvases include the superb series *Christ and the Apostles*. On the ground floor is a chapel with a fine Mudéjar ceiling and works of art by painters of the Toledan School, such as Luis Tristán.

Sinagoga de Santa María la Blanca

📍 Calle de los Reyes Católicos 4 🕐 10am-5:45pm daily (Mar-mid-Oct: to 6:45pm) 🚫 Jan 1, Dec 25 🌐 toledomonumental.com

The oldest of the city's original synagogues dates back to the 12th–13th century. Carved stone capitals and wall panels stand out against white horseshoe arches and plasterwork. In 1391, a massacre of Jews took place here, a turning point after years of religious tolerance in the city.

Elegant horseshoe arches at the Sinagoga de Santa María la Blanca ↓

↑ Segovia's aqueduct, built by the Romans in the 1st century

❸

Segovia

🏠 Segovia 🚋🚌 ℹ️ Plaza de Azoguejo 1; www.turismodesegovia.com

Segovia is one of the most spectacularly sited cities in the whole of Spain. The Old Town is set high on a rocky spur, surrounded by the Eresma and Clamores rivers. With its cathedral, ancient aqueduct, and castle dominating the skyline, the view of the town from the valley below at sunset is magical.

Perched on a rocky outcrop at the city's western end is the **Alcázar**, a fairy-tale castle featuring gabled roofs, turrets, and crenellations. Begun in the 12th century, the castle assumed its present form between 1410 and 1455, but did have to be largely rebuilt following a fire in 1862. The castle contains a museum of weaponry and several sumptuous apartments.

Dating from 1525, Segovia's **cathedral** was the last great Gothic church to be built in

Spain. The structure replaced the old cathedral, destroyed in 1520 when the Castilian towns revolted against King Carlos I. Other churches in the Old Town include the Romanesque San Juan de los Caballeros, which has an outstanding sculpted portico, San Esteban, and San Martín.

Segovia's impressive Roman aqueduct was constructed in the 1st century AD and stayed in use until the 19th century. Two tiers of arches, a total of 2,400 ft (728 m) in length, were needed to handle the gradient.

The **Palace of Riofrío**, 7 miles (11 km) southwest of the city, was built as a hunting lodge for Felipe V's widow,

Isabel Farnese, in 1752. Today, it houses a hunting museum.

Alcázar

◈ ◈ 🏠 Plaza de la Reina Victoria Eugenia ⏲ 10am–6pm daily (Apr–Oct: to 8pm) 🔒 Jan 5, Dec 25 & 31 🌐 alcazardesegovia.com

Cathedral

◈ ◈ 🏠 Calle Marqués del Arco 1 ⏲ Apr–Oct: 9am–9:30pm daily; Nov–Mar: 9:30am–6:30pm daily 🌐 catedralsegovia.es

Palace of Riofrío

◈ ◈ 🏠 Bosque de Riofrío ⏲ 10am–6pm Tue–Sun (Apr–Sep: to 8pm)

→ The imposing bulk of the 16th-century El Escorial palace

El Escorial

🏛 San Lorenzo de El Escorial 🚃🚌 🕙 10am–6pm Tue-Sun (Apr–Sep: to 8pm) 🚪 Public hols 🌐 patrimonio nacional.es

Felipe II's imposing palace of San Lorenzo de El Escorial was built in 1563–84 in honor of St. Lawrence. The austere, unornamented building, conceived as a mausoleum and contemplative retreat rather than a splendid residence, set a new architectural style – known as "Herreriano," after the palace's architect, Juan de Herrera.

Among the most impressive parts is the library, with a collection of more than 40,000 books and manuscripts. Its ceiling is decorated with 16th-century frescoes by Tibaldi. The ornate Royal Pantheon, a mausoleum made in marble, contains the funerary urns of Spanish monarchs, while some of the most important works of the royal Habsburg collections, including Flemish, Italian, and Spanish paintings, are housed in the Museum of Art, on the first floor. Other fine works of art can be found in the chapter houses, with their fresco-adorned ceilings, and in the basilica.

ST. TERESA DE ÁVILA

At the tender age of seven, Teresa de Cepeda y Ahumada (1515–82) ran away from home in hope of achieving martyrdom at the hands of the Moors, but was recaptured by her uncle on the outskirts of the city. She became a nun at 19 but rebelled against her order. From 1562, when she founded her first convent, St. Teresa traveled around Spain with her disciple, St. John of the Cross, founding more convents for the followers of her order, the Barefoot Carmelites. Her remains are kept in Alba de Tormes, near the town of Salamanca.

In contrast to the artistic wealth of other parts of the palace, the royal apartments are remarkably humble.

---

⑤

Avila

🏛 Avila 🚃🚌 ℹ Avenida de Madrid 39; www.avila turismo.com

The perfectly preserved medieval walls that encircle this historic city were built in the 12th century as a defense against the Moors. Of the nine gateways in the walls, the most impressive is the Puerta de San Vicente. Avila's cathedral, whose unusual exterior is carved with beasts and scaly wild men, also forms part of the city walls.

Avila is the birthplace of St. Teresa, one of the Catholic Church's greatest mystics and reformers. The Convento de Santa Teresa occupies the site of the home of this saint, who also lived for many years in the Monasterio de la Encarnación.

Among the city's finest churches are the 12th-century Iglesia de San Vicente and the Romanesque-Gothic Iglesia de San Pedro.

Beyond the town center, the Real Monasterio de Santo Tomás contains the tomb of Tomás de Torquemada, head of the Spanish Inquisition.

EAT

Zazu Bistro

This stylish restaurant located in the heart of Salamanca pays tribute to Mediterranean cuisine, with nods to classic French and Italian recipes. During the summer months, you can dine on the terrace.

⌂ Plaza Libertad 8, Salamanca

Ⓦ restaurantezazu.com

€€€

---

❻ Salamanca

⌂ Castilla y León ⓘ Plaza Mayor 32; www.salamanca.es

Home to one of the oldest universities in Europe, the city of Salamanca is also Spain's best showcase of Renaissance and Plateresque architecture. The city's famous **university** was founded by Alfonso IX of León in 1218. Its main building, on the Patio de las Escuelas, dates from the 16th century and is a splendid example of the Plateresque style. This form of early Spanish Renaissance architecture is so called because of its fine detail, which resembles ornate silverwork – *platero* in Spanish means silversmith.

The 16th-century New Cathedral and the 12th- to 13th-century Old Cathedral stand side by side. The west front of the New Cathedral has elaborate Late Gothic stonework, while the highlight of the Romanesque Old Cathedral is the richly colored, 53-panel altarpiece (1445) by Nicolás Florentino.

The magnificent Plaza Mayor was built by Felipe V in the 18th century to thank Salamanca for its support during the War of the Spanish Succession. Among the pretty, arcaded buildings here are the Baroque Town Hall and the Royal Pavilion, from where the royal family used to watch events in the square.

Other fine monuments located in the heart of the city include the 16th-century Iglesia-Convento de San Esteban, with its lovely ornamented facade, and the Convento de las Dueñas, which preserves Moorish and Renaissance features.

The **Museo Art Nouveau y Art Déco** holds an important collection of 19th- and 20th-century paintings, jewelry, ceramics, and stained glass.

On the city outskirts, the 1st-century AD Roman bridge, the Puente Romano, offers a good view over the entire city.

Universidad

⊘ ⌂ Calle Libreros ☏ 923-29 44 00 ⌂ Apr-mid-Sep: 10am-8pm Mon-Sat, 10am-2pm Sun; mid-Sep-Mar: 10am-7pm Mon-Sat ⌂ Dec 25

Museo Art Nouveau y Art Déco

⊘ ⊙ ⌂ Calle Gibraltar 14 ⌂ 11am-8pm Tue-Sun ⌂ Jan 1 & 6, Dec 25 Ⓦ museocasalis.org

↓ The Baroque town hall dominating Plaza Mayor, Salamanca

↑ Cow grazing in the Picos de Europa, and *(inset)* the Fuente Dé cable car

7
León

📍 León 🚍🚊 🛈 Plaza de la Regla 4; 987-23 70 82

Founded as a camp for the Romans' Seventh Legion, León became the capital of the kingdom of León in the Middle Ages and played a central role in the early years of the Reconquest.

The city's Gothic cathedral, on Plaza de la Regla, dates from the mid-13th century.

💬 **INSIDER TIP**
Iglesia de San Miguel de Escalada

To the east of León, the 10th-century Iglesia de San Miguel de Escalada is one of the finest surviving churches built by the Mozarabs – Christians influenced by the Moors.

In addition to some glorious stained glass – best appreciated on a sunny day – it also has a splendid west front, covered with a series of Gothic carvings from the 13th-century.

Other notable buildings in the city include the Colegiata de San Isidoro, built into the Roman walls that encircle the city, and the Romanesque Panteón Real (Royal Pantheon), decorated with carved capitals and 12th-century frescoes.

León's medieval old quarter is a maze of narrow alleyways, lined with bars, cafés, churches, and old mansions. The historic Hostal de San Marcos was founded in the 12th century as a monastery for pilgrims on route to Santiago *(p313)*. A gem of Spanish Renaissance architecture, the present building was begun in 1513 for the Knights of Santiago. Today, it houses a luxurious hotel and the **Museo de León**.

Museo de León

🏛 Plaza Santo Domingo 8
🕐 Hours vary, check website
📅 Main public hols 🌐 museodeleon.com

8
Picos de Europa

🗺 Asturias, Cantabria, and Castilla y León 🚍
🛈 Cangas de Onís; www.parquenacionalpicoseuropa.es

This beautiful mountain range – christened "Peaks of Europe" by returning sailors, as this was often the first sight of their homeland – offers superb upland hiking and supports a diversity of wildlife.

The two main gateways to the Picos are Cangas de Onís, northwest of the park, and Potes, on the eastern side. About 5 miles (8 km) southeast of the former, Covadonga is where, in 722, the Visigoth Pelayo is said to have defeated a Moorish army, inspiring the Christians to later reconquer the peninsula. The road south from Cangas de Onís follows the spectacular Desfiladero de los Beyes gorge.

The **Fuente Dé** cable car, in the heart of the park, climbs 2,950 ft (900 m) to a rocky plateau, offering magnificent panoramic views.

Fuente Dé

🕐 9am-7pm daily 📅 Jan 1 & 6, Dec 24, 25, & 31

STAY

AC Hotel Burgos

This stylish hotel is set right in the heart of Burgos. Fuel up at the restaurant's sumptuous breakfast buffet before exploring the sights. There's also a hotel bar to round off the day.

🏠 Paseo Isla 7
🌐 marriott.co.uk hotels/ travel/rgsbu-ac-hotel-burgos

NH Collection Palacio de Burgos

Centrally located, this 16th-century former convent offers spacious rooms, a charming Gothic cloister, and an excellent restaurant.

🏠 Calle de la Merced 13
🌐 nh-hotels.com/ burgos/palacio

9

Burgos

🏠 Castilla y León 🚊🚌
🛈 Plaza de Alonso Martínez 7; 947-20 31 25

Founded in 884, Burgos was the capital of the united kingdoms of Castile and León from 1073 until 1492. A few hundred years later, Francisco Franco chose Burgos as his headquarters during the Spanish Civil War.

Approaching the city via the Puente de Santa María, you enter the Old Town through the grand Arco de Santa María. The other main route into Burgos is the Puente de San Pablo, where a statue commemorates Burgos's most celebrated son, El Cid. This great 11th-century warrior was immortalized in the anonymous poem *El Cantar del Mío Cid* (1180).

Not far from the statue of El Cid stands the Casa del Cordón, a 15th-century former palace (now a bank). It was here, in 1497, that the Catholic Monarchs welcomed Columbus on his return from the second of his voyages to the Americas.

Burgos's **cathedral** is the city's most prominent landmark. Its lacy, steel-grey spires soar above a balustrade depicting Castile's early kings. As well as physically dominating the city, Spain's third-largest cathedral also commands its imagination. It was founded in 1221 by Bishop Don Mauricio under Fernando III and was named a UNESCO World Heritage Site in 1984. The ground plan – a Latin cross – measures 276 ft (84 m) by 194 ft (59 m). Its construction was carried out in several stages over three centuries, and involved many of the greatest architects and artists in Europe at the time. The style of the cathedral is almost entirely Gothic, and incorporates influences from Germany, France, and the Low Countries. The architects cleverly adapted the building to its sloping site, incorporating stairways inside and out. In the Middle Ages, the cathedral was a main stopping point for pilgrims on the road to Santiago *(p313)*. El Cid is buried in the cathedral, as is his wife.

Nearby, the Iglesia de San Nicolás has a fine 16th-century altarpiece, while the Iglesia

 The nighttime skyline of Burgos, dominated by the cathedral's Gothic spires

de San Lorenzo features a splendid Baroque ceiling. The **Museo de Burgos** contains archaeological finds from the Roman city of Clunia and a collection of fine art.

West of the city is the 12th-century **Real Monasterio de las Huelgas**, a Cistercian convent that houses an interesting textile museum.

Cathedral
◈ ◈ ◫ Plaza de Santa María
◷ Mid-Mar-Oct: 9:30am-7:30pm daily; Nov-mid-Mar: 10am-7pm daily ⊡ catedraldeburgos.info

Museo de Burgos
◈ ◫ Calle Miranda 13
◷ Hours vary, check website
⊡ museodeburgos.com

Real Monasterio de las Huelgas
◈ ◈ ◫ Plaza Compás
◷ 10am-2pm & 4-6:30pm Tue-Sat, 10:30am-3pm Sun & public hols ⊡ Jan 1 & 6, Good Fri, May 1, May 30, Dec 24, 25, & 31 ⊡ monasteriodelashuelgas.org

> **The cathedral's construction involved many of the greatest architects and artists in Europe.**

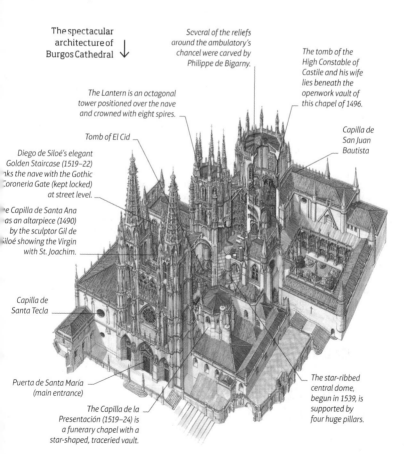

The spectacular architecture of Burgos Cathedral ↓

Several of the reliefs around the ambulatory's chancel were carved by Philippe de Bigarny.

The tomb of the High Constable of Castile and his wife lies beneath the openwork vault of this chapel of 1496.

The Lantern is an octagonal tower positioned over the nave and crowned with eight spires.

Tomb of El Cid

Capilla de San Juan Bautista

Diego de Siloé's elegant Golden Staircase (1519–22) links the nave with the Gothic Coroneria Gate (kept locked) at street level.

The Capilla de Santa Ana has an altarpiece (1490) by the sculptor Gil de Siloé showing the Virgin with St. Joachim.

Capilla de Santa Tecla

Puerta de Santa María (main entrance)

The Capilla de la Presentación (1519–24) is a funerary chapel with a star-shaped, traceried vault.

The star-ribbed central dome, begun in 1539, is supported by four huge pillars.

⑩

Oviedo

 Asturias 🚉🚌 ℹ️ **Marqués de Santa Cruz 1; www.turismoviedo.es**

Oviedo is the cultural and commercial capital of Asturias, and is best known for its Pre-Romanesque buildings. This style flourished in the 8th–10th centuries and was confined to a small area of the kingdom of Asturias, one of the few areas of Spain that escaped invasion by the Moors.

With its huge barrel-vaulted hall and arcaded galleries, the church of Santa María del Naranco, in the north of the city, was built as a summer palace for Ramiro I in the 9th century. Equally impressive are the church of San Miguel de Lillo and the 9th-century church of San Julián de los Prados, with its frescoes.

Did You Know?

Spain is one of only four countries in the world to have no official lyrics to its national anthem.

In the center of Oviedo, the Flamboyant Gothic **cathedral** and the 9th-century Iglesia de San Tirso are both worth taking some time to see.

The city has two museums of special note: the **Museo Arqueológico**, which contains local prehistoric, Roman, and Romanesque treasures, and the **Museo de Bellas Artes** (Museum of Fine Arts).

Cathedral

📍 Plaza Alfonso II El Casto
🕐 Hours vary, check website
🌐 catedraldeoviedo.com

Museo Arqueológico

📍 Calle San Vicente 5
🕐 Hours vary, check website
🌐 museoarqueologicode asturias.com

Museo de Bellas Artes

📍 Calle Santa Ana 1
🕐 Hours vary, check website
🌐 museobbaa.com

---

⑪

Rías Baixas

📍 **Pontevedra** 🚉🚌
ℹ️ **Praza da Verdura s/n, Pontevedra; 986-09 08 90**

The southern part of Galicia's west coast consists of four large *rias*, or inlets, between pine-covered hills. Known as

the Rías Baixas (Rías Bajas), they offer fine beaches, safe bathing, and lovely scenery.

The main town on the coast is lively Pontevedra, which has many historic monuments, such as the Gothic Convento de Santo Domingo, and an excellent provincial museum.

Many other areas along this stretch of coastline have become popular holiday resorts, such as Sanxenxo, west of Pontevedra. To the south, Baiona and Panxón both have good beaches, as well as facilities for sailing and a variety of watersports. In spite of tourism, much of the coastline – particularly the quieter northernmost part from Muros to Noia – remains unspoiled. Here you can visit many small fishing ports and watch the locals harvesting mussels and clams.

While in the Rías Baixas area, look out for the local *hórreos* – traditional stone-built granaries raised on stilts. The waterfront of picturesque Combarro is lined with these buildings, which are typical of the Galicia region.

The monumental clock tower of Santiago de Compostela's cathedral

← Colorful houses and open-air restaurants on a pedestrian street in Oviedo

 12

Santiago de Compostela

🏠 A Coruña 🚆🚉🚌 *i* Calle Rúa do Villar 63; www. santiagoturismo.com

In the Middle Ages, this fine city was Christendom's third most important place of pilgrimage after Jerusalem and Rome. In 813, the body of Christ's apostle James was supposedly discovered here, and in the following centuries, Santiago de Compostela attracted pilgrims from all over Europe.

On the Praza do Obradoiro stands the city's cathedral, built in honor of St. James. The present structure dates from the 11th to 13th century, but the Baroque west facade was added in the 18th century. The square's northern edge is flanked by the grand Hostal de los Reyes Católicos, built by the Catholic Monarchs as a resting place for sick pilgrims. It is now a Parador hotel. Nearby are the 9th-century Convento de San Paio de Antealtares, one of the city's oldest monasteries, and the Convento de San Martiño Pinario, whose Baroque church has a wonderfully ornate Plateresque facade.

The Convento de Santo Domingo de Bonaval, east of the center, is also worth visiting for its fine triple-helix staircase and adjoining church. Part of the monastery also houses a Galician folk museum.

 HIDDEN GEM
Go Goya

Head up to the third floor of the museum in Santiago de Compostela's cathedral to find an impressive textile arts collection, including tapestries by one of Spain's most famous artists, Francisco Goya.

Nearby is the **Centro Gallego de Arte Contemporáneo**, with works by leading Galician artists, as well as others from the rest of Spain, Portugal, and South America. The gallery also hosts various temporary exhibitions.

Centro Gallego de Arte Contemporáneo
🅰 🏠 Rúa de Ramón del Valle-Inclán 5 🕙 11am–8pm Tue–Sun 🌐 cgac. xunta.gal

Santander

⌂ Cantabria 🚆🚌🚢
🛈 Jardines de Pereda; www.turismo.santander.es

Cantabria's capital, Santander, is a busy port that enjoys a splendid site on a deep bay on Spain's north Atlantic coast. The cathedral was rebuilt in Gothic style, following a fire in 1941 that destroyed the entire town. The 12th-century crypt has been preserved. Nearby, the stately **Museo de Arte Moderno y Contemporáneo de Santander y Cantabria (MAS)** focuses on contemporary art, but also displays a portrait of Fernando VII by Goya and paintings by the 17th-century Portuguese artist Josefa D'Obidos. The **Museo de Prehistoria y Arqueología** displays local finds, including Neolithic axe heads, Roman coins, pottery, and figurines.

On the Península de la Magdalena stands the Palacio de la Magdalena, built for Alfonso XIII in 1912. To the north is the seaside resort of El Sardinero, which has a long beach, chic cafés, and a casino.

MAS

🅐 ⌂ Calle Rubio 6
🔒 For renovations until 2021
🆆 museosantandermas.es

Museo de Prehistoria y Arqueología

🅐🅐 ⌂ Calle Hernán Cortés 4
🕐 Hours vary, check website
🆆 museosdecantabria.es

Bilbao

⌂ Vizcaya 🚆🚌🚢
🛈 Plaza Circular 1; www.bilbaoturismo.net

Bilbao (Bilbo) is the center of Basque industry and Spain's leading commercial port, yet it also has numerous cultural attractions worth visiting. In the city's medieval quarter – the Casco Viejo – the Museo Arqueológico, Etnográfico e Histórico Vasco displays Basque art and folk artifacts, while in the newer town, the Museo de Bellas Artes is one of Spain's best art museums.

The jewel in Bilbao's cultural crown, however, is the **Museo Guggenheim Bilbao**, which has a superb collection of modern and contemporary art. It is just one of the city's many examples of modern architecture, which also include the striking Palacio de la Música y Congresos Euskalduna.

Museo Guggenheim Bilbao

🅐🅐🅐 ⌂ Av Abandoibarra
🕐 10am–8pm Tue–Sun (Jul & Aug: daily) 🔒 Public hols
🆆 guggenheim-bilbao.eus

BASQUE CULTURE

The Basques are one of the oldest peoples in Europe. Long isolated in their mountain villages, they have preserved their language (Euskera), myths, and art for millennia. Among the most popular exponents of Basque cultural life are the *bertsolaris*, oral poets, originally from rural areas, who improvise verses and who are still very popular among the younger generations. Though the Basque region has had its own parliament since 1975 (as all other Spanish regions), there has always been a strong separatist movement seeking to sever links with the government in Madrid.

↑ The distinctive architecture of Museo Guggenheim Bilbao

↑ Dining al fresco at a buzzing waterfront restaurant in San Sebastián

15

San Sebastián

🏛 Guipúzcoa 🚆🚌
ℹ Boulevard 8; www.san
sebastianturismoa.eus

San Sebastián (Donostia) became a fashionable seaside resort in the late 19th century. At the heart of the Old Town are the handsome Plaza de la Constitución and the church of Santa María del Coro, with its Baroque portal. Behind the Old Town, Monte Urgull offers superb views from its summit. At the foot of the hill, the **Museo de San Telmo** holds a number of works by El Greco.

Local beaches include the famous Playa de la Concha and Playa de Ondarreta, at the end of which is Eduardo Chillida's beautiful sculpture, the *Comb of the Winds*. The Palacio Miramar (1889), built for Queen María Cristina, is a venue for the city's film festival.

Museo de San Telmo
🎫♿ 🏛 Plaza Zuloaga
🕐 10am–8pm Tue–Sun
🌐 santelmomuseoa.eus

16

Pamplona

🏛 Navarra ✈🚆🚌
ℹ C/San Saturnino 2;
www.pamplona.es

Supposedly founded by the Roman general Pompey, Pamplona is most famous for the fiesta of Los Sanfermines, with its bull running.

West of the city's cathedral lies the old Jewish quarter, with the NeoClassical Palacio del Gobierno de Navarra and the medieval Iglesia de San Saturnino. Beneath the old town wall is the **Museo de Navarra**, a museum of regional history, archaeology, and art.

Museo de Navarra
🎫♿ 🏛 Calle Santo Domingo
🕐 Hours vary, check website
🌐 navarra.es

EAT

La Vinoteca
This fusion restaurant serves Spanish dishes with global influences.

🏛 Calle Hernan Cortes 38, Santander
📞 942 07 57 41

€€€

Bikandi Etxea
A friendly, good-value spot offering traditional Basque fare.

🏛 Paseo Campo Volantin 4, Bilbao
🌐 bikandietxea.wixsite.com

€€€

Arzak
Head to this three-Michelin-starred restaurant for fresh ingredients and Basque cooking. A tasting menu is available.

🏛 Avenida Alcade José Elosegui 273, San Sebastián 🌐 arzak.es

€€€

Borda Berri
This rustic spot serves traditional Basque *pintxos* (snacks). You may have to wait in line – but it's worth it.

🏛 Calle Fermin Calbeton 12, San Sebastián
📞 943 43 03 42

€€€

→

The medieval monastery of
Santa Maria de Poblet, part
of the Cistercian Triangle

Monestir de Poblet

⌂ Off N240, 6 miles
(10 km) from Montblanc
🚍🚌 ⏰10am-12:30pm &
3-5:25pm Mon-Sat (mid-
Mar-mid-Oct: to 5:50pm),
10:30am-12:25pm &
3-5:25pm Sun & public
hols ⧖Jan 1, Jul 6, Dec 25
& 26 🌐poblet.cat

A UNESCO World Heritage Site
since 1992, the Romanesque
monastery of Santa Maria
de Poblet was the first and
most important of three
medieval abbeys forming the
so-called "Cistercian Triangle,"
the others being at Santes
Creus and Vallbona de les
Monges. In 1835, during the
Carlist upheavals, the abbey
sustained serious damage and
was abandoned. Restoration
began in 1930, and monks
returned a decade later.

A haven of tranquility,
Poblet is enclosed by fortified walls that have hardly
changed since the medieval
era. Its evocative, vaulted
cloisters were built in the 12th
and 13th centuries. Beautiful,
carved scrollwork adorns the
capitals. Behind the stone
altar, an impressive alabaster
reredos, carved by Damià
Forment in 1527, fills the apse.
Other highlights include the
Royal Tombs, where many
Spanish monarchs are buried.
Begun in 1359, they were
reconstructed by Frederic
Marès in 1950.

**Parc Nacional
d'Aigüestortes**

⌂ Lleida 🚍🚌 ⓘ Boí; www.
aiguestortes.info

The pristine mountain scenery
of Catalonia's only national
park is among the most
spectacular in the Pyrenees.
Established in 1955, the park
covers an area of 40 sq miles
(102 sq km). The main access
towns are Espot, to the east,
and Boí, to the west. Dotted
around the park are waterfalls
and the sparkling, clear waters
of around 150 lakes.

The most beautiful scenery
is around Sant Maurici lake,
from where several picturesque walks lead north to the
towering peaks of Agulles
d'Amitges.

Early summer in the lower
valleys is marked by a mass of
pink and red rhododendrons,
while later in the year wild
lilies bloom in the forests.
The park is also home to an
impressive variety of wildlife,
including chamois, beavers,
otters, and golden eagles.

THE CATALAN LANGUAGE

A nation-within-a-nation, Catalonia has its own
semi-autonomous regional government, and its
own language. Catalan has recovered from the ban
it suffered under Franco's dictatorship and has sup-
planted Castilian (Spanish) as the language in everyday
use in the region. Spoken by more than 9.5 million people,
it is a Romance language akin to the Provençal of France.
Previously it was suppressed by Felipe V in 1717 and only
officially resurfaced in the 19th century, when the Jocs
Florals (medieval poetry contests) were revived during
the rebirth of Catalan literature.

 19

Tarragona

◻ Tarragona ⛖🚌🚆
◻ Carrer Major 39; www.tarragonaturisme.cat

Now a major industrial port, Tarragona still preserves many remnants of its Roman past, from the era when it was the capital of the Roman province Tarraconensis.

Among the town's extensive ancient ruins are the Anfiteatro Romano, an atmospheric amphitheater located close to the waterfront, and the **Praetorium**, a Roman tower that was later converted into a medieval palace. Also known as the Castell de Pilat (after Pontius Pilate), the tower now houses the Museu de la Romanitat, which contains Roman and medieval finds

and provides access to the cavernous passageways of the 1st-century-AD Roman circus. In the adjacent building is the **Museu Nacional Arqueològic**, containing the most important collection of Roman artifacts in Catalonia, including some beautiful frescoes. (The museum is currently closed for renovation until 2023.) Elsewhere, an archaeological walk follows part of the Roman city wall.

Tarragona's 12th-century cathedral was built on the site of a Roman temple and an Arab mosque, and exhibits a harmonious blend of styles.

Inside is an altarpiece of St. Tecla, carved in 1434.

Praetorium
⊛ ◻ Plaça del Rei 5 ◻ 977-24 22 20 ◻ Mid-Jun-Sep: 9am-9pm daily (to 3pm Sun & Mon); Oct-mid-Jun: 9am-7pm Tue-Sun (to 3pm Sun)

Museu Nacional Arqueològic
⊛ ◻ Avda de Ramón y Cajal 82 ◻ For renovation until 2023 ◻ mnat.cat

↑ Tarragona's Anfiteatro Romano, located close to the seafront

20

BARCELONA

⚑ Catalonia ✈🚊🚌 *i* www.barcelonaturisme.com

One of the Mediterranean's busiest ports, the capital of Catalonia rivals Madrid in culture, commerce, and sport. Although there are many historical monuments in the Old Town, the city is best known for the scores of superb buildings left behind by the artistic explosion of Modernisme at the turn of the 20th century.

① 🚲 🚇 🏛

Barcelona Cathedral

⚑ Plaça de la Seu Ⓜ Jaume I
🚌 17, V17, 45 🕗 8:30am-7:30pm daily 🌐 catedralbcn.org

Begun in 1298 under Jaime II, this compact Gothic cathedral was not finished until the late 19th century. The interior has beautiful Gothic cloisters and carved 15th-century choir stalls with painted coats of arms. Beneath the main altar, the crypt houses the sarcophagus of St. Eulalia, martyred in the 4th century AD. The nave has 28 side chapels, and a 85-ft (26-m) vaulted ceiling.

② 🚲 🚇

MUHBA Plaça del Rei

⚑ Plaça del Rei Ⓜ Jaume I
🕙 10am-7pm Tue-Sun (to 8pm Sun) 🚫 Jan 1, May 1, Jun 24, Dec 25
🌐 museuhistoria.bcn.cat

The Royal Palace, founded in the 13th century, was the residence of the count-kings of Barcelona. Today it is part

←

Barcelona's Old Town, dominated by the Gothic spire of the cathedral

of the Museu d'Història de Barcelona, with its exhibits including the vast Gothic Saló del Tinell and the Capella de Santa Àgata, with a painted-wood ceiling by Jaume Huguet. Entire streets of old Barcino are accessible via lifts and walkways suspended over the ruins of Roman Barcelona.

Did You Know?

Picasso's full name is 23 words long and includes the names of many saints.

③

Museu Picasso

🏛 Carrer Montcada 15-23
Ⓜ Jaume I Ⓗ 10am-8:30pm daily (to 5pm Mon, to 9:30pm Thu) Ⓗ Mon in Nov-Mar; Jan 1, May 1, 13 & 20, Jun 24, Dec 25
🌐 museupicasso.bcn.es

One of the most popular attractions in Barcelona, the Picasso Museum is housed in five adjoining palaces on the Carrer Montcada. It was founded in 1963, displaying works donated by artist and writer Jaime Sabartes, a great friend of Picasso. Later, Picasso himself donated paintings, including some graphic works left in his will. Several ceramic pieces were given to the museum by his widow, Jacqueline Roque.

The strength of the 3,000-piece collection is

💬 INSIDER TIP
Getting Around

The Old Town and the Barri Gòtic are well served by the metro. Line 5 takes you to the Sagrada Família. Set atop a steep hill, most of Montjuïc's attractions can be reached by bus from Plaça d'Espanya, or by funicular and cable car from Metro Paral·lel.

Picasso's early drawings and paintings, such as *The First Communion* (1896), produced when he was still an adolescent. The most famous work on show is the series *Las Meninas*, based on Velázquez's 1656 masterpiece in Madrid's Prado Museum *(p294)*.

Booking ahead is strongly recommended for this popular museum.

↑ An aerial view of the historic, tree-lined avenue of La Rambla in the Old Town

⑤

Basílica de Santa Maria del Mar

🅰 Plaza Sta Maria 1 Ⓜ Jaume I ⏱ 9am-1pm & 5-8:30pm Mon-Sat, 10am-2pm & 5-8pm Sun 🌐 santa mariadelmarbarcelona.org

This beautiful building, the only surviving example of an entirely Catalan Gothic-style church, took just 55 years to build. The speed of its construction – unrivaled in the Middle Ages – gave it a unity of style both inside and out. The west front has a 15th-century rose window of the *Coronation of the Virgin*. More stained glass, dating from the 15th to the 18th century, lights the wide nave and high aisles. The interior has superb acoustics for concerts.

---

④

La Rambla

Ⓜ Drassanes, Liceu, Catalunya

A stroll down this famous street's tree-shaded, central walkway to the seafront, taking in the mansions, shops, and cafés, makes a perfect introduction to Barcelona life.

The name comes from the Arabic *ramla*, meaning the dried-up bed of a seasonal river. Barcelona's 13th-century city wall followed the left bank of one such river. During the 16th century, monasteries, convents, and a university were built on the opposite bank. Later demolished, they have left their legacy in the names of the five sections of the street. Today, La Rambla is thronged with street vendors, tarot readers, musicians, and mime artists.

Among its many famous buildings is the **Palau Güell**, a Neo-Gothic mansion from 1889 that established the international reputation of inventive Catalan architect Antoni Gaudí.

Nearby, the Gran Teatre del Liceu, the city's fine opera house, has been restored twice after fires in 1861 and 1994. Farther along is the huge Mercat de Sant Josep, a colorful food market more popularly known by the nickname "La Boqueria."

On the opposite side of La Rambla is the Neo-Classical Palau Moja – pop inside the Baroque first-floor salon to learn more about Catalan culture. A little farther south, midway between the Liceu and Drassanes metro stations, is the Plaça Reial. This is the city's liveliest square and dates from the 1850s.

Palau Güell

♿ⓘ 🅰 Carrer Nou de la Rambla 3-5 Ⓜ Drassanes, Liceu ⏱ 10am-5:30pm Tue-Sun (Apr-Oct: to 8pm) 🚫 Jan 1, 3rd wk of Jan, Dec 25 & 26 🌐 palauguell.cat

⑥

Vila Olímpica

Ⓜ Ciutadella-Vila Olímpica

When Barcelona was made over for the 1992 Olympics, the most dramatic project was the demolition of the old industrial waterfront and the laying out of 2 miles (4 km) of promenade and pristine sandy beaches. Suddenly Barcelona seemed like a seaside resort, with a new estate of 2,000 apartments and parks called Nova Icària. The area is still popularly known as the Vila Olímpica because the buildings once housed Olympic athletes.

On the seafront, twin 44-floor towers stand beside the Port Olímpic, also built for the Olympics. Restaurants, stores, and nightclubs around the marina attract crowds at lunchtimes and on weekends.

> **Among La Rambla's famous buildings is the Palau Güell, a Neo-Gothic mansion that established the international reputation of inventive Catalan architect Antoni Gaudí.**

Fundació Joan Miró

🏛 Parc de Montjuïc
Ⓜ Espanya or Paral·lel, then bus 55 or 150
🕐 10am-6pm Tue-Sat (Apr-Oct: to 8pm), 10am-3pm Sun & public hols (Apr-Oct: to 6pm) 🚫 Jan 1, Dec 25 & 26 🌐 fmirobcn.org

Housed in a boldly modern building designed in 1975 by Josep Lluís Sert, this collection of paintings, sculptures, and tapestries by Catalan artist Joan Miró is lit by natural light.

An admirer of primitive Catalan art and Gaudí's Modernism, Miró developed a Surrealistic style, with vivid colors and fantastical forms that suggested dreamlike situations. Pieces on display include his *Barcelona Series* (1939–44), a set of 50 black-and-white lithographs. Temporary exhibitions of other artists' work are also held here.

Casa Batlló's beautiful stained-glass windows looking out over the Passeig de Gràcia

Casa Batlló

🏛 Passeig de Gràcia 43
Ⓜ Passeig de Gràcia 🕐 9am-9pm daily 🌐 casabatllo.es

The elegant Passeig de Gràcia is home to several Modernista buildings, among them Gaudí's Casa Batlló, a fantastical mansion completed in 1906. Covered in shimmering mosaics, its design is said to have been inspired by the legend of St. George, and the curving roof is covered in iridescent tiles recalling a dragon's scaly back. It is the centerpiece of a trio of neighboring Modernista mansions: the Casa Amatller, designed by Puig i Cadafalch, and the Casa Lleo i Morera, created by Domènech i Montaner. Nearby is another of Gaudí's creations, the **Casa Milà**, or La Pedrera, which has a creamy, rippling facade and is topped with a terrace that offers superb views.

Casa Milà/La Pedrera

🏛 Passeig de Gràcia 92
🕐 Hours vary, check website
🚫 25 Dec & 11-17 Jan
🌐 lapedrera.com

(9)

SAGRADA FAMÍLIA

Carrer de la Marina ⓜ Sagrada Família 🚌 19, 43, 51 🕒 Apr-Sep: 9am-8pm daily; Oct & Mar: 9am-7pm daily; Nov-Feb: 9am-6pm daily (to 2pm 1 & 6 Jan, 25 & 26 Dec); timed tickets only 🌐 sagradafamilia.org

Europe's most unconventional church, the Temple Expiatori de la Sagrada Família is an emblem of the city. Crammed with symbolism inspired by nature and striving for originality, it is Gaudí's greatest work and an icon of Modernisme.

The original commission for a Christian temple on the site was given to architect Francisco de Paula del Villar i Lozano, who drew up plans for a Gothic-style building. However, in 1883, a year after work had begun, the task of completing the church was given to the 31-year-old Antoni Gaudí, who changed everything, extemporizing as he went along. He designed it to be considered as a book in stone, with each element representing a biblical event or aspect of Christian faith. It became his life's work and he lived like a recluse on the site for 14 years. At his death, only one tower on the Nativity facade had been completed, but several more have since been finished according to his original plans. Work continues today, financed by public subscription.

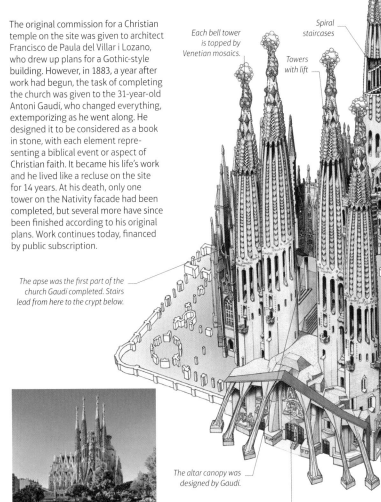

Each bell tower is topped by Venetian mosaics.

Spiral staircases

Towers with lift

The apse was the first part of the church Gaudí completed. Stairs lead from here to the crypt below.

The altar canopy was designed by Gaudí.

The bleak Passion facade, completed by Josep Maria Subirachs, has angular and somewhat sinister figures.

The crypt, where Gaudí is buried, was begun in 1882.

↑ The eye-catching exterior of Barcelona's most iconic landmark

2026

The date that the basilica is set to be completed.

↑ Soaring pillars branching out at the top to form a forest-like canopy

The most complete part of Gaudí's church, the Nativity facade has doorways which represent Faith, Hope, and Charity. Scenes of the Nativity and Christ's childhood are rich in symbolism.

↑ Stained-glass windows bathing the nave in multicolored pools of light

THE FINISHED CHURCH

Gaudí's initial ambitions have been kept over the years, using various new technologies to achieve his vision. Still to come is the central tower, which is to be encircled by four large towers representing the Evangelists. Four towers on the Glory (south) facade will match the existing four on the Passion (west) and Nativity (east) facades. An ambulatory (like an inside-out cloister) will run round the outside of the building.

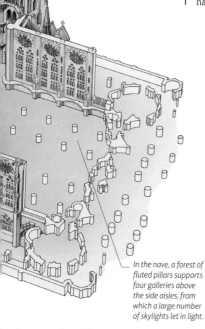

In the nave, a forest of fluted pillars supports four galleries above the side aisles, from which a large number of skylights let in light.

↑ A cross-section of the intricately designed cathedral interior

The gardens at Castell de Montjuïc, the former home of the Bourbon family

Montjuïc

M Espanya, Poble Sec, Paral·lel ▪ **13, 50, 150**

The hill of Montjuïc, rising above the commercial port on the south side of the city, is Barcelona's biggest recreation area. Its museums, art galleries, amusement park, and clubs make it popular night and day. The hill is also a spectacular vantage point from which to view the city.

There was probably a Celt-iberian settlement here before the Romans built a temple to Jupiter on the hill, which they called Mons Jovis (the Hill of Jove) – a possible source for Montjuïc's name. Another theory suggests that a Jewish cemetery on the hill inspired the name Mount of the Jews.

Many buildings here were constructed for the 1929 International Exhibition, and later for the 1992 Olympics. The **Museu Arqueològic** holds prehistoric finds from Catalonia and the Balearic Islands, while the Museu Etnològic houses artifacts from Oceania, Africa, Asia, and Latin America.

On the summit of Montjuïc, the huge 18th-century **Castell de Montjuïc**, built for the Bourbon family, has been converted into a center with exhibitions on the history of the castle and the Montjuïc mountain. In summer, it hosts outdoor film screenings.

Museu Arqueològic
⊗ 🚻 **Passeig Santa Madrona 39 M Espanya, Poble Sec** 🕐 9:30am–7pm Tue–Sat, 10am–2:30pm Sun & public hols 🚫 Jan 1, Dec 25 & 26 ✉ mac.cat

Castell de Montjuïc
⊗ ⊗ 🚻 **Parc de Montjuïc M Paral·lel, then funicular & cable car** 🕐 10am–8pm daily 🚫 Jan 1, Dec 25 ✉ ajuntament.barcelona. cat/castelldemontjuic

---

Museu Nacional d'Art de Catalunya

🚻 **Palau Nacional, Parc de Montjuïc M Espanya** 🕐 10am–6pm Tue–Sat (May–Sep: to 8pm), 10am–3pm Sun & public hols 🚫 Jan 1, May 1, Dec 25 ✉ museunacional.cat

Built for the 1929 International Exhibition, the austere Palau Nacional (National Palace) has been used to house the city's most important art collection since 1934.

The museum contains one of the greatest displays of Romanesque art in the world, its centerpiece being a series of magnificent 12th-century frescoes. These have been peeled from Catalan Pyrenean churches and pasted on to replicas of the original vaulted ceilings and apses they once adorned. The most remarkable are the wall paintings from the churches of Santa Maria de Taüll and Sant Climent de Taüll in Vall de Boí.

The museum's superb Gothic collection covers the whole of Spain, but is particularly good on Catalonia. Several outstanding works by El Greco, Velázquez, and Zurbarán are on display in the Renaissance and Baroque section. Call 93-622 03 75 to arrange a guided tour.

Tibidabo

🚻 **Plaça del Tibidabo 3–4 M Av Tibidabo, then Tramvia Blau & funicular, or TibiBus from Plaça Catalunya**

The heights of Tibidabo are reached by Barcelona's last surviving tram, the

---

 GREAT VIEW
Roof with a View

Don't miss the views of the city from the Museu Nacional d'Art de Catalunya's rooftop terraces. Access is included in the museum admission, or you can pay €2 if you just want to visit the rooftop.

Tramvia Blau, and a funicular railway. The name, inspired by the views of the city from the mountain, comes from the Latin *tibi dabo* ("I shall give you") – a reference to the Temptation of Christ, who was taken up a mountain by Satan and offered the world.

The amusement park at **Parc d'Atraccions** first opened in 1908. While the old rides retain their charm, the newer ones provide the latest in vertiginous experiences. Their hilltop location at 1,696 ft (517 m) adds to the thrill. Also in the park is the Museu dels Autòmats, which displays automated toys, jukeboxes, and gaming machines.

Tibidabo is crowned by the **Temple Expiatori del Sagrat Cor** (Church of the Sacred Heart), built with religious zeal by Enric Sagnier between 1902 and 1911. Inside, an elevator takes you up to an enormous statue of Christ.

Parc d'Atraccions

⊘ ⓥ ◖ Hours vary, check website ⓦ tibidabo.cat

Temple Expiatori del Sagrat Cor

◖ 11am–8pm daily
ⓦ tibidabo.salesianos.edu

⑬

Park Güell

🏠 Carrer d'Olot Ⓜ Lesseps
◖ Hours vary, check website ⓦ parkguell.barcelona

Designated a World Heritage Site by UNESCO, Park Güell is Gaudí's most colorful creation. He was commissioned in the 1890s by Count Eusebi Güell to design a garden city on 50 acres (20 hectares) of family estate. Little of Gaudí's grand plan for decorative buildings among landscaped gardens became reality, however; what we see today was completed between 1910 and 1914.

Most atmospheric is the Room of a Hundred Columns, a cavernous covered hall of 84 crooked pillars, which is brightened by glass and ceramic mosaics. Above it, reached by a flight of steps flanked by ceramic animals, is the Gran Plaça Circular – an open space with a snaking balcony of colored mosaics, said to have the longest bench in the world. It was executed by Josep Jujol, one of Gaudí's chief collaborators.

The **Casa-Museu Gaudí**, a pink villa where the architect lived from 1906 to 1926, was built by Francesc Berenguer. The drawings and furniture inside are all by Gaudí.

Casa-Museu Gaudí

⊘ ◖ Hours vary, check website ⓦ casamuseu gaudi.org

↑ View of the city and the distant sea from Antoni Gaudí's Park Güell

A SHORT WALK
BARRI GÒTIC

Distance 0.5 miles (700 m) **Nearest metro**
Jaume I **Time** 10 minutes

The Barri Gòtic (Gothic Quarter) is the true heart
of Barcelona. The oldest part of the city, it was the
site chosen by the Romans in the reign of Augustus
(27 BC–AD 14) on which to found a new *colonia* (town),
and has been the location of the city's administrative
buildings ever since. The Roman forum was
on the Plaça de Sant Jaume, where now
stand the medieval Palau de la Generalitat,
Catalonia's parliament, and the Casa de
la Ciutat, Barcelona's town hall. A walk
around the area also takes in the Gothic
cathedral and the royal palace, where
Columbus was received by Fernando
and Isabel on his return from his voyage
to the Americas in 1492.

*Built on the Roman city wall,
the Gothic-Renaissance **Casa de
l'Ardiaca** (archdeacon's residence)
now houses Barcelona's
historical archives.*

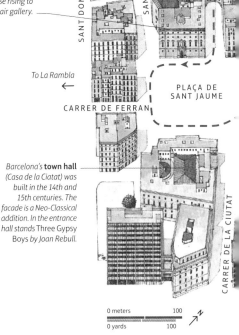

SANT SEVER

SANT DOMENEC DEL CALL

SANT HONORAT

CARRER DEL BISBE

PI

*The seat of Catalonia's
governor, the **Palau de la
Generalitat** has superb
Gothic features, such as
a stone staircase rising to
an open-air gallery.*

← To La Rambla

PLAÇA DE
SANT JAUME

CARRER DE FERRAN

*Barcelona's **town hall**
(Casa de la Ciatat) was
built in the 14th and
15th centuries. The
facade is a Neo-Classical
addition. In the entrance
hall stands Three Gypsy
Boys by Joan Rebull.*

CARRER DE LA CIUTAT

↑ The soaring Gothic
architecture of
Barcelona Cathedral

0 meters	100
0 yards	100

↗ N

← Vaulted arches and plant-filled courtyard in the Museu Frederic Marès

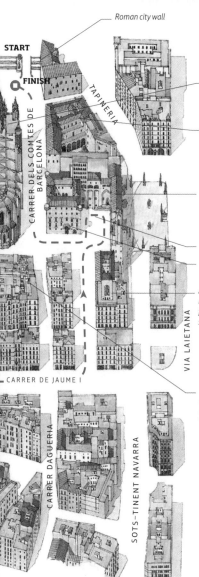

Roman city wall

START

FINISH

TAPINERIA

CARRER DELS COMTES DE BARCELONA

VIA LAIETANA

CARRER DE JAUME I

CARRER DAGUERIA

SOTS–TINENT NAVARRA

The **cathedral**'s facade and spire are 19th-century additions to the original Gothic building (p318). Among the artistic treasures inside are medieval Catalan paintings.

Museu Frederic Marès offers extraordinarily eclectic and high-quality collections, including an extensive display of Spanish sculpture.

The 14th-century **Capella Reial de Santa Àgata**, with a 1466 altarpiece, is one of the best surviving sections of the Palau Reial.

Plaça del Rei

Palau del Lloctinent

Accessed through this 14th-century mansion, **MUHBA Plaça del Rei** (p318) features the world's most extensive subterranean Roman ruins.

The **Centre Excursionista de Catalunya** displays in its entrance courtyard Roman columns from the Temple of Augustus, whose site is marked by a millstone in the street outside.

Did You Know?

The Temple of Augustus was discovered during building work in the 19th century.

MONESTIR DE MONTSERRAT

🏠 Montserrat, Barcelona province 🚠 Aeri de Montserrat, then cable car; Monistrol-Enllaç, then La Cremallera rack railway 🚌 ⏰ Basilica: 7:30am–8pm daily; Museum: 10am–6:45pm daily 🌐 montserratvisita.com

The "Serrated Mountain" *(mont serrat)*, its highest peak rising to 4,055 ft (1,236 m), is a magnificent setting for Catalonia's holiest place, the Monastery of Montserrat, which is surrounded by chapels and hermits' caves.

The earliest record of a chapel on this site is from the 9th century, but the monastery was not founded until the 11th century. In 1811, when the French attacked Catalonia in the War of Independence, the monastery was destroyed and the monks killed. Rebuilt and repopulated in 1844, it was a beacon of Catalan culture during the Franco years. Today, Benedictine monks live here. Visitors can hear the famous male choir singing the *Salve Regina* and the *Virolai* (the Montserrat hymn) in the basilica at 1pm Monday to Friday, or catch their renditions of *Vespers*, *Salve Montserratina*, and *Polyphonic Motet* at 6:45pm Monday to Thursday. They also sing at noon and 6:45pm on Sundays, except in the summer and during the Christmas period.

> ⛰ GREAT VIEW
> ## Natural Wonder
> Many locations in the Parc Natural de la Muntanya de Montserrat offer great views of Montserrat's rock formations. Bird-watchers will want their binoculars at the ready as birds of prey soar above.

Gothic cloister

The museum has a collection of 19th- and 20th-century Catalan paintings and many Italian and French works. It also displays liturgical items from the Holy Land.

Plaça de Santa Maria's focal points are two wings of the Gothic cloister built in 1476. The modern monastery facade is by Françesc Folguera.

Inner courtyard

Monestir de Montserrat, in its dramatic setting below the mountain ↑

The lofty mountain setting of Monestir de Montserrat

Looking toward the sanctuary in the domed basilica

Agapit Vallmitjana sculpted Christ and the apostles on the basilica's Neo-Renaissance facade.

The Black Virgin (La Moreneta) looks down from behind the altar. Protected behind glass, her wooden orb protrudes for pilgrims to touch.

Basilica interior

Cable car terminal

The rack railway follows a rail line built in 1880.

THE VIRGIN OF MONTSERRAT

The soul of Montserrat, the small wooden statue of La Moreneta ("the dark one") is said to have been made by St. Luke, brought here by St. Peter in AD 50, and later hidden from the Moors in the nearby Santa Cova (Holy Cave). Carbon dating suggests, however, that the statue was carved around the 12th century. The Black Virgin is the patroness of Catalonia.

The Basílica de Nuestra Señora del Pilar, on the Río Ebro, Zaragoza

22

Zaragoza

🏠 Zaragoza ✈🚉🚌 ℹ Plaza del Pilar; 976-20 12 00

The Roman settlement of Caesaraugusta gave Zaragoza its name. Located on the fertile banks of the Río Ebro, it grew to become Spain's fifth-largest city, and the capital of Aragón.

Badly damaged during the early-19th-century War of Independence, the old center nevertheless retains several fine monuments. Overlooking the vast Plaza del Pilar is the Basílica de Nuestra Señora del Pilar. With its 11 brightly tiled cupolas, it is one of the city's most impressive sights.

Also on the square are the Gothic-Plateresque Lonja

Did You Know?

Zaragoza's Roman name of Caesaraugusta honored the city's founder – Caesar Augustus.

(commodities exchange), the Palacio Episcopal, and Zaragoza's cathedral, La Seo, which displays a great mix of styles. Part of the exterior is faced with typical Mudéjar brick and ceramic decoration, while inside are splendid Flemish tapestries and a fine Gothic reredos. Nearby are the flamboyant Mudéjar bell tower of the Iglesia de la Magdalena, and the remains of the Roman forum.

Parts of the Roman walls can be seen on the opposite side of the Plaza del Pilar near the Mercado de Lanuza, a market with sinuous ironwork in Art Nouveau style. Nearby, the **Museo Goya** houses the eclectic collection of art historian José Camón Aznar, whose special interest was the locally born artist Goya. The top floor contains a collection of his etchings.

The Alfajería, a beautiful 11th-century Moorish palace with gardens and a mosque, lies on the main road linking Zaragoza to Bilbao.

Museo Goya

🕙 🏠 Calle Espoz y Mina 23 🕐 Hours vary, check website 🌐 museogoya.ibercaja.es

23

Costa Blanca

🏠 Alicante ✈🚉🚌🚢 ℹ Rambla Méndez Núñez 41, Alicante; www. comunitatvalenciana.com

The Costa Blanca occupies a prime stretch of Spain's balmy Mediterranean coastline. The main city, Alicante (Alacant), has an 18th-century Baroque town hall and a 16th-century castle, the Castillo de Santa Bárbara. The nearest beach to the city center is the popular Postiguet; slightly farther afield are the vast beaches of La Albufereta and Sant Joan.

The massive, rocky outcrop of the Penyal d'Ifach towers over Calp harbor, and is one of the Costa Blanca's most dramatic sights. Its summit offers spectacular views. A short drive inland, Castell de Guadalest is a pretty mountain village with castle ruins and a distinctive belfry perched precariously on top of a rock.

Also worth visiting are the whitewashed hilltop town of Altea; Denia, which has good snorkeling; and the cliffs and coves around Xabia. South of Alicante, Guardamar del

Segura has a quiet beach bordered by pine woods, while Torrevieja is a highly developed resort with sweeping, sandy shores.

㉔

Valencia

 Valencia 🛫🚍🚌🚆
ℹ Plaza del Ayuntamiento 1; www.visitvalencia.com

Valencia, Spain's third-largest city, is famous for its ceramics,

and for the spectacular fiesta of Las Fallas, marked by the erection and burning of elaborate papier-mâché monuments (fallas).

Among the city's finest buildings are **La Lonja**, an exquisite Late Gothic hall built between 1482 and 1498, and the cathedral (1262) on Plaza de la Reina. Other interesting monuments include the Gothic **Palau de la Generalitat**, with its splendidly decorated first-floor chambers, and the 17th-century Basílica de la Virgen de los Desamparados. Beyond the city center is the Torres de Serranos gateway, erected in 1391.

Valencia also has a number of fine museums. The **Museo de Bellas Artes** holds 2,000 paintings and statues, which range in date from antiquity to the 19th century – including

six paintings by Goya – while the Institut Valencià de Art Modern (IVAM) displays modern art in an eye-catching contemporary building. The **Ciudad de las Artes y las Ciencias** is a modern complex that includes a science museum and an aquarium.

Valencia's metro system stretches to the extensive beaches and quaint houses of La Malvarrosa and El Cabañal, east of the city.

La Lonja

✿🕙 📍 Plaza del Mercado s/n 📞 962-08 41 53 🕙 10am-7pm Mon-Sat, 10am-2pm Sun

Palau de la Generalitat

📍 Calle Caballeros 2 📞 963-42 46 36 🕙 By prior appointment only

Museo de Bellas Artes

🕙 📍 Calle San Pio V 9 🕙 10am-8pm Tue-Sun 🚫 Jan 1, Good Friday, Dec 25 🌐 museo bellasartesvalencia.gva.es

Ciudad de las Artes y las Ciencias

✿🕙😊 📍 Av del Professor López Piñero 7 🕙 Hours vary, check website 🌐 cac.es

Striking architecture at the Ciudad de las Artes y las Ciencias, Valencia

TOP 5 MALLORCA BEACHES

Cala Formentor
This beautiful beach in the northwest of Mallorca is surrounded by pine trees and forested mountains.

Cala Molins
A sandy Blue Flag beach in the old fishing village of Cala Sant Vicenç.

Cala Deià
Secluded and small, this rocky beach offers phenomenal views.

Santa Ponsa
A very popular sandy beach, Santa Ponsa has excellent amenities for families.

Playa d'Alcúdia
This enormous beach is lapped by shallow waters, making it particularly well-suited to families.

 25

The Balearic Islands

🏠 Balearic Islands 🚗🚌🛳
ℹ️ Plaça de la Reina 2, Mallorca; www.info mallorca.net

The Balearics are renowned for their chic resorts and glitzy nightclubs, but venture inland and you'll soon be rewarded with peaceful villages, awe-inspiring scenery, and a wealth of outdoor activities.

The largest of the Balearics is Mallorca, which has a varied landscape and a rich cultural heritage. Palma, the island's capital, has an atmospheric Old Town with a vast Gothic cathedral known locally as La Seu. Its interior was remodeled in the 20th century by Gaudí.

Also of interest in Palma are the Gothic Basílica de Sant Francesc, the Moorish Palau de l'Almudaina, and the modern Fundació Pilar i Joan Miró, housing Miró's studio and a collection of the artist's work.

Around the island, Andratx is a chic and affluent town, while Pollença is a popular tourist resort that has stayed relatively unspoiled. The Sanctuari de Lluc, high in the Sierra Tramuntana mountains, is regarded by many as the island's spiritual heart.

To the east of Mallorca is the island of Menorca, dotted with hundreds of Bronze Age villages. Menorca's capital, Maó, has a fine harbor, an 18th-century Carmelite church, and the Collecció Hernández Mora, which houses Menorcan art and antiques. The town of Ciutadella, meanwhile, features an impressive central square and a delightful Art Nouveau market.

Lying to the west of Mallorca are the islands of Ibiza and Formentera. The former is

Did You Know?

Ibiza's Sublimotion is the world's most expensive restaurant, charging €1,500 per head.

famed for its nightclubs, while the latter is is perhaps the most alluring island, with its white sands and crystal-clear waters. Formentera's capital, Sant Francesc, has a pretty 18th-century church and a folk museum.

Costa del Sol

🏛 Andalusia 🚇🚌🚗🛳
ℹ Plaza de la Marina 11, Málaga; www.visitcosta delsol.com

With its year-round sunshine and varied coastline, the Costa del Sol attracts crowds of vacationers every year. As well as relaxation, the area offers a full range of beach activities and watersports, and is home to more than 30 of Europe's finest golf courses.

The most stylish resort is Marbella, lined with smart villas and luxury hotels overlooking the area's 24 beaches. Its Old Town is home to the Museo de Grabado Contemporáneo, displaying works by Picasso.

In total contrast to Marbella, the quiet resort town of Estepona, 19 miles (31 km) southwest, is popular with families. Back behind the coastal road, old squares are shaded by orange trees and retain a charming Spanish atmosphere. At one end of town is a stylish marina with waterside restaurants, beyond which villa complexes stretch out along the coast.

Málaga

🏛 Andalusia 🚇🚌🚗🛳
ℹ Plaza de la Marina 11; 952-12 62 72

Málaga, the second-largest city in Andalusia, was a thriving port under Phoenician, Roman, and Moorish rule. It also flourished during the 19th century, when Málaga wine was one of Europe's most popular drinks.

At the heart of the Old Town is the cathedral; begun in 1528 by Diego de Siloé, it is a bizarre mix of styles. The half-built second tower, abandoned in

↑ Enjoying the sunshine at open-air tapas bars in Málaga's historic center

1765, gave the cathedral its nickname: La Manquita ("the one-armed one").

The Casa Natal de Picasso, where the painter spent his early years, is now the head-quarters of the international Picasso Foundation, while the **Museo Picasso Málaga** is home to about 300 of his works. By the port, the **Centre Pompidou Málaga** displays modern artworks.

The city's vast fortress – the **Alcazaba** – was built between the 8th and 11th centuries on the site of a Roman fortress. Its major attractions are Phoenician, Roman, and Moorish artifacts, as well as a Roman theater.

Museo Picasso Málaga
♿🕐🏛 C/San Agustín 8
🕐 10am-8pm daily
🚫 Dec 25, Jan 1 & 6
🌐 museopicassomalaga.org

Centre Pompidou Málaga
♿🕐🏛 Pasaje Doctor Carillo Casaux, Muelle Uno
🕐 9:30am-8pm Wed-Mon
🚫 Jan 1, Dec 25 🌐 centre pompidou-malaga.eu

Alcazaba
♿ 🏛 Calle Alcazabilla
📞 95-222 72 30 🕐 9am-6pm daily (Apr-Oct: to 8pm)

Ciutadella's city hall, overlooking the charming, boat-lined marina, Menorca

The close-packed houses of Granada, with the Alhambra on the hill above them ↑

28

GRANADA

 Granada 🚅🚌🚏 ℹ Santa Ana 4; www.granadatur.com

The guitarist Andrés Segovia (1893–1987) described Granada as a "place of dreams, where the Lord put the seed of music in my soul." It's not hard to see why as you explore the city's Moorish buildings – reminders of Granada's golden period during the rule of the Nasrid dynasty from 1238 to 1492. Following its fall to the Catholic Monarchs in 1492, the city subsequently blossomed in Renaissance splendor.

①
Cathedral

📍 Calle Gran Vía 5 📞 958 22 29 59 🕐 10am-6:30pm Mon-Sat, 3-5:45pm Sun

On the orders of the Catholic Monarchs, construction of Granada's cathedral began in 1523, with Enrique de Egas as the architect. The building works continued for over 180 years, with the Renaissance maestro Diego de Siloé taking on the job in 1529. De Siloé also designed the facade and the magnificent Capilla Mayor. Under its dome, 16th-century windows depict Juan del Campo's *The Passion*. The west front was designed by Alonso Cano, who was born in the city and whose tomb lies in the cathedral.

②
Capilla Real

📍 Calle Oficios 3 🕐 10:15am-6:30pm Mon-Sat, 11am-6pm Sun 🚫 1 Jan, Good Fri, 25 Dec 🌐 capillareal granada.com

The Royal Chapel was built for the Catholic Monarchs between 1506 and 1521 by Enrique de Egas, although both monarchs died before it could be completed. A magnificent *reja* (grille) by Maestro Bartolomé de Jaén encloses the high altar and the Carrara marble figures of Fernando and Isabel, their daughter Juana la Loca ("the Mad"), and her husband Felipe el Hermoso ("the Handsome"). Their coffins are in the crypt. Don't miss the sacristy, which is full of artistic treasures, including paintings by Botticelli, Perugino and Van der Weyden.

③
Monasterio de la Cartuja

📍 Paseo de la Cartuja 📞 958 16 19 32 🕐 Summer: 10am-8pm Mon-Fri, 10am-1pm & 3-8pm Sat, 10am-8pm Sun; winter: 10am-6pm Mon-Fri, 10am-1pm & 3-6pm Sat, 10am-6pm Sun

Founded in 1516 by Christian warrior El Gran Capitán, this monastery has a dazzling cupola by Antonio Palomino, and a Churrigueresque sacristy by Luis de Arévalo and Luis Caballo.

④
Casa de los Tiros

📍 Calle Pavaneras 19 📞 600 14 31 76 🕐 Mid-Sep-May: 10am-8:30pm Tue-Sat, 10am-5pm Sun; Jun-mid-Sep: 9am-3:30pm Tue-Sat, 10am-5pm Sun

Built in Mudéjar style in the 1500s, this palace owes its name to the muskets projecting from its battlements (*tiro* means "shot"). It originally belonged to the family that was awarded the Generalife after the fall of Granada. The facade features depictions of Trojan heroes.

---

 ⑤

Corral del Carbón

📍 Calle Mariana Pineda 📞 958 22 59 90 🕐 10:30am–1:30pm & 5–8pm Mon–Fri, 10:30am–2pm Sat

A relic of the Moorish era, this galleried courtyard was a theater in later times. Today it houses a cultural center.

---

 ⑥

Centro Cultural Caja Granada

📍 Avenida de la Ciencia 🕐 Hours vary, check website 🌐 cajagranada fundacion.es

Set in a stark, white, modern building, this cultural center is home to the superb Memoria de Andalucía Museum, which hosts temporary exhibitions, and a theater and restaurant.

---

 ⑦

Palacio de la Madraza

📍 Calle Oficios 14 📞 958 99 63 50 🕐 9am–2pm & 5–8pm Mon–Fri

Originally an Islamic school, this building later became the city hall and today is a part of Granada University. The Moorish hall has a finely decorated *mihrab* (prayer niche).

---

 ⑧

Generalife

📍 Calle Real de la Alhambra 🕐 8:30am–8pm daily (mid-Oct–mid-Mar: to 6pm daily) 🌐 alhambradegranada.org

From the northern side of the Alhambra (*p336*), a footpath leads to the Generalife, the country estate of the Nasrid kings. Here, they could escape palace intrigues and enjoy tranquility high above the city, a little closer to heaven. Today it provides a magical setting for an annual music and dance festival in late June and July.

EAT

Damasqueros
Order the tasty *guiso* (stew) at this tapas bar.

📍 Calle de Damasqueros 3 🌐 damasqueros.com

€€€

Mirador de Morayma
A delightful patio restaurant offering spectacular views.

📍 Calle de Pianista Gracia Carrillo 2 🌐 mirador demorayma.com

€€€

Tragaluz
This eatery is lit by a huge skylight.

📍 Calle Pintor López Mezquita 13 📞 958 20 46 81

€€€

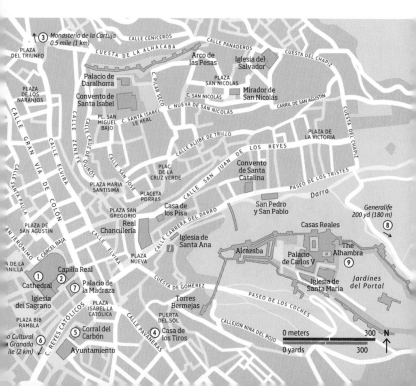

⑨ 🏃 🎽 🖐

THE ALHAMBRA

🏛 Calle Real de la Alhambra 🚌 C3, C4 ⏰ 8:30am–6pm daily
(Apr–mid-Oct: to 8pm); night visits: Apr–mid-Oct: 10–11:30pm Tue–
Sat, mid-Oct–Mar: 8–9:30pm Fri & Sat 🌐 alhambra-patronato.es or
alhambra-tickets.es

A visit to the Alhambra – arguably the pinnacle of Europe's
Moorish palaces – is a truly special experience. A magical
use of space, light, water, and decoration characterizes
this most sensual piece of architecture.

The Alhambra palace was built under Ismail I, Yusuf I, and Muhammad V,
caliphs when the Nasrid dynasty (1238–1492) ruled Granada. Seeking
to belie an image of waning power, they created their idea of paradise
on earth. Modest materials were used (plaster, timber, and tiles), but
they were superbly worked. Although the Alhambra suffered decay
and pillage, including an attempt by Napoleon's troops to blow it up,
it has been restored and its delicate craftsmanship still dazzles the eye.

💬 INSIDER TIP
Night Visit

For a truly magical
experience, visit the
Alhambra after dark,
when the honey-
colored walls are
lit with a warm glow.
It is recommended to
book well ahead to
avoid disappointment.

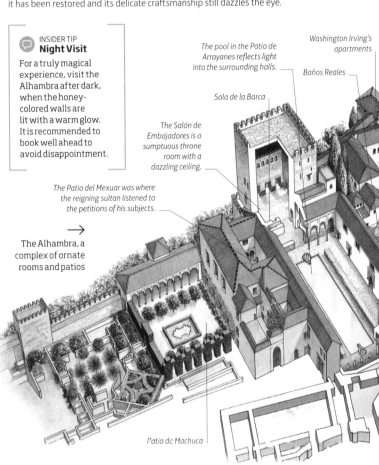

Washington Irving's apartments

The pool in the Patio de Arrayanes reflects light into the surrounding halls.

Baños Reales

Sala de la Barca

The Salón de Embajadores is a sumptuous throne room with a dazzling ceiling.

The Patio del Mexuar was where the reigning sultan listened to the petitions of his subjects.

→
The Alhambra, a
complex of ornate
rooms and patios

Patio de Machuca

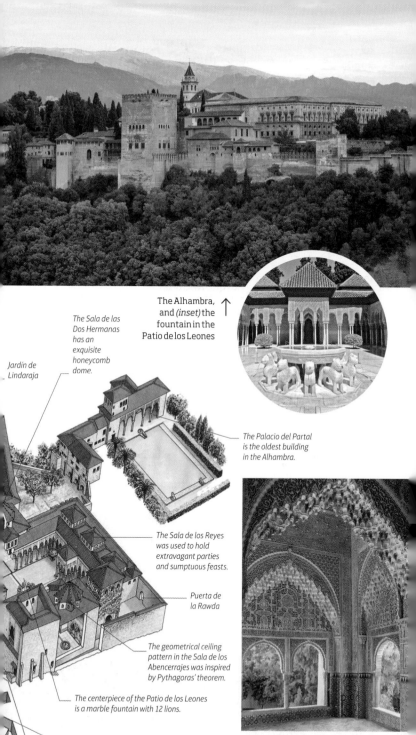

The Alhambra, and *(inset)* the fountain in the Patio de los Leones

The Sala de las Dos Hermanas has an exquisite honeycomb dome.

Jardín de Lindaraja

The Palacio del Partal is the oldest building in the Alhambra.

The Sala de los Reyes was used to hold extravagant parties and sumptuous feasts.

Puerta de la Rawda

The geometrical ceiling pattern in the Sala de los Abencerrajes was inspired by Pythagoras' theorem.

The centerpiece of the Patio de los Leones is a marble fountain with 12 lions.

The Palace of Charles V (1526) houses a collection of Spanish Islamic art.

Gorgeously intricate Moorish embellishments around a palace window

29
Ronda

🏠 Málaga 🚉🚌 ℹ️ Paseo Blas Infante; www.turismoderonda.es

Because of its impregnable position on a rocky outcrop, Ronda was one of the last Moorish bastions in Spain, finally falling to the Christians in 1485.

Among Ronda's many historic buildings are the Palacio Mondragón, adorned with original Moorish mosaics, and the 18th-century Palacio del Marqués de Salvatierra. From the Casa del Rey Moro, built on the site of a Moorish palace, 365 steps lead down to the river.

Across the Puente Nuevo, or "New Bridge," which spans the deep Tajo gorge, is one of Spain's oldest bullrings. Inaugurated in 1785, the **Plaza de Toros** and its bullfighting museum, the **Museo Taurino**, attract aficionados from all over the country.

Plaza de Toros & Museo Taurino

🏛 🏠 Calle Virgen de la Paz ⏰ Apr-Sep: 10am-8pm daily; Mar & Oct: 10am-7pm daily; Nov-Feb: 10am-6pm daily 🌐 rmcr.org

30 🚶 🌳
Parque Nacional de Doñana

🏠 Huelva & Sevilla ℹ️ Carretera A-483 km 1, La Rocina; Carretera A-483 Almonte-Matalascañas km 27.5, Palacio del Acebrón; Carretera A-483 del Rocío a Matalascañas km 12, El Acebuche; www.reddeparquesnacionales.mma.es

Doñana National Park is ranked among Europe's greatest wetlands, composed of more than 247,105 acres (100,000 hectares) of marshes and sand dunes. The area,

officially protected since 1969, was once a ducal hunting ground.

A road runs through part of the park, with information points located along it. There are also several self-guided walks on the park outskirts; however, the interior can be visited on official guided day tours only.

Doñana is home to wild cattle, fallow and red deer, and the lynx – one of Europe's rarest mammals. The greater flamingo and the rare imperial eagle can also be seen here, along with thousands of migratory birds that stop at the marshes in winter.

The Puente Nuevo, spanning the fearsome Tajo gorge at Ronda ↓

⓷ Jerez de la Frontera

🏛Cádiz ✈🚌🚆 ℹ️Alameda Cristina 7; www.turismo jerez.com

Jerez is the capital of sherry production and many *bodegas* (cellars) can be visited here, including **Bodegas Tio Pepe** and **Pedro Domecq**.

The city is also famous for its **Real Escuela Andaluza de Arte Ecuestre**, an equestrian school that arranges public-dressage displays and houses a museum of equestrian art. On the Plaza de San Juan, the 18th-century Palacio de Penmartín houses the Centro Andaluz de Flamenco, where exhibitions give a good introduction to this music and dance tradition. To its south are the 11th-century Alcázar, which encompasses a well-preserved mosque that is now a church, and the cathedral. The latter's most famous treasure is *The Sleeping Girl* by Zurbarán.

> **Because of its position on a rocky outcrop, straddling a precipitous cleft, Ronda was one of the last Moorish bastions in Spain, finally falling to the Christians in 1485.**

Bodegas Tio Pepe

🏛Calle Manuel María González 12 🕐Hours vary, check website 🌐bodegas tiopepe.com

Pedro Domecq

🏛Calle Puerta de Rota ☎956-15 15 52 🕐12am-6pm Mon-Sat

Real Escuela Andaluza de Arte Ecuestre

🏛Avenida Duque de Abrantes 🕐Hours vary, check website 🌐reale scuela.org

 The seafront at Cádiz, with the cathedral in the background

㉜ Cádiz

🏛Cádiz 🚌🚆 ℹ️Paseo de Canalejas; 956-24 10 01, or Avda José León de Carranza; 956-28 56 01

Surrounded almost entirely by water, Cádiz lays claim to being Europe's oldest city. After the Catholic reconquest, the city prospered on wealth brought from the New World.

Modern Cádiz is a busy port, with a pleasant waterfront and an Old Town with narrow alleys and lively markets. The Baroque and Neo-Classical cathedral, with its dome of golden-yellow tiles, is one of Spain's largest. Other attractions in the city include the **Museo de Cádiz**, which has a large art collection and archaeological exhibits, and the 18th-century Oratorio de San Felipe Neri, which has been a shrine to liberalism since 1812, when a provisional government assembled in the church to try to establish Spain's first constitutional monarchy. The Torre Tavira, an 18th-century watchtower with a camera obscura, offers spectacular views of the city.

Museo de Cádiz

🏛Plaza de Mina 🕐9am-9pm Tue-Sat, 9am-3pm Sun 🔒Public hols 🌐museosdeandalucia.es

㉝
Córdoba

🏠 Córdoba 🚌🚆 ℹ️ Plaza del Triunfo; www.cordoba turismo.es

With its glorious mosque and pretty Moorish patios, Córdoba is northern Andalusia's star attraction. In the 10th century, the city enjoyed a golden age as the western capital of the Islamic empire.

Córdoba's most impressive Moorish monument is the mighty **Mezquita**, with its many striped arches. Dating back 12 centuries, to a graceful age when Córdoba was a vibrant and diverse community, the Great Mosque embodied the power of Islam on the Iberian Peninsula. Abd al-Rahman I built the original mosque between 785 and 787, and the building evolved over the centuries, blending many architectural forms. In the 10th century, Al Hakam II made some of the most lavish additions, including the elaborate *mihrab* (prayer niche) and the *maqsura* (caliph's enclosure). During the 16th century, a cathedral was built inside the mosque, under the orders of Carlos V, to complete the city's "Christianization."

Did You Know?

The name Córdoba may have derived from "Kartuba", Phoenician for "prosperous city".

To the west of the Mezquita's towering walls, the **Alcázar de los Reyes Cristianos**, in the old Jewish quarter, is a stunning 14th-century palace-fortress built by Alfonso XI. It was the residence of the Catholic Monarchs during their campaign to wrest Granada from Moorish rule. Later, the Alcázar was used by the Inquisition, and then as a prison. The gardens are particularly lovely with their ponds and fountains. They are open in the evenings in July and August.

Elsewhere in the Jewish quarter, the small Mudéjar-style synagogue (c. 1315) has decorative plasterwork with Hebrew script. Nearby, the Museo Taurino, a bullfighting museum, contains a replica of the tomb of Manolete, a famous matador, and the hide of the bull that killed him.

A Roman bridge links the Old Town to the 14th-century Torre de la Calahorra. This defensive tower houses a small museum depicting life in 10th-century Córdoba.

In the newer part of the city, the Museo Arqueológico displays Roman and Moorish artifacts, while the Museo de Bellas Artes contains sculptures by local artist Mateo Inurria and paintings by Murillo and Zurbarán. Other notable buildings are the beautiful, art-filled Palacio de Viana, and the arcades of the Plaza de la Corredera.

Mezquita

⊘ 🏠 Calle Cardenal Herrero 1 🕐 Mar-Oct: 10am-7pm Mon-Sat, 8:30-11:30am & 3-7pm Sun; Nov-Feb: 8:30am-6pm Mon-Sat, 8:30-11:30am & 3-6pm Sun 🌐 mezquita-catedraldecordoba.es

Alcázar de los Reyes Cristianos

⊘ 🏠 Calle Caballerizas Reales s/n 🕐 Hours vary, check website 🔒 Jan 1, Dec 25 🌐 cultura.cordoba.es

Córdoba's Roman bridge crossing the Guadalquivir river, and the Mezquita

MOORISH ARCHES

The Moorish arch was developed from the horseshoe arch that the Visigoths used in the construction of their churches. The Moors modified the shape and used it as key feature in some of their greatest architectural endeavors - including Córdoba's Mezquita, which has striking Caliphal arches. Subsequent Moorish arches show more sophisticated ornamentation and the gradual demise of the basic horseshoe shape.

Caliphal arch, The Mezquita

Almohad arch, Real Alcázar (p342)

Mudéjar arch, Real Alcázar

Nasrid arch, the Alhambra (p336)

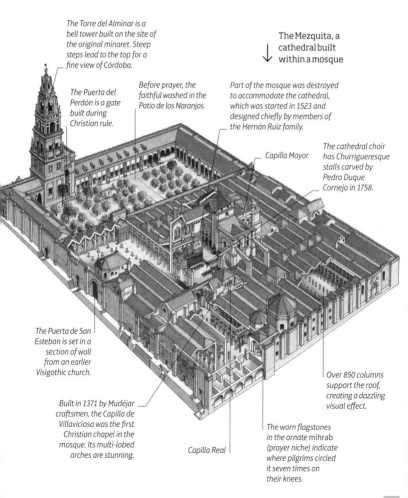

The Torre del Alminar is a bell tower built on the site of the original minaret. Steep steps lead to the top for a fine view of Córdoba.

The Puerta del Perdón is a gate built during Christian rule.

Before prayer, the faithful washed in the Patio de los Naranjos.

The Mezquita, a cathedral built within a mosque ↓

Part of the mosque was destroyed to accommodate the cathedral, which was started in 1523 and designed chiefly by members of the Hernán Ruiz family.

Capilla Mayor

The cathedral choir has Churrigueresque stalls carved by Pedro Duque Cornejo in 1758.

The Puerta de San Esteban is set in a section of wall from an earlier Visigothic church.

Built in 1371 by Mudéjar craftsmen, the Capilla de Villaviciosa was the first Christian chapel in the mosque. Its multi-lobed arches are stunning.

Capilla Real

The worn flagstones in the ornate mihrab (prayer niche) indicate where pilgrims circled it seven times on their knees.

Over 850 columns support the roof, creating a dazzling visual effect.

34

SEVILLE

 Andalusia 🚈🚌🚉 Ⓦ www.visitasevilla.es

The maze of narrow streets that makes up the Barrio de Santa Cruz is a good place to begin an exploration of Seville, since many of the city's best-known sights are located here. As well as souvenir shops, tapas bars, and strolling guitarists, there are plenty of picturesque alleys, hidden plazas, and flower-decked patios to reward the casual wanderer. Good restaurants and bars make the area well worth an evening visit.

①
Cathedral and La Giralda

 Avda de la Constitución
🕐 11am-5pm Mon-Sat (Jul & Aug: 10:30am-6pm), 2:30-6pm Sun (Jul & Aug: to 7pm)
Ⓦ catedralsevilla.es

Seville's imposing cathedral is an arresting sight not only for its size (it's the world's largest Gothic cathedral) but also for its mighty Moorish bell tower, La Giralda.

Officially named Santa María de la Séde, the cathedral occupies the site of a great mosque built by the Almohads in the late 12th century, which had been based on the Koutoubia Mosque of Marrakesh. Eclipsed by the Christian construction, La Giralda and the Patio de los Naranjos are the only lasting legacies of the original Moorish structure. Work on the Gothic cathedral began in 1401 and took just over a century to complete. La Giralda did not assume its present appearance until 1568.

The cathedral houses many fine works of art in its chapels and sacristy, including the stunning high altar reredos. Visitors can also ascend the ramps up to the top of La Giralda for stunning city views.

②
Real Alcázar

 Patio de Banderas
🕐 9:30am-5pm daily (Apr-Sep: to 7pm) 🚫 Jan 1 & 6, Good Fri, Sep 25 Ⓦ alcazar sevilla.org

In 1364, Pedro I of Castile ordered the construction of a royal residence within the palaces that had been built

AZULEJOS

Colorful *azulejos*, glazed ceramic tiles, are a striking feature of Seville. The craft was introduced to Spain by the Moors, who created fantastic mosaics in sophisticated patterns for palace walls - the word *azulejo* derives from the Arabic for "little stone." New techniques were introduced in the 16th century and later mass production extended their use to signs and shop facades.

La Giralda, originally a minaret and now the bell tower of Seville's cathedral

in the 12th century by the Moors. The result was a stunning complex of Mudéjar patios and halls, the Palacio Pedro I, now at the heart of Seville's Real Alcázar. Subsequent monarchs added their own touches: Isabel I dispatched navigators to explore the New World from her Casa de Contratación, while Carlos I (the Holy Roman Emperor Charles V) had grandiose apartments built.

The Salón de Embajadores (Ambassadors' Hall), with its dazzling dome of carved and gilded, interlaced wood, overlooks the elegant Patio de las Doncellas (Patio of the

Maidens), which features some exquisite plasterwork and has been restored to its function as a "floating garden," as it was during Pedro I's reign. Dramatized nocturnal tours take place May–September.

Laid out with terraces, fountains, and pavilions, the gardens of the Real Alcázar provide a delightful refuge from the bustle of Seville.

---

③

Hospital de los Venerables

🏠 Plaza de los Venerables 8
🕐 10am–6pm daily 🗙 Jan 1, Good Friday, Dec 25
🌐 hospitalvenerables.es

This late-17th-century home for elderly priests has been restored as a cultural center,

its upper floors, cellar, and infirmary serving as exhibition galleries. The hospital church is a showcase of Baroque splendors, with frescoes by both Juan de Valdés Leal and his son, Lucas Valdés.

EAT

La Quinta Brasería
Expect attentive service and excellent grilled meat at this stylish restaurant.

🏠 Plaza Padre Jerónimo de Córdoba 11
🌐 grupopanot.com

€€€

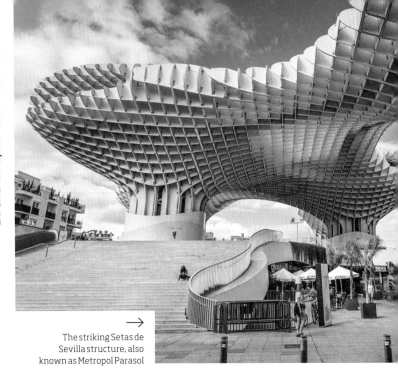

→

The striking Setas de Sevilla structure, also known as Metropol Parasol

④

Setas de Sevilla (Metropol Parasol)

🏠 Plaza de la Encarnación
🕐 Hours vary, check website
ⓦ setasdesevilla.com

German architect Jürgen Mayer's huge mushroom-shaped parasols are topped with a viewing platform and panoramic restaurant, while underneath there are Roman and medieval ruins (visible in the Antiquarium museum), shops, and a market.

⑤

Plaza de Toros de la Maestranza

🏠 Paseo de Cristóbal Colón 12 🕐 9:30am-7pm daily (Apr-Oct: to 9pm) 🚫 For bullfights, Dec 25 ⓦ real maestranza.com

Built between 1761 and 1881, Seville's famous bullring seats up to 14,000 spectators. Whatever your opinion is of bullfighting, this immense building has many interesting features. Visitors can take a

guided tour, which starts from the entrance on Paseo de Cristóbal Colón, and explore the small museum.

---

⑥

Museo de Bellas Artes

🏠 Plaza del Museo 9
🕐 9am-9pm Tue-Sat, 9am-3pm Sun & public hols w (Aug: 9am-3pm Tue-Sun)
ⓦ museosdeandalucia.es

The Convento de la Merced Calzada houses one of Spain's best fine art museums. Its delightful tree-filled patios and colorful *azulejos* make it a wonderful setting for the works of art.

The museum's collection of Spanish art and sculpture – which covers all periods from the medieval to the modern – focuses on the work of artists trained in Seville in the 16th and 17th centuries. Among the star attractions is Murillo's *La Servilleta*, a Virgin and Child (1665–8) that is said to be painted on a napkin *(servilleta)*.

FLAMENCO

The origins of this Andalusian art are hard to trace. The Romani may have been the main creators, mixing their own Indian-influenced culture with local folklore, and with Jewish and Christian music. Flamenco began to develop into its present form only in the 18th century. Dancers *(bailaores)* improvise from basic movements, following the rhythm of the guitar and their feelings.

houses the Museo de Artes y Costumbres Populares, with displays of traditional folk arts from Andalusia.

---

 (8)

Centro Andaluz de Arte Contemporáneo

🏛 Calle Americo Vespucio 2, Isla de la Cartuja ⏰ 11am-9pm Tue-Sat, 10am-3:30pm Sun 🌐 caac.es

Built in the 15th century, the Monasterio de Santa María de las Cuevas was inhabited by monks until 1836 and now houses the Centro Andaluz de Arte Contemporáneo, which contains works by Andalusian artists, plus Spanish and international art. It stands at the heart of the Isla de Cartuja, a sprawling complex of exhibition halls, museums, and entertainment and leisure spaces that was the site of Expo '92. The Isla Mágica theme park is also nearby.

---

(9)

Torre del Oro

🏛 Paseo de Cristóbal Colón 📞 95-422 24 19 ⏰ 9:30am-6:45pm Mon-Fri, 10:30am-6:45pm Sat & Sun 🚫 Aug

The Moors built the Torre del Oro (Tower of Gold) as

(7)

Parque María Luisa

In 1893, Princess María Luisa donated part of the grounds of the Palacio San Telmo to the city for this park. A leafy retreat from the heat of the city, its most extravagant feature is the semicircular Plaza de España, designed by Aníbal González and built for the 1929 Ibero-American Exposition. At the center of the park, the Pabellón Mudéjar

→ Dusk falling on the Torre del Oro, by the Guadalquivir river

a defensive lookout in 1220, but its distinctive turret was not added until 1760. The gold in the tower's name may refer to the gilded *azulejos* (ceramic tiles) that once clad its walls, or alternatively to treasures from the Americas unloaded here. The tower has had many uses, but now houses the Museo Marítimo, which exhibits an array of maritime maps and antiques.

PRACTICAL
INFORMATION

Here you will find all the essential advice and information you will need before and during your stay in Spain.

AT A GLANCE

CURRENCY
Euro (EUR)

TIME ZONE
CET/CEST. Central European Summer Time runs from the last Sunday in March to the last Sunday in October.

LANGUAGE
Spanish

ELECTRICITY SUPPLY
Power sockets are type F, fitting a two-prong, round-pin plug. Standard voltage is 230V.

EMERGENCY NUMBERS

GENERAL
EMERGENCY

112

TAP WATER
Unless stated otherwise, tap water in Spain is safe to drink.

Getting There

Madrid and Barcelona are the main airports for long-haul flights into Spain. European budget airlines fly to cities across Spain all year round at reasonable prices.

Spain's international rail services are operated by state-run **Renfe** (Red Nacional de Ferrocarriles Españoles). There are several routes to Spain from France, as well as connections with London, Brussels, Amsterdam, Zürich, Geneva, and Milan. The TALGO (Tren Articulado Ligero Goicoechea Oriol), a high-speed luxury train service (operated by Renfe), also serves many of these destinations. There are two main rail routes from Portugal to Spain: the Lusitania sleeper train from Lisbon to Madrid, and the Sud Express, which departs from Lisbon and terminates in the French town of Hendaye on the French-Spanish border, from where you can catch one of the regular services to a Spanish town or city.

Two car ferry routes link the Spanish mainland with the UK. Brittany Ferries sails from Plymouth and Portsmouth in the UK to Santander in Cantabria, and from Portsmouth to Bilbao. The crossings take more than 24 hours and advance reservations are essential in the summer months.
Renfe
w renfe.com

Personal Security

Spain is generally a safe country, but it is always a good idea to take sensible precautions against pickpockets. If you have anything stolen, report the crime as soon as possible to the nearest police station. Get a copy of the crime report in order to claim on your insurance.

Health

Medicinal supplies and advice for minor ailments can be obtained from a pharmacy *(farmacia)*, identifiable by a green or red cross. Each pharmacy displays a card in the window showing the address of the nearest all-night pharmacy.

EU citizens with a European Health Insurance Card (EHIC) are entitled to free emergency medical care in Spain, but it is also advisable to take out some form of supplementary health insurance. Visitors from outside the EU must arrange their own private medical insurance.

Passports and Visas

EU nationals may visit for an unlimited period,. Citizens of the US, Canada, Australia, and New Zealand can remain in Spain without a visa for up to 90 days. For visa information specific to your home country, consult your nearest Spanish embassy or check online.

Travelers with Specific Needs

The **Spanish National Tourist Office** has a number of helpful publications in English for travelers with specific needs, many of which are downloadable from their website *(see right)*. Most city tourist websites also offer a range of useful information for disabled travelers, as do Spain's Confederación Española de Personas con Discapacidad Física y Orgánica **(COCEMFE)** and **Accessible Spain**.

Accessible Spain
W accessiblespaintravel.com
COCEMFE
W cocemfe.es

Money

Most urban establishments accept major credit, debit, and prepaid currency cards. Contactless payments are common in cities, but it's always a good idea to carry cash for purchasing smaller items. ATMs are widely available, although many charge a small fee for cash withdrawals.

Cell Phones and Wi-Fi

Free Wi-Fi is reasonably common, particularly in libraries, large public spaces, restaurants, and bars. Some places, such as airports and hotels, may charge you to use their Wi-Fi.
Visitors traveling to Spain with EU tariffs can use their devices without being affected by data roaming charges. Visitors from other countries should check their contracts before departure in order to avoid unexpected charges.

Getting Around

A number of budget airlines offer good rates on regular internal flights within Spain.
Renfe is the country's national rail operator, from which you can buy tickets online or at stations. They, along with some regional companies, operate a good service throughout Spain. The fastest intercity services are the high-speed TALGO and AVE trains; *largo recorrido* (long-distance) trains are much cheaper, but they are so slow that you usually need to travel overnight. It is advisable to book tickets at least a month in advance. *Regionales y cercanías* (the regional and local services) are frequent and inexpensive.
Spain has no national long-distance bus company. The largest private company, **Alsa**, offers a variety of bus tours and sightseeing trips throughout the country; other companies operate in particular regions. Tickets and information for long-distance travel are available at main bus stations and from travel agents.
Spain's fastest roads are its *autopistas*, which are normally dual carriageways subject to *peajes* (tolls). *Autovías* are similar but do not have tolls. Smaller roads are less well kept but are a more relaxed way to see rural Spain.
All the major international car rental firms are represented in Spain. Spanish law requires drivers to carry at all times valid insurance and registration documents, a driver's license, and ID.
Trasmediterránea runs car ferry services from Barcelona and Valencia on the Spanish mainland to the Balearic Islands, and also operates frequent inter-island services.

Alsa
W alsa.com
Trasmediterránea
W trasmediterranea.es

Visitor Information

All major Spanish cities and towns have a tourist information office *(oficina de turismo)*, which will provide town plans, lists of hotels and restaurants, as well as details of local activities. There are branches of the **Spanish National Tourist Office** in several cities worldwide; its website is also a useful resource.
Spanish National Tourist Office
W spain.info

A tram winding its way through Lisbon's Alfama neighborhood

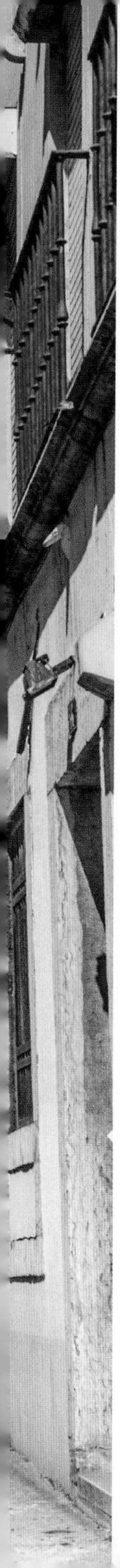

PORTUGAL

One of the oldest nation states in Europe, Portugal has experienced a dramatic rise and fall in its fortunes. The Romans arrived in the region in 216 BC, naming the province Lusitania after the Celtiberian tribe that lived there. After the collapse of the Roman Empire in the 5th century, it was overrun first by Germanic tribes, then by Moors from North Africa in 711. Reconquest by the Christian kingdoms of the north began in the 11th century. In the process, the small county of Portucale started to grow in stature, expanding south to the Algarve. Portuguese sailors began to explore the African coast and the Atlantic, leading to Vasco da Gama's voyage to India in 1498 and the colonization of Brazil in 1500. Exploitation of this expanding empire brought great wealth, but military defeat in Morocco, followed by Spanish rule from 1580 to 1640, meant that the prosperity was short-lived. A major earthquake in Lisbon in 1755 caused further devastation. In the late 18th century, the country began to modernize, but Napoleon's invasion in 1807 and the loss of Brazil in 1825 left Portugal impoverished and divided. Absolutists and Constitutionalists struggled for power, until, in 1910, a republican revolution overthrew the monarchy. The weakness of the economy led to a military coup in 1926 and a long period of dictatorship, which ended in 1974 with the bloodless Carnation Revolution. Democracy was restored in 1976, and Portugal has since enjoyed economic growth, largely through tourism and alternative forms of energy.

PORTUGAL

Camin

Viana do Caste

Póvoa de Var

Praia de M

Figueira da Foz

Leir

MOSTEIRO DE SANTA MARIA DA VITÓRIA
MOSTEIRO DE SANTA MARIA DE ALCOBAÇA 7

São Martinho do Porto

IC2

Peniche

Rio Maior

A8

Alenquer

Torres Vedras

Ericeira

Vila
de X

Atlantic

Ocean

SINTRA

PALÁCIO NACIONAL DA PENA 6 5

2 1 Alcoche

CASCAIS LISBON

Setúbal

Cabo Espichel Sesimbra

Santiago do Ca

Sines

Vila Nova de Milfont

Aljez

Vila do Bispo

Cabo de São Vicente LA

❶
LISBON

 **𝒊 www.visitlisboa.com**

One of Europe's oldest and most attractive capitals, Lisbon is a captivating city where history and tradition jostle with cutting-edge architecture and vibrant nightlife. Long lauded for its plentiful sunshine and excellent value, Lisbon is also home to a fast-developing foodie scene, and an array of rooftop bars that make the most of the hilly city's spectacular panoramas.

①
Sé

🏛 Largo da Sé 🚌 737
🚋 12, 28 ☎ 218-866 752
🕐 7am-7pm daily

Constructed in 1150 for the first bishop of Lisbon – Sé denotes the seat of a bishop – this cathedral was built by King Afonso Henriques on the site of a Moorish mosque.

Though much renovated over the centuries, the Sé has kept its solid Romanesque facade. The Capela de Santo Ildefonso, one of nine Gothic chapels in the ambulatory behind the altar, contains two fine 14th-century tombs, and in the Franciscan chapel by the entrance stands the font where St. Antony of Padua was baptized in 1195.

---

②
Museu Nacional do Azulejo

🏛 Rua da Madre de Deus 4
🚌 718, 728, 742, 759, 794
🕐 10am-6pm Tue-Sun
🚫 Jan 1, Easter Sun, May 1, Jun 13, Dec 25 🌐 museu doazulejo.gov.pt

The use of decorative tiles in Portugal was a legacy of the Moors. From the 16th century onward, the country started producing its own painted ceramic tiles *(azulejos)*, some of the finest of which are considered to be the blue-and-white tiles of the Baroque era.

The National Tile Museum is housed in the Convento da

← Sunset over Lisbon, seen from the Miradouro de Santa Luzia

today. Panels from churches, monasteries, and other sites around Portugal have been reassembled here. Highlights of the collection include a blue-and-white, 18th-century panorama showing Lisbon before the 1755 earthquake (*p356*), and colorful 17th-century carpet tiles (so-called because they imitated the patterns of Moorish rugs).

 INSIDER TIP
Getting Around

Lisbon's expanding metro system links the north of the city with sights in the center around Rossio square. Buses cover the whole city. Take the Santa Justa lift to reach the Bairro Alto district, and the 28 tram to climb the steep hill up through Alfama. Belém is served by tram, train, and bus.

Madre de Deus, founded by Dona Leonor (widow of João II) in 1509. The interior of the church has striking Baroque decoration, added by João V.

An important surviving feature of the original convent building is the Manueline cloister. Together with the larger Renaissance cloister, it provides a stunning setting for the museum. Decorative panels, individual tiles, and photographs trace tile-making from its introduction, through Spanish influence and the development of Portugal's own styles, to

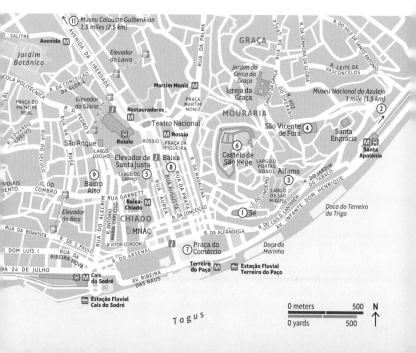

↑ Strolling through the colorful streets of the historic Alfama neighborhood

③

Alfama

 737 12, 28

A fascinating quarter at any time of day, the Alfama comes to life in the late afternoon and early evening when the small restaurants and bars start to fill and music, often *fado*, can be heard in the alleyways. The oldest part of Lisbon, this was once the most desirable quarter of the city. In the Middle Ages, wealthy residents began to move away, fearing earthquakes, leaving the quarter to fishermen and paupers. Ironically, the Alfama was spared by the earthquake of 1755 (*p356*). Today, the area is a warren of narrow streets and small, picturesque houses clinging to the hillside below the Castelo de São Jorge.

The best way to see this area is to start at the castle and work your way down. Interesting attractions on the way include the Museu de Artes Decorativas (Museum of Decorative Arts) and the views from the terrace of the Miradouro de Santa Luzia. On a Tuesday or Saturday, you can also pay a visit to the colorful Feira da Ladra (Thieves' Market) in Campo de Santa Clara, to the east of the castle.

④

São Vicente de Fora

 Largo de São Vicente 28 712, 734 218-824 400 10am-6pm Tue-Sat

St. Vincent was proclaimed Lisbon's patron saint in 1173, when his relics were brought to a church and monastery on this site. The present church was completed in 1627; its Italianate facade is adorned with statues of Saints Vincent, Augustine, and Sebastian over the entrance. Behind the church is the Bragança

Pantheon, housing the tombs of almost every Bragança king and queen, from João IV, who died in 1656, to Manuel II, last king of Portugal. Only Maria I and Pedro IV are not buried here. A stone mourner kneels at the tomb of Carlos I and his son Luís Felipe, assassinated in Praça do Comércio in 1908.

⑤

Elevador de Santa Justa

 Rua de Santa Justa and Largo do Carmo Rossio 709, 711, 736, & many others 213 613 000 7:30am-9:30pm daily (May-Sep: to 11pm)

Also known as the Elevador do Carmo, this Neo-Gothic lift was built at the turn of the 20th century by French architect Raoul Mesnier du Ponsard, a student of Gustave Eiffel. Made of iron and embellished with filigree, it links the Baixa with Largo do Carmo in the Bairro Alto, 105 ft (32 m) above. Passengers can travel up and down inside the tower in one of two smart wood-paneled cabins. The apex of the tower, reached via a spiral stairway, is given over to a viewing gallery – this vantage point commands splendid views of Rossio, the Baixa, the castle on the opposite hill, the river, and the nearby ruins of the Carmo church.

⑥

Castelo de São Jorge

Porta de S Jorge, Rua do Chão da Feira 737 28 9am-6pm daily (Mar-Oct to 9pm) castelodesao jorge.pt

Following the recapture of Lisbon from the Moors in 114 King Afonso Henriques transformed their citadel – which crowned Lisbon's eastern hill – into the residence of the Portuguese kings. In 151

TORRE DE ULISSES

Named after the Greek hero Ulysses, who supposedly founded Lisbon on his meander home from Troy, this tower in the Castelo de São Jorge contains a camera obscura – a complicated system of lenses and mirrors that projects 360° views of the city onto the walls in real time. Views are weather-dependent; sunny mornings, when the light is soft, yield the clearest images.

Manuel I built a more lavish palace beside the river, and in the centuries that followed the Castelo de São Jorge was used variously as a theater, a prison, and an arms depot. After the 1755 earthquake, the ramparts lay in ruins until 1938, when the castle was completely rebuilt.

The castle gardens and narrow streets of the old Santa Cruz district, which lies within the walls, are a pleasant place for a stroll, and the views are the finest in Lisbon. Visitors can climb the towers, walk along the reconstructed ramparts, or stand on the shaded observation terrace. Within the castle's outer walls there are also a museum and an archaeological site.

⑦ Praça do Comércio

Ⓜ Terreiro do Paço
🚌 711, 714, 732, 759, 794, & many others 🚋 15

More commonly known as Terreiro do Paço (Palace Square), this was the site of the royal palace for 400 years, after Manuel I moved the royal residence here in 1511. The first palace was destroyed in the 1755 earthquake, and its replacement was built around three sides of the square. After the 1910 revolution, it became government offices.

The south side looks across the Tagus and was once the finest gateway to Lisbon, with marble steps up from the river. In the center of the square is an equestrian statue of José I (1775). The triumphal arch on the north side, decorated with statues of historical figures, leads into Rua Augusta and the Baixa. Take the elevator to the top of the arch for sweeping views of the city.

The square has been the scene of several momentous events in Portuguese history. On February 1, 1908, King Carlos and his son, Luís Felipe, were assassinated here, ushering in the end of the monarchy. Then in 1974, it saw the first uprising of the Armed Forces Movement, which overthrew the Caetano regime in a bloodless coup known as the Carnation Revolution.

STAY

Solar do Castelo

A charming hotel by the castle walls, built on the site of the former palace kitchens. Expect original stone walls and intricate *azulejos*.

🏠 Rua das Cozinhas 2
 solardocastelo.com

€€€

Hotel Almalusa

Beautiful 18th-century building on a historic square. Many rooms have original features.

🏠 Praça do Município 21
 almalusahotels.com

€€€

As Janelas Verdes

This romantic hotel in a charming 18th-century townhouse offers stunning river views from its top.

🏠 Rua das Janelas Verdes 47 asjanelas verdes.com

€€€

Equestrian statue and triumphal arch on Praça do Comércio

THE EARTHQUAKE OF 1755

The first tremor of the devastating 1755 earthquake was felt at 9:30am on November 1. It was followed by a second, far more violent shock a few minutes later, which reduced over half the city to rubble. A third shock was followed by fires, which quickly spread. An hour later, huge waves came rolling in from the Tagus, flooding the lower part of the city. Most of Portugal suffered damage, but Lisbon was the worst affected: an estimated 15,000 people were killed.

Baixa

M Rossio, Restauradores, Terreiro do Paço ₪711, 714, 732, 736, 759, 794, & many others ₪15

After the 1755 earthquake, the Marquês de Pombal created an entirely new city center, one of Europe's first examples of town planning. Using a grid layout of streets, the Praça do Comércio was linked with the busy central square of Rossio.

The Baixa (Lower Town) is Lisbon's commercial hub, with banks, offices, and stores. By the Restauradores metro station is the Palácio Foz, an 18th-century palace. It was built by architect Francesco Savario Fabri for the Marquês de Castelo-Melhor and renamed after the Marquês de Foz, who lived here in the 19th century.

↑ The wide Rua Augusta, cutting through Lisbon's Baixa district

Visitors are naturally drawn to Rossio, an elegant square and social focal point with cafés and *pastelarias*. The Teatro Nacional stands on the north side. Just to the east of Rossio is the less attractive Praça da Figueira, the city's main marketplace during Pombal's time. Rua das Portas de Santo Antão, north of the two squares, is a lively pedestrian street full of restaurants.

Bairro Alto

M Baixa-Chiado ₪758, 773 ₪24, 28 (also Elevador da Glória, Elevador da Santa Justa & Elevador da Bica)

The hilltop Bairro Alto quarter dating from the 16th century, is one of Lisbon's most picturesque districts. Its narrow, cobbled streets house a traditional, close-knit community, with small workshops and family-run *tascas* (cheap restaurants). This predominantly residential area has become fashionable at night for its bars, nightclubs, and *fado* houses. Very different in character is the neighboring, elegant, commercial district, known as the Chiado, where affluent Lisboetas shop. On the main street, Rua Garrett, the Café Brasileira – once frequented by writers and intellectuals – is a popular meeting spot. The Chiado was devastated by fire in 1988, but a renovation project led by Portugeuese architect Álvaro Siza Vieira has restored many of the original facades.

The best way to reach the Bairro Alto from the Baixa is via the Chiado district or the Elevador de Santa Justa, a Neo-Gothic elevator (*p354*). Attractions to be found in Bairro Alto include the richly decorated São Roque church the ruined Igreja do Carmo, and the Museu Nacional de Arte Contemporânea (MNAC) a stylish space housing art from 1850 to 1950.

Displays in the Modern Collection at the Museu Calouste Gulbenkian

Museu Nacional de Arte Antiga

🏠 Rua das Janelas Verdes 🚌 713, 714, 727 🚋 15, 18 🕐 10am-6pm Tue-Sun 🗓 Jan 1, Easter Sun, May 1, Jun 13, Dec 25 🌐 museude arteantiga.pt

The national art collection, housed in a 17th-century palace, was inaugurated in 1770. In 1940, a modern annex (including the main facade) was built on the site of the St. Albert Carmelite monastery, largely destroyed in the 1755 earthquake. Its only surviving feature, the chapel, has been integrated into the museum.

The first floor houses 14th–19th-century European paintings, decorative arts, and furniture. Artists exhibited include Piero della Francesca, Raphael, Hieronymus Bosch, and Albrecht Dürer. East Asian and African art, Chinese ceramics, and the gold, silver, and jewelry collection are on the second floor. The top floor houses Portuguese works.

The pride of the Portuguese collection is the *Panels of St. Vincent* (c. 1467–70), attributed to painter Nuno Gonçalves.

This altarpiece, painted on six panels, features portraits of a wide range of contemporary figures – including beggars, sailors, bishops, and princes – all paying homage to the city's patron saint.

Museu Calouste Gulbenkian

🏠 Avda de Berna 45 Ⓜ Praça de Espanha, São Sebastião 🚌 716, 756, 726, 746 🕐 10am-6pm Wed-Mon 🗓 Jan 1, Easter Sun, May 1, Dec 24 & 25 🌐 gulbenkian.pt

Thanks to Armenian oil magnate Calouste Gulbenkian, who moved to the country in World War II, Portugal owns one of the finest personal art collections assembled during the 20th century. The works are split across two separately housed collections, linked by a park. The Founder's Collection – Gulbenkian's personal pieces – sits within a purpose-built museum, and features exhibits ranging from ancient Egyptian statuettes to Art Nouveau jewelry by René Lalique. South of the gardens stands the Modern Collection, widely considered to be the world's most complete collection of modern Portuguese art.

EAT

Confeitaria Nacional
This traditional café opened in 1829 and still serves a tempting array of pastries, teas, and strong coffee.

🏠 Praça da Figueira 18 📞 213 424 470

€€€

Time Out Market (Mercado da Ribeira)
Sample burgers, sushi, fine cheeses, *pastéis de nata*, and ice cream from some of Lisbon's best-known food outlets.

🏠 Avenida 24 de Julho 🌐 timeoutmarket.com

€€€

Cantina Zé Avillez
Enjoy tasty food by one of Lisbon's top chefs at this tiled restaurant.

🏠 Rua dos Arameiros 15 🌐 cantinazeavillez.pt

€€€

Páteo
Occupying a covered patio inside a former monastery, this lovely space specializes in quality fish and seafood.

🏠 Bairro do Avillez, 18 Rua Nova da Trindade 📞 215 830 290

€€€

A Baiuca
This tiny *tasca* has a good menu and even better *fado vadio* (amateur fado).

🏠 Rua de São Miguel 20 📞 218 867 284 🗓 Tue & Wed

€€€

LISBON: BELÉM DISTRICT

⑫

Museu Nacional dos Coches

🏛 Avda da Índia 136 🚌 714, 727, 728, 729, 751 🚊 15
🚉 Belém 🕙 10am-6pm Tue-Sun 🚫 Jan 1, Easter Sun, May 1, Jun 13, Dec 24 & 25
🌐 museudoscoches.pt

This museum's collection of coaches is arguably the finest in Europe. First established in the old Royal Riding School, the museum showcases a unique and opulent collection of coaches, carriages, and sedan chairs dating from the 17th, 18th, and 19th centuries. The collection was moved to a new, modern building by the Brazilian architect Paulo Mendes da Rocha in 2015.

The coaches on display span three centuries. The oldest is the comparatively plain 16th-century red leather and wood coach of Philip II of Spain. Later coaches become increasingly sumptuous, with interiors lined with red velvet and gold, and exteriors carved with allegorical figures. The most extravagant of all are three Baroque coaches made in Rome for the Portuguese

ambassador to the Vatican in the early 18th century. Also of note is the 18th-century Eyeglass Chaise, which has a black leather hood pierced with sinister eyelike windows. It dates from the era of Pombal, when the use of lavish decoration was discouraged.

⑬

Museu de Marinha

🏛 Praça do Império 🚌 714, 727, 728, 729, 751 🚊 15
🚉 Belém 🕙 10am-5pm daily (May-Sep: to 6pm)
🚫 Jan 1, Easter Sun, May 1, Dec 25 🌐 museu.marinha.pt

The Maritime Museum opened in 1962 in the west wing of the Jerónimos monastery (p360). A hall devoted to Portugal's Age of Discovery illustrates the rapid progress in ship design from the mid-15th century, from the bark and caravel to the Portuguese nau, or great ship. There is also a display of navigational instruments and replicas of 16th-century maps. The pillars carved with the Cross of the Order of Christ are replicas of various kinds of padrão, a stone marker set

↑ The Torre de Belém, a Manueline fortress on the Tagus River

up to denote sovereignty over the new lands encountered. Beyond the main hall are models of various modern Portuguese ships and the Royal Quarters, housing the exquisitely furnished wood-paneled cabin of King Carlos and Queen Amélia from the royal yacht Amélia.

⑭

MAAT

🏛 Avda Brasília 🚌 727, 728, 729 🚊 15 🚉 Belém 🕙 11am-7pm Wed-Mon 🚫 1 Jan, May 1 & 25 Dec 🌐 maat.pt

The stylish MAAT (Museu de Arte, Arquitetura e Tecnologia) is dedicated to contemporary, primarily Portuguese, art, along with modern architecture and technology. The award-winning building that houses the museum is a sharp contrast to the well-known Lisbon power station, which stands next door and forms an integral part of this complex. Visits to the MAAT include a tour of the iconic power station, and access to the building's undulating pedestrian roof, which affords stunning views of Lisbon.

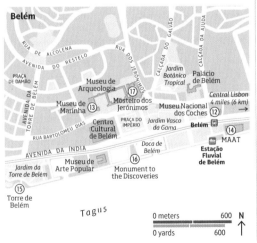

Belém

- Museu de Arqueologia ⑰
- Jardim Botânico Tropical
- Palácio de Belém
- Museu de Marinha ⑬
- Mosteiro dos Jerónimos
- Museu Nacional dos Coches ⑫
- Central Lisbon 4 miles (6 km) →
- Centro Cultural de Belém
- Jardim Vasco da Gama
- Belém 🚉
- ⑭ MAAT
- Doca de Belém
- Estação Fluvial de Belém
- Museu de Arte Popular
- Monument to the Discoveries ⑯
- Jardim da Torre de Belém
- ⑮ Torre de Belém

PRAÇA DE DAMÃO · RUA DE ALCOLENA · AVENIDA DO RESTELO · RUA DOS JERÓNIMOS · CALÇADA DO GALVÃO · CALÇADA DA AJUDA · AVENIDA DA TORRE DE BELÉM · RUA BARTOLOMEU DIAS · PRAÇA DO IMPÉRIO · AVENIDA DA ÍNDIA

Tagus

0 meters 600 | 0 yards 600 | N ↑

Torre de Belém

📍 Avenida da Índia 🚌 714, 727, 728, 729, 751 🚊 15 🚉 Belém ⏰ 10am-5:30pm Tue-Sun (May-Sep: to 6:30pm) 🚫 Jan 1, Easter Sun, May 1, Jun 13, Dec 25 🌐 torrebelem.pt

Commissioned by Manuel I, the tower was built as a fortress in the middle of the Tagus in 1515–21. Before nearby land was reclaimed in the 19th century, the tower stood much farther from the shore than it does today. As the starting point for the 16th-century navigators who set out to forge the trade routes to the east, this Manueline gem became a symbol of Portugal's era of expansion. On the terrace, facing the sea, stands a statue of Our Lady of Safe Homecoming, watching over the lives of Portugal's sailors.

The beauty of the tower lies in the exterior decoration: Manueline ropework carved in stone, openwork balconies, and Moorish-style watchtowers. The distinctive battlements are in the shape of shields, decorated with the squared cross of the Order of Christ, the emblem that also adorned the sails of Portuguese ships.

The space below the terrace is very austere, but the private quarters in the tower are worth visiting for the elegant arcaded Renaissance loggia and the wonderful panorama.

Monument to the Discoveries

📍 Padrão dos Descobrimentos, Avda de Brasília 🚌 714, 727, 728, 729, 751 🚊 15 🚉 Belém ⏰ Mar-Sep: 10am-7pm daily; Oct-Feb: 10am-6pm Tue-Sun 🚫 Jan 1, May 1, Dec 25 🌐 padrao dosdescobrimentos.pt

Standing prominently on the Belém waterfront, the Padrão dos Descobrimentos was built in 1960 to mark the 500th anniversary of the death of Henry the Navigator. The 170-ft- (52-m-) high monument resembles a caravel – the small, lateen-rigged ship used by Portuguese sailors to explore the coast of Africa in the 15th century. Henry the Navigator stands at the prow, with a caravel in hand, flanked by two lines of figures linked with the Age of Discovery.

In front of the monument is a huge mariner's compass cut into the paving. The central map, dotted with galleons and mermaids, shows the routes of the explorers in the 15th and 16th centuries. Inside the monument, an elevator whisks you to the sixth floor, where steps lead to the top for a splendid panorama.

EAT

Antiga Confeitaria de Belém

This famous café has been baking classic *pastéis de Belém* custard tarts since 1837, and you can see them being made right before your eyes here. The long queues are absolutely worth it.

📍 Rua de Belém 84-92 🌐 pasteisdebelem.pt

€€€

Sculptures decorating the Monument to the Discoveries ↓

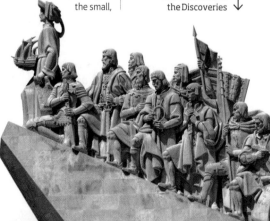

(17) ⚔

MOSTEIRO DOS JERÓNIMOS

📍 Praça do Império 🚌 714, 727, 728, 729, 751 🚋 15 🚉 Belém 🕐 10am–5:30pm Tue–Sun (May–Sep: to 6:30pm) 🚫 Jan 1, Easter Sun, May 1, Jun 13, Dec 25
🌐 mosteirojeronimos.pt

Belém's most popular attraction, this highly ornate monastery is a National Monument and was designated a UNESCO World Heritage Site in 1983.

A monument to the wealth of Portugal's Age of Discovery, the monastery is the culmination of the Manueline style of architecture. Commissioned by Manuel I in around 1501, soon after Vasco da Gama's return from his historic voyage, it was funded largely by "pepper money," taxes on spices, precious stones, and gold. Various master builders worked on the edifice, the most notable being Diogo Boitac, who was replaced by João de Castilho in 1517. The monastery was entrusted to the Order of St. Jerome (Hieronymites) until 1834, when all religious orders were disbanded.

The fountain is in the shape of a lion, the heraldic animal of St. Jerome.

The Refectory walls are tiled with 18th-century azulejos.

↑ The monastery's exterior, designed to emphasize the Portuguese empire's wealth

Did You Know?

Eighteenth-century *azulejos* in the refectory depict the Feeding of the Five Thousand.

The modern wing, built in 1850 in Neo-Manueline style, houses the National Museum of Archaeology.

Entrance to church and cloister

The West Portal was designed by the French sculptor Nicolau Chanterène.

[1] Slender pillars rise like palm trees to the spectacular vaulted roof in the church of Santa Maria.

[2] The marble tomb of navigator Vasco da Gama is festooned with seafaring symbols.

[3] João de Castilho's pure Manueline cloisters are adorned with delicate tracery and richly carved arches.

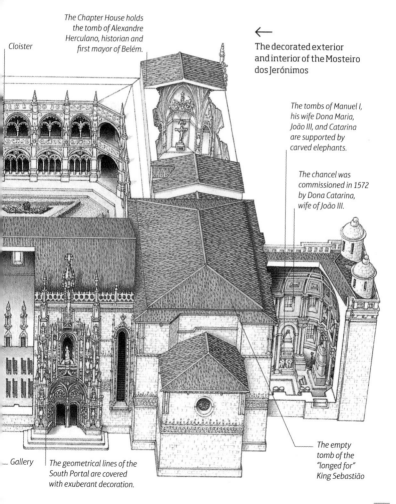

The Chapter House holds the tomb of Alexandre Herculano, historian and first mayor of Belém.

Cloister

← The decorated exterior and interior of the Mosteiro dos Jerónimos

The tombs of Manuel I, his wife Dona Maria, João III, and Catarina are supported by carved elephants.

The chancel was commissioned in 1572 by Dona Catarina, wife of João III.

Gallery | The geometrical lines of the South Portal are covered with exuberant decoration.

The empty tomb of the "longed for" King Sebastião

❷ Cascais

🏠 Lisbon 🚉🚌 🛈 Praça 5 de Outubro; www.visit cascais.com

Cascais became fashionable in the 1870s, when Luís I's summer palace was sited here. Today, it is a bustling resort, with many upscale stores in the pedestrian streets of the Old Town and a marina complex. Fishing is an important activity, and the day's catch is auctioned near the harbor in the afternoon.

Along the coast, 2 miles (3 km) to the east, the resort of Estoril has been home to exiled European royalty and has retained grand villas and hotels.

Guincho, 6 miles (10 km) north west of Cascais, has a sandy beach and is popular with surfers. Farther north is Cabo da Roca, the most westerly point of mainland Europe.

❸ Tomar

🏠 Centro 🚉🚌 🛈 Avda Dr. Cândido Madureira; 249-329 823

Founded in 1157 by Gualdim Pais, the first Grand Master of the Order of the Templars in Portugal, Tomar is dominated by the castle containing the **Convento de Cristo**. It was begun in 1162, on land given to the Templars for services in battle, and preserves many traces of its founders and the inheritors of their mantle, the Order of Christ. The nucleus of the castle is the 12th-century Charola, the Templars' octagonal oratory. In 1356, Tomar became the headquarters of the Order of Christ.

Cloisters were built in the time of Henry the Navigator, but it was in the reigns of Manuel I (1495–1521) and his successor, João III (1521–57), that the greatest changes were made, with the addition of the Manueline church and Renaissance cloisters. The church window (c. 1510) is probably the best-known example of the Manueline style of architecture.

Other fascinating features include the Terrace of Wax, where honeycombs were left to dry, and the "bread" cloister, where loaves were handed out to the poor.

The focal point of Praça da República, Tomar's main square, is the 15th-century Gothic church of São João Baptista. Tomar is also home to one of Portugal's oldest synagogues, now the Museu Luso-Hebraico de Abraham Zacuto, a Jewish museum.

Convento de Cristo

 🕘 9am–5:30pm daily (Jun–Sep: to 6:30pm) 🚫 Jan 1, Mar 1, Easter, May 1, Dec 24 & 25 🌐 conventocristo.gov.pt

❹ 🖐️

Mosteiro de Santa Maria da Vitória

🏠 Batalha 🚌 🕘 Apr–mid-Oct: 9am–6:30pm daily; mid-Oct–Mar: 9am–5:30pm daily 🚫 Jan 1, Easter Sun, May 1, Dec 25 🌐 mosteiro batalha.pt

The Dominican Abbey of Santa Maria da Vitória at Batalha is a masterpiece of Portuguese Gothic architecture and a UNESCO World Heritage Site. The pale limestone monastery was built to celebrate João I's historic victory at Aljubarrota in 1385. Today, the abbey still has military significance: two unknown soldiers from World War I lie in the Chapter House. João I, his English wife, Philippa of Lancaster, and their son, Henry the Navigator, are also buried here, in the Founder's Chapel

The abbey was begun in 1388 and work continued for the next two centuries. King Duarte, João's son, began an octagonal mausoleum for

←
Bathers enjoying the clear blue waters and sandy beach at Cascais

The Palácio Nacional de Sintra, and *(inset)* one of its splendid rooms

the royal house of Avis. The project was taken up again, but then abandoned by Manuel I. Consequently, it is known as the Unfinished Chapels. Much of the abbey decoration is in the Manueline style.

5

Sintra

⌂ Lisbon 🚆🚌 🚉 Praça da República 23; www.sintraromantica.net

Sintra's setting amid wooded ravines and fresh-water springs made it a favorite summer retreat for Portugal's kings, who built the fabulous **Palácio Nacional de Sintra** here. The main part of the palace – which is also known as the Paço Real – was built by João I in the late 14th century, on a site once occupied by the Moorish rulers. Additions to the building by the wealthy Manuel I in the early 16th century echo the Moorish

style. Gradual rebuilding of the palace has resulted in a fascinating mix of styles.

Present-day Sintra is a maze of winding roads, and exploring on foot involves much walking and climbing; for a more leisurely tour, take the hop-on, hop-off bus that loops around the sights. The Miradouro da Vigia in São Pedro offers impressive views, as does the cozy Casa de Sapa café, where you can sample *queijadas* – cheese tarts spiced with cinnamon. There are also many tranquil walks in the surrounding hills.

High above the town is the **Castelo dos Mouros**, an 8th-century Moorish castle. On a nearby hilltop stands the Palácio Nacional da Pena *(p364)*.

Palácio Nacional de Sintra

⊘ ⌂ Largo Rainha Dona Amélia 🕒 9:30am-7pm daily 🚫 1 Jan, 25 Dec 🌐 parquesdesintra.pt

Castelo dos Mouros

⊘ ⌂ Estrada da Pena, 3 miles (5 km) S 🚌 434 🕒 9:30am-8pm daily 🚫 Jan 1, Dec 25

⑥ 🚲 Ⓜ 🍴

PALÁCIO NACIONAL DA PENA

🏛 Estrada da Pena, 3 miles (5 km) S of Sintra 🚌 434 from Avenida Dr. Miguel Bombarda, Sintra ⏰ Apr-Oct: 9:45am-7pm daily; Nov-Mar: 10am-6pm daily 🚫 Jan 1, Dec 25 🌐 parquesdesintra.pt

On the highest peaks of the Serra de Sintra stands the spectacular palace of Pena. Built in the 19th century for Queen Maria II's flamboyantly creative husband, Ferdinand of Saxe-Coburg and Gotha, it comprises an eclectic medley of architectural styles.

The bright pink-and-yellow walls of the palace stand over the ruins of a Hieronymite monastery, founded here in the 15th century. Ferdinand appointed a German architect, Baron Von Eschwege, to build his dream summer palace, filled with international oddities and surrounded by a park. Construction started in 1840, and the extravagant project would ultimately last 45 years – the rest of the king's life. With the declaration of the Republic in 1910, the palace became a museum, preserved as it was when the royal family lived here.

Manuel II's bedroom is decorated with green walls and a stuccoed ceiling.

In the kitchen, the copper pots and utensils still hang around the iron stove.

1 The brightly painted hilltop palace is a UNESCO World Heritage Site.

2 *Trompe-l'oeil* frescoes cover the walls and ceiling of the Arab Room, one of the loveliest in the palace.

3 The exterior is adorned with intricate architecture, heavily inspired by European Romanticism.

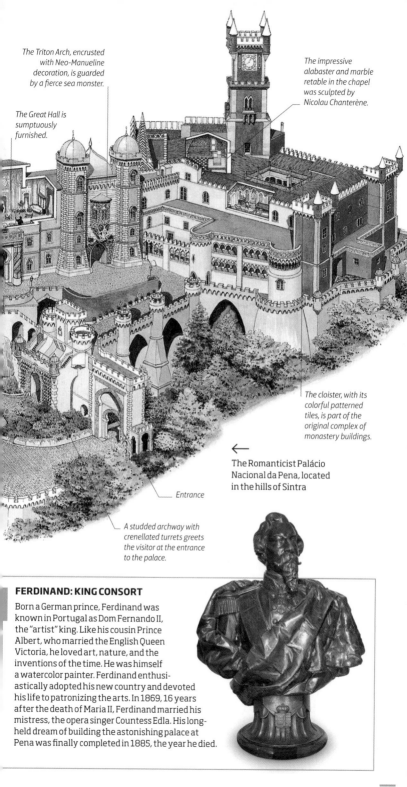

The Triton Arch, encrusted with Neo-Manueline decoration, is guarded by a fierce sea monster.

The impressive alabaster and marble retable in the chapel was sculpted by Nicolau Chanterène.

The Great Hall is sumptuously furnished.

The cloister, with its colorful patterned tiles, is part of the original complex of monastery buildings.

← The Romanticist Palácio Nacional da Pena, located in the hills of Sintra

Entrance

A studded archway with crenellated turrets greets the visitor at the entrance to the palace.

FERDINAND: KING CONSORT

Born a German prince, Ferdinand was known in Portugal as Dom Fernando II, the "artist" king. Like his cousin Prince Albert, who married the English Queen Victoria, he loved art, nature, and the inventions of the time. He was himself a watercolor painter. Ferdinand enthusiastically adopted his new country and devoted his life to patronizing the arts. In 1869, 16 years after the death of Maria II, Ferdinand married his mistress, the opera singer Countess Edla. His long-held dream of building the astonishing palace at Pena was finally completed in 1885, the year he died.

Mosteiro de Santa Maria de Alcobaça

🏛 Praça 25 de Abril, Alcobaça
🚌 🕐 9am–6pm daily (Apr–Sep: to 7pm) 🚫 Jan 1, Easter, May 1, Aug 20, Dec 25
🌐 mosteiroalcobaca.gov.pt

The Mosteiro de Santa Maria de Alcobaça is Portugal's largest church and a UNESCO World Heritage Site. Founded in 1153, the abbey is closely linked to the arrival of the Cistercian order in Portugal in 1138, as well as to the birth of the nation. In March 1147, Afonso Henriques conquered the Moorish stronghold of Santarém. To commemorate the victory, he gave land and money to build a church for the Cistercians. Completed in

1223, the church is a beautiful building of austere simplicity. Portugal's rulers continued to endow the monastery, notably King Dinis (1279–1325), who added the main cloister, known as the Cloister of Silence. In the Sala dos Reis, 18th-century tiles depict the founding of the abbey, and statues of Portuguese kings adorn the walls.

Among those buried here are the tragic lovers King Pedro (r. 1357–67) and his murdered mistress, Inês de Castro (died 1355), whose tombs face each other across the transept of the church.

One of Alcobaça's most popular features is the kitchen, so vast that whole oxen could be roasted on a spit inside the fireplace.

INÊS DE CASTRO

Reasons of state obliged Pedro, son and heir of Afonso IV, to marry Costanza, Infanta of Castile. On her death, Pedro went to live in Coimbra with Inês de Castro, a lady at court with whom he had fallen in love. Persuaded that Inês's family was dangerous, Afonso IV had her murdered in 1355. On Afonso's death, Pedro took revenge on two of the killers by having their hearts torn out. Claiming that he had been married to Inês, Pedro had her corpse exhumed and crowned.

8

Coimbra

🏛 Centro 🚌 🚆 ℹ️ Edifício da Biblioteca Geral da Universidade de Coimbra, 239-242 745; Largo da Portagem, 239-488 120

Afonso Henriques chose Coimbra as his capital in 1139, an honor it retained until 1256. Today, the city on the Mondego river is famous as the home of Portugal's oldest university. Most sights are within walking distance of each other.

Coimbra's two cathedrals, the Sé Velha ("old") and Sé Nova ("new"), lie in the shadow of the hilltop university. The Sé Velha, begun in 1064, is often viewed as the finest Romanesque building in Portugal. The Sé Nova was founded in 1598 by the Jesuits.

The **university**, a short walk away, was founded in 1290 by King Dinis. Originally, its location alternated between Lisbon and Coimbra, but it was finally installed in Coimbra's royal palace in 1537. Its oldest buildings are grouped around the Pátio das Escolas. The bell tower (1733) can be seen

→
A boat on the Mondego river, with Coimbra rising in the background

from all over the city. The library was a gift from João V (1706–50). Its rooms of gilt and exotic wood are lined with 300,000 books. Nearby is the similarly ornate Capela de São Miguel. Each May, at the end of the academic year, the Queima das Fitas takes place, at which students hold a ceremonial burning of their faculty ribbons, a tradition that dates back 700 years.

The **Museu Nacional Machado de Castro** holds some of Portugal's finest 15th- to 20th-century paintings and sculpture, which are displayed among the elegant 16th-century loggias and courtyards of the former bishops' palace.

A short walk away from this area (the "Upper Town") is the "Lower Town." Largo da Portagem is a good starting point for exploring, and river trips depart from nearby. In the Praça do Comércio, alongside buzzing coffee shops and bars, is the restored 12th-century church of São Tiago. North of this is Santa Cruz, founded in 1131, where Portugal's first two kings are buried.

In the southeast of the city are the gardens of the Jardim Botânico, created in 1772 and housing 1,200 plant species.

On the opposite bank of the Mondego are the convents of Santa Clara-a-Velha and Santa Clara-a-Nova; the latter was built to house the nuns after the former flooded in the 17th century. Nearby is the Portugal dos Pequenitos theme park.

Buçaco National Forest, 10 miles (16 km) north of Coimbra, was once the retreat of Carmelite monks. Part woodland and part arboretum, it is dotted with chapels and fountains.

The Roman town of **Conímbriga** lay south of modern Coimbra. Portugal's largest Roman site, it has villas with fine floor mosaics and an excellent museum.

💬 INSIDER TIP
Coimbra Fado

While Lisbon's music is melancholy and somber, Coimbra's is boisterous and romantic, ranging from serenades to drinking songs. Fado ao Centro (www.fadoao centro.com) holds daily concerts; make sure to cough rather than applaud the singers.

↑ Beautifully preserved central garden of Casa das Fontes in Conímbriga, near Coimbra

University
◈ 🏛 Largo da Porta Férrea
🕐 10:30am–7pm daily
🚫 Jan 1, 1st Sun in May, Dec 24, 25 🌐 visit.uc.pt

Museu Nacional Machado de Castro
◈ 🏛 Largo Dr José Rodrigues
🕐 10am–8pm Tue–Wed, 2–6pm Tue 🌐 museu machadocastro.gov.pt

Conímbriga
◈ 🚹 🏛 27 miles (17km) SE of Coimbra 📞 239-941 177
🕐 10am–7pm daily 🚫 Jan 1, Easter Sun, May 1, Jul 24, Dec 25

↑ Porto at dusk, looking across the Ponte de Dom Luís I

Porto

🏠 Norte ✈🚉🚌 ℹ Rua Clube dos Fenianos 25 or Terreiro de Sé; www. portoturismo.pt

The country's second city, Porto (sometimes referred to as Oporto) has never sat in Lisbon's shadow. Its remarkable cityscape – wedged into the Douro Valley – and museums, churches, and port wine lodges have put it firmly on the city-break circuit.

The commercial center and the Baixa ("lower") district attract fashionable shoppers. Most of the visitor attractions, however, are found elsewhere in the city.

High above the river, on Penaventosa Hill, is Porto's cathedral, or Sé, originally a fortress-church. A noteworthy 13th-century feature is the rose window, while the upper level of the 14th-century cloister affords splendid views.

Nearby are the Renaissance church of Santa Clara, and São Bento station, completed in 1916, decorated with spectacular *azulejo* panels.

Below the Sé is the hillside Barredo quarter, seemingly unchanged since medieval days. This leads down to the riverside quarter, the Ribeira, its houses decorated with tiled or pastel-painted facades. The district has been restored and is now a thriving area with restaurants and clubs.

Sights close to the river include the Palácio da Bolsa, the city's stock exchange, built in 1842. Its highlight is the Arabian Room decorated in the style of the Alhambra. Close by is the 14th-century São Francisco church. Its interior is richly covered in carved and gilded wood.

West of the Sé, in the Cordoaria district, stands the 18th-century Igreja dos Clérigos. The church tower offers superb views.

Situated in the lovely Serralves park, the **Fundação de Serralves** is dedicated to contemporary art. It presents temporary exhibitions in the Art Deco Casa de Serralves, and its art collection, from the 1960s to the present, in the Modernist Museu de Arte Contemporânea, designed by Álvaro Siza Vieira.

The oldest of the five bridges spanning the Douro are the Dona Maria Pia railroad bridge (1877), designed by Gustave Eiffel, and the two-tiered Ponte de Dom Luís I (1886), by one of Eiffel's assistants.

Across the river is the town of Vila Nova de Gaia, the center of port production, housing the lodges *(armazéns)* of over 50 companies. Many offer guided tours.

Fundação de Serralves
♿🅿🛍 🏠 Rua Dom João de Castro 210 ⏰ 10am–6pm Tue–Fri (to 7pm in summer), 10am–7pm Sat, Sun, & public hols (to 8pm in summer) 🚫 Jan 1, Dec 25 🌐 serralves.pt

---

THE STORY OF PORT

Port comes only from a demarcated region of the upper Douro Valley. Its "discovery" dates from the 1600s, when British merchants added brandy to Douro wine to stop it turning sour in transit. Over the years, methods of maturing and blending were refined and continue today in the port lodges of Vila Nova de Gaia. Much of the trade is still in British control. A classic after-dinner drink, port is rich and usually full-bodied. The tawnies are lighter in color than ruby or vintage but can be more complex. All ports are blended from several wines. White port, unlike the other styles, is drunk chilled as an aperitif.

⑩
Évora

🏛 Alentejo 🚌 ℹ Praça do Giraldo; 266-777 071

Rising dramatically out of the Alentejo plain, the enchanting city of Évora is set in Roman, medieval, and 17th-century walls. In 1986, UNESCO made it a World Heritage Site.

The fortress-like cathedral on the Largo do Marquês de Marialva, the Sé, was begun in 1186. Its portal is flanked by a pair of unmatched towers, while inside a Treasury houses sacred art. Beside it stands a 16th-century palace that houses the **Museu de Évora**, which has exhibits on the history of the city. Opposite the museum is a Roman temple – erected in the 2nd or 3rd century AD – which is believed to have once been dedicated to Diana.

Did You Know?

Évora was named Ebora by the Celts, meaning "of the yew trees."

From the Sé, the craft-store lined Rua de 5 Outubro leads to Praça do Giraldo, the main square, with its Moorish arcades and central fountain (1571). In 1573, the square was the site of an Inquisitional burning. Just outside the city's Roman walls stands the **university**, founded by the Jesuits in 1559. It was closed in 1759 by the Marquês de Pombal, but the building, with its notable *azulejos*, still forms part of the modern university.

Évora has more than 20 churches and monasteries, including the 15th-century São Francisco. The church's gruesome 17th-century Capela dos Ossos was created from the bones of 5,000 monks.

Northwest of the city stands the remaining 5 miles (9 km) of Évora's aqueduct, the Aqueduto da Água de Prata (1531–7).

Museu de Évora

⊛ 🏛 Largo do Conde de Vila Flor 📞 266-730 480 🕐 Apr-Oct: 10am–6pm Tue-Sun; Nov-Mar: 9:30am–5:30pm Tue-Sun 🚫 Jan 1, Easter Sun, May 1, Jun 29, Dec 25

University

⊛ 🏛 Largo dos Colegiais 📞 266-740 800 🕐 9am-8pm Mon-Sat 🚫 Public hols

↑ Évora's macabre Capela dos Ossos, constructed out of bones

EAT

Cantinho do Avillez
Renowned Portuguese chef José Avillez's outstanding restaurant serves innovative cuisine at highly affordable prices.

🏛 Rua Mouzinha da Silveira 166, Porto
🌐 cantinhodoavillez.pt

€€€

The Yeatman
The food here is every bit as memorable as the views of the city. Each dish is accompanied by fine wine.

🏛 Rua do Choupelo, Vila Nova de Gaia, Porto 🌐 the-yeatman-hotel.com

€€€

Fialho
This award-winning restaurant specializes in recreating traditional recipes, and it also has a good wine list. Book in advance.

🏛 Travessa das Mascarenhas 16, Évora
🚫 Mon 🌐 lawrences hotel.com

€€€

Momentos
The menu of the day here features local organic produce. Unlike much Portuguese cuisine, the fish and meat dishes come with salads or vegetables rather than fries.

🏛 Rua 5 de Outubro 61B, Évora 🚫 Mon & Wed-Fri lunch, Tue 📞 925 161 423

€€€

⑪ Faro

🏛 Algarve 🚉🚌 🅿 ℹ Rua da Misericórdia 8; 289-803 604

Faro has been the capital of the Algarve since 1756. It was damaged by the 1755 earthquake and, although some parts of the ancient city walls remain, most of the buildings date from the 18th and 19th centuries.

The old city is easy to explore on foot. At its heart is the Largo da Sé, lined with orange trees and flanked by the 18th-century bishops' palace, the Paço Episcopal.

The Sé itself is a mixture of Baroque and Renaissance styles and has a fine 18th-century organ. Next door is the **Museu Municipal**, which has Roman, medieval, and

> 🔺 GREAT VIEW
> ### City and Sea
> A brisk walk uphill to the highest point in Faro - Ermida de Santo António do Alto - grants a brilliant panorama of the city with the sea and saltpans to the south.

→
The coast at Praia de São Rafael, just outside Albufeira

Manueline archaeological finds from all over the region. On the other side of the old city wall is the impressive 18th-century church of São Francisco.

The lively center of modern Faro, along the Rua de Santo António, is stylish and pedestrianized, full of stores, bars, and restaurants. A little to the north is Faro's parish church, São Pedro. In the nearby Largo do Carmo is the impressive Igreja do Carmo. Its magnificent facade and richly decorated interior are in sharp contrast to its somber Capela dos Ossos (Chapel of Bones), built in 1816.

At the far northeast corner of the town is the Cemitério dos Judeus. The Jewish cemetery served from 1838 until 1932; most of the Jewish community has since moved away.

Museu Municipal

♿ 🏛 Largo Dom Afonso III 📞 289-870 827 🕐 Jun-Sep: 10am-7pm Tue-Fri, 11:30am-6pm Sat & Sun; Oct-May: 10am-6pm Tue-Fri, 10:30am-5pm Sat & Sun 🚫 Public hols

⑫ Albufeira

🏛 Algarve 🚌🚉 ℹ Rua 5 de Outubro; 289-585 279

This charming fishing port has become the holiday capital of the Algarve. The Romans built a castle here, and under the Arabs the town prospered from trade with North Africa. The oldest part of the town, around Rua da Igreja Velha, retains some original Moorish arches.

The coastline between Praia de São Rafael, 1 mile (2 km) west of Albufeira, and Praia da Oura, due east, is punctuated by small sandy coves set between eroded ocher rocks. East of Albufeira, the resort of Vilamoura is set to become one of Europe's biggest leisure complexes. It has a large marina with lively cafés, stores, and restaurants.

⑬ Portimão

🏛 Algarve 🚉🚌 ℹ Avda Tomás Cabreira, Praia da Rocha; 282-419 132

The Romans were attracted to Portimão by its natural

↑ Pretty purple jacaranda trees blooming in front of the whitewashed São Pedro church, Faro

THE ALGARVE'S ARAB LEGACY

The Algarve's fertile soil and strategic headlands and rivers have attracted visitors since the time of the Phoenicians. Five centuries of Arab rule, from AD 711, left a legacy that is still visible in the region's architecture, lattice chimneys, *azulejos*, orange groves, and almond trees. Place names beginning with Al are also of Moorish origin; Al-Gharb ("the West") denoted the western edge of the Islamic empire. When the Algarve was reclaimed by the Christians in 1249, the Portuguese rulers designated themselves kings "of Portugal and of the Algarves," emphasizing the region's separateness from the rest of the country.

harbor. It is still a flourishing fishing port and one of the largest towns in the Algarve.

The town center, around the pedestrianized Rua Vasco da Gama, dates mainly from the 18th century, since it was rebuilt after the 1755 earthquake. The 14th-century origins of the church of Nossa Senhora da Conceição are revealed in its portico. The interior contains 17th- and 18th-century *azulejo* panels.

Just 2 miles (3 km) south of Portimão is Praia da Rocha, a series of fabulous sandy coves. At its east end is the 16th-century castle, Fortaleza de Santa Catarina, with a superb view of the beach and cliffs – and a swathe of high-rise hotels. Inland from Portimão is the town of Silves, once the Moorish capital, Xelb. It has an impressive castle and picturesque groves planted with orange and lemon trees.

from 1576 to 1756. The town suffered badly in the 1755 earthquake; as a result, most of the buildings date from the late 18th and 19th centuries.

In the 15th century, Lagos became an important naval center, and a statue of Henry the Navigator stands in the town square. The town also has the unfortunate claim of being the site of the first slave market in Europe.

Lagos's parish church is the 16th-century Santa Maria. The 18th-century Santo António is worth a visit for its Baroque *azulejos* and carving. The statue of St. Anthony, kept in the church, accompanied the local regiment during the Peninsular War (1807–11).

The promontory of Ponta da Piedade shelters the bay of Lagos – with its dramatic rock formations and natural arches, it should not be missed. Praia de Dona Ana beach is 25 minutes' walk from the town center, but Praia do Camilo may be less crowded. Meia Praia, east of Lagos, stretches for 2 miles (4 km).

Lying 6 miles (10 km) north is the Barragem de Bravura reservoir. Another popular excursion is southwest to Sagres and the headland of Cabo de São Vicente.

Lagos

🏠 Algarve 🚉🚌 ℹ️ Praça Gil Eanes; 282-763 031

Lagos is set on one of the Algarve's largest bays; it was the region's capital

→
Statue of Henry the Navigator in Lagos town square

PRACTICAL
INFORMATION

Here you will find all the essential advice and information you will need before and during your stay in Portugal.

AT A GLANCE

CURRENCY
Euro (EUR)

TIME ZONE
CET/CEST. Central European Summer Time runs from the last Sunday in March to the last Sunday in October.

LANGUAGE
Portuguese

ELECTRICITY SUPPLY
Power sockets are type F, fitting a two-prong, round-pin plug. Standard voltage is 220–240V.

EMERGENCY NUMBERS
GENERAL EMERGENCY

112

TAP WATER
Unless stated otherwise, tap water in Portugal is safe to drink.

Getting There

Lisbon, Porto, and Faro are the main airports for long-haul flights into Portugal, and are also served by various European budget airlines.

There are two main routes into Portugal by train. The Sud Express departs daily from Irun on the French–Spanish border and splits near Coimbra, arriving into Lisbon and Porto. (Irun can be reached from Austerlitz station in Paris.) Alternatively, the overnight train from Madrid takes 10 hours. Both routes are operated by the Spanish state-run service **Renfe**. You can purchase tickets online or in person at a train station. It is advisable to book ahead in summer.

Traveling to Portugal by long-distance bus is cheap but very time consuming. **Flixbus** offer a variety of routes into Portugal from destinations across Western Europe.

Flixbus
W flixbus.com
Renfe
W renfe.com

Personal Security

Portugal is generally a safe country, but it is always a good idea to take sensible precautions against pickpockets. If you have anything stolen, report the crime as soon as possible to the nearest police station. Get a copy of the crime report in order to claim on your insurance.

Health

EU citizens with a European Health Insurance Card (EHIC) are entitled to free emergency medical care in Portugal, but it is also advisable to take out some form of supplementary health insurance. Visitors from outside the EU must arrange their own private medical insurance.

Seek medicinal supplies and advice for minor ailments from pharmacies (farmácias), identifiable by a green cross. Pharmacists can dispense some drugs that would normally be available only on prescription in other countries. Each pharmacy displays a card in the window showing the address of the nearest all-night pharmacy.

Passports and Visas

EU nationals may visit for an unlimited period, registering with local authorities after three months. Citizens of the US, Canada, Australia, and New Zealand can remain in Protugal without a visa for up to 90 days. For those arriving from other countries, check with your local Portuguese embassy.

Travelers with Specific Needs

The steep, winding streets in many of Portugal's historic towns and cities can be challenging for wheelchair-users and those with prams. Facilities in Portugal have improved greatly, however, with wheelchairs, adapted toilets, and reserved car parking available at airports and transport hubs. Ramps and lifts are installed in many public places and some buses (marked with a blue-and-white logo at the front) accommodate wheelchair-users. **Accessible Portugal** gives comprehensive advice on traveling with limited mobility.
Accessible Portugal
w accessibleportugal.com

Money

Most urban establishments accept major credit, debit, and prepaid currency cards. Contactless payments are gradually becoming more common in cities, but it's always a good idea to carry cash for smaller items, or when visiting markets. ATMs are widely available across cities.

Cell Phones and Wi-Fi

Free Wi-Fi is not yet widespread in Portugal, although it can be found in some restaurants and bars, specifically those aimed at tourists.

Visitors traveling to Portugal with EU tariffs can use their devices without being affected by data roaming charges. Visitors from elsewhere should check their contracts before departure in order to avoid unexpected charges.

Getting Around

CP (Comboios de Portugal) is the country's national rail operator, with routes spanning the length of the country. The new Alfa Pendular trains are fast, comfortable, and have free Wi-Fi, while Intercidades trains are older, cheaper, and stop more frequently. Trains should be pre-booked either online or at the station, except for journeys on urban rail networks *(urbanas)*. Tickets for *urbanas* can be bought at the station prior to departure and should be validated at the ticket machines on the platform before boarding the train.

Bus companies in Portugal are competitive and offer efficient, comfortable services. Some long-distance services – Lisbon to Évora for example – are quicker and more comfortable than going by train. **Rede Expressos** covers most of Portugal, linking Porto, Lisbon, and Faro, while **EVA** covers the Algarve particularly well.

Car hire agencies can be found in main towns and at airports. Driving can be a hair-raising experience – Portugal has one of the highest accident rates in Europe and traffic jams are a problem in and near cities – but a comprehensive freeway system allows for speedy travel between major cities (although some less-traveled rural roads may be in need of repair). Make sure you are familiar with the rules of the road and carry the necessary documentation with you at all times. Tolls are payable on highways and some bridges.
CP
w cp.pt
EVA
w eva-bus.com
Rede Expressos
w rede-expressos.pt

Visitor Information

The country is divided into tourist regions, separate from its administrative districts. All cities and large towns have a *posto de turismo* (tourist office), where you can obtain information about the region, lists of hotels, and details of regional events. Visitors can also consult overseas branches of the **Portuguese National Tourist Board**. In Lisbon, the convenient **Lisboa Card** entitles visitors to free public transportation, and free or reduced entry to museums.
Lisboa Card
w lisboacard.org
Portuguese National Tourist Board
w visitportugal.com

ITALY

Birthplace of much of the world's finest art and
architecture, Italy did not exist as a unified nation
state until the 19th century. Prior to this, the
only time the territory was united was under
the Romans, who emerged from scores of tribes
inhabiting ancient Italy to conquer the peninsula
by the 2nd century BC. Rome became the capital
of a huge empire, introducing its language, laws,
and calendar to most of Europe before falling to
Germanic invaders in the 5th century AD. Medieval
Italy saw a power struggle between various popes
and emperors, joined by waves of foreign invaders.
In the confusion, a number of northern city-states,
including Venice, asserted their independence.
Northern Italy became a prosperous and cultured
region, with Florence at the center of the 15th-
century Renaissance. Small, fragmented states,
however, could not compete with great powers,
and in the 16th century they fell prey to Spain. In
the 19th century, Napoleon conquered and briefly
united Italy, but it was soon redivided, with the
north falling to Austrian control and a small region
in the center coming under the rule of the papacy.
Piedmont managed to remain independent, and
became the focus for a movement toward a united
Italy – a goal that was achieved in 1870. In the
1920s, the Fascists seized power and, in 1946,
the monarchy was abolished. Business boomed
in the postwar era, despite a run of unstable political coalitions and corruption scandals, but the
economy has stagnated in the 21st century.

ITALY

0 kilometers 100

0 miles 100

N ↑

Cobbled Piazza Santa
Maria in Trastevere,
overlooked by the church ↑

❶

ROME

 *i* www.turismoroma.it

From its early days as a settlement of shepherds on
the Palatine hill, Rome grew to become the influential
headquarters of the mighty Roman Empire and then
of the Catholic Church. The legacy of this history can
be seen all over the city, from the ancient ruins of the
Centro Storico to the artistic treasures of the Vatican.
Hugely photogenic, with its spectacular piazzas,
cascading fountains, and exuberant street life, Rome
today remains a neighborly city, with a wealth of sidewalk bars and restaurants where you can join the
locals in enjoying *la dolce vita*.

①

Santa Maria in Trastevere

 Piazza Santa Maria in
Trastevere 📞 06-581 48
02 🚌 H, 23, 115, 125, 280
🕐 7:30am-9pm daily

Trastevere, which literally
translates as the area "across
the Tiber," is one of the city's
most attractive quarters:
a maze of narrow, cobbled
alleys. Once home to the city's
poor, the neighborhood has
witnessed a proliferation of
fashionable clubs, restaurants,
and boutiques.

At the heart of this charming
quarter, overlooking an attractive traffic-free square, stands
the Basilica of Santa Maria –
probably the first official
place of Christian worship in
Rome. It was founded by Pope
Callixtus I in the 3rd century,
when Christianity was still a
minority cult. According to
legend, the church was built
on the site where a fountain
of oil had sprung up miraculously on the day that Christ
was born.

The basilica became the
focus of devotion to the Virgin
Mary and today is famous
for its splendid mosaics. Both

the Madonna and Christ are
among the figures depicted
in the facade mosaics (c. 12th
century), while in the apse is a
stylized 12th-century mosaic
portraying the *Coronation of*

the Virgin. Below it are a series of realistic mosaic scenes from the life of Mary by the 13th-century Roman artist Pietro Cavallini. The oldest image of the Virgin is a 7th-century icon, which depicts her as a Byzantine empress flanked by a guard of angels. Another image of the Virgin and Child can be seen near the top of the campanile.

② ♿

Villa Farnesina

🏠 Via della Lungara 230
🚌 H, 280, 780 ⏰ 9am–2pm Mon–Sat, 9am–5pm 2nd Sun in month 🚫 Public hols
🌐 villafarnesina.it

The wealthy Sienese banker Agostino Chigi commissioned this villa in 1508 for his lavish banquets and for sojourns with the courtesan Imperia, who allegedly inspired one of the *Three Graces* painted by Raphael in the Loggia of Cupid and Psyche.

Designed by the Sienese architect Baldassare Peruzzi, the harmonious Farnesina, with a central block and projecting wings, is one of the first true Renaissance villas. Peruzzi decorated some of the interiors himself, such as the Sala della Prospettiva upstairs, in which illusionistic frescoes create the impression of looking out over Rome through a marble colonnade.

The painted vault of the Sala di Galatea shows the position of the stars at the time of Chigi's birth. After his death, the banking business collapsed, and in 1577 the villa was sold to the Farnese family.

↑ The frescoed Loggia of Cupid and Psyche, in the Villa Farnesina

③

ST. PETER'S

⌖ Piazza San Pietro Ⓜ Ottaviano - San Pietro 🚌 23, 34, 40, 49, 62, 64, 81, 492, 982 🕐 Basilica: 7am-7pm daily (Oct-Mar: to 6:30pm); Treasury: 9am-6pm daily (Oct-Mar: to 6pm); Grottoes: 9am-6pm daily (Oct-Mar: to 5pm); Dome: 7:30am-6pm daily (Oct-Mar: to 5pm) 🖥 vatican.va

Catholicism's most sacred shrine, the sumptuous, marble-caked Basilica of St. Peter draws pilgrims and tourists from all over the world.

A shrine was erected on the site of St. Peter's tomb in the 2nd century and the first basilica was commissioned by Constantine. Centuries later, in 1506, Pope Julius II laid the first stone of a new church while the original basilica was still in use. The present basilica, 623 ft (190 m) long, took more than a century to build and all the great architects of the Roman Renaissance and Baroque had a hand in its design. The dominant tone of the interior was set by Bernini, creator of the baldacchino below Michelangelo's magnificent dome. Bernini also created the *cathedra* in the apse, with four saints supporting a throne.

The 448 ft (137 m) dome, designed by Michelangelo, was not completed until 1590, long after his death.

The apse is dominated by Bernini's spectacular bronze monument containing the Throne of St. Peter in Glory.

Bernini's baldacchino, an extravagant Baroque canopy, stands above the Papal Altar, a plain slab of marble.

Bernini's monument to Alexander VII shows the pope surrounded by allegorical figures.

The Treasury houses ecclesiastical treasures, including reliquaries, tombs, and vestments.

The Papal Altar stands over the crypt where St. Peter is buried.

Many popes are buried in the Grottoes.

The 13th-century bronze statue of St. Peter is thought to be by Arnolfo di Cambio.

← *The grand facade of the basilica on St. Peter's Square*

Markings on the nave floor show the lengths of other churches.

AD 61
▼ Burial of
St. Peter

200
Altar built
marking grave
of St. Peter

1452
Nicholas V
plans program
of restoration

1547
Michelangelo named
as chief architect of
St. Peter's

324
Constantine
builds basilica

800
▲ Charlemagne
crowned Emperor
of the Romans
in St. Peter's

1514
Raphael named
director of
basilica works

1626
New Basilica
of St. Peter
consecrated

→
The grand, marble-
encrusted interior of
St. Peter's Basilica

*Two minor cupolas
by Vignola*

*Protected by glass since an
attack in 1972, Michelangelo's
Pietà stands in the first side
chapel on the right. He created
it in 1499, when he was only 24.*

*The facade (1614) is by
Carlo Maderno.*

POPE'S BLESSING

On Sundays (at noon),
religious festivals, and
special occasions such
as canonizations, the
pope stands on the
balcony at the Library
window and blesses
the faithful crowds
gathered in Piazza
San Pietro below.

*Entrance for
stairs to dome*

*From this window,
the pope blesses
the faithful
gathered in the
piazza below.*

Filarete door

Main entrance

←
St Peter's, center of
the Catholic faith

④ 〰 Ⓜ 🍴 🖥 🛍

VATICAN MUSEUMS

🏛 Città del Vaticano (entrance in Viale Vaticano) Ⓜ Ottaviano - San Pietro, Cipro 🚌 49 to entrance, 32, 81, 492, 982, 990 🕐 9am-6pm Mon-Sat, 9am-2pm last Sun of month 🚫 Religious and public hols 🌐 museivaticani.va

Home to the Sistine Chapel and the Raphael Rooms, as well as to one of the world's most important art collections, the Vatican Museums are housed in palaces originally built for wealthy Renaissance popes Julius II, Innocent VIII, and Sixtus IV. Most of the later architectural additions were made in the 18th century, when priceless works of art accumulated by earlier popes were first put on show. Strung along more than 4 miles (7 km) of corridors, these incredible collections form the basis of one of the world's largest museums.

Four centuries of papal patronage and connoisseurship have resulted in one of the world's great collections of Classical and Renaissance art. Among the Vatican's most impressive treasures are its Greek and Roman antiquities, together with the items brought to Rome in Imperial times and magnificent artifacts excavated from Egyptian tombs during the 19th century. The Etruscan Museum houses a superb collection, including the bronze throne, funerary bed, and funeral cart found in the 650 BC Regolini-Galassi tomb in Cerveteri. Some of Italy's leading Renaissance artists, such as Raphael, Michelangelo, and Leonardo da Vinci, are not only represented in the Pinacoteca (art gallery), but also in parts of the former palaces where they were employed by popes to decorate sumptuous apartments and galleries with wonderful frescoes.

→
The monumental spiral staircase designed by Giuseppe Momo in 1932

The Cortile della Pigna, with a spherical bronze sculpture by Arnaldo Pomodoro

Ancient Art

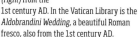

▷ The Egyptian collection includes the tomb of Iry, guardian of the Pyramid of Cheops (22nd century BC). The Pio-Clementine Museum houses a splendid *Laocoön (right)* from the 1st century AD. In the Vatican Library is the *Aldobrandini Wedding*, a beautiful Roman fresco, also from the 1st century AD.

GALLERY GUIDE

Visitors have to follow a one-way system. It is best to focus on a single collection or to follow one of the color-coded itineraries, which vary in length from 90 minutes to five hours. If you are planning a long visit, allow plenty of time to rest. The Sistine Chapel and the Raphael Rooms are 20–30 minutes' walk from the entrance, without allowing for any viewing time along the way.

Christian Art

The Pio-Christian Museum has Early Christian art from catacombs and basilicas. The first two rooms of the Pinacoteca house medieval art, including Giotto's *Stefaneschi Triptych* (c. 1300), while other rooms contain Renaissance works. Among the highlights from the 15th century are Leonardo da Vinci's unfinished *St. Jerome*. Exceptional 16th-century pieces include an altarpiece by Titian, a *Deposition* by Caravaggio, *St. Helen* by Paolo Veronese, and a whole room devoted to Raphael.

The Sistine Chapel

◁ The Sistine Chapel takes its name from Pope Sixtus IV, who commissioned it in 1473. Some of the finest artists of the age - including Botticelli, Ghirlandaio, and Perugino - frescoed its walls. In 1508-12, at the request of Pope Julius II, Michelangelo created the chapel ceiling. The main panels chart the *Creation of the World* and *Fall of Man*. They are surrounded by subjects from the Old and New Testaments.

Raphael Rooms

▷ Pope Julius II chose Raphael to redecorate four rooms of his apartments. The frescoes in the Room of the Segnatura (1508-11) include the famous *School of Athens*, which centers on a debate between Plato and Aristotle. The decoration of the Room of Heliodorus (1511-14) incorporates a famous portrait of Julius II, while the Room of the Fire in the Borgo (1514-17) was frescoed during the reign of Pope Leo X. All the frescoes here exalt the new pope or his earlier namesakes.

EAT

Casa Bleve
In a grand vaulted dining room, this *enoteca*-restaurant has an impressive wine list and gourmet offerings.

◻ Via del Teatro Valle 48
Ⓦ casableve.com

€€€

Osteria del Pegno
A romantic restaurant offering perfectly executed Italian dishes. Complimentary limoncello rounds off a meal nicely.

◻ Vicolo Montevecchio 8
☎ 06 68 80 70 25

€€€

Dal Toscano
This classic trattoria specializes in steak, but it also offers a superb thick Tuscan soup and a range of pasta dishes.

◻ Via Germanico 58
Ⓦ ristorantedal toscano.it

€€€

Lo Zozzone
A Roman institution, this spot near Piazza Navona serves *pizza bianca* stuffed with an array of fillings, from mozzarella to artichoke.

◻ Via del Teatro Pace
☎ 06 68 80 85 75

€€€

Franchi
A first-class deli with a tantalizing array of lunchtime snacks.

◻ Via Cola di Rienzo 200
☎ 06 686 55 64

€€€

⑤

Pantheon

◻ Piazza della Rotonda
☎ 06-68 30 02 30 🚌 116 & many others ⏰ 8:30am-7:30pm Mon-Sat, 9am-6pm Sun 🚫 Jan 1, May 1, Dec 25

The Pantheon, the Roman "temple of all the gods," is the most extraordinary and best-preserved ancient building in Rome. The present structure was built, and possibly even designed, by Emperor Hadrian in AD 118. The temple is fronted by a massive pedimented portico, screening what appears to be a cylinder fused to a shallow dome. Only from the inside can the true scale and beauty of the temple be appreciated; a hemispherical dome equal in radius to the height of the cylinder gives perfectly harmonious proportions to the building. A circular opening in the center of the coffered dome, the *oculus*, lets in the only light.

In the 7th century, Christians claimed that they were being plagued by demons as they passed by, and permission was granted to convert the Pantheon into a church. Today it is lined with tombs, which range from the restrained monument to Raphael to the huge marble and porphyry sarcophagi holding the bodies of Italian monarchs.

Did You Know?

The Pantheon's dome remains the largest unreinforced concrete dome in the world.

⑥

Castel Sant'Angelo

◻ Lungotevere Castello 50
🚌 23, 34, 40, 280 ⏰ 9am-7:30pm daily 🚫 Public hols
Ⓦ castelsantangelo.beniculturali.it

This large cylindrical fortress takes its name from the vision of the Archangel Michael, experienced by Pope Gregory the Great in the 6th century as he led a procession across the bridge, fervently praying for the end of the plague.

The castle started life in AD 139 as the mausoleum of Emperor Hadrian. Since then it has been a bridgehead in the Emperor Aurelian's city wall, a medieval citadel and prison, and a place of safety for popes during times of war or political unrest.

Visitors are given a glimpse into all aspects of the castle's history – from its dank prison cells to the lavish apartments of Renaissance popes.

↑ The formidable fortress of Castel Sant'Angelo, rising above the Tiber river

← Piazza Navona, with the Fontana dei Quattro Fiumi in the background

⑦
Galleria Doria Pamphilj

🏛 Via del Corso 305 Ⓜ Piazza Barberini, Colosseo 🚌 62, 85, 95, 175, 492, 630, 850 🕐 9am–7pm daily 🚫 3rd Wed of month, Jan 1, Easter Sun, Dec 25 🌐 doriapamphilj.it

The oldest parts of this vast stone edifice date from 1435. It was owned by the Della Rovere family and then by the Aldobrandini family, before the Pamphilj family took possession of it in 1647. The family art collection has over 400 paintings dating from the 15th to the 18th century, including a portrait of Pope Innocent X by Velázquez and works by Caravaggio, Titian, and Guercino. The private apartments retain many of their original furnishings, which include Brussels and Gobelins tapestries, Murano chandeliers, and a gilded crib.

In the first half of the 18th century, Gabriele Valvassori created a new facade along the Corso, using a highly decorative style known as *barocchetto*, which now dominates the building.

⑧
Gesù

🏛 Piazza del Gesù 🚌 H, 46, 62, 64, 70, 81, 87, 186, 492, 628 🕐 7:30am–12:30pm & 4–7:45pm daily 🌐 chiesa delgesu.org

The Gesù, built between 1568 and 1584, was Rome's first Jesuit church. The Jesuit order was founded in Rome in 1540 by a Basque soldier, Ignatius Loyola, who became a Christian after he was wounded in battle.

The design of the Gesù typifies Counter Reformation architecture: a large nave with side pulpits for preaching to crowds, and a main altar as the centerpiece for the Mass. The painting in the nave depicts the *Triumph of the Name of Jesus* and its message is clear: faithful, Catholic worshippers will be joyfully uplifted to heaven while Protestants and heretics are flung into the fires of hell. The message is reiterated in the Cappella di Sant'Ignazio, a rich display of lapis lazuli, serpentine, silver, and gold. The marble *Triumph of Faith over Idolatry* shows a female "Religion" trampling on the head of the serpent "Idolatry."

⑨
Piazza Navona

🚌 40, 46, 62, 64, 81, 87, 190, 492, 628

This spectacular Baroque piazza follows the shape of a 1st-century AD stadium, built by Domitian and used for athletic contests *(agones)* and chariot races. Traces of the ruined stadium are visible below the church of Sant' Agnese in Agone. The church, created by the architects Girolamo and Carlo Rainaldi and Francesco Borromini, is dedicated to the virgin martyr, St. Agnes. When she was stripped naked to force her to renounce her faith, her hair grew miraculously long, concealing her body.

The piazza began to take on its present appearance in the 1600s, when Pope Innocent X commissioned a new church, palace, and fountain. The Fontana dei Quattro Fiumi, Bernini's most magnificent fountain, has statues of four gods personifying the world's greatest known rivers at the time – the Nile, the Plate, the Ganges, and the Danube – sitting on rocks below an obelisk.

↑ The imposing Forum of Trajan, built in the early 2nd century

⑩

Trajan's Markets

🏠 Via IV Novembre 94
🚌 40, 60, 170 🕐 9:30am–7:30pm daily 🚫 Public hols
🌐 mercatiditraiano.it

Originally considered among the wonders of the Classical world, Trajan's Markets now display only a hint of their former splendor.

Emperor Trajan and his architect, Apollodorus of Damascus, built this visionary complex of 150 offices and shops in the early 2nd century AD. In their heyday, the markets sold everything from Middle Eastern silks and spices to fresh fish, fruit, and flowers. Shops opened early and closed about noon. Almost all the shopping was done by men and the traders were almost exclusively male.

The Forum of Trajan (AD 107–13) was built in front of the market complex. It was a vast colonnaded open space with a huge basilica, and included two libraries. Dominating the ruins today is Trajan's Column. Spiralling up its 98 ft (30 m) high stem are minutely detailed scenes depicting episodes from Trajan's successful military campaigns in Dacia (present-day Romania).

⑪

Roman Forum

🏠 Entrance: Via della Salara Vecchia 5-6 Ⓜ Colosseo
🚌 75, 81, 175, 204, 673
🚋 30 🕐 Hours vary, check website 🚫 Jan 1, Dec 25
🌐 coopculture.it

The Forum was the center of political, commercial, and judicial life in ancient Rome. As Rome's population grew the original Forum became too small, so Julius Caesar built a new one (46 BC). This move was emulated by successive emperors; their collective forums are known as the "Imperial Fora."

The layout of the Roman Forum is confusing, so it is a good idea to view it from the Capitoline Hill, before walking around. From there, you can make out the Via Sacra, the route of religious and triumphal processions.

Did You Know?

The female version of a Roman toga is known as a stola.

The best preserved of the complex's monuments are two triumphal arches. The Arch of Titus commemorates the crushing of the Jewish Revolt by Titus in AD 70; the Arch of Septimius Severus (AD 203) records the emperor's victories over the Parthians.

Most of the other ruins are temples or basilicas. The latter were huge public buildings that served as law courts and places of business. At the western end of the Forum are the scant remains of the Basilica Julia and the earlier Basilica Aemilia. Close to the latter stands the reconstructed Curia, where the Roman Senate once met.

The eastern end of the Forum is dominated by the shell of the Basilica of Constantine and Maxentius (4th century AD). Cross the Via Sacra from here to see the partly reconstructed Temple of Vesta and the House of the Vestal Virgins.

Farther east, past the Arch of Titus, are the extensive ruins of the Temple of Venus and Rome, built in AD 121 by

→ Assorted ruins of buildings dating from several eras in the Roman Forum

Hadrian. Attached to the ruined temple is the church of Santa Francesca Romana – patron saint of motorists. On March 9, drivers bring their cars here to have them blessed.

Note that admission to the Forum also includes entry to the Colosseum (p389) and the Palatine (p388).

Capitoline Museums

🏛 Piazza del Campidoglio 1
🚌 30, 51, 63, 81, & many others 🕐 9:30am–7:30pm daily 🚫 Jan 1, May 1, Dec 25
🌐 museicapitolini.org

When Emperor Charles V announced he was to visit Rome in 1536, Pope Paul III asked Michelangelo to give the Capitol a facelift.

↑ A 1st-century BC bronze on display in the Capitoline Museums

He redesigned the piazza, renovated the facades of its palaces, and built a new staircase, the Cordonata. This gently rising ramp is now crowned with the Classical statues of Castor and Pollux.

The Capitoline Museums, the Palazzo Nuovo and the Palazzo dei Conservatori, stand on opposite sides of the impressive Piazza del Campidoglio. Since 2000, they have been connected via a subterranean passage. In the center of the piazza is an equestrian statue of Marcus Aurelius (it is a copy; the original bronze is in the Palazzo Nuovo).

The Palazzo dei Conservatori had been the seat of the city's magistrates during the late Middle Ages. Its frescoed halls are still used occasionally for political meetings today, and the ground floor houses the municipal registry office. The current building was begun in 1536, constructed by architect and sculptor Giacomo della Porta, who also carried out Michelangelo's other designs for Piazza del Campidoglio.

A collection of Classical statues has been kept on the Capitoline Hill since the Renaissance. When the Palazzo Nuovo was completed, some of the statues were transferred

there. In 1734, Pope Clement XII decreed that the building be turned into the world's first public museum.

The museum is still devoted chiefly to sculpture. Most of its finest works, such as The Dying Galatian, are Roman copies of Greek masterpieces. There are also two collections of busts, which were assembled in the 18th century, featuring the philosophers and poets of ancient Greece and the rulers of ancient Rome.

The museum also houses a collection of porcelain, and its art galleries contain various works by Veronese, Titian, Caravaggio, Rubens, Van Dyck, and Tintoretto.

GREAT VIEW
Caffè Capitolino

The vast terrace of Caffè Capitolino (www.musei capitolini.org/it/oltre_il_museo/cafeteria), on the top floor of the Capitoline Museums, is a great spot for panoramic views over Rome's rooftops and ruins.

⑬

Santa Maria Maggiore

📍 Piazza di Santa Maria Maggiore Ⓜ Termini, Cavour 🚌 16, 70, 71, 714 🚋 5, 14 📞 06-69 88 68 00 🕐 7am–6:45pm daily

Santa Maria offers a successful blend of architectural styles. Its colonnaded triple nave is part of the original 5th-century building; the marble floor and Romanesque bell tower are medieval; the Renaissance saw a new coffered ceiling; and the Baroque gave the church twin domes and its imposing front and rear facades.

The mosaics in the nave and on the triumphal arch date from the 5th century. Medieval mosaics include a 13th-century enthroned Christ in the loggia and Jacopo Torriti's *Coronation of the Virgin* (1295) in the apse.

The gilded ceiling was a gift of Pope Alexander VI.

⑭

Trevi Fountain

📍 Piazza di Trevi 🚌 52, 53, 61, 62, 63, 71, 80, 119, & many others

Nicola Salvi's theatrical design for Rome's largest and most famous fountain was completed in 1762. The central figure is Neptune, flanked by two Tritons. One Triton is seen struggling to master a very unruly "sea-horse," while the other leads a far more docile animal. These symbolize the two contrasting moods of the sea.

The ever-popular Trevi Fountain, and *(inset)* statue of a Triton ↓

 INSIDER TIP
Gelateria Cecere

Around the corner from the Trevi Fountain, on Via del Lavatore, Cecere is famous for its ice cream, made to a secret family recipe. Try the Marsala-spiked *zabaglione* flavor, pistachio, or chocolate.

⑮

Palatine

📍 Entrance: Via di San Gregorio 30 Ⓜ Colosseo 🚌 75, 81, 175, 204, 673 🚋 30 🕐 Hours vary, check website 🚫 Jan 1, Dec 25 🌐 coopculture.it

The Palatine, the hill where Roman emperors built their palaces, is Rome's most pleasant ancient site. Shaded by pines and carpeted with flowers in the spring, it is dominated by the ruins of the Domus Augustana and the Domus Flavia, two parts of Domitian's huge palace (1st century AD).

Other remains here include the House of Augustus and the House of Livia, where the Emperor Augustus lived with his wife Livia; and the Cryptoporticus, a long underground gallery built by Nero.

The Huts of Romulus, not far from the House of Augustus, are Iron Age huts (10th century BC), which provide archaeological support for the area's legendary association with the founding of Rome. According to legend, Romulus and Remus grew up on this hill in the 8th century BC.

Tickets to the Palatine also include entry to the Forum (p386) and the Colosseum.

↑ The unmistakable facade of the Colosseum in the evening sun

Colosseum

🏠 Piazza del Colosseo Ⓜ Colosseo 🚌 75, 81, 175, 204, 673 🚋 30 🕐 Hours vary, check website 🚫 Jan 1, Dec 25 🌐 coopculture.it

Rome's great amphitheater, commissioned in AD 72 by the Emperor Vespasian, was

constructed on the marshy site of a lake in the grounds of Nero's palace.

It is likely that the arena took its name not from its own size, but from that of an enormous statue, the Colossus of Nero, that stood nearby.

The Colosseum was the site of deadly gladiatorial combats and wild animal fights, staged free of charge by the emperor and wealthy citizens. It was built to a very practical design, its 80 entrances allowing easy access for 70,000 spectators. Excavations carried out in the 19th century exposed a network of rooms under the arena, from which animals could be released.

The four tiers of the outside walls were built in differing styles. The lower three are arched; the bottom with Doric columns, the next with Ionic, and the third with Corinthian. The top level supported a huge awning, used to shade spectators from the sun.

Beside the Colosseum stands the Arch of Constantine, commemorating Constantine's victory in AD 312 over his co-emperor Maxentius. Most of the medallions, reliefs, and statues were scavenged from earlier monuments. Inside the arch are reliefs showing one of Trajan's victories.

Admission here also includes entry to the Palatine and the Forum (p386).

TOP 4 **BEST OF THE REST ANCIENT ROMAN SIGHTS**

Baths of Caracalla
🏠 Viale delle Terme di Caracalla 52 🌐 coopculture.it
Extensive ruins of a well-preserved bath complex built in AD 216.

Theater of Marcellus
🏠 Via del Teatro di Marcello
An Imperial theater that later housed a number of medieval shops. In the summer it is used as a venue for concerts.

Museo Nazionale Romano
🏠 Palazzo Massimo, Largo di Villa Peretti 1 🌐 museonazionaleromano. beniculturali.it
Sculpture, mosaics, wall paintings, and a Roman mummy. Another branch of the museum is across the road, at the Baths of Diocletian.

Palazzo Altemps
🏠 Piazza Sant'Apollinare 46 🌐 museonazionaleromano. beniculturali.it
Fine collection of Classical statuary set in a beautiful Renaissance palazzo.

The iconic Spanish Steps, leading up to the church of Trinità dei Monti ↑

⑰ 🚴 🎿

Villa Giulia

📍 Piazzale di Villa Giulia 9
Ⓜ Flaminio 🚌 3, 19, 982
🚊 2, 19 🕐 9am-8pm Tue-Sun 🚫 Jan 1, Dec 25
🌐 museoetru.it

Built as a country retreat for Pope Julius III in 1551–3, today Villa Giulia houses a renowned collection of Etruscan and pre-Roman remains, including jewelry, bronzes, mirrors, and a marvelous terra-cotta sarcophagus of a husband and wife from Cerveteri.

The delightful villa was the work of architects Vasari and Vignola, and the sculptor Ammannati. Michelangelo also contributed.

← Terra-cotta water jar, part of the Etruscan and pre-Roman collection in Villa Giulia

⑱

Spanish Steps

📍 Scalinata di Trinità dei Monti, Piazza di Spagna
Ⓜ Spagna 🚌 119

Linking the church of Trinità dei Monti with Piazza di Spagna below, the Spanish Steps were completed in 1725. They combine straight sections, curves, and terraces to create one of the city's most distinctive landmarks. To the right as you look at the steps from the square is the Keats-Shelley Memorial House, a small museum in the house where the poet John Keats died of consumption in 1821.

The steps are always filled with people taking photos, chatting, busking, or simply just watching the passers-by. Eating and sitting here are not allowed.

The steps overlook Via Condotti and the surrounding streets, which in the 18th century were full of hotels for foreigners doing the Grand Tour. They now contain the smartest shops in Rome.

KEATS AND SHELLEY

The Keats-Shelley Memorial House is where the poet John Keats stayed in 1820. He had been sent to Rome by his doctor, in the hope that it would help him recuperate from consumption. However, Keats died a few months later aged 25. His death inspired fellow poet Percy Bysshe Shelley to write the poem "Mourn not for Adonaïs." Shelley died the following year in a boating accident; both poets are buried in Rome's Protestant Cemetery.

⑲

Santa Maria del Popolo

📍 Piazza del Popolo 12
Ⓜ Flaminio 🚌 61, 89, 119, 120F, 150F, 160, 490, 495, 590 🚊 2 🕐 Hours vary, check website 🌐 santa mariadelpopolo.it

Santa Maria del Popolo was commissioned by Sixtus IV in 1472. After his death in 1484, the pope's family chapel, the

Della Rovere Chapel (first on the right), was frescoed by Pinturicchio. In 1503, Sixtus IV's nephew Giuliano became Pope Julius II and had Bramante build a new apse. Pinturicchio was called in again to paint its vaults with Sibyls and Apostles framed by freakish beasts.

In 1513, Raphael created the Chigi Chapel (second on the left) – a Renaissance fusion of the sacred and profane – for the banker Agostino Chigi. Bernini later added the statues of Daniel and Habakkuk. In the Cerasi Chapel, left of the altar, are two Caravaggios: *The Crucifixion of St. Peter* and *The Conversion of St. Paul*.

20

Galleria Borghese

🏠 Piazzale Scipione Borghese 5 🚌 52, 53, 910 🚋 3, 19 🕐 9am–7pm Tue–Sun (reservations obligatory) 🚫 Jan 1, Dec 25 🌐 galleria borghese.beniculturali.it

Villa Borghese and its park were designed in 1605 for Cardinal Scipione Borghese, nephew of Pope Paul V. The park was laid out with 400 pine trees, dramatic water features and sculptures by Bernini.

The villa was used for entertaining and displaying the cardinal's impressive collection of paintings and sculpture. Unfortunately, between 1801 and 1809, Prince Camillo Borghese, husband of Napoleon's sister Pauline, sold many of these to his brother-in-law. However, some Classical treasures remain, including fragments of a 3rd-century-AD mosaic of gladiators fighting wild animals.

The highlights of the collection are the sculptures by the young Bernini. *Apollo and Daphne* (1624) shows the nymph Daphne being transformed into a laurel tree to escape being abducted by Apollo. Other striking works are *The Rape of Proserpina* and a *David*, whose face is said to be a self-portrait of Bernini. The most notorious work is a sculpture by Canova of Pauline Borghese as *Venus Victrix* (1805), in which the semi-naked Pauline reclines on a *chaise longue*.

The Galleria Borghese, on the upper floor, houses some fine Renaissance and Baroque paintings. Among these are Raphael's *Deposition*, as well as works by Pinturicchio, Correggio, Caravaggio, Titian, and Rubens.

Within the Villa Borghese park are other museums and galleries, foreign academies, a zoo, schools of archaeology, an artificial lake, and an array of fountains and follies.

DRINK

American Bar
Nestled in greenery and offering stunning views of the Roman Forum, this rooftop bar is a lovely spot for a cocktail in the summer.

🏠 Hotel Forum, Via Tor de' Conti 25 🌐 hotelforum.com

Caffè Sant'Eustachio
Many Romans believe that this tiny bar serves the city's best coffee – hence the hordes of locals that throng it from morning till late.

🏠 Via Sant'Eustachio 82 🌐 santeustachio ilcaffe.com

Antico Caffè Greco
Founded in 1760, this café was once a meeting place for artists and intellectuals, and it still retains the feel of a refined salon.

🏠 Via dei Condotti 862 🌐 anticocaffegreco.eu

Enoteca Ferrara
This cosy *enoteca* has a vast wine list with a good selection of wines by the glass, helpful staff, and an abundant *aperitivo* buffet.

🏠 Piazza Trilussa 41 🌐 enotecaferrara.it

Ombre Rosse
This friendly bar's pleasant terrace is a great spot for a prosecco as you take in the pre-dinner Trastevere whirl. There's live music several nights a week.

🏠 Piazza Sant'Egidio 12 🌐 ombrerossein trastevere.it

↑ Bernini's masterful *Rape of Proserpina*, in the Galleria Borghese

The 15th-century Palazzo Ducale above the town of Urbino ↑

❷

Urbino

🅰Le Marche 🚌 🛈Piazza Rinascimento 1; www. provincia.pu.it

The charming hilltop town of Urbino traces its origins to the Umbrians, centuries before Christ, and became a Roman municipality in the 3rd century BC. The city's zenith, however, came in the 15th century under the rule of the philosopher-warrior Federico da Montefeltro, who commissioned the building of the **Palazzo Ducale** in 1444. This beautiful Renaissance palace features an extensive library, hanging gardens, and numerous fine paintings. Two great 15th-century works, *The Flagellation* by Piero della Francesca and *Ideal City* attributed to Luciano Laurana, are notable for their innovative use of perspective.

Of special interest in the city's Neo-Classical Duomo, built in 1789, is the painting of the *Last Supper* by Federico Barocci. The church's Museo Diocesano contains a fascinating collection of ceramics, glass, and religious artifacts.

Elsewhere, the **Casa Natale di Raffaello**, birthplace of Urbino's most famous son, the Renaissance painter Raphael, is also open to visitors.

PIADINA

Central Italy's most loved specialty is this simple and delicious flatbread. Cold cuts of cured ham, rocket, and soft cheese, particularly the tangy local kind called *squacquerone*, make an ideal accompaniment to the bread. Try *piadina* and other local specialties at Urbino's Piadineria L'Aquilone *(Via Cesare Battisti 23)*.

Palazzo Ducale

⊗ ⊙ 🅰Piazza Duca Federico 13 🕒8:30am-7:15pm Tue-Sun, 8:30am-2pm Mon 🚫Jan 1, Dec 25 🌐gallerianazionale marche.it

Casa Natale di Raffaello

⊗ 🅰Via di Raffaello 57 🕒Mar-Oct: 9am-1pm & 3-7pm Mon-Sat, 10am-1pm & 3-6pm Sun; Nov-Feb: 9am-2pm Mon-Sat, 10am-1pm Sun 🚫Jan 1, Dec 25 🌐casaraffaello.com

HIDDEN GEM
Perugina Chocolate Factory
Visit the Perugina Chocolate Museum and Factory *(Viale San Sisto 207C)* and enjoy tastings or a chocolate-making course. Every October, chocoholics gather here for the Eurochocolate festival.

3

Perugia

Umbria 🚉🚌 ℹ Piazza Matteotti 18, Loggia dei Lanari; www.turismo.comune.perugia.it

Perugia's old center hinges around Corso Vannucci, a thoroughfare named after the local painter Pietro Vannucci, more commonly known as Perugino. The street is dominated by Umbria's finest building, the monumental **Palazzo dei Priori.** Among its richly decorated rooms is the Sala dei Notari or Lawyers' Hall (c. 1295), vividly frescoed with scenes from the Old Testament. Superlative frescoes (1498–1500) by Perugino cover the walls of the Nobile Collegio del Cambio, which was the seat of the money-changers' guild in medieval times. The **Galleria Nazionale dell'Umbria** on the third floor displays a fine collection of paintings and statuary.

The Cappella del Santo Anello, in Perugia's 15th-century Duomo, houses the Virgin's agate "wedding ring," which is said to change color according to the character of its wearer. The third pillar in the south nave holds a Renaissance painting of the *Madonna delle Grazie* by Gian Nicola di Paolo.

Away from the Corso, on Piazza San Francesco, the Oratorio di San Bernardino, has a colorful facade (1457–61) by Agostino di Duccio. Beyond the old city walls, the 10th-century San Pietro is Perugia's most extravagantly decorated church. San Domenico (1305–1632), on Piazza Giordano Bruno, is Umbria's largest church. It houses the tomb of Pope Benedict XI (c. 1304) and an archaeological museum.

Palazzo dei Priori
Corso Vannucci 19 · 075 573 64 58 · Daily (Sun: am only) · 1st Mon of month, Jan 1, May 1, Dec 25

Galleria Nazionale dell'Umbria
Corso Vannucci 19 · 8:30am-7:30pm Tue-Sun (mid-Mar-Oct: also 12-7:30pm Mon) · Jan 1, May 1, Dec 25 · gallerianazionaledell umbria.it

Did You Know?
In Italy, *peperoni* refers to peppers - pepperoni salami was invented in America.

4 Ⓜ

BASILICA DI SAN FRANCESCO, ASSISI

⌂ Piazza San Francesco, Assisi 🚌🚆 ⏰ Hours vary, check website
🌐 sanfrancescoassisi.org

The burial place of St. Francis, this basilica was begun in 1228, two years after the saint's death. With its stunning frescoes by the great painters Giotto and Cimabue, the basilica remains among the most influential monuments of Western art today.

Over the course of the 13th and 14th centuries, the basilica's Upper and Lower Churches were decorated by the foremost artists of their day, among them Cimabue, Simone Martini, Pietro Lorenzetti, and Giotto, whose frescoes of the *Life of St. Francis* are some of the most renowned in Italy. The pictorial style created in Assisi was reproduced in numerous other Franciscan churches across the country. Many of the frescoes were damaged in the earthquake of 1997, but all have been restored. The basilica, which dominates Assisi, is one of the world's great Christian shrines and receives vast numbers of pilgrims throughout the year.

WHAT ELSE TO SEE IN ASSISI

With its geranium-hung streets and fountain-splashed piazzas, this pretty medieval town is heir to the legacy of St. Francis, who is buried in the Basilica di San Francesco.

The town has many other interesting churches. St. Clare – Francis's companion and the founder of the Poor Clares (an order of nuns) – is buried in the Basilica di Santa Chiara. Assisi's Duomo has a superb Romanesque facade, while the Oratorio dei Pellegrini, a 15th-century pilgrims' hospice, contains well-preserved frescoes by Matteo da Gualdo.

The Pinacoteca Comunale art gallery includes a *Maestà* painted by Giotto.

→ The basilica's simple facade *(inset)* belies its exquisite interior

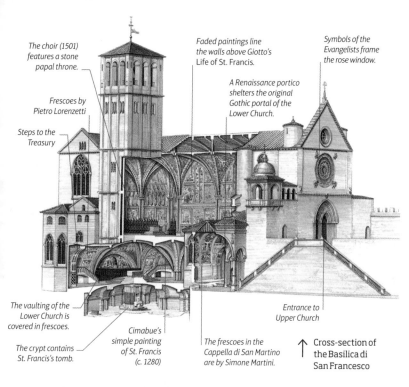

The choir (1501) features a stone papal throne.

Frescoes by Pietro Lorenzetti

Steps to the Treasury

Faded paintings line the walls above Giotto's Life of St. Francis.

A Renaissance portico shelters the original Gothic portal of the Lower Church.

Symbols of the Evangelists frame the rose window.

The vaulting of the Lower Church is covered in frescoes.

Cimabue's simple painting of St. Francis (c. 1280)

The crypt contains St. Francis's tomb.

The frescoes in the Cappella di San Martino are by Simone Martini.

Entrance to Upper Church

↑ Cross-section of the Basilica di San Francesco

❺

SIENA

🏠 Tuscany 🚉🚌 𝒊 Piazza Duomo 1;
www.terresiena.it

Siena is a city of steep medieval alleys surrounding
the Piazza del Campo. The buildings around this square
symbolize the golden age of the city, between 1260
and 1348, when wealthy citizens contributed to a
major program of civic building. Siena's decline began
in 1348 when the Black Death arrived, killing one-third
of the population; 200 years later, many more died
when the Florentines besieged and eventually won
the city. The victors repressed all further development
in Siena, and the city largely remains frozen in time,
crammed with renovated medieval buildings.

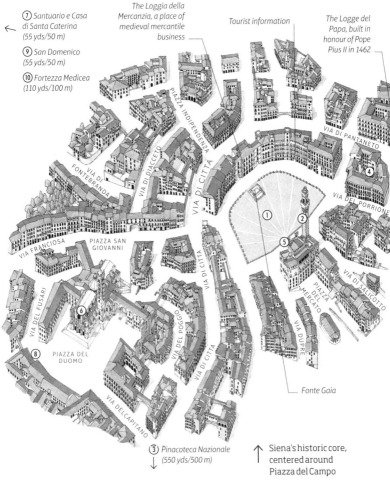

⑦ *Santuario e Casa
di Santa Caterina*
(55 yds/50 m)

⑨ *San Domenico
(55 yds/50 m)*

⑩ *Fortezza Medicea
(110 yds/100 m)*

*The Loggia della
Mercanzia, a place of
medieval mercantile
business*

Tourist information

*The Logge del
Papa, built in
honour of Pope
Pius II in 1462*

Fonte Gaia

③ *Pinacoteca Nazionale
(550 yds/500 m)*

Siena's historic core,
centered around
Piazza del Campo

↑ Siena's medieval townhouses, built up the city's gentle slopes

① Piazza del Campo

The shell-shaped, 12th-century Piazza del Campo is bordered by elegant *palazzi*. Its focal point is an elaborate fountain: the Fonte Gaia, a rectangular marble basin decorated with statues. The fountain that can be seen today is a 19th-century copy of the original, which was carved by Jacopo della Quercia in 1409–19. This was removed to preserve it from the ravages of the weather. The reliefs on the fountain depict Adam and Eve, the Madonna and Child, and the Virtues. Water is fed into it by a 15-mile- (25-km-) long aqueduct, which has brought fresh water into the city from the hills since the 14th century.

② Torre del Mangia

📍 Piazza del Campo 📞 0577 292 615 🕐 10am-7pm daily (mid-Oct-Feb: to 4pm)

The bell tower to the left of the Palazzo Pubblico is the second-highest in Italy, at 330 ft (102 m). Built by the brothers Muccio and Francesco di Rinaldo between 1338 and 1348, it is named after the first bell-ringer, who was nicknamed *Mangiaguadagni* (literally "eat the profits") because of his great idleness. (Since it was the bell-ringer's responsibility to warn the citizens of impending danger, this was worrisome.) There are 505 steps to the top of the tower, but climbers are rewarded with wonderful views across southeast Tuscany.

③ Pinacoteca Nazionale

📍 Via San Pietro 29 🕐 8:15am-7:15pm Tue-Sat, 9am-1pm Sun & Mon 🚫 Jan 1, Dec 25 🌐 pinacoteca nazionale.siena.it

Housed in the 14th-century Palazzo Buonsignori, this gallery contains key works by the Siena school. Lorenzetti's *Two Views*, produced in the 14th century, are early examples of landscape painting, and Pietro da Domenico's *Adoration of the Shepherds* (1510) shows how the art of the Siena school remained stylized long after Renaissance naturalism had influenced the rest of Europe. There is also a striking *Deposition from the Cross* (1502) by Sodoma.

④
Palazzo Piccolomini

📍 Via Banchi di Sotto 52
📞 0577 247145 🕐 By appt only; admission at 9:30am, 10:30am, & 11:30am Mon–Sat 🚫 1st two weeks in Aug & public hols

This imposing *palazzo* was built in the 1460s by Rossellino for the wealthy Piccolomini family. Today it houses the state archives, including the Tavolette di Biccherna – 13th-century municipal ledgers, with covers by Sano di Pietro, Ambrogio Lorenzetti, Domenico Beccafumi, and others.

⑤
Palazzo Pubblico

📍 Piazza del Campo 1
🕐 10am–6pm daily (mid-Mar–Oct: to 7pm) 🚫 Dec 25
🌐 comune.siena.it

The Palazzo Pubblico serves as the town hall, but the state rooms, which contain historic frescoes and works of art, are open to the public as part of the Museo Civico. The main council chamber is called the Sala del Mappamondo, after a map of the world painted in the early 1300s by Ambrogio Lorenzetti. One wall is covered by Simone Martini's *Maestà* (Virgin in Majesty; 1315). Opposite is Martini's fresco of the mercenary Guidoriccio da Fogliano (1330). The walls of the adjacent chapel are covered with frescoes by Taddeo di Bartolo, and the choir stalls (1428) feature wooden panels inlaid with biblical scenes.

The Sala della Pace contains the famous *Allegory of Good and Bad Government*, a pair of 1338 frescoes by Ambrogio Lorenzetti. The Sala del Risorgimento is covered with late-19th-century frescoes illustrating events leading up to the unification of Italy.

⑥
Duomo

📍 Piazza del Duomo
🕐 Hours vary, check website
🌐 operaduomo.siena.it

Siena's striking cathedral (1136–1382) is a spectacular example of Pisan-influenced Romanesque-Gothic architecture. Had the 14th-century plan to create a new nave come to fruition, it would have become the largest church in Christendom, but the idea was abandoned when the Black Death of 1348 virtually halved the city's population. Among the Duomo's treasures are sculptural masterpieces by Nicola Pisano, Donatello, and Michelangelo, an inlaid marble floor, and a magnificent fresco cycle by Pinturicchio. In the side aisle of the unfinished nave, which has been roofed over, is the **Museo dell'Opera del Duomo**. The museum is devoted mainly to sculpture removed from the exterior of the cathedral, including a circular relief of a Madonna and Child, most probably by Donatello. The highlight is Duccio's huge altarpiece, *Maestà* (1308–11), which shows the *Madonna and Child* on one side, and *Scenes from the Life of Christ* on the other.

> 🏔 GREAT VIEW
> ### Bird's-Eye View
>
> The small balcony of the San Paolo pub *(Vicolo San Paolo 2)*, directly opposite the Torre del Mangia, is the best place to go for views over the Campo. Come for a drink or a snack.

THE PALIO OF SIENA

The Palio is Tuscany's most celebrated festival. It's a bareback horse race, first recorded in 1238, that takes place in the Piazza del Campo each year on July 2 and August 16 at 7pm. The jockeys represent 10 of Siena's 17 *contrade* (districts), and horses are chosen by the drawing of lots. Preceded by days of colorful pageantry and heavy betting, the races themselves last only 90 seconds. Thousands come to watch, and rivalry is intense. The winner is rewarded with a silk *palio* (banner), and the victory celebrations can last for weeks.

Museo dell'Opera del Duomo

 ▢ Mar–Oct: 9:30am–7pm daily (Jun–Aug: to 8pm); Nov–Feb: 10am–5pm daily ▢ Jan 1, Dec 25 ▢ operaduomo.siena.it

---

⑦

Santuario e Casa di Santa Caterina

▢ Costa di Sant'Antonio 6 ▢ 9:15am–1pm & 3–7:30pm daily ▢ caterinati.org

Siena's patron saint, Catherine Benincasa, took the veil as a teenager and became known for her activism on behalf of the church. Her eloquence persuaded Gregory XI to return the seat of the papacy to Rome in 1376, after 67 years of exile in Avignon, France *(p230)*. She died in Rome and was canonized in 1461. Her house is surrounded by chapels and cloisters, and is decorated with paintings of her life by artists such as Pietro Sorri and Francesco Vanni.

←

Siena's Palazzo Pubblico, on the Piazza del Campo

⑧

Santa Maria della Scala

▢ Piazza del Duomo ▢ Hours vary, check website ▢ santamariadellascala.com

This former hospital is now a museum housing a collection of paintings and sculpture. In the Sala del Pellegrino, frescoes by Domenico di Bartolo depict hospital scenes from the 1440s.

---

⑨

San Domenico

▢ Piazza San Domenico ▢ Mar–Oct: 7:30am–6pm daily; Nov–Feb: 8:30am–6pm daily ▢ basilicacateriniana.it

This barn-like Gothic church was begun in 1226 and its bell tower was added in 1340. Inside is an exquisite chapel dedicated to St. Catherine. This was built in 1460 to store the saint's preserved head, which is now kept in a gilded marble tabernacle on the altar, encircled by frescoes depicting her.

Catherine experienced many visions and received her stigmata in the Cappella delle Volte, at the church's west end.

⑩

Fortezza Medicea

▢ Piazza Caduti delle Forze Armate ▢ Fortress: 24 hrs daily; theater: Nov–Apr, performances only

This huge red-brick fortress was built for Cosimo I by Baldassarre Lanci in 1560, following Siena's defeat by the Florentines in the 1554–5 war. The fortress now houses an open-air theater, and from the entrance bastions there are fine countryside views.

EAT

Taverna San Giuseppe
Exceptional food and service, plus an Etruscan wine cellar carved from the rock.

▢ Via Dupré 132 ▢ Sun ▢ tavernasangiuseppe.it

€€€

Grotta Santa Caterina da Bagoga
Charming trattoria run by an ex-Palio jockey.

▢ Via della Galluzza 26 ▢ Mon ▢ ristorantebagoga.it

€€€

Inside San Domenico is an exquisite chapel dedicated to St. Catherine, which was built in 1460 to store the saint's preserved head.

↑ A twilight view across Florence, from Piazzale Michelangelo

❻

FLORENCE

 **Tuscany** 🚆🚌🚲 ℹ️ **www.visitflorence.com**

Created in a whirlwind of artistic energy that can still be felt more than 500 years later, Florence is an exquisite monument to the Renaissance, the artistic and intellectual reawakening of the 15th century. The historic center is packed with art and architectural highlights, but the city is no mere museum piece: it is a lively place with bustling shops and markets, spirited street performers, and a plethora of tempting *gelateries*, restaurants, and cafés.

 INSIDER TIP
Getting Around

Buses are bright orange, and most can be taken at Santa Maria Novella station. Lines run until at least 9:30pm, the most popular until midnight or 1am. Information about routes can be found at www.ataf.net. Official taxis are white and are generally costly. The most enjoyable way to explore is on foot.

①

Galleria dell'Accademia

🏠 **Via Ricasoli 60** 🚌 **6, 10, 17, 20, 23** 🕐 **8:15am–6:50pm Tue–Sun** 🚫 **Public hols** 🌐 **galleriaaccademia firenze.beniculturali.it**

The Academy of Fine Arts in Florence, founded in 1563, was the first school in Europe set up to teach drawing, painting, and sculpture.

Since 1873, a number of Michelangelo's key works have been kept in the Accademia. Perhaps the most famous of all dominates the collection: his sculpture of *David* (1504).

This colossal nude depicts the biblical hero who killed the giant Goliath.

Michelangelo's other masterpieces include a statue of St. Matthew finished in 1506, and the *Quattro Prigioni* (Four Prisoners), sculpted around 1530. The muscular figures

Did You Know?

A replica *David* made for London's V&A Museum came with a detachable fig leaf for modesty.

struggling to free themselves are among the most dramatic of his works.

The gallery holds paintings by 15th- and 16th-century Florentine artists, and major works include the *Madonna del Mare* (1475–80) attributed to Botticelli; Pacino di Bona-guida's *Tree of Life* (1310–15); and *Venus and Cupid* (c. 1533) by Jacopo Pontormo. Also on display is a painted wooden chest, the *Cassone Adimari* (c. 1450) by Lo Scheggia. It was originally part of a bride's trousseau and is covered with details of Florentine daily life.

The Department of Musical Instruments contains about 50 items from the private collections of the grand dukes of Tuscany, the Medici and the Lorena. Among them are a violin, viola, and cello by Antonio Stradivari.

---

②

San Marco

🏛 Piazza di San Marco 🚌 6, 11, 17, 20, 23, 25 📞 055 28 76 28 🕐 7am–noon & 4-8pm daily

The church of San Marco and the monastery built around it date from the 13th century. Following the transfer of the site to the Dominicans of Fiesole by Pope Eugene IV in 1436, Cosimo the Elder paid a considerable sum for its reconstruction, overseen by Michelozzo. The single-naved church holds valuable works of art, and the funerary chapel of St. Antoninus is considered Giambologna's main work of architecture. To the right of the church, the oldest part of the monastery is now a **museum**. It contains a remarkable series of devotional frescoes by Fra Angelico. The former Pilgrims' Hospice houses *The Deposition* (1435–40), a scene of the dead Christ; his *Crucifixion* (1441–2) can be seen in the Chapter House. There are also over 40 cells adorned with frescoes by Fra Angelico, including *The Annunciation* (c. 1445).

The monastery houses Europe's first public library, in a light, airy colonnaded hall.

San Marco Museum
🏛 Piazza San Marco 3
🕐 Hours vary, check website
🌐 polomusealetoscana. beniculturali.it

↑ The striking and elaborately decorated interior of San Marco

> **Santa Maria Novella displays a number of superb frescoes, including Masaccio's *Trinity* (1425-6), renowned as a masterpiece of perspective and portraiture.**

③

San Lorenzo

🏛 Piazza di San Lorenzo 9
🚌 6, 17, 20, 25, 30 1A, 37 1A
🕙 10am-5:30pm Mon-Sat
🌐 basilicadisanlorenzo
firenze.com

San Lorenzo was the parish church of the Medici family. Rebuilt in Renaissance style in 1419, the outer facade was never finished.

The basilica's inner facade was designed by Michelangelo, while the bronze pulpits in the nave are the last works of Donatello. Cosimo the Elder, founder of the Medici dynasty, is buried by the High Altar.

The Biblioteca Medicea Laurenziana, which housed the family's manuscripts, was designed by Michelangelo and has an elaborate sandstone staircase, desks, and ceilings.

The Cappelle Medicee incorporate three sacristies which epitomize different periods of art. Donatello's decoration of the Old Sacristy contrasts with the design of the New Sacristy by Michelangelo. The latter's funerary figures are among his greatest works. The Chapel of the Princes (1604) is opulently decorated with inlaid semi-precious stones and bright frescoes.

④

Santa Maria Novella

🏛 Piazza di Santa Maria Novella 18 🚌 C1, C2, 6, 22
🕙 9am-5:30pm Mon-Thu, 11am-5:30pm Fri, 9am-5:30pm Sat, noon-5:30pm Sun 🔒 Jan 1 (am), Jan 6, Easter Sun, Aug 15, Nov 1, Dec 8, Dec 25 🌐 smn.it

The Gothic church of Santa Maria Novella, built by the Dominicans between 1279 and 1357, is the setting for the start of *The Decameron* by Renaissance writer Boccaccio. It also contains some of the most important works of art in Florence. The interior displays a number of superb frescoes, including Masaccio's *Trinity* (1425–6), which is renowned as a masterpiece of perspective and portraiture. The close spacing of the nave piers at the east end accentuates the illusion of length. The Tornabuoni Chapel contains Ghirlandaio's fresco cycle, *The Life of John the Baptist* (1485), and in the Filippo Strozzi Chapel are dramatic frescoes by Lippi that show St. John raising Drusiana from the dead and St. Philip slaying a dragon. The Strozzi Tomb (1493) was created by the local sculptor Benedetto da Maiano. The 14th-century frescoes in the Strozzi Chapel, meanwhile, are by two brothers (Nardo di Cione and Andrea Orcagna) and were inspired by Dante's *Divine Comedy*.

Beside the church is a walled cemetery with grave niches. The cloisters on the other side of the church form a museum. The Green Cloister's name derives from the green tinge to Uccello's *Noah and the Flood* frescoes, damaged by the floods of 1966. The adjoining Spanish Chapel contains frescoes on the theme of salvation and damnation.

💬 **INSIDER TIP**
Fine Fragrance

First opened in 1612 by Dominican friars at Santa Maria Novella, the Officina Profumo Farmaceutica di Santa Maria Novella (*www. smnovella.it*) has been selling perfumes for more than 400 years.

Bargello

⑤

🏛 Via del Proconsolo 4 🚌 C2 🕗 8:15am-2pm daily 🚫 1st, 3rd, & 5th Mon and 2nd & 4th Sun of each month, Jan 1, May 1, Dec 25 🌐 bargello musei.beniculturali.it

Florence's second-ranking museum after the Uffizi, the Bargello houses Italy's finest collection of Renaissance sculpture and some superb Mannerist bronzes. Begun in 1255, the fortress-like building was initially the town hall but later became home to the chief of police (the *Bargello*). The renovated building opened as one of Italy's first national museums in 1865.

The key exhibits range over three floors, beginning with the Michelangelo Room. Here, visitors can admire *Bacchus* (1497), the sculptor's first large free-standing work; a delicate circular relief depicting the *Madonna and Child* (1503–5); and *Brutus* (1539–40), his only known portrait bust. Among other sculptors' works in the same room is *Mercury* (1564), Giambologna's famous bronze. Across the courtyard, two more rooms contain exterior sculptures removed from sites around the city and an external staircase leads to a first-floor collection of bronze birds by Giambologna. To the right, the Salone del Consiglio Generale contains the cream of the museum's Early Renaissance sculpture collection, including Donatello's heroic *St. George* (1416) and his androgynous *David* (c. 1430). Restored in 2008, the latter is famous as the first free-standing nude created by a Western artist since antiquity.

Beyond the Salone, the Bargello's emphasis shifts to the applied arts, with room after room devoted to rugs, ceramics, silverware, and other *objets d'art*. The Sala dei Bronzetti on the second floor holds the finest collection of small bronzes in Italy. Benvenuto Cellini is among the artists featured.

EAT

Trattoria Mario
This historic eatery offers a lunch menu of typical local dishes.

🏛 Via Rosina 2R 🌐 trattoria-mario.com

€€€

Procacci
This deli/wine bar is famed for its truffle specialties.

🏛 Via de' Tornabuoni 64R 🌐 procacci1885.it

€€€

I Fratellini
This tiny establishment is a classic stop for a quick glass or a snack.

🏛 Via de' Cimatori 38R 🌐 iduefratellini.it

€€€

All'Antico Vinaio
Expect quality local produce at several locations on one street.

🏛 Via de' Neri 🌐 allanticovinaio.com

€€€

Mercato Centrale
Florence's busiest food market offers fresh produce on the ground floor and an appetizing array of dishes in the dining hall upstairs.

🏛 Via dell'Ariento 10-14 🌐 mercatocentrale.it

€€€

← The interior of the church of Santa Maria Novella, patterned with magnificent historic frescoes

DUOMO AND BAPTISTRY

📍 Piazza del Duomo 🚍 C1, C2, 6, 11, 14, 23
🕐 Hours vary, check website 🚫 Jan 1 & religious hols
🌐 ilgrandemuseodelduomo.it

Rising above the heart of the city, the richly decorated Duomo – Santa Maria del Fiore – and its revolutionary orange-tiled dome have become Florence's most famous symbols.

The Duomo's sheer size was typical of Florentine determination to lead in all things, and to this day no other building stands taller in the city. The Baptistry, with its celebrated doors, is one of Florence's oldest buildings, dating perhaps from the 4th century. In his capacity as city architect, Giotto designed the Campanile in 1334; it was completed in 1359, 22 years after his death.

↑ Mosaics in the interior of the Baptistry

Colorful 13th-century mosaics illustrating The Last Judgment decorate the ceiling above the large octagonal font where many famous Florentines were baptized.

The Baptistry doors demonstrate the artistic ideas that led to the Renaissance.

→ Florence's octagonal Baptistry

East doors

The south doors include sculpted panels showing The Baptism of St. John the Baptist.

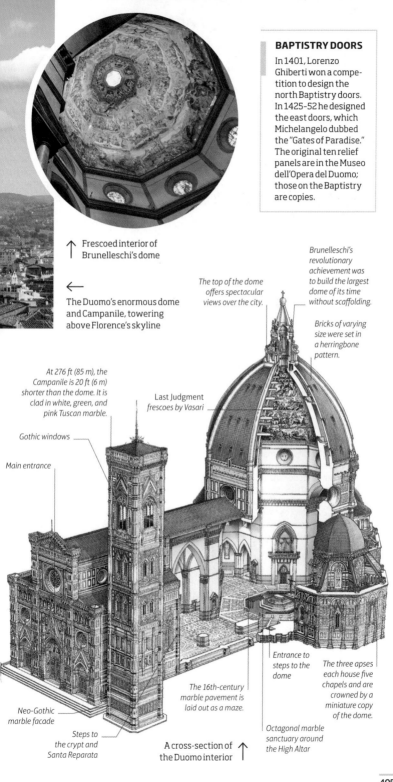

↑ Frescoed interior of Brunelleschi's dome

← The Duomo's enormous dome and Campanile, towering above Florence's skyline

The top of the dome offers spectacular views over the city.

Brunelleschi's revolutionary achievement was to build the largest dome of its time without scaffolding.

Bricks of varying size were set in a herringbone pattern.

At 276 ft (85 m), the Campanile is 20 ft (6 m) shorter than the dome. It is clad in white, green, and pink Tuscan marble.

Last Judgment frescoes by Vasari

Gothic windows

Main entrance

The 16th-century marble pavement is laid out as a maze.

Neo-Gothic marble facade

Steps to the crypt and Santa Reparata

A cross-section of the Duomo interior ↑

Entrance to steps to the dome

The three apses each house five chapels and are crowned by a miniature copy of the dome.

Octagonal marble sanctuary around the High Altar

↑ The beautifully decorated first courtyard of the Palazzo Vecchio

Palazzo Vecchio

◩ Piazza della Signoria
🚌 C1, C2 ◷ Hours vary, check website 🅦 cultura.comune.fi.it

Palazzo Vecchio, completed in 1322, has retained its external medieval appearance, and its imposing bell tower dominates the square on which it sits. The "Old Palace" still fulfils its original role as Florence's town hall. Much of the interior was remodeled for Duke Cosimo I in the mid-16th century by Vasari, whose work includes several frescoes.

The *palazzo* is entered via a courtyard, in which stands Verrocchio's *Putto* fountain. A staircase leads to the Salone dei Cinquecento, graced by Michelangelo's *The Genius of Victory* statue (1532–4), and to the tiny Studiolo decorated by 30 leading Mannerist painters.

Eleonora of Toledo, wife of Cosimo I, had a suite of rooms in the palace, decorated with scenes of virtuous women. Highlights of the palace include the paintings by Il Bronzino in the Cappella di Eleonora, and the loggia, with wonderful views over the city. The Sala dei Gigli (Hall of Lilies) contains frescoes of Roman heroes and Donatello's *Judith and Holofernes*.

There is also a Children's Museum, with storytelling sessions and tours in various languages. One tour takes in formerly secret stairways, hidden passages, and attics.

Piazza della Signoria

🚌 C1, C2

Piazza della Signoria has been at the heart of Florence's political and social life for

> 🔍 HIDDEN GEM
> **Michelangelo's Graffiti**
>
> Legend has it that the profile of a man's face etched into the facade of the Palazzo Vecchio (on the corner near the Uffizi) was carved by Michelangelo as part of a bet.

centuries. Citizens were once summoned to public meetings here, and the square's statues celebrate various events in the city's history. The sculpture of Grand Duke Cosimo I (1595) by Giambologna commemorates the man who subjugated all Tuscany, while Ammannati's impressive *Neptune Fountain* honors Tuscan naval victories. Michelangelo's original *David* stood here until 1873, when it was moved to the Galleria dell'Accademia *(p400)* and replaced by a copy. Donatello's original statue of the heraldic lion of Florence, known as the *Marzocco*, is now in the Bargello *(p403)*. Other notable statues include Cellini's bronze *Perseus*, and *The Rape of the Sabine Women* by Giambologna, carved from a single block of marble.

Museo Galileo

◩ Piazza dei Giudici 1
◷ 9:30am–6pm daily (to 1pm Tue) ◪ Jan 1, Dec 25
🅦 museogalileo.it

This lively museum devotes numerous rooms on two floors to different scientific themes, illustrating each with fine displays and beautifully made early scientific instruments. It is also something of a shrine to the Pisa-born scientist Galileo Galilei, and features two of his telescopes as well as large-scale reconstructions of his experiments into motion, weight, velocity, and acceleration. These are sometimes demonstrated by the attendants. Other exhibits come from the Accademia del Cimento (Academy for Experimentation), founded in memory of Galileo by Grand Duke Ferdinand II in 1657.

Some of the finest exhibits include early maps, antique microscopes, astrolabes, and barometers. Of equal interest are the huge 16th- and 17th-century globes illustrating the motion of the planets and

THE FLORENTINE RENAISSANCE

Fifteenth-century Italy saw a flowering of the arts and scholarship unmatched in Europe since ancient Greek and Roman times. This artistic and intellectual activity, later dubbed the Renaissance, was at its most intense in wealthy Florence. The patronage of the Medici, rulers of Florence from 1434, was lavished on the city, especially under Lorenzo the Magnificent. Architects turned to Classical models for inspiration, while the art world produced painters and sculptors that included such giants as Botticelli, Leonardo da Vinci, and Michelangelo.

stars. Be sure to see Lopo Homem's 16th-century map of the world, showing the newly charted coasts of the Americas, and the nautical instruments invented by Sir Robert Dudley, an Elizabethan marine engineer employed by the Medicis.

The second-floor rooms display calculators, fine old clocks, and weights and measures, as well as a horrifying collection of 19th-century surgical instruments and graphic anatomical models.

Santa Croce

📍 Piazza di Santa Croce 16
🚌 C1, C2, C3 🕐 9:30am-5:30pm Mon-Sat, 2pm-5:30pm Sun & religious hols 🌐 santacroceopera.it

The Gothic church of Santa Croce (1294) contains the tombs and monuments of many famous Florentines – among them Michelangelo, Galileo, and Machiavelli – as well as radiant early-14th-century frescoes by Giotto and his gifted pupil, Taddeo Gaddi. In 1842, the Neo-Gothic campanile of Santa Croce was added, and the coloured marble facade two decades later, in 1863. In the basilica, Rossellino's effigy (1447) of Leonardo Bruni, the great Humanist depicted in serene old age, is a triumph of realistic portraiture. Close by it is the 15th-century *Annunciation* by Donatello. The remainder of the monastic buildings scattered around the cloister form a museum of religious painting and sculpture. The museum houses Cimabue's *Crucifixion*, a 13th-century masterpiece damaged in the flood of 1966, and Gaddi's magnificent *Last Supper* (c. 1355–60).

The most famous of the church's many chapels is the Bardi Chapel, decorated by Giotto with frescoes of the *Life of St. Francis* (1325). The Peruzzi Chapel houses more Giotto frescoes. Gaddi's 1338 fresco in the Baroncelli Chapel, depicting an angel appearing to sleeping shepherds, is notable as one of the first night scenes in Western art.

In the cloister alongside the church is Brunelleschi's Cappella Pazzi (Pazzi Chapel), a masterpiece of Renaissance architecture with classical proportions. Its delicate gray stonework is strikingly offset by white plaster, which is inset with terra-cotta roundels of the Evangelists created by Luca della Robbia.

←
The distinctive marble facade of the church of Santa Croce

(11) ⚑ 🛍

THE UFFIZI

⌂ Piazzale degli Uffizi 6 🚍 C1 ⏰ 8:15am–6:50pm
Tue–Sun ⊘ Jan 1, May 1, Dec 25 🌐 uffizi.it

Florence's best-known gallery draws larger crowds
than any other art museum in Italy. The Uffizi's
notorious lines are almost unavoidable, but
once inside you'll forgive the wait.

The Uffizi was built in 1560–80 as a suite of offices *(uffici)*
for Duke Cosimo I's new Tuscan administration. The architect,
Giorgio Vasari, used iron reinforcement to create an almost
continuous wall of glass on the upper story. From 1581,
Cosimo's heirs used this well-lit space to display the Medici
family's art treasures, thus creating what is now the oldest
art gallery in the world.

The Uffizi houses some of the greatest art of the
Renaissance. The collection was born from the immense
wealth of the Medici family, who commissioned pieces
from many great Florentine masters. Francesco I was the
first to house the family collection at the Uffizi, and his
descendants added to it until 1737, when Anna Maria
Ludovica, the last of the Medici, bequeathed it to the people
of Florence (on the condition that it never leave the city).
Though the Renaissance collection is undoubtedly the
highlight, the works on display reach into the 20th century.

GALLERY GUIDE

The Uffizi art collection is
housed on the top floor.
Ancient Greek and Roman
sculptures are displayed
in the corridor running
round the inner side of the
building. The paintings are
hung in a series of rooms
off the main corridor, in
chronological order, to
reveal the development of
Florentine art from Gothic
to High Renaissance and
beyond. Most of the best-
known paintings are
grouped in rooms 7–18.
To avoid the long lines, be
sure to book your visiting
time in advance.

The museum's galleries
lining either side of the ↑
narrow Piazzale degli Uffizi

↑ Visitors marveling at Botticelli's famous masterpiece *Primavera*

← Raphael's serene yet boldly colored masterpiece *Madonna of the Goldfinch*

Gothic Art

▷ Following the collection of statues and antiquities in Room 1, the gallery's next six rooms are devoted to Tuscan art from the 12th to the 14th centuries, with notable works by Cimabue, Duccio, and Giotto, the three greatest artists of this period.

Early Renaissance

The famous Botticellis in Rooms 10–14 are the highlight of the gallery for most visitors. In *The Birth of Venus*, Botticelli replaces the Virgin with the goddess of love, while in *Primavera* (c. 1480), he breaks with Christian religious painting to show the pagan rite of spring.

High Renaissance and Mannerism

▽ Room 15 contains works attributed to the young Leonardo da Vinci, while Room 25 displays Michelangelo's influential *Holy Family* (1507; left). Nearby are works by Raphael and Titian.

Later Paintings

Rooms 41–45 of the Uffizi hold paintings acquired by the Medici in the 17th and 18th centuries. Three paintings by Caravaggio are in the Sala del Caravaggio.

Sculptures

The ancient Roman sculptures in the corridors and in Room 56 were mainly collected by the Medici in the 1400s. Their anatomical precision were much imitated by Renaissance artists, who saw themselves as giving rebirth to Classical perfection in art.

The Tribune

▷ Notable paintings in the Tribune include Bronzino's portrait of Bia de' Medici, Cosimo I's illegitimate daughter *(right)*. It was painted just before her early death in 1542.

Boboli Gardens

📍 Piazza de' Pitti 🚍 D, 11, 36, 37 ⏰ 8:15am–4:30pm daily (Mar & Oct: to 5:30pm; Apr, May, & Sep: to 6:30pm; Jun–Aug: to 6:50pm) 🚫 1st & last Mon of month, Jan 1, Dec 25 🌐 uffizi.it

Laid out behind Palazzo Pitti, the Boboli Gardens are a great example of stylized Renaissance gardening. Formal box hedges lead to peaceful groves of holly and cypress trees, interspersed with Classical statues.

Highlights include the stone amphitheater where early opera performances were staged and L'Isolotto (Little Island), with its statues of dancing peasants around a moated garden. The Grotta Grande is a Mannerist folly that houses several statues, including *Venus Bathing* (1565) by Giambologna and Vincenzo de' Rossi's *Paris with Helen of Troy* (1560).

Ponte Vecchio

🚍 C3, C4

The Ponte Vecchio, the oldest surviving bridge in the city, was designed by Taddeo Gaddi and constructed in 1345. The three-arched bridge rests on two stout piers with boat-shaped cutwaters. Its picturesque shops were originally occupied by blacksmiths, butchers, and tanners (who used the river as a convenient garbage dump). They were evicted in 1593 by Duke Ferdinando I and replaced by jewelers and goldsmiths, who were able to pay higher rents. A bust of Benvenuto Cellini, the most famous of Florence's goldsmiths, is located in the middle of the bridge.

The elevated Vasari Corridor runs along the eastern side of the bridge, above the shops. It was designed in 1565 to allow the Medici to move from the Palazzo Vecchio to Palazzo Pitti via the Uffizi, without having to mix with the public. The Mannelli family refused to demolish their tower to make way for the corridor, and it stands there defiantly to this day. The corridor passes around it, supported on brackets.

← *The Abundance*, one of many statues in the Boboli Gardens

 GREAT VIEW
Ponte Vecchio

One of Italy's most romantic spots, there are few better places than the Ponte Vecchio for enjoying Florence's river vistas. Buskers, portrait painters, and street traders all congregate on the bridge, creating an energetic, colorful scene.

The Ponte Vecchio, a popular spot for jewelry shoppers

The "Old Bridge," which is at its most attractive when viewed at sunset, was the only one to escape destruction during World War II. Visitors today come to admire the views and to browse among the antiques and specialized jewelry shops.

⑭

Palazzo Pitti

📍 Piazza de' Pitti 1 C3, C4
🕐 8:15am–6:50pm Tue–Sun
📅 Jan 1, Dec 25 W uffizi.it

Palazzo Pitti was originally built for the banker Luca Pitti, but his attempt to outrival the Medici backfired when costs of the building, begun in 1457, bankrupted his heirs. The Medici moved in and subsequent rulers of the city lived here. Today, the richly decorated rooms exhibit many treasures from the Medici collections.

The Palatine Gallery houses numerous works of art and ceiling frescoes glorifying the Medici. Raphael's *Madonna della Seggiola* (c. 1515) and Titian's *Portrait of a Gentleman* (1540) are among the exhibits.

On the first floor of the south wing, the royal apartments – Appartamenti Reali – are opulently decorated with gold-and-white stuccoed ceilings. The rooms are hung with portraits of the Medici family and are decorated with beautiful frescoes and Gobelins tapestries.

Other collections in the Palazzo include the Galleria d'Arte Moderna, with mainly 19th-century works of art; the Museo della Moda e del Costume (Museum of Fashion and Costume), which reflects changing taste in courtly fashions; and the Tesoro dei Granduchi (Treasury of the Grand Dukes), which displays the family's lavish tastes in silverware and furniture.

STAY

Hotel Brunelleschi
Part 15th-century tower, this unique hotel is furnished in opulent boutique style. Some rooms have views of Brunelleschi's dome.

📍 Piazza Santa Elisabetta
W brunelleschihotel florence.com

€ € €

SoprArno Suites
Vintage furnishings, original frescoes, and wooden floors characterize this stylish yet friendly small hotel.

📍 Via Maggio 35
W soprarnosuites.com

€ € €

Hotel AdAstra
Quiet but characterful, with a wide terrace overlooking gardens. Each of the 14 rooms has very individual and often quirky decor.

📍 Via del Campuccio 53
W adastraflorence.com

€ € €

Palazzo Guadagni
In a prime spot at the heart of the Oltrarno neighborhood, this 16th-century *palazzo* offers 15 comfortable rooms. The top-floor loggia is ideal for relaxing with a drink.

📍 Piazza Santo Spirito 9
W palazzoguadagni.com

€ € €

Masterpieces in the Palatine Gallery, part of the Palazzo Pitti

7

San Gimignano

Siena **Piazza del Duomo 1; www.san gimignano.com**

The 13 medieval towers that dominate San Gimignano's skyline were built by rival noble families in the 12th and 13th centuries, when the town's position on the main pilgrim route to Rome brought it great prosperity. The plague of 1348, and later the diversion of the pilgrim route, led to its economic decline and its miraculous preservation.

Full of good restaurants and shops, the town is also home to many fine works of art. The Museo Civico holds works by Pinturicchio, Benozzo Gozzoli, and Filippino Lippi, while the church of Sant'Agostino has a Baroque interior by Vanvitelli (c. 1740) and a fresco cycle by Benozzo Gozzoli (1465).

8

Lucca

Tuscany **Piazzale Verdi; www.turismo.lucca.it**

The city of Lucca is still enclosed within its 17th-century walls, and visitors can stroll along the ramparts, which were converted into a public park in the early 19th century. Within the walls, narrow lanes wind among dark medieval buildings, opening suddenly to reveal stunning churches and charming piazzas, including the vast Piazza Anfiteatro, which traces the outline of the old Roman amphitheater. The finest of the churches are all Romanesque: San Martino, the 11th-century cathedral; San Michele in Foro, built on the sight of the old Roman forum; and San Frediano.

9

Pisa

Tuscany **Piazza Duomo 7; www.turismo. pisa.it**

In the Middle Ages, Pisa's navy dominated the western Mediterranean. Trade with Spain and North Africa brought vast wealth, reflected in the city's splendid buildings.

The most notable structures are those of the **Campo dei Miracoli**, or "Field of Miracles," to the northwest of the city center. Pisa's world-famous Leaning Tower (Torre Pedente) is located here; begun in 1173 on sandy silt subsoil, it was completed in 1350. The Duomo, begun in 1064, is a magnificent example of Pisan-Romanesque architecture, its four-tiered facade an intricate medley of creamy colonnades and blind arcades. Inside, highlights include a pulpit (1302–11) by Giovanni Pisano and a mosaic of *Christ in Majesty* by Cimabue (1302). The graceful Baptistry was begun in 1152 and finished a century later by Nicola and Giovanni Pisano.

The **Museo Nazionale di San Matteo** holds Pisan and Florentine art from the 12th to the 17th centuries, including works by Masaccio and Donatello.

DRINK

Vernaccia di San Gimignano Wine Museum

Try San Gimignano's famous white wine and its lesser-known reds, rosés, and Vin Santo at this wine museum. A fascinating multimedia experience recounts the history and culture of the wines.

Via della Rocca 1, San Gimignano **sangimignano museovernaccia.com**

San Gimignano, nestled in the verdant hills of the Tuscan countryside ↑

↑ Pisa's Leaning Tower, with the Duomo and Baptistry behind

Campo dei Miracoli

⊛ ☐ Piazza dei Miracoli
🕒 Hours vary, check website
🅦 opapisa.it

Museo Nazionale di San Matteo

⊛ ☐ Piazza San Matteo 1
🕒 8:30am–7pm Tue–Fri 🚫 Jan 1, May 1, Dec 25 🅦 polomusea letoscana.beniculturali.it

⑩

Genoa

☐ Liguria ✈🚆🚌🛳
🛈 Via Garibaldi 12R;
www.visitgenoa.it

Genoa (Genova in Italian) rose to prominence as a sea-based power. As well as housing the most important commercial port in Italy, the city is also dotted with palaces, paintings, and sculptures that are among the finest in northwestern Italy.

The austere-looking **Palazzo Reale**, one-time residence of the Kings of Savoy, has a highly ornate Rococo interior, a collection of paintings, and an attractive garden. Opposite the palace is the old University (1634), designed by the architect Bartolomeo Bianco.

Palazzo Bianco, on Via Garibaldi, contains the city's prime collection of paintings, including works by Lippi, Van Dyck, and Rubens. Across the street, **Palazzo Rosso** houses works by Dürer and Caravaggio, and 17th-century frescoes by local artists.

Once the seat of the doges of Genoa and now an arts and cultural center, the Palazzo Ducale is located between San Lorenzo cathedral and Il Gesù, a Baroque church. All that remains of the Gothic church

of Sant'Agostino, bombed in World War II, is the bell tower, decorated with colored tiles. Two surviving cloisters of its surrounding monastery are now the **Museo di Sant' Agostino**, which contains the city's collection of sculptural and architectural fragments.

Palazzo Reale

⊛ ☐ Via Balbi 10 🕒 9am–2pm Tue–Fri (to 7pm Wed & Thu), 1:30–7pm Sat & Sun 🚫 Jan 1, Apr 25, Dec 25 🅦 palazzorealegenova. beniculturali.it

Palazzo Bianco

⊛ ☐ Via Garibaldi 11
🕒 Hours vary, check website
🅦 museodigenova.it

Palazzo Rosso

⊛ ☐ Via Garibaldi 18
🕒 Hours vary, check website
🅦 museodigenova.it

Museo di Sant'Agostino

⊛ ☐ Piazza Sarzano 35
🕒 Hours vary, check website
🚫 Public hols 🅦 museodi genova.it

VESPA MUSEUM

Visitors staying in Pisa should not miss the opportunity to visit this great museum in Pontedera, just a 15-minute train ride away. Vespa scooters have been made in Pontedera since the 1940s. The collection includes custom and race versions of the iconic motorbikes (*Viale Rinaldo Piaggio 7; closed Mon & Sun*).

⑪

Portofino Peninsula

🏛 Liguria 🚌🚤 ❼ Piazza della Libertà 13B; www. comune.portofino. genova.it

Portofino is one of the most exclusive harbor and resort towns in Italy, its marina crammed with the elegant yachts of VIPs and wealthy jet-setters. Cars are not allowed in the village, but boats run regularly between here and the nearby resort of Santa Margherita Ligure. Boats also run to the Abbazia di San Fruttuoso, an 11th-century abbey situated on the other side of the peninsula.

Above Portofino are the church of San Giorgio, containing relics said to be those of the dragon-slayer, and a castle. Farther west along the coast is Punta Chiappa, a rocky promontory famous for the changing colors of the sea. Other attractive resorts along the Ligurian coast include the fishing village of Camogli,

Sunset over the waterfront in Camogli, near Portofino

Other attractive resorts along the Ligurian coast include romantic Portovenere, with its narrow streets lined with pastel-colored houses.

Rapallo and its patrician villas, and romantic Portovenere, with its narrow streets lined with pastel-colored houses.

---

⑫

Turin

🏛 Piedmont ✈🚆🚌 ❼ Piazza Castello; www. turismotorino.org

Home of the Fiat car company, the famous Shroud, and the Juventus football team, Turin (Torino to the Italians) is also a town of grace and charm, with superb Baroque architecture.

Many of Turin's monuments were erected by the House of Savoy (rulers of Piedmont and Sardinia) from their capital here, before Italian unification in 1861 made the head of the House of Savoy King of Italy.

The **Museo Egizio** – one of the world's great collections of Egyptian artifacts – was amassed by Bernardo Drovetti, Napoleon's Consul General in Egypt. Wall and tomb paintings and a reconstruction of the 15th-century BC Rock Temple of Ellesiya are among its marvels.

The artworks in the Galleria Sabauda, in the same building, are from the House of Savoy's main painting collection, and include an array of works by Italian, French, Flemish, and Dutch masters.

Other notable buildings include San Lorenzo, the former Royal Chapel designed by Guarino Guarini, which boasts an extraordinary geometric dome. The **Palazzo Reale**, seat of the Savoys, holds a vast arms collection.

Did You Know?

Turin was the first capital of Italy when the country was unified in 1861.

Kha and his wife Merit adoring Osiris, in Turin's Museo Egizio ↑

The Duomo (1497–8), Turin's cathedral dedicated to St. John the Baptist, is the only example of Renaissance architecture in the city. Just outside, the Cappella della Sacra Sindone houses the famous Turin Shroud.

Inside the Palazzo Madama, the Museo Civico d'Arte Antica contains Classical and antique treasures. Turin's unmissably tall Mole Antonelliana, meanwhile, hosts the excellent **Museo Nazionale del Cinema**.

In the countryside near Turin, two superb monuments to the House of Savoy are worth visiting. About 5 miles (9 km) southwest of Turin, **Stupinigi** is a sumptuously decorated hunting lodge. It has a vast collection of 17th- and 18th-century furniture.

The **Basilica di Superga**, east of Turin, offers good views of the city. Its mausoleum commemorates kings of Sardinia and other royals.

Museo Egizio
⊗ 🖤 🖬 Via Accademia delle Scienze 6 🕒 9am-6:30pm daily 🔒 Mon pm, Jan 1, Dec 25 🔗 museoegizio.it

Palazzo Reale
⊗ ⊗ ⊗ 🖤 🖬 Piazzetta Reale 1 🕒 9am-7pm Tue-Sun 🔒 Jan 1, May 1, Dec 25 🔗 residenzereali.it

Museo Nazionale del Cinema
⊗ ☺ 🖤 🖬 Via Montebello 20 🕒 9am-8pm Wed-Mon (to 11pm Sat) 🔒 Jan 1, Dec 25 🔗 museocinema.it

Stupinigi
⊗ 🖬 Piazza Principe Amedeo 7 🕒 10am-5:30pm Tue-Fri, 10am-6:30pm Sat & Sun 🔗 residenzereali.it

Basilica di Superga
⊗ 🖬 Strada Basilica di Superga 73 🕒 10am-6pm daily (Mar-Oct: to 7pm) 🔗 basilicadisuperga.com

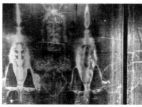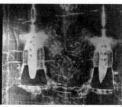

THE TURIN SHROUD

The most famous - and most dubious - holy relic of them all is kept at Turin's Duomo. The shroud, said to be the sheet in which the body of Christ was wrapped after the Crucifixion, bears the imprint of a man with a side wound, and bruises, possibly from a crown of thorns.

The shroud's early history is unclear, but the House of Savoy was in possession of it around 1450, and displayed it in Guarini's chapel in the Duomo from 1694. The shroud sits in a silver casket inside an iron box within a marble coffer. This has been placed inside an urn on the chapel altar. A replica shroud is on view. Tests carried out in 1988 claiming the shroud to be only a 12th-century relic were discredited by a US scientist in 2005, while a study released in 2019 strengthens the hypothesis that the man of the shroud was really crucified.

↑ The interior and *(inset)* exterior of the Galleria Vittorio Emanuele II

⑬

Milan

⌂ **Lombardy** ✈🚉🚌
ℹ **Piazza Duomo 14;**
www.turismo.milano.it

A thriving center of fashion and business, Milan (Milano in Italian) also has a wealth of impressive sights reflecting its long and checkered history.

Milan has been an important trading center since its foundation by the Romans in 222 BC. The city's central position made it a favored location for Rome's rulers, who made it capital of the Western Empire. It was here that Emperor Constantine declared that Christianity was officially recognized, following his own conversion (known as the Edict of Milan, AD 313).

By the Middle Ages, Milan was one of many cities in Lombardy that opposed the power of the Holy Roman Emperor. A period of local dynastic rule followed the fall of the region in 1277 to the Visconti family, who were themselves succeeded by the Sforzas during the Renaissance. These dynasties became great patrons of the arts, with the result that Milan has acquired a host of artistic treasures. Today this chic, bustling, and prosperous metropolis also offers opportunities for designer shopping and gastronomic pleasures.

Situated at the very heart of Milan, the giant **Duomo** is one of the largest Gothic churches in the world. The roof is extraordinary, with 135 spires and innumerable statues and gargoyles. Inside, there are remarkable stained-glass windows, bas-reliefs, and a medieval treasury. More religious artifacts can be seen in the Museo del Duomo, located in the Palazzo Reale.

An ornate shopping arcade completed in 1878, the Galleria Vittorio Emanuele II links the Piazza del Duomo with the Piazza della Scala. It boasts a superb metal-and-glass roof crowned with a central dome, mosaic floors, and stylish shops and restaurants.

The Neo-Classical Teatro alla Scala opened in 1778 and is among the most prestigious opera houses in the world. Its stage is one of the largest in Europe. The adjoining Museo Teatrale displays past sets and costumes and offers a glimpse of the auditorium.

The **Castello Sforzesco**, a symbol of Milan, was initially

> In the beautiful Santa Maria delle Grazie you will find the *Last Supper* of Leonardo da Vinci, one of the key images of Western civilization

the palace of the Visconti family. Francesco Sforza, who became Lord of Milan in 1450, embellished the building, turning it into a magnificent Renaissance residence. Its forbidding exterior belies the delightful interior, which contains an impressive collection of furniture, antiquities, and paintings. Michelangelo's unfinished sculpture, known as the *Rondanini Pietà*, can also be seen here.

Milan's finest art collection is held in the imposing 17th-century Palazzo di Brera, home to the 38 rooms of the **Pinacoteca di Brera**. Major works of Italian Renaissance and Baroque painters hang here, including *The Marriage of the Virgin* by Raphael, and Mantegna's *Dead Christ*. A number of works by some of Italy's 20th-century artists are also on display.

The city's most famous artwork, however, is located in the beautiful 15th-century Renaissance convent of **Santa Maria delle Grazie**. Here you will find the *Last Supper* (or *Cenacolo*) of Leonardo da Vinci, one of the key images of Western civilization. The large wall

painting has deteriorated badly but remains an iconic work of great subtlety.

Sant'Ambrogio is a mainly 10th-century Romanesque basilica dedicated to the patron saint of Milan, whose tomb lies in the crypt. The 4th-century church of San Lorenzo has a collection of Roman and early Christian remains.

Duomo
⊛ 🏛 Piazza del Duomo
🕐 8am–7pm daily
🌐 duomomilano.it

Castello Sforzesco
🏛 Piazza Castello 🕐 9am–5:30pm Tue–Sun 🚫 Public hols 🌐 milanocastello.it

Pinacoteca di Brera
⊛ 🅟 🍴 🏛 Via Brera 28
🕐 8:30am–7:15pm Tue–Sun (to 10:15pm Thu) 🚫 Jan 1, May 1, Dec 25 🌐 pinacotecabrera.org

Santa Maria delle Grazie
⊛ 🏛 Piazza Santa Maria delle Grazie 2 🕐 Basilica: hours vary, check website; *Last Supper*: 8:15am–6:45pm Tue–Sun, booking compulsory 🚫 Public hols 🌐 legraziemilano.it

STAY

Camperio House
Stylish residence with its own restaurant.

🏛 Via Manfredo Camperio 9, Milan
🌐 camperio.com

€€€

Hotel Viu
This chic hotel has a rooftop swimming pool.

🏛 Via Aristotile Fioravanti 6, Milan
🌐 hotelviumilan.com

€€€

The Yard Milano
Boutique hipster hotel with 32 suites.

🏛 Piazza XXIV Maggio 8, Milan
🌐 theyardmilano.com

€€€

SHOP

Bi
A curated space stocking designers such as Alexander Wang, Marni, and more.

🏛 Corso Genova 6, Milan

Dictionary
Cool mid-price clothes by young European designers.

🏛 Corso di Porta Ticinese 46, Milan

Fiera di Sinigaglia
Popular flea market stocked with vintage clothes, furniture, books, vinyl records, and accessories.

🏛 Ripa di Porta Ticinese, Milan

→ Mantua's old center, seen from across one of the lakes that surround the city

Lake Garda

🄰 Lombardy, Veneto, & Trentino-Alto Adige 🚌🚆 ⓘ Corso Repubblica 1, Gardone Riviera; www. visitgarda.com

Garda, the largest of Northern Italy's lakes, borders three regions: Trentino to the north, Lombardy to the west and south, and the Veneto to the south and east.

Hydrofoils and catamarans ply its waters, offering stops at charming lakeside towns like Sirmione, site of a medieval castle; Gardone, with the

DRINK

Villa Calicantus
Bardolino, on Lake Garda, has long been famous for its light red wine, and this little winery in the Bardolino hills produces some of the best in the region. Booking is essential.

🄰 Via Concordia 13, Bardolino 🕔 Sun & Mon 🌐 villacalicantus.it

curiosity-filled Vittoriale degli Italiani villa; and Salò, where Mussolini established a short-lived Republic in 1943.

Mantua

🄰 Lombardy 🚌🚆 ⓘ Piazza Andrea Mantegna 6; www. turismo.mantova.it

A striking city of fine squares and aristocratic architecture, Mantua (Mantova in Italian) is bordered on three sides by lakes. It was the birthplace of the poet Virgil and playground for three centuries of the Gonzaga dukes. Mantua was also the setting for Verdi's opera *Rigoletto*, and is referenced in Shakespeare's *Romeo and Juliet*. These theatrical connections are celebrated in local street names and monuments, and are reinforced by the presence of the 18th-century Teatro Scientifico Bibiena, a masterpiece of Late Baroque theater architecture.

Mantua is focused on three attractive main squares: Piazza Sordello, Piazza delle Erbe, and Piazza Broletto,

named after the 13th-century building adorned with a statue of the poet Virgil. Piazza Sordello is the site of the vast **Palazzo Ducale**, the former home of the Gonzaga family which also incorporates a 14th-century fortress and a basilica, and the Duomo, which has an 18th-century facade and fine interior stuccoes by Giulio Romano.

Piazza delle Erbe, meanwhile, is dominated by the Basilica di Sant'Andrea (15th century), designed largely by the early Renaissance architect and theorist, Alberti.

→ Aerial view of the beautiful town of Varenna, on Lake Como

GREAT VIEW
Castello di Vezio

For unobstructed Lake Como views, climb up to the medieval Castello di Vezio *(www.castellodi vezio.it)*. Check for events before you visit - once a year volunteers pose as eerie ghost-like statues around the grounds.

Across town is the early-16th-century Palazzo Tè, designed as the Gonzaga family's summer retreat. This extraordinary palace is decorated with frescoes by Giulio Romano and has rooms lavishly painted with horses and signs of the zodiac.

Palazzo Ducale

 Piazza Sordello 40
8:15am-7:15pm Tue-Sun
Jan 1, May 1, Dec 25
mantovaducale.
beniculturali.it

16
Lake Como

Lombardy i Via Albertolli 7, Como; www.lakecomo.is

Set in an idyllic landscape, Como has long attracted visitors who come to walk in the hills or go boating. The northern stretches, in particular, are shrouded in an almost eerie calm. The long, narrow lake, also known as Lario, is shaped like an upside-down Y, and offers fine views of the Alps.

In the heart of the town of Como lies the elegant Piazza Cavour. The beautiful 14th-century Duomo nearby has 15th- and 16th-century reliefs and paintings, and fine tombs.

Bellagio, at the junction of the "Y," has spectacular views, and is one of the most popular spots on the lake.

In the lakeside town of Tremezzo, the 18th-century Villa Carlotta is adorned with sculptures and celebrated for its terraced gardens.

17
Lake Maggiore

Lombardy & Piedmont i Piazza Marconi 16, Stresa; www.illago maggiore.com

Lake Maggiore, the second-largest Italian lake after Lake Garda, is a long expanse of water that nestles right against the mountains and stretches away into Alpine Switzerland. In the center lie the exquisite Borromean islands, named after the chief patron of the lake, St. Carlo Borromeo, of whom there is a giant statue in Arona.

Farther up the western coast of the lake is Stresa, the chief resort and main jumping-off point for visits to the islands. From here, Monte Mottarone – a snow-capped peak offering spectacular panoramic views – can be reached by cable car.

↑ Statue of St. Carlo Borromeo in the town of Arona, on Lake Maggiore

↑ Bridge across the Adige river, with the Duomo in the background, Verona

18

Verona

🏠 Veneto ✈️🚃🚌
🛈 Via degli Alpini 9; www. veronatouristoffice.it

A large and prosperous city of the Veneto region, Verona boasts magnificent Roman ruins, second only to those of Rome itself, as well as fine *palazzi* built of *rosso di Verona*, the local pink-tinged limestone.

The **Arena**, Verona's Roman amphitheater completed in AD 30, is the third largest in the world. Concerts, plays, and opera productions are staged here. Other Roman sites in the city include the Roman Theater, and artifacts from Roman times can be seen in the Museo Archeologico.

The tragic story of Romeo and Juliet, immortalized by Shakespeare, has inspired several local monuments, including Juliet's balcony,

Romeo's House, and the so-called Tomb of Juliet. Verona's focal point is Piazza Erbe, scene of colorful markets for 2,000 years.

The ornate tombs of the Scaglieri family, who ruled the city for 127 years from 1263, are situated beside the entrance to the church of Santa Maria Antica. A further legacy of the family is **Castelvecchio**, an impressive castle built by Cangrande II between 1355 and 1375. It houses a fine art gallery with a collection of 15th-century Late Renaissance Madonnas.

Built in 1125–35 to house the shrine of Verona's patron saint, San Zeno Maggiore is the most ornate Romanesque church in Northern Italy, famed for its unusual medieval bronze door panels. The city's Duomo also dates from the 12th century and displays Titian's lovely *Assumption*.

Arena

 🏠 Piazza Brà 🕐1:30–7:30pm Mon, 8:30am–7:30pm Tue–Sun 🚫 Jan 1, Dec 25–26 🌐 arena.it

Castelvecchio

 🏠 Corso Castelvecchio 2 🕐1:30–7:30pm Mon, 8:30am–7:30pm Tue–Sun 🌐 museodicastel vecchio.comune.verona.it

19

Vicenza

🏠 Veneto 🚃🚌 🛈 Piazza Matteotti 12; www. vicenzae.org

Vicenza is celebrated for its splendid, varied architecture. Known as the city of Andrea Palladio, stonemason turned architect, it offers a unique opportunity to study the evolution of his style.

Piazza dei Signori at the heart of Vicenza is dominated by the **Palazzo della Ragione**, known also as the Basilica. This building has a roof like an upturned boat and a balustrade bristling with statues. Beside it stands the 12th-century Torre di Piazza. The Loggia del Capitaniato, to the northwest, was built by Palladio in 1571. Its upper rooms contain the city's council chamber.

Europe's oldest surviving indoor theater, the **Teatro Olimpico**, was begun by Palladio in 1580 and completed by his pupil, Vincenzo Scamozzi. It was Scamozzi who created the stage, built of wood and plaster and painted to look like marble. It represents Thebes, a Greek city, and uses perspective to create an illusion of depth.

Palladio also designed the Palazzo Chiericati, which houses the Museo Civico, but the epitome of his work can be seen in the **Villa Rotonda**, in the countryside to the south of Vicenza.

Palazzo della Ragione
⊘ 🏠 Piazza dei Signori
🕐 Hours vary, check website
🌐 museicivici vicenza.it

Teatro Olimpico
⊘ 🏠 Piazza Matteotti
🕐 9am–5pm Tue–Sun 🚫 Jan 1, Dec 25 🌐 teatrolimpico vicenza.it

Villa Rotonda
⊘ 🏠 Via della Rotonda 45
🕐 Mid-Mar–late Nov: 10–noon & 3–6pm Tue–Sun; late Nov–mid-Mar: 10–noon & 2:30–5pm Tue–Sun 🌐 villalarotonda.it

---

Padua

🏠 Veneto 🚍🚌 ℹ Vicolo Pedrocchi; www.turismo padova.it

Padua (Padova in Italian) is an old university town with an illustrious academic history. It has two major attractions: the Basilica di Sant'Antonio, one of Italy's most popular pilgrimage sites, and the **Cappella degli Scrovegni**, a beautifully decorated chapel. The exotic Basilica was built from 1232 to house the remains of the great Franciscan preacher St. Anthony of Padua.

The chapel (1303) features a series of frescoes by Giotto depicting the life of Christ. The Museo Civico Eremitani on the same site has a coin collection and an art gallery.

Other attractions include the Duomo and Baptistry – which contains an impressive medieval fresco cycle (painted by Giusto de' Menabuoi in 1378) – and the Palazzo della Ragione, constructed in 1218 to serve as Padua's council chamber and law court.

Cappella degli Scrovegni
⊘ 🏠 Piazza Eremitani 8
🕐 9am–7pm daily (advance booking necessary) 🚫 Jan 1, Dec 25 & 26 🌐 cappella degliscrovegni.it

---

The Palazzo della Ragione in Vicenza, designed by Palladio ↓

VENICE

⌂ Veneto ✈ 🚆 🚌 🚢 **ℹ www.veneziaunica.it**

Constructed on a series of mud banks in a lagoon, with canals in place of roads, this magical city is truly unique. Once a powerful commercial and naval force in the Mediterranean, Venice has found a new role in the modern age. Its palazzi have become museums, shops, hotels, and apartments, while its convents have been turned into leading centers for art restoration.

①

Santa Maria Gloriosa dei Frari

⌂ Campo dei Frari 🚢 **San Tomà** 🕘 **9am–6pm Mon–Sat, 1–6pm Sun** 🚫 **Jan 1 & 6, Easter, Dec 25** 🌐 **basilicadeifrari.it**

More commonly known as the Frari (a corruption of *frati*, meaning brothers), this vast Gothic church dwarfs the area

of San Polo with its 230-ft (70-m) campanile. The first church on the site was built by the Franciscans in 1250–1338, but was replaced by a larger building completed in the mid-15th century. The airy interior is striking for its sheer size and for its works of art. The sacristy altarpiece, *The Madonna and Child* (1488) by Bellini, is one of Venice's most beautiful Renaissance paintings, while the main

altarpiece is *The Assumption of the Virgin*, a spectacular, glowing work by Titian (1518). Between the altar and the screen is the Monks' Choir (1468), its three-tiered stalls lavishly carved with saints and Venetian city scenes.

The marble, pyramidal Tomb of Canova was built after Canova's death in 1822 by his pupils, as was the Titian monument opposite, in the shape of a triumphal arch.

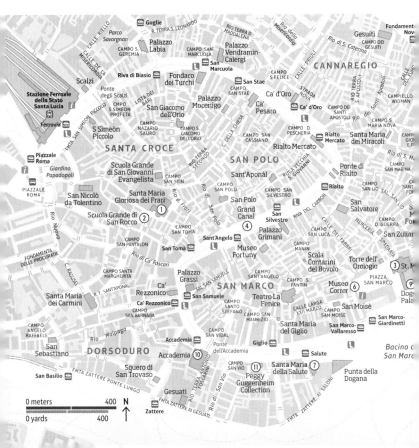

The Madonna and Child (1488) by Bellini is one of Venice's most beautiful Renaissance paintings.

② 🏃 Ⓜ 👜

Scuola Grande di San Rocco

🏛 Campo San Rocco
🚏 San Tomà ⏰ 9:30am–5:30pm daily ⛔ Jan 1, Dec 25 🌐 scuolagrande sanrocco.org

Founded in honor of San Rocco (St. Roch), a saint who dedicated his life to helping the sick, the Scuola started out as a charitable confraternity. Construction began in 1515, and in 1564 its members decided to commission Tintoretto to decorate its walls and ceilings. His earliest paintings, the first of over 50 works the artist eventually created for the Scuola, fill the small Sala dell'Albergo, off the Chapter House. His later paintings are found in the Ground Floor Hall, just inside the entrance.

The ground floor cycle was executed in 1583–7, when Tintoretto was in his sixties, and consists of eight episodes from the life of Mary. They are remarkable for the tranquil serenity of paintings such as *The Flight into Egypt* and *St. Mary of Egypt.*

Scarpagnino's great staircase (1544–6) leads to the Chapter Room, which was decorated by Tintoretto in 1575–81. The ceiling is covered with scenes from the Old Testament. The three large square paintings in the center show episodes from the Book of Exodus, all alluding to the charitable aims of the Scuola in alleviating thirst, sickness, and hunger. The vast wall paintings feature episodes from the New Testament, linking with the ceiling paintings. Two of the most striking are *The Temptation of Christ*, which shows a young Satan offering Christ two loaves of bread, and *The Adoration of the Shepherds.*

In the Sala dell'Albergo is Tintoretto's breathtaking *Crucifixion* (1565). Henry James once remarked of it: "No single picture in the world contains more of human life: there is everything in it, including the most exquisite beauty."

↑ Gondolas cruising along Venice's famous Grand Canal

 INSIDER TIP
Getting Around

On land, the only way to get around is on foot. *Vaporetti* (water buses) ply the canals and go to the lagoon islands. Gondolas are very expensive, but *traghetti* (gondola ferries) are more reasonable. The speediest means of travel is water taxi.

③ 〈〉 Ⓜ 🛍

ST. MARK'S

🏛 Piazza San Marco 328 🚉 San Marco 🕐 Mid-Apr-Oct: 9:35am-5pm Mon-Sat, 2-5pm Sun; Nov-mid-Apr: 9:45am-4:45pm Mon-Sat, 2-4:30pm Sun 🌐 basilicasanmarco.it

Venice's dark and mysterious basilica blends the architectural and decorative styles of East and West to create one of Europe's greatest buildings. Inside, this Byzantine extravaganza is embellished with golden mosaics, icons, and ornate marble carvings.

Built on a Greek-cross plan and crowned with five huge domes, it is the third church to stand on this site. The first, built to enshrine the body of St. Mark in the 9th century, was destroyed by fire. The second was pulled down in the 11th century to make way for a spectacular edifice reflecting the growing power of the Republic and its links with Byzantium. Many treasures – such as the famous horses – were brought to St. Mark's after the fourth Crusade had plundered Constantinople in 1204.

The Ascension Dome features a magnificent 13th-century mosaic of Christ surrounded by angels, the 12 Apostles, and the Virgin Mary.

The dome above the nave is decorated with the 12th-century Pentecost Mosaic, showing the Holy Spirit descending on the Apostles.

The statues of St. Mark and the angels crowning the central arch were added in the early 15th century.

The porch, or narthex, contains many fine mosaics, notably those of the Genesis Cupola showing the Creation.

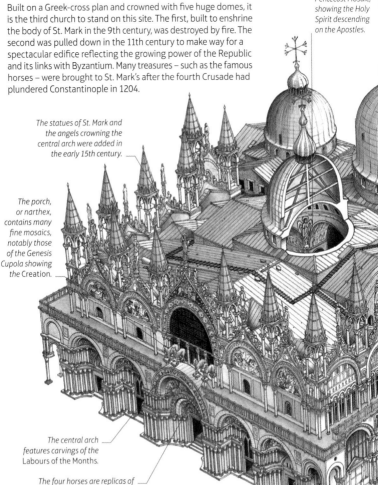

The central arch features carvings of the Labours of the Months.

The four horses are replicas of the gilded bronze originals, kept in the Museo Marciano, reached from the atrium.

The facade mosaics are either heavily restored or replacements of the originals.

Baptistry

978–1117

▽ The church is replaced by a grand basilica, "the House of St. Mark," reflecting Venice's growing power.

1807

▽ The doge's private chapel until 1807, St. Mark's succeeds San Pietro di Castello as the cathedral of Venice.

828–978

△ A church is built to house relics of St. Mark, stolen from Alexandria. It burns down in 976 and is rebuilt in 978.

1117–c.1300

△ 45,600 sq ft (4,240 sq m) of gleaming golden mosaics are added to the domes, walls, and floors of the basilica.

The altar canopy, or baldacchino, has alabaster columns that are carved with New Testament scenes.

↑ Stunning mosaic of Christ in Glory in the vast Ascension Dome

St. Mark's body, thought to have been lost in the fire of 976, reappeared when the new church was consecrated in 1094. The remains are housed below the altar.

←

Cross-section of the splendid St. Mark's Basilica

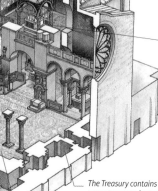

The Treasury contains many treasures looted from Constantinople by the Venetians in 1204.

Allegorical mosaics decorate the floor of the south transept.

On the facade is a porphyry sculptural group (4th-century Egyptian) known as The Tetrarchs, which may represent the four joint rulers of the Roman Empire c. AD 300.

↑ View across St. Mark's Square to the exuberant Byzantine basilica

↑ The Grand Canal, lined with moored gondolas and colorful houses

Grand Canal

🚊 1 from Ferrovia & many others

The best way to view the Grand Canal as it winds through the heart of the city is from a *vaporetto*, or water bus. There are several lines traveling the length of the canal. The palaces lining the waterway were built over a span of five centuries and present a panoramic survey of the city's history, almost all bearing the name of some once-great Venetian family.

Nearly 2.5 miles (4 km) long, the Grand Canal varies in width from 98 to 230 ft (30 to 70 m) and is spanned by four bridges: the Scalzi, the Rialto, the Accademia, and the Costituzione. After passing the Rialto, the canal doubles back on itself along a stretch known as La Volta (the bend). It then widens out and the views become more spectacular approaching San Marco. Facades may have faded and foundations rotted, yet the canal remains, in the words of the French ambassador in 1495, "the most beautiful street in the world."

> ### SAVE VENICE!
>
> Venice is a dreamlike city, but its delicate microcosm is under threat from rising waters and mass tourism. Wave-induced erosion caused by speeding motorboats is a serious problem, so limit your impact by opting for public transport whenever possible. Cruise ships are a particularly contentious issue: the average cruise liner pollutes as much as do 14,000 cars and damages the already fragile lagoon environment.

⑤
Santi Giovanni e Paolo

🏛 Campo Santi Giovanni e Paolo (also signposted San Zanipolo) 🚊 Fondamenta Nove, Ospedale Civile ⏰ 9am–6pm daily 🔔 Sun am for Mass 🌐 basilica santigiovanniepaolo.it

Known colloquially as San Zanipolo, Santi Giovanni e Paolo vies with the Frari as the city's greatest Gothic church. Constructed by the Dominicans in the 14th century, it is striking for its vast scale and architectural austerity. Also called the Pantheon of Venice, it houses monuments to 25 doges. Among these are several fine works of art by the Lombardo family and other leading sculptors. Pietro Lombardo created the magnificent tombs of the doges Nicolò Marcello (died 1474) and Pietro Mocenigo (died 1476). Lombardo's masterpiece, the Tomb of Andrea Vendramin (died 1478), takes the form of a Roman triumphal arch.

The main doorway, which is decorated with Byzantine reliefs, is one of Venice's earliest Renaissance architectural works. On the right as you enter is a polyptych by Giovanni Bellini (c. 1460–65) showing St. Vincent Ferrer, a Spanish cleric, flanked by St. Sebastian and St. Christopher.

118

small islands make up the body of land on which Venice sits.

---

⑥

Museo Corror

⬜ Piazza San Marco (entrance in Ala Napoleonica) ⬛ San Marco ⬜ 10:30am-5pm daily ⬜ Jan 1, Dec 25 ⬜ correr.visitmuve.it

Teodoro Correr bequeathed his extensive collection of works of art to Venice in 1830, thus forming the core of the city's fine civic museum.

Its first rooms form a suitably Neo-Classical backdrop for early statues by Antonio Canova. The rest of the floor covers the history of the Venetian Republic, with maps, coins, armor, and a host of doge-related exhibits.

The second floor contains the picture gallery. Works are hung chronologically, enabling one to trace the evolution of Venetian painting. The most famous include the *Portrait of a Young Man in a Red Hat* (1490–5), once attributed to Vittore Carpaccio but now thought to be by an artist

from the Ferrara/Bologna area, and Carpaccio's *Two Venetian Ladies* (1490–5).

---

⑦

Santa Maria della Salute

⬜ Campo della Salute ⬛ Salute ⬜ Church: 9:30am-noon & 3-5:30pm daily; sacristy: 10am-noon & 3-5pm Mon-Sat, 3-5pm Sun ⬜ basilicasalutevenezia.it

The great Baroque church of Santa Maria della Salute, standing at the entrance of the Grand Canal, is an imposing architectural landmark. Construction of the church, which began in 1631 under the architect Baldassare Longhena, was not completed until 1687, five years after his death.

The comparatively sober interior of Santa Maria della Salute consists of a large octagonal space below the cupola and six chapels radiating from the ambulatory. The sculptural group around the grandiose high altar is by Giusto Le Court and represents the Virgin and Child protecting the city of Venice from the plague.

In the sacristy to the left of the altar, Titian's early altarpiece *St. Mark Enthroned with St. Cosmas, St. Damian, St. Roch, and St. Sebastian* (1511–12) and his dramatic ceiling paintings of *David and Goliath*, *Cain and Abel*, and *The Sacrifice of Isaac* (1540–9) are considered the finest paintings in the church. *The Wedding at Cana* (1551) on the wall opposite the entrance, is a major work by Jacopo Tintoretto.

The church was named *Salute*, which means both "health" and "salvation,"

→

Carpaccio's *Calling of St. Matthew*, Scuola di San Giorgio degli Schiavoni

in thanksgiving for the deliverance of the city from the plague epidemic of 1630. Each November, in a moving ceremony of remembrance, worshipers light candles and approach the church across a bridge of boats that spans the mouth of the Grand Canal.

---

⑧

Scuola di San Giorgio degli Schiavoni

⬜ Calle Furlani 3259A ⬛ San Zaccaria ⬜ 9:30am-5:30pm daily ⬜ Mon am, Sun pm ⬜ scuoladalmata venezia.com

Within this small Scuola, established in 1451 and rebuilt in 1551, are some of the finest paintings of Vittore Carpaccio. Commissioned by the Schiavoni, or Dalmatian Slav trading community in Venice, Carpaccio's exquisite frieze (1502–10) shows scenes from the lives of three saints: St. George, St. Tryphon, and St. Jerome. Each episode of the narrative cycle is remarkable for its vivid coloring and minutely observed detail of Venetian life. *St. George Slaying the Dragon* and *The Vision of St. Jerome* are both outstanding.

⑨ 🗾 📵 🖥 🏛

DOGE'S PALACE

🏠 Piazza San Marco 1 🚏 San Marco 🕐 8:30am–7pm daily 🚫 Jan 1, Dec 25
🌐 palazzoducale.visitmuve.it

A magnificent combination of Byzantine, Gothic, and Renaissance architecture, the Doge's Palace was for almost 1,000 years the official residence of the doges who ruled Venice. Artists such as Titian, Tintoretto, and Bellini vied with each other to embellish the palace with painting and sculpture, not to mention architects Antonio Rizzo and Pietro Lombardo, the latter responsible for the ornate western facade.

The Doge's Palace was founded in the 9th century, when a fortress-like structure stood on this spot. The present palace owes its external appearance to the building work of the 14th and early 15th centuries. To create their airy Gothic masterpiece, the Venetians broke with tradition by perching the bulk of the palace (built of pink Veronese marble) on top of an apparent fretwork of loggias and arcades (built of white Istrian stone). A tour of the palace leads through a succession of richly decorated chambers and halls, ending with the Bridge of Sighs and the prisons.

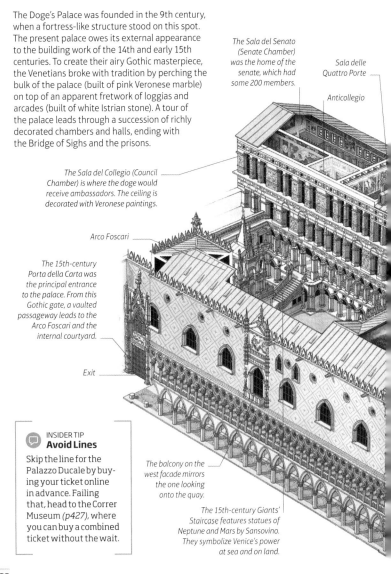

The Sala del Senato (Senate Chamber) was the home of the senate, which had some 200 members.

Sala delle Quattro Porte

Anticollegio

The Sala del Collegio (Council Chamber) is where the doge would receive ambassadors. The ceiling is decorated with Veronese paintings.

Arco Foscari

The 15th-century Porta della Carta was the principal entrance to the palace. From this Gothic gate, a vaulted passageway leads to the Arco Foscari and the internal courtyard.

Exit

The balcony on the west facade mirrors the one looking onto the quay.

The 15th-century Giants' Staircase features statues of Neptune and Mars by Sansovino. They symbolize Venice's power at sea and on land.

> 💬 INSIDER TIP
> ## Avoid Lines
>
> Skip the line for the Palazzo Ducale by buying your ticket online in advance. Failing that, head to the Correr Museum *(p427)*, where you can buy a combined ticket without the wait.

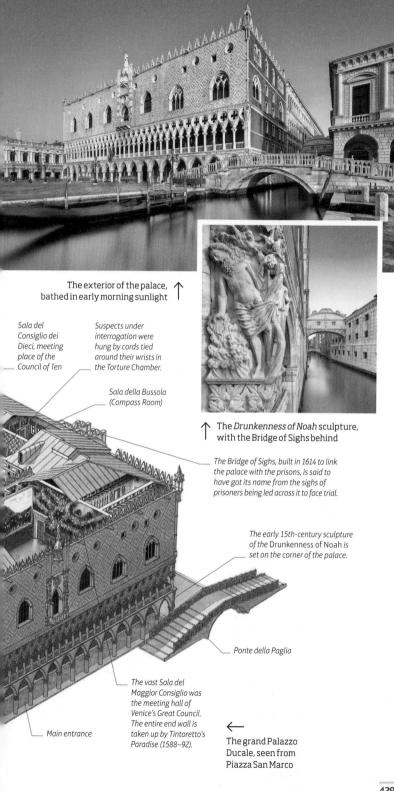

The exterior of the palace, ↑
bathed in early morning sunlight

Sala del Consiglio dei Dieci, meeting place of the Council of Ten

Suspects under interrogation were hung by cords tied around their wrists in the Torture Chamber.

Sala della Bussola (Compass Room)

↑ The *Drunkenness of Noah* sculpture, with the Bridge of Sighs behind

The Bridge of Sighs, built in 1614 to link the palace with the prisons, is said to have got its name from the sighs of prisoners being led across it to face trial.

The early 15th-century sculpture of the Drunkenness of Noah *is set on the corner of the palace.*

Ponte della Paglia

The vast Sala del Maggior Consiglio was the meeting hall of Venice's Great Council. The entire end wall is taken up by Tintoretto's Paradise *(1588–92).*

Main entrance

←

The grand Palazzo Ducale, seen from Piazza San Marco

Accademia

🏛 Campo della Carità
🚉 Accademia 🕐 8:15am-
7:15pm daily (Mon: am
only) 🚫 Jan 1, Dec 25
🌐 gallerieaccademia.it

Spanning five centuries, the
Accademia's art collection
provides a complete spectrum
of the Venetian school, from
the Byzantine period through
the Renaissance and on to the
Baroque and later.

The basis of the collection
was the Accademia di Belle
Arti, founded in 1750 by the
painter Giovanni Battista
Piazzetta. In 1807, Napoleon
moved the academy to its
present premises, greatly
enlarging the collection with
artworks from churches and
monasteries he suppressed.

The gallery is currently
being enlarged and some
rooms may be closed.

A highlight of the Byzantine
and Gothic section is Paolo
Veneziano's *Coronation of the
Virgin* (1325), which contrasts
with the delicate naturalism
of Giambono's painting of
the same name (1448).

CARNEVALE

The Venetian gift for intrigue comes
into its own during Carnevale, a
vibrant, playful festival preceding
the abstinence of Lent. Masks and
costumes play a key role in this
anonymous world; social divisions
are dissolved, participants delight
in playing practical jokes, and
anything goes. The tradition
of Carnevale in Venice
began in the 11th century
and reached its peak in
popularity and outrageous-
ness in the 18th century.

The Bellini family played a
dominant role in the early
Venetian Renaissance, and
outstanding examples of their
work include Giovanni Bellini's
*Madonna and Child Between
St. John the Baptist and a Saint*
(c. 1504). Bellini's student
Giorgione painted the atmospheric *Tempest* (c. 1505–09).
Among Renaissance works on
display are *Feast in the House
of Levi* (1573) by Veronese,
and Tintoretto's *Miracle of
the Slave* (1548).

The long gallery of Baroque,
genre, and landscape paintings alongside Palladio's inner

courtyard (1561) features
works by Giambattista
Tiepolo, as well as a view of
Venice (1765) by Canaletto.

Peggy Guggenheim
Collection

🏛 Palazzo Venier dei Leoni
🚉 Accademia 🕐 10am-
6pm Wed-Mon 🚫 Dec 25
🌐 guggenheim-venice.it

Intended as a four-story
palace, the 18th-century
Palazzo Venier dei Leoni

in fact never rose beyond the ground floor – hence its nickname "The Unfinished Palace." In 1949, the building was bought by Peggy Guggenheim, an American collector and patron of the arts. Her collection consists of 200 fine paintings and sculptures, representing the 20th century's most influential modern art movements. The dining room has notable Cubist works of art, including *The Poet* (1911) by Pablo Picasso, and an entire room is devoted to Jackson Pollock, who was "discovered" by Guggenheim. There are also works by Braque, Chagall, Dalí, Klee, Mondrian, and Magritte, whose Surreal *Empire of Light* (1953–4) shows a night scene of a darkened house with bright daylight above.

The sculpture collection, which includes Constantin Brancusi's elegant *Bird in Space* (1932–40), is laid out in the house and the garden. On the canal terrace, Marino Marini's provocative *The Angel of the City* (1948) shows a man sitting on a horse, erect in all respects.

Murano

🚊 N, LN, 4.1, & 4.2 from Fondamenta Nove; N & 5.2 from Ferrovia & Piazzale Roma

Like Venice, Murano consists of a cluster of small islands connected by bridges. In the 15th and 16th centuries, Murano was the main glass-producing center in Europe, and today most tourists visit to tour the furnaces and buy traditionally designed glass.

The **Museo del Vetro** houses a fine collection of antique pieces. The prize exhibit is the dark blue wedding cup (c. 1470) with enamelwork by Angelo Barovier.

The 12th-century **Basilica dei Santi Maria e Donato** has a lovely colonnaded apse. Also of note are its Gothic ship's-keel roof and the medieval mosaic floor, from 1140.

Museo del Vetro

♿ 📷 🏛 Fondamenta Marco Giustinian 8 🚊 Museo ⏰ 10:30am-4:30pm daily (Apr-Oct: to 6pm) 🚫 Jan 1, May 1, Dec 25 🌐 museovetro. visitmuve.it

Basilica dei Santi Maria e Donato

🏛 Campo San Donato ⏰ 9am-6pm Mon-Sat, 12:30-6pm Sun 🌐 sandonato murano.it

---

Gallery in the Accademia, and *(inset)* Bellini's *Madonna and Child*

EAT

Osteria Alla Ciurma
Locals come to this cosy *osteria* for the fried *cicchetti* (tapas) and Venetian wines.

🏛 Calle Galiazza 406A 📞 340 686 3561 🚫 Sun

€€€

Alla Palanca
This unassuming café does a great tagliatelle with *funghi porcini* (dried mushrooms).

🏛 Giudecca 448 📞 041 528 7719 🚫 Dinner & Sun

€€€

La Zucca
Head to this family-run *osteria* for vegetarian takes on Italian classics, such as courgette and almond lasagne.

🏛 Santa Croce 1762 🚫 Sun 🌐 lazucca.it

€€€

Trattoria dalla Marisa
Don't expect a menu here; rather, it's plates of whatever the chef has made that day.

🏛 Cannaregio 652 📞 041 720 211

€€€

Osteria Santa Marina
A splurge-worthy local restaurant offering an excellent seafood-based tasting menu.

🏛 Campo Santa Marina 5911 🚫 Sun 🌐 osteria disantamarina.com

€€€

㉒

Ferrara

🅰 **Emilia-Romagna** 🔼📶
ℹ️ **Castello Estense, Piazza Castello; www.ferrara info.com**

The D'Este dynasty has left an indelible mark on Ferrara, in the Emilia-Romagna region. The family took control of the walled town under Nicolò II in the late 13th century, holding power until 1598. **Castello Estense**, the family's dynastic seat, with its moats and towers, looms over the town center.

Bronze statues of Nicolò III and Borso d'Este, one of Nicolò's reputed 27 children, adorn the medieval Palazzo del Comune. The family's summer retreat was the Palazzo Schifanoia (currently closed for renovation). Begun in 1385, the palace is famous for its Salone dei Mesi, whose walls are covered with murals by Cosmè Tura and other Ferrarese painters.

Ferrara's cathedral has an excellent museum, with marble reliefs of the *Labours of the Months* (late 12th century), two painted organ shutters (1469) by Tura, and *Madonna of the Pomegranate* (1408) by Sienese sculptor Jacopo della Quercia.

Castello Estense

◈ 🅰 Piazza Castello
🕘 9:30am–5:30pm Tue–Sun (Mar–Sep: daily) 🚫 Dec 25
🌐 castelloestense.it

___

㉓

Ravenna

🅰 **Emilia-Romagna** 🔼📶
ℹ️ **Piazza S. Francesco 7; www.turismo.ravenna.it**

Ravenna rose to power in the 1st century BC, under Emperor Augustus. As Rome's power declined, the city was made capital of the Byzantine Empire in AD 402. It was during this later era, in the 5th and 6th centuries, that many of the city's superb early Christian mosaics were created. The most spectacular examples include those in the church of **San Vitale**, where apse mosaics (526–47) show the saint being handed a martyr's crown and another mosaic depicts Emperor Justinian, who ruled from 527 to 565. Next door, the tiny **Mausoleo di Galla Placidia** is adorned with a mosaic of *The Good Shepherd*. (Galla Placidia ran the Western Empire for 20 years after the death of her husband, the Visigothic King Altauf.) The 6th-century church of **Sant'Apollinare Nuovo** is dominated by two rows of mosaics which depict processions of martyrs and virgins bearing gifts.

Travelers in Ravenna can also visit Dante's Tomb – the great writer died here in 1321.

San Vitale and Mausoleo di Galla Placidia

◈ 🅰 Via Argentario 22
🕘 9am–7pm daily 🚫 Dec 25
🌐 ravennamosaici.it

___

BYZANTINE ITALY

By the 5th century AD, the Roman Empire was split into two. The Western Empire could not stem the tide of Germanic invaders, and Italy fell to the Goths. After 535, however, the Eastern Empire reconquered most of it. Its stronghold, Ravenna, became the richest, most powerful Italian city. Most of the peninsula was later lost to the Lombards, who invaded in 564, but Ravenna, protected by marshes and lagoons, held out until 752.

←
Cycling past majestic Renaissance buildings in central Ferrara

The apse of Ravenna's basilica of San Vitale, covered in mosaics ↑

Sant'Apollinare Nuovo

 Via di Roma 52
9am–7pm daily Jan 1, Dec 25 ravennamosaici.it

24

Bologna

Emilia-Romagna Piazza Maggiore 1/e; www.bologna welcome.com

The prosperous capital of Emilia-Romagna, Bologna has a rich cultural heritage, ranging from medieval palaces and churches to leaning towers. The city was celebrated in the Middle Ages for its university – believed to be the oldest in Europe.

The two central squares, Piazza Maggiore and Piazza del Nettuno, are bordered to the south by the churches of San Petronio and San Domenico. The former ranks among the greatest of Italy's brick-built medieval buildings. Founded in 1390, its construction was halted halfway due to financial constraints. Twenty-two chapels open off the nave of the Gothic interior, many with fine works of art.

San Domenico is the most important of Italy's Dominican churches, housing the tomb of St. Dominic himself. A magnificent composite work, the tomb features statues and reliefs by Nicola Pisano, while the figures of angels and saints are early works by Michelangelo.

The **Torri degli Asinelli e Garisenda** are among the few surviving towers of the 200 that once formed the skyline of Bologna. Both were begun in the 12th century. The Garisenda tower (closed to the public) leans some 10 ft (3 m), while the Asinelli tower has a 500-step ascent and offers fine views.

The Romanesque-Gothic church of San Giacomo Maggiore, begun in 1267 but since altered substantially, is visited mainly for the superb Bentivoglio family chapel, decorated with frescoes by Lorenzo Costa. The Bentivoglio tomb is among the last works of Jacopo della Quercia.

Highlights of Bologna's **Pinacoteca Nazionale** art gallery include Perugino's *Madonna in Glory* (c. 1500) and Raphael's famous *Ecstasy of St. Cecilia*, painted in 1518.

Torri degli Asinelli e Garisenda

 Piazza di Porta Ravegnana 9am–7pm daily

Pinacoteca Nazionale

 Via delle Belle Arti 56 Hours vary, check website pinacotecabologna. beniculturali.it

㉕
Naples

🏛 Campania 🚐🚗🚆🚌
ℹ Piazza del Gesù;
www.visitnaples.eu

Chaotic yet spectacular, Naples (Napoli) sprawls around the edge of a beautiful bay in the shadow of Mount Vesuvius.

Originally a Greek city named Neapolis, founded in 600 BC, Naples became an "allied city" of Rome two centuries later. It then had many foreign rulers. The French House of Anjou controled Naples between 1266 and 1421, when power passed to Alfonso V of Aragón. A colony of Spain by 1503, in 1707 Naples was ceded to Austria, and in 1734 Charles III of Bourbon took over. In 1860, Naples became part of the new kingdom of Italy.

The centuries of occupation have left Naples with a rich store of ancient ruins, churches, and palaces, many of which can be seen in the Old City. The **Museo Archeologico Nazionale** holds treasures excavated from Pompeii and Herculaneum, including fine glassware, frescoes, mosaics, and the fabulous Farnese Classical sculptures. Nearby, the church of San Giovanni a Carbonara houses some glorious medieval works of art, such as the tomb of King Ladislas of Naples. The French Gothic Duomo holds the relics of San Gennaro, martyred in AD 305. Next to it is the Monte della Misericordia, a 17th-century octagonal church housing Caravaggio's huge *Seven Acts of Mercy* (1607), and a little farther east is the Porta Capuana, one of Italy's finest Renaissance gateways, completed in 1490.

Central Naples is particularly rich in 14th- and 15th-century churches. Some fine Renaissance sculpture is contained in San Domenico

↑ A typical narrow street in the famous Spanish Quarter of Naples

Maggiore, while Santa Chiara houses the tombs of the Angevin monarchs and a museum whose exhibits include the ruins of a Roman bathhouse. Southeast Naples is home to the city's castles and the royal palace of Castel Nuovo, built for Charles of Anjou in 1279–82. Another star sight, the Palazzo Reale has a superb library, richly adorned royal apartments, and a court theater.

The Palazzo Reale di Capodimonte, once a hunting lodge, now houses the **Museo di Capodimonte**, with its magnificent collection of Italian paintings, including works by Titian, Botticelli, and Raphael. This part of Naples is also known for its "Spanish Quarter," or Quartieri Spagnoli, a neighborhood of narrow, cobbled alleys often used to represent the archetypal Neapolitan street scene.

A trip by funicular railway up Vomero hill brings you to the Certosa di San Martino. This 14th-century charterhouse has been lavishly redecorated over the centuries. Just behind the Certosa lies the Castel Sant Elmo, which offers fine views.

Boat excursions can be taken along the Posillipo coast, and to the islands of Capri, Ischia, and Procida. Inland, Caserta has its own Palazzo Reale, with over 1,000 sumptuously decorated rooms. The town of Santa Maria Capua Vetere has a Roman amphitheater.

Museo Archeologico Nazionale

⊘ 🏠 Piazza Museo Nazionale 19 🕓 9am-7:30pm Thu-Wed 🗓 Jan 1, Dec 25 🌐 museoarcheologico napoli.it

Museo di Capodimonte

⊘ 🏠 Parco di Capodimonte 🕓 8:30am-7:30pm Thu-Tue 🌐 museocapodimonte. beniculturali.it

←

Statue of Frederick II in Naples' Palazzo Reale, built for the viceroy Ruiz de Castro

---

THE STORY OF PIZZA

Deeply engrained in Naples' gastronomic identity, pizza first emerged in southern Italy in the late 1700s, quickly becoming a working-class staple. In 1889, Queen Margherita of Savoy developed a taste for this peasant delicacy while she was touring the kingdom. After she summoned chef Raffaele Esposito to the royal palace, pizza Margherita was born. In recognition of the skill of pizza-making, in 2017 the culinary art was awarded UNESCO Intangible Cultural Heritage status. Try it in Naples at Da Michele (www. damichele.net), Sorbillo (www. sorbillo.it), and Concettina (www. pizzeriaoliva.it).

26

Amalfi Coast

🏠 Campania 🚍🚊 🛈 Via delle Repubbliche Marinare 19-21, Amalfi; www. amalfituristoffice.it

The most enchanting and most visited route in the Campania region skirts the southern flank of Sorrento's peninsula: the Amalfi Coast (Costiera Amalfitana). Among the popular pleasures here are dining on locally caught grilled fish and sipping icy Lacrima Christi from Vesuvian vineyards, interspersed with beach-hopping.

From the well-developed holiday resort of Sorrento, the road winds down to Positano, a village clambering down a vertiginous slope to the sea. Farther on, Praiano is another fashionable resort.

Amalfi – the coast's largest town – was a maritime power before it was subdued in 1131 by King Roger of Naples. Its most illustrious citizens were buried in the 13th-century Chiostro del Paradiso, flanking the 9th-century Duomo. Above Amalfi, Ravello offers peace and quiet, in addition to superb views of the coast.

STAY

Constantinopoli 104
Impeccably appointed boutique hotel.

🏠 Via Santa Maria di Costantinopoli 104, Naples 🌐 costantinopoli104.it

€€€

Hotel Romeo
Luxurious rooms in the Old Town.

🏠 Via C. Colombo 45, Naples 🌐 romeohotel.it

€€€

Decumani
Tasteful furnishings in a 20th-century *palazzo*.

🏠 Via del Grande Archivio 8, Naples 🌐 decumani.com

€€€

↑ The spectacular city of Matera, a UNESCO World Heritage Site

㉗ Matera

 Basilicata ᚎ ⊠ ᵢ Via de Viti de Marco 9; www. materaturismo.it

Fused to a cave-ridden outcrop above a deep ravine, Matera is one of the most extraordinary cities in the Italian south. Cave dwellings, churches, houses, stepped streets, and twisting pavements form an astonishing maze of limestone. Declared a UNESCO World Heritage Site in 1993, and European Capital of Culture in 2019, Matera is now a thriving destination with numerous boutique cave hotels and excellent restaurants.

The Sassi district is made up of a labyrinth of cave dwellings on the eastern slope of Matera (the literal translation of *sassi* is "stones"). It is divided into two quarters: Sasso Caveoso, to the south, and Sasso Barisano, to the north. Highlights include the **Casa Grotta di Vico Solitario**, a traditional cave dwelling that has been reconstructed with the help of a family who lived there until the 1950s, and **Madonna de**

Idris, a church carved right into the rock of conical Monte Errone. To the south is the **Convincinio Sant'Antonio**, four interlinked churches that were used as wine cellars in the 18th century. There are great views from outside the church right over the ravine.

The center of the historic town, perched on the higher slopes of Matera above the Sassi, is Piazza Vittorio Veneto, a spacious square that is at its liveliest in the early evenings, when traffic is banned. At the far end of Via del Corso is the elliptical facade of the Chiesa del Purgatorio, a 17th-century church ghoulishly decorated with a chequerboard of screaming skull and skeleton sculptures reminiscent of Edvard Munch's *The Scream*.

Casa Grotta di Vico Solitario

🏠 Vicinato di Vico Solitario 11 🕙 9am–6pm Mon–Sat, 9:30am–6:40pm Sun ⍈ casagrotta.it

Madonna de Idris

🏠 Via Madonna dell'Idris 🕙 10:30am–1:30pm daily (Apr–Nov: also 2:30–7pm) ⍈ sassiweb.it

Convincinio Sant'Antonio

🏠 Rione Casalnuovo 📞 930 5715 0778 🕙 Hours vary, call ahead

___

㉘ Pompeii

🏠 Porta Marina, Via Marina 6 ᚎ ⊠ 🕙 Apr–Oct: 9am–7:30pm daily; Nov–Mar: 9am–5pm daily 🗓 Jan 1, May 1, Dec 25 ⍈ pompeiisites.org

The ancient city of Pompeii, which was destroyed in AD 79 by an eruption of Vesuvius, lay buried under rock and ash until the 18th century. When excavations began in 1748, a city frozen in time was revealed. Many buildings survived the devastating eruption, some complete with paintings and sculptures. Among the most notable are the villa of the wealthy patrician Casii, known as House of the Faun after its bronze statuette, and the House of the Vettii, which contains rich wall decorations.

The original layout of the city can be clearly observed. The Forum was the center of public life, with administrative and religious institutions grouped around it. Theaters, the marketplace, temples, stores, and even brothels can be visited. It is believed that around 2,000 people died at Pompeii, and casts of numerous recumbent figures have been made.

Much of our knowledge of the daily lives of the ancient Romans has been derived from the excavations conducted here and at nearby Herculaneum. The baths were divided into separate sections for men and women, but the citizens of Pompeii were not prudish – graphic frescoes reveal the services offered by male and female prostitutes in the *lupanares*, or brothels.

A large number of works of art, domestic items, and other artifacts that were preserved by the mud and ash are now on permanent display in the excellent Museo Archeologico Nazionale in Naples (p434).

Ruins of Pompeii against the backdrop of Mount Vesuvius

MOUNT VESUVIUS

Vesuvius is the most volatile volcano in Europe, with an estimated 700,000 people living in the danger zone. Consequently, the volcano - which last erupted in 1944 - is constantly monitored. To experience the volcano close-up, take a minibus from Ercolano Scavi train station to the Mount Vesuvius car park, from where it's a half-hour climb to the steaming crater. For more volcanic experiences, head to the Solfatara, 30 minutes' drive west of Naples, where you can have the unforgettably bizarre experience of walking on the hot, spongy, stinking fields of sulphur in another volcanic crater.

㉙

Palermo

⌂ Sicily 🚆🚌🚍 ℹ Palazzo Galletti, Piazza Marina; www.turismo.comune.palermo.it

Capital of Sicily and situated along the bay at the foot of Monte Pellegrino, Palermo was originally known as Panormos, or "port," by the Phoenicians. A prosperous Roman town, Palermo's golden age came later, while under Arab domination. The Baroque period (17th–18th centuries) has also left a lasting mark on the city's civic and religious buildings. Palermo suffered heavy bombardment by the Allies in World War II, but despite chaotic rebuilding, the city remains an exotic mix of the Oriental and the European.

The old Arab quarter can be found in north Palermo, typified by Vucciria, one of the city's lively markets. On Piazza Marina, the focal point of north Palermo, the Palazzo Abatellis houses the **Galleria Regionale di Sicilia**, which has a fine collection of art.

In south Palermo, the **Palazzo Reale** – a focus of power since Byzantine rule – is now the home of Sicily's regional government. Its splendid **Cappella Palatina** is adorned with mosaics. The Duomo, founded in 1184, has a Catalan Gothic portico (1430) and a cupola in Baroque style.

The **Museo Regionale Salinas** is considered one of Italy's most important archaeology museums.

A few miles away inland, the cathedral at **Monreale**, founded in 1172, is one of the great sights of Norman Sicily, with its glittering mosaics and Saracenic-style cloisters.

Galleria Regionale di Sicilia
⊗ ⌂ Via Alloro 4 ☎ 091-623 00 11 🕐 9am-6pm Tue-Fri, 9am-1pm Sat & Sun

Palazzo Reale & Cappella Palatina
⊗ ⌂ Piazza Indipendenza 🕐 8:15am-5:40pm daily (to 1pm Sun) 🚫 Jan 1, Dec 25 🌐 federicosecondo.org

Museo Regionale Salinas
⊗ ⌂ Piazza Olivella 24 ☎ 091-611 68 07 🕐 9am-6pm Tue-Sat, 9am-1:30pm Sun & hols

Monreale
⊗⊗ ⌂ Piazza Guglielmo II 🕐 8:30am-12:45pm & 2:30-4:45pm Mon-Sat 🌐 enteoperemonreale.it

THE GODFATHER

Several scenes from Francis Ford Coppola's iconic Mafia-inspired *Godfather* movies were filmed in the remote Sicilian hilltop villages of Savoca and Forza d'Agro, between Messina and Taormina. Aficionados can sit at the table at Bar Vitelli in Savoca, where Al Pacino's character, Michael Corleone, sat and asked the owner for his daughter's hand in marriage.

㉚ Taormina

 Messina, Sicily 🚉🚌
🚆 Palazzo Corvaja, Piazza Santa Caterina; 0942-232 43

Sicily's most popular tourist resort has sandy beaches and numerous restaurants. Its most illustrious relic is the 3rd-century BC Theater, begun by the Greeks and rebuilt by the Romans. Among other Classical ruins are the Odeon (a musical theater) and the Naumachia (a manmade lake for mock battles).

The 14th-century Palazzo Corvaja and the 13th-century Duomo are also worth visiting.

㉛ Piazza Armerina

 Sicily 🚌 Via Maestranza 33 🚆 Via F. Guccio 24b; www.piazzaarmerina.org

This active town is half medieval and half Baroque. The most interesting of the Baroque buildings is the 17th-century Duomo, situated at the town's highest point.

Many visitors are attracted to Piazza Armerina by the lively Palio dei Normanni festival in August, but the undisputed star sights here are the spectacular mosaics in the UNESCO-listed **Villa Romana del Casale**, 3 miles (5 km) southwest of the town. It is thought that this huge, sumptuous villa, with its public halls, private quarters, baths, and courtyards, once belonged to Maximianus Herculeus, Diocletian's coemperor from AD 286 to 305. His son and successor, Maxentius, probably carried on its decoration, with Constantine taking over on Maxentius's death in 312.

Although little remains of the building fabric, the floors have some of the finest surviving mosaics from Roman antiquity. Highlights include a circus scene showing a chariot race, ten female athletes dressed in bikinis, and a 197-ft- (60-m-) long hunting scene featuring tigers, ostriches, elephants, and a rhino being trapped and transported to games at the Colosseum.

Villa Romana del Casale

 Contrada Casale 🕐 May-Oct: 9am-6pm daily (Jul-Aug: to 11pm Fri & Sun); Nov-Aug: 9am-4pm daily 🔲 villa romanadelcasale.it

㉜ Syracuse

 Sicily 🚉🚌🚆 🚆 Via Maestranza 33; www.comune.siracusa.it

Syracuse (Siracusa in Italian) was the most important and powerful Greek city from 400 to 211 BC, when it fell to the Romans.

The peninsula of Ortigia is the hub of the Old City. A highlight here is the 18th-century Duomo, with a Baroque facade masking the Temple of Athena (5th century BC) that was absorbed into it. Nearby, the Chiesa di Santa Lucia alla Badia houses Caravaggio's *Burial of St. Lucy* (1608).

At Ortigia's farthest point are the Castello Maniace, built by Frederick II around 1239, and the **Galleria Regionale di Palazzo Bellomo**.

One of the most important examples of ancient theater architecture, the 5th-century BC

Greek Theater has a 67-tier auditorium, or *cavea*. The great Greek playwrights staged their works here.

At Tyche, north of Syracuse, the **Museo Archeologico Regionale Paolo Orsi** houses artifacts excavated from local digs, which date from the Paleolithic to the Byzantine era.

Galleria Regionale di Palazzo Bellomo

 Palazzo Bellomo, Via Capodieci 14-16
0931-69511 ⏰9am-7pm Tue-Sat, Sun am

Museo Archeologico Regionale Paolo Orsi

 Viale Teocrito 66 ☎0931-48 95 11 ⏰9am-6pm Tue-Sat, 9am-1pm Sun

---

33
Mount Etna

 Catania, Sicily �)To Linguaglossa or Randazzo; Circumetnea 🚌To Nicolosi
ℹ️Piazza Vittorio Emanuele, Nicolosi; www.parcoetna.it

One of the world's largest active volcanoes, Mount Etna was thought by the Romans to have been the forge of

↑ A plume of smoke rising from the crater of snow-covered Mount Etna

Vulcan, the god of fire. The Circumetnea railroad runs around its base from Catania to Riposto. Now a protected area, approximately 22 sq miles (58 sq km) in size, Etna offers numerous opportunities for excursions. Guides accompany visitors on foot as far as the authorities allow according to volcanic activity.

34
Agrigento

 Sicily 🚍🚌🚆 ℹ️Via Empedocle 73; 0922-203 91

Modern Agrigento occupies the site of Akragas, an important city of the ancient Greeks.

After the Roman conquest of 210 BC, Agrigento was renamed and successively occupied by Byzantines, Arabs, and Normans. The historic medieval core of the city focuses on Via Atenea. The 13th-century abbey complex of Santo Spirito houses stuccoes by Giacomo Serpotta (1695).

South of Agrigento, the Valley of Temples is the principal sacred site of ancient Akragas. The mainly 5th- and 6th-century BC ruins rank among the most impressive complexes of ancient Greek buildings outside Greece. Agrigento's **Museo Regionale Archeologico** houses outstanding artifacts from the site.

Museo Regionale Archeologico

 Contrada San Nicola, Viale Panoramica ⏰9am-7:30pm daily (to 1:30pm Sun)
🌐lavalledeitempli.it

💬 INSIDER TIP
Scala dei Turchi

Eroded by sea and wind into a magnificent natural white staircase, the marl cliffs of Scala dei Turchi, on the south coast of Sicily, descend into a crystalline turquoise sea and beaches of glinting quartz. The beach is ideal for a swim after visiting Agrigento's Valley of the Temples.

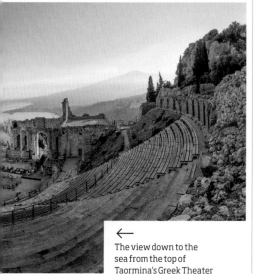

← The view down to the sea from the top of Taormina's Greek Theater

PRACTICAL
INFORMATION

Here you will find all the essential advice and information you will need before and during your stay in Italy.

AT A GLANCE

CURRENCY
Euro (EUR)

TIME ZONE
CET/CEST. Central European Summer Time runs from the last Sunday in March to the last Sunday in October.

LANGUAGE
Italian

ELECTRICITY SUPPLY
Power sockets are type F and L, fitting two- and three- pronged plugs. Standard voltage is 220–230V.

EMERGENCY NUMBERS

GENERAL EMERGENCY

112

TAP WATER
Unless stated otherwise, tap water in Italy is safe to drink.

Getting There

Rome's Leonardo da Vinci (Fiumicino) and Milan's Malpensa are the main airports for long-haul flights into Italy. Many budget airlines fly to cities across Italy year round.

Regular high-speed international trains connect Italy to the main towns and cities in Austria, Germany, France, and Eastern Europe. Reservations for these services are essential and tickets are booked up quickly.

Eurolines offers a variety of bus routes to destinations in Italy from other European cities. Fares are very reasonable, with discounts available for students, children, and seniors.

International ferries operate regular services to the main ports in Italy from Spain, France, Corsica, Malta, Tunisia, Morocco, Slovenia, Croatia, and Greece.

Personal Security

Italy is generally a safe country, but it is a good idea to take precautions against pickpockets. If you have anything stolen, report the crime to the nearest police station. Get a copy of the crime report in order to claim on your insurance.

Health

Seek medicinal supplies and advice for minor ailments from pharmacies *(farmacia)*. You can find details of the nearest 24-hour service on all pharmacy doors. EU citizens with a European Health Insurance Card (EHIC) are entitled to free emergency medical care in Italy, but it is also advisable to take out some form of health insurance. Visitors from outside the EU must arrange their own private medical insurance.

Passports and Visas

Citizens of the EU, US, Canada, Australia, and New Zealand do not require a visa for stays of up to three months. Most EU visitors need only a valid identity document to enter Italy. Citizens from other countries should contact their Italian consulate for visa information.

LGBT+ Safety

Homosexuality is legal and widely accepted in Italy, particularly in cosmopolitan cities such as Rome and Milan. However, smaller towns and rural areas are often traditional in their views, and overt displays of affection may receive a negative response from locals.

Travelers with Specific Needs

Italy's historic towns and cities are ill-equipped for disabled access. Many buildings do not have wheelchair access or lifts. The **SuperAbile** website provides useful information and tips on accessible tourism, and lists the latest online aids such as maps showing wheelchair access. **Rete Ferroviaria Italiana** (RFI) offers services to disabled people to assist them during their train journey; these services can be arranged through the Sale Blu (Blue Room) service.

Rete Ferroviaria Italiana
W rfi.it
SuperAbile
W superabile.it

Money

Northern Italy is generally more expensive than the south. Most establishments accept major credit, debit, and prepaid currency cards, but carry cash for smaller items.

Cell Phones and Wi-Fi

Wi-Fi is generally widely available throughout Italy, and cafés and restaurants will usually give you the password for their Wi-Fi on the condition that you make a purchase.

Visitors traveling to Italy with EU tariffs can use their devices without being affected by data roaming charges. Visitors from other countries should check their contracts before departure in order to avoid unexpected charges.

Getting Around

There are regular domestic flights between many Italian cities, but these can be expensive, and busy at peak periods. Flights to airports in the north can also be disrupted by fog in the winter months.

Trenitalia (FS) is the main train operator in Italy. Tickets can be bought online, but there are only a fixed number available so book ahead. **Italo Treno** (NTV) also offers a high-speed service between major train stations throughout Italy; reservations are essential, whichever company you travel with. Train tickets must be validated before boarding by stamping them in machines at the entrance to platforms.

Long-distance buses (*pullman* or *corriere*) operate between towns and can be less expensive and more frequent than trains. Tickets can be purchased on board, and services usually depart from a town's train station or main square.

A car is invaluable for touring the Italian countryside. However, driving can also be a hair-raising experience: Italians have a reputation for driving erratically, particularly in the south. Make sure you are familiar with the rules of the road and have all the necessary documentation, as traffic police *(carabinieri)* carry out routine checks. Italy has a good network of highways, but most have toll-booths, which often leads to congestion. Car rental is expensive in Italy, and should be organized in advance. Visitors from outside the EU need an international license, but in practice not all rental firms insist on this.

Italy's large number of off-shore islands means that it has a well-developed network of ferries. Boats of various kinds also operate on the Italian Lakes. Ferries depart for Sicily from Naples and Reggio di Calabria. They also run from the mainland and from Sicily to surrounding islands and archipelagos, for example from Naples to Capri and Ischia.

Italo Treno
W italotreno.it
Trenitalia
W trenitalia.com

Visitor Information

The national tourist board, **ENIT**, has branches in cities worldwide and offers general information on Italy. Locally, there are two types of tourist office: an EPT (Ente Provinciale per il Turismo) has information on its town and surrounding province, whereas an APT (Azienda di Promozione Turistica) or a PIT (Punto d'Informazione Turistica) deals exclusively with an individual town.

ENIT
W enit.it

GREECE

The home of Europe's first civilizations and its oldest living language, as well as the birthplace of philosophy, drama, and democracy, Greece has had an enduring impact on European culture. Early Greek history featured a series of internal struggles, from the Mycenaean and Minoan cultures of the Bronze Age to the competing city-states of the 1st millennium BC. In spite of warfare, the 5th and 4th centuries BC were the high point of ancient Greek civilization, an apex of creativity in philosophy and the arts. In 338 BC, Greece was absorbed into the Macedonian Empire, before being made a province of Rome in 146 BC. As part of the Eastern Roman Empire, it was ruled from Constantinople and became a vital element in the Orthodox Christian, Byzantine world. After the Ottomans' capture of Constantinople in 1453, the Greek mainland was ruled by the Turks, while Crete and the Ionian islands were governed by the Venetians. Eventually, the Greeks rebelled, emerging victorious from the War of Independence (1821–30). During the 19th century, Greece reasserted its sovereignty over many of the islands, but the country's territorial gains largely ceased in 1922, after a failed attempt to seize western Anatolia. The ensuing, unstable years saw the arrival in Greece of over one million Greek refugees from Turkey. The Metaxás dictatorship was followed by Axis occupation during World War II, then civil war. Greece's present boundaries date from 1948, when the Dodecanese were finally ceded by Italy. Today, Greece is a stable democracy and has been a member of the EU since 1981.

GREECE

1. Athens
2. Soúnio
3. Monastery of Dafní
4. Monastery of Osios Loukás
5. Ancient Delphi
6. Metéora
7. Thessaloníki
8. Pílio
9. Royal Macedonian Tombs, Vergína
10. Ancient Pélla
11. Mount Athos
12. Mount Olympos
13. Ancient Corinth
14. Epidauros
15. Mycenae
16. Náfplio
17. Monemvasiá
18. Ancient Olympia
19. Máni Peninsula
20. Mystrás
21. Loúsios Gorge
22. Corfu and the Ionian Islands
23. Cyclades
24. Rhodes and the Dodecanese
25. Crete

↑ Early evening in Platía Monastirakíou, overlooked by the Acropolis

❶

ATHENS

 **ⓘ www.thisisathens.org**

Sprawling Athens is an incredibly vibrant city. This bustling capital, overlooked by the ancient temples on the Acropolis, has been inhabited for 7,000 years and is the birthplace of philosophy, Classical art, and democracy – a tradition that continues through lively student protests and activism. But there's more to the city than the treasures of its Classical era: the streets here are alive with open-air markets and walls decorated with some of the best street art on the globe. Hidden histories lie in wait at every street corner, amid the buzz of bars and tavernas that bring locals flocking out after dark.

 INSIDER TIP
Getting Around

Athens' major sights are closely packed, and the best way of getting around is on foot. Bus and trolley bus routes crisscross the city, and the metro is useful for getting to the port of Piraeus and the airport.

①
Pláka

Ⓜ **Monastiráki, Akropoli**
🚎 **1, 2, 4, 5, & many others**

Even though only a handful of buildings in Pláka date back to before the Ottoman period, this is the historic heart of Athens. One probable explanation of its name comes from the word used by Albanian soldiers in the service of the Ottomans who settled here in the 16th century – *pliaka* (old) was how they described the area. Despite the constant flow of tourists and locals, who come to eat in charming tavernas or browse in the antique and icon shops, Pláka still retains the atmosphere of a traditional neighborhood.

The Lysikrates Monument in Platía Lysikrátous is one of a number of monuments that were built to commemorate the victors at the annual choral and dramatic festival at the Theater of Dionysos. Taking its name from a 4th-century BC sponsor of the winning team, it is the only such monument still intact in Athens.

Many churches here are worth a visit: on the outside of the 11th-century Agios Nikólaos Rangavás you can see ancient columns built into the walls.

The Tower of the Winds, in the west of Pláka, lies in the grounds of the Roman Agora. It was built during the 1st century BC by astronomer Andronikos Kyrrhestes as a weather vane and water clock. The name comes from external friezes on each of its marble sides, depicting the eight mythological winds.

②
Monastiráki

Ⓜ **Monastiráki**

This lively and atmospheric area, which is named after the little monastic church in Platía

Monastirakíou, is next to the Ancient Agora. It is bounded by Sarrí in the west and Eólou in the east. The streets of Pandrósou, Iféstou, and Areos leading off Platía Monastirakíou are packed with shops selling an eclectic assortment of goods, including expensive antiques, jewelry, leather items, and tourist trinkets.

The area is synonymous with Athens' famous **flea market**. The heart of the market is in Platía Avyssinías, west of Platía Monastirakíou, where on weekend mornings dealers arrive with pieces of furniture and various odds and ends. During the week, the shops and stalls are filled with antiques, second-hand books, rugs, leatherware,

taverna chairs, army surplus gear, and tools. On Sunday mornings, the market flourishes along Adrianoú and at the end toward Thisío. There are always bargains to be had, in particular used vinyl, backgammon sets, and copper items. Normánou, a lane perpendicular to Iféstou, is good for old engravings.

↑ Souvenirs for sale in the eclectic stores around Monastiraki

Flea Market
🕐 8am–6pm daily

③ ⟨⟩ ⟨M⟩

ACROPOLIS

🏛 Dionysíou Areopagítou (main entrance), Pláka; ticket booth at tourist office on Dionysíou Areopagítou Ⓜ Akropoli 🚍 230, X80 🕐 Apr–Oct: 8am–8pm daily; Nov–Mar: 8am–4:30pm daily 🚫 Jan 1, Mar 25, Easter Sun, May 1, Dec 25 & 26 🌐 acropolisofathens.gr

One of the most famous archaeological sites in the world, the Acropolis and its temples stand as a monument to the political and cultural achievements of Greece. The Acropolis overlooks the city from a plateau that has been in use for 5,000 years.

In the mid-5th century BC, after the Athenians had defeated the invading Persian Empire, Athenian leader Perikles persuaded Athens' citizens to begin a grand program of building work in the city, sparking a new political and cultural golden age. This work, constructed by Athens' leading architects, sculptors, and painters, transformed the Acropolis with three contrasting temples – two dedicated to Athena and one shared between Athena and Poseidon – and a monumental gateway called the Propylaia. The best-known structure is the Parthenon, a massive temple to the city's patron goddess Athena, which is being restored. The Theater of Dionysos on the south slope was developed further in the 4th century BC, and the Odeon of Herodes Atticus was added in the 2nd century AD.

INSIDER TIP
Early Bird

Your best chance to catch the Acropolis before the large crowds descend in summer is at 8am, immediately after the complex opens to visitors.

THE ACROPOLIS MUSEUM

Located in the historic Makrigiánni district, at the foot of the Acropolis, this €130-million showpiece was designed by Bernard Tschumi and constructed over excavations of an early Christian settlement; a glass walkway hovers over the ruins. The collection has been installed in chronological order and begins with finds from the slopes of the Acropolis, including statues and reliefs from the Shrine of Asklepios. The skylit Parthenon Gallery on the top floor is the highlight, showcasing the parts of the Parthenon frieze that remain in Greece, displayed in their original order.

The awe-inspiring columns ↑ of the Parthenon, with restoration under way

3000 BC

▽ First settlement on the Acropolis during the Neolithic period.

447–438 BC

▽ Construction of the Parthenon begins under noted Athenian leader Perikles.

510 BC

△ Delphic Oracle declares the Acropolis a holy place of the gods, banning habitation by mortals.

AD 1985

△ Restorations begin on the Acropolis site, starting with the Erechtheion.

Exploring the Acropolis

Once through the Propylaia, the grand gateway built between 437 and 432 BC, the eye is immediately drawn to the Parthenon. The other fine temples here include the Erechtheion, the temple dedicated to both Athena and Poseidon, and the Temple of Athena Nike. The Erechtheion is particularly notable for the Porch of the Caryatids, statues of women used in place of columns on the south porch. Visitors are not allowed to enter the temples.

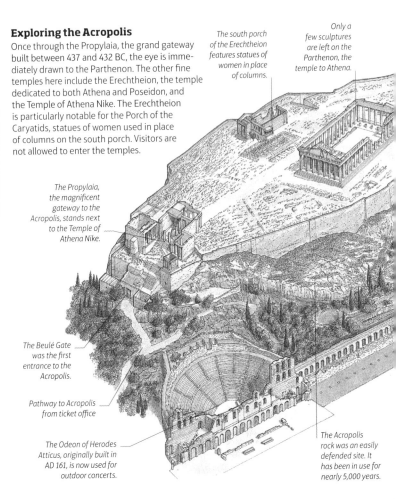

The south porch of the Erechtheion features statues of women in place of columns.

Only a few sculptures are left on the Parthenon, the temple to Athena.

The Propylaia, the magnificent gateway to the Acropolis, stands next to the Temple of Athena Nike.

The Beulé Gate was the first entrance to the Acropolis.

Pathway to Acropolis from ticket office

The Odeon of Herodes Atticus, originally built in AD 161, is now used for outdoor concerts.

The Acropolis rock was an easily defended site. It has been in use for nearly 5,000 years.

THE PARTHENON MARBLES

These famous – and controversial – sculptures were acquired from the Ottoman authorities by Lord Elgin in 1801–11. He sold them to the British nation, and they are now in the British Museum in London (p102). While some say that they are more carefully preserved there, the Greek government does not accept the legality of the sale and believes they belong in Athens.

The partially restored Odeon of Herodes Atticus, now used for summer festivals ↑

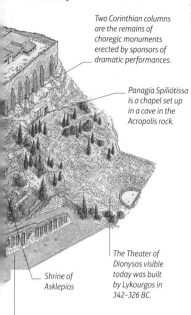

Illustration of the
Acropolis rock as it
looks today

*Two Corinthian columns
are the remains of
choregic monuments
erected by sponsors of
dramatic performances.*

*Panagía Spiliótissa
is a chapel set up
in a cave in the
Acropolis rock.*

*The Theater of
Dionysos visible
today was built
by Lykourgos in
342–326 BC.*

*Shrine of
Asklepios*

Stoa of Eumenes

The Parthenon

▶ One of the world's most recognizable structures, the Parthenon was started in 447 BC, when the sculptor Pheidias was entrusted with supervising the building of a magnificent new Doric temple to Athena, the patron goddess of the city. It was designed primarily to house the Parthenos, Pheidias's impressive 39-ft- (12-m-) high cult statue of Athena, covered in ivory and gold. Taking nine years to complete, the temple was dedicated to the goddess during the Great Panathenaia festival of 438 BC. The famous Parthenon Marbles consist of the pediments, metopes, and friezes that decorated the temple. These marbles show a range of scenes from both mythology and daily life. The magnificent frieze that ran around the four walls of the structure depicted the ancient Panathenaic procession, which happened every four years in the city on Athena's birthday.

Temple of Athena Nike

The second sacred structure dedicated to Athena, this particular temple on the west side of the Propylaia worships Athena as goddess of victory. It was built between 427 and 424 BC.

Theater of Dionysos

◀ Nestled on the southeastern flank of the Acropolis, the Theater of Dionysos - dedicated to the local cult of Dionysos Eleutherios - was originally erected during the 5th century BC and upgraded in about 330 BC to seat 17,000. The first performances of many works by Sophocles, Aristophanes, and Euripides took place here. The most interesting architectural details are the ancient front-row thrones for VIPs, including one with lion-paw details for the priest of Dionysos. The stage building shows scenes from the life of the god.

Odeon of Herodes Atticus

Herodes Atticus was a wealthy Athenian scholar and Roman consul who endowed the giant odeon (building for musical performances) that bears his name, completed in AD 161, to the city of Athens. The orchestra area would have been roofed in cedar, though seating was apparently open to the sky, as no supports for a roof have been found. Extending to three storys in places, the odeon is immensely tall - particularly compared to the more modest odeons found in other sites across the islands. Restored during the 20th century, it is now one of the main venues for the summer Hellenic Festival, and is not normally open during daylight hours.

Ancient Agora

📍 Main entrance at Adrianoú 24, Monastiráki 📞 210-32 10 185 Ⓜ Thisío, Monastiráki ⏰ 8am–8pm daily (winter: to 3pm) 🚫 Main public hols

The American School of Archaeology commenced

TOP 3 GREEK TEMPLE STYLES

Doric
Doric temples were surrounded by sturdy columns, plain or fluted, with plain capitals and no bases.

Ionic
Ionic temples tended to have more columns than Doric temples. The capital has a pair of volutes, like rams' horns.

Corinthian
Corinthian temples were built under the Romans in Athens, Corinth, and Kos. They feature columns with capitals decorated with acanthus leaves.

excavations of the Ancient Agora in the 1930s, and since then a complex array of public buildings and temples has been revealed. From about 3000 BC, the Agora was the political and religious heart of ancient Athens. Also the center of commercial and daily life, it abounded with schools and elegant stoas, or roofed arcades, filled with shops. The state prison was here, as was the city's mint. Even the remains of an olive oil mill have been found.

The main building standing today is the impressive two-story Stoa of Attalos. This was rebuilt in the 1950s on the original foundations, using ancient building materials. Founded in the 2nd-century BC by King Attalos II of Pergamon, the stoa dominated the eastern quarter of the Agora until it was destroyed in AD 267 by the Herulians. The building is used as a museum, exhibiting the finds from the Agora. These include a *klepsydra* (a water clock that was used for timing plaintiffs' speeches),

bronze ballots, and items from everyday life such as some terra-cotta toys and leather sandals.

The best-preserved ruins on the site are the Odeon of Agrippa, a covered theater, and the Hephaisteion (or Theseion), a temple to Hephaistos.

Temple of Olympian Zeus

📍 Corner of Amalías & Vasilíssis Olgas, Záppio 📞 210-92 26 330 🚌 2, 4, 11 ⏰ 8am–3pm daily (summer: to 8pm) 🚫 Main public hols

This vast temple is the largest in Greece, exceeding even the Parthenon in size. The tyrant Peisistratos allegedly initiated the building of the temple in the 6th century BC to gain public favor. It was not completed until 650 years later.

In AD 132, the Roman Emperor Hadrian dedicated the temple to Zeus Olympios

The center of ancient Athens' commercial and daily life, the Agora abounded with schools and elegant stoas, or roofed arcades, filled with shops.

The temple stands next to Hadrian's Arch, built in AD 131 and marking the boundary between the ancient city and the Roman Athens of Hadrian.

↑ The imposing Stoa of Attalos, on the site of the Ancient Agora

and set up a statue of the god inside, a copy of the original by Greek sculptor Pheidias at Olympia (p466). Next to it he placed a huge statue of himself. Both statues have since been lost.

Only 15 of the original 104 columns remain, but they are sufficient to give a sense of the once enormous size of this temple – approximately 315 ft (96 m) long and 130 ft (40 m) wide. Roman-style Corinthian capitals were added to the original Doric columns in 174 BC.

Benaki Museum

🏛 Corner of Koumbári & Vasilíssis Sofías, Kolonáki 🚌 3, 7, 8, 13 🕐 9am–5pm Wed–Sat (to midnight Thu & Sat), 9am–3pm Sun 🔒 Public hols 🌐 benaki.gr

The Benaki Museum contains a superb collection of Greek art and crafts, jewelry, regional costumes, and political memorabilia spanning from the 3rd century BC to the 20th century. It was founded by art collector Andonios Benakis, who became interested in Greek, Persian, Egyptian, and Ottoman art at an early age and started accumulating pieces while living in Alexandria in Egypt. On moving to Athens in 1926, he donated his collection to the Greek state. The family home, an elegant 19th-century Neo-Classical mansion, was adapted as a museum and opened to the public in 1931.

A major part of the Benaki collection consists of gold jewelry dating from as far

back as 3000 BC. Also on display are icons, liturgical silverware, Egyptian artifacts, and Greek embroideries.

Byzantine and Christian Museum

🏛 Vasilíssis Sofías 22 Ⓜ Evangelismos 🕐 12:30–8pm Tue, 8am–8pm Wed–Mon (winter: to 3pm) 🌐 byzantine museum.gr

This is one of Athens' must-see museums, for both the quality of its displays and the clarity of their presentation. It features religious artifacts from the early Christian, Byzantine, medieval, post-Byzantine, and later periods. Treasures on display include a reconstructed frescoed church from inland Attikí and the gold Hoard of Mytilene, which was buried during 7th-century Saracen raids.

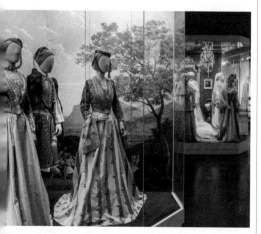

↑ Exhibition of traditional Greek costumes at the Benaki Museum

The National Archaeological Museum's airy interior and *(inset)* facade

EAT

Ama Lachei
Dine in an old house in winter or a large tiered garden in summer. Rakí by the carafe.

Kallidromíou 69
210 38 45 978

€€€

Diporto
Popular with locals, who come here for grilled fish and stews. There is limited seating available, so you share tables with other diners.

Sokrátous 9, crn Theátrou, basement; no sign 210 32 11 463

€€€

National Archaeological Museum

Patisíon 44 Omónia
Apr-Oct: 12:30-8pm Tue, 8am-8pm Wed-Mon; Nov-Mar: 1-8pm Tue, 9am-4pm Wed-Mon
namuseum.gr

When it opened in 1891, this museum brought together pieces that had previously been stored in different places all over the city. New wings were added in 1939, but during World War II, the museum's priceless exhibits were dispersed and buried underground to protect them from possible damage. The museum reopened in 1946, but it has taken another 60 or so years of renovation and reorganization to finally do justice to its formidable collection, which can be claimed as one of the finest in the world. It is a good idea to plan ahead and be selective when visiting the museum and not attempt to cover everything in one go.

The museum's exhibits can be divided into six main collections: Neolithic and Cycladic; Mycenaean, Geometric and Archaic sculpture; Classical sculpture; Roman and Hellenistic sculpture; the pottery collections; and the ancient Thera frescoes. There are also several other smaller collections that are well worth seeing. These include the stunning Eleni

Stathatou jewelry collection and the Egyptian rooms.

High points of the museum include the unique finds from the grave circle at Mycenae (p464), in particular the gold Mask of Agamemnon. Also not to be missed are the Archaic *kouroi/korai* statues and the unrivaled collection of Classical and Hellenistic statues. Three of the most important and finest of the bronzes are the *Horse with the Little Jockey*, the *Ephebe of Antikythera*, and *Poseidon*. One of the world's largest collections of ancient ceramics can also be found here, comprising a vast array of elegant red- and black-figure vases from the 6th and 5th centuries BC, as well as some Geometric funerary vases that date back as far as 1000 BC.

The Library of Archaeology holds a large collection of rare books, including the diaries of 19th-century German archaeologist Heinrich Schliemann, who uncovered the remains of Mycenae and Troy (at Hisarlık, in modern-day Turkey).

Museum of Cycladic Art

🏛 Neofýtou Doúka 4 (new wing at Irodótou 1), Kolonáki ⏫ 3, 7, 8, 13 🕙 10am–5pm Wed–Mon (to 8pm Thu, from 11am Sun) 🚫 Main public hols 🌐 cycladic.gr

A magnificent selection of ancient Greek art, including the world's most important collection of Cycladic figurines, is on view here. The displays start on the first floor, with the Cycladic collection. Dating back to the 3rd millennium BC, the Cycladic figurines were found mostly in graves, although their exact purpose remains a mystery. Ancient Greek art is exhibited on the second floor and the

GREAT VIEW
Lykavittós Hill

Athens' highest point at 910 ft (277 m), this hill north of the Museum of Cycladic Art offers the best city views. You can hike to the top along the pleasant footpaths or take the funicular up and saunter down at your leisure.

Charles Polítis collection of Classical and Prehistoric art on the fourth floor. The third floor displays some excellent ancient Cypriot art. Another wing in the adjoining Stathátos Mansion is used for temporary exhibits, many unrelated to Cycladic art.

← Marble idol on display in the Museum of Cycladic Art

Soúnio

🏛 5.5 miles (9 km) S of Lávrio, Attica ☎ 22920-39363 🚌 ⏰ 9am-sunset daily (winter: from 9:30am) 🔒 Main public hols

The temple of Poseidon, at the top of sheer cliffs tumbling into the Aegean Sea at Soúnio (Cape Sounion), was ideally located as a place to worship the powerful god of the sea. Its pale beige marble columns have been a landmark for ancient and modern mariners alike.

The present temple, built in 444 BC, stands on the site of older ruins. Marble from the quarries at Agriléza was used for the temple's 34 slender Doric columns, of which 15 survive today. In 1810, the British Romantic poet Lord Byron carved his name on one of the columns, setting an unfortunate precedent of vandalism at the temple.

---

❸
Monastery of Dafní

🏛 6 miles (10 km) NW of Athens, Attica ☎ 210-581 58 🚌 ⏰ 8am-3pm Wed-Sat

Taking its present form during the 11th century AD, this leafy monastery is named after the

Did You Know?

The official name of Greece is the Hellenic Republic.

laurels (dáfnes) that once grew here. It was built into the remains of an ancient sanctuary of Apollo, which had occupied the site until it was destroyed in AD 395. In the early 13th century, Otto de la Roche, the first Frankish Duke of Athens, bequeathed it to Cistercian monks in Burgundy. Greek Orthodox monks took the site in the 16th century, erecting the elegant cloisters just south of the church. Today, the monastery is still undergoing restoration following a 1999 earthquake.

Byzantine church architecture was concerned almost exclusively with decoration, and Dafní is no exception: one of the principal attractions here are the beautiful gold-leaf Byzantine mosaics in the *katholikón* (main church). Mosaics and frescoes portraying Christian figures and scenes from the Bible had a dual purpose: they gave inspiration to worshipers and represented

windows into the spiritual world. The most impressive mosaics at Dafní are those in the esonarthex, which include the *Last Supper*, the *Washing of the Feet*, and the *Betrayal of Judas*. Equally magnificent is the *Christ Pantokrátor*, a mosaic of Christ the Ruler of All that fills the church's huge dome.

---

❹
Monastery of Osios Loukás

🏛 5 miles (8 km) E of Dístomo, Stereá Elládos ☎ 22670-22228 🚌 ⏰ 10am-5pm daily

Dedicated to a local hermit and healer, Osios Loukás ("Holy Luke"), who died in AD 949, this splendid monastery was one of Greece's most important Byzantine buildings architecturally. Extending an earlier church dating from AD 942, it was completed around 1040 during the reign of Constantine IX Monomakhos. The octagonal shape of the main church – the *katholikón* – became a hallmark of Late Byzantine church design, while the mosaics inside lifted Byzantine art into its final great period.

One of the most impressive features of the monastery is the frescoed 10th-century crypt, which was part of the

original church and contains the sarcophagus of Holy Luke and a mosaic of the *Niptir (Washing of the Apostles' Feet)*. This 11th-century work, based on a style dating back to the 6th century, is the finest of numerous mosaics found in the narthex, the western entrance hall. On the supports under the main dome are several other fine mosaics, including *The Nativity, The Presentation of Jesus,* and *The Baptism.*

ORACLE OF DELPHI

The ancient Oracle of Delphi delivered divine prophecies through a priestess who practised consciousness-altering rituals – such as chewing laurel leaves and poppies. She then communicated the prophecies in a series of inarticulate cries, which priests translated into verse.

Ancient Delphi

🏠 Mount Parnassós, Stereá Elládos 📞 22650-82313 🚌 ⏰ 8am–8pm daily (winter: to 3pm) 🚫 Main public hols

In ancient times, Delphi was believed to be the center of the earth. The site was renowned as a dwelling place of Apollo, and from the late 9th century BC people came here to worship and seek advice from the god. With the political rise of Delphi in the 6th century BC, and the establishment of the Pythian Games – a cultural, religious, and athletic festival – the site entered a golden age

that lasted until the arrival of the Romans in 191 BC. The Oracle of Delphi was eventually abolished in AD 391 after Christianity was introduced as the state religion.

The Sanctuary of Apollo (also known as the Sacred Precinct) forms the heart of the complex, and one of its most impressive sights is the Temple of Apollo. A temple has stood on this spot since the 6th century BC, but the remains visible today date from the 4th century BC. Leading from the sanctuary entrance to the Temple of Apollo is the Sacred Way, once lined with some 3,000 statues and treasuries. Also of note is the well-preserved stadium. The present structure

dates from Roman times, and the majority of the seating is still intact.

The Marmaria ("marble quarry") Precinct is where the Sanctuary of Athena Pronaia is found. Here, the most remarkable monument is the *tholos*, which dates from the 4th century BC. The purpose of this circular structure, originally surrounded by 20 columns, remains a mystery.

A **museum** houses a vast collection of sculptures and architectural remains.

Museum
⏰ 8am–8pm daily (to 5pm Tue)

← Exploring the ruins of Ancient Delphi, home of the famous Oracle

6

METÉORA

🏠 Kalambáka 🚌 ℹ️ Patriárhou Dimitríou & Vladáva streets, Kastráki;
24323 50245 🕐 Megálo Metéoro: summer: 9am-3pm Wed-Mon, winter:
9am-2pm Fri-Mon; Varlaám: summer: 9am-4pm Sat-Thu, winter: 9am-
3pm Sat-Wed; Agíou Nikoláou: 9am-4pm Sat-Thu; Rousánou: 9am-5pm
Thu-Tue (winter: to 2pm); Agías Triádas: summer: 9am-5pm Fri-Wed,
winter: 10am-4pm Fri-Wed; Agíou Stefánou: summer: 9am-1:20pm &
3:30-5:30pm Tue-Sun, winter: 9:30am-1pm & 3-5pm Tue-Sun

The imposing rock formations of Metéora – topped by a
remarkable complex of gravity-defying monasteries –
are one of Greece's most spectacular sights.

The extraordinary sandstone towers of Metéora were formed
around 30 million years ago. They were first used as a religious
retreat in AD 985, when a hermit named Barnabas occupied
a cave here, and subsequently became the setting for a
series of precipitous monasteries – the name Metéora
means "things in mid-air" in Greek. The first monastery,
Megálo Metéoro, was founded in 1344 by the monk
Athanasios from Mount Athos. A further 23 monasteries were built on top of other pinnacles, though
most had fallen into ruin by the 19th century.
The remaining six – Megálo Metéoro, Varlaám,
Rousánou, Agía Triádas, Agíou Nikoláou, and Agíos
Stefánou – were made more accessible in the
1920s, when stairs were cut in the rock faces.
Today, walking trails access all monasteries
from Kastráki village.

Monastic
cells

Outer walls

The refectory contains
a small icon museum.

Dedicated to Agii Pándes
(All Saints), the Katholikón
church is adorned with frescoes,
including one of Theophanes
and Nektarios, its founders.

←

The frescoed interior
of the 16th-century
monastery at Varlaám

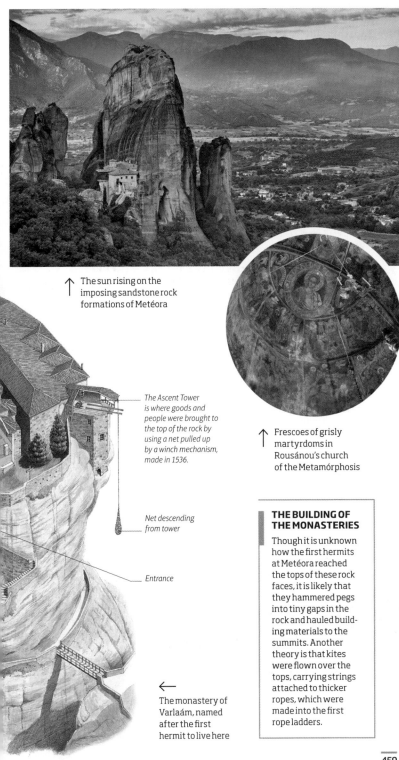

↑ The sun rising on the imposing sandstone rock formations of Metéora

The Ascent Tower is where goods and people were brought to the top of the rock by using a net pulled up by a winch mechanism, made in 1536.

Net descending from tower

Entrance

↑ Frescoes of grisly martyrdoms in Rousánou's church of the Metamórphosis

THE BUILDING OF THE MONASTERIES

Though it is unknown how the first hermits at Metéora reached the tops of these rock faces, it is likely that they hammered pegs into tiny gaps in the rock and hauled building materials to the summits. Another theory is that kites were flown over the tops, carrying strings attached to thicker ropes, which were made into the first rope ladders.

←
The monastery of Varlaám, named after the first hermit to live here

7

Thessaloníki

🏛 Central Macedonia
✈🚇🚌🚆 ℹ 136 Tsimiski;
www.thessaloniki.travel

Thessaloníki, also known as Salonika, is Greece's second city, and was founded by King Kassandros in 315 BC. The capital of the Roman province of Macedonia Prima from 146 BC, it later became part of the Byzantine Empire. In 1430 it was captured by the Ottomans, who held it until 1912. Today, Thessaloníki is a bustling cosmopolitan city and a major cultural center.

On the *paralía*, the city's attractive waterfront, stands one of Thessaloníki's most famous sights: the White Tower. Built by the Byzantines and then modified by the Ottomans, it formed a critical corner defense of the city's now-vanished medieval walls. Today it houses a permanent exhibition on the city's history.

The Arch of Galerius was built in AD 303 by the Emperor Galerius to celebrate victory over the Persians, and is the principal architectural legacy of Roman rule. Standing north of the arch is the Rotónda, believed to have been constructed as a mausoleum for

Did You Know?

The Greek national anthem, "Hymn to Liberty," has 158 verses.

Galerius. It has been used in the past as both a church and a mosque, and is worth a visit for its magnificent mosaics.

Thessaloníki has a number of fine museums, including the **Museum of Byzantine Culture** and the Folk and Ethnological Museum, housed in an ornate, 1906-built mansion. The star attractions at the city's **Archaeological Museum** are its Roman floor mosaics and the splendid Dervéni Krater, a 4th-century BC bronze wine-mixing bowl. You should also make time to see the museum's stunning collection of Macedonian gold.

Among the city's rich array of UNESCO-listed Byzantine churches is the 5th-century Agios Dimítrios – the largest church in Greece – and the mid-8th century Agía Sophía, an important building known for its mosaics and for its role in influencing future

architectural development. The 14th-century Agios Nikólaos Orfanós contains the best-preserved Late Byzantine frescoes in the city.

Museum of Byzantine Culture

🏛 Stratoú 2 🕐 Mid-Apr-Oct: 8am-8pm daily; Nov-mid-Apr: 9am-4pm daily 🌐 mbp.gr

Archaeological Museum

♿🅿 🏛 Manóli Androníkou 6 🕐 Late Apr-Oct: 8am-8pm daily; Nov-late Apr: 9am-4pm daily 🚫 Main public hols 🌐 amth.gr

---

8

Pílio

🏛 Thessaly 🚆🚌 Vólos
ℹ Platía Riga Feraíou, Vólos; www.volosinfo.gr/en

The Pílio Peninsula is one of the most beautiful areas of the mainland. The mountain air is sweet with the scent of herbs, which in ancient times were renowned for their healing properties. The area was first populated in the 13th century by Greeks retreating from Latin Crusaders and the Ottomans. Today, Pílio is known for its strong local

→ Thessaloníki's centuries-old White Tower, close to the waterfront

↑ A picturesque street in Makrinitsa, a village on the Pílio Peninsula

cuisine and for its network of hiking trails, many of which are cobbled.

The gateway town to the peninsula, Vólos, has an excellent Archaeological Museum. From here you can make a tour of the many traditional hillside villages and fishing ports. Particularly worth visiting are Miliés, with its Folk Museum and fresco-adorned church, and picturesque Vyzítsa. The largest settlement in the south of the

peninsula is Argalastí. For sandy beaches and excellent seafood, visit the popular coastal resorts of Plataniás or Agios Ioánnis.

9

Royal Macedonian Tombs, Vergína

🚗 10 miles (16 km) SE of Véria ⏰ 8am–8pm daily (from noon Tue) 🔒 Public hols 🌐 aigai.gr

Discovered in autumn 1977, these tombs settled the long-disputed location of ancient Aigai, and proved to be the resting place of King Philip II and other members of the Macedonian royal family. You can explore several of the subterranean burial chambers. The treasures found here are divided between on-site exhibits and Thessaloníki's archaeological museum.

10

Ancient Pélla

🚗 24 miles (38 km) NW of Thessaloníki 📞 23820-32963 🚌 ⏰ 8:30am–5pm Wed–Mon (Nov–Mar: to 3:30pm) 🔒 Main public hols

This small site was once the flourishing capital of

Macedonia. The court was moved here from Aigai (near modern Vergína) in 410 BC by King Arkhelaos, who ruled from 413 to 399 BC. It is here that Alexander the Great was born in 356 BC, and was later tutored by the philosopher Aristotle. Some sense of the existence of a city can be gained from a plan of the site, which shows where the main street and stores were located. The palace, believed to have been north of the main site, is still being excavated.

Throughout the site, and in the museum, are some of the best-preserved pebble mosaics in Greece. Dating from about 300 BC, many of them depict vivid hunting scenes. One of the most famous mosaics is of two huntsmen preparing to kill a lion; it is housed in the now-covered House of the Lion Hunt. Originally comprising 12 rooms around three open courtyards, this building was constructed at the end of the 4th century BC.

THE MACEDONIAN ROYAL FAMILY

The gold burial casket found at Vergína is emblazoned with the Macedonian Sun, the symbol of the king. Philip II was the first ruler to unite the whole of Greece as it existed at that time. His son, Alexander the Great, was just 20 when Philip was assassinated in 336 BC. He inherited a large empire and his father's ambition to conquer the Persians, which he did in 334 BC, when he crossed the Dardanelles, advancing as far as the Indus Valley in Asia. When Alexander died aged 33, the Macedonian empire divided into three kingdoms.

Mount Athos, and *(inset)* walkers on the southwest coast of the Athos Peninsula ↑

Mount Athos

🏛 **Athos Peninsula**
🚢 **Dáfni** 🚌 **To Karyés**

Also known as the Holy Mountain, Mount Athos is the highest point on the Athos Peninsula – an autonomous republic, ruled by the 2,000 monks who live in its 20 monasteries and numerous smaller colonies. Only adult males may visit the peninsula, but it is possible to see many of the monasteries from a boat trip along the coast. They include some fine examples of Byzantine architecture and provide a fascinating insight into Orthodox monastic life.

For the monks who live here, the day begins at 3 or 4am with solitary meditation and morning services. They eat two meals a day, fasting for 159 days in the year.

Ouranoúpoli is the main town of secular Athos and is the departure point for boat trips along the peninsula's

west coast. Among the monasteries that can be viewed from the water are the 10th-century Doheiaríou, Agios Pantelímonos, a Russian Orthodox monastery always busy with pilgrims, and Agios Pávlou. On the east coast, Megístis Lávras was the first monastery to be founded on Athos, while 10th-century Vatopedíou, farther north, is one of the largest and best-preserved buildings. Adult males wishing to visit any of the monasteries must obtain a written entrance permit from the Holy Executive of the **Mount Athos Pilgrims' Bureau** in Thessaloníki up to six months in advance; the final permit is collected in person in Ouranoúpoli, and grants the bearer a stay of up to four nights, one in each of four monasteries. Monastic

hospitality is free – and very frugal – but donations are always appreciated.

Mount Athos Pilgrims' Bureau
w agioritikiestia.gr

Mount Olympos

🏛 **10 miles (16 km) W of Litóhoro** 🚊 **Litóhoro** 🚌
ℹ **EOS: Evángelou Karavákou 20, Litóhoro; www.olympusfd.gr**

The mythological home of the Greek gods, Mount Olympos is actually a range of mountains, 12 miles (20 km) across. The highest peak in the range is Mytikas, at 9,570 ft (2,917 m). The entire area constitutes the Olympos National Park, an area of outstanding natural beauty whose rich flora and

> **Olympus National Park is an area of outstanding natural beauty whose rich flora and fauna include around 1,700 plant species.**

fauna include around 1,700 plant species, in addition to chamois, boars, and roe deer. A series of walking trails are accessible from Litóhoro, which has many hotels and tavernas.

Not far from Litóhoro is **Ancient Dion**, considered a holy city by the ancient Macedonians. The flat plains were used as a military camp by King Philip II of Macedon in the 4th century BC. The ruins visible today – which include mosaics, baths, and a theater – date mainly from the Roman era. A museum in the adjacent modern village shows finds from the site.

Ancient Dion
 ⬙ **Dion** ☏ 23510 43484 🕒 May–Oct: 8am–8pm daily (Sep: to 7pm, Oct: to 6pm)

Ancient Corinth

⬙ 4 miles (7 km) SW of modern Corinth ☏ 27410-31207 🚌 🕒 Apr–Oct: 8am–8pm daily (Sep: to 7pm, Oct to 6pm); Nov–Mar: 8:30am–3:30pm Wed–Mon (Mar: to 4pm) 🗓 Main public hols

A settlement since Neolithic times, Ancient Corinth was razed in 146 BC by the Romans, who rebuilt it a century later. Under the patronage of the Roman emperors, the town gained a reputation for licentious living, which St. Paul attacked when he came here in AD 52. Excavations have revealed the vast extent of the ancient city, which was destroyed by earthquakes in Byzantine times. The ruins constitute the largest Roman township in Greece.

Among the most impressive remains are the Lechaion Way, the marble-paved road that linked the nearby port of Lechaion with the city, and the Temple of Apollo, with its striking Doric columns. The temple was one of the few buildings preserved by the Romans when they rebuilt the city in 44 BC. All that remains of the Temple of Octavia, once dedicated to the sister of Emperor Augustus, are three ornate Corinthian columns, overarched by a restored architrave. The Odeon is one of several buildings endowed to the city by Herodes Atticus, the wealthy Athenian and friend of the Emperor Hadrian.

Close to the Odeon, the museum houses a collection of exhibits representing all periods of the town's history. The Roman gallery is particularly rich, containing some spectacular 2nd-century AD mosaics lifted from the floors of nearby villas.

Near to Ancient Corinth is the bastion of **Acrocorinth**. Held and refortified by every occupying power in Greece from Roman times onward, it was one of the country's most important fortresses in medieval times. The summit affords one of the most sweeping views in Greece.

Acrocorinth
 ⬙ 2 miles (4 km) S of Ancient Corinth 🕒 8:30am–3pm daily

↑ The atmospheric setting of the Temple of Apollo, Ancient Corinth

↑ Taking in the wonderful view from the theater of Epidauros
seats at the stone

14

Epidauros

🏛19 miles (30 km) E of Náfplio 🚌27530-22009 🚍
🕐8am-7pm daily (winter: 8:30am-3pm) 🚫Main public hols

Active from the 6th century BC until at least the 2nd century AD, the important Sanctuary of Epidauros (also Epidaurus) was an extensive therapeutic and religious center, dedicated to the healing god Asklepios.

The site is known for its magnificent theater, featuring a 66-ft (20-m) diameter *orchestra* (stage), the only circular stage to have survived from antiquity. Designed in the late 4th century BC, the theater is renowned for its near-perfect acoustics.

💬 INSIDER TIP
Athens/ Epidauros Festival

Together with Athens' Odeon of Herodes Atticus, the theater of Epidauros hosts an annual summer festival of ancient drama *(www. greekfestival.gr)*.

Most of the Asklepieion, or Sanctuary of Asklepios, has been re-excavated. Accessible remains include the *propylon* (monumental gateway), the Colonnade of the Enkimitirion, where patients slept and hoped for cures to be revealed in a dream, and the Tholos of Polykleitos – a circular building, thought to have been used either as a pit for sacred serpents or as the setting for religious rites.

15

Mycenae

🏛1 mile (2 km) N of Mykínes 🚌27510-76585 🚍 🕐Apr-Oct: 8am-8pm daily (Sep: to 7pm, Oct: to 6pm); Nov-Mar: 8:30am-3:30pm daily (Mar: to 4pm) 🚫Main public hols

Discovered in 1874, the fortified palace complex of Mycenae is an early example of citadel architecture. The Mycenaeans were a Bronze Age culture that existed

between 1700 and 1100 BC. Only the ruling class inhabited the palace, with artisans and merchants living outside the city walls. The citadel was abandoned in 1100 BC after much disruption in the region.

The tombs at Mycenae are one of the most famous attractions of the site. The city's nobles were entombed in shaft graves, such as those at Grave Circle A, or, later, in *tholos* ("beehive") tombs, so-called because of their shape.

→ The forbidding rock of Monemvasiá, on the east coast of the Peloponnese

Found outside the palace walls, the *tholos* tombs were buried under an earth mound, only accessible via a *dromos*, or open-air corridor. The most outstanding example of these burial structures is the 14th-century BC Treasury of Atreus, where a Mycenaean king was buried with his weapons and enough food and drink for his journey to the underworld.

Also of interest at the site are the remains of the Royal Palace; the Secret Stairway, which leads down to a cistern deep beneath the citadel; and the 13th-century BC Lion Gate, which formed the grand entrance to Mycenae.

Náfplio

⌂ Peloponnese 🚌 🚇 *i* Town Hall, Vasiléos Konstantínou; 27520-24444

One of the most elegant towns in mainland Greece, Náfplio emerged in the 13th century and later endured numerous sieges during the struggles between the Ottomans and the Venetians for the ports of the Peloponnese. From 1829 to 1834, it was the first capital of liberated Greece.

A number of fortifications testify to the town's checkered history. The island fortress of Boúrtzi is a legacy of the second Venetian occupation (1686–1715). Akronafplía, also known as Its Kale ("Inner Castle" in Turkish), was the site of the Byzantine and early medieval town, while the Venetian citadel of Palamídi was built in the early 1700s.

Near Platía Syndágmatos, the hub of public life in Náfplio, are three mosques built by the Ottomans. These are now an occasional cinema, the former first Greek parliament (now used for concerts), and the cathedral, Agios Geórgios, which before Ottoman times was a Catholic church.

The town has two museums of note: the award-winning **Folk Art Museum**, and the **Archaeological Museum**, which houses mainly local Mycenaean artifacts.

Folk Art Museum

⊗ ⏲ ⌂ Vasiléos Alexándrou 1 ⏰ 9am-2:30pm Mon-Sat, 9:30am-3pm Sun 🌐 pli.gr

Archaeological Museum

⊗ ⏲ ⌂ Platía Syndágmatos 📞 27520-27502 ⏰ 8:30am-4pm Wed-Mon (Nov-Feb: to 3:30pm) 🔒 Main public hols

Monemvasiá

⌂ Laconia 🚌🚇 *i* 27320-61210

This fortified town is built on two levels on a rock rising 1,150 ft (350 m) above the sea. Monemvasiá was for centuries a semi-autonomous city-state, which prospered thanks to its position astride the sea lanes from Italy to the Black Sea. After a protracted siege, the town was finally surrendered by the Ottomans in 1821 during the War of Independence.

In the restored lower town, enclosed by formidable 16th-century walls, are a number of mosques and churches, such as the 18th-century Panagía Myrtidióssa and the 13th-century cathedral Christós Elkómenos, with its Venetian belfry. Also in the lower town are the birthplace of Yiannis Ritsos, the 20th-century Greek poet and Communist, and his grave.

Originally fortified in the 6th century, the oldest part of Monemvasiá is the now-uninhabited upper town, which lies largely in ruins. Here, the most impressive sight is the still-intact cliff-top church of Agía Sophía, founded by Emperor Andronikos II and modeled on the Monastery of Dafní (p456). Visitors can also see the remains of a 13th-century fortress.

↑ Visitors in Ancient Olympia's excellent Archaeological Museum

Ancient Olympia

🅐Peloponnese 📞26240-22517 🚉🚌 ⏰8am-8pm daily (mid-Oct-mid-Apr: earlier closure) 🚫Main public hols

The sanctuary of Olympia enjoyed over 1,000 years of renown as a religious and athletics center. Its historic importance dates to the coming of the Dorians, at the start of the first millennium BC. They brought the worship of Zeus, after whose abode on Mount Olympos the site was named. The first Olympian Games, the forerunner of the Olympic Games, took place here in 776 BC, but were later banned in AD 393 by Emperor Theodosios I, who took a dim view of all pagan festivals.

The most important ruins include the 5th-century BC Doric Temple of Zeus and the partly reconstructed Palaestra, which was a training center for athletes. The workshop of ancient Greek artist Pheidias was where an enormous statue of Zeus – one of the Seven Wonders of the World – was sculpted in the 5th century BC.

The superb Archaeological Museum has exhibits from prehistory, through to the Classical period and the Roman era, including the pediment and metope sculpture from the Temple of Zeus and the Hermes of Praxiteles.

19

Máni Peninsula

🅐Peloponnese 🚌Gýthio 🚌Kalamáta (Outer Máni), Areópoli (Inner Máni) 🛈Vasiléos Georgiou 20, Gýthio; 27330-24484

This harsh, remote peninsula is divided into two areas: Outer Máni, encompassing the region to the north of the village of Oítylo, and Inner Máni, covering the area to the south. The peninsula is famous for its history of internal feuding.

From the 15th century, rival clansmen built many fine tower houses, from where they would shoot at their opponents. After years of bloodshed, the clans finally united, instigating the Greek Independence uprising in 1821.

The main places of interest in the more fertile Outer Máni are Oítylo, with its elegant 19th-century mansions, and Kardamýli, the lair of the Troupákis family, one of the main Maniot clans. Near Kardamýli are the stunning Vyrós Gorge and the resort of Stoúpa. Inland, Mount Taygetus offers several days of wilderness trekking.

In Inner Máni, bustling Gýthio is an attractive coastal town with an 18th-century fortress housing the Museum of the Máni. The town of Areópoli was where the Maniot uprising against the Ottomans was declared; nearby is the 17th-century Ottoman Kelefá Castle. Other attractions in Inner Máni include the Pýrgos Diroú cave system and the Byzantine churches scattered along the west coast. Built between the 10th and 14th centuries, the finest churches include Taxiarhón, at Haroúda; Agios Theódoros, at Vámvaka; and, near Ano Boulárii village,

> The workshop of ancient Greek artist Pheidias was where an enormous statue of Zeus - one of the Seven Wonders of the World - was sculpted in the 5th century BC.

Agios Panteleímon, containing 10th-century frescoes. All are locked, so locate the warden to get in. Farther south, in a dramatic location overlooking Cape Ténaro, Váthia is of interest for its tower houses.

Mystrás

🏛 3 miles (5 km) W of Spárti 📞 27310-83377 🚇
🕐 Summer: 8am–8pm daily (Sep: to 7:30pm, Oct: 6pm); winter: 8:30am–4pm daily
🚫 Main public hols

Majestic Mystrás occupies a panoramic site on a spur of the Taygetus range. Founded by the Franks in 1249, the town soon passed to the Byzantines and, after 1348, became the seat of the Despots of Morea. By the 15th century, Mystrás had become the last major Byzantine cultural center, attracting scholars and artists from Italy, Constantinople, and Serbia. One result was the cosmopolitan decoration of Mystrás's churches, whose pastel-colored frescoes, filled with detail, reflect the influence of the Italian Renaissance.

Now in ruins, Mystrás consists of an upper and lower town, with churches, monasteries, and palaces lining its narrow streets. Among the churches and monasteries worth visiting are Mitrópoli, the oldest church in Mystrás, dating from 1291; Moní Perivléptou (1310); and Moní Pandánassas (1428). The Vrontóhion, a 13th-century monastic complex, was the cultural heart of medieval Mystrás. Visitors can also explore the ruins of the Despots' Palace and the Kástro, a fortification at the summit of the upper town that offers expansive views of the entire site.

21
Loúsios Gorge

🏛 Peloponnese
🚇 Dimitsána, Karýtena, & Stemnítsa

Although merely a tributary of the Alfiós river, the Loúsios stream has one of the most impressive canyons in Greece. Scarcely 3 miles (5 km) long, the Loúsios Gorge is nearly 985 ft (300 m) deep at its narrowest section. Hiking trails connect the area's highlights, which include several churches and **monasteries** clinging to the steep cliffs of the gorge. Of these, the most impressive are Moní Emyalón, founded in 1605 and containing some magnificent frescoes; the 17th-century Néa Moní Filosófou; and the 10th-century Moní Agios Ioánnou Prodrómou, wedged into the canyon's east flank. Occupying a sunken excavation on the stream's west bank, the therapeutic center of Ancient Gortys contains the foundations of a 4th-century BC temple to Asklepios, the god of healing. Accessible from here, or by road from Karýtena, the cliffside monastery of Paleoú Kalamioú has excellent frescoes.

Overlooking the gorge are the hillside towns of Karýtena, Dimitsána, and Stemnítsa, all of which make good bases to explore the area.

Monasteries
🕐 Dawn to dusk daily
🚫 Moní Emyalón: 2–5pm

↑ Moní Agios Ioánnou Prodrómou, a monastery in the Loúsios Gorge

↑ Corfu Town, with the Byzantine fortress and Agios Spyrídon's belfry

22

CORFU AND THE IONIAN ISLANDS

The Ionian Islands are the greenest and most fertile of all of Greece's island groups. Lying off the west coast of mainland Greece, they have been greatly influenced by periods of rule by the Venetians, French, and British, who left their mark in the mixed architecture of places like Corfu Town. The Ionians first became a holiday destination during the Roman era, and the beaches here still draw numerous visitors today.

①

Corfu

 ☒ 🛏 🚌 ℹ **Platía Saróko; www.corfu-kerkyra.eu**

The island of Corfu offers secluded coves, bustling resorts, and traditional hill villages. Part of the Roman Empire from 229 BC to AD 337, it remained under Byzantine rule until the 14th century, when the Venetians took control. French and British occupation followed, before unification with Greece in 1864.

The checkered history of the island is reflected in Corfu Town's varied architecture. The Palace of St. Michael and St. George was built by the British between 1819 and 1824 to serve as the residence of a high commissioner. Used for a short time by the Greek royal family after the British left the island, the palace is now home to the eclectic **Museum of Asian Art**.

The palace overlooks the Spianáda, a mixture of park and town square, and the site of a cricket ground developed by the British (now used only for children's matches). The Liston, a parade of cafés built in 1807 as a copy of the Rue de Rivoli in Paris, lines one side of the square.

Look out for the 16th-century Agios Spyrídon church, with its red-domed belfry, the tallest on Corfu; the Town Hall, a grand Venetian building flanking Platía Dimarhíou; the Byzantine (Andivouniótissa) Museum; and the town's fascinating **Archaeological Museum**. The latter's center-piece exhibit is a stunning Gorgon frieze.

On the town's eastern side, an originally Byzantine fortress offers great views extending along the island's east coast. The New Fortress,

Did You Know?
—
Britain's Prince Philip, the Duke of Edinburgh, was born on Corfu in 1921.

on the west side of town, is a 16th-century Venetian construction. The town's market is held in the former moat.

Northern Corfu's entire coastline is a busy vacation destination lined with resorts and beaches. Set around a fishing harbor, Kassiópi has retained its character despite its popularity. Near the village center are the ruins of a 13th-century castle, and the church of Kassópitra, which occupies the site of a former temple of Zeus.

The bustling vacation center of Sidári is famous for its sandy beaches and rock formations, while picturesque Paleokastrítsa has safe swimming and watersports, as well as boat trips to nearby grottoes.

Mount Pandokrátor, a short drive north of Corfu Town, is the highest point on Corfu. It offers fine views over the whole island and across to the Epirot mainland.

In southern Corfu, tranquil hillside villages, such as Pélekas and Sinarádes, offer a taste of traditional Greece with their rural architecture and local crafts.

Peaceful spots in the south include the Korisíon Lagoon, a Venetian-built stretch of water separated from the sea by dunes and beaches. It provides a habitat for many species of birds and wild flowers.

The **Achílleion Palace** was built between 1890 and 1891 as a personal retreat for Empress Elizabeth of Austria. After a tour of the palace and its gardens, visit the Vasilakis Distillery, opposite, and sample its kumquat liqueur.

Museum of Asian Art

⊛ ⊚ ⬛ Palace of St. Michael & St. George 📞 26610-30443 ⬛ Apr-Oct: 8am-8pm Wed-Mon (Nov-Mar: 8:30am-3:30 or 4pm) ⬛ Main public hols

Archaeological Museum

⊛ ⬛ Vráila 1 📞 26610-30680 ⬛ 8am-8pm Wed-Mon (Nov-Mar: earlier closure) ⬛ Main public hols

Achílleion Palace

⬛ 7 miles (10 km) SW of Corfu Town ⬛ ⬛ Hours vary, check website ⬜ achillion-corfu.gr

---

② Kefaloniá

⬛⬛⬛ ℹ️ Waterfront, Argostóli; 26710-22248

The largest island in the Ionians, Kefaloniá has a range of attractions, from busy beach resorts to areas of outstanding natural beauty.

The capital, Argostóli, is a busy town located by a bay. Its traditional appearance is deceptive, as the town was destroyed in an earthquake in 1953 and rebuilt with donations. The main sights of interest here are the Archaeological Museum and the Historical and Folk Museum.

The liveliest places around the rest of the island are Lássi, just outside Argostóli, and the south-coast resorts, but elsewhere there are quiet villages and stunning scenery. Don't miss fir-covered Mount Énos and its national park, in the south, and the subterranean Melissáni cave-lake on the east coast. Kefaloniá's prettiest village is Fiskárdo, with its 18th-century Venetian houses clustered by the harbor.

From Kefaloniá, there are ferry services to Lefkáda from Fiskárdo and to Ithaca from Sámi or Póros; there is also a summer link to Zákynthos from Pessáda.

---

③ Zákynthos

⬛⬛⬛ ℹ️ Tourist Police, Lomvárdou Quay 62, Zákynthos Town; 26950-24482

Zákynthos is a verdant island with good beaches and beautiful scenery. The main point of arrival is Zákynthos Town, where the impressive church

of Agios Dionysios and the Byzantine Museum – which houses a breathtaking array of frescoes – are both deserving of a visit.

Tourism on Zákynthos is concentrated in Laganás and its 6 mile (9 km) sweep of soft sand, where the hectic nightlife continues until dawn. Quiter spots can be found on the island's northeast coast, at the beach resorts of Tsiliví and Alykés; the latter of these is especially good for windsurfing. At the northernmost tip of the island are the spectacular and unusual Blue Caves, which can be visited by boat from below the lighthouse at Cape Skinári.

EAT

The Venetian Well
This classy bistro serves imaginative cuisine in a delightful spot beside the eponymous well.

⬛ Platía Kremastí, Corfu Town ⬜ venetianwell.gr

€€€

↑ Sunset over Firá's whitewashed cliff homes, Santoríni

23

CYCLADES

The most-visited island group, the Cyclades embody the Greek island ideal, with their whitewashed cliff-top villages, blue-domed churches, and stunning beaches. The islands vary greatly, from the quiet and traditional to the more nightlife-oriented, but nearly all have important archaeological sites, such as those on Santoríni and Delos.

①
Santoríni

 ✈🚌🚢 ❱ Firá; www.santorini.gr

Colonized by the Minoans in 3000 BC, this volcanic island erupted in about 1630 BC, forming Santoríni's distinct crescent shape. Today, this stunning island is as famous for its archaeological sites as for its whitewashed villages, cliffs, and black sand beaches.

Founded in the late 18th century, the capital Firá is packed with hotels, bars, and restaurants, and its streets enjoy magnificent views out to sea. The tiny cruise-ship port of Skála Firón, 890 ft

(270 m) below, is connected to the town by cable car or by mule up 580 steps.

Among Firá's main sights are the Lignos Folklore Museum in the Kondohóri suburb and the **Museum of Prehistoric Thera**, with compelling finds from the Ancient Akrotíri site, including vivid Minoan frescoes and a golden ibex figurine. Akrotíri itself can be visited at the south of the island; unearthed in 1967, the Minoan settlement is still preserved after some 3,500 years of burial under volcanic ash.

Also within easy reach of Firá, on the headland of Mésa Vounó, are the ruins of the Dorian town of **Ancient Thera**. Most of the ruins here date

from the Ptolemies, who built temples to the Egyptian gods in the 3rd century BC. There are also Hellenistic and Roman remains. Below the site are the popular beach resorts of Oeríssa and Kamári.

Museum of Prehistoric Thera

⊗ ❱ Mitropóleos St █ 22860-23217 ❍ 8am-3pm Wed-Mon ❱ Main public hols

Ancient Thera

⊗ ❱ 7 miles (11 km) SW of Firá █ 22860-23217 ❍ 8:30am-4pm Wed-Mon (Nov-mid-Apr: to 3pm) ❱ Main public hols

②
Mýkonos

 ✈🚌🚢 ❱ Harbourfront, Mýkonos Town; www.mykonos.gr

Although Mýkonos is dry and barren, its sandy beaches and dynamic nightlife make it one of the most popular destinations in the Cyclades. A premier LGBT resort, Mýkonos thrives on its reputation as one of Greece's glitziest islands.

It is also a good base to visit the impressive ancient archaeological site on Delos.

Mýkonos Town (or Hóra) is a tangle of dazzling white alleys and cube-shaped houses. The bustling old port is particularly picturesque. At the south end of its quayside is the island's most famous church, Panagía Paraportianí, comprising four chapels in one building, and to the northeast of the port is the **Archaeological Museum**. The latter has a fine collection of ancient pottery, including finds from the excavations of the ruins on Delos.

Above the oldest part of town, known as the *kástro*, is a working windmill. From there, the lanes run down into pretty Aléfkandra, the artists' quarter. Also referred to as "Little Venice," the area is dotted with bars and boutiques, as well as attractive houses with painted balconies that jut out over the sea.

Mýkonos is popular primarily for its beaches, including long Kalafátis in the east and clubber's mecca Paradise, south of Mýkonos Town. There are also a few gay and/or nudist beaches, including Super Paradise, Liá, and Eliá.

Inland, the traditional village of Ano Merá remains relatively unspoiled by tourism. The main attraction here is the Panagía Tourlianí monastery, with its marble tower.

Accessible by boat from the old port in Mýkonos Town, the tiny island of **Delos** is one of Greece's most important archaeological sites. The legendary birthplace of Artemis and Apollo, from 1000 BC it was home to the annual Delian Festival, held in honor of the god Apollo. In addition to some impressive mosaics and temple ruins from the 2nd century BC, the most important remains on Delos are the magnificent 7th-century BC Lion Terrace, the theater, built in 300 BC to hold 5,500 people, and the Theater Quarter, with some villa mosaics in situ.

Archaeological Museum

◈ ⌂ Harborfront ☎ 22890-22325 🕒 Apr-Oct: 8:30am-4pm Sun, Mon & Wed, 10am-9pm Thu-Sat; Nov-Mar: 9am-4pm Wed-Mon 🚫 Public hols

Delos

◈◈ ⌂ 6 nautical miles SW of Mýkonos Town ☎ 22890-22259 ⛴ 10-11:30am daily from Mýkonos Town, returning 2-4pm 🕒 Apr-Oct: 8am-1pm daily 🚫 Main public hols

---

③
Náxos

🚌🚍🚐 ℹ Náxos Town; www.naxos.gr

The largest of the Cyclades, Náxos was a major center of the Cycladic civilization. The Venetians, who arrived in the 13th century, built many fortifications that still stand on the island today.

Overlooking Náxos Town's bustling harbor is the huge, marble, 6th-century BC Portára gateway, built as the entrance to an unfinished Temple of Apollo. To the south, Agios Geórgios is the main tourist district. The old town divides into the Venetian Kástro area, housing 13th-century fortifications, and the medieval Boúrgos lower down. The 18th-century Orthodox cathedral, the Mitrópoli Zoödóhou Pigís, stands in Boúrgos, which also has arcaded lanes of shops. In the Kástro, the **Archaeological Museum** has one of the best collections of Cycladic marble figurines in the Greek islands.

South of Náxos Town are many fine beaches, including Agía Anna and Kastráki – the latter good for watersports – and tranquil Pláka.

Inland, the Trageá Valley is a walkers' paradise. It is dotted with charming villages such as Halkí, with its tower-mansions. Beyond Ano Sangrí, at Gyroúla, a reconstructed Demeter temple is the most interesting ancient monument on Náxos.

Archaeological Museum

◈ ⌂ French Jesuit School ☎ 22850-22725 🕒 8am-3:30pm Wed-Mon (Oct-mid-Apr: to 3pm) 🚫 Public hols

Did You Know?

Although he was born in a cave on Crete, the king of the gods, Zeus, was brought up on Náxos.

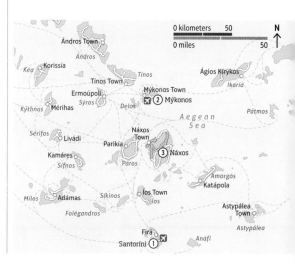

RHODES AND THE DODECANESE

EXPERIENCE Greece

The hot climate and fine beaches of the Dodecanese attract many visitors, but the islands also feature lush, fertile valleys and craggy, wooded mountains. The most southerly group of Greek islands, the Dodecanese have been subject to several invasions, and this history is still apparent in the islands' impressively varied architecture and wealth of historical sites.

① Rhodes

 ℹ Crn Platía Megálou Alexándrou & Ippotón or at international jetty, Rhodes Town; www. rhodes.gr/tourist-guide

An important Dorian center from the 7th to 3rd centuries BC, the island of Rhodes was later part of both the Roman and Byzantine empires. It was subsequently conquered by the Knights of St. John, an order founded to tend Christian pilgrims in Jerusalem, who occupied Rhodes from 1309 to 1522 and built a medieval walled city. Ottoman and Italian rulers followed, leaving their own traces of occupation.

First founded in 408 BC, the town of Rhodes is split into two distinct parts: the medieval walled city of the Old Town and the more modern New Town. The Old Town is divided into the Collachium (the Knights' quarter) and the Boúrgos (home to the rest of the population), and is dominated by the 14th-century **Palace of the Grand Masters**, the seat of 19 Grand Masters of the Knights. The palace houses several mosaics from sites in Kos, plus exhibitions about ancient and medieval Rhodes on the ground floor.

South of the Collachium, the Mosque of Süleyman commemorates the Sultan's victory over the Knights in 1522. The Library of Hafız

Ahmet (opposite), the now-disused public baths, and four large mosques provide further reminders of the town's Ottoman past.

Beyond the citadel walls, the New Town of Rhodes is made up of several areas, including Néa Agora (new market), with its whimsical fishmongers' gazebo, and Mandráki harbor in the eastern half of town. Near the harbor is the Mosque of Murad Reis, with its graceful minaret.

A few miles southwest of Rhodes Town are the well-preserved remains of **Ancient Kámeiros**, which include a 3rd-century BC Doric temple. To its east is Petaloúdes, or Butterfly Valley, which teems with Jersey tiger moths from June to September.

Halfway along Rhodes' east coast, Líndos is a magnet for visitors seeking sun, sea, and sand, but it is also famous for its cliff-top **acropolis**, crowned by the 4th-century BC Doric Temple of Lindian Athena.

A short drive from Líndos, south of Láerma village, the church of Moní Thárri shelters the finest frescoes on Rhodes, dating from 1300 to 1450.

Palace of the Grand Masters

⊛ ⌂ Platía Kleovoúlou
☎ 22413-25500 ⌚ Apr-Oct: 8am-8pm daily; Nov-Mar: 8am-3pm Tue (ground floor closes at 3pm year round)
🗓 Main public hols

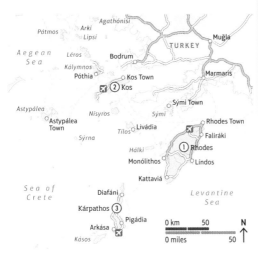

Agathónisi
Pátmos · Arkí · Lipsi · Muğla
A e g e a n   S e a · Léros · Bodrum · TURKEY
Kálymnos
Póthia · Kos Town · Marmaris
② Kos
Astypálea · Nísyros · Sými Town
Astypálea Town · Sými · Rhodes Town
Tílos · Livádia · Faliráki
Sýrna · ① Rhodes
Hálki · Líndos
Monólithos
Kattaviá
S e a   o f   C r e t e · Diafáni · L e v a n t i n e   S e a
Kárpathos ③ · Pigádia
Arkása
Kásos

0 km 50
0 miles 50
N ↑

↑ Strolling at dusk in a pedestrianized square in Rhodes' Old Town

Ancient Kámeiros

 22 miles (36 km) SW of Rhodes Town ⏰ May–Oct: 8am–8pm daily; Nov–Apr: 8am–3pm Tue–Sun 🚫 Main public hols

Acropolis at Líndos

E of Líndos village 📞 22440-31258 ⏰ Mid-Apr–Oct: 8am–8pm daily; Nov–mid-Apr: 8am–3pm Wed–Mon 🚫 Main public hols

---

② Kos

🚗🚌 ℹ Artemisías, crn Epiharmoú, Kos Town; www.kos.gr

Mainly flat and fertile, Kos is the second largest island in the Dodecanese. It has a wealth of archaeological sites: Hellenistic and Roman ruins, as well as Byzantine and Crusader castles. Many of these can be found in Kos Town – the 15th-century Castle of the Knights, the Ancient Agora,

and the Roman remains should not be missed. Most visitors, however, come for the sandy beaches. The best of these lie between the airport and Kamári, on the island's southwest coast. Kardámena is Kos's biggest and brashest resort, while north-coast beaches like Marmári and Tingáki are ideal for watersports. In spite of tourist development, remnants of Kos's traditional lifestyle can be found inland.

Kos is a good base from which to explore the northerly Dodecanese islands, including Pátmos, home to the 11th-century Monastery of St. John, and Léros, with its Italian-built Rationalist townscape.

---

③ Kárpathos

🚗🚌🚢 ℹ Pigádia; www.karpathos.gr

Despite an increase in tourism since the late 1990s, rugged Kárpathos is largely unspoiled.

> **Many archaeological sites can be found in Kos town – the 15th-century Castle of the Knights, the Ancient Agora, and the Roman remains should not be missed.**

Its capital, Pigádia (also known as Kárpathos Town), is a busy center, with hotels, cafés, and restaurants around its bay. South of here is the resort of Ammopí, arranged around three sand-and-gravel coves.

In addition to some magnificent beaches northwest of the capital, including Lefkós and Ápella, the island is also home to an archaeological site at Vroukoúnda, with ancient walls and rock-cut tombs dating back to the Hellenistic and Roman eras. Nearby is the attractive hillside village of Ólymbos, where traditional Greek life and customs can still be observed.

←

A picturesque back street draped in flowers in Réthymno's Old Town

Crete. In 1900–4, excavations unearthed two palaces here. Remains of the first palace, destroyed by an earthquake in 1700 BC, are still visible, but most of the present ruins are of the second palace. They include the Grand Staircase, which was the main entrance to the palace, and the Central Court. In the 2nd century BC, Phaistos was destroyed by the ancient city-state of Gortys, the remains of which lie a few miles east of Phaistos.

③
Iráklio

☐ Iráklio 🚤🚌🚗
ⓘ Xanthoudídou 1; 2810-246298

A sprawling town of concrete buildings, Iráklio nevertheless has much of interest for visitors. Four centuries of Venetian rule have left a rich architectural legacy, evident in the imposing 16th-century fortress overlooking the harbor, and the 17th-century Loggia, a former meeting place for the island's nobility. The most noteworthy of Iráklio's many churches are 13th-century Agios Márkos, now the city's main picture gallery, and 16th-century Agios Títos.

The **Iráklio Archaeological Museum** displays Minoan artifacts from all over Crete. Its most magnificent exhibits include a rock-crystal *rhyton* (drinking horn) and the clay Phaistos Disk. Inscribed with pictorial symbols, the disk's meaning and origin remain a mystery. Among the museum's many other treasures are the Snake Priestesses, two faïence figurines dating from around 1600 BC.

The heart of the town is Platía Eleftheríou Venizélou, a bustling pedestrianized zone

㉕
CRETE

🚤🚌🚗 ⓘ www.incrediblecrete.gr

Rugged mountains, sparkling seas, and ancient history make Crete an idyllic vacation destination. The center of the Minoan civilization, it has also been influenced by the legacy of various occupying forces.

①
Réthymno

☐ Réthymno 🚌 ⓘ Sofokli Venizélou, Delfini Bldg; 28310-29148

Despite modern development, Réthymno has retained much of its historic charm. Venetian and Ottoman architecture in the old quarter includes the elegant 16th-century Lótzia (Loggia, now a gift shop) and the Nerantzés Mosque, a converted church that is now a concert hall. Below the huge Fortétsa, built by the Venetians in the 1500s to defend the port, is a pretty harbor, lined

with cafés and bars. Also of interest here is the **Historical and Folk Art Museum**.

Historical and Folk Art Museum
☐ Vernárdou 30 ⏰ Summer: 10am–3pm Mon-Sat

②
Phaistos

☐ 40 miles (65 km) SW of Irákleio 📞 28920-42315 🚌
⏰ 8am–8pm daily (winter: to 5pm) ☐ Main public hols

Phaistos was one of the most important Minoan palaces on

of cafés and shops. Farther afield are the beach resorts of Mália and Hersónisos, just a short drive east of the town.

South of Iráklio, Knossos was the largest of Crete's Minoan palaces. Built around 1900 BC, the first **Palace of Knossos** was destroyed by an earthquake in about 1700 BC but soon rebuilt. The ruins visible today are largely from this second palace. They were restored by British archae-ologist Sir Arthur Evans in the early 1900s; although the sub-ject of academic controversy, his reconstructions give a good impression of life in Minoan Crete. Highlights of the site include the Giant Pithos, one of over 100 *pithoi* (storage jars) unearthed here, the Throne Room, and the Royal Apartments. The original frescoes from the palace are now on display in Iráklio's Archaeological Museum.

Iráklio Archaeological Museum

⊘ ⌂ Cnr of Xanthoudídou 2 & Bofór, Platía Eleftherías ☎ 2810-279086/279000 🕐 Mid-Apr-Oct: 8am-8pm daily (from 10am Tue); Nov-mid-Apr: 8:30am-3:30pm Wed-Mon, 10am-5pm Tue

Palace of Knossos

⊘⊘ ⌂ 3 miles (5 km) S of Iráklio ☎ 2810-231940 🕐 8am-8pm daily (winter: to 5pm) ⌧ Main public hols

---

④

Agios Nikólaos

⌂ 40 miles (65 km) W of Iráklio ▦ 🛈 Koundoúrou 21; 28410-22357

The main transport hub for the east of the island, Agios Nikólaos is a thriving vacation center with an attractive port and fine beaches to the east, as well as an interesting Folk Museum. A few miles north, the resort of Eloúnda has a good range of accommodations and boat trips to Spinalónga islet, with its Venetian fortifications.

---

⑤

Haniá

⌂ Haniá ✕▦ 🛈 Kydonías 29 (inside the town hall); www.chania.eu

Ruled by Venice from 1204 to 1645, Haniá is dotted with elegant houses, churches, and fortifications from this period, especially in the Venetian quar-ter around the harbor, and in the charming Splántzia district. The Küçük Hasan Mosque, on one side of the harbor, was built in 1645–8 and is the old-est Ottoman building on Crete. The nearby covered market is also interesting to explore.

Some 2 miles (4 km) west of Haniá is the popular sandy beach of Agii Apóstoli.

---

⑥

Samariá Gorge

⌂ 27 miles (44 km) S of Haniá ▦ To Xylóskalo ⛴ To Agía Rouméli 🕐 May-mid-Oct: 6am-4pm daily; Apr 10-30 & Oct 16-31: if weather permits

Crete's most spectacular scenery lies along the Samariá Gorge, the longest ravine in Europe. Starting from the Xylóskalo (Wooden Stairs), a 10-mile (16-km) trail leads to the seaside resort of Agía Rouméli. A truly impressive sight along the route is the Sideróportes, or Iron Gates, where the path squeezes between two towering walls of rock. Upon reaching Agía Rouméli, walkers can take a boat to Hóra Sfakíon, Soúgia, or Paleóhora to join the road and buses back to Haniá.

PRACTICAL
INFORMATION

Here you will find all the essential advice and information you will need before and during your stay in Greece.

Getting There

There are around 20 international airports in Greece that can be reached directly from Europe, including Athens and Thessaloníki on the mainland, plus Crete, Rhodes, Kos, Santoríni, Mýkonos, Kefaloniá, Zákynthos, and Corfu among the islands. From outside Europe, all scheduled flights to Greece arrive in Athens, and only a few airlines offer direct flights.

International buses connect Greece with Eastern Europe; there are no longer any services to northwestern Europe. There are also regular, year-round ferry crossings from Italy and Turkey to the Greek mainland and islands.

Personal Security

Greece is generally a safe country to travel in, but it is always a good idea to take sensible precautions against pickpockets. If you have anything stolen, report the crime as soon as possible to the nearest police station. Get a copy of the crime report in order to claim on your insurance.

Health

Pharmacies, indicated by a green cross, have medicinal supplies available at accessible prices without prescriptions. When they are shut, a notice on the door will list the nearest duty pharmacist.

EU citizens with a European Health Insurance Card (EHIC) are entitled to free emergency medical care in Greece, but it is also advisable to take out some form of supplementary health insurance. Visitors from outside the EU must arrange their own private medical insurance.

Passports and Visas

Visitors from the US, Canada, Australia, and New Zealand do not need visas for stays of up to three months. EU nationals can stay in the country indefinitely. For visa information specific to your home country, consult your nearest Greek embassy.

LGBT+ Safety

Homosexuality is legal and widely accepted in Greece. However, smaller towns and rural areas are often more traditional in their views, and overt displays of affection may receive a negative response from locals.

Travelers with Specific Needs

Greece has made some progress in meeting the needs of travelers with accessibility requirements. All hotels must by law provide at least one wheelchair-adapted en-suite room, but compliance will vary. Most newer museums have disabled access. Many towns have ramps at pedestrian crossings but announcements for the visually impaired to cross safely are rare.

Money

Major credit and debit cards are accepted in most shops and restaurants, while prepaid currency cards are accepted in some, as are contactless credit cards. It is worth carrying some cash, as many smaller businesses and markets still operate on a cash-only policy.

Cell Phones and Wi-Fi

Visitors traveling to Greece with EU tariffs can use their devices without being affected by data roaming charges. If on Corfu (opposite Albania), or any Northeast Aegean or Dodecanese island (opposite Turkey), make sure that your phone does not use the non-EU network. Visitors from elsewhere should check their contracts before departure for potential charges.

All hotels and most *domátia* (rooms) or apartments have Wi-Fi, which is often free. Most cafés, tavernas, and bars have password-protected Wi-Fi.

Getting Around

A number of airlines offer internal flights in Greece, including to or between the islands. Fares, if booked far enough in advance, can cost little more than a bus or ferry journey.

Greece's rail network is operated by the state-owned **OSE** (Organismós Sidirodrómon Elládos). Limited to the mainland, it is fairly skeletal. First- and second-class tickets are less expensive than the equivalent bus journey, but services tend to be slower. The pricier intercity express trains are worth it for the time they save. Super-express "Silver Arrow" trains between Athens and Thessaloníki opened in 2019.

The long-distance bus network within Greece is extensive, with frequent express services on all major routes. From Athens, there are regular departures to all the larger mainland towns, apart from those in Macedonia and Thrace, which are served by buses from Thessaloníki.

Car rental agencies are found in every tourist resort and major town. The mainland's express highways are very fast, but expensive tolls are charged for their use. Roads on the islands can be poorly surfaced, particularly in more remote areas. Greece has a high accident rate, so take extra care when driving.

Athens' Piraeus port has ferry routes to most islands. Between them, **Hellenic Seaways** and **Blue Star** cover most of the Aegean, with **ANEK** and **Minoan Lines** serving Crete. All fares except first class are set by the Ministry of Transport, so a journey should cost the same whichever company you choose. In the off-season services may be reduced or suspended. Catamarans also ply the Argo-Saronic islands, the Cyclades, and the Dodecanese; they tend to be faster, but more expensive.

ANEK
W anek.gr
Blue Star
W bluestarferries.com
Hellenic Seaways
W hellenicseaways.gr
Minoan Lines
W minoan.gr
OSE
W trainose.gr

Visitor Information

The **Greek National Tourism Organization** (GNTO) has many resources for trip planning on its website. In Greece, tourist information is widely available from government-run EOT offices (Ellinikós Organismós Tourismoú), municipally run tourist offices, the local tourist police, or privately owned travel agencies.

Greek National Tourism Organization
W visitgreece.gr

GERMANY

Divided into small states for much of its history, the area that is now Germany has experienced a turbulent journey to unification. Germanic tribes initially became established in the region during the 1st millennium BC, going on to both clash and trade with the Romans. As the Roman Empire collapsed, the largest portion of land was inherited by the Franks, whose king was made emperor by the Pope. The power and wealth of the Catholic Church gave rise in 1517 to the 95 Theses of theologian Martin Luther, challenging the abuses of the clergy and setting in motion the Reformation. Religious differences were again a major factor in the Thirty Years' War (1618–48), which laid waste to most of Germany. In the 17th and 18th centuries Germany remained a patchwork of small states, but by 1871 Prussia had united the country and declared the start of the Second German Reich. The economy flourished, but imperialist tendencies began to grow, and tensions in European politics led to World War I. The humiliation of defeat and the terms of the Treaty of Versailles (1919) left Germany in economic chaos. The Weimar Republic struggled on until 1933 when Hitler seized power; his territorial ambitions led the country into World War II and a second defeat. The country subsequently became the theater for the Cold War, divided into East and West by the Berlin Wall. The fall of the Wall in 1989 marked the start of the process of reunification, and Germany's rise as one of today's major economic powers, with a prominent position in the EU.

GERMANY

1. Berlin
2. Potsdam
3. Dresden
4. Leipzig
5. Bayreuth
6. Weimar
7. Bamberg
8. Würzburg
9. Rothenburg ob der Tauber
10. Nürnberg
11. Munich
12. Passau
13. Neuschwanstein
14. Bodensee
15. Schwarzwald
16. Freiburg im Breisgau
17. Stuttgart
18. Trier
19. Mosel Valley
20. Mainz
21. Heidelberg
22. Rhine Valley
23. Bonn
24. Koblenz
25. Köln
26. Frankfurt am Main
27. Bremen
28. Münster
29. Hannover
30. Lübeck
31. Hamburg

↑ The Neo-Classical architecture of the Brandenburg Gate, topped by the *quadriga* chariot

❶
BERLIN

❌🏠🚗 ℹ️ www.visitberlin.de

Few European cities have witnessed as much upheaval and renewal as Berlin. From Prussian powerhouse and Nazi bastion to Cold War zombie and revitalized capital of a reunited Germany – Berlin has seen it all, and then some. Today the city thrums with a vibrant alternative spirit, thrillingly manifest in edgy nightlife and exciting art scenes. The main sights are located around Unter den Linden and Museuminsel in the historic center, leading out to cool neighborhoods such as Kreuzberg and leafy green spaces such as Tiergarten.

①
Brandenburg Gate

🏛 Pariser Platz
🚇/Ⓢ Brandenburger Tor
🚌 100, TXL

The Brandenburg Gate is the quintessential symbol of Berlin. This Neo-Classical structure was designed by Carl Gotthard Langhans and modeled on the Propylaea of the Acropolis in Athens (*p448*). It was erected between 1788 and 1791, although the sculptural decorations were not completed until 1795.

Pavilions frame its simple Doric colonnade, and bas-reliefs on the entablature above the columns depict scenes from Greek myth. The structure is crowned by the famous sculpture of a *quadriga* – a chariot drawn by four horses – designed by local sculptor Johann Gottfried Schadow.

The Brandenburg Gate has witnessed many key historical events. Military parades and demonstrating workers have marched under its arches, and it was the site of celebrations marking the birth of the

Deutsches Reich in 1871. It was here, too, that the Soviet flag was raised in 1945.

Restored between 1956 and 1958, for the next 30 years the gate stood watch over the divided city, until the fall of the Berlin Wall in 1989. It was renovated once again in 2002.

Unter den Linden

 Brandenburger Tor
100, 200, TXL

Unter den Linden was once the route to the royal hunting grounds that became the Tiergarten. In the 1600s, it was planted with lime trees, to which it owes its name ("under the lime trees").

In the 18th century, Unter den Linden became the main thoroughfare of the westward-growing city. The street gradually filled with prestigious buildings, such as the Baroque

---

> 💬 **INSIDER TIP**
> **Getting Around**
>
> U- and S-Bahn trains are the quickest way of getting around, as buses are reliable but slow. Trams are another useful option, especially in the east of the city. The same tickets are valid on buses, trams, and S-Bahn lines.

Zeughaus, a former arsenal now home of the Deutsches Historisches Museum, and the Humboldt Universität (1753). Next door, the Neue Wache memorial commemorates the victims of war and dictatorship.

---

③

Reichstag

🏛 **Platz der Republik**
Brandenburger Tor, Bundestag Ⓢ **Brandenburger Tor** **100, 200, TXL** 🕐 **Dome & Assembly Hall: 8am–midnight daily** 🚫 **Dec 24 & 31** 🌐 **bundestag. de/en/visittheBundestag**

Constructed to house the German parliament, the Reichstag was built between 1884 and 1894 to a Neo-Renaissance design by Paul Wallot. In 1933 fire destroyed the main hall, and World War II delayed rebuilding for years. The structure underwent a partial restoration in the 1960s, which included the controversial removal of most of the ornamentation

↑ Inside the Reichstag's glass dome, designed by Norman Foster

on the facade. After German reunification in 1990, the Reichstag once again became the home of the German parliament. The magnificent glass dome was added in 1999 by British architect Norman Foster.

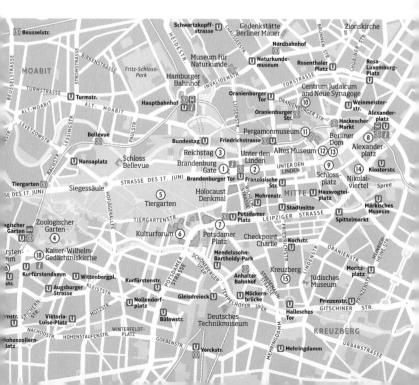

④

Zoologischer Garten

📍Hardenbergplatz 8/
Budapester Straße 34
Ⓤ/Ⓢ Zoologischer Garten
🚌100, 200, 204, 249, & many
others ⏰Hours vary, check
website 🌐 zoo-berlin.de

The Zoological Garden forms
part of the Tiergarten. Its
attractions include the mon-
key house, which contains a
family of gorillas, and a darkened pavilion for observing
nocturnal animals. A glazed
wall in the hippopotamus
pool enables visitors to watch
these enormous creatures
moving through the water.
The aquarium contains sharks,
piranhas, and unusual animals
from coral reefs. There is also
a huge terrarium with an over-
grown jungle that is home to
a group of crocodiles.

⑤

Tiergarten

Ⓢ Tiergarten, Bellevue
🚌100, 200

Situated at the heart of the
city, the Tiergarten bursts to
life with gardens, meadows,
and lakes threaded together
with pleasant pathways. Once
a hunting reserve, the area
was transformed into a landscaped park in the 1830s, with
a triumphal avenue – lined
with statues of the nation's
rulers and statesmen – added
at the end of the 19th century.
The park sustained serious
damage during World War II,
but has since been restored
by replanting.

The Tiergarten's southern
fringe borders the bustling
areas of Potsdamer Platz and
the Kulturforum, while the
northern edge runs parallel
to important sights like the
Reichstag. Beyond the park's
eastern edge is the moving
Holocaust Denkmal. Designed
by architect Peter Eisenman,
this wave-like monument
symbolizes the overwhelming
scale of the Holocaust.

⑥

Kulturforum

📍Matthäikirchplatz
Ⓤ/Ⓢ Potsdamer Platz
🌐 smb.museum

The idea of creating a new
cultural center in West Berlin
was first mooted in 1956. The
first building to go up was the
Philharmonie concert hall,
built to an innovative design
by Hans Scharoun in 1961.
Most of the other plans for
the Kulturforum were realized
between 1961 and 1987.

The **Kunstgewerbemuseum**
(Museum of Arts and Crafts)
holds a lavish collection of
decorative art and crafts that
date from the early Middle
Ages to the modern day.
Goldwork is very well represented, as is Late Gothic and
Renaissance silver, with many

Relaxing on a summer
day at the Café am Neuen
See, in the Tiergarten ↓

The night-time
neon illuminations
of Potsdamer Platz

Potsdamer Platz

U/⑤Potsdamer Platz 🚌200

There is no better place to experience the vibrant energy of Berlin than Potsdamer Platz. Originally a green park, the square evolved into a major traffic hub in the 19th century, with the construction of a railroad station. During the Roaring Twenties it was Europe's busiest plaza and a bustling entertainment center, frequented by famous artists and authors. The square was almost completely destroyed during World War II and was left as a derelict wasteland for decades. Redevelopment began in 1992, with a total investment of $25 billion.

Today the city's old hub is a thriving financial and business complex. It features an array of entertainment, shopping, and dining opportunities in splendid modern buildings designed by architects such as Renzo Piano, Helmut Jahn, and Arata Isozaki. Highlights include the Sony Center and the Kohloff Tower.

fine pieces from Lüneburg. The fashion gallery contains costumes and accessories from the 18th to 20th centuries.

The **Gemäldegalerie**'s fine art collection is in a modern building designed by Heinz Hilmer and Christopher Sattler, with galleries stretching over 1 mile (2 km). Works by German Renaissance artists, including Hans Holbein and Albrecht Dürer, dominate the exhibition space, but there are also pieces by Van Dyck, Raphael, Velázquez, and Caravaggio, plus one of the world's largest Rembrandt collections.

Housed in an eye-catching building designed by Mies van der Rohe, the **Neue National-galerie** contains mainly 20th-century art. German art is well represented in the collection: as well as pieces produced by the Bauhaus movement, the gallery shows works by exponents of a crass realism, such as Otto Dix. The sculpture garden houses figurative and abstract works.

Philharmonie
🅦 berliner-philharmoniker.de

Kunstgewerbemuseum
⊛ ⊜ 🄰 🄲 ⏰10am–6pm Tue–Fri, 11am–6pm Sat & Sun
🗓Dec 24 & 31

Gemäldegalerie
⊛ ⏰10am–6pm Tue–Fri (to 8pm Thu), 11am–6pm Sat & Sun 🗓Dec 24 & 31

Neue Nationalgalerie
🗓For renovations

BERLIN WALL

Initially the border between East and West Berlin consisted of barbed wire, but this was replaced by a tall concrete wall and a second border wall. Alongside ran the so-called "death zone," controlled by guards with dogs, with 293 watchtowers, 57 bunkers, and alarms. The longest surviving stretch of the Berlin Wall is the East Side Gallery - it is also the most colorful, thanks to the many paintings that adorn its surface.

GREAT VIEW
Fernsehturm

By far the best view of Berlin is from the viewing gantry of the TV tower. It's Europe's highest publicly accessible building and provides panoramic views of the German capital in its entirety.

 ⑧

Alexanderplatz

Ⓤ/Ⓢ Alexanderplatz
🚊 M2, M4, M5, M6 🚌 100, 200, M48, TXL

Alexanderplatz, or "Alex" as it is known locally, has a long history, although it is difficult now to find any visible traces of the past. Once the site of a cattle and wool market, it was later renamed after Czar Alexander I, who visited Berlin in 1805. Houses and stores sprang up along with a market hall and rail station, and by the early 20th century it was one of the city's busiest spots. World War II erased most of the square's older buildings and it is now surrounded by 1960s edifices, including the Park Inn and the Fernsehturm. The area bustles with stores, cinemas, and restaurants, as well as seasonal markets.

 ⑨

Schlossplatz

Ⓢ Hackescher Markt
🚌 100, 200

This square was once the site of a vast residential complex known as the Stadtschloss (City Palace), which served as the main residence of the Brandenburg rulers. The palace partly burned down during World War II and was demolished in 1950–51. The square was renamed Marx-Engels-Forum while it was under East German control, but reverted to its original name of Schlossplatz in 1989.

After a lengthy debate, it was decided to rebuild the palace as the **Humboldt Forum**, a museum complex with three reconstructed historical facades and a modern one. Opening in 2020, it will eventually house the Dahlem Museums' overseas collections, the Humboldt Laboratory research center, and the Berlin Exhibition, featuring interactive displays on the city's history.

The complex was named after two of Berlin's most prominent intellectuals: Wilhelm and Alexander von Humboldt.

Humboldt Forum
🌐 humboldtforum.com

 ⑩

Centrum Judaicum and Neue Synagoge

🏛 Oranienburger Straße 28 & 30 Ⓢ Oranienburger Straße 🚊 1, M1, M5 🕐 Apr-Sep: 10am-6pm Sun-Fri (to 7pm Sun); Oct-Mar: 10am-6pm Sun-Fri (to 3pm Fri); 🚫 Jewish hols 🌐 centrum judaicum.de

Housed in the former premises of the Jewish community council, the Centrum Judaicum (Jewish Center) contains an extensive library, archives, and a research center devoted to the history and cultural heritage of the Jews of Berlin. The Center also uses the restored rooms of the adjoining Neue Synagoge as a museum, exhibiting material relating to the local Jewish community.

The history of the New Synagogue dates back to 1859. Its narrow facade – flanked by a pair of towers and crowned with a gilded dome – was a response to the asymmetrical plot of land on which it sits. The structure was Berlin's largest synagogue until it was damaged first during the infamous

↓ The Fernsehturm, visible from almost any point in Berlin

↑ Visitors in front of the Pergamon Altar, which gives the Pergamonmuseum its name

"Kristallnacht" ("Night of the Broken Glass") in 1938 and then by Allied bombing in 1943. Eventually demolished, it was rebuilt in 1995.

Pergamonmuseum

🏛 Bodestraße (entrance from Am Kupfergraben) 🚇 Friedrichstrasse 🚈 Hackescher Markt, Friedrichstrasse 🚌 100, 200, TXL 🕙 10am–6pm daily (to 8pm Thu) 🚫 Dec 24 🌐 smb.museum

Built between 1912 and 1930 to a design by Alfred Messel and Ludwig Hoffmann, the Pergamonmuseum is one

of Berlin's major attractions. Its three large independent collections together form one of Europe's most famous archives of antiquities.

A highlight of the Greek and Roman antiquities collection (Antikensammlung) is the huge Pergamon Altar from the acropolis of ancient Pergamon in Turkey. Also impressive is the 2nd-century market gate from the Roman city of Miletus.

Major excavations begun in the 1820s form the basis of the Museum of Near Eastern Antiquities (Vorderasiatisches Museum). One particularly striking exhibit is the Ishtar Gate, built during the reign of Nebuchadnezzar II (604–562 BC) in ancient Babylon. There are also pieces from Persia, Syria, and Palestine, including a basalt sculpture of a bird from Tel Halaf and a glazed wall relief from Artaxerxes II's palace in Susa, capital of the Persian Empire.

The final collection here is that of the Museum of Islamic Art (Museum für Islamische Kunst). It began in 1904, with a large collection of carpets donated by Wilhelm von Bode – who also brought a 150-ft (45-m) section of the facade of a Jordanian desert palace. Today the museum displays a diverse array of fascinating objects, including pages of the Koran, prayer rugs, and a beautiful 13th-century *mihrab* (Islamic prayer niche).

Altes Museum

🏛 Am Lustgarten 🚇 Friedrichstrasse 🚈 Hackescher Markt 🚊 M4, M5, M6 🚌 100, 200 🕙 10am–6pm Tue–Sun (to 8pm Thu) 🚫 Dec 24 & 31 🌐 smb.museum

The Altes Museum, designed by Karl Friedrich Schinkel, is one of the world's finest Neo-Classical structures.

Officially opened in 1830, this was one of the earliest purpose-built museums in Europe, designed to house the royal collection of paintings and antiquities. Since 1998, the Altes Museum has housed a portion of the Antiken-sammlung, a magnificent collection of Greek, Etruscan, and Roman antiquities. Among the highlights are a colorful floor mosaic from Hadrian's Villa near Tivoli, and Perikles' Head, a Roman copy of the sculpture by Kresilas that stood at the entrance to the Acropolis in Athens.

> ### TREASURE ISLAND
>
> At the eastern end of Unter den Linden lies Museuminsel (Museum Island), home to some of the world's greatest museums, including the Altes Museum and the Pergamonmuseum. Museumsinsel is the northern part of the island in the River Spree, where the city was first settled. The idea for the museums came from King Friedrich Wilhelm III who, in 1830, commissioned what would become the Altes Museum to make his personal art collection available to the public. More museums followed to host finds from German archaeological digs in Egypt, Turkey, and Asia Minor.

⑬ ⌖

BERLINER DOM

🏠 Am Lustgarten Ⓢ Hackescher Markt 🚌 100, 200 🕐 9am-8pm
Mon-Sat, noon-8pm Sun (Oct-Mar: to 7pm) 🌐 berlinerdom.de

Picturesquely located on the east bank of the River Spree, the exquisitely restored Berlin Cathedral is the largest and most lavish church in the city.

Designed by Julius Raschdorf and constructed between 1894 and 1905, this cathedral is unusually ornate for a Protestant church. The building incorporates the crypt of the powerful Hohenzollern dynasty, which ruled Berlin for nearly 500 years, and their aspirations to power are reflected in lavish features such as the black marble imperial staircase. Following severe damaged sustained in World War II, the cathedral has been restored in a simplified form, but still contains some original features like the pulpit and altar, and beautiful reconstructed mosaics.

The mosaics of the Four Evangelists in the smaller niches were designed by Woldemar Friedrich.

Figures of the Apostles

At the base of the arcade stand statues of church reformers and princes who supported the Reformation.

The impressive, richly decorated interior was designed by Julius Raschdorff at the turn of the 20th century.

Wilhelm Sauer's organ has an exquisitely carved case. The instrument contains some 7,200 pipes.

270

The number of steps up to the dome's walkway, with great views over Museumsinsel.

Main entrance

The imperial Hohenzollern family crypt contains 100 sarcophagi, including that of Prince Friedrich Ludwig.

Neo-Baroque pulpit

EXPERIENCE Germany

GREAT VIEW
Light Show

For ten days in October, Berlin gets a kaleidoscopic remix during the annual Festival of Lights, when famous sights like the Berliner Dom become canvases for creative light shows.

The stained glass in the windows of the apses, designed by Anton von Werner, shows scenes from the life of Jesus.

↑ Changing light and video projections on the facade of the cathedral during the annual Festival of Lights

The main altar, saved from the previous cathedral, is the work of Friedrich August Stüler and dates from 1850.

The sarcophagi of Friedrich I and his wife were designed by Andreas Schlüter.

↑ A cross-section of the richly decorated interior of the Berliner Dom

↑ The impressive Neo-Renaissance interior, featuring some extravagant furnishings and impressive decorations

DOME MOSAICS

Look up at the interior of the dome to marvel at Anton Von Werner's intricate mosaics. All but destroyed during World War II, von Werner's original designs were used by Tuscan company Ferrari & Bacci to reproduce the mosaics between 1975 and 2002.

⑭
Nikolaiviertel

🚇 Alexanderplatz, Kloster-
straße 🚆 Alexanderplatz
🚌 100, 200, 248, M48, TXL
🌐 berlin.nikolaiviertel.com

This small area on the bank
of the Spree, known as the
Nikolaiviertel (St. Nicholas
Quarter), is a favorite strolling ground for both Berliners
and visitors. Some of Berlin's
oldest houses stood here until
they were destroyed in World
War II. The redevelopment of
the area in the 1980s proved
to be an interesting, if somewhat controversial, attempt at
recreating a medieval village.
Today, the area consists mostly
of replicas of historic buildings, along narrow streets
filled with small shops, cafés,
bars, and restaurants.

⑮
Kreuzberg

Kreuzberg is an area
full of contrasts,
with luxury apart-
ments standing
alongside
dilapidated
buildings.
This

CLUBBING IN
BERLIN

Berlin and electronic
music have gone
hand in hand since
the Berlin Wall fell
to the bass-heavy
sound of underground
techno. House and
techno still rule the
roost, with clubs like
Berghain, Watergate,
and Villa Renate in the
area around Kreuzberg
now legendary for
hosting parties that
can last for days.

dynamic district is packed
with restaurants and Turkish
bazaars, as well as theaters,
cinemas, and galleries.

Key sights here include
Checkpoint Charlie, the
notorious border crossing
between East and West Berlin,
which witnessesed several
dramatic events during the
Cold War. The museum close
by, **Mauermuseum – Museum
Haus am Checkpoint Charlie**,
houses exhibits connected
with the ingenious
attempts by
East Germans
to escape to
the West.

Also in this neighborhood
is the **Jüdisches Museum**,
Europe's largest museum
dedicated to Jewish history
and art. Designed by Daniel
Libeskind, a Polish-Jewish
architect based in the United
States, the museum's imaginative architecture conveys
something of the tragic history of the millions of Jews
who lost their lives in the
Holocaust. The zigzag layout
recalls a torn Star of David,
while the interior is dominated by a long empty area,
which symbolizes the void
left in Europe by the exile
and murder of countless
thousands of Jews.

**Mauermuseum -
Museum Haus am
Checkpoint Charlie**
♿🚾 📍 Friedrichstraße
43-45 🚇 Kochstraße
🚌 M29, N6 🕐 9am-10pm
daily 🌐 mauer museum.de

Jüdisches Museum
♿🚊🚾🅿 📍 Lindenstraße
14 🚇 Hallesches Tor, Kochstraße 🚌 248 🕐 10am-8pm
daily 🌐 jmberlin.de

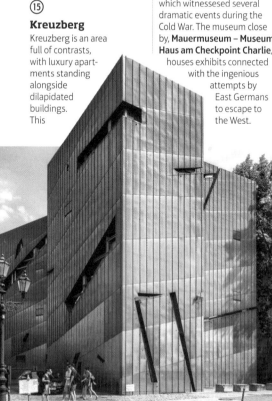

←
The stark metal facade
of the Jüdisches Museum,
in the Kreuzberg district

Christ figure in the Kaiser-Wilhelm-Gedächtniskirche, and *(inset)* its iconic ruined tower

⑯ Kurfürstendamm

 Kurfürstendamm
🚌 204, 249, M0, M19, M29, M46, N9, X10

Established in the 1880s, this wide avenue was the site of a former track that led to the Grunewald forest *(p492)*. It quickly acquired many imposing buildings and grand hotels. In the 20 years between World Wars I and II, the Ku'damm, as it is popularly called, was renowned for its cafés, which were visited by famous film directors, writers, and painters.

After World War II, new buildings replaced the damaged houses, but this did not change the character of the street. Elegant shops and pretty cafés still attract a chic crowd.

⑰ Museum Berggruen

🏛 Schlossstraße 1
 Richard-Wagner-Platz, Sophie-Charlotte-Platz
Ⓢ Westend 🚌 109, 309, M45 🕐 10am–6pm Tue–Sun
🌐 smb.museum

This museum's collection of artworks, dating from the late 19th and first half of the 20th centuries, was assembled by the German collector Heinz Berggruen. A highlight is the array of paintings, drawings, and gouaches by Pablo Picasso. There is also a display of more than 20 works by Paul Klee and paintings by Van Gogh, Braque, and Cézanne.

The Sammlung Scharf-Gerstenberg, opposite, exhibits pieces by the Surrealists and their predecessors.

⑱ Kaiser-Wilhelm-Gedächtniskirche

🏛 Breitscheidplatz
Ⓤ Zoologischer Garten, Kurfürstenstraße
Ⓢ Zoologischer Garten
🚌 100, 200, X9 🕐 9am–7pm daily 🌐 gedaechtnis kirche-berlin.de

The damaged roof of this former church has become one of the best-known symbols of postwar Berlin. The vast Neo-Romanesque building was consecrated in 1895, but was almost completely destroyed by Allied bombs in 1943. After World War II, the ruins were removed, leaving only the huge front tower. In 1963, it was joined by a new octagonal church in blue glass, designed by German architect Egon Eiermann. His freestanding hexagonal bell tower stands on the site of the former nave of the destroyed church.

At the base of the remains of the original tower is the Gedenkhalle (Memorial Hall). This exhibition space documents the history of the church and contains some of the original ceiling mosaics, marble reliefs, and liturgical objects. The latter include the Coventry Crucifix, a modest cross fashioned from nails found in the ashes of Coventry Cathedral, England, which was destroyed in the bombing raids of the 1940s.

Schloss Charlottenburg

🏛 Spandauer Damm
Ⓤ Richard-Wagner-Platz, Sophie-Charlotte-Platz
Ⓢ Westend 🚌109, 309, M45 🚌 Schlossbrücke
🕐 Hours vary, check website 🌐 spsg.de/charlottenburg

The large, elegant palace in Charlottenburg was intended as a summer residence for Sophie Charlotte, Elector Friedrich III's wife, who died aged 36 in 1705. Construction began in 1695 to a design by Johann Arnold Nering. Between 1701 and 1713, the palace was enlarged, and an orangery and a Baroque cupola were added. Further extensions were undertaken by Frederick the Great (King Friedrich II), who added the Neuer Flügel (New Wing) between 1740 and 1746.

Restored to its former elegance after World War II, the palace's richly decorated

A romantic bridge in the gardens of Schloss Charlottenburg ↓

interior is unequalled in Berlin. In the central section of the palace, the mirrored gallery of the Porzellankabinett has walls lined with fine Japanese and Chinese porcelain.

The Neuer Flügel used to house the Galerie der Romantik. The former private apartment of Friedrik the Great, it now has displays of the king's exquisite furniture. (This wing has a separate entrance from the main section of the palace, and requires a separate ticket.)

The Orangery was originally used to protect rare plants during the winter, but in the summer months was used as a setting for court festivities and entertainment. It has been rebuilt and is now a concert and events venue.

The park surrounding the palace is one of the most picturesque places in Berlin. Among the fine monuments dotted around the grounds are the Neo-Classical Neuer Pavillon (New Pavilion, 1824–5), whose interior is furnished in period style, and the Belvedere (1788), housing a large collection of porcelain. Note that the Belvedere is only accessible to the public from April to October.

Grunewald

Ⓢ Grunewald 🚌115

Just a short S-Bahn ride from central Berlin lie the vast forests of the Grunewald, bordering some of the city's most elegant suburbs. Once the haunt of politicians, wealthy industrialists, and renowned artists, some of the villas here now serve as the headquarters of Berlin's academic institutes.

On the shore of the picturesque Grunewaldsee is the **Jagdschloss Grunewald**, one of the oldest civic buildings in Berlin. Built by Elector Joachim II in 1542, this hunting lodge was reconstructed in the Baroque style around 1700. Inside the diminutive palace is Berlin's only surviving Renaissance hall, which houses canvases by Rubens and Van Dyck, among others. Opposite the Jagdschloss, the **Jagdzeugmagazin** (Hunting Museum) holds displays of historic hunting equipment. Just 2 miles (4 km) away is the Waldmuseum, the only museum devoted to forest life in the Berlin area.

↑ Paintings by Karl Schmidt-Rottluff lining the walls at the Brücke-Museum, Dahlem

To the southwest of the Grunewaldsee is Forsthaus Paulsborn. This picturesque former hunting lodge, which now houses a restaurant, was constructed in 1905.

Jagdschloss Grunewald & Jagdzeugmagazin

 Apr–Oct: 10am–7:30pm Tue–Sun; Mar, Nov, & Dec: 10am–4pm Sat & Sun ◷ Jan & Feb ⓦ spsg.de/jagdschloss-grunewald

---

㉑

Dahlem

Ⓤ Dahlem Dorf 🚌 101, 110, X11, X83

First mentioned in 1275, by the 19th century Dahlem had grown from a small village into an affluent suburb. In the early 20th century, a number of museums, designed by Bruno Paul, were built. They were extended in the 1960s, when the Museumszentrum was created to rival East Berlin's Museuminsel.

This cluster of museums, which includes the Museum of Ethnography and the Exhibition of Native North American Cultures, plus the Museum of Asian Art, are in the process of moving to the Humboldt Forum (p486).

What will remain in Dahlem is the **Museum Europäischer Kulturen**, which specializes in European culture and folk art.

Domäne Dahlem is an oasis of country life in the Berlin suburbs. This Baroque manor house (c. 1680) has splendid period interiors, and its 19th-century farm buildings and courtyard host regular artisans' markets. There is also a petting zoo for children.

The elegant Functionalist building occupied by the **Brücke-Museum** was built by Werner Düttmann in 1966–7. Today, the museum houses German Expressionist paintings by members of the artistic group known as *Die Brücke* (The Bridge), which originated in Dresden in 1905.

Museum Europäischer Kulturen

⊕ ⊕ Arnimallee 25 ◷ 10am–5pm Tue–Fri, 11am–6pm Sat & Sun ◷ Dec 24 & 31 ⓦ smb.museum

Domäne Dahlem

⊕ ⊕ ⊕ Königin-Luise-Straße 49 ◷ Hours vary, check website ⓦ domaene-dahlem.de

Brücke-Museum

⊕ Bussardsteig 9 ◷ 11am–5pm Wed–Mon ⓦ bruecke-museum.de

Looking over the main square in Potsdam's historic center ↑

②

POTSDAM

 Brandenburg ⑤ S1, S7 🚌🚋 Ⓦ potsdam.de

An independent city close to Berlin, Potsdam has almost 160,000 inhabitants and is the capital of Brandenburg. The city was a splendid center of the Enlightenment, which reached its architectural and artistic climax in the 18th century with Frederick the Great's palace of Sanssouci – today a UNESCO World Heritage Site that draws millions of visitors. Elsewhere, this former garrison town has plenty of lower-key delights, including small palaces, old churches, idyllic parks, and historic immigrant settlements.

① 🏃

Marmorpalais

🏛 Am Ufer des Heiligen Sees (Neuer Garten) 🚌 692, 695 Ⓒ Hours vary, check website Ⓦ spsg.de/marmorpalais

The Marmorpalais (Marble Palace) is located on the edge of the lake in the Neuer Garten, a park northeast of Potsdam's center. Completed in 1791, the grand Neo-Classical building owes its name to the Silesian marble that decorates its facade. The rooms in the main part of the palace contain Neo-Classical furnishings from the late 18th century, including Wedgwood porcelain and furniture from the workshops of Roentgen. The concert hall in the right wing, whose interior dates from the 1840s, is particularly impressive.

② 🏃

Schloss Cecilienhof

🏛 Am Neuen Garten 🚌 692, 695 Ⓒ Hours vary, check website Ⓦ spsg.de/cecilienhof

Schloss Cecilienhof was built for the Hohenzollern family between 1914 and 1917. It was designed by Paul Schultze-Naumburg in the style of an English country manor and is a sprawling, asymmetrical building with wooden beams that make a pretty herring-bone pattern on its walls. In July 1945, the palace played an important role in history, when it served as the venue for the Potsdam Conference. Today, the palace houses a museum as well as a hotel.

③

Alexandrowka

🏛 Russische Kolonie Allee/Puschkinallee 🚌 604, 609, 629 🚋 92 Ⓒ Apr-Oct: 10am-6pm Thu-Tue; Mar: 10am-6pm Fri-Sun Ⓦ alexandrowka.de

A trip to the charming village of Alexandrowka, north of Potsdam's center, takes visitors into the world of Pushkin's fairy-tales. Wooden log cabins, set in their own gardens, form a delightful residential estate. The houses were built in 1826 for singers in a Russian choir established to entertain military troops. Peter Joseph Lenné was responsible for the overall look of the estate, which was named after a Prussian princess.

THE POTSDAM CONFERENCE

On July 17, 1945 the heads of government of Great Britain, the United States, and the Soviet Union met in Schloss Cecilienhof to confirm the decisions made earlier that year at Yalta. They decided to abolish the Nazi Party, limit the size of the German militia, punish war criminals, and establish reparations. The conference played a major part in establishing a political balance of power in Europe.

④
Holländisches Viertel

🏠 Friedrich-Ebertstraße/Kurfürstenstraße/Hebbelstraße/Gutenbergstraße
🚌 138, 601, 602, 603, 604, & many others

The Dutch Quarter features stores, galleries, cafés, and beer cellars, especially along Mittelstraße. The area was built up in the early 18th century, when Dutch workers, invited by King Friedrich Wilhelm I, began to settle in Potsdam. Today, you can still see the pretty red-brick, gabled houses that were built for them.

---

⑤
Filmpark Babelsberg

🏠 Großbeerenstraße
🕐 Hours vary, check website
🔒 Mon & Fri in May & Sep
🌐 filmpark-babelsberg.de

This park was laid out on the site of the studios where Germany's first movies were made in 1912. From 1917, the studios belonged to Universum-Film-AG, which produced some of the most renowned movies of the silent era, such as Fritz Lang's futuristic *Metropolis* (1927). Later, Nazi propaganda films were also made here.

The studio is still in operation today, but part of the complex is open to the public. There are plenty of sets from old films to explore, as well as behind-the-scenes professionals who demonstrate their skills to visitors.

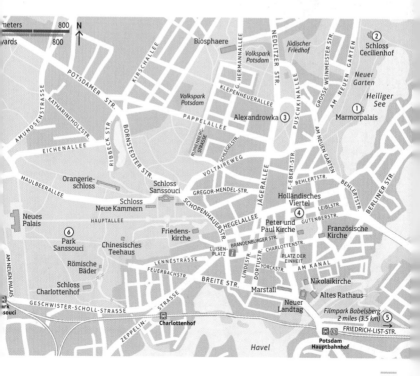

PARK SANSSOUCI

🏛 Schopenhauerstraße/Zur Historischen Mühle 🚌 605, 606, 612, 614, 695 🚊 91, 94, 96 🕐 Park: 8am–dusk daily; buildings: hours vary, check website 🌐 spsg.de

The enormous Park Sanssouci, covering an area of 709 acres (287 hectares), is among the most beautiful palace complexes in Europe. Built for Frederick the Great in 1745–7, its setting is straight out of a Romantic landscape painting.

It was Frederick himself who made the original sketches for this enchanting Rococo palace, whose name – *sans souci* is French for "without a care" – gives an indication of the building's flamboyant character. Over the years, the park has been enriched by several other palaces and pavilions. These include the Baroque Neues Palais, begun at the request of Frederick the Great in 1763, and Schloss Charlottenhof, a small Neo-Classical palace designed by Friedrich Schinkel and Ludwig Persius in 1829, in the style of a Roman villa. Today, the park is made up of small gardens dating from different eras, all maintained in their original style. The collection of buildings and gardens has been declared a UNESCO World Heritage Site.

It was Frederick the Great who made the original sketches for this Rococo palace, whose name – *sans souci* is French for "without a care" – hints at its flamboyant character.

← A tree-lined avenue in Park Sanssouci, with stairs leading to the palace

Neues Palais

▶ Decorated with hundreds of sculptures, this vast two-story building contains more than 200 richly adorned rooms. Especially unusual is the Grottensaal (Grotto Salon), where man-made stalactites hang from the ceiling.

Schloss Sanssouci

Schloss Sanssouci was built in 1745-7. The walls of the Konzertzimmer (Concert Hall) are lined with paintings by Antoine Pesne, but the greatest treasures are the paintings of *fêtes galantes* by Antoine Watteau, a favorite artist of Frederick the Great.

Orangerieschloss

◀ The highlight of this palace-cum-guest house is the Raphael Hall, decorated with copies of works by the great Italian Renaissance artist. The view from the observation terrace extends over Potsdam.

Schloss Charlottenhof

The rear of this diminutive palace has a portico that opens out onto the garden terrace. Some of the wall paintings, produced by Schinkel, are still in place.

Schloss Neue Kammern

▶ Originally built as an orangery for Schloss Sanssouci in 1747, the Neue Kammern (New Chambers) was remodeled as guest accommodations in 1777. The most impressive of its four elegant Rococo halls is the Ovidsaal, with its rich reliefs, vast mirror, and marble floors.

Bildergalerie

Constructed between 1755 and 1764 to a design by J. G. Buring, the Bildergalerie holds an exhibition of paintings once owned by Frederick the Great. Highlights of the collection include Caravaggio's *Doubting Thomas* (1597) and Guido Reni's *Cleopatra's Death* (1626), as well as a number of works by Rubens and Van Dyck.

❸

Dresden

⌂ Saxony ✕🚋🚌🚊
ℹ Neumarkt 2, QF passage, near Frauenkirche; www. dresden.de

Once one of Germany's most beautiful cities, Dresden blossomed during the 18th century, when it acquired many magnificent buildings. Almost all of these, however, were destroyed during Allied bombing raids in World War II. Today, restoration work is still in progress to return the city to its former glory.

The most celebrated building in Dresden is the Frauenkirche. The landmark Church of Our Lady (1726–43) was left in ruins during the Communist era to serve as a reminder of World War II damage, but reconstruction began after reunification. The church was finally reconsecrated in 2005, and now serves as a symbol of reconciliation between former warring nations.

The imposing Zwinger is a Baroque building constructed in 1709–32, with a spacious courtyard that is surrounded on all sides by galleries housing several

museums, including the **Gemäldegalerie Alte Meister**. This contains a particularly fine art collections, with works by Antoine Watteau, Rembrandt, Van Eyck, Vermeer, Velázquez, Raphael, Titian, and Albrecht Dürer.

Built in the 19th-century, the Sächsische Staatsoper (Saxon State Opera) has been the venue for many world premieres, including *The Flying Dutchman* and *Tannhäuser* by Wagner, as well as works by Richard Strauss.

Dresden's **Residenzschloss** was built in stages from the late 15th to the 17th centuries. The palace now houses some of the most beautiful art collections in eastern Germany, as well as the famous Grünes Gewölbe, a vast royal treasury. The nearby **Verkehrsmuseum**, originally designed as royal stables, has been a museum of transportation since 1956.

Once part of the town's fortifications, the Brühlsche Terrasse was subsequently transformed into magnificent gardens by Heinrich von Brühl. Today dubbed "the balcony of Europe," it is a popular place to promenade and people-watch, and to admire the splendid views over the Elbe river.

REBUILT FROM THE ASHES

Once known as the "Florence of the north," Dresden was one of Europe's most beautiful cities. Then, on the night of February 13, 1945, 800 British aircraft launched the first of five massive Allied firebomb raids on the city. The raids completely destroyed the greater part of Dresden, killing over 35,000 people, many of whom were refugees. Soon after the war, it was decided to restore the Zwinger palace and other historic buildings, and create a new city of modern developments on the leveled land around the old city center. Much of Dresden has now been reconstructed, though some reminders of the city's destruction remain.

← The Baroque Frauenkirche in Dresden, rebuilt after World War II

The Neo-Renaissance Albertinum houses several magnificent art collections, including the **Gemäldegalerie Neue Meister**, which holds paintings from the 19th century to the present day. These include landscapes by Caspar David Friedrich and works by Degas, Van Gogh, Manet, and Monet.

On the banks of the Elbe stands Schloss Pillnitz, the charming summer residence of Augustus the Strong. The main attraction here is the park, laid out in English and Chinese styles.

Meissen, 12 miles (19 km) northwest of Dresden, is noted for its porcelain manufacture. Overlooking the town is the **Albrechtsburg**, a vast fortified hilltop complex with a cathedral and a palace once used by the Electors. Europe's first porcelain factory was set up in the palace in 1710 but moved to Talstrasse in 1865. Documents relating to the history of the factory and examples of its products are on display in the palace rooms.

Gemäldegalerie Alte Meister

⊛ ◧ Theaterplatz 1 ◱ 10am–5pm Tue–Sun ⓦ skd.museum

Residenzschloss

⊛ ◧ Taschenberg 2 ◱ 10am–6pm Wed–Mon ⓦ skd.museum

Verkehrsmuseum

⊛ ◧ Augustusstrasse 1 ◱ 10am–5pm Tue–Sun ⓦ verkehrsmuseum-dresden.de

Gemäldegalerie Neue Meister

⊛ ◧ Tzschirnerplatz 2 ◱ 10am–6pm Tue–Sun ⓦ skd.museum

Albrechtsburg

⊛ ◧ Domplatz 1 ◱ 10am–6pm daily (Nov–Feb: to 5pm) 🗓 Jan 7–19, Dec 24 & 25 ⓦ albrechtsburg-meissen.de

④
Leipzig

◧ Saxony ✈🚆🚌
🛈 Katharinenstr 8; www.leipzig.de

One of Germany's leading commercial towns, Leipzig is an important center for the German book trade. Most of the interesting sights here can be found in the Old Town.

Lovers of Johann Sebastian Bach's music can visit the Thomaskirche (1482–96),

↑ The Mädler Passage Arcade in Leipzig's charming Old Town

where he was choirmaster from 1723 until his death in 1750. It now contains his tomb. The Bacharchive und Bachmuseum houses items relating to the composer.

Other notable attractions include the 16th-century Nikolaikirche (Church of St. Nicholas), the elegant Mädler Passage shopping arcade, and the grand Renaissance Altes Rathaus (Old Town Hall), which is now the municipal museum. The nearby **Museum der Bildenden Künste** has an excellent collection of German masters, including works by Caspar David Friedrich, Lucas Cranach the Elder, Van Eyck, Rubens, and Rodin.

The Grassimuseum complex to the east of the center houses three collections: a museum of ethnography, a museum of applied arts, and a museum of musical instruments.

Museum der Bildenden Künste

⊛⊛ ◧ Katharinenstr 10 ◱ Noon–8pm Wed, 10am–6pm Thu–Sun ⓦ mdbk.de

RICHARD WAGNER

The German composer is inseparable from Bayreuth, where he enjoyed his greatest triumphs. Wagner's career began in Magdeburg, Königsberg, and Riga. From there he fled to Paris to evade creditors, before his reputation was established by performances of his operas in Dresden. From 1872, Wagner lived in Bayreuth, where the Festspielhaus (Festival Theater) was built specifically for his operas.

5 Bayreuth

 Bavaria 🅿
ℹ Opernstrasse 22; www. bayreuth-tourismus.de

The German composer Richard Wagner lived in Bayreuth from 1872. The Villa Wahnfried, built for him by Carl Wölfel, today houses a museum dedicated to the musician. Nearby, the Franz-Liszt-Museum occupies the house where the Hungarian composer died in 1886.

Other sights of interest here include the Markgräfliches Opernhaus, the lavish Baroque opera house, and the Neues Schloss palace, constructed for Margravine Wilhelmine in the 1700s. The latter has fine Baroque and Rococo interiors and English-style gardens.

6 Weimar

 Thuringia 🅿🚌 ℹ Markt 10; www.weimar.de

Weimar was a significant center for German culture during a period that became known as the Golden Age, from 1758 to 1832. It continued to play a part in the lives of many influential artists and thinkers, and it was here that the Bauhaus School was founded in 1919. The city also gave its name to the Weimar Republic, the democratic German state which lasted from World War I to 1933.

Weimar is fairly small, and most of its museums are in the town center. To the north stands the Neues Museum, which holds a large collection of modern art. The nearby Stadtmuseum is devoted to Weimar's history, while the Goethe-Museum displays items associated with the famous writer.

The Neo-Classical Deutsches Nationaltheater, erected in 1906–7, was the venue for the world premiere of Wagner's *Lohengrin*. It was also here, in 1919, where the National Congress sat to pass the new constitution for the Weimar Republic government.

The ducal castle, Weimar Schloss (currently closed), was built for Duke Karl August and has original interiors and fine paintings by Dürer, Rubens, and Monet. Nearby is the Herzogin-Anna-Amalia Bibliothek, also known as the Grünes Schloss (Green Castle), which was converted into the duchess's library in 1761–6. It has a splendid Rococo interior. Farther south is the ducal summer residence of Schloss Belvedere (1724–32), set in an attractive park and containing fine collections of Rococo decorative art and vintage vehicles.

Bamberg

🏛 Bavaria ▣
ℹ Geyerswörth-straße 5;
www.bamberg.info

Bamberg's most interesting historical monuments are clustered around Domplatz, including the magnificent Cathedral of St. Peter and St. George. Begun around 1211, the cathedral combines the Late Romanesque and Early French-Gothic styles. The eastern choir contains the equestrian statue of the "Bamberg Rider" (1225–30), whose identity remains a mystery to this day.

The west side of Domplatz is flanked by the Alte Hof-haltung, the former bishop's residence. Built in the 15th and 16th centuries, it houses a museum of local history. The more recent Baroque Bishop's Palace (1763) stands behind the cathedral.

Also on Domplatz is the **Neue Residenz** (1695–1704), with its richly decorated apartments. Inside, the Staatsgalerie displays a collection of German Old Masters.

On the east side of the town is the Altes Rathaus (Old Town Hall). Originally Gothic in style, it was remodeled in 1744–56 by Jakob Michael Küchel. It has a striking facade of timbered beams and frescoes.

Neue Residenz

⊛ 🏛 Domplatz 8 🕒 Apr-Sep: 9am-6pm daily; Oct-Mar: 10am-4pm daily 🗺 residenz-bamberg.de

---

Würzburg

🏛 Bavaria ▣
ℹ Falkenhaus, Marktplatz 9; www.wuerzburg.de

On the bank of the Main river, Würzburg is an important cultural and commercial center, and home of the excellent Franconian wine.

The city's most impressive landmark is the **Residenz**, where Würzburg's prince-bishops lived from 1744. A highlight of this lavish Baroque palace is the huge Treppenhaus (staircase), by Balthasar Neumann, capped by a glorious ceiling fresco by Giovanni Battista Tiepolo.

Before the Residenz was built, the city's prince-bishops resided in the fortress known

↑ Looking toward the spires of Würzburg's charming Old Town

as the **Festung Marienberg**, which has stood on a hill over-looking the river since 1210. Inside the fortress is the **Main-fränkisches Museum**, which illustrates the history of the town and holds works by the German sculptor Tilman Riemenschneider.

Würzburg's cathedral, the Dom St. Kilian, dates from 1045 and is one of Germany's largest Romanesque churches. North of it is the 11th-century Basilica Neumünster. Its imposing Baroque dome and sandstone facade are 18th-century additions. The pictur-esque Rathaus (Town Hall) dates from the 13th century.

Residenz

⊛ 🏛 Residenzplatz 2 🕒 Apr-Oct: 9am-6pm daily; Nov-Mar: 10am-4:30pm daily 🗓 Jan 1, Shrove Tue, Dec 24, 25 & 31 🗺 residenz-wuerzburg.de

Festung Marienberg

⊛ ⊛ 🕒 Apr-Oct: 10am-4pm Tue-Fri; Nov-Mar: 11am-3pm Sat & Sun 🗺 schloesser. bayern.de

Mainfränkisches Museum

⊛ 🕒 10am-4pm Tue-Sun (Mar-Oct: to 5pm) 🗺 museum-franken.de

←
The orangery in the splendid park of the 18th-century Neues Schloss, Bayreuth

9

Rothenburg ob der Tauber

 Bavaria 🚗 ℹ️ Marktplatz 2; www.tourismus. rothenburg.de

Encircled by ramparts, Rothenburg is a perfectly preserved medieval town in a picturesque setting on the banks of the Tauber river.

At the heart of the town is Marktplatz, whose focal point is the Rathaus (Town Hall), which combines Renaissance and Gothic styles. Off the main square, St. Jakobs Kirche and the Franziskanerkirche both contain a variety of historical treasures.

Two museums of note here are the Reichsstadtmuseum, devoted to the town's history, and the Mittelalterliches Museum, which contains a large collection of medieval instruments of torture.

East of Marktplatz, through the Burgtor (a gate in the city walls), is Burggarten – a pretty garden with great views.

10

Nürnberg

Bavaria ✈️ 🚗 ℹ️ Königstraße 93; www. tourismus.nuernberg.de

The largest city in Bavaria after Munich, Nürnberg (known as Nuremberg in English) is loved for its delicious gingerbread and sausages. The town is also a symbol of Germany's long history, with its earliest records dating from 1050, when it was a trading settlement.

The city is divided in two by the Pegnitz river. In the southern half, the mighty Frauentor is one of several gateways along the massive 15th and 16th-century ramparts. A short walk away is the **Germanisches National-museum**. Founded in 1852, the museum houses a superb collection of antiquities from the German-speaking world, including masterworks by the sculptor Tilman Riemen-schneider, as well as paintings by Lucas Cranach the Elder and Albrecht Dürer.

 INSIDER TIP
Christmas Market

Each year, Nürnberg's Hauptmarkt provides a picturesque setting for the town's festive Christkindlesmarkt. Throughout Advent you can buy gingerbread, enjoy the taste of German sausages, warm yourself with a glass of mulled wine spiced with cloves, and buy a range of locally made souvenirs.

Overlooking the bustling Lorenzer Platz, the Gothic **St. Lorenz-Kirche** is one of the city's most important churches. Begun in 1243, it posseses some glorious stained-glass windows.

As you cross over the Pegnitz to the north side of town, look out for the Heilig-Geist-Spital (Hospital of the Holy Spirit), which dates from 1332 and spans

the river. Today it houses a restaurant serving local Frankish cuisine.

A major landmark north of the river is the Frauenkirche, commissioned by the Holy Roman Emperor Charles IV in the mid-14th century. Also of importance is the **Albrecht-Dürer-Haus**, where the celebrated Renaissance painter lived in 1509–28.

A climb up Burgstraße brings you to the Kaiserburg, the imperial castle complex. The oldest surviving part is a pentagonal tower, the Fünfeckturm, which dates from 1040. At its foot is the Kaiserstallung (Imperial Stables), now a youth hostel.

Nürnberg is famous for the Christkindlesmarkt, the lively Christmas fair held during Advent in the Hauptmarkt. Here you can warm yourself with a glass of hot red wine spiced with cloves and buy locally made crafts.

Germanisches Nationalmuseum
Kartaüsergasse 1
10am–6pm Tue–Sun (to 9pm Wed) gnm.de

St. Lorenz-Kirche
Burgstraße 1–3 9am–5:30pm Mon–Sat (to 7pm Thu), 10am–3:30pm Sun lorenzkirche.de

Albrecht-Dürer-Haus
Albrecht–Dürer–Straße 39 Hours vary, check website Dec 24 & 25 museen.nuernberg.de/duererhaus

←

Half-timbered buildings in the charming Old Town of Rothenburg ob der Tauber

↑ Nürnberg's Christmas market, illuminated by festive lights

TOP 3 NÜRNBERG CHURCHES

St. Martha
Königstraße 79
The small church of St. Martha dates from the 14th century. Despite being almost devoid of furnishings, it is worth a visit for the magnificent Gothic stained-glass windows.

Sebalduskirche
Winklerstraße 26
Completed in 1273, Sebalduskirche is the oldest church in Nürnberg. It houses many beautiful relics, including the bronze tomb of St. Sebald.

Frauenkirche
Hauptmarkt 14
Dating back to the 14th century, the Frauenkirche is renowned for the Männleinlaufen, a mechanical clock from 1509. Its plays a scene every day at noon.

 ⑪

MUNICH

 🏛Bavaria 🚇🚍🚃 ℹ️ www.muenchen.de

Founded in 1158, Munich became the capital of Bavaria in the 16th century. Its period of greatest growth was in the 19th century, when the city was developed along Neo-Classical lines – many of the grand buildings around Königsplatz and along Ludwigstrasse date from this time. As well as historic monuments, Munich has first-class museums and excellent shopping. It also hosts a world-famous annual beer festival, Oktoberfest.

① Marienplatz

Ⓤ/Ⓢ Marienplatz

In medieval times, this square was Munich's salt- and corn-market. In the center stands a column with a statue of the Virgin Mary dating from 1623. The walls of the Neo-Gothic Neues Rathaus (New Town Hall), built in 1867–1909, are adorned with statues of saints, Bavarian rulers, mythological figures, and gargoyles. At 11am and 5pm, the bells of the clock tower ring out a carillon, while figures of knights fight and a crowd dances. At the eastern end of the square is the Altes Rathaus (Old Town Hall), originally built in the late 15th century, but rebuilt many times since. The high tower, next to it, above the old city gate, was rebuilt in 1975 to a design based on pictures from 1493. Since 1983, the tower has been the home of the city's **Spielzeugmuseum** (Toy Museum).

Spielzeugmuseum
 ✎ 📞089-29 40 01
🕙10am–5:30pm daily

↑ The impressive Neues Rathaus, dominating Munich's Marienplatz

② Frauenkirche

🏛Frauenplatz 1
Ⓤ/Ⓢ Karlsplatz,
Marienplatz 🚋18, 19
🕙Church: 7:30am–8:30pm
daily ⏰ Tower: for resto-
ration and rebuilding
🌐muenchner-dom.de

Built by the architects Jörg von Halspach and Lukas Rottaler, the Frauenkirche (or Dom) was completed in 1488, although the copper onion domes were not added to its towers until 1525. The church is one of southern Germany's largest Gothic structures and can accommodate about 2,000 people. Its triple-naved hall has no transept and features long rows of side chapels and a gallery surrounding the choir. For a good view of central Munich, take an elevator to the top of one of the towers.

Partly demolished in 1944–5, the church was rebuilt after

World War II. Treasures held here include a painting of the Virgin by Jan Polack (c. 1500), the altar of St. Andrew in the Chapel of St. Sebastian, and Hans Krumpper's monumental tomb of Ludwig IV the Bavarian, the first member of the house of Wittelsbach to be elected Holy Roman Emperor.

💬 INSIDER TIP
Getting Around

Munich has efficient U- and S-Bahn train networks, plus buses and trams. There is a large pedestrianized zone at the heart of the city, making walking a pleasant alternative to public transportation.

③

Asamkirche

📍 Sendlinger Straße 32
Ⓤ Sendlinger Tor 🚌 52, 62
🚋 16, 17, 18, 27 🕐 9am–6pm daily

This extraordinary Rococo church is dedicated to St. John Nepomuk, but is known as the Asamkirche after the brothers Cosmas Damian and Egid Quirin Asam, who built it as a private family church. Completed in 1746, the tiny church is a riot of decoration with a dynamically shaped single nave, where no surface is left unembellished. The eye is drawn to the altar and its sculptural group of the Holy Trinity. The house next door to the church was the residence of Egid Quirin Asam, who was a stuccoist and sculptor.

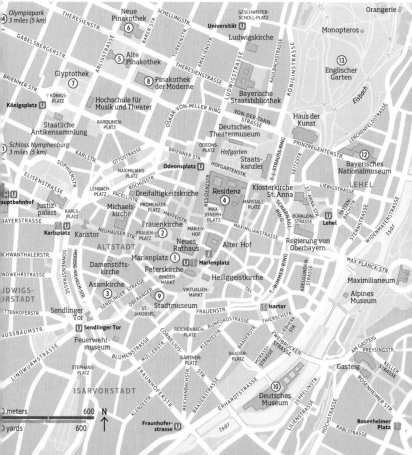

RESIDENZ

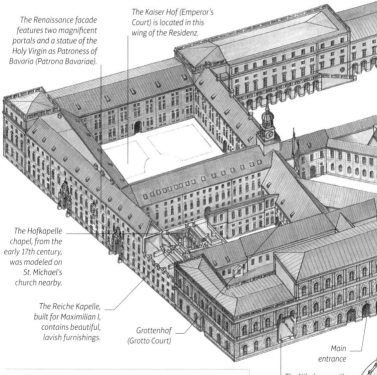

🏛 Residenzstrasse 1 Ⓤ Odeonsplatz 🕐 Apr-mid-Oct: 9am-6pm daily; mid-Oct-Mar: 10am-5pm daily 🚫 Jan 1, Shrove Tue, Dec 24, 25, & 31 🌐 residenz-muenchen.de

The largest city palace in Germany, this former residence of Bavarian kings has housed a museum since 1920 and is today one of the most eminent palace museums in Europe. Its attractions include a beautiful Renaissance facade, a splendid banqueting hall, and a range of gold and silver treasures.

The origins of Munich's Residenz go back to the 14th century, when a castle was built here for the Wittelsbach dynasty. In the following centuries, the fortress was replaced by a palace complex, which in turn was gradually modified and extended. Major work in the 17th century included the addition of two chapels, the Reiche Kapelle and the Hofkapelle. The Königsbau, containing the superb Nibelungensäle, was added by Leo von Klenze in the first half of the 1800s. In addition to the Residenzmuseum and the Schatzkammer (Treasury), there is a museum of Egyptian art, the Staatliches Museum Ägyptischer Kunst.

The center-piece of the Brunnenhof is an ornate fountain dedcated to the Wittelsbachs.

The Renaissance facade features two magnificent portals and a statue of the Holy Virgin as Patroness of Bavaria (Patrona Bavariae).

The Kaiser Hof (Emperor's Court) is located in this wing of the Residenz.

The Hofkapelle chapel, from the early 17th century, was modeled on St. Michael's church nearby.

The Reiche Kapelle, built for Maximilian I, contains beautiful, lavish furnishings.

Grottenhof (Grotto Court)

Main entrance

The Nibelungensäle, or Halls of the Nibelungs, is named for the wall paintings depicting the German epic, the Nibelungenlied.

STATUETTE OF ST. GEORGE

The most dazzling work in Room III of the Schatzkammer (Treasury) is a small equestrian statue of St. George (1586-97). The work of Friedrich Sustris, it was commissioned to house a relic of the saint. In the 17th century it was displayed in the Residenz on important feast days.

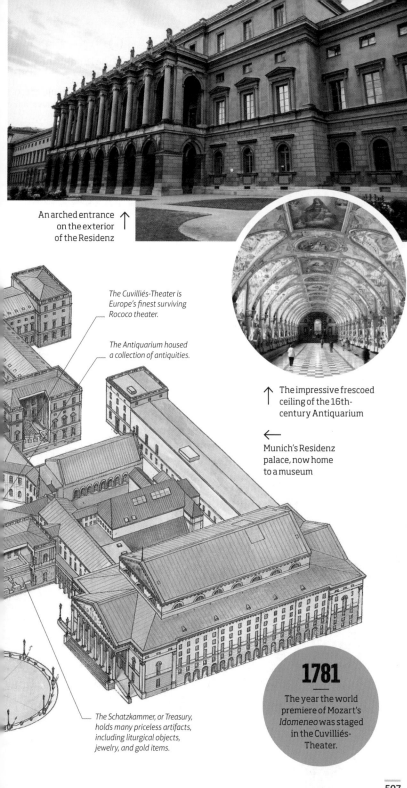

An arched entrance on the exterior of the Residenz →

The Cuvilliés-Theater is Europe's finest surviving Rococo theater.

The Antiquarium housed a collection of antiquities.

↑ The impressive frescoed ceiling of the 16th-century Antiquarium

← Munich's Residenz palace, now home to a museum

The Schatzkammer, or Treasury, holds many priceless artifacts, including liturgical objects, jewelry, and gold items.

1781

The year the world premiere of Mozart's *Idomeneo* was staged in the Cuvilliés-Theater.

⑤ Alte Pinakothek

Barer Straße 27
U Königsplatz 100
27, 28 10am-6pm
Tue-Sun (to 8pm Tue)
w pinakothek.de

This magnificent gallery is filled with masterpieces of European art, ranging from the Middle Ages to the mid-18th century. Started by Wilhelm IV the Steadfast, who ruled from 1508 to 1550, the collection was amassed by the Wittelsbach rulers of Bavaria. In the 19th century Ludwig I commissioned the Alte Pinakothek (Old Picture Gallery) to showcase the collection; it was designed in the form of a Florentine Renaissance *palazzo*. The ground floor is devoted to the works of German and Flemish Old Masters from the 16th and 17th centuries and on the first floor are Dutch, Flemish, French, German, Italian, and Spanish pieces.

Did You Know?

The Alte Pinakothek has the second-largest collection of Rubens paintings after Madrid's Prado Museum.

Of the German works, pride of place goes to Albrecht Dürer's famous *Self-Portrait* (1500) and two panels of an altarpiece showing *Four Apostles*. Among the other German artists represented are Lucas Cranach the Elder and Grünewald. Early Flemish masterpieces include *St. Luke Painting the Madonna* by Rogier van der Weyden, and works by Hans Memling and Pieter Brueghel the Elder.

Of later artists, the one with most works on display is the prolific Rubens. There are also interesting works by El Greco, Rembrandt, Raphael, Titian, and Tintoretto.

⑥ Neue Pinakothek

Barer Straße 29
U Theresienstraße 100
27, 28 For renovation
w pinakothek.de

Bavaria's collection of late-18th- and 19th-century European painting and sculpture usually occupies the purpose-built Neue Pinakothek, completed in 1981. However, while this gallery is being renovated, a selection of its artworks will be on display in the east wing of the Alte Pinakothek.

In addition to German paintings from various artistic movements of the 19th century – including the "Nazarenes," Romanticism, Biedermeier, and Impressionism – there are also a number of works by French Realists, Impressionists, and Symbolists. These were purchased when the gallery's director was art historian Hugo von Tschudi.

The grassy space between the Neue Pinakothek and Alte Pinakothek buildings is now a sculpture park.

---

⑦
Glyptothek

🏛 Königsplatz 3 Ⓤ Königsplatz ⏳ For renovation until 2020; check website for details 🌐 antike-am-koenigsplatz.mwn.de

On the northern side of Königsplatz stands the Glyptothek, a collection of Greek and Roman sculpture (currently closed for renovations). The museum's imposing facade, with the portico of an Ionic temple at the center, is part of a kind of Neo-Classical forum created in the first half of the 19th century to house the archaeological finds acquired by King Ludwig I of Bavaria. On the opposite side of the square, the **Staatliche Antikensammlung** (open during the Glyptothek's renovations) houses smaller treasures, in particular a vast array of Greek vases.

Staatliche Antikensammlung

🎨 🏛 Königsplatz 1 ⏳ 10am–5pm Tue–Sun (to 8pm Wed)

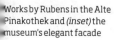

← Works by Rubens in the Alte Pinakothek and *(inset)* the museum's elegant facade

⑧
Pinakothek der Moderne

🏛 Barer Straße 40 Ⓤ Königsplatz 🚌 100 🚋 27, 28 ⏳ 10am–6pm Tue–Sun (to 8pm Thu) 🌐 pinakothek-der-moderne.de

Designed by the German architect Stephan Braunfels, this sleek contemporary museum brings together the collections of four previously separate museums, including the Staatliche Graphische Sammlung, the design collection of Die Neue Sammlung, and the models, drawings, and objects of the Architekturmuseum.

---

⑨
Stadtmuseum

🏛 St. Jakobsplatz 1 Ⓤ/Ⓢ Marienplatz Ⓤ Sendlinger Tor ⏳ 10am–6pm Tue–Sun 🌐 muenchner-stadtmuseum.de

The fascinating City Museum has been housed in this former arsenal building since 1880. Exhibits illustrate daily life in Munich throughout the ages. One of the greatest treasures is the "Dancing Moors" by Erasmus Grasser (1480). Originally, there were 18 highly expressive limewood carvings of dancing figures surrounding the figure of a woman, but only ten survive.

The Waffenhalle has a fine collection of arms and armor. There are also paintings, prints, photographs, furniture, and musical instruments. The doll collection includes paper dolls from India and China, as well as automata and puppets.

Also located in the square is the cube-shaped Judisches Zentrum Jakobsplatz (Jewish Center). It has three floors of exhibitions, a library, and a learning center offering extensive information on Jewish culture and history.

↑ Contemporary designs at the Pinakothek der Moderne

A display showcasing the Deutsches Museum's transportation collection

built in 1663–4 for Electress Henrietta-Adelaide. The palace became the summer residence of the Wittelsbachs, and during the following century several additions were made, including four pavilions, connected to the original villa by arcaded passageways.

The palace's interior features some magnificent examples of the Rococo style, like the Festsaal, a sumptuous ballroom designed by father and son Johann Baptiste and Franz Zimmermann, and the elegant Schönheitengalerie (Gallery of Beauties), decorated with 38 portraits of beautiful women – favorites of King Ludwig I. The old stables now house the Marstallmuseum, a collection of ornate carriages that once belonged to Bavarian rulers.

The approach to the palace is dominated by a broad canal, bordered by immaculately presented gardens. On the edge of the gardens is the Porcelain Factory, established in 1741, and one of the oldest factories of its type in Europe. The palace's Porzellanmuseum offers a record of the famous Nymphenburg porcelain.

Behind the palace stretches the Schlosspark, an English-style country park dotted with lakes and royal lodges. The most notable of these structures is François de Cuvilliés' Amalienburg, a hunting lodge with a lavish Rococo interior. Its highlight is the splendid Spiegelsaal (Hall of Mirrors). Joseph Effner, the principal architect of the palace's extensions, was also responsible for designing the Pagodenburg, used for entertaining, and the Baroque bathing house, the Badenburg.

⑩

Deutsches Museum

🏛 Museuminsel 1 Ⓢ Isartor
🚊 18 ⏰ 9am–5pm daily
🌐 deutsches-museum.de

Reputed to be the world's largest science and technology museum, the Deutsches Museum was founded in 1904. Its collection features more than 28,000 exhibits across a wide variety of subject areas, ranging from agriculture to telecommunications.

The aeronautics section holds a plane that belonged to the Wright brothers and a

1936 Messerschmitt ME 109. A hall charting the history of seafaring houses a 14th-century cog, a ship used by the Hanseatic League, and a 19th-century fishing vessel.

⑪

Schloss Nymphenburg

🏛 Schloss Nymphenburg
Ⓤ Rotkreuzplatz 🚊 12
⏰ Hours vary, check website 🌐 schloss-nymphenburg.de

Schloss Nymphenburg grew up around an Italianate villa,

North of the palace, the city's large **Botanischer Garten** (Botanical Garden) holds many rare and exotic species.

Botanischer Garten

 Hours vary, check website ◻ Jan 1, Shrove Tue, Dec 24, 25, & 31 ⓦ botmuc.org

---

⑫

Bayerisches Nationalmuseum

◻ Prinzregentenstraße 3 🚌 100 🚊 17 ◻ 10am–5pm Tue–Sun (to 8pm Thu) ⓦ bayerisches-national museum.de

Founded in 1855 by King Maximilian II, the Bavarian National Museum holds a collection of fine and applied arts and historical artifacts. Since 1900, the museum has occupied an impressive building designed by Gabriel von Seidl. The ground floor contains a mix of works from the Gothic, Romanesque, Renaissance, Baroque, and Neo-Classical periods. Star exhibits are German sculptor Conrat Meit's *Judith* (1515) and a beautiful sculpture of the Madonna by Tilman Riemenschneider. The first-floor collections include German porcelain, clocks, glassware, ivory carvings, textiles, and items of gold.

In the basement rooms are Christmas Nativity scenes by Bavarian and Italian artists.

---

⑬

Englischer Garten

Ⓤ Giselastraße 🚌 54

First opened in 1808, the Englischer Garten (English Garden) covers an area of 914 acres (370 ha). Buildings dotted about the gardens include the Monopteros, a Neo-Classical temple (1837) by Leo von Klenze, and the Chinese Tower (1789–90). Demonstrations on the art of tea brewing are held in the Japanese Teahouse. Also within the grounds are three beer gardens, where locals and tourists come to drink and listen to live music. Visitors can also take out rowing boats on the park's lake, the Kleinhesseloher See.

---

⑭

Olympiapark

Ⓤ Olympia-zentrum 🚊 20, 21, 27 ⓦ olympiapark.de

Built for the 1972 Olympic Games, the Olympiapark is identifiable by the 950-ft- (290-m-) high television tower, the Olympiaturm, which affords bird's-eye views of the city. The site has three main facilities: the Olympic Stadium, which can seat

EAT

Wirtshaus in der Au
Waitresses at this inn wear traditional dress. Try the spinach and beetroot dumplings.

◻ Lilienstrasse 51 ⓦ wirtshausinderau.de

€€€

Trader Vic's
Creative Polynesian food and cocktails in the cellar-bar of the plush Hotel Bayerischer Hof.

◻ Promenadenplatz 2–6 ⓦ bayerischerhof.de

€€€

over 60,000 spectators, the Olympic Hall arena, and the Swimming Hall. All three are covered by a vast transparent canopy, stretched between several tall masts to form an irregular-shaped pavilion. Also within the complex are an indoor skating rink, a cycle racing track, and tennis courts. As well as sporting occasions, the Olympiapark hosts many popular cultural events, such as fireworks displays and open-air rock and pop concerts during the summer months.

The Olympiapark grounds, with the iconic Olympiaturm

FOR THE LOVE OF BEER

Although fine wines are produced in Germany, beer is without doubt the country's favorite alcoholic drink. Germans drink an average of 22 gallons (100 liters) of beer annually, and during Munich's Oktoberfest a staggering 1.5 million gallons (7 million liters) are served. The country's oldest brewery, established in 1040, is the Weihenstephan Benedictine monastery in Freising, believed to be the oldest working brewery in the world. Today, Bavaria has over 700 breweries, producing around 40 types of beer.

WHERE TO DRINK

For a local brew, head to a *Bierkeller* (beer cellar) or *Bierstube* (pub) or - if the weather's good - a *Biergarten* (beer garden). Bavaria has plenty of each, including Munich's Hirschgarten, which can cater for up to 8,000 patrons, and the city's hugely popular Hofbräuhaus, established in 1589 as a court brewery for Bavarian Duke Wilhelm V.

THE ULTIMATE BEER FESTIVAL

Attracting millions of visitors every year, Oktoberfest is one of the biggest folk festivals in the world. A celebration of all things beer and Bavaria - with many attendees clad in *dirndls* or *lederhosen* - the event runs in Munich from the end of September to early October. The festival opens with a colorful parade, launching over two weeks of raucous revelry.

TOP 5 GERMAN BEERS TO TRY

Dunkel
Ranges from dark amber to red-brown in color, and from malty to chocolatey in taste.

Helles
A lager whose gold color is matched to a light, medium-bodied taste.

Eisbock
A strong beer with a hoppy character and a sweet to fruity taste.

Weissbier
A translucent lager whose specialized yeast content gives it a sweet flavor.

Maibock
Has a toasty or even spicy taste thanks to the kind of hops used.

← Inside the Hacker Festzelt during Munich's famous Oktoberfest

↑ Neuschwanstein, rising amid magnificent mountain scenery

Passau

🏠 Bavaria 🚉🚌
ℹ️ Rathausplatz 2; www.passau.de

Passau lies on a peninsula between the Danube and the Inn rivers, near the Austrian border. In 739, the Irish monk St. Boniface founded a major bishopric here. After two destructive fires in 1662 and 1680, the town was rebuilt by Italian architects, who left many fine Baroque buildings, including the cathedral, St. Stephans Dom. However, the town retains a medieval feel in its narrow alleys and archways. Opposite the Gothic town hall, the Passauer Glasmuseum has a fine collection of glass.

Neuschwanstein

🏠 Neuschwansteinstrasse 20, Schwangau 🚌 ⏰ Apr-mid-Oct: 9am-6pm daily; mid-Oct-Mar: 10am-4pm daily 🚫 Jan 1, Dec 24, 25, & 31 🌐 neuschwanstein.de

Set on the shores of the Alpsee, this fairy-tale castle was built in 1869–86 for the eccentric Bavarian King Ludwig II, to a design by the theater designer Christian Jank. Its pinnacled turrets have provided the inspiration for countless models, book illustrations, and film sets.

The walls of the vestibule and other rooms in the castle are lavishly decorated with paintings of scenes from German myths and legends. The gilded interior of the throne room is reminiscent of a Byzantine basilica, while the dining room has intricately carved panels and fabulous pictures and furniture. The pale-gray granite castle, which draws on a variety of historical styles, is a 20-minute walk from the village of Schwangau.

In Schwangau itself there is another castle, **Schloss Hohenschwangau**, built in 1832 by Maximilian, heir to the throne of Bavaria, over the ruins of a medieval castle. A tour of the Neo-Gothic castle gives a fascinating insight into the history of the Wittelsbach family, rulers of Bavaria from 1180 to 1918. There are also some fine 19th-century furnishings and the castle's terraced gardens afford magnificent views.

Schloss Hohenschwangau
⏰ Apr-mid-Oct: 7:30am-5pm daily; mid-Oct-Mar: 8:30am-3pm daily 🚫 Dec 24 & 31 🌐 hohenschwangau.de

Bodensee

🏠 Baden-Württemberg
🚉 Konstanz 🚌 ℹ️ Bahnhofsplatz 43, Konstanz; www.konstanz-tourismus.de

Bodensee (Lake Constance) lies on the borders of Germany, Austria, and Switzerland. The best time to visit is summer, when local fishermen stage colorful festivals and there are plenty of opportunities for watersports and cruises.

Konstanz (Constance) is the largest town in the region, and its main attraction is the magnificent 11th-century Romanesque cathedral. The town is in two parts: the Old Town (Altstadt) is a German enclave in Switzerland, while the newer part stands on a peninsula between the two main arms of the lake.

The romantic old towns and beautiful islands of Bodensee attract visitors every summer. The exquisite little town of Meersburg, opposite Konstanz, is a popular destination. So too is Mainau, the "Island of Flowers." The most beautiful gardens on the island are in the park of the Baroque palace (1739–46). At the northeastern (Bavarian) end of the lake, the medieval island town of Lindau is the major draw.

↑ Snow-dusted hills of the Black Forest, and *(inset)* hikers near Todtnau

15

Schwarzwald

🏠 Baden-Württemberg
🚆🚌 ℹ Wehratalstrasse 19, Todtmoos; www.todtmoos.de or www.hochschwarzwald.de

The expansive Schwarzwald (Black Forest), named for its dense woodland canopies, stretches from the spa town of Baden-Baden as far as the Swiss border. It is one of Germany's most picturesque regions, containing scenic valleys, towering mountains, and sprawling meadows, as well as beautiful lakes and numerous hiking trails. Located in the southwest corner of Baden-Württemberg, the area is famous not just for its unspoilt landscapes, cuckoo clocks, *Kirschwasser* (schnapps) and *Schwarzwälder Kirschtorte* (Black Forest

gâteau), but also for the therapeutic qualities of the local spring waters. (The sources of the rivers Danube and Neckar are here.)

The entire area, especially in and around the national park created in 2014, is also a haven for skiers, kayakers, climbers, hang-gliders and sailors – not to mention hikers and cyclists, who have a vast 18,000 miles (30,000 km) of trails to pick from. If time is limited, take a scenic drive along the Schwarzwald-Hochstrasse route.

16

Freiburg im Breisgau

🏠 Baden-Württemberg
🚆🚌 ℹ Rathausplatz 2-4; www.freiburg.de

Freiburg is a natural gateway to the Black Forest. The counts Von Zähringen first established the town in 1120, and since 1805 it has been part of Baden. From the Middle Ages, fast-flowing canals, or *bächle*, have run through the town, providing water to help extinguish the once frequent fires.

The cathedral was built in the 13th century in Gothic style. Münsterplatz, the picturesque cathedral square, is lined with houses from various architectural periods.

BLACK FOREST RAILWAY

The Black Forest Railway offers one of Europe's most scenic train journeys. Running between Offenburg and Singen, the 93-mile (149-km) route passes through dense pine forests, over mountains, and past fairy-tale villages, at times running alongside rivers such as the Kinzig and the Brigach, and crossing high viaducts. A Eurail Pass valid for travel within Germany can also be used for a journey on this line.

Completed in 1520, with ground-floor arcades and richly adorned gables, the Kaufhaus was used by merchants for meetings and conferences.

Stuttgart

🏛 Baden-Württemberg
🚆 🚍 🚌 ℹ Königstraße 1A;
www.stuttgart-tourist.de

Stuttgart grew from humble beginnings as a stud farm to become the ducal and royal capital of Württemberg. Beautifully situated among picturesque hills, the town is a major industrial and cultural center, with a ballet company, chamber orchestra, splendid art collections, and a modern, airy library.

When Württemberg Castle burned down in 1311, the family seat was moved to Stuttgart. The ducal residence, the Altes Schloss, was given its present square layout in 1553–78. The palace now houses the Württembergisches Landesmuseum, which holds vast collections of art and jewelry. On the east side of Stuttgart's main square is a huge palace complex, the Neues Schloss, built in 1746–1807. The palace gardens still have much of their original charm, with neat avenues and a collection of impressive sculptures.

The **Staatsgalerie** grew from a fine art museum containing King Wilhelm I of Württemberg's private collection. Among the Old Masters on display are Bellini and Rembrandt, while modern artists include Monet, Picasso, and Modigliani.

Yet more art is on view at Kunstmuseum Stuttgart (Stuttgart Art Museum), which is housed in a spectacular glass cube designed by the Berlin architects Hascher & Jehle. A short distance away is the equally eye-catching Liederhalle, a cultural center that successfully synthesises tradition and modernism.

The Linden Museum is one of Germany's finest ethnology museums, containing exhibits from all over the world. Figures from the Indonesian theater of shadows and a 6th–8th-century mask from Peru are among the eclectic items on display.

To the east of the center is the **Mercedes-Benz-Museum**. Its splendid collection illustrates the development of automobile production with over 70 historic vehicles, all

> **Beautifully situated among picturesque hills, Stuttgart is a major industical and cultural center, with splendid art collections.**

in immaculate condition. Stuttgart's other famous car manufacturer has created the Porsche-Museum, which includes around 50 examples of these high-speed vehicles.

Once a separate health resort, Bad Cannstatt is now a district of Stuttgart. Set in a beautiful park, it has a Late-Gothic church, a Neo-Classical town hall, and a *kursaal* (spahouse). One of the area's main attractions is the magnificent Schloss Rosenstein, which was built in 1824–9 and now hosts a natural history museum.

Staatsgalerie

♿ 🏛 Konrad-Adenauer-Str 30-32 🕐 10am–5pm Tue–Sun (to 8pm Thu) 🌐 staats galerie.de

Mercedes-Benz-Museum

♿ 🏛 Mercedesstraße 100 🕐 9am–6pm Tue–Sun 🌐 mercedes-benz.com/de/classic/museum

↑ Stuttgart's inviting and light-filled Stadtbibliothek (public library)

18

Trier

⌂ Rhineland-Palatinate
🚉 🚌 🛈 An der Porta Nigra;
www.trier.de

Germany's oldest town, Trier was founded by the Roman Emperor Augustus in 16 BC. Its monumental Roman gateway, the Porta Nigra (Black Gate), was built in the 3rd century AD. Among the city's other Roman relics are the 4th-century Kaiserthermen (Imperial Baths), the third-largest bathing complex in the Roman world, and the Aula Palatina (Konstantin-Basilika), a vast, austere building that dates from AD 310. It originally served as the throne hall of the Roman emperor, before later being incorporated into a Baroque palace for the archbishop-electors of Trier in the 17th century; since 1856 it has served as the church of St. Saviour. Nearby, a superb collection of Roman artifacts and other historical items is held in the **Rheinisches Landesmuseum**.

Rheinisches Landesmuseum

⊘ ⌂ Weimarer Allee 1
🕙 10am–5pm Tue–Sun
🌐 landesmuseum-trier.de

19

Mosel Valley

⌂ Rhineland-Palatinate
🚉 🚌 🛈 Am Gestade 6,
Bernkastel-Kues; www.
mosellandtouristik.de

This scenic stretch of the Mosel between Trier and Koblenz is lined with romantic castles towering above lush vineyards. The best way to explore the area is by taking a boat trip along the river – a variety of day trips and longer cruises are available between May and October. A tour by car or bus or a cycle ride makes a pleasant alternative. Popular excursions include those from Trier to Bernkastel-Kues and from Koblenz to Cochem.

The Mosel Valley is home to hundreds of vineyards, mainly producing Riesling. Many of the wineries here have tasting rooms where you can sample the local wares.

Of the many castles that line the river, be sure to visit **Burg Eltz**, a short walk from the town of Wierschem – its core has survived more or less intact since it was built in the 12th century.

Burg Eltz

⊘ ⌂ Wierschem 🕙 Apr–Oct:
9:30am–5:30pm daily
🌐 burg-eltz.de

The attractive
↓ Hauptmarkt in Trier,
Germany's oldest town

20
Mainz

⬗ Rhineland-Palatinate
🚆🚌 🛈 Im Brückenturm,
Rheinstrasse 55; www.
mainz-tourismus.com

Mainz enjoyed power and influence under the Holy Roman Empire, as the city's archbishop was one of the electors. The Kaiserdom, the Romanesque cathedral, dates back to the 11th century and has a choir at each end – one for the emperor and one for the clergy. The nave is filled with the splendid tombs of the archbishops, ranging in date from the 13th to the 19th centuries. The St. Gotthard-Kapelle beside the cathedral was the private chapel of the archbishops. It has a fine 12th-century arcaded loggia.

Other attractions include the well-preserved old half-timbered houses of the Kirschgarten area and the Renaissance Kurfürstliches Schloss, now a museum of Roman and other relics (note that some sections may be closed for renovation work).

Mainz is also famous as the home of Johannes Gutenberg, who invented the printing press in the 1440s. The **Gutenberg Museum** has a recreation of his studio and a copy of his 42-line Bible.

Gutenberg Museum

⬗ Liebfrauenplatz 5 🕘 9am-5pm Tue-Sun (from 11am Sun) 🚫 Public hols 🌐 gutenberg-museum.de

---

21
Heidelberg

⬗ Baden-Württemberg
🚆🚌 🛈 Willy-Brandt-Platz 1;
www.heidelberg.de

Situated on the banks of the Neckar river, Heidelberg was for centuries a center of political power, with a lively and influential cultural life. In 1386, Germany's first university was established here by the Elector Ruprecht I. The construction of the town's palace began during his reign, continuing until the mid-17th century. French incursions in the late 17th century completely destroyed medieval Heidelberg, however, and the town was rebuilt in the 18th-century in Baroque style.

Towering over the town, the Heidelberger Schloss was built and repeatedly extended from the 13th to the 17th centuries. Once a well-fortified Gothic castle, it is now mostly ruined.

↑ The imposing ruins of the Heidelberger Schloss, on a forested hill

The Universitätsbibliothek (University Library), erected in 1901–5, has one of the largest book collections in Germany.

The French Count Charles de Graimberg's collection of fine drawings, paintings, arms, and other curios forms the core of the **Kurpfälzisches Museum**, which also has a fascinating archaeology section.

Other city landmarks include the Baroque domes of the Heiliggeistkirche. Former canons of the college were university scholars, and the church aisle features extensive galleries of books.

Kurpfälzisches Museum

⊘ ⬗ Hauptstraße 97 🕘 10am-6pm Tue-Sun 🚫 Shrove Tue, May 1, Dec 24, 25, & 31 🌐 museum-heidelberg.de

---

 GREAT VIEW
Terrace Treat

Heidelberger Schloss's gardens - created by architect Salomon de Caus in tribute to the town's natural surroundings - feature a great terrace that offers panoramic views over the city and the Neckar river.

㉒
Rhine Valley

🏛 North Rhine-Westphalia, Rhineland-Palatinate, & Hesse 🚉🚌🚢
ℹ Zentralplatz 1 (in the Forum Confuentes), Koblenz; 0261-194 33

Cruises on the Rhine are available along much of its length, but the most scenic and popular stretch is the Rhine Gorge between Mainz and Bonn. The gorge starts at Bingen, where the Nahe joins the Rhine on its 825-mile-(1,320-km-) journey from Switzerland to the North Sea. Popular sights along the route include Bacharach, a pretty town on the left bank with the ruins of the Gothic Werner's Chapel, and the striking white-walled island castle of Pfalzgrafenstein, which once levied tolls on passing ships. Past the town of Kaub on the right bank is the rock of the Lorelei, a legendary siren who lured sailors to their deaths with her song and her beauty. A modern statue marks the spot. Back on the left bank, a little farther north, is the town of St. Goar, dominated by the ruined Burg Rheinfels, blown up by French troops in 1797. On the opposite side of the river, Burg Katz offers one of the best-known views of the Rhine Valley. At Boppard, the attractions include the 13th-century church of St. Severus and more spectacular views. Just south of Koblenz stands Schloss Stolzenfels, constructed in the early 19th century for King Friedrich Wilhelm IV. There are no bridges along this stretch of the river, but if you are exploring by car, there are ferries at various points. However, the best way to enjoy the Rhine's magnificent scenery is by boat.

㉓
Bonn

🏛 North Rhine-Westphalia
✈🚉🚌 ℹ Windeckstraße 1; www.bonn.de

There has been a crossing over the Rhine at Bonn since pre-Roman times, but the settlement first rose to prominence under the Archbishops of Köln in the 13th century. Bonn later entered the world stage as the capital of the Federal Republic of Germany from 1949 to reunification in 1990.

The central market square is surrounded by a mixture of modern and Baroque architecture, including the Late-Baroque Rathaus (Town Hall), built in 1737–8. Just north of

Festung Ehrenbreitstein in Koblenz, standing on the bank of the Rhine ↓

A romantic view of the Rhine and the castle of Burg Katz, at St. Goarshausen

the market square stands the 18th-century Baroque house where Beethoven was born. The **Beethovenhaus** is now a museum housing an impressive collection of memorabilia on the composer.

Bonn has many other fine museums. The Rheinisches Landesmuseum has a vast collection of archaeological exhibits dating back to Roman times, as well as displays of medieval and modern art. The **Kunstmuseum Bonn**, a museum of modern art, has a superb array of Expressionist paintings. Next door stands the Bundeskunsthalle, which holds temporary exhibitions relating to art and culture.

Beethovenhaus

 🏠 Bonngasse 20 & 24-26 🕐 Hours vary, check website 🌐 beethoven.de

Kunstmuseum Bonn

🏠 Museum Mile, Helmut-Kohl-Allee 2 🕐 11am–6pm Tue–Sun (to 9pm Wed) 🌐 kunstmuseum-bonn.de

---

㉔
Koblenz

🏠 Rhineland-Palatinate 🚊 ℹ️ Zentralplatz 1; www.koblenz-touristik.de

The city of Koblenz is situated at the confluence of the Mosel and Rhine rivers. On the Deutsches Eck, the spur of land between the two rivers, stands a huge equestrian statue of Emperor Wilhelm I.

The old town's Florinsmarkt takes its name from the Romanesque-Gothic church of St. Florin, which dates from the 12th century. Nestling among the square's historic buildings is the **Mittelrhein Museum**, with paintings, sculptures, and applied arts from the Middle Ages onward. The present appearance

 INSIDER TIP
Maria Laach

Northwest of Koblenz, the Benedictine abbey of Maria Laach *(www.maria-laach.de)* is a Romanesque masterpiece. It was begun in 1093 on the orders of Count Palatine Heinrich II, who lies buried here.

of the Alte Burg, with its fine Renaissance facade, dates from the 17th century, but a fortress has stood on this site since the early Middle Ages.

Other sights of interest are the Liebfrauenkirche, which has a beautiful Gothic choir, the Kurfürstliches Schloss (the Electors' Palace), and Festung Ehrenbreitstein, where the archbishops of Trier resided from 1648 to 1786.

Mittelrhein Museum

🏠 Zentralplatz 1 🕐 10am–6pm Tue–Sun 🌐 mittelrhein-museum.de

Köln

North Rhine-Westphalia
Kardinal-Höffner-Platz 1; www.koeln tourismus.de

Originally founded by the Romans, Köln (Cologne) is one of the oldest settlements in Germany. The present-day city is an important cultural and ecclesiastical center, possessing several excellent museums, historic buildings, and superb galleries, as well as 12 Romanesque churches and the famous **Kölner Dom** (cathedral) by the river.

Köln's cathedral is one of the finest example of Gothic architecture in the world. The foundation stone was laid on August 15, 1248, the chancel

GREAT VIEW
Towering Above

Climb the 533 steps of the cathedral's South Tower to find the wide observation deck. From here, at a height of 300 ft (100 m), sweeping panoramic views take in the city, the Rhine, and the Siebengebirge hills.

was consecrated in 1322, and building work continued until about 1520. The cathedral then stood unfinished until the 19th century, when the original Gothic designs were rediscovered. It was finally completed in 1842–80. Precious works of art include the fabulous Shrine of the Three Kings, the Altar of the Magi, and an Early-Gothic carving of the Virgin Mary (c. 1290) known as the Mailänder (Milanese) Madonna.

Museums in the city include the **Wallraf-Richartz-Museum**, which contains 14th- to 19th-century paintings organized by artistic school. Featured artists include Rubens, Dürer, Munch, and Max Liebermann. The Römisch-Germanisches Museum houses archaeological finds from Köln and the Rhine Valley, with displays of Roman weapons, tools, and decorative objects, as well as the superb Dionysus mosaic from around 250 BC. The Museum Ludwig, meanwhile, has one of Europe's best collections of modern art. German Expressionists, Surrealists, and American Pop Artists are all represented.

The 12th-century Groß St. Martin, with its distinctive tower, is built on the site of a Roman sports arena. Remains

The spiky Gothic structure of the Kölner Dom ↓

The North Tower, at 516 ft (157 m), is slightly higher than the South Tower.

Built out of porous sandstone, the facade is susceptible to environmental impurities, such as traffic fumes.

Main entrance

The Petrusportal is the only entrance built in the Middle Ages.

The Gothic spires of Köln's cathedral, seen from across the Rhine

of the baths of this complex have been uncovered underneath the church crypt.

Another notable building is Köln's Rathaus (Town Hall), its irregular-shaped appearance the result of successive waves of modifications made after 1330. Under a glass pyramid at the front of the building are the remains of 12th-century Jewish baths.

Highlights of the Late-Gothic Parish church of St. Peter, built in 1515–39, are its stained-glass windows and the magnificent painting

of the *Crucifixion of St. Peter* (c. 1637) by Peter Paul Rubens.

The southern chamber of the Basilica of St. Ursula is lined with numerous shrines. According to legend, they hold the remains of St. Ursula and 11,000 virgins, all of whom were reputedly killed at the hands of the Huns in the 4th century.

KÖLN'S ROMANESQUE CHURCHES

Köln's 12 Romanesque churches are set in a semicircle around the city center. Built between 1150 and 1250 on the graves of martyrs and early bishops of the city, these churches influenced the development of Romanesque architecture well beyond the Rhineland. Almost all the churches were damaged in World War II; some, such as the church of St. Kolumba, have not been restored, but most were returned to their former glory.

Kölner Dom

♦ ♦ 🚪 Domkloster 4
⏰ Hours vary, check website
🌐 koelner-dom.de

Wallraf-Richartz-Museum

♦ 🚪 Obenmarspforten
⏰ 10am–6pm Tue–Sun
🚫 Carnival days, Dec 24, 25, & 31 🌐 wallraf.museum

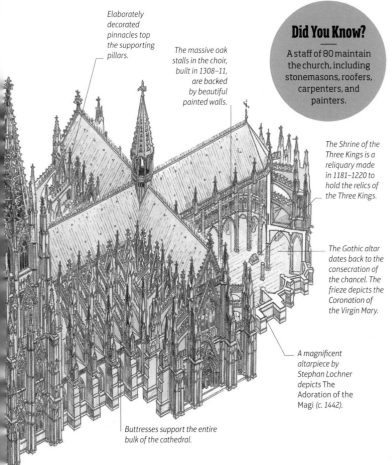

Elaborately decorated pinnacles top the supporting pillars.

The massive oak stalls in the choir, built in 1308–11, are backed by beautiful painted walls.

Did You Know?

A staff of 80 maintain the church, including stonemasons, roofers, carpenters, and painters.

The Shrine of the Three Kings is a reliquary made in 1181–1220 to hold the relics of the Three Kings.

The Gothic altar dates back to the consecration of the chancel. The frieze depicts the Coronation of the Virgin Mary.

A magnificent altarpiece by Stephan Lochner depicts The Adoration of the Magi (c. 1442).

Buttresses support the entire bulk of the cathedral.

26

Frankfurt am Main

Hesse 🚈🅿️🚊🚢
ℹ️ Hauptbahnhof; www.
frankfurt-tourismus.de

Frankfurt am Main is one of the main economic and cultural centers of Europe. The headquarters of many major banks and newspaper publishers are based here, and the city's International Book Fair is the world's largest event of its kind.

Since 1878, the **Städelsches Kunstinstitut** (also known as the Städel Museum) has occupied a Neo-Renaissance building on Schaumainkai, the picturesque "museum embankment." The ground floor houses a collection of Dutch and German prints and drawings, the first floor is devoted to 19th- and 20th-century art, and the second floor displays masterpieces

DRINK

Adolf Wagner

Dating from 1931, this traditional tavern is full of warm wooden decor and Art Deco accents. It specializes in Hesse's regional *Apfelwein* (apple wine) but offers lots of local fare, as well.

🏠 Schweizer Strasse 71,
Frankfurt am Main
🌐 apfelwein-
wagner.com

Wein-Dünker

Popular with locals, this tiny, family-run wine cellar has a wonderfully authentic atmosphere and serves some of Germany's best wines.

🏠 Berger Strasse 265,
Frankfurt am Main
🌐 wein-duenker.de

by Old Masters including Botticelli, Van Eyck, Vermeer, and Rembrandt.

Another interesting museum in the Schaumainkai complex is the Deutsches Architektur-museum, which concentrates mainly on developments in 20th-century architecture.

Nearby is the Deutsches Filmmuseum, which holds documents and objects related to the art of movie-making and the development of film technology. The museum also has its own cinema, which screens old and often long-forgotten movies.

On the other side of the river is the Goethehaus, where the great German poet, novelist, and dramatist Johann Wolfgang von Goethe was born in 1749. The house was totally destroyed in World War II, but later lovingly restored, with its interior reconstructed in typical mid- to late-18th-century style. The desk at which Goethe wrote his early works, such as *The Sorrows of Young Werther* (1774), has been carefully preserved.

Located in the center of the Old Town, the Römer is a collection of 15th- to 18th-century houses, including

the Altes Rathaus (Old Town Hall), rebuilt after World War II. Opposite is a group of half-timbered houses known as the Ostzeile.

On the banks of the Main stands Leonhardskirche (Church of St. Leonard), a fine example of Gothic and Romanesque architecture. Built in stages in the 13th and 15th centuries, the church contains many treasures, including a copy of Leonardo da Vinci's *Last Supper* by Hans Holbein the Elder, from 1501.

East along the river, the **Historisches Museum** has an interesting display of items relating to Frankfurt's history, including a fascinating model of the medieval town, a collection of local prehistoric finds, and several decorative fragments from buildings destroyed during World War II. Behind the museum is the twin-naved Alte Nikolaikirche, or Church of St. Nicholas, popular for its fine statues of St. Nicholas and the 47-bell carillon, which plays German folk songs twice a day.

Frankfurt's Kaiserdom, an imperial cathedral, was constructed between the 13th and 15th centuries. It has

← The impressive skyline of Frankfurt am Main lit up at sunset

INSIDER TIP
Fairy Trails

East of Frankfurt, Hanau is the birthplace of the brothers Wilhelm and Jakob Grimm. The town marks the starting point of the German Fairy-Tale Route, a 375-mile (603-km) trail through villages linked to the brothers' work.

several priceless masterpieces of Gothic artwork, including the magnificent 15th-century Maria-Schlaf-Altar.

Contemporary artworks can be viewed at the **Museum für Moderne Kunst** (Museum of Modern Art), covering all the major artistic trends from the 1960s until the present day, with works by Andy Warhol and Roy Lichtenstein.

The Liebieghaus, a museum of sculpture, displays works ranging from ancient times through to Mannerism and Rococo. There are also some superb examples of ancient Egyptian and Far Eastern art, as well as splendid works from the Middle Ages and the Renaissance.

Städelsches Kunstinstitut

🏛️⊘ 🅰 Schaumainkai 63 🕐 10am–6pm Tue–Sun (to 9pm Thu & Fri) 🌐 staedel museum.de

Historisches Museum

⊘ 🅰 Saalhof 1 🕐 10am–6pm Tue–Fri (to 9 pm Wed), 11am–7pm Sat & Sun 🌐 historisches-museum- frankfurt.de

Museum für Moderne Kunst

⊘🚆 🅰 Domstraße 10 🕐 10am–6pm Tue–Sun (to 8pm Wed) 🌐 mmk.art

㉗
Bremen

🅰 Bremen 🚆🚌 🛈 Böttcherstrasse 4 & Hauptbahnhof; www. bremen-tourism.de

Bremen is one of Germany's three former city-states. The town has been a thriving seaport since the Middle Ages, and still has many attractive buildings from the medieval era in its Old Town.

Bremen's **Rathaus** (Town Hall), on Marktplatz, was built in 1405–10 and boasts a

splendid Renaissance facade, added to the original Gothic structure 200 years later. Opposite is the 11th-century Romanesque Dom, which contains some fine bas-reliefs. In Marktplatz itself stand a tall statue of Charlemagne's knight Roland (1404) and a sculpture of the *Musicians of Bremen* (1953), recalling the Grimm fairy-tale.

Two museums worth a visit are the Kunsthalle, exhibiting European art from the Middle Ages to the 20th century, and the Focke Museum of local history and decorative arts.

Rathaus

🏛️⊘ 🅰 Am Markt 21 🕐 For guided tours only; 11am, noon, 3pm & 4pm Mon–Sat, 11am & noon Sun 🌐 rathaus. bremen.de

Did You Know?

The European contribution to the International Space Station was built in Bremen.

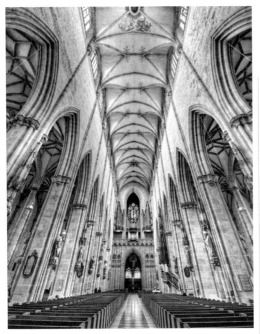

 The imposing interior of the Gothic, five-nave Ulm Münster

Among the city's most notable landmarks are the Opernhaus (Opera House), built 1845–52 in Neo-Classical style, and the early-20th-century Neues Rathaus. The latter's massive central dome offers fine views of the city.

On Marktplatz, in the Old Town, are many restored, 15th-century half-timbered houses, as well as the stately Marktkirche St. Georg und St. Jacobus with its 14th-century nave and fine Gothic altar. The **Sprengel Museum** holds modern art by Munch, Chagall, Picasso, and Christo. Also worth visiting is the eclectic **Niedersächsisches Landesmuseum** (Lower Saxony State Museum), whose picture gallery has German medieval and Renaissance paintings; Dutch and Flemish works by Rubens, Rembrandt, and Van Dyck; and 19th- and 20th-century German art.

West of the city center, the Herrenhäuser Gärten are among the most beautiful Baroque gardens in Germany.

Sprengel Museum

 Kurt-Schwitters-Platz ◷ 10am–6pm Tue–Sun (to 8pm Tue) 🅦 sprengel-museum.de

Niedersächsisches Landesmuseum

Willy-Brandt-Allee 5 ◷ 10am–5pm Tue–Sun (to 6pm Sat & Sun) 🅦 landesmuseum-hannover.de

---

㉘

Münster

🏠 North Rhine-Westphalia ✈🚊 ℹ Heinrich-Brüning-Straße 9; www.tourismus.muenster.de

Münster's main sights of interest are located in the Altstadt, the historic heart of the city. The imposing Gothic Rathaus (Town Hall), carefully restored following damage during World War II, dates from the late 12th century. In 1648, the Treaty of Westphalia was signed here, ending the Thirty Years' War.

Münster's great cathedral, the Dom St. Paulus, was built in 1225–65. Its best-known treasure is the astronomical clock (1540). Also on the square is the Westfälisches Landesmuseum (Westphalian State Museum), specializing in Gothic art. Nearby, the Lambertikirche (1375–1450) is a fine example of the hall-churches typical of Westphalia.

West of the center stands the Residenzschloss. Built in 1767–87, the splendid Baroque palace, now the headquarters of Münster's university, overlooks pleasant gardens.

㉙

Hannover

🏠 Lower Saxony 🚊 ℹ Ernst-August-Platz 8; www.hannover.de

Hannover is the capital of Lower Saxony, and for more than a century, from 1714 to 1837, it shared a succession of rulers with Britain. The city was heavily bombed during World War II, but it has been largely rebuilt.

> **The most important town in the Baltic basin at the end of the Middle Ages, Lübeck is known for its beautifully restored medieval architecture.**

㉚

Lübeck

🏠 Schleswig-Holstein 🚊 ℹ Holstentorplatz 1; www.luebeck-tourism.de

The most important town in the Baltic basin at the end of the Middle Ages,

Lübeck is today known for the beautifully restored medieval architecture of its cobbled historic center.

The city's 13th-century Marienkirche (St. Mary's Church) has the highest vaulted brick nave in the world. A short walk away, the turreted Rathaus dates from 1226 and is a fine example of Lübeck's distinctive Gothic brick architecture. The older Gothic cathedral was begun in 1173. Nearby, a former Augustinian nunnery houses the St. Annen-Museum, which displays historical artifacts dating from the 13th to the 18th centuries. Another famous monument is the Holstentor (1464–78), the western gateway to the city.

The **Buddenbrookhaus** is a museum devoted to the great writers Thomas and Heinrich Mann, whose family lived here from 1841 to 1891.

Buddenbrookhaus

Heinrich-und-Thomas-Mann-Zentrum, Mengstrasse 4 ◻ Jan: 11am-5pm Tue-Sun; Feb-Mar: 11am-5pm daily; Apr-Dec: 10am-6pm daily ◻ Jan 1, Dec 24, 25, & 31 W buddenbrookhaus.de

Cranes and ships at the St. Pauli pier in the busy port of Hamburg ↓

MARZIPAN FROM LÜBECK

Marzipan has been popular throughout Europe since the 19th century. Its name was recorded as Martzapaen for the first time in Lübeck in 1530. It is made from two-thirds sweet almonds from Venice and one-third sugar and aromatic oils. In 1806, Lübeck's Niederegger patisserie perfected the recipe, and their Breite Strasse premises still operate today.

Hamburg

◻ Hamburg ✈ 🚗 🚌
🛈 Hauptbahnhof, Kirchenallee; www. hamburg.com

For many years, Hamburg, Germany's second largest city, was a leading member of the Hanseatic League. In 1945, it became a city-state of the Federal Republic.

Hamburg sustained considerable damage during World War II, and little of the Old Town remains. The ruined tower of the Neo-Gothic Nikolaikirche serves as a monument to the tragic

---

consequences of war. Nearby, the Jakobikirche (1340) has been rebuilt in its original style; inside is a massive 17th-century organ. The tower of the Baroque Michaeliskirche gives splendid views of the city.

Just north of Hamburg's Neo-Renaissance town hall, on the Rathausmarkt, is the Binnenalster recreational lake. Also nearby, the **Kunsthalle** traces the history of European art from medieval times to the 20th century, with an excellent section devoted to the 19th-century German Romantics.

The best example of the city's collection of Expressionist buildings is the Chilehaus (1922–4) in Kontorhausviertel.

Hamburg is the second largest port in Europe after Rotterdam, and a tour of this area is highly recommended. There are two museum ships moored here: the freighter **Cap San Diego** and the sailing boat **Rickmer Rickmers** (1896).

Kunsthalle

◻ Glockengießerwall ◻ 10am-6pm Tue-Sun (to 9pm Thu) W hamburger-kunsthalle.de

Cap San Diego

◻ Port ◻ 10am-6pm daily W capsandiego.de

Rickmer Rickmers

◻ Port ◻ 10am-6pm daily W rickmer-rickmers.de

PRACTICAL
INFORMATION

Here you will find all the essential advice and information you will need before and during your stay in Germany.

AT A GLANCE

CURRENCY
Euro (EUR)

TIME ZONE
CET/CEST. Central European Summer Time runs from the last Sunday in March to the last Sunday in October.

LANGUAGE
German

ELECTRICITY SUPPLY
Power sockets are type F, fitting two-pronged plugs. Standard voltage is 230V.

EMERGENCY NUMBERS

GENERAL EMERGENCY	AMBULANCE
112	**112**

FIRE SERVICE	POLICE
112	**110**

TAP WATER
Unless otherwise stated, tap water in Germany is safe to drink.

Getting There

Germany's major airports are Frankfurt, Munich, Berlin Schönefeld and Düsseldorf. These airports are outside the city centers, but are well-connected by public transport or buses that can take you from the airport into the heart of the city. Frankfurt is Germany's largest airport and one of the busiest in Europe.

Germany has an efficient high-speed rail network, and there are regular services into Germany from many European cities, particularly those in neighboring countries.

Flixbus also runs many international bus services to Germany from across Europe; tickets are cheapest when bought in advance. Bus travel is cheaper than using high-speed trains but journeys can be longer and less comfortable.
Flixbus
W flixbus.de

Personal Security

Germany is generally a safe country, but it is always a good idea to take sensible precautions against pickpockets. If you have anything stolen, report the crime as soon as possible to the nearest police station. Get a copy of the crime report in order to claim on your insurance.

Health

EU citizens with a European Health Insurance Card (EHIC) are entitled to free emergency medical care in Germany, but it is also advisable to take out some form of supplementary health insurance. Visitors from outside the EU must arrange their own private medical insurance.

Pharmacies (apotheke) are indicated by a red stylized letter "A." Details of the nearest 24-hour service are posted in all pharmacy windows or can be found online.

Passports and Visas

Citizens of countries that are members of the EU, as well as citizens from the US, Canada, Australia, and New Zealand, do not need a

visa to visit Germany, so long as their stay does not exceed three months. Visitors from South Africa must have a visa. Visitors from EU countries do not require a passport to enter Germany, as long as they have a national ID card. For visa information specific to your home country, consult your nearest German embassy or check online.

Travelers with Specific Needs

Germany is generally a very straightforward destination to navigate if you have accessibility requirements. Most public transport, sights, and accommodation facilities throughout the country cater for wheelchairs, although it's always best to check in advance (especially at cheaper hotels and guesthouses). Guide dogs are allowed on all forms of public transport.

Money

Major credit, debit, and prepaid currency cards are accepted in most shops and restaurants. Contactless payments are becoming more widely accepted, occasionally even on public transport. However, it is always worth carrying some cash, as many smaller businesses don't accept card payments. ATMs are widespread throughout Germany – even in villages you'll find at least one. All vending and ticket machines take notes up to €20.

Cell Phones and Wi-Fi

Visitors traveling to Germany with EU tariffs can use their devices without being affected by data roaming charges. Visitors from other countries should check their contracts before using their phone in Germany in order to avoid unexpected charges.

Free Wi-Fi hotspots are widely available in big cities. Hotels usually offer free Wi-Fi to their guests; cafés and restaurants are often happy to permit the use of their Wi-Fi on the condition that you make a purchase.

Getting Around

There are a number of airlines offering regular domestic flights on internal routes. However, train is the best way to travel around Germany,

thanks to an efficient high-speed network and a reliable local service. **Deutsche Bahn** (DB) operates the vast majority of services in Germany. The fastest trains – InterCity Express (ICE) – connect the largest cities and can travel at more than 125 mph (200 km/h). This means that crossing almost the entire country on a journey from Hamburg to Munich takes only 6 hours. Somewhat slower but less expensive are the InterCity (IC) trains. When traveling over shorter distances it is often quicker to take the Regional Express (RE) trains. The S-Bahn (Schnellbahn) is a fast commuter rail network that operates in some of the major German cities.

Germany's excellent network of toll-free highway routes guarantees fast journeys over long distances, while a well-maintained system of smaller roads means that many interesting places throughout the country are within easy reach. On smaller roads and in remote areas, filling stations may be few and far between. The German Autobahn (highway) is indicated by the letter "A", while a Bundesstraße (main road) has the letter "B."

There is a good network of intercity bus services in Germany, though journeys are generally no cheaper than traveling by train. Most towns have a Zentraler Omnibus Bahnhof (ZOB) close to the train station, from where most bus services originate.

Deutsche Bahn
🅦 bahn.com

Visitor Information

The **German National Tourist Board** website is helpful for pre-trip planning, and in Germany there is a good network of tourist information centers. These are usually run by the city or regional tourist authorities, Verkehrsamt. They provide advice on accommodations, opening hours of monuments, museums, tours, and excursions, as well as brochures covering the most important tourist attractions. They may also be able to find and book you a hotel room.

German National Tourist Board
🅦 germany.travel

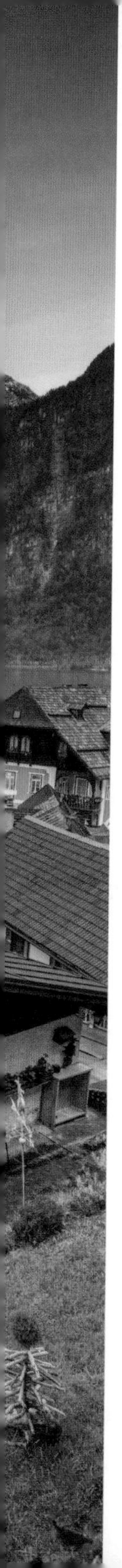

AUSTRIA

Although landlocked, Austria has thrived over the centuries thanks to its geographical position at the heart of Europe. The strategic benefits of this location were recognized early by Celtic and Germanic tribes, who both populated and repeatedly raided the Austrian territory from the 7th century BC onward. The Romans occupied the region by the end of the 1st century BC, but were later chased off by Germanic tribes. Bavarian settlers then held sway in the 7th and 8th centuries, before being eventually crushed by Charlemagne, King of the Franks. In the 10th century, the Babenbergs acquired the territory, and it was appointed a hereditary fief of the Holy Roman Empire in 1156. The lands came under the control of the Habsburg dynasty in the 13th century, and from that point on their domains steadily grew. Military success against the Ottomans meant that by the 18th century Austria was a major power, but the rise of Prussia, Napoleon's occupation of Vienna in 1809, and the growth of nationalist movements saw the empire begin to weaken. Creatively, however, the country thrived, with Vienna as a leading center for intellectuals, artists, and musicians. The assassination of the Habsburg heir, Franz Ferdinand, in 1914 was the catalyst for World War I, after which the defeated Austrian Empire was dismembered – struggles for control of the new republic ensued between left and right. The country was annexed by Germany in 1938 and then came under Allied control until 1955, when it became a sovereign state once more. Austria has since flourished economically, but old political divisions have re-emerged in the 21st century.

AUSTRIA

1. Vienna
2. Graz
3. Eisenstadt
4. Melk and the Wachau Valley
5. Linz
6. Innsbruck
7. Hallstatt
8. Salzburg

❶

VIENNA

 𝒊 www.wien.info/en

Once the capital of a great empire, with Baroque pomp at every turn to prove it, modern Vienna remains a city at the very heart of Europe. A cornucopia of culture, it puts art, architecture, music, and theater at center stage. The city's most famous sights are encircled by the grand Ringstrasse boulevard, but there are visitor-friendly enclaves to discover all over.

> **Did You Know?**
>
> The croissant was invented in Vienna – it originated from the Austrian *kipfel*.

① 🏛 🎭

Burgtheater

🏛 Universitätsring 2
Ⓤ Schottentor 🚋 D, 1, 71
🕐 For performances and guided tours 🔒 Good Fri, Dec 24; Jul & Aug (except for guided tours) 🌐 burg theater.at

The Burgtheater is one of the most prestigious stages in the German-speaking world. The original theater, commissioned by Empress Maria Theresa in the 1730s, was replaced in 1888 by today's Italian Renaissance-style building. It closed for refurbishment in 1897 after the discovery that several

seats had no view of the stage. At the end of World War II, a bomb devastated the building, leaving only the side wings. Now restored, the theater today stages a diverse range of plays performed by its famed in-house ensemble.

Stephansdom

🏛 Stephansplatz Ⓤ Steph-ansplatz 🚌 1A, 2A, 3A
🕐 Hours vary, check web-site 🌐 stephanskirche.at

Situated in the very center of the city, the Stephansdom, with its glazed-tile roof, is the

heart and soul of Vienna. It is no mere coincidence that the urns containing the entrails of some of the Habsburgs lie in a vault beneath its main altar.

A church has stood on the site for over 800 years, but all that remains of the original 13th-century Romanesque church are the Heathen Towers and the Giants' Doorway. The Gothic nave, the choir, and the side chapels are the result of rebuilding in the 14th and 15th centuries, while some of the outbuildings are Baroque additions. The North Tower, begun in 1450, was never finished; according to legend, this is because its master builder broke a pact he made with the devil and consequently fell to his death.

The lofty vaulted interior of Stephansdom holds a collection of art spanning centuries.

← Views over Vienna from the magnificent tiled roof of the Stephansdom

Masterpieces of Gothic sculpture include the fabulously intricate pulpit, several of the figures of saints adorning the piers, and the canopies over many of the side altars. To the left of the High Altar is the 15th-century winged Wiener Neustädter Altar, bearing the painted images of 72 saints. The altar panels open out to reveal delicate sculpture groups. The most spectacular Renaissance work is the tomb of Friedrich III, and a flamboyant Baroque note is added by the 17th-century High Altar.

Staatsoper

🏠 **Opernring 2** Ⓤ **Karlsplatz**
🚌 **59A** 🚋 **D, 1, 2, 62, 71**
⌚ **For performances**
🌐 **wiener-staatsoper.at**

Vienna's opera house, the Staatsoper, was the first of the grand buildings on the Ringstrasse to be completed; it opened on May 25, 1869 to the strains of Mozart's *Don Giovanni*. Though built in elaborate, Neo-Renaissance style, it initially failed to impress the Viennese. However, when the building was hit by a bomb in 1945 and largely destroyed, the event was seen as a symbolic blow to the city. The Opera House reopened in

💬 INSIDER TIP
Getting Around

The center of the city is easily explored on foot. Trams 1, 2, 71, and D take you along parts of the Ringstrasse past many of the main sights. To see these in old-world style, hire a horse-drawn *Fiaker*. The suburbs are served by the U-bahn (subway) and S-bahn services.

1955 with a performance of Beethoven's *Fidelio* in a brand new auditorium. Today it hosts over 350 performances of classical music, opera, and ballet each season.

The grand Hofburg entrance, Michaelertor, topped with gilded domes ↑

④

HOFBURG

🏠 Michaelerplatz 1 🚇 Stephansplatz, Herrengasse, Volkstheater
🚌 48A, 57A 🚋 D, 1, 2, 71 🌐 hofburg-wien.at

The vast Hofburg, Vienna's former imperial palace, is a lavish complex of buildings in the city center. The seat of Austrian power since the 13th century, it is an awe-inspiring reminder of the glory of the Habsburg Empire.

What began as a small fortress in 1275 grew over the centuries into a vast palace, the Hofburg. It was the seat of Austrian power for over six centuries, and successive rulers were all anxious to leave their mark. The various buildings range in style from Gothic to late-19th-century Neo-Renaissance. The complex was still expanding up until a few years before the Habsburgs fell from power in 1918. The presence of the imperial court had a profound effect on the surrounding area, with noble families competing to site their palaces as close as possible to the Hofburg. Complementing the buildings are the Burggarten and Volksgarten, whose sublime gardens make for a welcome respite and a chance to recharge your batteries.

Did You Know?

The oldest surviving part of the Hofburg is the Schweizerhof, which dates back to the 13th century.

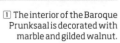

1 The interior of the Baroque Prunksaal is decorated with marble and gilded walnut.

2 Visitors stroll the pathways beside the Burggarten's vast Jugendstil greenhouses.

3 The Albertina now houses a priceless collection of modern art.

Exploring the Hofburg Complex

The vast Hofburg complex contains the former Imperial Apartments and Treasury (Schatzkammer) of the Habsburgs, several museums, a chapel, a church, the Austrian National Library, the Spanish Riding School, and the President of Austria's offices. The entrance to the Imperial Apartments and the Treasury is through the Michaelertor on Michaelerplatz.

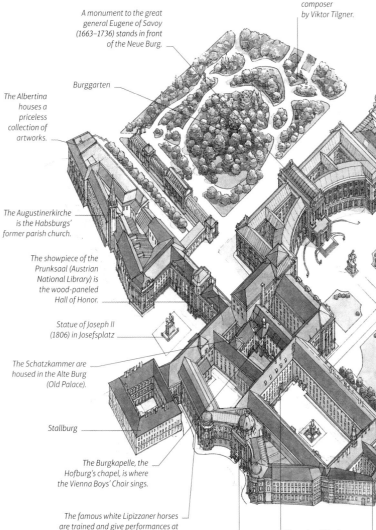

A monument to the great general Eugene of Savoy (1663–1736) stands in front of the Neue Burg.

The Mozart Memorial (1896) is a statue of the composer by Viktor Tilgner.

Burggarten

The Albertina houses a priceless collection of artworks.

The Augustinerkirche is the Habsburgs' former parish church.

The showpiece of the Prunksaal (Austrian National Library) is the wood-paneled Hall of Honor.

Statue of Joseph II (1806) in Josefsplatz

The Schatzkammer are housed in the Alte Burg (Old Palace).

Stallburg

The Burgkapelle, the Hofburg's chapel, is where the Vienna Boys' Choir sings.

The famous white Lipizzaner horses are trained and give performances at the Spanish Riding School.

The Michaelertor is the gate through which visitors reach the older parts of the palace.

The red and black Schweizertor (Swiss Gate) leads to the Schweizerhof.

Imperial Apartments

The grand imperial buildings of the Hofburg Complex ↑

Neue Burg

▶ The massive Neue Burg was added to the Hofburg in 1881-1913. Archaeological finds from Ephesus are on display in the Ephesos Museum, while pianos that belonged to Beethoven, Schubert, and Haydn are housed in the musical instrument museum. The weapons collection in the Hofjagd und Rüstkammer is one of the finest in Europe, and there is also an excellent ethnological collection.

Augustinerkirche

The church has one of the best-preserved 14th-century Gothic interiors in Vienna. In the Loreto Chapel are a series of silver urns that contain the hearts of the Habsburg family. The church is also celebrated for its music, with Masses by Schubert or Haydn performed here on Sundays and holidays.

Imperial Apartments

◀ The Imperial Apartments (Kaiserappartements) in the Reichskanzleitrakt and the Amalienburg include the rooms used by Franz Joseph from 1857 to 1916, Empress Elisabeth's apartments from 1854 to 1898, and those where Czar Alexander I stayed during the Congress of Vienna in 1815.

Burgkapelle

From the Schweizerhof, steps lead up to the Burgkapelle, founded in 1296. The interior has Gothic statues in canopied niches. The Wiener Sängerknaben, the Vienna Boys' Choir, performs here on Sundays.

The Burgtor, or outer gate, was built to a design by Peter Nobile in 1821–4.

Heldenplatz

↓
N

Schatzkammer

Treasures amassed during centuries of Habsburg rule are displayed in 21 rooms known as the Schatzkammer, or Treasury. They include relics of the Holy Roman Empire, the crown jewels, and liturgical objects of the imperial court.

Spanish Riding School

▶ The Spanish Riding School is believed to have been founded in 1572 to cultivate the classic skills of *haute école* horsemanship. Today, shows take place in the building known as the Winter Riding School, built in 1729-35 to a design by Josef Emanuel Fischer von Erlach.

Did You Know?

Lipizzaner horses take their name from the stud farm at Lipizza in Slovenia, founded in 1580.

Burggarten and Volksgarten

Some of the space left around the Hofburg after Napoleon had razed part of the city walls was transformed by the Habsburgs into gardens. The Volksgarten opened to the public in 1820, but the Burggarten was the palace's private garden until 1918.

Albertina

The Albertina is named after Duke Albert of Sachsen-Teschen, the son-in-law of Empress Maria Theresa. Its vast art collection includes one million prints, over 65,000 watercolors and drawings, and some 70,000 photographs.

↑ Young visitors captivated by the displays in the Hall
of the Dinosaurs at the Naturhistorisches Museum

EXPERIENCE Austria

EAT

TIAN Wien
Expect fresh flavors
and innovative
vegetarian dishes at
this modern, Michelin-
starred eatery.

🏠 Himmelpfortgasse 23
🌐 tianrestaurant.com

€€€

Figlmüller
Try the fabulously large
schnitzel at this cosy
traditional dining spot.

🏠 Wollzelle 5
🌐 glmueller.at

€€€

Stomach
Sample wholesome
Central European food
and vegetarian dishes
at this authentic and
friendly restaurant.

🏠 Seegasse 26 📞 01 310
2099 🚫 Mon & Tue

€€€

Restaurant Vestibül
This upsclae restaurant
in the Burgtheater
serves traditional
dishes with a modern
twist, such as roasted
tafelspitz with almond-
garlic purée.

🏠 Universitätsring 2
🌐 vestibuel.at

€€€

Café Central
Enjoy a Grand Café
experience at this
Vienna institution,
where the likes of Freud
and Loos once sipped
their coffee. Opens early
for breakfast.

🏠 Herrengasse 14
🌐 cafecentral.wien

€€€

⑤

Naturhistorisches Museum

🏠 Burgring 7 🚇 Volks-
theater 🚌 48A 🚊 D, 1, 2,
46, 49, 71 🕐 9am–6:30pm
Thu–Mon (to 9pm Wed)
🚫 Jan 1, Dec 25 🌐 nhm-
wien.ac.at

The Natural History Museum
was built in the late 19th
century as a pair with the
Kunsthistorisches Museum.
The collections at this palatial-
style institution include
archaeological, anthropo-
logical, mineralogical, zoological, and geological displays.
The exhibits comprise over
30 million fascinating objects;
there are casts of dinosaur
skeletons, the world's largest
display of skulls illustrating
the history of man, one of
Europe's most comprehensive
collections of gems, prehistoric
sculpture, Bronze Age items,
and extinct birds and mammals. In the archaeological
section, look out for the celebrated Venus of Willendorf,
a 25,000-year-old Paleolithic
fertility figurine, as well as a
number of fascinating finds
from the early Iron Age settlement at Hallstatt *(p546)*.

THE VENUS OF WILLENDORF
Found in Willendorf in
1908, this 4-in (11-cm)
limestone figure is one
of the most important
prehistoric artifacts in
the world. It is thought
to be approximately
30,000 years old,
and its purpose is
unknown, although it
has been speculated
that the figure was
used during ancient
fertility rituals.

⑥

Museums-Quartier Wien

🏠 Museumsplatz 1–5
🚇 MuseumsQuartier,
Volkstheater 🚌 48A 🚊 49
🕐 MQ Point Visitor Center:
10am–7pm daily 🌐 mqw.at

This arts and museum complex
is one of the largest cultural
centers in the world, housed
in what were once the imperial
stables and carriage houses.
The compound houses a
diverse array of facilities, from
art museums to a venue for
contemporary dance to a

children's creativity center. The visitor center is a good starting point to get your bearings.

Among the attractions are the Leopold Museum, which focuses on Austrian art, and the Museum of Modern Art Ludwig Foundation Vienna, which showcases modern art from around the world. ZOOM Kinder-museum offers interactive creative workshops for kids, while Architekturzentrum is dedicated to 20th- and 21st-century architecture.

Kunsthistorisches Museum

🏛 Maria-Theresien-Platz
Ⓤ MuseumsQuartier, Volkstheater 🚌 57A 🚊 D, 1, 2, 71
🕙 10am–6pm Tue–Sun (Jun–Aug: daily); picture gallery also 6–9pm Thu 🚫 Jan 1, May 1, Nov 1, Dec 25
🌐 khm.at

The Museum of the History of Art attracts over one-and-a-half million visitors each year. Its collections are based largely on those built up over several centuries by the Habsburgs.

The picture gallery occupies the first floor. The collection focuses on Old Masters from the 15th to the 18th centuries, with a fine selection of Flemish paintings thanks to the links between the Habsburgs and the Netherlands. About half the surviving works of Peter Brueghel the Elder are held by the museum, including most of the cycle of *The Seasons*. The Dutch paintings range from genre scenes of great domestic charm to magnificent landscapes. All the Rembrandts on show are portraits, while the only Vermeer is his enigmatic *The Artist's Studio* (1665). The Italian galleries have a strong collection of 16th-century Venetian paintings, with works by Titian, Giovanni Bellini, and Tintoretto. Also on show are the bizarre vegetable portrait heads made for Emperor Rudolf II by Giuseppe Arcimboldo.

The German section is rich in 16th-century paintings, with several works by Dürer. The most interesting of the Spanish works are the portraits of the Spanish royal family by Diego Velázquez.

On the ground floor are the Greek, Roman, Egyptian, and Near Eastern collections, with new rooms devoted to Greek and Roman antiquities. Among the Egyptian and Near Eastern antiquities are an entire 5th-Dynasty tomb chapel from Giza (c. 2400 BC) and a bust of King Tuthmosis III (c. 1460 BC).

The sculpture and decorative arts collection (Kunstkammer Wien) houses some Late-Gothic religious statues by artists such as Tilman Riemenschneider, and curiosities such as automata and scientific instruments owned by various Habsburg monarchs.

The Egyptian Collection at the *(inset)* Kunsthistorisches Museum ↑

⑧
Freud Museum

⌂ Berggasse 19
Ⓤ Schottentor 🚌 40A
🚋 D, 37, 38, 40, 41, 42
🕐 Moving Freud Museum:
10am–6pm daily 🌐 freud-
museum.at

A Vienna resident for more
than 50 years, Sigmund Freud,
the father of psychoanalysis,

STAY

DO & CO
At this central boutique
hotel, guests can enjoy
rooms with fine views
of the Stephansdom.
There is a sleek bar and
restaurant on-site, too.

⌂ Stephansplatz 12
🌐 docohotel.com

€€€

Hotel ViennArt am MuseumsQuartier
This stylish 60-room
design hotel is located
mere steps from the
main attractions.

⌂ Breite Gasse 9
🌐 austrotel.at

€€€

---

is as synonymous with the
Austrian capital as coffee
houses and the waltz. His
former home on Berggasse
differs little from any other
19th-century apartment
building in Vienna, yet it is
one of the city's most famous
addresses and something of
a shrine. Freud lived, worked,
and received patients here
from 1891 until his sudden
departure from Vienna in
1938, when the Nazis forced
Freud and his family to leave
the city. The apartment has
been preserved as a museum
to his life and work, and is also
home to an extensive library.

The museum is closed for
renovation until May 2020, but
until this time some exhibits
are on display in the temporary "Moving Freud Museum,"
housed in nearby Berggasse
13 and Leichtensteinstrasse 19.

---

⑨
MAK (Museum für angewandte Kunst)

⌂ Stubenring 5
Ⓤ Stubentor, Landstrasse
🚌 3A, 74A 🚋 2 🕐 10am–
10pm Tue, 10am–6pm Wed–
Sun 🗓 Jan 1, May 1, Nov 1,
Dec 25 🌐 mak.at

The Museum of Applied Arts, or
MAK, was founded in 1864 as a
collection of art and architecture. It has since expanded
and diversified to include

↑ Panels focusing on the
life and work of Sigmund
Freud at the fascinating
Freud Museum

objects representing new
artistic movements and
contemporary design. The
museum has a fine collection
of textiles, glass, Islamic and
East Asian art, Renaissance
jewelry, and various items of
furniture – including a room
full of Biedermeier pieces.

The most important
Austrian artistic movement
was the Secession, formed
by artists who seceded from
the Vienna academy in 1897.
Their style, which was greatly
influenced by the German
Jugendstil, is represented
through the many and varied
items produced by the Wiener
Werkstätte (Viennese Workshops), a cooperative arts and
crafts studio founded in 1903.

---

⑩
Secession Building

⌂ Friedrichstrasse 12
Ⓤ Karlsplatz 🕐 10am–6pm
Tue–Sun 🌐 secession.at

Austrian architect Joseph
Maria Olbrich designed the
unusual Secession Building
in *Jugendstil* style in 1898 as
a showcase for the Secession
movement's artists. The
almost windowless structure

TOP 4 FEATURES OF THE SECESSION BUILDING

Gorgons' Heads
The mythical demons sit above the legend "Painting, Architecture, and Sculpture."

Dome
The great dome is made from 2,500 gilt laurel leaves and 311 berries.

Planters
Look out for the turtles that support massive plant pots on either side of the entrance.

Owl Reliefs
Koloman Moser's wise birds can be found on the side of the building.

↑ Gorgons' heads, adorning the facade of the Secession Building

is a squat cube with four towers, topped by a filigree globe of entwined laurel leaves – a feature that gave rise to the building's nickname: "The Golden Cabbage." Inside, Gustav Klimt's famous *Beethoven*

Frieze of 1902 covers three walls and is one of the finest works of the movement.

Karlskirche

🏛 Karlsplatz ⓤ Karlsplatz
🚌 4A 🚋 D, 1, 2 ⏰ 9am–6pm Mon-Sat, noon–7pm Sun
🌐 karlskirche.at

During a plague epidemic in Vienna in 1713, Karl VI vowed that, as soon as the city was delivered, he would build a church dedicated to St. Charles

Borromeo, a patron saint of the plague. The result was Johann Bernhard Fischer von Erlach's Baroque masterpiece, which borrows elements from Classical architecture.

The interior was embellished with carvings and altarpieces by leading artists of the day. Johann Michael Rottmayr's huge fresco in the cupola depicts St. Charles in heaven interceding for deliverance from the plague.

Henry Moore's *Hill Arches* (1973) in the pond in front of the Karlskirche

Schönbrunn Palace and Gardens

🏠 Schönbrunner Schloss Strasse 47, Schönbrunn Ⓤ Schönbrunn 🚌 10A 🚊 10, 60 ⏱ Hours vary, check website 🌐 schoenbrunn.at

The former summer residence of the imperial family, this magnificent palace takes its name from a "beautiful spring" that was found nearby. It is one of Vienna's most popular attractions and a UNESCO World Heritage Site.

After an earlier hunting lodge was destroyed by the Ottomans, Leopold I asked Johann Bernhard Fischer von Erlach to design a Baroque residence here in 1695. The project was finally completed by Nikolaus Pacassi in the mid-18th century, under Empress Maria Theresa. The strict symmetry of the architecture is complemented by the extensive formal gardens, with their neat lawns and careful planting. The gardens contain a huge tropical Palm House with a collection of exotic plants, a small zoo, a butterfly house, an orangery, and the Gloriette – a large Neo-Classical arcade that crowns the hill behind the palace.

The Rococo decorative schemes inside the palace were devised by Pacassi. The rooms vary from the highly sumptuous – such as the Millionen-Zimmer, paneled with fig-wood inlaid with Persian miniatures – to the plainer apartments of Franz Joseph and Empress Elisabeth.

The Memorial Room contains the portrait and effigy of the Duke of Reichstadt, the son of Napoleon and Princess Maria Louisa. A virtual prisoner in the palace after Napoleon's fall from power, the duke died here in 1832 aged 21. Alongside the palace is a museum of imperial coaches and sleighs.

Prater

🏠 Prater Ⓤ Praterstern 🚊 0, 5 ⏱ 10am–midnight daily 🌐 praterwien.com

Originally an imperial hunting ground, this huge area of woods and meadows between the Danube and the Danube Canal was opened to the public by Joseph II in 1766. The central avenue, or Hauptallee, stretches for 3 miles (5 km) through the center of the Prater, and was for a long time the preserve of the nobility and their footmen. During the 19th century, the northern end of the Prater became a massive funfair, dominated by the iconic Wiener Riesenrad Ferris wheel. (Access to the Prater itself is free, but each ride is charged individually.) There is also a planetarium, an exhibition center, and a racing track nearby.

The southern side of the Prater contains extensive woodland, interlaced with cycle paths and a municipal

---

INSIDER TIP
Take in a Show

Puppet shows at the Marionetten Theater at Schönbrunn will delight children and adults alike. A version of Mozart's *The Magic Flute* is an undisputed highlight, featuring a feather-clad Tamino and a superbly vicious snake *(www. marionettentheater.at)*.

The Ehrenhof fountain in front of the magnificent Schönbrunn Palace

golf course. The miniature Prater Train runs for almost 2 miles (4 km) around the park from March to October.

---

⑭ 🚲 Ⓜ 🖥 🏛

Belvedere

📍 Upper Belvedere: Prinz-Eugen-Strasse 27; Lower Belvedere: Rennweg 6
Ⓢ Quartier Belvedere
🚌 13A, 69A 🚊 D, 0, 18, 71
🕐 Hours vary, check wesbite 🌐 belvedere.at

The Belvedere was built by Johann Lukas von Hildebrandt as the summer residence of Prince Eugene of Savoy, the brilliant military commander whose strategies helped vanquish the Ottomans in 1683. Situated on a gently sloping hill, the Belvedere consists of two palaces linked by a French-style formal garden. The huge garden is sited on three levels, joined by two elaborate cascading waterfalls. Different areas of the garden have been designed to convey a complicated series of Classical allusions: the lower part of the garden represents the realm of the Four Elements, the center is Parnassus (a sacred mountain), and the upper section is Olympus (home of the gods).

Standing at the highest point of the garden, the Upper Belvedere has an elaborate facade, with lavish stone ornamentation, balustrades, and statues. The domed copper roofs of the end pavilions were designed to resemble Turkish tents – an allusion to Prince Eugene's military victories. In fact, the whole palace was intended to be a symbolic reflection of the prince's power and glory. The many impressive interiors include the Sala Terrena, with four Herculean figures supporting the ceiling, the ornately decorated chapel, and the opulent Marble Hall.

Masterpieces from the Baroque collection are displayed on the first floor of the east wing in the Upper Belvedere. These include the character heads by Franz Xaver Messerschmidt and sculptures by Georg Raphael Donner, as well as paintings by J. M. Rottmayr, Martino Atomonte, and Paul Troger. The ground floor houses some masterpieces of Austrian Medieval Art, including the Znaimer Altar – the seven panels painted by Rueland Frueauf the Elder that show

> **In fact, the whole Belvedere was intended to be a symbolic reflection of Prince Eugene of Savoy's power and glory.**

the Passion taking place in an Austrian setting – and the 12th-century Romanesque Stammerberg Crucifix, one of the oldest surviving examples of Tyrolean woodcarving.

The building also houses the collections of 19th- and 20th-century paintings that belong to the Austrian Gallery. Many of the works are by Austrian painters, with an excellent collection by Gustav Klimt that includes his celebrated canvas *The Kiss*. There are also works by Ferdinand Georg Waldmüller, Schiele, and Van Gogh.

The Lower Belvedere was used by Prince Eugene for day-to-day living, and the building itself is less elaborate than the Upper Belvedere. Many of the rooms are just as grand, however, such as the ornate, golden Hall of Mirrors. A museum here shows temporary exhibitions. Next door to the Lower Belvedere is the handsome Orangery.

↑ Visitors admiring Klimt's glittering *The Kiss* (1907-8) at the Belvedere

❷

Graz

🏠 Styria ✈️ 🚉 🚌
ℹ️ Herrengasse 16;
www.graztourismus.at

Almost entirely surrounded by mountains, Graz is Austria's second largest city. During the Middle Ages, its importance rivaled that of Vienna. In the late 14th century, the Habsburg Duke Leopold III chose Graz as his base, and in the following century, the town played a vital strategic role in the war against the invading Ottomans.

The city is dominated by the Schlossberg, the huge hill on which the town's medieval defenses were built. During the Napoleonic Wars, Graz was occupied by French troops, who blew up most of the fortifications in 1809. Among the ruins visible today are a clock tower – the Uhrturm – which dates from 1561, and the 1588 Glockenturm (bell tower). The former houses the Schlossbergmuseum, with exhibits illustrating the history of Graz. From the summit of the hill, there are splendid views.

Beneath the Schlossberg lies the Old Town, a UNESCO World Heritage Site. Its medieval Burg (fortress) was built in several stages and completed in 1500. To the south are the Late-Gothic Cathedral of St. Ägydius, with its striking Baroque interior, and the Mausoleum of Ferdinand II, designed by the Italian Pietro de Pomis in the 17th century.

The **Universalmuseum Joanneum** incorporates 18 museums in and around Graz, including the Neue Galerie (New Gallery), displaying 19th- and 20th-century art; the Naturkundemuseum (Natural History Museum), with exhibits on Earth-science and biology; and the eye-catching Kunsthaus Graz, showcasing Austrian and international contemporary art. Also of interest is the Landeszeughaus, with its array of over 30,000 weapons and pieces of armor.

Universalmuseum Joanneum

◈ 🕐 Hours vary, check website 🌐 museum-joanneum.at

---

❸

Eisenstadt

🏠 Burgenland 🚉 🚌
ℹ️ Hauptstrasse 21; www.eisenstadt-tourismus.at

The main attraction of the pleasant town of Eisenstadt, the capital of Burgenland

↓ Looking over Graz from the city's 16th-century clock tower

INSIDER TIP

Schloss Eggenberg

While in Graz it is worth making a trip to Schloss Eggenberg, a few miles west of the city. Open daily, the Baroque palace houses an archaeology museum, a collection of local prehistoric finds, and a rich selection of paintings.

---

state, is **Schloss Esterházy**. This grand residence was built in 1663–73 for Prince Paul Esterházy, a member of the Esterházy family of Hungarian aristocrats who claimed to be descendants of Attila. In the palace's Haydnsaal – a huge hall of state decorated with 18th-century frescoes – the family orchestra was conducted by famous composer Joseph Haydn. Haydn himself lived in a house on Haydngasse, which is now a museum. He is buried in the Bergkirche, west of the palace.

Until World War II, Eisenstadt had a large Jewish community, and there is a Jewish Museum near the palace.

Schloss Esterházy

◈ 🏠 Esterházyplatz 🕐 Apr-Oct: 10am–5pm daily (May-Sep: to 6pm); Nov-Mar: 10am-5pm Fri–Sun 🌐 esterhazy.at/en/esterhazypalace

← The gilded interior of Melk's Benedictine abbey, which sits perched on a brush-covered hilltop *(inset)*

❹ Melk and the Wachau Valley

🏛 Lower Austria 🚌🚆 Melk
ℹ Kremserstrasse 5, Melk; www.stiftmelk.at

The town of Melk lies at the western end of one of the loveliest stretches of the River Danube, the Wachau. Dotted with Renaissance houses and old towers, Melk itself is most famous for its abbey.

A boat trip is the best way to enjoy the picturesque scenery of the Wachau Valley, but for the energetic there are cycle paths along the banks of the river. Landmarks to look out for while traveling downstream include the pretty castle of **Schönbühel** and the ruined medieval fortress at Aggstein. Though not visible from the river, nearby Willendorf is the site of famous prehistoric finds *(p538)*.

At the eastern end of the Wachau are the well-preserved medieval towns of Dürnstein and Krems. The latter's tiny hillside streets offer fine views across the Danube to the Baroque Göttweig Abbey.

---

❺ Linz

🏛 Upper Austria ✈🚌🚆
ℹ Hauptplatz 1; www.linztourismus.at

Austria's third city, Linz has been inhabited since Roman times. In the early 16th century, it developed into an important trading center, and is still a busy industrial city today.

The attractive Old Town contains many historic buildings and monuments. The Hauptplatz, one of the largest medieval squares in Europe, is bordered by splendid Baroque facades, including that of the town hall.

In the southeast corner of the square is the church of St. Ignatius. Also known as the Alter Dom, it was built in the 17th century in Baroque style and features a wonderfully ornate pulpit and altarpiece.

The streets west of here lead up to Linz's hilltop castle, built for Friedrich V (Holy Roman Emperor Friedrich III) in the 15th century. Today the castle houses the vast Schlossmuseum, displaying paintings, sculptures, and historical artifacts.

On the other side of the river is the **Ars Electronica Center**, a superb center for electronic arts that allows visitors to experiment with the latest technological innovations. Hidden away in a shopping mall is the **Lentos Kunstmuseum**, containing a fine collection of 19th- and 20th-century Austrian art, including works by Egon Schiele and Gustav Klimt.

For splendid views of Linz, hop on the Pöstlingbergbahn train, which climbs to the top of nearby Pöstlingberg Hill. Various river cruises along the Danube, meanwhile, depart from the quay at the Nibelungen Bridge.

Ars Electronica Center
♿ 🏛 Ars-Electronica-Strasse 1 🕐 9am–5pm Tue–Fri (to 7pm Thu), 10am–6pm Sat & Sun 🌐 aec.at

Lentos Kunstmuseum
♿ 🏛 Ernst-Koref-Promenade 11 🕐 10am–6pm Tue–Sun (to 9pm Thu) 🌐 lentos.at

← The marble interior of the Hofkirche in Innsbruck

❼
Hallstatt

 Upper Austria 🏠🚌🚆
ℹ Seestrasse 99; www.hallstatt.net

This pretty village on the bank of the Hallstätter See lies in the Salzkammergut, a stunning region of lakes and mountains. The area takes its name from the rich deposits of salt *(salz)* that have been mined here since the 1st millennium BC. Salt mining is still a major industry in Hallstatt, and it is possible to visit a working mine, the **Salzwelten Hallstatt**, by taking a cable car from the southern end of the village up to the mine entrance on the Salzberg mountain.

Back in town, the **Museum Hallstatt** contains Iron Age artifacts discovered near the mines, from the Celtic culture that flourished here from the 9th to the 5th century BC.

North of the museum, behind the Pfarrkirche – the town's Late-Gothic parish church – the Beinhaus (Charnel House) has been used to store human remains since 1600.

❻
Innsbruck

🏠 Tyrol ✈🏠🚌
ℹ Burggraben 3; www.innsbruck.info

Capital of the Tyrol region, Innsbruck grew up at the crossroads of trade routes between Vienna, Germany, Italy, and Switzerland.

One of Innsbruck's finest pieces of architecture is the Goldenes Dachl (Golden Roof), commissioned by Emperor Maximilian I, who chose the city as his imperial capital at the end of the 15th century. Made of gilded copper tiles, the roof was constructed in the 1490s to cover a balcony used by members of the court to observe events in the square below. Beneath the balcony is the **Museum Goldenes Dachl**, which focuses on the life of Maximilian I, who ruled the Habsburg Empire from 1493 to 1519.

The neighboring **Hofburg** (Imperial Palace) also dates from the 15th century, but was rebuilt in Rococo style in the 18th century by Empress Maria Theresa. On either side of it are two churches. Built in 1555–65, the Hofkirche contains the impressive mausoleum of Maximilian I. The highlight of the Domkirche St. Jakob (1717–22), meanwhile, is Lucas Cranach the Elder's painting of the Madonna and Child adorning the high altar.

Innsbruck's many museums include the **Tiroler Landesmuseum Ferdinandeum** (Tyrolean State Museum), which has European art from the 15th to the 20th centuries, and the **Tiroler Volkskunstmuseum** (Museum of Tyrolean Regional Heritage), with exhibitions of local folk art and crafts.

Museum Goldenes Dachl

⊛ 🏠 Herzog-Friedrichstrasse 15 📞 0512-5360 1441 🕐 May-Sep: 10am–5pm daily; Oct-Apr: 10am–5pm Tue-Sun

Hofburg

⊛ 🏠 Rennweg 1 🕐 9am–5pm daily 🌐 hofburg-innsbruck.at

Tiroler Landesmuseum Ferdinandeum

⊛ 🏠 Museumstrasse 15 🕐 9am–5pm Tue-Sun 🌐 tiroler-landesmuseen.at

Tiroler Volkskunstmuseum

⊛ 🏠 Universitätsstrasse 2 🕐 9am–5pm daily 🌐 tiroler-landesmuseen.at

→ The historic city of Salzburg, overlooked by the Hohensalzburg fortress

Elsewhere, the mountains and the crystal waters of the Hallstätter See offer many opportunities for swimming, watersports, scuba diving, hiking, and cycling. At the southern end of the lake are the Dachstein limestone caves, open daily from May to mid-October. A cable car from south of Obertraun climbs to their entrance, giving superb views of the lake and surrounding mountains.

Salzwelten Hallstatt

 Mar-mid-Dec: tours daily 🆆 salzwelten.at

Museum Hallstatt

Seestrasse 56A Apr-Oct: 10am-4pm daily (May-Sep: to 6pm); Nov-Mar: 11am-3pm Wed-Sun 🆆 museum-hallstatt.at

---

8
Salzburg

Salzburg 🆇🆁✉
ℹ Mozartplatz 5; www. salzburg.info

Salzburg rose to prominence around AD 700, when a church and a monastery were established here. Until 1816, when Salzburg became part of the Habsburg Empire, it was an independent city-state ruled by a succession of prince-archbishops, with its wealth stemming from salt mines.

Today, Salzburg is best known as the birthplace of Wolfgang Amadeus Mozart, and the city is still home to a thriving musical tradition. Each summer, large numbers of visitors arrive to attend the Salzburger Festspiele, a festival of opera, classical music, and theater. Throughout the rest of the year, the composer's birthplace can be visited at Mozarts Geburtshaus,

and audio-visual exhibits at the Mozart Wohnhaus tell the story of his life.

Salzburg's medieval fortress, the **Festung Hohensalzburg**, looms over the city from its hilltop position. The castle dates from the 11th century, but the state apartments are an early 16th-century addition.

The **Residenz**, where the prince-archbishops lived, is Early Baroque in appearance. In addition to its state rooms, the palace also contains the Residenzgalerie – a collection of European art of the 16th to 19th centuries. Opposite, the **Salzburg Museum** in the New Residenz relates the history of Salzburg and also hosts temporary exhibitions.

On the right bank of the Salzach, Schloss Mirabell and its Baroque garden were built by Archbishop Wolf Dietrich for his mistress. Away from the city center is the Renaissance palace of Hellbrunn.

Festung Hohensalzburg

Mönchsberg 34 Hours vary, check website 🆆 salzburg-burgen.at

Residenz

Residenzplatz 1 Hours vary, check website 🆆 domquartier.at

Salzburg Museum

Mozartplatz 1 9am-5pm Tue-Sun Nov 1, Dec 25 🆆 salzburgmuseum.at

PRACTICAL
INFORMATION

Here you will find all the essential advice and information you will need before and during your stay in Austria.

AT A GLANCE

CURRENCY
Euro (EUR)

TIME ZONE
CET/CEST. Central European Summer Time runs from the last Sunday in March to the last Sunday in October.

LANGUAGE
German

ELECTRICITY SUPPLY
Power sockets are type F, fitting type C and type F plugs. Standard voltage is 230V.

EMERGENCY NUMBERS

GENERAL EMERGENCY	AMBULANCE
112	**144**

FIRE	POLICE
122	**133**

TAP WATER
Unless stated otherwise, tap water in Austria is safe to drink.

Getting There

Major airports include Vienna Schwechat International Airport, Innsbruck Airport, and Salzburg Airport W. A. Mozart. A number of smaller airports, including Graz, Klagenfurt, and Linz, also serve destinations within Europe.

Situated at the heart of Europe, Austria has excellent international rail links. Regular high-speed trains connect the country to major cities in neighboring countries. The fastest train, the Railjet, can travel at speeds of up to 143 mph (230 km/h) and links major Austrian cities with hubs across Germany, Italy, Switzerland, the Czech Republic, and Hungary.

FlixBus and Eurolines offer a variety of inter-national bus routes to Austria from most major European cities, including Berlin, Budapest, London, and Paris.

A number of cruise companies offer trips through Austria along the Danube between Germany and the Black Sea, including **Scenic** and **Viking**, which stop at Vienna, Linz, Melk, and other destinations along the way.
Scenic
W scenic.co.uk
Viking
W viking.co.uk

Personal Security

Austria is generally a safe country, but it is always a good idea to take sensible precautions against pickpockets. If you have anything stolen, report the crime as soon as possible to the nearest police station. Get a copy of the crime report in order to claim on your insurance.

Health

EU citizens with a European Health Insurance Card (EHIC) are entitled to free emergency medical care in Austria, but it is also advisable to take out some form of supplementary health insurance. Visitors from outside the EU must arrange their own private medical insurance.

For minor ailments, seek medical supplies and advice from a pharmacy *(apotheke)*.

Passports and Visas

Citizens of the US, Canada, Australia, and New Zealand just need a passport to visit Austria. No visa is required for stays of up to three months. Most EU visitors need only a valid identity card to enter the country. For visa information specific to your home country, consult your nearest Austrian embassy or check online.

LGBT+ Safety

LGBT+ rights in Austria are less progressive than in many European countries, although same-sex marriage has been legal since 2019. The LGBT+ scene is best in Vienna, which celebrates two weeks of EuroPride Vienna festivities annually, climaxing with its Rainbow Parade.

Travelers with Specific Needs

Austria offers a high standard of facilities for travelers with disabilities. Most hotels and major museums are wheelchair accessible (except in some older buildings) and most of the transport system is equipped for disabled use. Guide dogs are allowed on public transport. Österreichische Bundesbahnen (ÖBB; see right) has mobility aids at around 100 train stations and offers discounted tickets and travel assistance. For further information on accessible travel, contact the Austrian National Tourist Office (see right).

Money

Major credit, debit, and prepaid currency cards are accepted in most shops and restaurants, and contactless payments are becoming more widely accepted. However, it is always worth carrying some cash for smaller items.

Cell Phones and Wi-Fi

Visitors traveling to Austria with EU tariffs can use their devices without being affected by data roaming charges. Visitors from other countries should check their contracts before departure in order to avoid unexpected charges.

Wi-Fi is widely available throughout Austria, and cafés and restaurants will usually permit the use of their Wi-Fi on the condition you make a purchase.

Getting Around

Austria's reliable rail network is run by the state-owned **Österreichische Bundesbahnen (ÖBB)**, and is one of the best ways to travel from town to town. The railroad timetable is well coordinated with buses and other forms of public transport.

Although train is the most popular way of traveling between cities in Austria, ÖBB postbuses offer reasonably priced bus travel throughout the country, and are especially useful for reaching mountainous regions and ski resorts. **FlixBus** also provides a popular low-cost inter-city bus network, with easy online booking and direct services between Vienna, Salzburg, Linz, Graz, and Klagenfurt.

Autobahns (highways) link all the major cities and even in winter, Austrian road conditions are good. Highways are subject to a toll, which is paid by buying a windshield sticker valid for a certain period of time. Stickers can be bought at the border or at post offices, gas stations, and tobacconists throughout the country. Tolls are also payable on certain mountain roads and tunnels. All drivers in Austria must carry their driver's license, car registration documents, and insurance documents.

Flixbus
W flixbus.com
ÖBB
W oebb.at

Visitor Information

Austria has a wide network of local and regional tourist offices and the **Austrian National Tourist Office** has branches in many countries abroad. In the busier ski resorts in winter, local offices often stay open as late as 9pm. In Vienna, **Wiener Tourismusverband** is a very helpful organization, especially with regard to forthcoming events and booking accommodations.

Austrian National Tourist Office
W austria.info
Wiener Tourismusverband
W wien.info

The iconic peak of the Matterhorn, bathed in dawn light

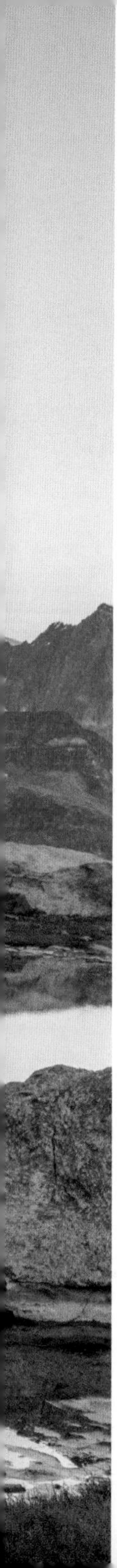

SWITZERLAND

Switzerland's story has been of a gradual coming together of diverse languages, cultures, and religions, making what is today viewed as a haven of peace and reason. It was first inhabited over 50,000 years ago, and by the start of the Christian era there were Celtic peoples living in western Switzerland and Germanic tribes in the north and east. Many of these were under the control of the expanding Roman Empire, whose rule lasted until the 5th century AD. Different factions then fought over the territory until it was swallowed into the Holy Roman Empire in the 9th century, although it continued to be a battleground for powerful feudal families – notably the Habsburgs, Savoys, and Zähringens – up to the 13th century. In 1291, the "Three Forest Cantons" – Uri, Schwyz, and Unterwalden – came together to form the independent Swiss Confederation, which was joined by more cantons over the next 200 years. Protestantism took root in the 16th century; Swiss cities embraced the new doctrines, whereas rural cantons remained mostly Catholic. There were tensions between the two communities and, apart from a brief period at the turn of the 19th century when Napoleon established the Helvetic Republic, these issues were not resolved until the adoption of a federal constitution in 1848. With stability came development – railroads were built, agriculture diversified, and resorts developed. In the 20th century, Switzerland remained neutral during the two world wars, and concentrated on furthering its economic development, notably in finance and pharmaceuticals. Today it remains outside the EU, but continues to play a prominent role in world affairs.

SWITZERLAND

1 Geneva
2 Lake Geneva
3 Basel
4 Bern
5 Interlaken and the Jungfrau
6 Neuchâtel
7 Zermatt
8 Zürich
9 Lucerne
10 Chur
11 Ticino
12 Swiss National Park

← Evening illuminations at one of the squares in Geneva's Old Town

Geneva

⌂ Geneva ✈🚆🚌 🛈 Rue du Mont-Blanc 18; www. geneve.com

Geneva's origins go back to Roman times. The Old Town, situated on a craggy hill above the western end of Lake Geneva, is the most

---

EAT

Le Jardin
Artfully presented French cuisine.
⌂ Rue Adhémar-Fabri 8-10
🌐 lerichemond.com

Café-Restaurant de l'Hôtel de Ville
Exceptional traditional Genevois fare.
⌂ Grand-Rue 39
🌐 hdvglozu.ch

Ananda Café-Boutique
Himalayan food in a vintage setting.
⌂ Fbg de l'Hôpital 31, Neuchâtel 📞 032 721 34 44

---

attractive part of the city, with narrow cobbled lanes and streets, fountain-filled squares, and an array of galleries, shops, and cafés.

In the heart of the Old Town stands the Cathédrale St-Pierre. Built from 1160 to 1230, with later additions, this vast cathedral is a mishmash of styles, from the Gothic to the Neo-Classical with a mix of Catholic and Protestant symbolism. Close by is the Maison Tavel, a splendid 14th-century townhouse that gives a good insight into life in the city as it evolved through the centuries. Around the corner, in Rue Jean-Calvin, the Barbier-Müller Museum displays a mesmerizing collection of beautiful carvings, jewelry, and textiles from traditional societies in Africa and the Asia-Pacific region.

At the eastern end of the Old Town is Geneva's grandest museum, the **Musée d'Art et d'Histoire**, housing some 650,000 objects. Its collections range from applied and fine arts to archaeology, and are presented alongside regular temporary exhibitions.

North of the museum, the Rue de Rive – Geneva's main shopping street – runs parallel to the lake shore. The quays on either side of the lake are pleasant places to stroll, with the Jardin Anglais and the Jet d'Eau (one of the world's largest fountains) on the left bank, and the Quai du Mont-Blanc on the right. It is from the latter that ferries and paddle-steamers operate pleasure cruises and regular services to towns along the lake. Farther along the right

bank are the city's botanic gardens; take the road that borders them and you will come to the international quarter of the city. Here, the **Palais des Nations** – the UN office of Geneva – runs frequent guided tours through the day (ID documents are mandatory). Opposite, the International Red Cross and Red Crescent Museum offers a moving testimony to the need for such an organization.

Musée d'Art et d'Histoire
🅰️🛈🏛 ⌂ Rue Charles-Galland 2 🕐 11am-6pm Tue-Sun 🌐 ville-ge.ch/mah

Palais des Nations
♿🅰️ ⌂ Avenue de la Paix 14 🕐 Hours vary, check website 🌐 unog.ch

---

Lake Geneva

⌂ Vaud 🚆🚌🚌 🛈 Avenue d'Ouchy 60, Lausanne; www.region-du-leman.ch

While most of Lake Geneva's southern shore is French territory, the greater part of

→ The imposing Château de Chillon, perched on the shore of Lake Geneva

---

the lake lies within Switzerland. The region around it offers a string of charming settlements in a landscape replete with rolling hills, pretty stone-built villages, vine-clad slopes, and palm-fringed esplanades.

Just north of Geneva is the quaint medieval village of Coppet. The 17th-century Château de Coppet was the home of French-Swiss writer Madame de Staël, whose literary soirées and opposition to Napoleon enhanced the popularity of the château in the 18th century. Farther along the lake is the charming town of Nyon, commanding a fine hilltop view over the water with its fortress-like château. Nyon itself dates from Roman times, a heritage displayed at the excellent Roman Museum.

Lausanne, 38 miles (60 km) east of Geneva, is a bustling city with a fine Old Town, a beautiful Gothic cathedral, and excellent shopping. The city is also home to the headquarters of the International Olympic Committee – the Musée Olympique, in the lakeside district of Ouchy, is a must for all sports enthusiasts. Farther east still is the resort of

Montreux, with a palm-lined promenade and a busy marina. As well as grand *belle-époque* hotels and health resorts, the town is also home to one of Switzerland's top attractions, the **Château de Chillon**. This enchanting medieval castle is the former bastion of the dukes of Savoy, and has all the accoutrements you might expect – dungeons, weaponry, and huge banqueting halls.

North of Montreux, the well-preserved medieval walled town of Gruyères is also a major tourist attraction. Its cobbled main street is flanked by numerous tempting restaurants, many of which serve the famous cheese – you can see it being made in the traditional way in the Moléson-sur-Gruyères.

Another holiday resort in this area is Vevey, whose culture and climate have long attracted rich expats. The comedian Charlie Chaplin spent the last 25 years of his life here, and the Chaplin's World museum in his former home is dedicated to his life and work.

Château de Chillon
⊗⊗⊗⊗ 🏠 Avenue de Chillon 21, 1820 Veytaux ⏱10am–5pm daily 🚫Jan 1, Dec 25 🌐chillon.ch

↑ Basel's riverside Old Town, beneath the twin spires of the cathedral

③

Basel

 Basel ⊠🚃 🚌 **i** Basel Tourismus, Stadt-Casino, Barfüsserplatz; www. basel.com

Straddling the Rhine, Basel is a city of contrasts, with a reputation for both industry and art. As the country's only port, Basel has long been a center of commercial activity, particularly for the chemical and pharmaceutical industries. More recently, the city has developed a vibrant cultural scene as the host of Art Basel, the world's largest contemporary art fair. Basel is also famous for its festivals, the largest of which, Fasnacht, is an exuberant masked carnival.

The Old Town remains the heart of the city and is a maze of fine streets and squares, including Marktplatz, with its daily fruit and vegetable market. The red-painted Rathaus (Town Hall) stands here, on the southern bank of the Rhine.

The twin sandstone towers of the Gothic cathedral are major landmarks. This imposing 12th-century building stands in a grand square – site of the famous autumn fair that has been an annual event since the 15th century.

Basel's modern side can be seen in the city's collection of art museums. The most notable of these are the **Kunstmuseum**, which features an impressive range of 20th-century artists, and the Kunsthalle, with a rolling programme of exhibitions by leading contemporary artists. The **Museum Tinguely** is devoted to the outlandish mechanical sculptures of Switzerland's most famous artist, Jean Tinguely.

Kunstmuseum

⊛⊘ 🏠 St Alban-Graben 16 🕐 10am–6pm Tue–Sun (to 8pm Wed) 🔲 kunstmuseum basel.ch

Museum Tinguely

⊛ 🏠 Paul Sacher Anlage 2 🕐 11am–6pm Tue–Sun 🔲 tinguely.ch

---

④

Bern

 Bern ⊠🚃🚌 **i** Bahnhofplatz 10a; www.berninfo.com

The capital of Switzerland, Bern is arguably the country's most attractive city, with a beautifully preserved medieval town center. It is located

> 💬 INSIDER TIP
> **Museum Pass**
>
> Valid for a full year, the Museum Pass is a good option if you plan to visit a few of Basel's 37 museums. It can be bought at the tourist information office at the SBB station, or from the Stadtcasino at Barfüsserplatz.

on raised land in a bend of the Aare river, with spectacular views over the river and across to the peaks of the distant Alps.

The city was founded at the end of the 12th century by the Duke of Zähringen, and allegedly named after the first animal – a bear – killed in the forests that previously covered the area. The bear has been the city's emblem ever since. Most of the center of Bern, with its fine stone Renaissance houses and covered arcades, dates from the 16th and 17th centuries.

Bern was made capital of the Swiss Confederation in 1848. The city's vast Bundeshaus (Parliament House) is the home of the Swiss Parliament, and the building is open to visitors when parliament is not in session. It is situated at the end of the city's main market squares – Bärenplatz and Bundesplatz. These adjoining squares are also the site of the annual onion market that takes place on the fourth Monday in November, when the local onion harvest is traditionally celebrated.

The attractive Old Town at the heart of Bern is a UNESCO World Heritage Site, famous for its arcaded streets, which offer broad protection in the event of bad weather. The main streets – Kramgasse, Spitalgasse, Marktgasse, and Gerechtigkeitsgasse – are all lined with tempting shops, galleries, and cafés.

The city's famous clock tower stands where Kramgasse meets Marktgasse. The clock dates from 1530, and on the hour a sequence of figures – including bears, a jester, and a rooster – play out a performance. The Old Town is filled with magnificent fountains, each of which depicts a well-known historical or legendary figure. A wander around the city center will reveal the likenesses of Bern's founder, the Duke of Zähringen, Moses, and the gruesome child-eating ogre, the Kindlifresser.

The imposing cathedral on Münstergasse was built in the 15th century and is a beautiful example of Late Gothic architecture. The building's most magnificent element is the main portal – a masterpiece of carved and painted stone, with a depiction of the Last Judgment; the tall spire was only added in the late 19th century. To the right of the cathedral is a delightful small park overlooking the Aare flowing far below, which makes a good picnic spot in summer.

On the shore of the Aare, just below the old Bärengraben, or bear pits, is a huge bear park. Its caves, pools, and forest provide a more natural home than the 19th-century pits.

Across the Kirchenfeldbrücke, opposite the Old Town, is the city's **Historical Museum**. It provides a great introduction to the city's history with some 500,000 artifacts, including wonderful Flemish tapestries. The site is also home to the Einstein Museum, which offers an engaging account of Albert Einstein's life and ground-breaking discoveries.

Another of the city's notable residents is celebrated at the **Zentrum Paul Klee**, on Monument im Fruchtland. The center is an incredible wave-like structure that was designed by Italian architect Renzo Piano, who intended it to blend in with the surrounding landscape. Inside are around 4,000 works by the renowned artist, who was influenced by Expressionism, Cubism, and Surrealism.

To the southeast of Bern is the Emmental Valley. This verdant agricultural region is famous for the cheese of the same name. A drive around the region can make an ideal half-day tour, taking in some of the delightful towns and villages – Burgdorf, Affoltern, and Langnau im Emmental – and the rolling hills dotted with covered wooden bridges and gabled farmhouses.

Historical Museum
⊘ ⊘ 🅰 Helvetiaplatz 5 🕐 10am–5pm Tue–Sun 🗓 4th Mon in Nov, Dec 25 🌐 bhm.ch

Zentrum Paul Klee
⊘ ⊘ ⓘ ⓘ 🅰 Monument im Fruchtland 3 🕐 10am–5pm Tue–Sun 🌐 zpk.org

Bern's wave-like Zentrum Paul Klee, designed by Renzo Piano

ALPINE WILDLIFE

Marmots

Often difficult to spot but quite easy to hear, marmots live in burrows high on the valley slopes. Found throughout the Alps, they're especially abundant around Ticino and Graubünden *(p564)*.

Chamois

Adept at scaling high mountain ridges, these goat-like antelopes were once hunted for their soft leather hides. Today, however, hunting quotas are imposed.

Alpine Chough

A lively, crow-like bird, the alpine chough spends the summer above the tree line, but descend to the valleys and villages in winter.

5

Interlaken and the Jungfrau

🏠 Bern 🚉🚌 ℹ Marktgasse 1; www.interlaken.ch

As suggested by its name, Interlaken lies between two lakes – the Thunersee and the Brienzersee – in the foothills of the Alps. To the south is the classic landscape of the Jungfrau mountains – one of the first regions of Switzerland to be opened up to tourism in the mid-19th century. Tourism is virtually the only industry in town, which caters for skiers in winter and sightseers by the busload in summer. A funicular, built in 1906, transports visitors up to the summit of the Heimwehfluh (2,230 ft/680 m), a wonderful vantage point above the town. From here, you can walk along woodland paths, visit an open-air model railroad, or take the bob-run all the way down to the base station in Interlaken.

One of the Alps' most famous peaks, the 13,642-ft (4,158-m) Jungfrau lies 12 miles (20 km) to the south of Interlaken. The Aletsch Glacier in this area is the longest in the Alps, and can be traversed on a breathtaking guided walk. Nearby, the turquoise Oeschinensee is one of Switzerland's most stunning glacial lakes.

West of the Jungfrau massif, the village of Kanderstag is an excellent winter ski resort, while in summer it becomes a popular base for hiking, biking, and paragliding. The Mönch and Eiger mountains are also neighbors of the Jungfrau, and the stretch between Interlaken and the mountains is full of pretty Alpine valleys and villages. From Grindelwald or Lauterbrunnen, you can take a train up to Kleine Scheidegg, and another to Jungfraujoch, which at 11,332 ft (3,454 m) is Europe's highest train station. A thrilling cable-car ride from the Stechelberg parking area in the Lauterbrunnen Valley

rises to the Schilthorn peak. The region is perfect skiing and hiking territory, with a range of walking trails to suit all ability levels.

A few miles east of the town of Brienz lies the **Ballenberg** (Swiss Open Air Museum). This interesting living museum displays a variety of local building types from all over the country.

Ballenberg

 2 miles (3 km) E of Brienz Apr–Oct: 10am–5pm daily **w** ballenberg.ch

---

6

Neuchâtel

Neuchâtel **i** Hôtel des Postes; www.neuchateltourisme.ch

Neuchâtel, an old religious center and university town, lies at the eastern end of Lake Neuchâtel, at the base of the Jura mountains. It has an

←

Colorful market stalls lining the streets of Interlaken's charming Old Town

attractive Old Town, with a market square that is bounded by elegant 17th-century buildings. The surrounding area is known for its wines, including Perdrix Blanche.

Northwest of Neuchâtel lies La Chaux-de-Fonds, the largest of Switzerland's watch-making towns. Located 3,255 ft (992 m) above sea level, it is set out in a rigid grid pattern – adopted when the town was rebuilt following a devastating 18th-century fire. The **Musée International d'Horlogerie** here has a wonderful watch collection, and is well worth a visit.

Musée International d'Horlogerie

 Rue des Musées 29 10am–5pm Tue–Sun Jan 1, Dec 24–25 & 31 **w** chaux-de-fonds.ch/musees/mih

---

7

Zermatt

Valais **i** Bahnhofplatz 5; www.zermatt.ch

Switzerland's most famous resort, Zermatt sits directly below the Matterhorn, a peak

↑ Mountaineers making their way through a carpet of snow towards the Matterhorn, near Zermatt

of 14,688 ft (4,478 m) that has been a legend of mountain-climbing for the best part of two centuries. In addition to mountaineering, Zermatt offers top-quality skiing and hiking. Skiing is possible all year round here – at the highest of Switzerland's resorts – and there are also miles of well-marked trails accessible to all walkers.

The most scenic way to reach Zermatt is aboard the Glacier Express from St. Moritz, but most visitors arrive by train from Täsch, 3 miles (5 km) down the valley. Taxis from Täsch to car-free Zermatt cost about the same as the train.

The most historic part of town is Hinterdorf. The parish church and cemetery contain some poignant reminders of the dangers of the mountains, while the displays at the interesting Matterhorn Museum – Zermatlantis – located near the church – reflect the importance of the region's mountaineering tradition.

Gornergrat is probably the best viewing point for the Matterhorn – it can be reached via a four-hour hike or a less-strenuous ride on the cog-wheel railroad.

EXPERIENCE Switzerland

⑧
Zürich

⌂ Zürich 🚊🚆🚌
ℹ Hauptbahnhof;
www.zuerich.com

Zürich's dominant position in the nation's economy dates back centuries – in medieval times the guilds ruled the city and, boosted by the Reformation, Zürich and its inhabitants developed a talent for hard work and accumulating wealth. The stock exchange opened in 1877, and today Swiss bankers control the purse strings of many international companies and organizations.

Despite this tradition, the city also knows how to enjoy itself, and the medieval town center, which stretches either side of the Limmat river, is a hive of cafés, bars, and hip boutiques. On the east bank, the warren of streets and alleys lies close to the university, whose students add to the district's buzz. Also on the east bank is the extremely austere Grossmünster, which dominates the city. This was the church from which religious leader Ulrich Zwingli launched the Reformation

←
A globe by Jost Bürgi (1552-1632), on display at the Swiss National Museum

Did You Know?

Singer-songwriter Tina Turner lives in Zürich and became a Swiss citizen in 2013.

on the receptive burghers of Zürich in 1520. Along Limmat Quai, you can see the Rathaus (Town Hall) built out on supports over the river, opposite one of Zürich's guildhalls. Its facade is ornmented with friezes, and the marble doorway has gilt decoration.

There are also a number of interesting sights on the other side of the river. Lindenhof, a small tree-covered hill, was where Zürich was founded in the 1st century BC. Today, an observation platform here provides views over the city. Nearby are the churches of Fraumünster and St. Peter's;

← The striking Fraumünster church, and *(inset)* one of the Bodmer frescoes in its cloisters

the former in particular is worth a visit, with its Romanesque cloisters and stained-glass windows by Marc Chagall.

Leading down from St. Peter's is Augustinergasse, a delightful street with traces of medieval storefronts. It is a world away from Zürich's main shopping street of Bahnhofstrasse, which it meets at one end. Mostly pedestrianized, Bahnhofstrasse is a wide, tree-lined avenue with trams running along its length. There are plenty of high-priced emporia, especially towards the southern lake end, but interesting and reasonably priced shops and department stores can still be found here or in the streets nearby. At Füsslistrasse 4, Orell Füssli is Switzerland's largest English-language bookshop, while nearby on Löwenplatz, you will find delicious coffee and chocolate delights at the celebrated confectioner Confiserie Sprüngli.

Just behind the main train station at the top of Bahnhofstrasse, housed in a suitably impressive building, the **Swiss National Museum** contains a comprehensive collection of art and artifacts detailing the history and cultural diversity of the country, with items dating from prehistoric times through to the present day.

Winterthur, 15 miles (25 km) northwest of Zürich, is an interesting and little-visited Swiss town. Its history as an industrial center in the 19th century has left a legacy of old factory and mill architecture and it also has some excellent museums; the best of these are the Oskar Reinhart Collection am Römerholz and the Fotomuseum.

The nucleus of medieval Stein-am-Rhein, 25 miles (40 km) northeast of Zürich, is unchanged since the 16th century. Rathausplatz and Understadt, at its heart, are

EAT

Haus Hiltl
Sample the delicous saffron gnocchi at this pioneering vegetarian buffet.

🏠 Sihlstrasse 28
🌐 hiltl.ch

Conditorei Schober
Impossible-to-resist handmade chocolates and delicate pastries tempt all who enter this lavish cakebox of a café.

🏠 Napfgasse 4
🌐 peclard-zurich.ch

lined with buildings covered in colorful frescoes, with oriel windows and window boxes.

Swiss National Museum
🏛️🏛️🏠 Museumstrasse 2
⏰ 10am–5pm Tue–Sun (to 7pm Thu) 🌐 landesmuseum.ch

Lucerne

🏠 Lucerne 🚲🚌
ℹ️ Zentralstrasse 5; www.
luzern.com

The city of Lucerne makes a good base for touring most of central Switzerland. The local countryside is stereotypically Swiss: crystal lakes ringed with snow-capped mountains, hemmed by lush pastures in summer, and crisscrossed with cog-wheel railroads. This is also the heartland of the Swiss Confederation – the three forest cantons of Uri, Schwyz, and Unterwalden, which swore the original Oath of Allegiance in 1291, border the shores of Lake Lucerne. Today, the region remains one of the most conservative parts of the country.

The town's historic center stands on the north bank of the Reuss river. Stretches of the ancient city wall and its watchtowers can be clearly seen bounding a ridge that marks the northern edge of the lively, cobbled Old Town.

The city's most famous symbol is the Kapellbrücke. This covered wooden bridge was built in 1333, and formed part of the city's original boundary, though much of it had to be renovated following a destructive fire in 1993. Nearby is the **Rosengart Collection**, with over 300 Modernist works collected by the art dealers Siegfried Rosengart and his daughter, Angela. As well as 125 works by Paul Klee, the museum has a fabulous collection of watercolors and sculptures by Pablo Picasso. There are also Impressionist paintings by Cézanne and Monet, plus pieces by Chagall, Matisse, and Kandinsky.

East from the central train station is the most-visited museum in the country, the **Swiss Museum of Transport**. Great for families, the museum has both plane and helicopter flight simulators, as well as trains, boats, and cable cars.

About 17 miles (28 km) east of Lucerne is Schwyz, the capital of one of the first three forest cantons and the origin of Switzerland's name. The town's Bundesbriefmuseum displays the charter detailing the 1291 Oath of Allegiance,

💬 INSIDER TIP
Lucerne's Markets

The markets of Lucerne are dazzling in their array of goods. Farmers' markets generally take place on Tuesdays, while on weekends you'll find a selection of crafted goods and vintage gems.

Panoramic views from the top of Pilatus, which can be accessed via cable car *(inset)*

↑ Sunlight bathing the vineyards on the hills surrounding the historic town of Chur

but perhaps more interesting is the Ital Reding Hofstatt, a fine 17th-century mansion that was built on the proceeds of one of Switzerland's first exports – mercenaries. The fighting skills of the men of Schwyz were highly prized by warring European rulers until well into the 18th century.

The whole area is overlooked by the Pilatus and Rigi mountains, both of which are easily accessible. Rigi was the first peak in Europe to have a rail line constructed to its summit; Pilatus is higher, and has unrivaled views of the Alps. Its peak can be reached by cable car or cog-wheel railroad.

Rosengart Collection

◉ ◉ ☐ Pilatusstrasse 10 ☐ Apr-Oct: 10am–6pm daily; Nov-Mar: 11am–5pm daily ☐ During carnival (dates vary) ⓦ rosengart.ch

Swiss Museum of Transport

◉ ☐ Lidostrasse 5 ☐ 10am–5pm daily (summer: to 6pm) ⓦ verkehrshaus.ch

---

Chur

☐ Graubünden ☐ ☐ Bahnhofplatz 3; www.chur tourismus.ch

Chur, the capital of the largest Swiss canton Graubünden, is a quiet town with origins that go back 2,000 years. Located on the upper reaches of the Rhine, it has long been both a religious center – the bishop of Chur controls dioceses as far away as Zürich – and a commercial center, and is famous throughout the country for the Passugger mineral water that is bottled just outside the town.

Chur's pedestrianized historic center is a pleasant maze of cobbled streets and small squares. The area is dominated by the late-Romanesque cathedral, at the southern tip of the Old Town. Its highlight is the intricately carved 15th-century altarpiece, depicting Christ stumbling under the weight of the cross alongside several scenes from the life of St. Catherine. Unfortunately, lighting levels are so low inside the building that its full glory is hard to discern.

Next to the cathedral stands the Bishop's Palace (closed to the public), and at the bottom of the small flight of steps leading to the cathedral square is the **Rätisches Museum**, which focuses on the history and culture of the canton of Graubünden.

To the east of Chur, there are a number of world-class ski resorts. The best-known two are Klosters and Davos. The former, famous for its associations with British royalty, is a small traditional resort filled with charming chalets. Davos, on the other hand, is a big, brash town, offering plenty of diversions away from the slopes. It has steadily grown from a 19th-century mountain health resort to a major year-round sporting center, and is also the host city of the annual meeting of the World Economic Forum.

Rätisches Museum

◉ ☐ Hofstrasse 1 ☐ 10am–5pm Tue–Sun ⓦ rm.gr.ch

EAT

Luz

A perfect pit-stop, this tiny coffee joint serves delicious snacks along with idyllic lake views.

☐ Landungsbrücke 1, Lucerne ⓦ luzseebistro.ch

Taube

The go-to place for local Lucerne dishes, cooked just like your grandmother would do.

☐ Burgerstrasse 3, Lucerne ⓦ taube-luzern.ch

Bündner Stube

Candlelit meals of fresh, seasonal fare, much of it grown in the on-site kitchen garden.

☐ Reichsgasse 11, Chur ⓦ stern-chur.ch

Calanda

A trendy spot with a popular lunch menu and new specials every day.

☐ Postplatz, Chur ⓦ calanda-chur.ch

⓫ Ticino

🏠 Ticino 🚆🚌 🛈 Via C. Ghiringhelli 7, Bellinzona; www.ticino.ch

Ticino, Switzerland's most southerly canton, feels much more Italian than Swiss, with its mild climate and Italian cuisine and language. It lies south of the Alps, bordering the Italian lakes, and is traversed by routes up the Alpine passes of St. Gotthard and San Bernadino. The three main towns of Bellinzona, Locarno, and Lugano all make good bases for exploring the area, with numerous attractions, cafés, and restaurants. Beyond, Ticino's valleys offer top sightseeing opportunities.

Bellinzona is the capital of the canton. Lying on the main north–south route between the Alps and Italy, it provides the first hint of Italian life with its elegant piazzas, hilltop fortresses, and Renaissance churches. Bellinzona is particularly appealing on Saturdays, when its Old Town comes alive with the bustle of tempting market stalls.

The three castles here – Castelgrande and Montebello on either side of the Old Town, and Sasso Corbaro on top of the hill – are a UNESCO World Heritage Site. Castelgrande, with its imposing battlements,

↑ The incredible blue waters of Lake Lugano, glimpsed from Monte Bre in Ticino

is the oldest of the trio and was the stronghold of the Visconti family in medieval times. Montebello houses an archaeological museum, while Sasso Corbaro commands wide views across the Ticino Valley.

Locarno is located at the northern end of Lake Maggiore (p419). The Piazza Grande is the heart of town, and for two weeks in August becomes a giant open-air cinema during the International Film Festival. The festival aims to keep alive experimentation, eclecticism, and passion for auteur cinema. Film buffs of all nationalities and ages gather here in the square to watch movies on one of the world's biggest open-air screens.

Winding lanes filled with restaurants and boutiques radiate off the piazza. Above the town, the sanctuary of **Madonna del Sasso** is a major tourist and pilgrimage site. There has been a church here since 1480, when a vision of the Virgin Mary appeared to a local monk. The Baroque church is filled with marvelous frescoes and commands a fantastic view over the lake.

Probably the most charming of the three main centers of this region is Lugano, with its palm-lined lakeside location and attractive historic center of elegant piazzas. The pretty arcaded streets are full of interesting local shops.

Away from the main towns, there are plenty of quaint villages along the Maggiore and Lugano lakes, such as Ascona and Gandria. These are both filled with waterside restaurants and arts and crafts shops. For more rural pursuits, the valleys to the

→ A pair of hikers negotiating the rugged terrain of the Swiss National Park

---

GREAT VIEW
The Tibetan Bridge

From the Bellinzona suburbs, a funicular carries passengers through chestnut woods up into Monte Carasso. A pleasant hike leads to the spectacular Carasc wooden Tibetan bridge, anchored with flexible cables. It hangs above the Sementina Valley, and offers sweeping views over the treetops to the town.

north offer great hiking and beautiful, peaceful scenery. Val Verzasca, north of Locarno, is particularly picturesque, with the photogenic stone hamlet of Corippo and the pretty villages of Brione and Sonogno toward the head of the valley.

Madonna del Sasso

🏠 Via Santuario 2, Orselina
📞 091-743 6265 ⏰ 7am-6:30pm daily

Swiss National Park

🏠 Graubünden 🚇 ⏰ Jun-Oct: 8:30am-6pm daily; Nov-May: 9am-5pm daily
ℹ️ National Park Center, Zernez; www.national park.ch

Switzerland has many small nature reserves but only one national park. Established in 1914, this was the first national park to be created in the Alps. By international standards, it is relatively small, covering only 66 sq miles (170 sq km), but it is an area where conservation measures have been strictly enforced since the park was first inaugurated.

The Ofenpass road, which links Switzerland with Austria, cuts through the center of the park and affords good views of one of the park's valleys. Otherwise, the best way to see the park is to walk some of the 50 miles (80 km) of marked trails – visitors should note that hikers are not allowed to deviate off the paths. A free app has detailed maps and park information, including where to find accommodations in the park.

The landscape is one of wooded lower slopes and jagged, scree-covered ridges, including the park's highest peak at 10,414 ft (3,174 m) –

Did You Know?

Switzerland is the only sovereign state in the world that has a square flag.

Piz Pisoc. Among the park's abundant wildlife, you may see chamois, ibex, marmots, and glorious bearded vultures, which are very rare in Europe and were reintroduced into the park in 1991. From June to August, with the retreat of the snows at higher altitudes, a carpet of beautiful alpine flowers appears.

A viewing platform at Piz Nair offers incredible vistas. The Schmelzra Museum, in the former headquarters of a mining company, has an interesting bear exhibition.

PRACTICAL
INFORMATION

Here you will find all the essential advice and information you will need before and during your stay in Switzerland.

AT A GLANCE

CURRENCY
Swiss Franc
(CHF)

TIME ZONE
CET/CEST. Central
European Summer
Time runs from the last
Sunday in March to the
last Sunday in October.

LANGUAGE
French, German, Italian, and Romansh

ELECTRICITY SUPPLY
Power sockets are type
J, fitting type J (3-pin)
plugs and type C (2-pin)
plugs. Standard voltage is 230V.

EMERGENCY NUMBERS

GENERAL EMERGENCY	AMBULANCE
112	**144**

FIRE	POLICE
118	**117**

TAP WATER
Unless otherwise
stated, tap water
in Switzerland is
safe to drink.

Getting There

Zürich and Geneva airports are the main hubs for long-haul flights into Switzerland. Smaller airports at Bern, Basel, and Lugano also serve destinations within Europe.

Switzerland has excellent international rail links. Regular high-speed trains connect the country to all major cities in the neighboring countries of France, Germany, Austria, and Italy, and beyond. Train journeys can often compete with flights on price, and, for some short-haul routes, are not much longer door to door.

Eurolines offer several bus routes between Swiss destinations and other European cities.

Personal Security

Switzerland is generally a safe country, but it is a wise to take precautions against pickpockets. If you have anything stolen, report the crime to the nearest police station.

Health

Switzerland has no national health service, so medical treatment of any kind must be paid for. A reciprocal agreement exists with all EU nations, so if you have an EHIC card, present this as soon as possible. Private health insurance is recommended. For minor ailments, seek medical supplies and advice from pharmacies.

Passports and Visas

Visitors must have a valid passport to enter Switzerland. A visa is not required for visitors from the EU, US, Canada, Australia, and New Zealand for stays of up to 90 days. For visa information specific to your home country, consult your nearest Swiss embassy or check online.

LGBT+ Safety

LGBT+ rights in Switzerland are progressive, but smaller towns and rural areas can be more conservative, and overt displays of affection may be met with a negative response from locals.

Travelers with Specific Needs

Switzerland offers a high standard of facilities for travelers with specific needs. Most sights and public buildings have wheelchair access, but amenities in rural areas may be more limited.

For assistance at stations on the Swiss rail network, phone **SBB Call Centre Handicap** one hour before departure (or three working days beforehand for international travel). **Mietauto** has details on adapted hire vehicles.

Switzerland Tourism (*see right*) can provide full details of suitable hotel facilities. The website of **Mobility International Switzerland (MIS)** is also a helpful source of information.

Mietauto
w mietauto.ch
Mobility International Switzerland (MIS)
w mis-ch.ch/reiseinfos
SBB Call Centre Handicap
☎ 0800 007 102 (within Switzerland, toll-free),
+41 51 225 78 44 (from abroad, subject to charge)

Money

Major credit and debit cards are accepted in most shops and restaurants, and prepaid currency cards and American Express are accepted in some. It is advisable to carry cash for smaller items. Contactless payments are becoming more widely accepted.

Language

Switzerland has four national languages – French, German, Italian, and Romansh. Although English is not an official language, it is often used to bridge the language divides. German is spoken mostly in the east, French mostly in the west, and Italian mostly in the southern canton of Ticino and the southern parts of Graubünden. Romansh is spoken only in Graubünden.

Cell Phones and Wi-Fi

Wi-Fi is widely available, and cafés and restaurants usually permit customers to use their Wi-Fi.

Visitors traveling with EU tariffs can use their devices in Switzerland without being affected by data roaming charges. Visitors from elsewhere should check their contracts before departure in order to avoid unexpected charges.

Getting Around

Switzerland's comprehensive rail network is operated by Swiss Federal Railways or **SBB/CFF/FFS** (Schweizerische Bundesbahnen/Chemins de Fer Fédéraux Suisses/Ferrovie Federali Svizzere). Trains are modern, clean, and comfortable; services are frequent and dependably punctual; and connections tie in well with tram, bus, boat, and cable car services. When traveling to a major city, ask for a ticket that covers your destination's transportation network too – this usually costs only a small amount more. The **Swiss Travel System** provides a range of discount offers; the most popular of these is the Swiss Travel Pass, which allows unlimited travel on trains, lake ferries, and many mountain railroads.

Most of the international car rental firms have offices at airports and in the major towns. The majority of roads are generally free of congestion, but driving around major cities can be more difficult. Many mountain passes are closed from November to June; a sign at the foot of the pass will indicate whether the road is open.

Switzerland has an extensive network of routes covered by local buses and **Swiss Post's** distinctive yellow postbuses. The latter are useful for reaching alpine locations inaccessible by rail and also carry unaccompanied luggage, which is handy for hikers.

SBB/CFF/FFS
w sbb.ch
Swiss Post
w swisspost.ch
Swiss Travel System
w swisstravelsystem.com

Visitor Information

Most large cities have at least one central tourist information office – Verkehrsverein, Tourismus, or Office du Tourisme – offering a wide range of information and facilities. Even the smallest towns and resorts have tourist offices, but the opening hours of those in ski resorts may be limited in summer. **Switzerland Tourism** produces or partners a number of excellent free apps including Family Trips, SwitzerlandMobility, Swiss Events, and various city guides.

Switzerland Tourism
w myswitzerland.com

Gamla Stan, Stockholm's attractive Old Town

SWEDEN

Once a nation of mighty conquerors, Sweden has transformed through the centuries into a beacon of peace and social welfare. The 8th-century Vikings were the country's first traders, opening up routes along the Russian rivers to the east. Their reign ended, however, with the Christianization of Sweden at the end of the 11th century, and the unification of the country's tribes under King Olaf Skötkonung. The 14th century was dominated by trade with the German merchants of the Hanseatic League, but this ceased with the Kalmar Union of 1397, which sought to block German expansion by bringing the crowns of Denmark, Norway, and Sweden under Danish rule. This uneasy alliance continued until the Swedes rebelled, naming Gustav I king of an independent Sweden in 1523. Sweden's strength grew in the 17th and early 18th centuries under kings Gustav II Adolf and Karl XII, whose military conquests made the country more power-ful than its old rival, Denmark. However, decades of warfare and an outbreak of plague weakened the empire, and by 1809 the country was forced to surrender its Finnish territories to Russia, and draw up a new constitution that transferred power from the king to Parliament. The country was also suffering from stagnation in agriculture and trade, and over the course of the 19th century, nearly one million Swedes migrated, mostly to America. Their departure was a sobering lesson to those that remained, inspiring the welfare state of the 20th century. The country remained neutral in both world wars, and by the 21st century, Sweden had grown from a poor rural economy to a leading industrial nation. Today, Sweden's economy remains strong, with an emphasis on sustainability.

SWEDEN

*Norwegian
Sea*

*North
Sea*

Molde

Ålesund

Måløy   Stryn

Lavik   Sogndal

Bergen   Gol

NORWAY

Haugesund

Notodden

Stavanger

Arendal

Flekkefjord
Kristiansand

Hirtsha

Aalbor

Holstebro   Aarh

DENMARK

Kolding

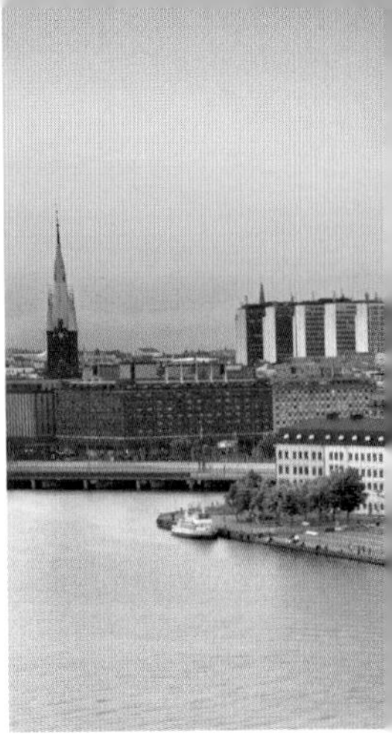

1

STOCKHOLM

www.visitstockholm.com

Stockholm was founded around 1250 on a small island in a narrow channel between the Baltic Sea and Lake Mälaren. Today, the Swedish capital stretches across 14 islands. As well as a stunning location, Stockholm has a rich cultural heritage, with buildings like the Royal Palace and Drottningholm – symbols of Sweden's great power in the 17th and early 18th centuries.

①

Storkyrkan

Trångsund 1 Gamla Stan 55, 57, 76, 96, & many others 9am-4pm daily storkyrkan.nu

Stockholm's cathedral, the Storkyrkan (literally, "big church") is of great national religious importance. From here, the Swedish reformer Olaus Petri spread his Lutheran message around the kingdom.

A small church built on this site in the 13th century, probably by the city's founder Birger Jarl, was replaced in 1306 by a much bigger basilica, St. Nicholas. The 15th-century Gothic interior was revealed in 1908 during restoration work. The late Baroque period provided the cathedral's so-called "royal chairs," the pews nearest the chancel, which were designed by Nicodemus Tessin the Younger to be used by royal guests on special occasions. The 216-ft- (66-m-) high tower was added in 1743.

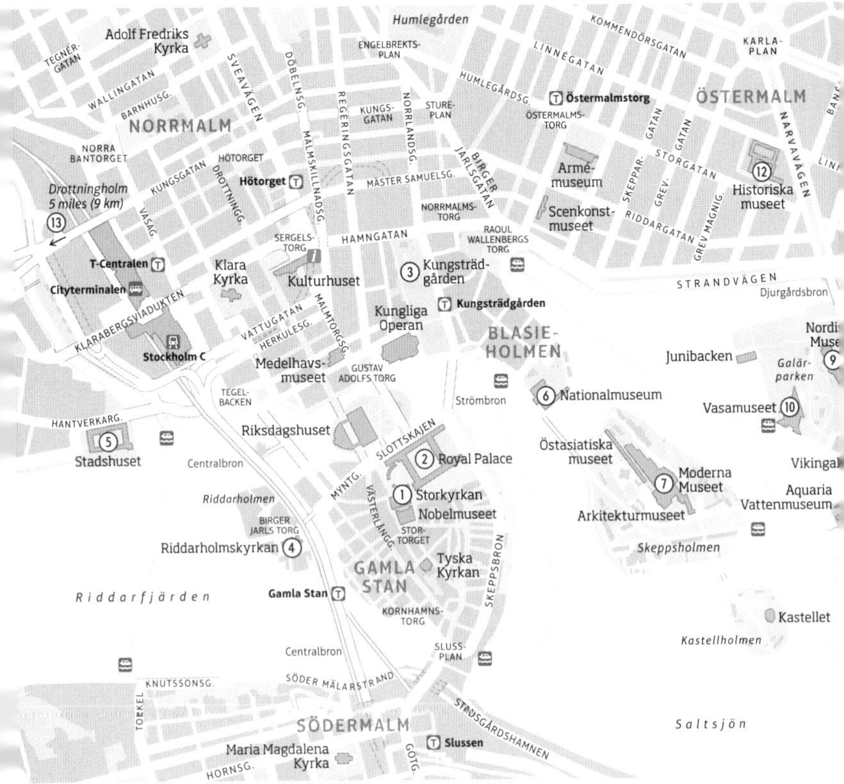

↑ Stockholm's waterfront buildings and church spires at twilight

The cathedral houses some priceless artifacts, such as Bernt Notke's Late-Gothic sculpture of *St. George and the Dragon* (1489), celebrating Sten Sture the Elder's 1471 victory over the Danes, and the silver altar (1650s).

②

Royal Palace

⌂ Kungliga Slottet
Ⓣ Gamla Stan, Kungsträd-
gården 🚌 55, 57, 76, 96, &
many others ⏱ Hours vary,
check website 🌐 kungliga
slotten.se

Completed in the mid-13th century, the Tre Kronor (Three Crowns) fortress was turned into a royal residence by the Vasa kings during the following century. In 1697, it was destroyed by fire. In its place, architect Nicodemus Tessin the Younger created a new palace with an Italianate exterior and a French interior with Swedish influences.

Although the palace is no longer the king's residence, the State Apartments are still used for official functions. Banquets for visiting heads of state are often held in the magnificent Karl XI's Gallery, which is modeled on the Hall of Mirrors at Versailles outside Paris (*p204*), and is a fine example of Swedish Late Baroque. Look out in particular for the exquisite ivory and silver salt cellar, designed by Flemish painter Peter Paul Rubens. The two-story Hall of State, designed by Tessin and Carl Hårleman, combines Rococo and Classical elements, and contains one of the palace's most valuable treasures: the

INSIDER TIP
Getting Around

Most of Stockholm's sights can be reached by subway (Tunnelbana has 100 stations) or bus. The best sightseeing routes are 3, 4, 46, 62, and 69. Boats and ferries are another great way of getting to know the city.

silver coronation throne of Queen Kristina, who reigned from 1633 to 1654.

Below the Hall of State is the Treasury, where the state regalia are kept, including King Erik XIV's crown, scepter, and orb. Other priceless artifacts, such as two crystal crowns belonging to the present monarchs, King Carl XVI Gustaf and Queen Silvia, are on view in the Royal Chapel.

Within the palace are two museums. Gustav III's Museum of Antiquities opened in 1794, two years after the king was assassinated, and contains his personal collection of classical sculptures. The Museum Tre Kronor illustrates the palace's 1,000-year history, and has relics rescued during the palace fire of 1697.

The daily changing of the guard – a particularly popular event with visitors – takes place at midday in the palace's Outer Courtyard.

③
Kungsträdgården

 Kungsträdgården
🚌 2, 54, 55, 57, 69, 76, 96

The city's oldest park, the King's Garden takes its name from when it was a royal kitchen garden in the 15th century. The space was later transformed into a Renaissance garden in the 16th century, and in the 17th century the summer house for Queen Kristina was constructed on the park's western flank.

Today, open-air theater, dancing, concerts, and food festivals take place here during the summer, while in winter, the ice rink is popular with skaters. At the center of the park is a bronze fountain (1866) by J. P. Molin, who also designed the statue of Karl XII (1868) at the park's southern end. Overlooking this part of the park is the city's royal opera house, the **Kungliga Operan** (1898), whose ornate interior includes the Gold Foyer, with ceiling paintings by Carl Larsson.

Kungliga Operan

Ⓐ Ⓑ Ⓒ 🕐 Ticket office: 3–6pm Mon–Fri, noon–3pm Sat 🅦 operan.se

④
Riddarholmskyrkan

 Birger Jarls Torg 🚇 Gamla Stan 🚌 3, 53, 59 🕐 Mid-May–mid-Sep: 10am–5pm daily 🅦 kungahuset.se

This majestic brick church is best known for its ornate burial vaults. Dating back to the 17th century, the vaults hold the remains of all the Swedish sovereigns from Gustav II Adolf, with two exceptions: Queen Kristina, buried at St. Peter's in Rome in 1689, and Gustav VI Adolf, who was interred at Haga, on the city outskirts in 1973. Especially moving are the graves of royal children, including the many small tin coffins that surround the tombs of Gustav II Adolf and his queen Maria Eleonora.

---

⑤
Stadshuset

Ⓐ Hantverkargatan 1 🚇 Rådhuset 🚌 3, 50 🕐 For guided tours 🕐 Some public hols 🅦 international. stockholm.se/the-city-hall

Probably Sweden's biggest architectural project of the

 PICTURE PERFECT
Capture the City Hall

One of the best times to photograph the Stadshuset is at night, when the exterior is lit with an atmospheric glow. Position yourself across the water, to the east, so you can also capture the light reflecting in the ripples.

20th century, the Stadshuset (City Hall) was completed in 1923 and has become a symbol of Stockholm. It was designed by Swedish architect Ragnar Östberg and displays influences of both the Nordic Gothic and Northern Italian schools. Many leading Swedish artists contributed to the rich interior design, including Einar Forseth, who created the stunning Byzantine-inspired gold-leaf wall mosaics that decorate the Golden Room banqueting hall.

The building contains the Council Chamber and 250 offices for administrative staff. As well as a work place for the city's councillors, the Stadshuset also provides a venue for special events.

↑ Blossoming cherry trees lining an avenue in the Kungsträdgården

Nationalmuseum

📍 Södra Blasieholms-hamnen 🚇 Kungsträd-gården 🚌 2, 55, 57, 65, 76, 96 🕐 11am–5pm Tue–Sun (to 9pm Thu; to 7pm Fri) 🌐 nationalmuseum.se

The location of the National-museum, on the Strömmen channel, inspired the 19th-century German architect August Stüler to design a building in the Venetian and Florentine Renaissance styles. Renovated in 2018, it houses some 500,000 paintings, sculp-tures, prints, and drawings from the 15th to the early 20th centuries. The focus of the painting and sculpture section is 18th- to early 20th-century Swedish art, but the 17th-century Dutch and Flemish, and 18th-century French schools are also rep-resented. Highlights include Rembrandt's *The Conspiracy of the Batavians under Claudius Civilis* (1661–2) and *The Lady with the Veil* (1769) by Swedish portrait painter Alexander Roslin. The decorative arts department contains Scandi-navia's largest display of porcelain, glass, silverware, and furniture.

↑ Visitors studying a sculpture in one of the Nationalmuseum's galleries

All the works on display date from between 1900 and the present day. Two of the star exhibits are *The Child's Brain* (1914) by Italian artist Giorgio de Chirico, widely considered a precursor to the Surrealists, and *Monogram* (1955–9) by the late American painter and sculptor Robert Rauschenberg. Among the fine collection of Swedish works is Nils Dardel's Expressionistic painting *The Dying Dandy* (1918).

Moderna Museet

📍 Exercisplan 4, Skepps-holmen 🚇 Kungsträd-gården 🚌 65 🕐 10am–8pm Tue–Fri (to 6pm Wed & Thu), 11am–6pm Sat & Sun 🚫 Jan 1, Easter Mon, Whit Mon, Midsummer eve, Dec 24, 25, & 31 🌐 modernamuseet.se

The Museum of Modern Art is a contemporary building designed by Catalan architect Rafael Moneo. The airy venue provides a perfect setting for the world-class collection of modern art, photography, and film. Built partly underground, the museum includes a movie theater and auditorium.

ABBA Museum

📍 Djurgårdsvägen 68 🚋 7 🕐 Hours vary, check website 🌐 abbathe museum.com

Few cultural entities have put Stockholm – and Sweden – on the map like ABBA did in the 1970s and 1980s, when they ruled the global pop charts. Fans of the band will love this museum, which has exhibits of their costumes, gold records, and other memorabilia.

Interactive experiences on offer include the chance to sit at a piano that is connected to Benny Andersson's own piano in his music studio; when the composer tinkles the ivories, the museum piano also starts playing. Visitors can also put on stage costumes and sing alongside hologram illusions of the band, as well as listen to the band members' stories from their amazing careers.

↑ An exhibit on the Northern Lights, or aurora borealis, at the Nordiska museet

⑨

Nordiska museet

🏠 Djurgårdsvägen 6-16
🚇 Karlaplan 🚌 67 🚊 7
⛴ Djurgårdsfärja, Allmänna Gränd 🕐 10am-5pm daily 🚫 Midsummer eve, Dec 24, 25, & 31
🌐 nordiskamuseet.se

Housed in a Renaissance-style building, the Nordiska museet's collection was started in the 19th century by Artur Hazelius, founder of the Skansen open-air museum, with the aim of reminding future generations of the old Nordic farming culture. Today, the museum has over 1.5 million exhibits portraying everyday life in Sweden from the 1520s to the present day. Items range from priceless jewelry to furniture, dolls' houses, and replicas of period rooms, such as the splendid 17th-century state bedchamber from Ulvsunda Castle. Highlights include the

Did You Know?

Sweden is fast becoming a cashless society, with only one per cent of payments made with cash.

monumental gilded oak statue of King Gustav Vasa (1924), and 16 paintings by the Swedish author and dramatist August Strindberg.

⑩

Vasamuseet

🏠 Galärvarvsvägen 14, Djurgården 🚌 69, 76 🚊 7
⛴ Djurgårdsfärja 🕐 Jun-Aug: 8:30-6pm daily; Sep-May: 10am-5pm daily (to 8pm Wed) 🚫 Jan 1, Dec 23-25 & 31 🌐 vasamuseet.se

The centerpiece of this popular maritime museum is the massive royal warship *Vasa*, which capsized in Stockholm harbor on its maiden voyage in 1628. Rediscovered in 1956, the vessel has been painstakingly restored to 95 per cent of its original appearance.

The warship is decorated with around 700 sculpted figures and carved ornaments, designed as a type of war propaganda. King Gustav II Adolf, who commissioned *Vasa*, was known as the Lion of the North, so a springing lion was the obvious choice for the figurehead on the ship's prow.

Although visitors cannot board the ship, full-scale models of *Vasa*'s upper gun deck and the Admiral's cabin

provide a glimpse of what life on board was like. There is also a fascinating display of items retrieved from the salvage operation, including medical equipment, an officer's backgammon set, and a chest still neatly packed with clothing and various other personal belongings.

Moored in the dock alongside the museum are two other historic vessels, collectively referred to as the **Museifartygen**. The lightship *Finngrundet* was built in 1903 and worked for 60 years before becoming a museum. *Sankt Erik* was commissioned in 1915 and was Sweden's first seagoing icebreaker.

Museifartygen

🕐 Mid-Jun-Aug: 11am-6pm daily
🌐 sverigedagarna.se

⑪

Skansen

🏠 Djurgårdsslätten 49-51
🚊 7 ⛴ Djurgårdsfärja
🕐 Hours vary, check website 🌐 skansen.se

The world's oldest open-air museum opened in 1891 to show an increasingly industrialized society how people once lived. Around 150 buildings were assembled from all over Scandinavia, to portray the life of peasants and landed gentry, as well as Lapp (Sami) culture.

In the Town Quarter, glass-blowers and other craftsmen demonstrate their skills. Two of Skansen's oldest "exhibits" are a 650-year-old wooden farmhouse from Dalarna, and a 14th-century storehouse from Norway. Nordic flora and fauna can be also seen, with moose, bears, and wolves in natural habitat enclosures.

Not far from Skansen is Sweden's oldest amusement park, Gröna Lund, which opened in 1883 and features attractions including a love tunnel and a haunted house.

(12)

Historiska museet

🏛 Narvavägen 13-17
🚇 Karlaplan, Östermalms-
torg 🚌 67, 68 🕐 Jun-Aug:
10am-5pm daily; Sep-May:
11am-5pm Tue-Sun (to 8pm
Wed) 🚫 Some major hols
🌐 historiska.se

Sweden's National Historical
Museum was opened in 1943.
It originally made its name
with relics from the Viking
era, as well as its outstanding
collections from the Middle
Ages. The latter include one
of the museum's star exhibits:
a gilded wooden Madonna
figure, from Sweden's early
medieval period. In the prehistoric collection is the Alunda
Elk, a ceremonial stone ax,
discovered in 1920 at Alunda
and thought to have been
made around 2000 BC.

The museum's priceless
collection of gold and silver,
dating from the Bronze Age
to the Middle Ages, is on display in the Guldrummet (Gold
Room). Look out for the jewel-
encrusted Elisabeth Reliquary,
an 11th-century goblet, with
a silver cover made in 1230
to enclose the disembodied
skull of St. Elisabeth.

Sitting by the water in
the gardens of the royal
palace of Drottningholm ↓

(13)

Drottningholm

🏛 5 miles (9 km) W of
Stockholm 🚇 Brommaplan,
then bus 176, 177, 301,
323 ⛴ May-Sep from
Stadshusbron 🕐 Hours
vary, check website
🚫 Public hols 🌐 royal
palaces.se

With its sumptuous palace,
theater, park, and Chinese
pavilion, the whole of the
Drottningholm estate has
been designated a UNESCO
World Heritage Site. Begun
in the 1660s on the orders of
King Karl X Gustav's widow,
Queen Hedvig Eleonora, it
was designed by Nicodemus
Tessin the Elder and com-
pleted by Tessin the Younger.
Today, the royal family still
uses parts of the palace as
a private residence.

The Baroque and Rococo
gardens and lush parkland
surrounding the palace are
dotted with several splendid
buildings. The blue and gold
Chinese Pavilion (Kina Slott)
was built for Queen Lovisa
Ulrika in the latter half of the
18th century, and contains
interesting artifacts from
China and Japan. Its designer,
Carl Fredrik Adelcrantz, was
also responsible for the

Drottningholm Court Theater
(Slottsteatern, 1766). This simple wooden building is the
world's oldest theater still
preserved in its original form.

❷ Lake Mälaren

⊞ Svealand 🚗🚢

To the west of Stockholm lies the vast Lake Mälaren, whose pretty shores and islands offer several day excursions from the city. A variety of sightseeing tours are run by boat operator Strömma Kanalbolaget, leaving from Stadshusbron.

Sweden's first town, Birka, was founded on the island of Björkö in the 8th century, although archaeological finds indicate that trading activity was taking place here 200 years earlier. In the 9th and 10th centuries, Birka grew into a busy Viking center. The **Birkamuseet** has displays of local archaeological finds and provides a fascinating insight into the daily lives of the town's early inhabitants. There are also guided tours of ongoing excavations.

A few miles southwest of Birka is the pretty town of Mariefred, whose most striking feature is the majestic **Gripsholms Slott**, built for King Gustav Vasa in 1537 and later modified under Gustav III in the 18th century. The palace is known for its well-preserved interiors, including an 18th-century theater, and also houses the National Portrait Gallery, with more than 4,000 paintings spanning 500 years.

Mariefred itself has a lovely 17th-century church and an 18th-century timber Rådhus (Town Hall), as well as several specialist stores, galleries, and antique shops. In summer, one of the most enjoyable ways to travel to the town from Stockholm is aboard

the **S/S Mariefred**, a historic, coal-fired steamboat. The trip takes around three and a half hours and allows passengers to enjoy the spectacular scenery along the route.

Birkamuseet

⊛ ⊕ ⊞ Birka ⊙ Late Mar-late Sep: 11:30am-3pm daily (Jun 30-Aug 11: 11am-5pm) ⓦ birkavikingastaden.se

→ Mariefred's Gripsholms Slott, and *(inset)* the National Portrait Gallery

← The leafy surrounds of the Fyrisån river, running through Uppsala

Gripsholms Slott

♿ⓧ🅿 ⌂Mariefred
🕐Hours vary, check website ⏲Dec 18-Jan 2
🌐kungligaslotten.se

S/S Mariefred

🕐May & Sep: Sat & Sun; Jun-Aug: Tue-Sun
🌐mariefred.info

3
Uppsala

⌂Uppland 🚆🚌🚲
🚉Uppsala Central Station; www.destination uppsala.se

One of Sweden's oldest settlements, Uppsala, on the banks of the Fyrisån river, is also a lively university town. Each year, on the last day of April, crowds of students wearing white caps parade through the town for the traditional spring season celebrations.

Dominating the town's attractive medieval center is the imposing Domkyrkan, Scandinavia's largest Gothic cathedral. Its chapel contains the relics of Sweden's patron saint, St. Erik. Opposite the cathedral stands the onion-domed **Gustavianum**, which dates from the 1620s and now houses the Uppsala University Museum. The museum's exhibits include a 17th-century anatomical theater and a variety of Egyptian, Classical, and Nordic antiquities. Just a short walk away stands the stately Carolina Rediviva, the main university library.

Uppsala Slott, the town's hilltop fortress, was built in the 16th century by King Gustav Vasa, although it was later destroyed by fire. Now restored, the complex houses the **Uppsala Art Museum**. Tours of the castle are also available during the summer.

A short bus ride north of the town center, Gamla Uppsala is the site of the Kungshögarna, royal burial mounds believed to date from the 6th century. This was a center for worshipping the Norse gods long into the 11th century, with a temple that was reputedly clad entirely in gold and contained images of Odin, Thor, and Frey. The **Gamla Uppsala Museum**, also known as the Historiskt Centrum, acquaints visitors with the history, legends, and lore surrounding the burial mounds and contains displays of local archaeological finds.

Gustavianum

♿ⓧ🅿 ⌂Akademigatan 3
🕐11am-4pm Tue-Sun (Jun-Aug: from 10am)
🌐gustavianum.uu.se

Uppsala Art Museum

♿ ⌂Slottet, entrance E
🕐11:30am-4pm Tue-Sun (to 8pm Thu) 🌐uppsalakonst museum.se

Gamla Uppsala Museum

♿♿ ⌂Disavägen
🕐Hours vary, check website 🌐raa.se

Did You Know?

Every night at 10pm, students in Uppsala's Flogsta district let out a cry known as the Flogsta Scream.

4
Gothenburg

🏛 Västergötland and Bohuslän 🚋🚌🚗🚆
ℹ Mässans gata 8; www.goteborg.com

Sweden's second-largest city, Gothenburg (Göteborg), has a distinctive character, with beautiful architecture, café-lined boulevards, a bustling harbor, and a dynamic cultural life.

The largest seaport in the whole of Scandinavia, the city is dominated by the lofty Göteborgsutkiken, a huge lookout tower that provides stunning panoramic views of the city and its surroundings. A short walk west along the quayside are the industrial-style Göteborgsoperan (Opera House), built in 1994, and the **Maritiman**, reputedly the world's largest floating ship museum. Moored in the dock are a dozen different types of vessel, all of which are open to the public. They include a destroyer, a lightship, and a submarine.

The pulse of the city is Kungsportsavenyn, simply known as Avenyn, or "The Avenue." This lively boulevard is lined with restaurants, pubs, and cafés, and is a favorite haunt of Gothenburg's street musicians and hawkers.

On a side street off Avenyn is **Röhsska museet**, a museum devoted to arts, crafts, and industrial design from around the world and throughout history. At the southern end of the avenue is Götaplatsen, a square whose focal point is the famous Poseidon fountain by the Swedish sculptor Carl Milles. It is flanked by the fine **Konstmuseet** (Art Museum), which exhibits a selection of Scandinavian art from the 19th and 20th centuries.

Southeast of Götaplatsen is Liseberg, a hugely popular amusement park packed with rides and various different performance venues.

Maritiman
⊘⊘🕐 🏛 Packhusplatsen 12 ⏰ Hours vary, check website 🔳 maritiman.se

Röhsska museet
⊘⊘🕐 🏛 Vasagatan 37-39 ⏰ 11am-5pm Tue-Sun (to 6pm Tue & Wed; to 8pm Thu) 🔳 rohsska.se

Konstmuseet
⊘⊘🕐 🏛 Götaplatsen 6 ⏰ 11am-5pm Tue-Sun (to 6pm Tue & Thu; to 8pm Wed) 🔳 goteborgskonstmuseum.se

5
Dalarna

🏛 Svealand 🚋🚌
ℹ visitdalarna.se/en/touristinformations

With its proud traditions of music, dance, and handicrafts, the province of Dalarna is Sweden's folklore hub. In particular, the area is famous for its Midsummer festivals – in the towns of Leksand and Rättvik, it is not unusual to see traditionally dressed locals dancing and playing musical instruments or rowing on the lake in wooden longboats during the celebrations.

Dalarna's charming rural landscape, dotted with red, wooden cottages, attracts many visitors seeking a quiet country retreat in the summer. In winter, the area's mountain resorts, Sälen and Idre, are packed with skiers. The main sights of interest are located

Dusk falling over the city of Gothenburg, Scandinavia's largest seaport

↑ Traditionally dressed people in procession during a Midsummer festival in Leksand, Dalarna

around Lake Siljan. Mora, the largest of the lakeside towns, was home to one of Sweden's best-known artists, Anders Zorn. Open daily, the Zorn Museum, at No. 36 Vasagatan, holds paintings by the artist, and you can also visit his former home and studio.

Around 9 miles (15 km) from the provincial capital and largely industrial town of Falun is Sundborn, where Swedish painter Carl Larsson and his wife Karin, a textile artist, lived in the early 20th century. Their work still has a big influence on contemporary Swedish design. The couple's lakeside house is open to the public.

Gotland and Visby

🏛 Gotland ✈🚢
ℹ Donnerska Huset, Donners Plats 1, Visby; www.gotland.com

The island of Gotland, Sweden's most popular holiday destination, has a stunning coastline, a rich cultural heritage, and a superb climate, enjoying more hours of sunshine than anywhere else in the country.

In the Viking Age, Gotland – the largest island in the Baltic Sea – was a major trading post and its capital, Visby, later became a prosperous Hanseatic port. Surrounded by very-well-preserved city walls, Visby has pretty step-gabled houses and a web of narrow cobbled streets and small squares. The original Hanseatic harbor is now a park, while the Burmeisterska Huset (Burmeister's House), dating from 1645, is an excellent surviving example of the architecture of the post-Hanseatic period. Some of Visby's most attractive historic buildings can be found along Strandgatan, lined with the former homes of wealthy merchants. The street also houses the historical museum **Gotlands Fornsal**, which holds a collection of artifacts spanning 8,000 years. The Domkyrkan (Cathedral of St. Maria) below Kyrkberget is the only medieval church still intact and in use in Visby.

Away from Visby, the rest of Gotland is dotted with many unspoilt farmhouses, old medieval churches, and secluded beaches. Among the most impressive sights are the subterranean limestone caves of **Lummelundagrottans**, with a fantastic show of stalactites and stalagmites, and, off the northeastern tip of the island, Fårö. This island, known for its severe beauty, can be reached by ferry from Fårösund. Besides old fishing hamlets such as Helgumannen, visitors can enjoy the long stretch of white sandy beach and the swimming at Sudersands. Look out for Fårö's spectacular *raukar* – huge limestone rock formations, rising out of the sea on the west side of the island.

Gotlands Fornsal

♿🧥♿ 🏛 St. Hansgatan 2, Visby ⏰ 9am-6pm daily
🌐 gotlandsmuseum.se

Lummelundagrottans

♿ 🏛 8 miles (13 km) N of Visby ⏰ Jun-Aug: 9am-6pm daily; May & Sep: 10am-3pm
🌐 lummelundagrottan.se

TOP 5 SWEDISH FOODS

Swedish Meatballs
The classic Swedish *köttbullar* are made with beef and served with mashed potato and lingonberry jam.

Cinnamon Buns
Kanelbullar, the perfect accompaniment to coffee or tea, are found in almost every café.

Pytt i Panna
A classic Swedish "hash" based around diced, fried potatoes, with meat or a vegetarian meat substitute.

Västerbotten Cheese
The king of Swedish cheeses is a hard, salty, cow's milk cheese. Look out, too, for mature Prästost and Grevé.

Cloudberries
A delicacy that flourishes only in cold climates. Cloudberry jam is best enjoyed with ice cream or waffles.

↑ Colorful vase produced by Orrefors, a glassworks in the Växjö area

❼
Växjö

⌂ Småland 🚆🚌
ⓘ Residenset, Stortorget; www.vaxjoco.se

Located right at the heart of the verdant province of Småland, Växjö is an ideal base from which to explore the Glasriket, or "Kingdom of Glass," Sweden's world-famous region of glassworks. The town's main attraction is the **Smålands Museum**, which tells the story of 400 years of glassmaking, and provides a fascinating introduction to a visit to any one of the many local glassworks.

The best-known glassworks are located at Orrefors and **Kosta**, within 56 miles (90 km) of Växjö, but other factories worth visiting include Åfors and Strömbergshyttan. Most of the factories have excellent glass-blowing demonstrations, and all have a shop with a wide selection of products.

In the past, Småland's glassworks were more than just a place of work. Locals used to meet here in the evenings to bake herrings and potatoes in the furnace, while music was provided by a fiddler. Today several glassworks (including Kosta) arrange similar forms of entertainment, known as *hyttsill* evenings. The **Kingdom of Glass** website has detailed information on these events.

Visitors to Växjö should not miss the **Utvandrarnas Hus** (House of Emigrants). This interesting museum recounts the story of the one million Swedes who, in the face of famine in the late 19th and early 20th centuries, left Småland in search of a better life in America.

Smålands Museum

❸❸❸ ⌂ Södra Järnvägsgatan 2 🕐 Jun–Aug: 10am–5pm daily; Sep–May: 10am–5pm Tue–Fri, 11am–4pm Sat & Sun 🌐 kulturpark ensmaland.se

Kosta Glassworks

❸❸ ⌂ Stora vägen 96, Kosta, on route 28 🕐 8:30am–3:30pm Mon–Fri, 10am–4pm Sat & Sun 🌐 kostaboda.co.uk

Kingdom of Glass

🌐 glasriket.se

Utvandrarnas Hus

❸ ⌂ Vilhelm Mobergsgatan 4 🕐 Jun–Aug: 10am–5pm daily; Sep–May: 10am–5pm Tue–Fri, 11am–4pm Sat & Sun 🌐 kulturparkensmaland.se

❽
Malmö

⌂ Skåne 🚈🚆🚌🚢 ⓘ Across from Central Station; 040-341200

Malmö is the capital of the province of Skåne, in south-western Sweden. In the 16th century, the city was a major fishing port, competing with Copenhagen as Scandinavia's most influential city. Today, Malmö is well known for its busy harbor, as well as for its rich architectural heritage.

The centre of Malmö, where most of the main sights are located, is compact and easy to explore on foot. The imposing 16th-century Malmöhus was built by the Danish King Christian III, when Skåne was part of Denmark. Today it contains the **Malmö Museer** (Malmö Museums), which include the Art Museum, the Museum of Natural History, the City Museum, the Science and Maritime Museum, and a photograph gallery contained in the Kommendants Hus (Commander's House).

↑ Malmö's Rådhus (right), overlooking the city's attractive main square

The Dutch Renaissance style is evident in Malmö's impressive **Rådhus** (Town Hall), which dates from 1546 and dominates the city's main square, Stortorget. Northeast of here is the 14th-century St. Petri's Kyrka, built in the Baltic Gothic style. The church's most beautiful features include its altarpiece (1611), one of the largest in Scandinavia, and a wonderfully ornate pulpit. Amid the city's maze of café-lined pedestrianized streets is Lilla Torg (Little Square), with its cobblestones and charmingly restored houses. Another lively square can be found in the multicultural district of Möllevångstorget, where there is a daily farmers' market and many small shops, bars, and cafés.

Located south of Lilla Torg is **Malmö Konsthall**, a vibrant museum of modern art that opened in 1975. Its vast contemporary exhibition space houses an excellent international collection of avant-garde and experimental art and installations, as well as photography and sculpture.

THE ÖRESUND BRIDGE

Despite a legacy of mutual warfare and rivalry, in May 2000 the close ties between Denmark and Sweden were strengthened with the inauguration of the Öresund Bridge. A 10-mile- (16-km-) long combined suspension bridge and tunnel now connects the Danish capital, Copenhagen, with the Swedish city of Malmö, on either side of the channel of water known as the Öresund. The bridge is one of the strongest cable stay bridges in the world, designed to carry the combined weight of a motorway and a dual-track railroad. Trade, science, industry, and culture have prospered since it opened, and the structure itself has attained worldwide fame thanks to its role in the crime television series *The Bridge*.

Malmö Museer

⊛ ⊜ ⊕ ⧉ Malmöhus, Malmöhusvägen 6 ⏲ 10am–5pm daily ⏰ Dec 24, 25, & 31, Jan 1 ⊠ malmo.se/museer

Malmö Konsthall

⊛ ⊜ ⊕ ⧉ St. Johannesgatan 7 ⏲ 11am–5pm daily ⏰ Dec 24, 25, & 31, Jan 1 ⊠ konsthall.malmo.se

PRACTICAL
INFORMATION

Here you will find all the essential advice and information you will need before and during your stay in Sweden.

AT A GLANCE

CURRENCY
Swedish krona (SEK)

TIME ZONE
CET/CEST. Central European Summer Time runs from the last Sunday in March to the last Sunday in October.

LANGUAGE
Swedish

ELECTRICITY SUPPLY
Power sockets are type C and F, fitting two-pin plugs. Standard voltage is 220V.

EMERGENCY NUMBERS

GENERAL EMERGENCY

112

TAP WATER
Unless otherwise stated, tap water in Sweden is safe to drink.

Getting There

Most major European cities have direct flights to Stockholm. Many of the world's leading airlines serve Arlanda Airport, located about 25 miles (40 km) north of the city center; Stockholm Skavsta Airport, or Nyköping Airport, 62 miles (100 km) south of Stockholm, is Sweden's main airport for low-cost, no-frills carriers. International flights also serve Gothenburg and Malmö.

Rail travel to Sweden from mainland Europe is fast and comfortable. Copenhagen to Malmö, for example, takes less than 40 minutes.

Ferries to Gothenburg from Fredrikshavn in Denmark (2–3 hours) and from Kiel in Germany (20–22 hours) are operated by **Stena Line**. Large passenger and car ferries sail to Stockholm from Finland; both **Viking Line** and **Tallink Silja Line** operate daily services from Helsinki (about 15 hours) and Turku-Åbo (about 11 hours).

Stena Line
W stenaline.co.uk
Tallink Silja Line
W tallinksilja.com
Viking Line
W vikingline.com

Personal Security

Sweden is generally a safe country to travel around, but it is always a good idea to take sensible precautions against pickpockets. If you have anything stolen, report the crime as soon as possible to the nearest police station. Get a copy of the crime report in order to claim on your insurance.

Health

Swedish hospitals are excellent. EU citizens with a European Health Insurance Card (EHIC) are entitled to free emergency medical care in Sweden, but it is also advisable to take out some form of supplementary health insurance. Visitors from outside the EU must arrange their own private medical insurance.

Prescription and non-prescription medicines can be obtained from a pharmacy (apotek), but

note that a prescription is often required to purchase certain medicines that can be bought over the counter in many other countries.

Passports and Visas

Passports are not required for visitors from most EU countries, but visitors from the US, Canada, the UK, Ireland, Australia, and New Zealand still need a valid passport. Citizens of almost all countries can enter Sweden with-out a visa.

Travelers with Specific Needs

Stockholm prides itself on being one of the most accessible capital cities in the world. The subway is adapted for disabled users with access at all stations, and buses "kneel" at stops to help travelers board and disembark. All buses have wheelchair ramps. Most of the major tourist attractions have disabled access and disabled toilets. For more detailed information visit the **De Handikappades Riksförbund** (National Disabled Association).

De Handikappades Riksförbund
w dhr.se

Money

Few people and businesses use cash in Sweden. Credit cards and debit cards are often the only accepted mode of payment, and are used even for small transactions in shops, museums, bars, and restaurants. Avoid taking out large amounts of cash in advance of your trip – you may find yourself unable to spend it.

Cell Phones and Wi-Fi

Free Wi-Fi access is available almost everywhere, including cafés, bars, restaurants, and hotels. Visitors traveling to Sweden with EU tariffs can use their devices without being affected by data roaming charges. Visitors from other countries should check their contracts before departure in order to avoid unexpected charges.

Getting Around

Within Sweden, the state-owned rail company **Statens Järnvägar** (SJ) operates many of the long-distance trains. Some routes are run by private companies – Tågkompaniet runs trains from Stockholm to Narvik, Umeå, and Luleå in the far north. The journey time by high-speed train from Malmö to Stockholm is about five hours; the journey from Gothenburg to the capital takes about three hours.

Travel by long-distance bus is inexpensive and hassle-free. There is an excellent network of express services, such as those run by **Flixbus**, between the larger towns and cities in south and central Sweden, and between Stockholm and towns in the north.

Most of the international car rental firms have offices at airports and in the major towns. Fines for speeding in Sweden are high, and even if the limit is only slightly exceeded, you can lose your license. The maximum permitted blood alcohol level is so low that drinking is effectively banned for drivers. When driving in the Swedish countryside, be particularly cautious, as moose and deer may appear unexpectedly in the middle of the road.

Ferries to Visby in Gotland leave from Nynäshamn, about 45 miles (75 km) south of Stockholm, and Oskarshamn, about 155 miles (250 km) south of Stockholm. Daily crossings are run by **Destination Gotland**.

Destination Gotland
w destinationgotland.se
Flixbus
w flixbus.co.uk
Statens Järnvägar
w sj.se

Visitor Information

Tourist information offices are located throughout the country, and the **Visit Sweden** website is also a useful tool. Check out **Totally Stockholm** for information in English about places to eat, things to do, and concerts, arts, and current events in the capital.

Totally Stockholm
w totallystockholm.se
Visit Sweden
w visitsweden.com

NORWAY

Norway may be relatively small, but it has a history of epic proportions. The success of the country's early agricultural groups led to over-population and clan warfare, and from the 8th century AD the Norwegian Vikings traveled to find new lands, reaching the British Isles, Iceland, Greenland, and even America. Norway's tribes battled under their various leaders until around 890, when Viking chieftain Harald the Fairhaired united the country. The 11th and 12th centuries were marked by dynastic conflicts and the rising influence of the church, but the 13th century saw Norway flourish under strong, centralized government, with both Iceland and Greenland coming under Norwegian rule. However, terrible losses in the Black Death saw Norway's status diminish, and from 1380 to 1905 it was under the rule first of Denmark and then of Sweden. Following independence from Sweden in 1905, the government set about industrializing the country and establishing a welfare state. Norway pursued a policy of neutrality in both world wars, although half of its merchant fleet was sunk by the Germans in World War I and it was occupied by Germany during World War II. Norway's part in the war helped it gain in status and it became a founding member of the UN in 1945 and joined NATO in 1949. The main issue of the postwar years has been whether to join the EU. Twice Norway has refused, but the economy thrives regardless, thanks largely to revenues from North Sea oil.

NORWAY

① Oslo
② Stavanger
③ Bergen and the Fjords
④ Trondheim
⑤ Tromsø

0 kilometers 150

0 miles 150

N

Arctic Circle

Sørvåge

Norwegian Sea

Mosjøen
Trofors
Rorvik
Namsos
Grong
Steinkjer
Brekstad
Levanger
Stjørdal
TRONDHEIM ④ 14
Kristiansund
Støren
Molde
Åndalsnes
Oppdal
39
Ålesund
Hjerkinn
Røros
Hede
Måløy
Stryn
Tynset
Florø
Lom 15
Otta
Drevsjø
39
Sogndal
Koppang
Sognefjord
Vang
26
THE FJORDS ③
16
Lillehammer
39
Flåm
Osterfjord
Gol
3
Hamar
BERGEN ③
Ulvik
7
16
7
16
6
2
Hardangerfjord
Odda
Rødberg
Hønefoss
Kongsvinger
Haugesund
Drammen
① OSLO
North Sea
Notodden
Hjelmeland
Valle
Sandefjord
Karlstad
STAVANGER ②
9
41
Skien
Sandnes
Byglandsfjord
Vänern
18
Flekkefjord
Arendal
Uddevalla
39
Kristiansand
Kiel, Copenhagen
Hirtshals
Hirtshals

❶

OSLO

⊠ ⌂ ≡ ≡ **f** www.visitoslo.com

Founded around 1048, Oslo is the oldest of the Scandinavian capitals. The heart of the city is largely made up of Neo-Classical buildings, wide avenues, and landscaped parks, and most of the sights are within walking distance of each other. The city is a cultural hotspot, with many museums and art galleries.

①

Opera House

⌂ Kirsten Flagstads Plass 1 Ⓣ Jernbanetorget 🚌 32, 74, 81B, 83 🕐 10am–11pm Mon-Fri, 11am-11pm Sat & Sun 🌐 operaen.no

The home of the Norwegian National Opera and Ballet is situated on the waterfront in the Bjørvika neighborhood, and much of the building is positioned in or under the sea. Its central feature is its sloping roof, which is covered in white marble and granite, creating the illusion of glistening ice, like a glacier rising from the Oslofjord. There are three main performance spaces, though concerts are also held on the roof.

②

Akershus Festning

⌂ Festningsplassen Ⓣ Stortinget 🚊 12 📞 23 09 39 17 🕐 May-Aug: 10am-4pm Mon-Sat, noon-4pm Sun; Sep-Apr: noon-5pm Sat & Sun 🚫 Public hols

A dramatic contrast to the modern complexes along Oslo's waterfront, this medieval fortress was built in 1299 to safeguard the city. Over the years it has been the site of battles, housed criminals, and witnessed executions.

Today, Akershus Festning is the government's main venue for state functions. It is open to the public, and comprises a mix of museums, historic buildings, and defense installations.

The **Hjemmefrontmuseet** (Resistance Museum), by the gates of the castle, provides a moving account of World War II in Norway, from Nazi occupation through resistance to liberation.

Hjemmefrontmuseet

Jun-Aug: 10am-5pm Mon-Sat, 11am-5pm Sun; Sep-May: 10am-4pm Mon-Sat • Public hols • forsvaretsmuseer.no/Hjemmefrontmuseet

---

③

Rådhus

Fridtjof Nansens Plass • Nationaltheatret, Stortinget • 30, 31, 32, 45, 81, 83 • 12, 13, 19 • 9am-4pm Mon-Fri (Jul: daily) • Public hols • oslo.kommune.no

Oslo's twin-towered City Hall has become a landmark since it opened in 1950, despite many locals initially disliking the design of its grandiose facade. Inside, the Rådhus is a treasure trove of vibrant murals and sculptures that celebrate Norwegian artistic and intellectual achievements. This is also where the Nobel Peace Prize is presented.

←

The unusual sloping roof of the dramatic, glacier-like Opera House

---

④

Aker Brygge and Astrup Fearnley Museet

Astrup Fearnley Museet, Strandpromenaden 2 • Nationaltheateret • 21, 32, 33, 54, 122, 129, 132 • 12, 16 • Noon-5pm Tue-Sun (to 7pm Thu), 11am-5pm Sat & Sun • afmuseet.no

The historic Aker Brygge shipyard has been transformed to provide a major shopping and entertainment center, with residential apartments and the city's biggest concentration of restaurants. Bold new architecture blends with the old, creating a delightful setting by the quayside.

Farther along the waterfront is vibrant Tjuvholmen, where the striking Astrup Fearnley Museet houses artworks by the likes of Damien Hirst, Jeff Koons, and Takashi Murakami.

HENRIK JOHAN IBSEN (1828–1906)

Born in the southern town of Skien, Ibsen was brought up in poverty. In 1864, he left for Germany and Italy, where he spent the next 27 years. One of the founders of modern drama, Ibsen wrote about the alienation of the individual from a morally bankrupt society, loss of religious faith, and women's desire to free themselves of their roles as wives and mothers. His plays include *Peer Gynt* (1867), *A Doll's House* (1879), and *Hedda Gabler* (1890).

⑤ Munchmuseet

🏠 Kirsten Flagstads Plass
🚇 Jernbanetorget/Oslo S
🚌 34, 37, 54 🚋 11, 12, 13, 17, 28, 29 ⏰ Check website
🌐 munchmuseet.no

Artist Edvard Munch led a troubled life, plagued by melancholy and depression; this had a profound influence on his work, which remains a great cornerstone of early Expressionist art. Highly prolific, he left an amazing 1,100 paintings, 4,500 drawings, and 18,000 graphic works to the city of Oslo when he died.

In 1963, the Munchmuseet opened in Tøyen to display the collection, but it soon became clear that the donation exceeded its home. As part of the regeneration of Oslo's waterfront, the Munchmuseet will move to a brand new building in Bjørvika, next to the Opera House. Known as Lambda, this new structure is due to open in June 2020 and its bold 16-story glass tower, designed by architect Juan Herreros, will be a striking sight. The museum will contain works from every aspect of Munch's life, from versions of his iconic *The Scream* to the sensuous

Kiss (1897). The Munchmuseet in Tøyen will remain open with limited artworks and capacity during the transition.

⑥ Kongelige Slottet

🏠 Slottsplassen 1
🚇 Nationaltheatret 🚌 30, 31, 32, 34, 45, 81, 83 🚋 11, 13, 17, 18, 19 ⏰ Jun 22–Aug 25: by guided tour only
🌐 kongehuset.no

The Neo-Classical Royal Palace stands in the freely accessible palace gardens (Slottsparken). Without gates or walls, the gardens symbolize Norway's "open" monarchy. The palace was built in 1825–48 for King Karl Johan. Every day at 1:30pm, the ceremony of the changing of the guard takes place. On Norway's National Day on May 17, the palace becomes the focal point of celebrations. The palace is open only for guided tours; check the website for details.

⑦ Nationaltheatret

🏠 Johanne Dybwads Plass 1
🚇 Nationaltheatret
🚌 30, 31, 32, 34, 45, 81, 83
🚋 11, 13, 17, 18, 19 ⏰ For performances and tours
🌐 nationaltheatret.no

Constructed in 1899, Norway's Neo-Classical National Theater is flanked by imposing statues of the nation's two greatest 19th-century playwrights – Henrik Johan Ibsen and Bjørnstjerne Bjørnson. The latter is little known outside Scandinavia these days, but was a prolific writer of plays and poetry. The theater has four stages, and a varied program, with all performances given in Norwegian. Visitors can arrange to have a guided tour of the interior, which also contains many fine works of art.

→ An equestrian statue of King Karl Johan in front of the Kongelige Slottet

Nasjonalmuseet

⬛ Brynjulf Bulls Plass
🚇 Nationaltheatret
🚊 12 🕐 Opening in 2020; check website 🌐 nasjonal museet.no

This powerhouse of art will bring together the National Gallery, the Museum of Contemporary Art, and the Museum of Decorative Arts and Design under one roof. The new Nasjonalmuseet is a sleek, modern building that celebrates Oslo's evolving architectural scene, from its waterfront projects to the brown-brick Rådhus, which stands near the site (p591). The ground and first floors will house the permanent collection, with further exhibition spaces on the lower and upper levels. A terrace is being constructed on the roof, providing stunning views towards the harbor and the fjord. A tree-lined square and outdoor seating, 200-capacity auditorium, and restaurant will provide public spaces for visitors to linger and reflect.

The National Gallery will be the last of the three museums to close its doors before its artworks are transferred to the Nasjonalmuseet, opening in early 2020. Check online to learn more about this project, or visit Mellomstasjonen (Brynjulf Bulls Plass 2), next to the Nobel Peace Center, which provides more information about the new museum and offers guided tours of the site.

Vigelandsparken

⬛ Kirkeveien 🚇 Majorstuen
🚌 20, 45 🚊 12 🕐 24 hrs daily

Vigelandsparken lies within the larger green expanse of Frognerparken. Free to enter, it takes its name from the larger-than-life sculptures of Gustav Vigeland, which form extraordinary tableaux of fighting, play, and love. Works on display include a series of 58 bronzes of men, women, and infants, flanking the footbridge over the river and leading up to his most famous creation, a 56-ft (17-m) granite obelisk of no fewer than 121 intertwined figures depicting the cycle of life.

One of Oslo's most-visited attractions, the park is a massive artistic creation that took Vigeland 40 years to complete. Some other examples of his work can be seen at Vigelandsmuseet near the park or at the Nasjonalmuseet.

INSIDER TIP
Getting Around

Oslo has around 60 bus and tram routes. Bus 30 goes to the Bygdøy Peninsula, which you can also reach by ferry from the boarding point by the Rådhus (mid-Mar–mid-Oct). The T-bane subway is most useful for reaching the suburbs.

⑩

Vikingskipshuset

📍 Huk Aveny 35 🚌 30 🚢 ⏰ May–Sep: 9am–6pm daily; Oct–Apr: 10am–4pm daily 🚌 Public hols 🌐 khm.uio.no

Norway is famous for its Viking explorers, and this museum contains three of the world's best-preserved Viking long-ships. They were unearthed from burial mounds in Norway, and funeral goods from each of the vessels are on display, including ceremonial sleighs, chests, and tapestries. Viewing platforms allow visitors to study the magnificent 72 ft by 16 ft (22 m by 5 m) Oseberg ship and the slightly larger Gokstad boat, both of which were discovered on the western side of the Oslofjord. The smaller Tune was found on the eastern bank.

↑ A remarkably well-preserved Viking ship at the Vikingskipshuset

⑪

Kon-Tiki Museum

📍 Bygdøynesveien 36 🚌 30 🚢 ⏰ Mar–Apr & Sep–Oct: 10am–5pm daily; Jun–Aug: 9:30am–6pm daily; Nov–Feb: 10am–4pm daily 🚌 Public hols 🌐 kon-tiki.no

On display at this museum are the fragile-looking vessels used by Thor Heyerdahl to make his legendary journeys across the Pacific and Atlantic Oceans. The balsawood *Kon-Tiki* raft carried Heyerdahl and a crew from Peru to Polynesia in 1947. In 1970, he sailed *Ra II*, a papyrus boat, from Morocco to the Caribbean to prove that the ancient peoples of Africa or Europe might have had contact with South America.

⑫

Norsk Folkemuseum

📍 Museumsveien 10 🚌 30 🚢 ⏰ 11am–4pm daily (May–Sep: 10am–5pm) 🚌 Jan 1, May 17, Dec 24, 25, & 31 🌐 norskfolkemuseum.no

Established in 1894, this attraction is devoted largely to Norwegian rural life, with over 150 restored buildings.

↑ Walking past a traditional wooden hut at the Norsk Folkemuseum

These include storehouses, barns, and a splendid stave church (c. 1200) with typical steep, shingle-covered roofs and dramatic dragon finials. The indoor collections consist of displays of folk art, toys, and folk dress, as well as the playwright Ibsen's study and a pharmacy museum. On Sundays in the summer there are displays of folk dancing, and guides demonstrate skills such as weaving tapestries or baking traditional flatbread.

⑬

Frammuseet

📍 Bygdøynesveien 36 🚌 30 🚢 ⏰ 10am–6pm daily 🌐 frammuseum.no

The *Fram* is best known as the ship that carried Norwegian explorer Roald Amundsen on his epic journey to the South Pole in 1911. It was an ideal vessel for this undertaking – its sides are perfectly smooth, making it impossible for ice to get a grip on the hull. Visitors can ease themselves between the remarkable array of beams in the ship's hull and marvel at the assortment of equipment – ranging from a piano to surgical instruments – that the crew took with them. Fascinating displays relate the history of Arctic exploration.

↑ Illustration of a 10th-century Viking raid on the English coast

THE VIKINGS

From the 8th to the 11th centuries, the Vikings sailed from their overpopulated fjords in Scandinavia and made their way across Europe, plundering, looking for trade, and offering mercenary service – some even traveled to the coast of North America. Fear of the Viking raid unified many otherwise disparate tribes and kingdoms, and many new political states were created by the Vikings themselves. Despite profiting from the spoils of war, their greatest achievement was their success as settlers and traders.

RELIGION

Viking religion was dominated by the supreme gods Odin (god of war), Thor (thunder), and Frey (fertility). Valhalla was their equivalent of heaven. Warriors were buried with items for the afterlife, and the rich were entombed in ships. Most Vikings had converted to Christianity by the late 10th century, but Sweden remained pagan into the 11th century.

↑ A small bronze statue of Thor, the Viking god of thunder

↑ A replica set of 10th-century armor, including helmet and ax

↑ Brooches richly decorated with animals and people

LONGSHIP

The longship was the main vessel of the Viking raid. Longer, slimmer, and faster than the usual Viking ship, it had a large rectangular sail and between 24 and 50 oars. Navigation was achieved by taking bearings from the stars.

WEAPONS AND ARMOR

Weapons and armor were the backbone of Viking culture. Bronze and iron swords were endlessly produced (many of which followed their bearers to the grave), and arrows, axes, shields, helmets, and coats of mail were standard military gear.

JEWELRY

Jewelry design often showed Arab and Eastern European influence, illustrating the extent of the Viking trading network. Gold and silver were a sign of prestige, but many ornaments were made of bronze, pewter, colored glass, jet, and amber.

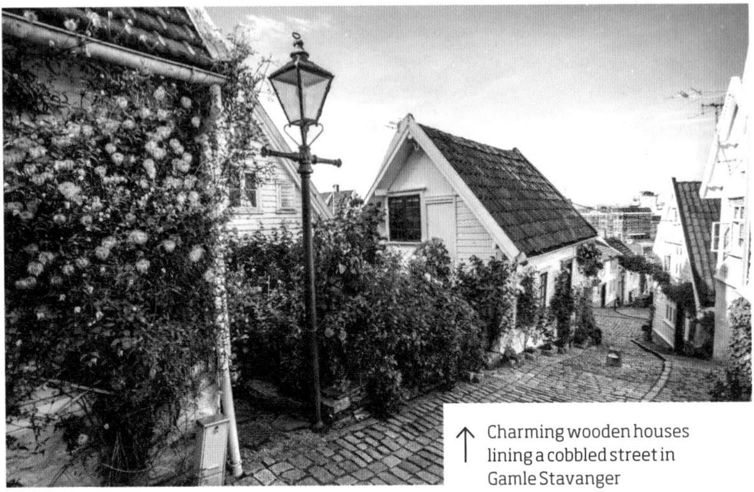

Charming wooden houses lining a cobbled street in Gamle Stavanger

2 Stavanger

Rogaland
Strandkaien 61; www.regionstavanger-ryfylke.com

For much of its early history, Stavanger was little more than a fishing village. The town prospered in the 1960s when oil was discovered off the North Sea coast, and today it is Norway's fourth-largest city, with a reputation as a thriving foodie destination.

Small enough to be seen on foot, much of the center of Stavanger is modern. One notable exception to this is the cathedral, the Stavanger Domkirke, which dates back to the 12th century but has been restored several times since. Later 17th-century additions include a flamboyant pulpit and a number of huge, richly carved memorial tablets hanging in the aisles.

Stavanger's main attraction is the area of Gamle Stavanger (Old Stavanger), west of the harbor. Visitors can wander down the narrow cobblestone streets of this old city quarter, amid the painted wooden houses, and imagine life here in the 19th century. At No. 88 Øvre Strandgate, in an old cannery, the interesting Norsk Hermetikkmuseet (Norwegian Canning Museum) tells the story of Stavanger's fisheries. Overlooking the harbor, meanwhile, the ultra-modern Norsk Oljemuseum (Norwegian Petroleum Museum) gives an insight into the town's more recent source of prosperity: North Sea oil exploration.

3 Bergen and the Fjords

Hordaland
Strandkaien 3; www.visitbergen.com

Surrounded by mountains, Bergen offers visitors plenty to do and see, although it rains relentlessly here. The city is one of the prettiest in the whole of Norway, with a medieval quarter dating back to the days when Bergen's port was an important hub of European trade for the

The landscape at Lustrafjord, an arm of Sognefjord, the world's deepest fjord

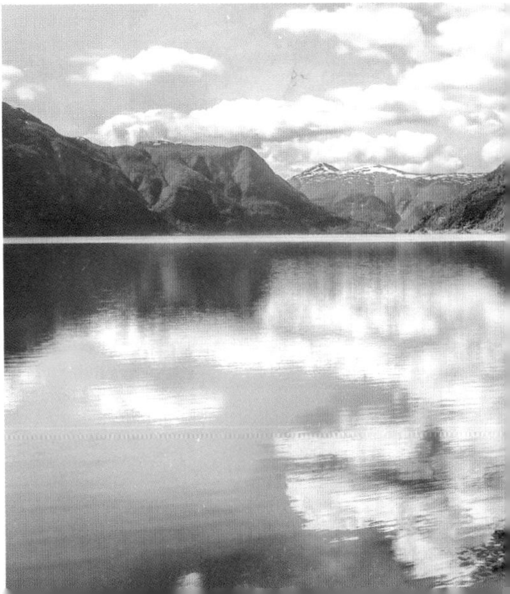

all-powerful German Hanseatic League. Many of the surviving Hanseatic buildings are found on the Bryggen (quay), where brightly painted old wooden warehouses – now museums, shops, and restaurants – make up an attractive harborside. Close to the harbor is the busy Fisketorvet (Fish Market), where fresh fish, produce, and local crafts can be found. Also nearby are the 11th-century Mariakirken (St. Mary's Church) and the **Hanseatic Museum and Schøtstuene** – a well-preserved late Hansa house from the 18th century.

Around Lille Lungegårds-vannet, the city's central lake, are four world-class art galleries, which together form the **KODE** museum.

Just outside the city is **Troldhaugen**, an enchanting villa filled with paintings, prints, and other memorabilia, where Norway's most famous composer, Edvard Grieg, spent the later years of his life and composed much of his work. A short way beyond is Fantoft Stavkirke, a traditional, ancient wooden church, originally built in Sognefjord.

Bergen also makes a good base for viewing the western fjord scenery, which extends from south of Bergen up to Kristiansund in the north.

THE WORLD'S MOST BEAUTIFUL VOYAGE

What began in 1893 as a means of mail delivery and transport has matured into an awe-inspiring coastal journey. The *Hurtigruten* cruise takes six days, calling at 35 ports, to travel from Bergen to the far north Kirkenes. It sails through emerald fjords, past rugged mountain scenery and tiny island villages. Halfway through the voyage, *Hurtigruten* passes the Arctic Circle. A round trip takes 11 days to cover 3,230 miles (5,200 km). In summer, the expedition can feel like a Mediterranean cruise with endless midnight sun. In winter, you're likely to see the Northern Lights across the night sky; if you do not, *Hurtigruten* will book you another cruise for free.

Boat trips leave from Bergen throughout the summer (a few run year-round), visiting local fjords. One of the closest fjords in the area is Osterfjord, but Hardangerfjord, with its majestic waterfalls, is perhaps the most spectacular. To the north, the vast Sognefjord, at 127 miles (205 km) long and 4,291 ft (1,308 m) deep, is the deepest and longest fjord in the world.

Hanseatic Museum and Schøtstuene

⊕ 🏠 Øvregaten 50 🕐 Hours vary, check website 📅 Dec 24–26 🌐 hanseatiske museum.museumvest.no

KODE

⊕ ⊗ ⊕ ⊕ ⊕ 🏠 Around Lars Hilles gate 🕐 Hours vary, check website 📅 May 1 & 17, Dec 24–Jan 4 🌐 kode bergen.no

Troldhaugen

⊕ ⊗ ⊖ ⊕ 🏠 Troldhaug-veien 65, Paradis 🕐 May–Sep: 9am–6pm daily; Oct–Apr: 10am–4pm daily 📅 Dec 14–Jan 5 🌐 grieg museum.no

---

 GREAT VIEW
Fløyen Funicular

For spectacular views of Bergen, ride the Fløibanen funicular 1,050 ft (320 m) to the top of Mount Fløyen. Once up, have pancakes at Fløistuen Café or, if you're feeling energetic, take a forest hike.

The awe-inspiring spectacle of the Northern Lights over the town of Tromsø ↑

❹

Trondheim

🏠 Trøndelag
ℹ️ Nordre gate 11; www.
trondheim.com

Called Nidaros (meaning "the mouth of the Nid river") until the 16th century, Trondheim has benefited from having a good harbor and being situated in a wide and fertile valley. Founded in AD 997, the city was for many centuries the political and religious capital of Norway, with the earliest Parliament (or *Ting*) being held here. This period saw the construction of the Nidaros Cathedral – Trondheim's most beautiful building and one of Norway's architectural highlights – which was established around 1077. Until the Reformation in the 16th century, the cathedral drew pilgrims from all over Scandinavia. Notable features of this huge building include the Gothic-style great arched nave and a magnificent stained-glass rose window above the entrance. Since 1988, the cathedral has been home to the Norwegian crown jewels and the modest but beautiful regalia of the king, queen, and crown prince, which are on display in one of the side chapels.

Another reminder of Trondheim's medieval past is provided by the wharves alongside the harbor and the narrow streets that wind between brightly painted warehouses. Although the buildings you see today only date back to the 18th century, the layout of the area is much as it was in earlier times, when fishing and timber were the main sources of the town's wealth.

SCANDI STYLE

Scandi fashion and interiors are known for their sleek designs and quality materials. When shopping in Trondheim, Olav Tryggvasons gate is a good starting point. At No. 19, Livid Jeans sells hand-crafted trousers *(www.livid jeans.com)*. Up the road, at No. 10, Ting is a one-stop-shop for Scandi homewares *(www. ting.no)*, and Småting, at No. 6, designs toys and clothing for kids *(www.smaating.no)*.

←
Beautiful buildings in Trondheim, reflected in the waters of the Nidelva

Other attractions include the Stiftsgården, built in 1774–8 as a private home and now serving as the king's official residence in Trondheim. The red-brick **Nordenfjeldske Kunstindustrimuseum**, or Museum of Decorative Arts, houses an extensive collection of furniture, tapestries, silver, ceramics, and glassware from the 16th to the 20th centuries, including a fine range of Art Nouveau pieces, plus contemporary arts, crafts, and design.

Nordenfjeldske Kunstindustrimuseum

 Munkegaten 3-7 ⏰ Hours vary, check website ✖ Some public hols 🌐 nkim.no

---

5

Tromsø

🏛 Troms 🚇🚌🚍 𝒊 Samuel Arnesens gate 5; www. visittromso.no

Situated inside the Arctic circle, Tromsø, the so-called capital of northern Norway, is a lively university town. There are not many specific attractions in the town itself, but its fine mountain and fjord setting make it well worth a visit – a trip on the aerial tramway (Fjellheisen) up the mountain behind the city gives a real sense of the setting of this polar town. The most spectacular time to stay is in the summer, during the period of the midnight sun – due to the high latitude, the sun remains above the horizon from May 21 to July 21, and the sky often glows red throughout the night. Tromsø is also a good place to view the Northern Lights in winter.

The compact center sits on a small hilly island reached by a bridge, and it is possible to stroll through the area in around 15 minutes. The most impressive sight here is the striking white Ishavskatedralen

💬 INSIDER TIP
Northern Lights

Chase the aurora in Tromsø on a 7-hour tour with Polar Adventures (www.polaradventures. no), or learn how to photograph them with the Arctic Guide Service (www.arcticguide service.com).

↑ The modern, tent-like structure of the Arctic Cathedral in Tromsø

(Arctic Cathedral), intended to represent the type of tent used by the Sami, the region's indigenous semi-nomadic people. The **Polarmuseet** (Polar Museum) documents the history of the local economy – seal-trapping played a big part until the 1950s – and polar expeditions, in particular the voyages of Norwegian explorer Roald Amundsen. Tromsø is a famous starting point for Arctic expeditions, and Amundsen made his last expedition from here to the Arctic ice cap, where he died in 1928.

Polarmuseet

 Søndre Tollbugata 11B 📞 77 62 33 60 ⏰ 11am-5pm daily (Jun 15-Aug 15: 9am-6pm) ✖ Public hols

PRACTICAL
INFORMATION

Here you will find all the essential advice and information you will need before and during your stay in Norway.

AT A GLANCE

CURRENCY
Norwegian
Krone (NOK)

TIME ZONE
CET/CEST. Central
European Summer
Time runs from the last
Sunday in March to the
last Sunday in October.

LANGUAGES
Norwegian

ELECTRICITY SUPPLY
Power sockets are
type F, also accommo-
dating two-prong type
C and E plugs. Standard
voltage is 220–230V.

EMERGENCY NUMBERS

AMBULANCE	FIRE
113	**110**

POLICE
112

TAP WATER
Unless stated
otherwise, tap
water in Norway
is safe to drink.

Getting There

Most international flights arrive at Oslo's airport, Gardermoen, 37 miles (60 km) north of the city, although some carriers also fly to Stavanger, Bergen, and Tromsø.

Norway is integrated with other European rail networks via Sweden. There are no high-speed trains, but the standard of comfort and service on board is high. The major point of entry from mainland Europe is Copenhagen, where trains cross the Øresund Bridge before heading to Oslo.

Car ferries from Kiel in Germany, Hirtshals in Denmark, and Strømstad in Sweden arrive in four Norwegian ports: Oslo, Larvik, Kristiansand, and Sandefjord. **Color Line** is Norway's biggest car ferry operator.

Color Line
🅦 colorline.com

Personal Security

Norway is generally a safe country, but it is always a good idea to take sensible precautions against pickpockets. If you have anything stolen, report the crime as soon as possible to the nearest police station. Get a copy of the crime report in order to claim on your insurance.

Health

In case of accident or emergency, treatment is swift in Norway's excellent hospitals. EU citizens with a European Health Insurance Card (EHIC) are entitled to free emergency medical care in Norway, but it is also advisable to take out some form of supplementary health insurance. Visitors from outside the EU must arrange their own private medical insurance.

Each town has one pharmacy *(apotek)* that is always open or "on call."

Passports and Visas

Citizens of the EU, the US, Canada, Australia, and New Zealand do not require a visa for stays of less than three months. Citizens of most EU countries can use a national identity card

instead of a passport for entry to Norway. For visa information specific to your home country, consult your nearest Norwegian embassy or check online.

Travelers with Specific Needs

Few countries are better equipped for wheelchair access. However, some rural parts of Norway and older transport systems, such as trams and ferry boats, can pose problems. Note that guide dogs can be denied access to buses if there are passengers with allergies. **Visit Norway** provides useful information on traveling around Norway. Otherwise, check ahead for access information at specific sights.
Visit Norway
w visitnorway.com/plan-your-trip

Money

Credit cards, debit cards, and prepaid currency cards are accepted in almost all shops and restaurants. Contactless payments are also common. Cash is used only for small purchases – Norway is increasingly becoming a cashless society. Not every bank provides money exchange services involving cash.

Cell Phones and Wi-Fi

European travelers can use up to 15GB of their data allowance without being charged an additional fee. Visitors from other countries should check their contracts before departure in order to avoid unexpected charges.

Most businesses and institutions have Wi-Fi open to everyone.

Getting Around

Domestic flights can be useful if you are short on time – especially if you wish to visit the far north – and are operated by a variety of carriers.

Vy (Norway's state railroad) operates a more extensive network in the south than in the north, but there are routes to all the major towns. A Norway Rail Pass allows unlimited travel on all trains in Norway for a specified number of days in a given period. The pass is available from rail ticket agents in Norway and abroad. In Oslo and Akershus county, the **Ruter** system covers the

bus, tram, and T-bane subway. Tickets for all of these services are interchangeable and can be purchased online.

Buses cover the length and breadth of Norway, and are useful for getting to places the train network does not reach. Most long-distance buses are operated by the national company, **NOR-WAY Bussekspress**.

Car rental is fairly costly, although Norway's main roads are fast and very well maintained. Road regulations are strictly enforced, particularly those relating to drink driving. Speeding can incur hefty fines, even if you are driving only a few miles above the limit; most main roads have cameras. Due to poor visibility and bad weather, many minor roads in Norway close during the dark winter months.

Local ferries are an invaluable means of transportation across the fjords. **Hurtigruten**, the Norwegian Coastal Express service, sails from Bergen to Kirkenes, far above the Arctic Circle, putting in at 35 ports en route. It is a superb way to see Norway's dramatic coastline.
Hurtigruten
w hurtigruten.co.uk
NOR-WAY Bussekspress
w nor-way.no
Ruter
w ruter.no
Vy
w vy.no

Visitor Information

Norway has around 350 local tourist offices, as well as almost 20 regional offices. Visitors to the capital can use the **Oslo Visitor Center** in the heart of town. For brochures and more general information on all parts of the country, contact the **Norwegian Tourist Board** before you leave home. As well as providing useful information on hiking routes and guided mountain tours, **Den Norske Turistforening** (The Norwegian Mountain Touring Association) sells a range of maps and hiking gear, and maintains more than 300 mountain huts throughout the country.
Den Norske Turistforening
w dnt.no
Norwegian Tourist Board
w visitnorway.com
Oslo Visitor Center
w visitoslo.com

DENMARK

Despite a history of pillaging, invasion, and plague, Denmark has evolved through centuries of religious and social conflict into one of the world's most enviable and egalitarian democracies. The first mention of the Danes as a distinct people dates to AD 590. Their strategic position made them a central power in the Viking expansion and by 1033 the Danes controlled much of Britain and Normandy, as well as most trading routes in the Baltic Sea. In the 14th century, the kingdoms of Sweden and Norway came under Danish rule, leading to the Kalmar Union, the first Scandinavian federation. The disintegration of this alliance and a series of disastrous religious wars meant that the next period of Danish prosperity did not occur until the 16th century, when the country profited from a tax on ships traversing the channel between Denmark and Sweden. By the 18th century, Denmark had discovered lucrative trading opportunities in the Far East, ushering in a new sense of Danish nationalism, and inspiring a series of social reforms. In spite of a British attack on Copenhagen at the start of the 19th century, Denmark experienced an unprecedented flourishing of culture. This era also saw the rise of the social democrats and the trade unions, with parliamentary democracy established in 1901. Denmark was neutral in both world wars, but during World War II was occupied by the Nazis. In 1972, Denmark became the first Scandinavian country to join the European Community and today it is ranked one of the world's most desirable places to live, with a reputation as a tolerant society with high standards of living.

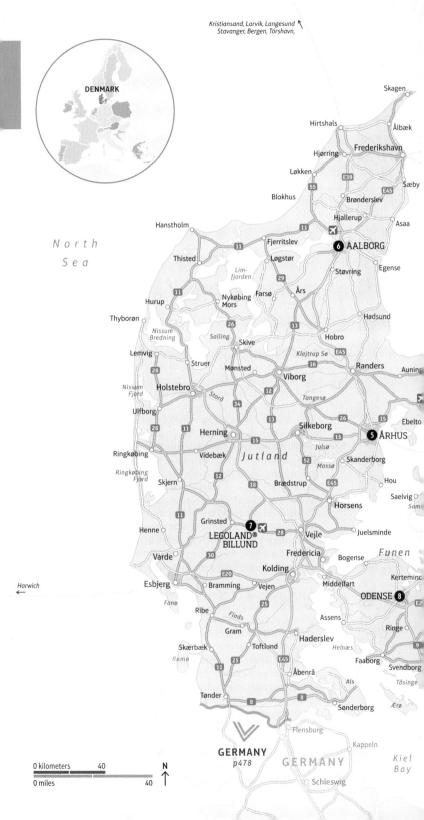

DENMARK

1. Copenhagen
2. Roskilde
3. Frederiksborg Slot
4. Helsingør
5. Århus
6. Aalborg
7. LEGOLAND® Billund
8. Odense

↑ Oslo

Gothenburg

Vesterø
Havn

Læsø

Varberg

Falkenberg

Anholt

SWEDEN
p568

Grenå

Kattegat

Halmstad

Osby

Ängelholm

Hässleholm

Helsingborg

SWEDEN

Gilleleje

Höör

Kristianstad

Tisvildeleje

Helsingør

4 HELSINGØR

Odden
Færgehavn

FREDERIKSBORG
SLOT

3 Fredensborg

Hörby

Hundested

Birkerød

Landskrona

Sejerø

Frederikssund

Rungsted

Zealand

Ballerup

E47

Lund

Holbæk

COPENHAGEN

1

Nørre Jernløse

Kalundborg

57

21

Lejre

Malmö

2 ROSKILDE

Tissø

Stenlille

14

Amager

E20

Sorø

E20

Ringsted

Køge

22

Trelleborg

Slagelse

Ystad

Korsør

Nyborg

Store Heddinge

Skælskør

Fakse

Agersø

Næstved

E47

Langeland

22

Præstø

Femø

Møn

→

Fejø

Vordingborg

Rønne

Rudkøbing

Stege

Baltic

Nakskov

Stubbekøbing

Sea

Sakskøbing

Falster

Lolland

E47

Nykøbing Falster

Rødbyhavn

Nysted

Sassnitz

Gedser

Puttgarden

Rügen

Bergen auf Rügen

↑ Pedestrianized streets in Copenhagen's delightful Old Town district

❶

COPENHAGEN

 www.visitcopenhagen.com

Denmark's capital is an icon of Scandi cool. Locals navigate their famously laid-back city by bicycle, stopping to chat, drink coffee, and revel in the art of *hygge* (cosiness). Peppering the city are green spaces and superb restaurants, not to mention a wealth of art galleries, design-led stores, and regal buildings.

①

Ny Carlsberg Glyptotek

🏛 Dantes Plads 7
Ⓜ København H 🚌 1A, 2A, 9A, 37 🕐 11am-6pm Tue-Sun (to 9pm Thu)
📅 Jan 1, Jun 5, Dec 24 & 25
🌐 glyptoteket.com

Copenhagen's most elegant art gallery was opened in 1897 by Carl Jacobsen, son of the founder of the Carlsberg Brewery, to give more people the chance to see Classical art. Housed in a magnificent Neo-Classical building, the Glyptotek is best known for its exquisite antiquities, in particular its collections of Etruscan and Roman art.

The main building showcases an array of Egyptian, Greek, Roman, and French sculpture, as well as works from the "Golden Age" of Danish painting (1800–50). A modern wing, designed

by acclaimed Danish architect Henning Larsen, contains a selection of Impressionist paintings by Monet, Sisley, Pissarro, Gauguin, and works by David and Bonnard.

②

Tivoli Gardens

🏛 Vesterbrogade 3
Ⓜ København H 🚌 2A, 5C, 9A, 34, 37, 66, 250S
🕐 Hours vary, check website 🌐 tivoli gardens.com

Opened in 1843, this highly popular entertainment park combines all the fun of fairground rides with fountains and fireworks, concerts and ballets, alongside top-quality restaurants and fast-food outlets. Based on the ornamental gardens popular in Europe at the time, this verdant wonderland features Chinese-style pagodas and

Moorish pavilions, as well as modern additions, such as the Hanging Gardens.

Among the many fairground rides are a traditional roller coaster, a Ferris wheel, a "freefall" tower, and the Star Flyer, an 262 ft (80 m) carousel that provides a unique view over the city. There are also amusement arcades, shooting galleries, and children's rides.

The gardens are at their most enthralling after dusk, when thousands of tiny lights illuminate the park. At night, open-air theaters host all forms of entertainment, from big bands to Friday night rock concerts, and – during the summer season – performances of traditional Danish pantomimes in the Peacock Theater.

 INSIDER TIP
Getting Around

All the city's attractions are within walking distance of each other. Copenhagen has an excellent cycling infrastructure, with dedicated cycle lanes and bikes for hire across the city. There are also numerous buses. The metro has three lines: M1 runs from Vanløse to Vestamager, M2 goes from Vanløse to the airport, and M3 runs in a loop around the center.

A good time to visit Tivoli is between late November and Christmas, when the gardens are transformed into a bustling Christmas fair. You can sample traditional Danish seasonal fare, buy specialty Christmas gifts, and try the toboggan run.

National Museum

🏠 Ny Vestergade 10
Ⓜ Gammel Strand 🚌 1A, 2A, 9A, 14, 26, 37 🕐 10am–5pm Tue–Sun 🚫 Dec 24, 25, & 31 🌐 natmus.dk

The extensive ethnographic and antiquities collections at this museum detail Danish history from prehistoric to modern times, and include some fascinating exhibits of Viking life.

Many of the items on display come from the Danish isles, such as items of jewelry, bones, and even several bodies found preserved in peat bogs, as well as imposing rune stones with inscriptions dating from around AD 1000. The restored 18th-century royal residence also houses a children's museum and offers a host of educational activities. Close by, and part of the museum, is a Danish home with authentic interiors from the 1890s, complete with decorated panels and elaborately carved furniture (view by guided tour at noon on Saturday June–August only; book in main museum).

Rådhuset

🏠 Rådhuspladsen 📞 33 66 33 66 Ⓜ Rådhuspladsen 🚌 2A, 10, 12, 14, 26, 250S, & many others 🕐 9am–4pm Mon–Fri, 9:30am–1pm Sat

At the edge of the city center, in the middle of a wide open square, is the Baroque-style Rådhuset, or City Hall, built in the early 1900s. Climb the 300-step staircase to the top of the bell tower for a view of the city. On the way, check out the First World Clock, a super-accurate timepiece designed by Jens Olsen. It took three years to design and 12 to produce. Guided tours take place at 1pm during the week and 10am on Saturday.

↑ Admiring classical statuary at Thorvaldsens Museum, Christiansborg Palace

(5)

Christiansborg Palace

◨ Slotsholmen Ⓜ Gammel Strand 🚌 1A, 2A, 9A, 26, 37 🕐 Hours vary, check website 🌐 royalpalaces.dk

Situated on the island of Slotsholmen, Christiansborg Palace has been the seat of the Danish Parliament since 1928. It also houses the Royal Reception Rooms, the Queen's Library, the Supreme Court, and the Prime Minister's Office. Built on the site of a fortress constructed in 1167 by Copenhagen's founder Bishop Absalon, the palace has twice burnt down and been rebuilt, then altered and extended. Much of this work was carried out in the 18th century under Christian VI, whose elaborate visions were realized in both the architecture and the lavish interiors. The current palace dates mostly from the early 20th century. Today, it is possible to visit the Royal Reception Rooms, the Harness Room, the Stables and Coach House, and some ruins from the original fortress.

Above the riding stables is the Royal Court Theater, built by Christian VI in 1767. Now the **Teatermuseet**, much of it has been restored to its original

18th-century appearance. Exhibits illustrate the history of Danish theater up to the present day. The auditorium, with its plush red furnishings and small, gold side boxes, houses a wealth of memorabilia – including costumes, theater programs, wigs, and even old make-up boxes and a reconstructed dressing room. The whole theater is dominated by the grand royal box, built for King Frederik VII in 1852. Situated at the back of the auditorium, it seems almost to upstage the stage itself. The king's wife, the former ballet dancer Louise Rasmussen, had a private box to the right of the royal box, where she sat if she was alone.

Along the north side of the palace, the **Thorvaldsens Museum** houses the work of the country's most celebrated sculptor, Bertel Thorvaldsen, who spent much of his career

Did You Know?

Denmark's national flag is the oldest in the world. It dates back to 1625.

in Rome. As well as his own impressive Neo-Classical sculptures, the museum houses Thorvaldsen's collection of antiquities and 19th-century Danish art.

Teatermuseet

 Christiansborg Ridebane 18 🕐 Noon–4pm Tue–Sun 🔒 Jan 1, Dec 24, 25, & 31 🌐 teatermuseet.dk

Thorvaldsens Museum

 Bertel Thorvaldsens Plads 2 🕐 10am–5pm Tue–Sun 🌐 thorvaldsensmuseum.dk

---

(6)

Designmuseum Danmark

◨ Bredgade 68 Ⓜ Marmorkirken 🚌 1A, 15 🕐 11am–6pm Tue, Thu–Sun; 10am–9pm Wed 🌐 designmuseum.dk

Copenhagen's reputation for cool design is reflected in this museum, which celebrates the history of applied arts and industrial design. Housed in a former hospital, the extensive collection includes fashion, textiles, and poster art, and celebrates Danish innovators such as Arne Jacobsen, Kaare Klint, and Poul Henningsen. The star attraction is an exhibit on the humble chair, a key example of design evolution.

---

(7)

Strøget

◨ Frederiksberggade to Østergade Ⓜ Kongens Nytorv 🚌 1A, 2A, 26

Running between Rådhuspladsen (City Hall Square) and Kongens Nytorv (King's New Square), Strøget (pronounced

→ Sailing boats moored on Nyhavn, a narrow canal lined with colorful houses

> **Since the 1970s, Nyhavn has gentrified and is now one of the cities most-loved districts, packed with bars, restaurants, and cafés.**

"Stroll") is Europe's longest pedestrian street. Located at the center of a large traffic-free zone in the heart of the city, Strøget consists of five streets – Frederiksberggade, Nygade, Vimmelskaftet, Amagertorv, and Østergade. The area is home to several exclusive stores, including top international designers Louis Vuitton and Gucci. Other stores sell the best in Danish porcelain, modern design, glass, and furnishings – all areas in which Denmark has a world-class reputation.

The best selection can be found on Plaza Amagertorv, where an interesting twin-gabled house, built in 1616 in the style of the Dutch Renaissance, houses the Royal Copenhagen Porcelain Shop. Adjacent to it is the showroom of Georg Jensen, which specializes in upscale silverware. There are also many bustling restaurants and cafés, as well as street performers and musicians, making it a lively place for walking or for relaxing with a coffee and pastry.

Nyhavn

🏛 **Kongens Nytorv**
Ⓜ **Kongens Nytorv** 🚌 **1A, 26, 66, 350S** 🚆 **991, 992**

Lined with colorful houses, this short canal, known as the New Harbor, was originally intended to enable small ships to sail into the center of Copenhagen. Today it is one of the city's most iconic and attractive spots, with stylish yachts and wooden sailing boats moored along its quays.

For much of its history, the area had a rather seedy reputation thanks to its cheap bars, rough-and-ready hotels, tattoo parlors, and numerous brothels. Since the 1970s, Nyhavn has gentrified and is now one of the city's most-loved districts, packed with bars, restaurants, and cafés targeting a more salubrious clientele. It is also a good spot to take a stroll or pick up a canal tour. The area is especially popular on warm evenings, and many of the restaurants and bars can fill up quickly, particularly on the north side of the harbor.

EAT

Torvehallerne
A food hall with everything from a bottle shop to gourmet food stalls.

🏛 Frederiksborggade 21
 torvehallernekbh.dk

Ⓚ Ⓚ Ⓚ

Schønnemanns
The most revered of the traditional *smørrebrød* lunch restaurants.

🏛 Hauser Plads 16
 restaurant schonnemann.dk

Ⓚ Ⓚ Ⓚ

Studio
Nordic-French gourmet restaurant tucked into the Standard Hotel.

🏛 Havnegade 44
 thestandardcph.dk

Ⓚ Ⓚ Ⓚ

Amalienborg

Amaliegade Marmor-kirken 1A, 26 991, 992 Hours vary, check website Dec 23–25 royalpalaces.dk

The stately Amalienborg consists of four identical Rococo buildings arranged symmetrically around a large cobbled square, with an imposing equestrian statue of Frederik V in the middle. Changing of the guard takes place every day at noon outside the palace of the present queen, Margrethe II.

Originally intended as mansions for four wealthy families, the buildings have housed the Danish royal family since 1874. Only Christian VII's palace is currently open to the public. It houses the Amalienborg museum – the museum of the Danish monarchy – which contains part of the Royal Collection (the bulk of which is housed at Rosenborg Slot), and also has a selection of official and private rooms on view. The highlights are the study of King Christian IX and the drawing room of his wife, Queen Louise, which are filled with family presents, photographs, and the occasional Fabergé treasure.

There are two attractive but contrasting views from the square. On the harborside is Amaliehaven, a garden dating from 1983 with a fountain in its center; in the opposite direction is Marmorkirken, a white marble church officially known as Frederikskirken, which has one of Europe's largest domes, inspired by St. Peter's in Rome (p380). Its construction was begun in 1749 with expensive Norwegian marble, but it was not completed until 150 years later (with less expensive Danish limestone) owing to the huge costs incurred.

Christiania

Bådsmandsstræde 43 Christianshavn 9A www.christiania.org

Originally set up in 1971 on the site of a former military barracks, this "free town" is an enclave of an alternative lifestyle: colorful, anarchic, and self-governing. Though it has a salacious reputation thanks to its bohemian attitude, the settlement is actually a fairly pastoral enclave defined by its slef-built houses, workshops, galleries, music venues, and organic eateries.

HYGGE

You may have heard of hygge, pronounced "hew-ga." The word has been literally translated as "cosiness," but talk to any Dane and you'll see it means much more. Hygge refers to inner contentment, usually when enjoying the companionship of others and almost always in ambient, sociable surroundings. Look around and you'll see how Danish design facilitates the art of hygge, from friends wrapped in blankets at ultra-modern cafés, to parents conversing while cycling, their kids stowed safely in their cargo bikes.

Little Mermaid

Langelinie Østerport 1A, 26, 27, then a short walk 991, 992

The iconic Little Mermaid statue (Den Lille Havfrue) has become the unofficial emblem of Copenhagen. Sitting on a stone by the promenade at Langelinie and looking out over the Øresund, she is much smaller than her pictures would have you believe. Sculpted by Edvard Erichsen and first unveiled in 1913, this bronze statue was inspired by the Hans Christian Andersen character, who left the sea after falling in love with a prince. The mermaid has suffered over the years at the hands of mischievous pranksters, even losing her head and an arm. Happily, she is currently in possession of all her "parts."

←

Vibrant mural in the self-governing enclave of Christiania

Rosenborg Slot

🏠 Øster Voldgade 4A
Ⓜ Nørreport 🚌 6A, 15E, 42, 150S, 184, 185 🕐 Hours vary, check website
📅 Jan 1, Dec 22-26 & 31
🌐 royalpalaces.dk

Originally built by Christian IV as a summer residence in the early 17th century, Rosenborg Slot took inspiration from the Renaissance architecture of the Netherlands. The "builder king" continued to add to it over the next 30 years until the castle looked much as it does today – a playful version of a fortress. The interiors are particularly well preserved and its sumptuous chambers, halls, and ballrooms are full of objects, including amber chandeliers, life-size silver lions, tapestries, thrones, portraits, and gilded chairs.

The impressive Porcelain Cabinet includes examples from the famous *Flora Danica* dinner service made for 100 guests, created by the Royal Copenhagen porcelain factory between 1790 and 1803. The colorful Glass Cabinet – the only known cabinet of its kind – houses nearly 1,000 examples of old Venetian glass as well as

The stately interior and (inset) facade of Rosenborg Slot ↑

glass from the Netherlands, the Czech Republic, England, and Germany.

Statens Museum for Kunst

🏠 Sølvgade 48-50
Ⓜ Nørreport, Østerport 🚌 6A, 15E, 26, 42, 150S, 184, 185 🕐 10am-6pm Tue-Sun (to 8pm Wed)
📅 Jan 1, Dec 24, 25, & 31
🌐 smk.dk

The extensive Statens Museum for Kunst (State Art Museum) holds Danish and European art from the 14th century to the present. Among its many artworks are paintings by Titian, Rubens, Rembrandt, El Greco, Picasso, and Matisse. Danish artists are particularly well represented in the modern art wing. There is also a vast collection of prints and drawings. The gallery offers a number of interesting guided tours; check online for details.

Frederiksberg Have

🏠 Roskildevej 32 🚉 Valby 🚌 4A, 6A, 18, 26

Copenhageners could not imagine their city without Frederiksberg Have, a romantic pleasure garden designed for King Frederik IV in the 18th century. The public received access to the park in 1865 and the rambling English-style gardens have been a favorite spot for picnickers ever since. There is much to explore in this idyllic green space, from woodlands and waterfalls to the Chinese Pavilion and zoological garden. Crowning the scene is Frederiksberg Slot, King Frederik IV's summer retreat, now used by the Military Academy. It is open for guided tours at 11am and 1pm on the last Saturday of the month (except in July and December).

A reconstructed longboat at Roskilde's light-filled Vikingeskibsmuseet

surrounded by an artificial lake. Created for Frederik II, the castle was rebuilt in the Dutch Renaissance style by his son, Christian IV. Highlights include the vaulted black marble chapel, where monarchs were once crowned, and the Great Hall, with its fine tapestries, paintings, and reliefs. The castle also houses the National History Museum.

EXPERIENCE Denmark

Roskilde

⌂ Zealand 🚃🚌
🛈 Stændertorvet 1; www.visitroskilde.com

The settlement of Roskilde first came to prominence in AD 980, when Viking king Harald Bluetooth constructed Zealand's first Christian church here. Once the center of Danish Catholicism, the town declined after the Reformation. Today, it is a quiet town, except when it hosts Roskilde Festival, Northern Europe's largest annual music festival, in July.

The magnificent Roskilde Domkirke stands on the site of Harald Bluetooth's original church. Begun by Bishop Absalon in 1170, the building is now a mix of architectural styles. The cathedral also functions as Denmark's royal

> **INSIDER TIP**
> **Be a Viking**
>
> Between April and October, Roskilde's Vikingeskibsmuseet runs special events and workshops. These cover a range of activities, including painting shields, shadowing a blacksmith, chatting to rope-makers, carving Viking symbols into wood, visiting the jewelry workshop, and sailing on a Viking ship.

mausoleum – some 39 Danish kings and queens are buried here. The remains of Harald Bluetooth are said to be inside one of the columns to the side of the main altar.

Overlooking Roskilde Fjord is the **Vikingeskibsmuseet**. This Viking ship museum contains five reconstructed Viking ships, originally built around AD 1000 and excavated from the bottom of the fjord in 1962. In the waterside workshops, Viking ship replicas are built using period tools and traditional techniques; visitors can sail on them from April to October (booking essential).

Vikingeskibsmuseet
🅿♿🚻☕ ⌂ Vindeboder 12
⌚ 10am–4pm daily (summer: to 5pm) 🚫 Dec 24, 25, & 31
🌐 vikingeskibsmuseet.dk

Frederiksborg Slot

⌂ Hillerød, Zealand
🚂 To Hillerød, then bus 301, 302 ⌚ 10am–5pm daily 🌐 dnm.dk

One of Scandinavia's most magnificent royal castles, the Frederiksborg Slot is built across three small islands

Helsingør

⌂ Zealand 🚂🚃🚌
🛈 Havnepladsen 3; www.visitnorthsealand.com

Helsingør, or Elsinore, lies at the narrowest point of

→ The spacious courtyard of Kronborg Slot, and (inset) the William Shakespeare Monument, Helsingør

HAMLET

Although William Shakespeare probably never visited Helsingør's Kronborg Slot, he set *Hamlet*, one of his most famous plays, here. The prototype for the fictional Danish prince was Amleth, whose story is told by the 12th-century Danish writer Saxo Grammaticus in his *Historia Danica*. Shakespeare might have come across the tale of murder and revenge via François de Belleforest's *Histoires Tragiques* (1570).

the Øresund, the waterway dividing Denmark and Sweden. Its attractive medieval quarter is dotted with many well-preserved merchants' and ferrymen's houses. On the waterfront stands the Museet Sofart, the Maritime Museum of Denmark, built around an old dry dock. Next door is the Kulturværftet, or "culture yard" – a glittering, modern complex of geometric glass blocks that hosts drama and music performances, festivals, exhibitions, and countless other art-based events.

Standing over all this is **Kronborg Slot** (Kronborg Castle), which rests on a spit of land overlooking the sea. Famous as the setting of *Hamlet*, the fortress actually dates from 1574–75 – contemporary with Shakespeare, but considerably later than the era in which his play was set. Highlights include the 62-m (210-ft) banqueting hall. A statue of the Viking chief Holger Danske slumbers in the castle cellars – according to legend he will awaken to defend Denmark if needed.

Kronborg Slot

♿ ⊛ ⓘ 🚗 Kronborg 🕐 Mar, Apr, & Oct: 11am–4pm daily; Jun–Sep: 10am–5:30pm daily; Nov–Mar: 11am–4pm Tue–Sun 🌐 royalpalaces.dk

> **Next door is the Kulturværftet, or "culture yard" – a glittering modern complex of geometric glass blocks that hosts performances and countless other art-based events.**

⑤ Århus

🛫🏛️🚌🚆 Jutland
🛈 Dokk1, Hack Kampmanns Plads 2; visitaarhus.com

Denmark's second city and a major center for wind energy, Århus has a thriving cultural scene, with the eye-catching ARoS art museum and an annual summer arts festival, Aarhus Festuge. In 2017, the city was designated European Capital of Culture.

Århus divides clearly into two parts. The Old Town is a cluster of medieval streets with several fine churches. The city's open-air Old Town Museum, **Den Gamle By**, consists of around 60 historic half-timbered houses and a watermill, transported from locations all over Jutland and carefully reconstructed.

In the modern part of the city, the Rådhus (City Hall) is a prime example of Danish

PICTURE PERFECT
Møllestien

In Århus in summer, head to Møllestien. Roses grow around the doorways of the 18th-century cottages – painted pink, blue, and orange – that line this cobbled lane. Perfect Instagram fodder.

Modernism, designed by Arne Jakobsen and Erik Møller in 1941. Its rectangular clock tower affords a good view of the city.

Den Gamle By

 🏠 Viborgvej 2
🕐 Hours vary, check website
🌐 dengamleby.dk

⑥ Aalborg

🛫🏛️🚌🚆 Jutland
🛈 Kjellerups Torv 5, Kedelhallen; www.visitaalborg.com

Founded by the Vikings, the port of Aalborg spreads across both sides of the Limfjord, which slices through the tip of the Jutland peninsula. Aalborg is the leading producer of the spirit aquavit, the fiery Danish national drink.

The well-preserved Old Town has several sights of interest, including the suitably dark and atmospheric dungeons of the town castle, Aalborghus Slot (1539). The nearby Budolfi Domkirke, a 16th-century Gothic cathedral, houses a collection of portraits depicting Aalborg merchants from the town's prosperous past.

Designed by Finnish architect Alvar Aalto in conjunction with Danish architect Jean-Jacques Baruël, the striking

marble Kunsten (Museum of Modern Art Aalborg) houses a collection of Danish modern art, as well as works by foreign artists such as Max Ernst.

On the edge of Aalborg is the historical site of **Lindholm Høje**. Set on a hilltop overlooking the city, it contains more than 650 marked graves from the Iron Age and Viking Age. A museum depicting the site's history stands nearby.

Lindholm Høje

 🏠 Vendilavej, Nørresundby 📞 99 31 74 40
🕐 Site: daily until dusk; Museum: 10am–5pm Tue–Sun (Nov–Mar: to 4pm)
🔒 Dec 24–Jan 1

⑦

LEGOLAND® Billund

🏠 Billund, Jutland 🛫
🚌 To Vejle, then bus 🕐 Apr–Oct: hours vary, check website 🌐 legoland.dk

The LEGOLAND® Billund theme park celebrates the tiny plastic blocks that have become a household name worldwide. The park opened in 1968, and more than 45 million LEGO® bricks were used in

→

Children and adults enjoying themselves at Legoland® Billund

 ←

Olafur Eliasson's rainbow-colored walkway atop the ARoS art museum, Århus

Looking like a storybook village, the Old Town contains some fine museums, including three art museums, one of which, Brandts, is dedicated to photography. The city's showpiece, however, is the **Hans Christian Andersen Museum**, where the story-teller's life is detailed through drawings, photographs, letters, and personal belongings. A library contains his works in more than 90 languages. The H. C. Andersen's Childhood Home shows where the writer lived with his parents.

Hans Christian Andersen Museum

⊛ ⊛ ⌂ Claus Bergs Gade 11 ⊙ Hours vary, check website ⊠ hcandersensodense.dk

> **HANS CHRISTIAN ANDERSEN (1805-75)**
>
> Denmark's most internationally famous writer, Hans Christian Andersen was born in Odense, the son of a poor cobbler. Andersen made his debut as an author with his first novel in 1833. Several plays and other novels followed, but he is best known for his children's fairy-tales, published between 1835 and 1872. Andersen used everyday language, thus breaking with the literary tradition of the time. Some of his tales, such as "The Little Mermaid" *(p610)*, are deeply pessimistic. A strong autobiographical element runs through these sadder tales; throughout his life, Andersen saw himself as an outsider.

its construction. By 2016, this total had increased to in excess of 58 million bricks.

Aimed primarily at 3–13 year olds, LEGOLAND® is divided into different zones. As well as LEGO® sculptures of animals, buildings, and landscapes, there are numerous rides and stage shows. Highlights include Miniland, a collection of miniature LEGO® towns that represent places around the world, and a driving track where children can take a safety test in a LEGO® car.

 8

Odense

⌂ Funen 🚍🚌 ℹ Rådhus, Vestergade; www. visitodense.com

Odense lies at the heart of an area dubbed the "Garden of Denmark" for the variety of produce grown here. The town is most famous, however, as the birthplace of writer Hans Christian Andersen.

Odense's historic center is easily explored on foot.

PRACTICAL
INFORMATION

Here you will find all the essential advice and information you will need before and during your stay in Denmark.

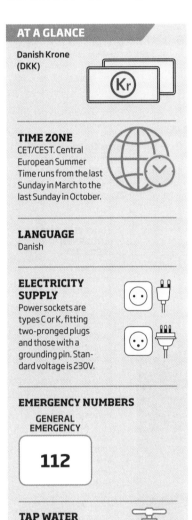

AT A GLANCE

Danish Krone (DKK)

TIME ZONE
CET/CEST. Central European Summer Time runs from the last Sunday in March to the last Sunday in October.

LANGUAGE
Danish

ELECTRICITY SUPPLY
Power sockets are types C or K, fitting two-pronged plugs and those with a grounding pin. Standard voltage is 230V.

EMERGENCY NUMBERS

GENERAL EMERGENCY

112

TAP WATER
Unless stated otherwise, tap water in Denmark is safe to drink.

Getting There

Most international flights arrive at Copenhagen Airport, 5 miles (8 km) from the city center. Billund (closest to LEGOLAND®) is increasingly used by budget airlines, and Aalborg, Aarhus, Esbjerg, and Sønderborg also have their own international airports.

Denmark can be accessed by rail from any major city in Europe via the country's national DSB rail network.

It is possible to travel to Denmark by bus from London, via Brussels, in under 24 hours with Flixbus. Eurolines operates more frequent bus services from the main cities in Germany. Both firms travel extensively within Denmark.

International car ferries run services to Denmark from Germany, Sweden, and Norway.

Personal Security

Denmark is generally a safe country, but it is wise to take precautions against pickpockets. If you have anything stolen, report the crime to the nearest police station. Get a copy of the crime report in order to claim on your insurance.

Health

Denmark's healthcare service is excellent, but note that not all hospital emergency rooms are open 24 hours a day. EU citizens with a European Health Insurance Card (EHIC) are entitled to free emergency medical care in Denmark, but it is also advisable to take out some form of supplementary health insurance. Visitors from outside the EU must arrange their own private medical insurance. Pharmacists are readily available and can give advice and over-the-counter medication. Pharmacies are generally open 24 hours; look for the *apotek* sign.

In an urgent situation that does not quite require an ambulance, call 1813 before going to an emergency room. This alerts an on-call physician or an appropriate hospital to your arrival. The 1813 service can also issue medical prescriptions, which can be picked up at a nearby pharmacy.

Passports and Visas

Visitors who are not citizens of a Scandinavian country require a valid passport to enter Denmark. Citizens of the EU may use a national identity card in lieu of their passport. No visa is required for visitors from the US, Canada, the UK, Ireland, Australia, or New Zealand. For visa information specific to your home country, consult your nearest Danish embassy or check online.

Travelers with Specific Needs

Denmark is constantly improving its access to both buildings and services, but it does not yet offer full accessibility. A number of buses provide wheelchair access, and all taxis accept collapsible wheelchairs. Travelers can phone the national train company, Danske Statsbaner (**DSB**), for information on specific stations or to arrange for assistance. **Visit Denmark** lists accessible sites, and **God Adgang** is also a great resource, listing and rating venues and service providers across Denmark.

DSB
📞 70 13 14 15
God Agang
ⓦ godadgang.dk
Visit Denmark
ⓦ visitdenmark.com

Money

Credit, debit, and prepaid currency cards are accepted almost everywhere. Contactless payment is also common. ATMs can be found in all tourist areas, though may not be available 24 hours a day. It is the custom to pay in cash for transactions under 100Kr.

Cell Phones and Wi-Fi

European travelers can use up to 15GB of their data allowance without being charged an additional fee. Visitors from other countries should check their contracts before departure in order to avoid unexpected charges.

Libraries and many businesses offer free Wi-Fi, as do all trains. Free hotspots can be found quickly on **Wi-Fi Space**.

Wi-Fi Space
ⓦ wifispc.com/Denmark

Getting Around

All regions of Denmark are served by the national railroad company, **DSB**. Standard tickets are valid for travel at any hour, on the day specified. They also include free travel for two children under 12 per adult ticket. Business class tickets include reserved seats and complimentary snacks. Considerable discounts can be had by purchasing "orange tickets," available online only and up to two months in advance; they cannot be changed or refunded, and do not include a seat reservation.

Budget flights and train travel are the most popular means for getting between cities, but long-distance buses do still operate. Buses are cheaper than trains, if not as comfortable. However, they are useful for traveling to remote areas not covered by the rail network.

Denmark is one of the most pleasant countries in Europe for driving. Distances are comfortable, traffic is relatively light, the roads are extremely well maintained and flat, and local drivers are not aggressive. However, car rental in Denmark is expensive. Note that the Danish authorities conduct random breath tests, and penalties for driving under the influence of alcohol are severe.

Ferries link all of the Danish islands and range in size from the car- and bus-carrying catamarans and ferries of **Molslinjen**, which travel between Zealand and Jutland, to tiny vessels serving small settlements off the mainland and major islands.

DSB
ⓦ dsb.dk
Molslinjen
ⓦ molslinjen.dk

Visitor Information

General and location-specific information on all parts of Denmark can be obtained from the **Danish Tourist Board**, which has offices in many countries, including the US and the UK. Visitors to the capital can obtain brochures, maps, and other useful information at the **Copenhagen Visitor Center**.

Copenhagen Visitor Center
ⓦ visitcopenhagen.com
Danish Tourist Board
ⓦ visitdenmark.com

FINLAND

Straddling East and West both geographically and economically, Finland's history has been deeply intertwined with that of its Nordic neighbors and Russia. Little is known of early Finnish history, although it is believed that the ancestors of the Sami first arrived in Finland about 9,000 years ago. Even before the Viking age (8th–11th century AD), Swedes had settled on the southwest coast of Finland, and in 1216, Finland became part of Sweden. From the 13th to the 18th century, the country was a battleground for power struggles between Sweden and Russia. In 1809, Sweden ceded Finland to Russia, and the territory became an autonomous Grand Duchy of Russia. When Czar Nicholas II unwisely removed Finland's autonomous status, a determination to achieve independence took root – this independence was finally won in 1917. Between the two world wars, Finland was dominated by a controversy over language: the Finns fought for the supremacy of their native tongue, and the use of Swedish declined sharply. Despite Finland's independent status, tensions between it and the Soviet Union remained, culminating in conflict during World War II. Suspicion of the Soviet Union continued for decades, but after the demise of the USSR in 1991, Finland reached an agreement with Russia that pledged to end disputes peacefully. In recent years, Finland has carved for itself a peace-brokering reputation, and has expanded economically through membership of the EU and the efforts of its entrepreneurs.

FINLAND

1 Helsinki
2 Savonlinna
3 Turku

Andenes

Harstad

Narvik

Bognes

Bodø

*Norwegian
Sea*

Mo i Rana

Arjeplog

Mosjøen

Hemavan

Sorsele

Storuman

Rorvik

Vilhelmina

Namsos

Åsele

Brekstad

Strömsund

Stjørdal

Trondheim

Sollefteå

Molde

NORWAY

Östersund

Härnösand

Ålesund

Oppdal

Røros

Hede

Sundsvall

Sveg

Drevsjø

SWEDEN

Hudiksva

FINLAND

Mora

Hamar

Gävle

Borlänge

Uppsala

Oslo

Västerås

Stockholm

Karlstad

Örebro

HELSINKI

✕ 🚇 🚌 ⛴ ℹ www.myhelsinki.fi

Finland's capital since 1812, Helsinki is called the "White City of the North," a reference to the white Neo-Classical buildings commissioned by its Russian rulers in the 19th century. It also features impressive modern architecture, from the copper, glass, and rock Temppeliaukio Church to the futuristic Kiasma center. The city is at its best in summer, when long days and clear light draw lively crowds to parks and waterfront cafés.

→

The distinctive architecture of Uspenski Cathedral

①
Market Square

🏠 Head of South Harbor
🚌 16 🚊 1, 1A, 2, 4, 4T

Located near South Harbor, the cobbled Market Square (Kauppatori) has long been a center of trade. A market is held here throughout the year, taking place daily in summer and from Monday to Saturday in winter. Finnish craftsmen sell a variety of handmade wares alongside fish, fruit, and vegetable stalls. During the city's annual Baltic Herring Market in October, fishermen come by boat from the archipelago region of Aland to sell salted herrings and seasonal delicacies in a tradition dating back to 1743.

Among the various fine buildings lining the square are the blue-painted City Hall, by Carl Ludwig Engel, and the 19th-century red- and yellow-brick Old Market Hall, which contains several gourmet and specialist food shops.

Leading westward from Market Square is Esplanadi park, a favorite gathering place for locals, who stroll up and down its grand wide boulevards. At the eastern end of the park, a bronze

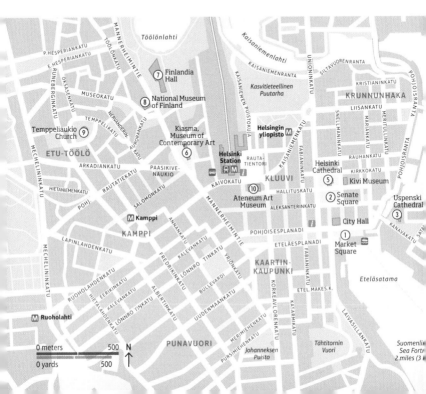

statue of a nude, *Havis Amanda* (1905) by Ville Vallgren, stands in the middle of a fountain. The statue is now a symbol of the city.

② Senate Square

 16 🚋 2, 4, 5, 7

Senate Square (Senaatintori) is the masterpiece of German architect Carl Ludwig Engel. It was commissioned by Finland's Russian rulers in the early 1800s, and a statue of Czar Alexander II of Russia stands in the center.

The best place to survey the square is from the top of the steps up to Helsinki Cathedral. From here, the Senate Building lies to the left and the University of Helsinki to the right. Adjacent to the square is Sederholm House (1757), the oldest stone building in Helsinki.

③ Uspenski Cathedral

 Kanavakatu 1 📞 09-8564 6200 🚋 4, 4T 🕐 9:30am-4pm Tue-Fri, 10am-3pm Sat, noon-3pm Sun

With its dark red-brick exterior, this Russian Orthodox cathedral is a colorful landmark in the ubiquitous white of the historic city center. Its green copper roof and gold onion domes make it stand out on Helsinki's skyline.

Designed in the Byzantine-Russian architectural style by A. M. Gornostayev of St. Petersburg, the cathedral was constructed between 1862

 ←

Detail at the base of Czar Alexander II's statue, Senate Square

💬 INSIDER TIP
Getting Around

The center of Helsinki is easily explored on foot. The city's efficient transportation network consists of buses, trams, and a metro system, although the latter is of limited use for sightseeing. Virtually all bus and tram routes converge on the streets around Helsinki Central Station. Suomenlinna Sea Fortress can be reached by ferry only, from Market Square.

and 1868. Uspenski is the biggest Russian Orthodox church in Scandinavia, and its spacious interior is resplendent in gold, silver, red, and blue – its sheer exuberance forms a sharp contrast to the Lutheran austerity of Helsinki Cathedral *(p624)*. The terrace offers great views over the surrounding Katajanokka district, peppered with well-preserved Art Nouveau buildings and former warehouses that have been converted into shops and restaurants.

↑ Suomenlinna Sea Fortress, a UNESCO World Heritage Site in the Helsinki Bay

the exhibition spaces. Created as a space for post-1960s art, it hosts mixed-media shows, art installations, and drama.

Finlandia Hall

🏛 Mannerheimintie 13E
🚌 40 🚊 4, 5, 10
🌐 finlandiatalo.fi/en

In the tranquil setting of Hesperia Park, this hall is one of architect Alvar Aalto's best-known works. It hosts music and dance performances, as well as conferences.

⑧

National Museum of Finland

🏛 Mannerheimintie 34
🚌 40 🚊 4, 5, 10 🕐 11am-6pm Tue-Sun (May-Aug: daily) 🚫 Public hols
🌐 kansallismuseo.fi

One of Helsinki's most notable examples of Finnish National-Romantic architecture, this museum explores the history of Finland, from prehistory to

④

Suomenlinna Sea Fortress

🚢 From Market Square
🌐 suomenlinna.fi

Constructed by the Swedes between 1748 and 1772, this island fortress is the biggest in Scandinavia, and is now a UNESCO World Heritage Site. Designed to defend the Finnish coast, Suomenlinna offered security to Helsinki's burghers, enabling the city to flourish. The fortress contains about 200 buildings and until the early 19th century, it had more residents than Helsinki.

Eight hundred people still live on the group of islands that make up Suomenlinna, which house many restaurants, galleries, and museums. They receive more than one million visitors a year.

⑤

Helsinki Cathedral

🏛 Unioninkatu 29, Senaatintori 🚌 16 🚊 2, 4, 5, 7 🕐 9am-6pm daily, except during services
🌐 helsinginseurakunnat.fi

The five green cupolas of the gleaming white Lutheran Cathedral are among the

most iconic sights in Helsinki. Designed by German architect Carl Ludwig Engel, the Neo-Classical building sits at the top of a steep flight of steps.

White Corinthian columns decorate the exterior, while the inside is rather spartan. There are, however, statues of the 16th-century Protestant reformers Martin Luther, Philip Melanchthon (the humanist scholar), and Mikael Agricola (translator of the Bible into Finnish). Beneath the cathedral is a **crypt**, now used for concerts and exhibitions.

Crypt
🕐 Jun-Aug: 11am-5pm Mon-Sat, 12-5pm Sun

⑥

Kiasma, Museum of Contemporary Art

🏛 Mannerheiminaukio 2
🚊 4, 4T, 7A, 7B, 10, & many others 🕐 10am-8:30pm Tue-Sun (to 6pm Tue & Sat; to 5pm Sun) 🚫 Public hols
🌐 kiasma.fi

This glass and metal-paneled building, designed by US architect Steven Holl, was completed in 1998. With its fluid lines and white interior, the museum is built in a curve to maximize natural light in

the present day. One of the highlights is the throne of Czar Alexander I from 1809.

The striking wall painting by Akseli Gallen-Kallela in the entrance hall depicts scenes from Finland's national epic, a poem known as the *Kalevala*.

Temppeliaukio Church

 Lutherinkatu 3 🚌14, 18, 39, 39B, 41, 42, 45, 70T, 205 🚊1, 2 ⏰Hours vary, check website 🌐temppeliaukion kirkko.fi

Built into a granite outcrop with walls of stone, this circular "Church in the Rock" is an

> 💬 INSIDER TIP
> **Traditional Sauna**
>
> A wood-fired sauna is the ideal place to relax and unwind. There are more than a million throughout Finland; in Helsinki, try Kotiharjun Sauna *(www.kotiharjun sauna.fi)*.

astonishing piece of modern architecture. Consecrated in 1969, it is the work of architect brothers Timo and Tuomo Suomalainen. The ceiling is an enormous, domed, copper disk, separated from the rough-surfaced rock walls by a ribbed ring of glass that allows light to filter in from outside. The austere interior is relatively free of iconography and religious symbolism.

This popular church is also used for organ concerts and choral music.

---

⑩

Ateneum Art Museum

📍Kaivokatu 2 🚊2, 4, 5, 7 ⏰10am–6pm Tue & Fri, 10am–8pm Wed & Thu, 10am–5pm Sat & Sun 🌐ateneum.fi/en

Part of the Finnish National Gallery, this museum houses the biggest collection of art in Finland, with over 20,000 works spanning two centuries (1750s–1950s), plus temporary exhibitions. The building was designed by Theodor Höijer and completed in 1887.

EAT

Gran Delicato

This popular, brightly decorated café in the center of town serves excellent sandwiches and salads, plus its own blends of coffee.

📍Kalevankatu 34 🌐grandelicato.fi

€€€

Sea Horse

In business since the 1930s, this restaurant is as renowned for its dish of 16 fried herrings as it is for its reindeer steak. A winning recipe of serving hearty Finnish food in simple surroundings has long attracted celebrity diners and rave reviews.

📍Kapteeninkatu 11 🌐seahorse.fi

€€€

↑ Ice rink in front of the 19th-century Ateneum Art Museum building

EXCURSION TO ST. PETERSBURG

Easily accessible by air, train, and boat, St. Petersburg makes an excellent excursion from Helsinki. Situated at the meeting of the Neva river and the Gulf of Finland, Russia's second city was founded in 1703 by Peter the Great. Dubbed the "Venice of the North," the city comprises a bewitching mix of grand Neo-Classical and Baroque architecture, sparkling waterways, and majestic bridges. St. Petersburg's center is easy to explore on foot, but a boat trip along the rivers and canals is one of the undoubted highlights of a visit.

INSIDER TIP
Peterhof

Just a 45-minute trip by hydrofoil from the Hermitage, Peter the Great's sprawling Baroque residence, Peterhof, sits at the center of a magnificent park. The lavish palace of Tsarskoe Selo also lies within easy reach.

(1)

SS Peter and Paul Fortress

🏛 Petropavlovskaya krepost Ⓜ Gorkovskaya
🕐 10am–8pm daily
🌐 spbmuseum.ru

The founding of the SS Peter and Paul Fortress on May 27, 1703, on the orders of Peter the Great, is considered to mark the beginning of the city. Its history is a gruesome one, with hundreds of forced laborers dying during the construction of the fortress. Its bastions were later used to guard and torture many political prisoners, including Peter's own son Aleksey. The former cells are open to the public, along with the magnificent **cathedral**, which contains the tombs of the royal Romanov family.

Cathedral
🕐 10am–6pm daily

(2)

The Hermitage

🏛 Dvortsovaya Naberez-hnaya 34 🚌 7, 10, K-141, K-187, K-209, K-228 🚊 1, 7, 10, 11 🕐 10:30am–6pm Tue–Sun (to 9pm Wed & Fri)
🌐 hermitagemuseum.org

This grand ensemble of buildings on the bank of the Neva river houses one of the world's greatest art collections. Built up by successive czars, the museum has masterpieces by Leonardo da Vinci, Picasso, and Rembrandt, as well as pre-historic, Classical, and Oriental art exhibits. The complex includes the Winter Palace, the former residence of the czars and headquarters for the Provisional Government after the 1917 Revolution.

↓ The Winter Palace, part of the impressive Hermitage complex

(3)

Russian Museum

🏛 Inzhenernaya ulitsa 4 Ⓜ Nevskiy Prospekt, Gostinyy Dvor 🚌 3, 7, 22, 24, 27, 191, K-212, K-289 🚊 1, 5, 7, 10, 11, 22 🕐 Hours vary, check website
🌐 rusmuseum.ru

The Neo-Classical Mikhaylovskiy Palace, built in 1819–25, is the setting for a truly outstanding collection of Russian art, ranging from medieval icons to contemporary painting, sculpture, and applied art.

(4)

Church of the Savior on Spilled Blood

🏛 Naberezhnaia Kanala Griboedova 26 📞 315 1636 Ⓜ Nevskiy Prospekt, Gostinyy Dvor 🕐 10am–5pm Thu–Tue

A cacophony of color, this Russian Revival-style church stands out against the city's Baroque and Neo-Classical buildings. It was built as a memorial to Alexander II in 1881, on the site of his assassination in March of that year.

(5)

Nevskiy Prospekt

Ⓜ Nevskiy Prospekt, Gostinyy Dvor

A stroll along Nevskiy Prospekt is a journey through time,

↑ An aerial view of the city and the SS Peter and Paul Fortress

from czsarist-era splendors to the cafés and chic boutiques of modern-day St. Petersburg. Immortalized in Russian literature, this 3-mile (4.5-km) stretch has been the hub of the city's social life since the 18th century.

---

⑥

St. Isaac's Cathedral

🏛 Isaakievskaya ploshchad
Ⓜ Admiralteyskaya, Sadovaya 🚌 3, 10, 22, 27, 71, 100, K-169, K190, K-289
🕐 10:30am-6pm Thu-Tue
Ⓦ eng.cathedral.ru

One of the world's largest cathedrals, St. Isaac's was designed in 1818 by Auguste de Montferrand. The construction of the colossal building was a major feat of engineering: thousands of wooden piles were sunk into the marshy ground to support its 330,000 tons. The cathedral opened in 1858 but was designated a museum of atheism during the Soviet era. Still a museum today, the church is filled with a variety of impressive 19th-century works of art.

⑦

Mariinskiy Theater

🏛 Teatralnaya ploshchad 1
🚌 2, 3, 6, 22, 27 🕐 Shows at 7pm Ⓦ mariinsky.ru/en

A St. Petersburg institution, the Mariinskiy Theater has long been one of the world's most respected venues for opera and ballet. It has seen premieres by such greats as Tchaikovsky and Prokofiev, while the dance school produced Nureyev and Nijinsky. Watching a performance in the sumptuous 19th-century auditorium is a truly memorable experience.

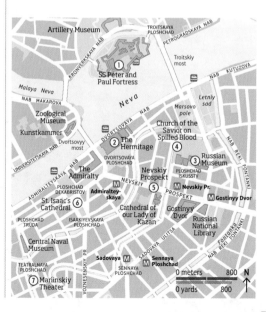

GREAT VIEW
Lovely Lakes

The Haapavesi and Pihlajavesi lakes, near Savonlinna, are widely considered Finland's most beautiful scenery. Hop on board a steamship from Savonlinna harbor for an excursion around their islands.

Savonlinna

⬜ Southern Savonia
🚌🚆🚤 ℹ️ Riihisaari; www.visitsavonlinna.fi/en/

Savonlinna is a good base from which to make excursions into the island-dotted Saimaa Lakelands, but the town – which is spread over several islands – also has numerous charms of its own. Savonlinna's main attraction is the castle of **Olavinlinna** (St. Olav's Castle), one of the best-preserved medieval strongholds in Scandinavia.

↓ The impressive Olavinlinna castle at Savonlinna

In July and August, it provides an atmospheric setting for the acclaimed, month-long Savonlinna International Opera Festival.

Founded in 1475, the castle consists of three towers and a bailey with an encircling wall reinforced by more towers. There are two museums: the Castle Museum illustrates the history of the castle, while the Orthodox Museum displays items of Russian Orthodox iconography originating from both Finland and Russia.

Olavinlinna

 ⏰ 10am–4pm Mon–Fri, 11am–4pm Sat & Sun (Jun–mid-Aug: 11am–6pm daily) 🔒 Some public hols 🌐 kansallismuseo.fi

---

③
Turku

⬜ Varsinais-Suomi
✈️🚌🚆🚤 ℹ️ Aurakatu 4; www.visitturku.fi

Lying on the southwest coast of Finland, Turku (Åbo in Swedish) is a bustling port with a modern city center. Originally settled in the 13th century, it was Finland's principal city during the sovereignty of Sweden, and remains to this day the center of Finland's second language, Swedish.

Completed in 1300, **Turku Cathedral** is the principal place of worship for the Evangelical-Lutheran Church of Finland. Its museum holds many ecclesiastical treasures, from sculptures to silverware.

Work on **Turku Castle** also began in the late 13th century, but the building reached its prime in the mid-1500s with the addition of the Renaissance halls. A permanent exhibition offers an insight into the history of Turku and the castle, and during the summer there are interesting guided tours.

Other attractions in Turku include **Aboa Vetus and Ars Nova**, a double museum with exhibitions on life in medieval Turku and 20th-century Finnish and international art. The west bank of the River Aura – with its many cafés, restaurants, and river boats – is also well worth a visit, as is the old Market Hall, which has been in business since 1896. Scenic cruises

↑ The central aisle of Turku Cathedral, an airy building consecrated in 1300

of the beautiful archipelago are available in summer.

Just west of Turku lies the popular seaside resort of Naantali, which offers cruises from its harbor. The town is also home to **Moominworld**, a childrens' theme park based on Tove Jansson's creations.

> **A good base from which to make excursions into the island-dotted Saimaa Lakelands, Savonlinna also has many charms of its own.**

Turku Cathedral
⊜ ⬕ 🏠 Tuomiokirkkokatu 1 ⏱ 9am–6pm daily 🖩 turunseurakunnat.fi

Turku Castle
⊛ ⊛ 🎔 ⬕ 🏠 Linnankatu 80 ⏱ 10am–6pm Tue–Sun (Jun–Aug: daily) 🛇 Public hols 🖩 turku.fi/en/turkucastle

Aboa Vetus and Ars Nova
⊛ ⊛ 🏠 Itäinen Rantakatu 4–6 ⏱ 11am–7pm daily 🛇 Public hols 🖩 aboavetus arsnova.fi

Moominworld
⊛ 🎔 ⊜ ⬕ 🏠 Naantali 🚌 6, 7 from Turku ⏱ Hours vary, check website 🖩 moominworld.fi

PRACTICAL
INFORMATION

Here you will find all the essential advice and information you will need before and during your stay in Finland.

AT A GLANCE

CURRENCY
Euro (EUR)

TIME ZONE
EET/EEST. Eastern European Summer Time runs from the last Sunday in March to the last Sunday in October.

LANGUAGE
Finnish and Swedish

ELECTRICITY SUPPLY
Power sockets are type F, also accommodating two-prong type C and E plugs. Standard voltage is 220–240V.

EMERGENCY NUMBERS

GENERAL EMERGENCY

112

TAP WATER
Unless otherwise stated, tap water in Finland is safe to drink.

Getting There

Most international flights arrive in Finland at Helsinki Airport, situated 12 miles (19 km) north of the city. There are regular direct flights to locations around the world, including London, Amsterdam, Copenhagen, and New York.

State-of- the-art luxury ferry services run between Stockholm in Sweden and the Finnish ports of Helsinki and Turku, operated by **Tallink Silja Line** and **Viking Line**. The crossing takes about 17 hours.

Tallink Silja Line
🇼 tallinksilja.com
Viking Line
🇼 vikingline.com

Personal Security

Finland is generally a safe country, but it is always a good idea to take sensible precautions against pickpockets. If you have anything stolen, report the crime as soon as possible to the nearest police station. Get a copy of the crime report in order to claim on your insurance.

Health

EU citizens with a European Health Insurance Card (EHIC) are entitled to free emergency medical care in Finland, but it is also advisable to take out some form of supplementary health insurance. Visitors from outside the EU must arrange their own private medical insurance.

Finnish pharmacies *(apteekki)* are well stocked with basic medicines for minor ailments.

Passports and Visas

Visitors who are not citizens of Norway, Sweden, Denmark, or Iceland must have a passport to enter Finland, though members of most EU countries may use an official EU identity card in lieu of their passport. Visas are not required for visitors from the UK, Ireland, the US, Canada, Australia, or New Zealand. For visa information specific to your home country, consult your nearest Finnish embassy or check online.

Travelers with Specific Needs

Finland is making great strides in improving access for those with specific needs. Many museums and cultural venues have mobility-friendly facilities, and often also provide tactile signs and hearing induction loops. Historic buildings can be more problematic, but work is ongoing to improve accesst. Ramps, lifts, wheelchair seats, audio announcements, and stop display boards are becoming increasingly common on trains, buses, and the metro; all Intercity trains are equipped for wheelchair users and a personal assistant may travel on them for free. Note, however, that some of the country's older buses and trams remain difficult for those with limited mobility.

Money

Most establishments accept major credit, debit, and prepaid currency cards, but carry cash for smaller items. ATMs are found at banks and at various points in town and city centers.

Language

Finland has two official languages – Finnish, which is spoken by the vast majority of the population, and Swedish, which is spoken by 5 per cent of Finns, mainly on the western and southern coast.

Cell Phones and Wi-Fi

Visitors traveling to Finland with EU tariffs can use their devices without being affected by data roaming charges. Visitors from other countries should make sure to check their contracts before departure in order to avoid unexpected charges.

Wi-Fi access is widely available at cafés, bars, restaurants, and hotels, often for free. Helsinki has a useful free Wi-Fi network with hotspots throughout the city.

Getting Around

Long-distance journeys in Finland can be very time-consuming, so it is worth considering the relatively inexpensive domestic flights if on a tight schedule.

Finland's national rail network is run by the State Railroads of Finland (Valtion Rautatiet, or VR), and connects all of the major cities. Trains are reliable and clean, and can be a relaxing way to see the countryside. Advance reservations are recommended for long-distance, intercity (IC), and some express (EP) trains.

Finland's long-distance bus network, run by **Matkahuolto**, is extremely comprehensive, encompassing towns not accessible by train. Buses in rural areas are infrequent (but reliable), while intercity buses are fast and efficient.

With light traffic and toll-free roads in good condition, driving in Finland is relatively stress-free. However, driving conditions can be slippery in winter, and elk and reindeer are a serious road danger, so do pay attention to animal hazard signs. There are numerous car rental companies, but the cost of car hire can be expensive. Laws about driving under the influence of alcohol are rigidly enforced, as are speed restrictions.

Matkahuolto
w matkahuolto.fi
VR
w vr.fi

Visiting St. Petersburg

Flights from Helsinki to St. Petersburg's Pulkovo Airport take around one hour. Regular ferries run between Helsinki and St. Petersburg (10 hours), operated by **St. Peter Line**. There are also daily express trains (3 hours and 30 minutes) between the two cities, which can be booked via VR.

Ferry passengers are entitled to stay in St. Petersburg for up to 72 hours without a visa. Visitors arriving by other modes of transport should obtain a visa from a Russian visa center in their home country before traveling to Russia.

St. Peter Line
w stpeterline.com

Visitor Information

For general and location-specific information, contact the **Finnish Tourist Board**, which has offices in major cities all over the world. The Finnish Tourist Board office in Helsinki has information about different parts of Finland in several languages. Helsinki, Turku, and Savonlinna all have a local tourist office.

Finnish Tourist Board
w visitfinland.com

CZECH REPUBLIC

The Czechs' strategic position at the heart of Europe has caused their history to be a turbulent one, shaped by religious strife and bitterly resented rule from elsewhere. From 500 BC, the area now known as the Czech Republic was settled by Celtic tribes, who were later joined by Germanic peoples and Slavs. The Přemyslids emerged as the ruling dynasty at the start of the 9th century, and their kingdom of Bohemia became part of the Holy Roman Empire in 950. This culminated in a golden age in the 14th century, when Emperor Charles IV chose Prague as his residence. The city subsequently became a hotbed of the religious reform movement thanks to reformist cleric Jan Hus; his execution for heresy in 1415 initiated a series of fierce wars. At the start of the 16th century, the Austrian Habsburgs assumed control of the country. Revolt against their rule in 1618 marked the start of the Thirty Years' War, which ultimately strenghtened the Habsburg hold on Bohemia and ended in a Germanization of the country's institutions. The 19th century saw a national revival, with Czech re-established as the official language, but it was not until 1918 that the independent republic of Czechoslovakia was declared. World War II brought German occupation, followed by four decades of Communism. Reform was attempted in 1968 with the quashed "Prague Spring," but Communism was not overthrown until the non-violent "Velvet Revolution" of 1989. In 1993, Czechoslovakia was peacefully divided into Slovakia and the Czech Republic, with the Czech Republic going on to join the EU in 2004. In 2016, the country changed its short-form name to Czechia, but it is still commonly known by its full title.

CZECH REPUBLIC

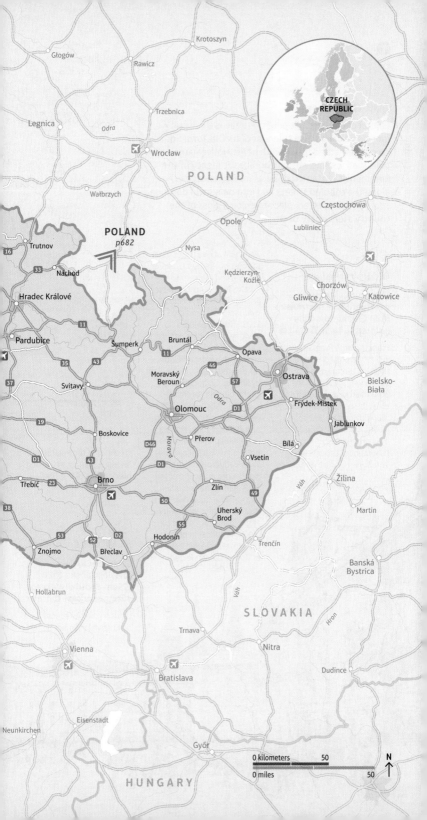

❶

PRAGUE

✈ 🚆 🚌 𝑓 www.prague.eu

Capital of the Czech Republic, Prague is a cultural mosaic. The medieval splendor of its Old Town Square is complemented by a wealth of Art Nouveau masterpieces, all jostling with the bombastic legacy of the Communist era. A rich classical music heritage echoes along the cobbled streets and into delightful Baroque squares – the perfect place to enjoy a glass of the country's legendary beer.

①

Old Royal Palace

🏛 Prague Castle, third courtyard Ⓜ Malostranská 🚊 22 🕒 9am–5pm daily (winter: to 4pm) 🌐 hrad.cz

From the time Prague Castle was first fortified in stone in the 11th century, the Royal Palace was the seat of the Bohemian kings. Altered over time, the building consists of four different architectural layers. A Romanesque palace, built around 1135, forms the basement of the present structure; two further palaces were built above the original – the first by Přemysl Otakar II in 1253, and the second by Charles IV in 1340. On the top floor is the massive Gothic Vladislav Hall, completed in 1502, with its splendid rib vaulting. The Riders' Staircase, just off the hall, is a flight of steps with a glorious Gothic rib-vaulted ceiling. It was used by knights on horseback to get to jousting contests.

Under Habsburg rule, the palace housed government offices, courts, and the old Bohemian parliament. The Bohemian Chancellery, the former royal offices of the Habsburgs, is the site of the 1618 defenestration, when two Catholic Governers were thrown out of a window by angry Protestant nobles. In 1619, the nobles deposed Emperor Ferdinand II as King of Bohemia and elected

Frederick of the Palatinate in his place, leading to the first major battle of the Thirty Years' War.

___

②

St. Vitus's Cathedral

🏛 Prague Castle Ⓜ Malostranská 🚊 22 🕒 9am–5pm daily (except during services) 🌐 hrad.cz

Work on the city's most distinctive landmark began

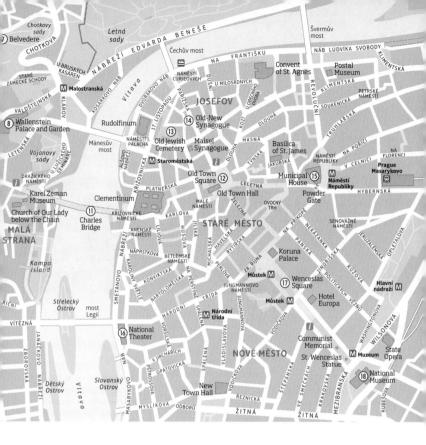

Chotkovy sady
Belvedere
Letná sady
Švermův most
CHOTKOVA
NÁBŘEŽÍ EDVARDA BENEŠE
Čechův most
NA FRANTIŠKU
NÁB LUDVÍKA SVOBODY
KLIMENTSKÁ

U BRUSKÝCH KASÁREN
STARÉ ZÁMECKÉ SCHODY
Malostranská
NÁMĚSTÍ CURIEOVYCH
DUŠNÍ
U MILOSRDNÝCH
Convent of St. Agnes
Postal Museum
KLIMENTSKÁ
PETRSKÉ NÁMĚSTÍ
REVOLUČNÍ
SOUKENICKÁ

VALDŠTEJNSKÁ
KLÁROV
KOSÁRKOVO NÁB.
DVOŘÁKOVO NÁB.
11 LISTOPADU
PAŘÍŽSKÁ
JOSEFOV
KOŽÍ
U OBECNÍHO DVORA
DLOUHÁ
TRUHLÁŘSKÁ
NA POŘÍČÍ
NA FLORENCI

Wallenstein Palace and Garden
Rudolfinum
Old-New Synagogue
Maisel Synagogue
MASNÁ
Basilica of St. James
JAKUBSKÁ
NÁMĚSTÍ REPUBLIKY
V CELNICI
Prague Masarykovo

LETENSKÁ
Vojanovy sady
U LUŽICKÉHO SEMINÁŘE
Mánesův most
NÁMĚSTÍ J. PALACHA
Old Jewish Cemetery
Staroměstská
DLOUHÁ
DLOUHÁ
TÝNSKÁ
Municipal House
Náměstí Republiky
HYBERNSKÁ

DRAŽICKÉHO NÁMĚSTÍ
Karel Zeman Museum
Clementinum
ALŠOVO NÁBŘEŽÍ
KŘIŽOVNICKÁ
PLATNÉŘSKÁ
Old Town Square
Old Town Hall
MALÉ NÁMĚSTÍ
CELETNÁ
ŽELEZNÁ
OVOCNÝ TRH
Powder Gate
SENOVÁŽNÉ NÁMĚSTÍ

Church of Our Lady below the Chain
MALÁ STRANA
Charles Bridge
KŘIŽOVNICKÉ NÁMĚSTÍ
KARLOVA
STARÉ MĚSTO
NA PŘÍKOPĚ
NEKÁZANKA
PANSKÁ
JINDŘIŠSKÁ
POLITICKÝCH VĚZŇŮ
RŮZOVÁ
OPLETALOVA
JERUZALÉMSKÁ

ANENSKÉ NÁMĚSTÍ
LILIOVÁ
HUSOVA
JILSKÁ
MICHALSKÁ
RYTÍŘSKÁ
Koruna Palace

Kampa Island
NÁPRSTKOVA
BETLÉMSKÉ NÁMĚSTÍ
KAROLINY SVĚTLÉ
KONVIKTSKÁ
BARTOLOMĚJSKÁ
NA PERŠTÝNĚ
PERLOVÁ
Můstek
Wenceslas Square
Hlavní nádraží

Střelecký Ostrov
most Legii
SMETANOVO NÁBŘEŽÍ
VORŠILSKÁ
NÁRODNÍ TŘÍDA
JUNGMANNOVO NÁMĚSTÍ
JUNGMANNOVA
Můstek
Hotel Europa

ŘÍČNÍ
VÍTĚZNÁ
JANÁČKOVO NÁBŘEŽÍ
National Theater
Národní třída
VODIČKOVA
VLADISLAVOVA
NOVÉ MĚSTO
ŠTĚPÁNSKÁ
Communist Memorial
St. Wenceslas Statue
Muzeum
State Opera

ZBOROVSKÁ
Dětský Ostrov
Slovanský Ostrov
V JIRCHÁŘÍCH
OPATOVICKÁ
ŠTĚPÁNSKÁ
 VE SMEČKÁCH
KRAKOVSKÁ
MEZIBRANSKÁ
WASHINGTONOVA
WILSONOVA
National Museum

MASARYKOVO NÁBŘEŽÍ
VLTAVA
New Town Hall
VODIČKOVA
ŽITNÁ
ODBORŮ
ŘEZNICKÁ
ŽITNÁ

in 1344 on the orders of John of Luxembourg. The Gothic cathedral replaced an earlier Romanesque basilica that stood on the site of a small rotunda dating back to the time of St. Wenceslas (c. 925). The first architect

of the new Gothic structure, Matthew of Arras, was French; after his death, Peter Parler of Swabia took over. The eastern end of the cathedral dates from this period, when the entrance was the Golden Portal on the south side of the building. The present entrance, the western end of the nave, and the facade with its twin spires were added in 1873–1929.

In addition to religious services, the coronations of Czech kings and queens took place here. The Bohemian crown jewels are housed in a safe chamber, while a number of royal tombs can be seen in the chapels. The tomb of "Good King" Wenceslas stands

in the St. Wenceslas Chapel, which is decorated with Gothic frescoes. Another spectacular memorial is the huge silver tomb (1736) of St. John Nepomuk, who was thrown off the Charles Bridge in 1393 by Wenceslas IV.

←

Locals and tourists strolling across the square in front of the Old Royal Palace

> 💬 INSIDER TIP
> ### Getting Around
>
> Prague's subway, known as the metro, is the fastest way of getting around the city. It has three lines – A, B, and C – and 61 stations. Line A covers all the main areas of the city center. Trams are the city's oldest method of public transport, and a number run into the night. Routes 14, 17, 18, and 22 pass many major sights on both banks of the Vltava.

3

St. George's Basilica and Convent

◪ Prague Castle, Jiřské náměstí Ⓜ Malostranská ☲ 22 ◷ 9am–5pm daily (winter: to 4pm) ▥ hrad.cz

The elegant St. George's Basilica was founded in 920 by Prince Vratislav, father of the "good king" St. Wenceslas. Enlarged in 973 by the addition of St. George's Convent and rebuilt following a fire in 1142, it is the best-preserved Romanesque church in the city. Throughout the Middle Ages, the pair of buildings formed the heart of Prague's castle complex. Today, the basilica's huge twin towers and austere interior have been restored to give an idea of the church's original appearance, while the rusty-red facade is a 17th-century Baroque addition. Buried in the church is St. Ludmila, who became Bohemia's first female Christian martyr when she was strangled while praying.

The former Benedictine nunnery is the oldest convent building in Bohemia. It was founded in 973 by Princess Mlada, sister of Boleslav II, and today houses a collection of Bohemian art.

4

Schwarzenberg Palace

◪ Prague Castle, Hradčanské náměstí 2 Ⓜ Malostranská ☲ 22 ◷ 10am–6pm daily (to 8pm Wed & Sat) ▥ ngprague.cz

From a distance, the facade of this grand Renaissance palace appears to be clad in pyramid-shaped stonework. On closer inspection, this turns out to be an illusion created by sgraffito patterns incised on a flat wall. Built originally for the Lobkowicz family by the Italian architect Agostino Galli in 1545–76, the gabled palace is Florentine rather than Bohemian in style. It passed through a few hands before the Schwarzenbergs, a leading family in the Habsburg Empire, bought it in 1719. Much of the interior decoration has survived, including four painted ceilings dating from 1580. Following renovation, the palace became a branch of the National Gallery, housing its collection of Old Masters. Highlights among the works include Albrecht Dürer's *The Feast of the Rosary* (1506) and Rembrandt's *Scholar in His Study* (1634).

KAFKA'S PRAGUE

In an ironic twist, the most famous literary figure to emerge from the cobbled streets of Prague isn't regarded by the locals as a Czech writer at all. Franz Kafka (1883-1924) wrote in German, but his novels are quintessential Central European tales, set in a city he never names, but which is easily recognizable as Prague. Few of his works were published during his lifetime and his dying wish was to have his unfinished work destroyed, but fellow Prague writer Max Brod acted against Kafka's request. Brod had classics such as *The Castle*, which Kafka wrote while he lived at No. 22 Golden Lane, and *The Trial* published after his death, and many others followed to huge acclaim. Visit the excellent Kafka Museum (www.kafkamuseum.cz) to discover the full story of his life and work.

Interior of the Romanesque St. George's Basilica, the city's second-oldest church

Sternberg Palace

🏛 Hradčanské náměstí 15 Ⓜ Hradčanská, Malostranská 🚊 22 🕐 Closed until 2020; check website 🌐 ngprague.cz

Franz Josef Sternberg founded the Society of Patriotic Friends of the Arts in Bohemia in 1796. Fellow noblemen would lend their finest pictures and sculpture to the society, which had its headquarters in the early-18th-century Sternberg Palace. The fine Baroque building is undergoing renovations in 2020, and will be used to host major exhibitions of art from the National Gallery collection.

↑ Statue of a cherub riding a lion in the Royal Garden of Prague Castle

⑥

Golden Lane

Ⓜ Malostranská 🚊 22 🕐 9am–5pm daily (winter: to 4pm) 🌐 hrad.cz

Named after the goldsmiths who lived here in the 17th century, this is one of the most picturesque streets in Prague. The tiny, brightly painted houses that line one side of it were built in the late 1500s for Rudolph II's castle guards. A century later, the goldsmiths moved in. By the 19th century, however, the area had degenerated into a slum, populated by Prague's poor and the criminal community. In the 1950s, the area was restored to something like its original state, and most of the houses were converted into shops selling books, Bohemian glass, and other souvenirs for the visitors who flock here. The house at No. 20 is the oldest and the least altered in appearance.

Golden Lane has been home to a number of well-known writers, including Franz Kafka, who stayed at No. 22 for a few months between 1916 and 1917, and the Nobel Prize-winning Jaroslav Seifert.

⑦

Royal Garden and Belvedere

🏛 Prague Castle, Královský letohrádek Ⓜ Hradčanská, Malostranská 🚊 22 🕐 Garden: Apr–Oct: 6am–10pm daily; Belvedere: for exhibitions only 🌐 hrad.cz

Prague's well-kept Royal Garden was created in 1535 for Ferdinand I. Its appearance has been altered over time, but some fine examples of 16th-century architecture have survived, including the Belvedere, a beautiful arcaded summerhouse with slender Ionic columns and a blue-green copper roof. Also known as the Royal Summer Palace, the building was commissioned in the mid-16th century for Ferdinand's beloved wife Anne, and is considered one of the finest Italian Renaissance structures north of the Alps. The main architect was Paolo della Stella, a sculptor who was also responsible for the ornate reliefs inside. Today, the building is used to host art exhibitions.

In front of the Belvedere is the Singing Fountain, cast by bell founder Tomáš Jaroš, which owes its evocative name to the musical sound the water makes as it hits the bronze bowl. Also in the garden is the Ball Game Hall, built in 1569 and used primarily for playing a form of real tennis. At the entrance to the garden is the Lion Court, where Rudolph II had his zoo (now a restaurant). The garden is beautiful to visit in spring, when thousands of tulips burst into bloom.

↑ A row of colorful small houses built into Prague Castle wall on Golden Lane

EXPERIENCE Czech Republic

⑧
Wallenstein Palace and Garden

🏛 Valdštejnský palác, Valdštejnské náměstí 4 Ⓜ Malostranská 🚋 12, 18, 20, 22 🕐 Palace: 10am–5pm Sat & Sun; Garden: 10am–6pm daily (Jun–Sep: to 7pm) 🌐 senat.cz

The first large secular building of the Baroque era in Prague, this palace stands as a monument to the fatal ambition of military commander Albrecht von Wallenstein (1581–1634). His string of victories in the Thirty Years' War made him vital to Emperor Ferdinand II. Although he was already showered with titles, Wallenstein started to covet the crown of Bohemia, and when he dared to independently enter into negotiations with the enemy, he was killed on the emperor's orders by a group of mercenaries in 1634.

The Wallenstein Palace stands as a monument to the fatal ambition of military commander Albrecht von Wallenstein.

Wallenstein's intention was to overshadow even Prague Castle with his vast palace, built between 1624 and 1630. The magnificent main hall has a ceiling fresco of the commander portrayed as Mars, Roman god of war, riding in a triumphal chariot. The palace is now used by the Czech Senate, but the State Rooms are open to the public.

Dotted with bronze statues and fountains, the gardens are laid out as they were when Wallenstein lived here. Their most unusual feature is the Grotesquery – an imitation of the walls of a cave, covered in stalactites – and there is also a fine frescoed pavilion. The old Riding School is today a branch of the National Gallery.

⑨
Church of St. Nicholas

🏛 Malostranské náměstí Ⓜ Malostranská 🚋 12, 15, 20, 22 🕐 Hours vary, check website 🌐 stnicholas.cz

Dominating Little Quarter Square, at the heart of Malá Strana, is the church of St. Nicholas. Begun in 1702, it is the acknowledged masterpiece of architects Christoph and Kilian Ignaz Dientzenhofer, who were responsible for the greatest examples of Jesuit-influenced Baroque architecture in Prague. Neither lived to see the completion of the church – their work was finished in 1761 by Kilian's son-in-law, Anselmo Lurago.

Among the many works of art inside the church is Franz Palko's magnificent fresco *The Celebration of the Holy Trinity*, which fills the 165-ft (50-m) dome. A fresco of St. Cecilia, patron saint of music, watches

Wallenstein Palace Garden and *(inset)* the statue of Hercules ↓ by Dutch sculptor Adriaen de Vries

↑ Pedestrians meandering along the snaking slope of Nerudova Street

over the church's splendid Baroque organ. Built in 1746, it was played by Mozart in 1787 and has more than 4,000 pipes. Another star feature is the ornate 18th-century pulpit, adorned with golden cherubs. The impressive statues of the Church Fathers that stand at the four corners of the crossing are the work of Ignaz Platzer, as is the statue of St. Nicholas that graces the high altar.

Nerudova Street

Ⓜ Malostranská 🚋 12, 15, 20, 22

A narrow, picturesque street leading up to Prague Castle, Nerudova is named after the 19th-century poet and journalist Jan Neruda, who wrote many short stories set in this part of Prague. He lived in the

house known as At the Two Suns (No. 47) between 1845 and 1857.

Before the introduction of house numbers in 1770, the city's residences were distinguished by signs. Nerudova's houses have a splendid selection of heraldic beasts and emblems. On your way up the steep slope make sure to look out for the Red Eagle (No. 6), the Three Fiddles (No. 12), the Golden Horseshoe (No. 34), the Green Lobster (No. 43), and the White Swan (No. 49), as well as the Old Pharmacy museum (No. 32).

Nerudova Street also has a number of grand Baroque buildings, including the Thun-Hohenstein Palace (No. 20) – now the Italian embassy – and Morzin Palace (No. 5) – home of the Romanian embassy. The latter has an interesting facade featuring two massive statues of Moors.

EAT

La Degustation
The excellent Czech-inspired menus at this upscale eatery have earned it one of Prague's rare Michelin stars.

🏠 Haštalská 18
🌐 ladegustation.cz

Století
Enjoy dishes named after Czech artists, writers, and singers in a simple but stylish dining room.

🏠 Karoliny Svetlé 21
🌐 stoleti.cz

Villa Richter
Located just outside the castle, this stylish place has two eateries: one serving Italian dishes, the other specializing in Czech food and wine.

🏠 Staré zámecké schody 6 🌐 villarichter.cz

Krcma
A medieval-themed tavern just off Parížská, Krcma offers reasonably priced food, draft beer, and low-lit ambience.

🏠 Kostecná 4
🌐 krcma.cz

Barácnická rychta
A wood-paneled beer hall in a 1930s building, this bar serves an excellent selection of no-nonsense Czech food and beer.

🏠 Na tržište 23
🌐 baracnickarychta.cz

Charles Bridge

 Staroměstská (for Old Town side) 🚊 12, 15, 20, 22 (for Little Quarter side); 17, 18 (for Old Town side)
🕐 Towers: Mar & Oct: 10am-8pm daily; Apr-Sep: 10am-10pm daily; Nov-Feb: 10am-6pm daily

One of the most familiar sights in Prague, the Charles Bridge connects the Old Town with the Little Quarter (Malà Strana). Although it is now pedestrianized, at one time it took four carriages abreast. The bridge was commissioned

HIDDEN GEM
Statue of Bruncvik

Peer over the bridge's southern edge to see the Czech answer to King Arthur. Bruncvik, a mythical Bohemian knight, is said to have sworn to awaken and save Prague at the city's most desperate hour.

by Charles IV in 1357 to replace the Judith Bridge, which was destroyed by floods in 1342.

The bridge's original decoration consisted of a simple wooden cross. In 1683, a statue of St. John Nepomuk was added – the first of the many Baroque statues that line the bridge. A number of finely worked reliefs depict the martyrdom of this saint, a vicar-general who was arrested in 1393 for having displeased King Wenceslas IV. He died under torture and his body was thrown from the bridge. Rubbing the brass relief on his statue to attract good luck is an old local tradition.

More statues were erected between 1683 and the latter half of the 19th century. One of the most artistically remarkable is the statue of St. Luitgard, sculpted by Matthias Braun at the age of 26.

Another splendid piece of decoration is the 17th-century *Crucifixion*, which bears the Hebrew inscription "Holy, Holy, Holy Lord." It was paid for by a local Jewish leader who had been subjected to accusations of blasphemy.

At the Little Quarter end of the bridge stand two bridge towers. The shorter of these is the remains of the Judith Bridge and dates from the early 12th century. The taller pinnacled tower was built in 1464. It offers a magnificent view of the city, as does the late-14th-century Gothic tower at the Old Town end.

---

⑫
Old Town Square

Ⓜ Staroměstská, Můstek 🚊 17, 18

Free of traffic and ringed with historic buildings, Prague's enormous Old Town Square (Staroměstské náměstí) ranks among the finest public spaces of any European city.

One of its most striking buildings is the Old Town Hall, established in 1338. Consisting of a row of Gothic and Renaissance buildings, it features a tower with an astronomical clock that not only tells the time, but displays the movement of the sun, moon, and planets.

↑ Looking toward Prague Castle from the Charles Bridge

Dominating the east side of the square is the church of Our Lady before Týn, with its magnificent multiple Gothic steeples. Begun in 1365, it was Prague's main Hussite church from the early 15th century until 1620.

Also on the east side of the square is the House at the Stone Bell, which has been restored to its former appearance as a Gothic town palace. Next door stands the splendid 18th-century Rococo Kinský Palace, which is today one of several branches of the National Gallery. Outside the front of the building is a huge monument to the reformist Jan Hus, who was burnt at the stake for heresy in 1415.

At the northern end of the square is the church of St. Nicholas, standing on the site of a former 12th-century church. The present building has a dramatic facade studded with statues by Antonín Braun and is a popular venue for classical music concerts.

A colorful array of arcaded buildings with fascinating house signs grace the south side of the square – the block between Celetná and Železná is especially attractive. There are also many shops, restaurants, and cafés, whose tables and chairs spill out onto the square in summer.

---

⑬ 🖼 🖼

Old Jewish Cemetery

🅰 Široká 3 (main entrance) Ⓜ Staroměstská 🚊 17, 18 🕐 Hours vary, check website 🖥 jewish museum.cz

Founded in 1478, for over 300 years this was the only burial ground permitted to Jews in Prague. Because of the lack of space, people had to be buried on top of each other, up to 12 layers deep. Today, over 12,000 gravestones are visible, but around 100,000 people are thought to have been buried here – the last person in 1787. The most visited grave is that of Rabbi Löw (p645).

The Old Jewish Cemetery is part of the Jewish Museum, along with four neighboring historical synagogues, the Ceremonial Hall, and the Robert Guttman Gallery. The Maisel Synagogue provides a good introduction to Jewish life in Prague, with displays of a wide variety of ritual objects.

The Spanish Synagogue has an intricately decorated interior that contains further historical exhibitions, while the Pinkas Synagogue is possibly the most memorable, with the names of 80,000 Czech Jews who died in the Holocaust inscribed on the walls. Nearby, the Klausen Synagogue has an exhibit on Jewish rituals and the Ceremonial Hall, next door, contains an illuminating exhibit on death and Jewish funerals. Finally, the Robert Guttman Gallery hosts temporary exhibits.

↑ The ornate Spanish Synagogue, which is part of the Jewish Museum

⑭ ⟨⟩

OLD-NEW SYNAGOGUE

📍 Červená 2 Ⓜ Staroměstská 🚊 2, 17, 18 to Staroměstská,
17 to Law Faculty (Právnická fakulta) 🚌 194, 207 🕐 9am–5pm
Sun–Fri (Apr–Oct: to 6pm) 🔒 Jewish holidays 🌐 synagogue.cz

Built around 1270, this is the oldest synagogue in Europe and one of the earliest Gothic buildings in Prague. The interior, with its antique furnishings, looks much as it did in the 15th century.

The synagogue has survived fires, 19th-century slum clearances, and many Jewish pogroms. Residents of the Jewish Quarter have often sought refuge within its walls, and today it is still the religious center for Prague's Jews. Its name may come from the fact that another synagogue was built after this one, taking the title "new," but was later destroyed. Legend has it that the stones used in the construction of the synagogue came from the Second Temple in Jerusalem, which was destroyed in AD 70.

Did You Know?

Apart from during the Nazi occupation of 1942–5, services have been held here continuously for over 700 years.

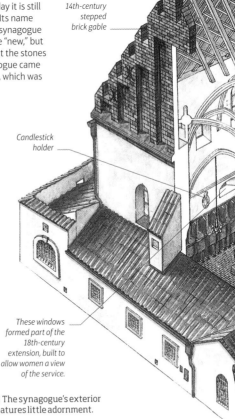

14th-century stepped brick gable

Candlestick holder

These windows formed part of the 18th-century extension, built to allow women a view of the service.

↑ Cross-section of the Gothic Old New Synagogue

① The synagogue's exterior features little adornment.

② The tympanum above the entrance portal is decorated with clusters of grapes and vine leaves growing on twisted branches.

③ Bronze chandeliers light the seats of worshippers and the cantor's platform.

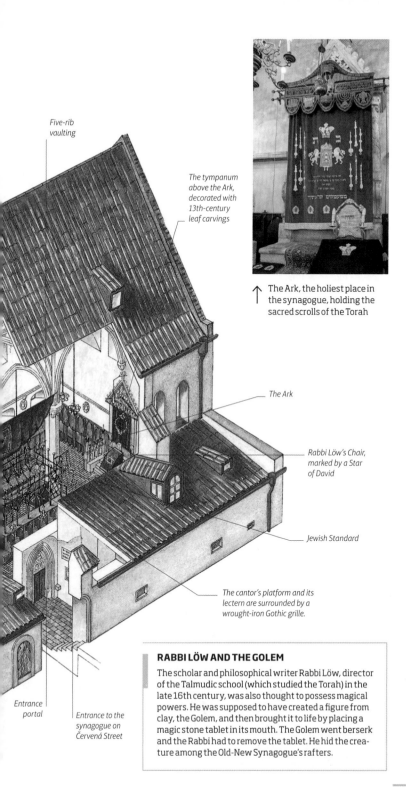

Five-rib vaulting

The tympanum above the Ark, decorated with 13th-century leaf carvings

↑ The Ark, the holiest place in the synagogue, holding the sacred scrolls of the Torah

The Ark

Rabbi Löw's Chair, marked by a Star of David

Jewish Standard

The cantor's platform and its lectern are surrounded by a wrought-iron Gothic grille.

Entrance portal

Entrance to the synagogue on Červená Street

RABBI LÖW AND THE GOLEM

The scholar and philosophical writer Rabbi Löw, director of the Talmudic school (which studied the Torah) in the late 16th century, was also thought to possess magical powers. He was supposed to have created a figure from clay, the Golem, and then brought it to life by placing a magic stone tablet in its mouth. The Golem went berserk and the Rabbi had to remove the tablet. He hid the creature among the Old-New Synagogue's rafters.

⑮ Municipal House

🏠 Náměstí Republiky 5
Ⓜ Náměstí Republiky 🚊 5, 8, 24, 26 ⏰ For guided tours; check website for details 🌐 obecnidum.cz

Prague's most prominent Art Nouveau building occupies the site of the former Royal Court palace, the king's residence between 1383 and 1484. The magnificent exterior is embellished with allegorical statuary, and above the main entrance there is a mosaic by Karel Špillar entitled *Homage to Prague*.

Inside – topped by an elegant glass dome – is Prague's principal concert venue, the Smetana Hall, which is also used as a ballroom. The interior is decorated with works by leading Czech artists of the early 20th century, including Alfons Mucha, one of the most successful exponents of the Art Nouveau style.

On October 28, 1918, the Municipal House was the scene of the momentous proclamation of the new independent state of Czechoslovakia.

⑯ National Theater

🏠 Národní divadlo, Národní třída Ⓜ Národní třída 🚊 2, 9, 18, 22, 23 ⏰ Performances only or by arrangement (22 49 01 506) 🌐 narodni-divadlo.cz

The gold-crested National Theater has always been an important symbol of the Czech cultural revival. Work began on the building in 1868, funded largely by voluntary contributions. The original Neo-Renaissance design was by the Czech architect Josef Zítek. After it was completely destroyed by fire – just days before the official opening – Josef Schulz was given the job of rebuilding the theater, and all the best Czech artists of the period contributed toward its lavish decoration. The western facade is particularly magnificent, with statues representing the Arts. During the late 1970s and early 80s, the theater underwent restoration work and the New Stage was built by architect Karel Prager.

The theater's auditorium has an elaborately painted ceiling adorned with allegorical figures representing the arts. Equally impressive are the sumptuous gold-and-red stage curtain and the ceiling fresco in the lobby. The fresco is the final part of a triptych entitled the *Golden Age of Czech Art*, painted by Czech artist František Ženíšek in 1878. Two of the most fitting operas to see at the theater are Smetana's *Libuše*, which debuted here in 1883, and Dvořák's *The Devil and Kate*.

The theater's vivid sky-blue roof, covered with stars, is said to symbolize the summit that all artists should aim for.

Did You Know?

The narrowest street in Prague is just 20 in. (50 cm) wide – but still has its own traffic light.

⑰ Wenceslas Square

M Můstek, Muzeum 🚊 3, 5, 6, 9, 14, 24

Originally a medieval horse market, today Wenceslas Square remains an important commercial center. More of a gently sloping avenue than a grand piazza, it is nevertheless the epicenter of the city, and is lined with shops, hotels, restaurants, and clubs.

Many of the buildings date from the early 20th century and have lovely Art Nouveau facades, such as the Hotel Europa (1906). Also of note is the church of Our Lady of the Snows, a towering Gothic building that is part of a vast church planned in the 14th century but never completed.

Wenceslas Square has witnessed many important events in the course of Czech history, having been the location of numerous marches, political protests, and celebrations. In November 1989, a protest rally against police brutality took place here, leading to the Velvet Revolution and the overthrow of Communism.

↑ The striking Municipal House building, with its iconic glass dome

↑ The richly decorated pillared hall of the National Museum, with its impressive marble stairway

⑱ National Museum

A Václavské námestí 68
M Muzeum 🚊 11, 13
O 10am–6pm Tue–Sun
W nm.cz

Rising majestically at the upper end of Wenceslas Square is the Neo-Renaissance building of the National Museum, a grand, purpose-built affair that even has its own metro station. The entrance fee is worth it, if only to see the spectacular marble stairway, the Pantheon, and the interior paintings by artists Václav Brožík, František Ženíšek, and Vojtech Hynais.

The stern edifice, until recently sporting its 1968 bullet holes, was built in the late 1880s to accommodate the growing collection of the National Museum, which was then spread across various locations. Alongside the National Theater, it is one of the greatest symbols of the Czech National Revival. Both buildings are the work of the same architect, Josef Schulz.

The museum has a central pillared lobby with a glass-covered courtyard on either side. On the first floor is the Pantheon, a hall containing busts of famous Czech scholars, writers, and artists. The yard on the right houses the fantastic permanent exhibition, which features sculptures and monuments from the museum's collection. Other artifacts on display are devoted mainly to mineralogy, archaeology, anthropology, and natural history. On the ground floor there are halls for temporary exhibits, while the left yard has a café, a shop, and a children's playroom. The dome's observation platform has great city views.

Outside the museum is a huge statue of St. Wenceslas, the work of 19th-century sculptor Josef Myslbek.

MARKET STREETS

Some of the most wonderful places to browse in the Czech capital are interwar *pasáže* – stylish Functionalist and Art Deco shopping passages, mostly located in the New Town. Top among them is the Pasáž Lucerna, an Art Nouveau complex. There are about 20 others to discover around the Wenceslas Square area.

↑ The grand Italian Court, Kutná Hora's former Royal Mint and palace

❷ Kutná Hora

 Central Bohemia 🚗🚌
ℹ Palackého náměstí 377;
www.kutnahora.cz

After deposits of silver were found here in the 13th century, Kutná Hora grew from a small mining community into the second most important town in the kingdom of Bohemia, after Prague. The Prague *groschen*, a silver coin that was in circulation all over Europe, was minted at the Italian Court, so-called because Florentine experts were employed to set up the mint. Strongly fortified, the Italian Court was also the seat of the town's ruler. In the late 14th century, a palace was added, containing reception halls and the Chapel of St. Wenceslas and St. Ladislav. Both the mint and the palace can be visited by guided tour.

Other attractions in the town include Kutná Hora's Mining Museum, in a former fort called the Hrádek, and the splendid 14th-century Gothic Cathedral of St. Barbara.

❸ Český Krumlov

 South Bohemia 🚗🚌
ℹ Náměstí Svornosti 2;
www.ckrumlov.info

Of all the Czech Republic's medieval towns, Český Krumlov ranks as one of the very finest. Almost entirely enclosed by a bend in the River Vltava, the beautifully preserved inner town seems to have changed very little in the last few hundred years, although some buildings suffered from flood damage in 2002. A maze of narrow cobbled streets radiates out from the main square, which is lined with elegant arcaded Renaissance buildings, including the former town hall. On one of these streets – Horní – is the magnificent 16th-century sgraffitoed Jesuit College (now a hotel), as well as a museum explaining the town's history. On the east side of the inner town is the Schiele Centrum, with an excellent collection of works by the Austrian painter Egon Schiele, housed in a 15th-century former brewery.

Český Krumlov's best-known sight is its 13th-century castle – the **Krumlovský zámek** – in the Latrán quarter. In the older, lower part of the castle complex, the splendidly restored castle tower can be climbed for superb views of the whole town. Other highlights of the castle include a Rococo chapel, a lavishly decorated ballroom – the Maškarní sál – and the ornate 18th-century Rococo theater. The castle grounds provide a tranquil spot to sit and relax, while performances of opera and ballet take place in the gardens' open-air theater in July and August.

In summer, renting a canoe from one of the many outlets in the town is a good way to enjoy the fine views of Český Krumlov from the river.

Krumlovský zámek
⊛⊛ Latrán ◔ Apr–Oct: 9am–5pm Tue–Sun 🆆 zamek-ceskykrumlov.cz

❹ Karlovy Vary

 Karlovy Vary ✈🚗🚌
ℹ Lázeňská 14; www.karlovyvary.cz

Legend has it that Charles IV discovered one of the sources of mineral water that would make Karlovy Vary's fortune when one of his staghounds fell into a hot spring. By the end of the 16th century, more than 200 spa buildings had been built in the town, and

→ The River Ohře, running through the pretty spa town of Karlovy Vary

today there are 13 hot mineral springs. The best-known of these is the Vřídlo, which, at 162°F (72°C), is also the hottest. Its waters are said to be good for digestive disorders

Among the town's most appealing historic monuments are the 18th-century Baroque parish church of Mary Magdalene and the elegant 19th-century Mill Colonnade by Josef Zítek, architect of the celebrated National Theater in Prague (p646).

Karlovy Vary is also known for its Karlovy Vary china and Moser glass, and for summer concerts and cultural events. The Karlovy Vary International Film Festival, for example, has been running since 1946 and remains a major draw, with thousands of film buffs and celebrities descending upon the town in July each year.

Around 38 miles (60 km) southwest of Karlovy Vary is another of Bohemia's delightful spa towns, Mariánské Lázně. Here, the cast-iron colonnade, with frescoes by 20th-century artist Josef Vyleťal, is a grand sight. There are also many pleasant walks in the local countryside, especially in the spruce-dotted protected land of the Slavkov Forest.

5

Karlštejn Castle

⌂ 16 miles (25 km) SW of Prague 🚆 🕐 For guided tours only; see website for times 🌐 hrad-karlstejn.cz

With its turrets, towers, and immaculate interiors, Karlštejn Castle is one of the most visited historic sites in the Czech Republic. Once a purely 14th-century fortress, built by Charles IV as a country retreat and a treasury for the imperial crown jewels, the castle was given a Neo-Gothic makeover in the late 19th century by Czech architect Josef Mocker. It was then that the castle got its ridge roofs, a feature typical of medieval architecture.

Access to the building is by guided tour only. The one-hour-long basic tour leads you through the historic interiors of the first and second floors of the Imperial Palace – including the royal audience hall and bedchamber of Charles IV – and also visits the treasury. The 100-minute special tour takes in the Chapel of the Holy Cross, one of the most ornate and precious chapels in the country. It features a gilded vaulted ceiling studded with glass stars and 129 portraits of saints and monachs by Master Theodori. Numbers are limited on this tour, so book well ahead.

CZECH BEERS

The best-known Czech beer is Pilsner, which is made by the lager method: fermented and matured at low temperatures. The name "Pilsner" derives from Plzeň, a town where this type of beer was first brewed in 1842. Guided tours of the original brewery are available (www. prazdrojvisit.cz). České Budějovice is the other famous brewing town – home to the country's biggest selling export beer, Budweiser Budvar.

PRACTICAL INFORMATION

Here you will find all the essential advice and information you will need before and during your stay in the Czech Republic

AT A GLANCE

CURRENCY
Czech Koruna
(CZK)

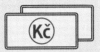

TIME ZONE
CET/CEST. Central
European Summer
Time runs from the last
Sunday in March to the
last Sunday in October.

LANGUAGE
Czech

ELECTRICITY SUPPLY
Power sockets are
type E, fitting two-
pronged plugs.
Standard voltage
is 230V.

EMERGENCY NUMBERS

GENERAL
EMERGENCY

112

TAP WATER
Unless stated
otherwise, tap
water in the Czech
Republic is safe
to drink.

Getting There

More than 60 international airlines fly to Prague's Václav Havel Airport. There are also smaller international airports in Brno, Ostrava, Karlovy Vary, and Pardubice.

Prague is connected by high-speed train to all the major capitals of Europe, although journeys can be time-consuming. Regular international trains arrive and depart from Prague's Hlavní Nádraží and Nádraží Holešovice stations; reservations for these services are essential as seats book up quickly.

Traveling by bus to Prague from other major European cities can also be slow, but is signif-icantly less expensive than rail or air travel. As with the trains, seats get booked up very quickly, especially in summer, so reserve well in advance. Flixbus and RegioJet are the main operators of international bus routes to Prague.

Personal Security

The Czech Republic is generally a safe country, but it is wise to take sensible precautions against pickpockets. If you have anything stolen, report the crime as soon as possible to the nearest police station. Get a copy of the crime report in order to claim on your insurance..

Health

EU citizens with a European Health Insurance Card (EHIC) are entitled to free emergency medical care in the Czech Republic, but it is also advisable to take out some form of supplementary health insurance. Visitors from outside the EU must arrange their own private medical insurance.

For minor ailments and medication, visit a pharmacy *(lékárna)*. Closed pharmacies will usually display details of the nearest 24-hour service in their windows.

Passports and Visas

Citizens of the US, EU, Australia, New Zealand, and countries of the European Free Trade

Association need a valid passport to enter the Czech Republic, and can stay for up to 90 days without needing a visa. For visa information specific to your home country, consult your nearest Czech embassy or check online.

Travelers with Specific Needs

Travelers with limited mobility seeking advice on transportation, accommodations, and sightseeing tours will find a variety of helpful resources available from the **Czech National Disability Council**, the **Prague Wheelchair Association**, or **Accessible Prague**.

Information on disabled travel on public transportation can be found on the websites of the **Prague Public Transport Company** (buses, trams, and metro) and **České Dráhy** (trains; see right).

Accessible Prague

W accessibleprague.com

Czech National Disability Council

W nrzp.cz

Prague Public Transport Company

W dpp.cz

Prague Wheelchair Association

W presbariery.cz

Money

Most establishments accept major credit, debit, and prepaid currency cards. Contactless payments are becoming increasingly common in the Czech Republic, but it's a good idea to carry some cash for smaller items and local markets.

Cell Phones and Wi-Fi

Visitors traveling to the Czech Republic with EU tariffs can use their devices without being affected by data roaming charges. Visitors from other countries should check their contracts before departure to avoid unexpected charges.

Free Wi-Fi is available in many public places, and can also often be found in restaurants, cafes, and hotels.

Getting Around

The Czech Republic's state-run rail company, **České Dráhy** (ČD), operates several types of domestic routes. Supercity (SC) trains are the fastest and most expensive; express trains (*rychlík*) stop only at the major towns and cities; and slow trains, or *osobní*, stop at every station. Some intercity services are operated by **Leo Express** and **RegioJet** – note that tickets for ČD services are not valid on these trains.

Long-distance bus services within the Czech Republic are run by RegioJet and other local companies. There is an extensive route network, and buses are often a less expensive way of traveling between towns than trains. For popular routes, buy your ticket in advance from the bus station. The main bus terminal in Prague is Florenc, which serves all international and long-distance domestic routes.

There are several freeways in the Czech Republic, but to travel on them you must buy a special highway sticker (*dálniční známka*), valid for 10 days, one month, or a year, and available at the border or from post offices and gas stations. Most of the major car rental firms have offices in Prague and at Václav Havel Airport, but renting is relatively expensive.

České Dráhy

W cd.cz

Leo Express

W leoexpress.com

RegioJet

W regiojet.com

Visitor Information

The **Czech Tourist Authority** has an informative website, and most towns and visitor destinations in the Czech Republic have a tourist information center run by the local municipality. Many employ English speakers and offer a variety of English-language publications, maps, and guides. The efficient **Prague City Tourism** is the best source of tourist information for visitors to the capital. It has offices in the city center and at the airport, providing information in several languages, including English.

Czech Tourist Authority

W czechtourism.com

Prague City Tourism

W praguecitytourism.cz

HUNGARY

Hotly fought over due to its strategic location in Central Europe, Hungary has survived various occupations with its rich indigenous culture intact. The Romans ruled the area corresponding roughly to Hungary from AD 100 to the arrival of the Huns in the early 5th century. After the death of Attila the Hun in 453, the region was ruled by the Goths, the Longobards, and the Avars. The ancestors of the modern Hungarians, the Magyars, migrated from the Urals in 896 and ruled until 1301, when their line ended. The throne then passed to a series of foreign kings, under whom the country flourished, and by the 15th century Hungary was a major cultural and military power. These achievements were eclipsed by a series of Ottoman invasions, however, and in 1541, Buda became the capital of Ottoman Hungary. Christian armies led by the Habsburgs of Austria fought to recapture Buda, finally defeating the Turks in 1686. Economic prosperity came with Austrian rule, but national sovereignty was suppressed, culminating in a major uprising in 1848–9. After crushing the rebellion, Emperor Franz Joseph I united the two nations by creating the Dual Monarchy of Austro-Hungary in 1867. This was dissolved following World War I, and Hungary lost two-thirds of its territory. Hungary backed Germany in World War II to regain this land, but in 1945, Budapest was taken by the Russians. Communist rule was ruthlessly upheld, and free elections did not take place until 1990. Since then, Hungary has joined the EU and grown its economy through tourism and investment in infrastructure projects.

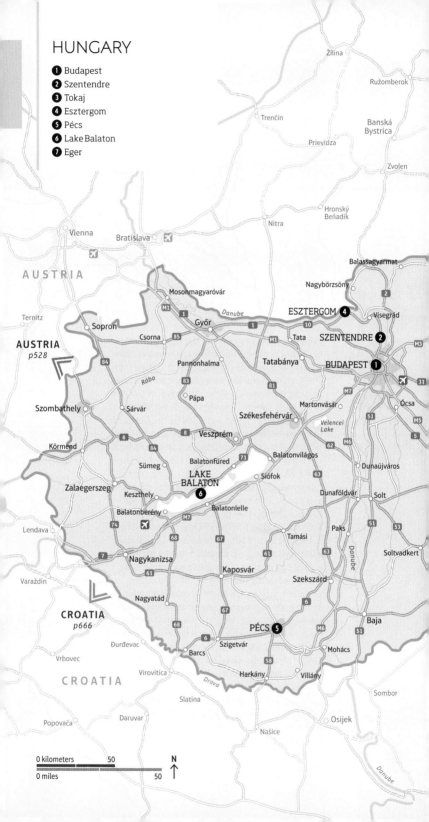

↑ The Danube river in Budapest, illuminated along its banks

❶

BUDAPEST

✈🏨🚋 **ℹ️** www.budapestinfo.hu

Exuding a *fin de siècle* elegance, Budapest is two cities for the price of one. Gazing at each other across the Danube, the city's two halves - Buda and Pest - have distinctive characters. Hilly Buda is dominated by the city's medieval quarter, while buzzing Pest is bursting with historic cafés and cool pubs. Dotted across both sides is a rich cornucopia of compelling museums, astounding architecture, and restorative thermal baths.

①

Mátyás Church

🏠 Szentháromság tér 2
🚌 16, 16A, 116 🕐 Hours vary, check website
🌐 matyas-templom.hu

The profusion of architectural styles in Mátyás church reveals the troubled history of both the building and the city itself. The church is mainly a Neo-Gothic reconstruction dating from 1874 to 1896. Most of the original church (13th–15th centuries) was lost when the Ottomans turned it into their Great Mosque in 1541, and the building had to be restored again following damage in World War II. Nevertheless, the great rose window over

the main portal has been faithfully reproduced in its original Gothic style.

The tombs of King Béla III (13th century) and his wife can be seen in the Trinity Chapel, and the Mary Portal (near the main altar) contains the finest example of Gothic stone carving in Hungary. Also fascinating is a Baroque statue of the Madonna that, according to legend, was set into a wall during the Ottoman occupation. When the church was virtually destroyed in 1686, the Madonna made a miraculous reappearance, which the Ottomans took as an omen of defeat.

Mátyás church stands in the heart of Buda's Old Town, which developed to the north

of the Royal Palace from the 13th century onward.

In front of the church is Holy Trinity Square, with a memorial column to those who died in the plague of 1691. On the square stands the Old Town Hall, an elegant Baroque building with an onion-domed clock tower.

---

②

Gellért Hotel and Bath Complex

🏠 Szent Gellért tér 1
Ⓜ Szent Gellért tér 🚌 7, 107, 109, 133, 233 🚋 19, 41, 47, 49, 56 🕐 6am–8pm daily
🌐 gellertbath.hu

The earliest reference to the presence of healing waters on this site dates from the 13th

> 💬 INSIDER TIP
> **Getting Around**
>
> Trams are a convenient means of transportation for visitors, especially the 18, 19, and 61 on the Buda side and the 2, 4, and 6 in Pest. There are also around 200 bus routes. The four metro lines and the HÉV suburban rail lines link the center with the suburbs.

century. A hospital stood here in the later Middle Ages, and then, during the Ottoman occupation, baths were built – they are, perhaps, the finest of all the great bathhouses in the city. The area takes its name from Bishop Gellért, whose monument on the hill is visible from many parts of the city. He was martyred here in 1046 by a mob of citizens opposed to the introduction of Christianity. From the top of the hill, one can admire a beautiful view of the whole of Budapest.

The Gellért Hotel, with its famous spa, was built between 1912 and 1918 in the Secession style, at the foot of the hill. It features elaborate mosaics, stained-glass windows, statues, and fanciful balconies. Its Eastern-style towers and turrets offer superb views.

The complex houses an institute of water therapy, which features plunge pools, a sauna, and a steam bath. The facilities have been modernized, but the glorious Secession interiors remain. There is also an outdoor pool with a wave machine, installed in 1927 and still in operation. The baths and health spa, with their sun terraces and restaurants, are open to both the public and hotel guests.

↑ The Neo-Classical main pool at the Gellért bath complex, which lies beneath a curved glass roof

③

Royal Palace

🏛 Színház utca 🚌 16, 16A, 116

A royal castle was first built in Buda by King Béla IV (1235–70), but its exact location is unknown. Around 1400, it was replaced by a Gothic palace, which was subsequently remodeled in Renaissance style by King Mátyás in 1458. Under Ottoman rule, the palace was used to stable horses and store gunpowder, leading to its destruction in 1686 during the reconquest. A new palace, begun in 1719 by the Habsburgs, grew in size and grandeur under Empress Maria Teresa, but in 1849 this, too, was destroyed, and had to be rebuilt in the second half of the 19th century.

When the Habsburg palace was again razed to the ground in February 1945, remains of the 15th-century Gothic palace were uncovered. These were incorporated into the restored palace that visitors see today.

Various statues, gateways, and fountains have survived from the 19th-century palace.

Did You Know?

Budapest has the oldest subway line in mainland Europe - it opened in 1896.

In the northwest courtyard stands the Mátyás Fountain (1904), depicting Mátyás Corvinus (1458–90) and his legendary love, the peasant girl Ilonka. In front of the palace's rebuilt dome stands an equestrian statue (1900) of Prince Eugene of Savoy, victor of the Battle of Zenta against the Ottomans in 1697.

Today, the palace houses the exquisite collection of the **Hungarian National Gallery** and the **Castle Museum**. The National Gallery, which is part of the Museum of Fine Arts, has a superb array of Hungarian art from medieval times to the 20th century. The permanent exhibits include the Lapidarium, a section of sculpture and stonework. Highlights from the gallery's collection include a carved stone head of King Béla III from c. 1200, religious artifacts spanning several centuries, and a superb selection of 19th- and 20th-century Hungarian works. Notable early works include *The Madonna of Bártfa* (1465–70), and the folding St. Anne Altarpiece (1510–20). Among the 19th-century pieces to look out for are the historical scenes by Bertalan Székely and the landscapes of Mihály Munkácsy, widely held to be Hungary's greatest artist.

The Castle Museum, part of Budapest History Museum, illustrates the city's evolution from its origins under the Romans. In the basement are recreations of chambers dating from the Middle Ages, which were uncovered in the south wing of the palace following bomb damage in World War II. The ground floor exhibits cover the period from Roman times to the 15th century, including some Gothic statues discovered here in 1974, while the first floor traces the history of the city from 1686 (the end of Ottoman rule) to the present.

As part of a large-scale reconstruction program, several buildings in the palace area are undergoing major renovations that will result in changes in their

↑ The richly decorated interior of the Hungarian National Museum

function during the coming years. Check online for the latest updates.

Hungarian National Gallery

 Royal Palace A-B-C-D Wings, Szent György tér 2
○10am-5pm Tue-Sun
Ⓦmng.hu

Castle Museum (Budapest History Museum)

Royal Palace E Wing, Szent György tér 2 ○10am-6pm Tue-Sun (Nov-Feb: to 4pm Tue-Fri) Ⓦbtm.hu

←

A lively nighttime festival within the grounds of the Royal Palace

④

Hungarian National Museum

Ⓐ Múzeum körút 14-16
Ⓜ Kálvin tér, Astoria 🚌7, 9
🚃47, 49 ○10am-6pm Tue-Sun Ⓦhnm.hu

A vast treasure trove of art and artifacts, this expansive museum is dedicated to the country's compelling – and sometimes turbulent – past. Founded in 1802, the museum owes its existence to Count Ferenc Széchényi, who offered his huge collection of coins, books, and documents – numbering over 20,000 items in total – to the nation. Among other things, the museum's ever-expanding collection includes archaeological finds, works of art, weapons, textiles, and photographs.

The museum is housed in an impressive Neo-Classical building, constructed between 1837 and 1847. It was from the museum's steps, in 1848, that the poet Sándor Petőfi first read his *National Song*, which sparked the uprising against Habsburg rule. This day is commemorated each year on 15 March, when a reenactment is performed.

⑤

Inner City Parish Church

Ⓐ Március 15 tér 2 Ⓜ Ferenciek tere 🚌5, 7, 15, 112 ○9am-4:30pm daily (to 10pm Sun) Ⓦbelvarosi plebania.hu

The Inner City Parish Church was first established during the reign of St. István, the first king of Hungary, on the burial site of the martyred St. Gellért; fragments of the building's original walls can still be seen. During the 14th century, a large Gothic church was built on this spot, which was then used as a mosque under the Ottomans – a prayer niche is all that remains from this time. Damaged by the Great Fire of 1723, the church was partly rebuilt in the Baroque style in 1725–39. The interior features Neo-Classical and Gothic elements, plus some 20th-century works – the Gothic chapel and Neo-Gothic pulpit are particular highlights. The church sometimes hosts free organ concerts.

←
A packed audience in the city's spectacular State Opera

location in 1906. As well as great European paintings and sculptures from every era from the Middle Ages to the 1800s, there are Egyptian, Greek, and Roman antiquities. There are also paintings by Holbein and Dürer, and seven works by El Greco.

⑨
Great Synagogue

🏛 Dohány utca 2 Ⓜ Astoria ⏰ Hours vary, check website 🌐 greatsynagogue.hu

Built in Byzantine style by Viennese architect Ludwig Förster in 1854–9, this is the largest synagogue in Europe, able to hold over 3,000 worshippers. It is home to the Jewish Museum, which chronicles the long history of the city's Jewish residents.

At the rear of the synagogue is the Raoul Wallenberg Memorial Park, which features the *Tree of Life*, a Holocaust memorial. Designed by Imre Varga, each leaf of this silver weeping willow bears the

⑥
Museum of Applied Arts

🏛 Ulloi út 33-37 Ⓜ Corvin-Negyed 🔒 For renovations 🌐 imm.hu

Founded in 1872, this striking Art Nouveau museum houses a cornucopia of outstanding arts and crafts objects. Items on display include furniture, ceramics, glasswear, costumes and textiles, and metalwork. Adorned with eye-catching Zsolnay ceramics, the remarkable Secession building is itself a work of art.

The museum is currently undergoing renovations that are expected to last at least three years. In the meantime, a selection of objects from its collection will be available to view at the György Ráth Villa on Városligeti Avenue.

> 💬 INSIDER TIP
> **Bath Time**
>
> After a trip to the Museum of Fine Arts, why not relax with a soak at the nearby Széchenyi Baths *(www. szechenyibath.com)*. Its steamy pools are some of the city's hottest.

⑦
State Opera

🏛 Andrássy út 22 Ⓜ Opera ⏰ Daily; tours only 🌐 opera.hu

The State Opera (Magyar Állami Operaház), which opened in 1884, was the life's work of architect Miklós Ybl. The facade expresses musical themes, with statues of two of Hungary's most prominent composers: Ferenc Erkel and Franz Liszt. The opulence of the foyer, with its chandeliers, murals, and vaulted ceiling, is echoed in the grandeur of the sweeping main staircase and of the three-story auditorium. The opera house is currently closed until 2021, but partial tours can be booked.

⑧
Museum of Fine Arts

🏛 Hősök tere Ⓜ Hősök tere 🚌 20E, 30, 30A, 105 🚋 72, 75, 79 ⏰ 10am-6pm Tue-Sun 🌐 szepmuveszeti.hu

In 1870, the state bought a magnificent collection of paintings from the Esterházy family. Enriched by donations and acquisitions, the collection moved to its present

The State Opera facade expresses musical themes, with statues of two of Hungary's most prominent composers.

name of one of the 600,000 Hungarian Jews killed during the Holocaust.

St. Stephen's Basilica

🏠 Szent István tér 1 Ⓜ Deák Ferenc tér 🕒 9am-5pm Mon-Fri, 9am-1pm Sat, 1-5pm Sun 🌐 bazilika.biz

This impressive basilica is dedicated to St. Stephen, or István, Hungary's first Christian king (1001–38). Built in 1851–1905 on a Greek cross floor plan, it is the country's most sacred place of worship for Catholic Hungarians.

On the main altar is a statue of St. Stephen; scenes from his life are depicted

St. Stephen's Basilica, which is topped by a beautifully decorated cupola *(inset)* ↓

behind it. A painting to the right of the main entrance shows István dedicating Hungary to the Virgin Mary. His mummified forearm is famously kept in the Chapel of the Holy Right Hand.

The main entrance to the basilica is a massive door, decorated with carved heads of the 12 Apostles. The dome reaches 315 ft (96 m) and in good weather you can enjoy one of the best panoramas of Budapest from the look-out in the cupola.

Vajdahunyad Castle

🏠 Városliget Ⓜ Széchenyi fürdő 🕒 10am-5pm Tue-Sun 🌐 mmgm.hu

This fantastical structure stands surrounded by trees at the edge of a lake in the City Park (Városliget). Contrary

to appearances, it is not a genuine castle – it is in fact a complex of pavilions illustrating the evolution of Hungarian architecture. Created for the 1896 Millennium Celebrations as a temporary exhibit, it proved so popular that it was rebuilt permanently, in brick.

The pavilions are grouped in chronological order of style, but the elements are linked to suggest a single, cohesive design. Details from more than 20 of Hungary's best-loved buildings are reproduced.

The site is also home to the engaging Museum and Library of Hungarian Architecture.

Parliament

🏠 Kossuth Lajos tér 1-3 Ⓜ Kossuth tér 🚌 70, 78 🚋 2, 2A 🕒 Apr-Oct: 8am-6pm daily; Nov-Mar: 8am-4pm daily 🚫 During ceremonies and plenary sessions 🌐 parlament.hu

Rising from the banks of the Danube, Hungary's majestic Parliament (Országház) has become a symbol of Budapest. Built between 1884 and 1902, it was based on London's Houses of Parliament *(p94)*. Although the facade is Neo-Gothic, the ground plan follows Baroque conventions, with a magnificent dome at the center. Beneath it is the Domed Hall, off which is the Gobelin Hall, with a Gobelin tapestry of Árpád and his fellow Magyar chiefs taking a blood oath. The greatest artists of the day decorated the interior of the building, and there are some amazing ceiling frescoes by Károly Lotz and György Kiss.

Between the Domed Hall and the south wing is the National Assembly Hall. Opposite it is the Congress Hall, a virtual mirror image. Both have public galleries. Since 2000, the royal insignia have been displayed here.

Szentendre

🏠 Szentendre 🚗🚌🚆
ℹ️ Dumtsa Jenő utca 22;
www.szentendre
program.hu

Szentendre was settled by Serbian refugees in the 14th century. More Serbs arrived after the Ottoman occupation of Belgrade in 1690, ushering in a period of great prosperity.

The Slavic interiors of the town's many churches are filled with incense, icons, and candlelight. Look out for the magnificent iconostasis at Blagovestenska church on Fő tér, the main square. Nearby, the Museum of Serbian Art has displays of religious artifacts.

Many artists have made their home in Szentendre, including Hungarian ceramic artist Margit Kovács. Her work can be seen at the **Kovács Margit Ceramics Museum**.

Kovács Margit Ceramics Museum
🎨🖐 🏠 Vastagh György utca 1 🕐 10am-6pm daily
🌐 muzeumicentrum.hu

Tokaj

🏠 Tokaj 🚗🚌 ℹ️ Serház utca
1; www.tokaj-turizmus.hu

Tokaj is located at the center of one of Hungary's most important wine-growing areas. Tokaji dessert wines owe their full-bodied flavor to the volcanic soil in which the vines grow, and a type of mold peculiar to the region. The best cellars to visit are the **Rákóczi Cellar** and the privately owned Hímesudvar.

Tokaj has a synagogue and a Jewish cemetery, relics of the period before World War II, when the town had a large Jewish population.

Rákóczi Cellar
🖐 🏠 Kossuth tér 15 📞 (47) 352 408 🕐 Apr-Oct: daily (call in advance)

 Esztergom

🏠 Esztergom 🚗🚌🚆

St. István, Hungary's first Christian king, was baptized

A pier jutting into ↑ Lake Balaton from Keszthely

in Esztergom and was later crowned here on Christmas Day in AD 1000. Dominating the city's skyline is the huge Catholic Cathedral, built in the early 19th century on the site of a 12th-century church. In the treasury are religious artifacts from the original church. The 16th-century marble Bakócz chapel, next to the southern entrance, was built by Florentine craftsmen.

South of the cathedral, are the remains of Esztergom's Castle, dating from the 10th century. The central square in the pretty Old Town is bordered by lively outdoor cafés.

Pécs

🏠 Pécs 🚗🚌 ℹ️ Széchenyi tér 7; www.pecs.hu

First a Celtic, then a Roman settlement, Pécs was later ruled by the Ottomans from 1543 until 1686. Several monuments testify to these various periods of Pécs' history.

The city's expansive main square, Széchenyi tér, is overlooked by a Catholic church,

 ←

The soaring interior of Esztergom's cathedral

formerly the Mosque of Gazi Kasim Pasha, built under Ottoman occupation. Inside, a delicately decorated *mihrab* (prayer niche) serves as a reminder of the building's origins. Behind the church is the **Archaeological Museum**, whose collection of exhibits dates from prehistoric times to the Magyar conquest.

On Dom tér are Pécs' four-towered, Neo-Romanesque cathedral, which stands on the foundations of an 11th-century basilica, and the Neo-Renaissance Bishop's Palace (1770). South of here, on Szent István tér, a stairway leads to the ruins of a 4th-century underground chapel, decorated with wonderful frescoes. On nearby Apáca utca, excavations unearthed a collection of Roman tombs, which were declared a UNESCO World Heritage Site in 2000.

Remains of Pécs' medieval walls, erected after an invasion by the Mongols in the 13th century, include a 15th-century barbican. Elsewhere, the city's museums include the Vasarely Museum, which is dedicated to Hungarian Op artist Victor Vasarely.

Archaeological Museum
 Széchenyi tér 12
(72) 312 719 10am–6pm Tue–Sat

⑥
Lake Balaton

Transdanubia 🚌🚈🚲
Siófok: Fő tér 11, (84) 696 236; Balatonfüred: Blaha Lujza utca 5

Every summer, Lake Balaton – Europe's largest freshwater lake – attracts thousands of vacationers. The southern shore is the more developed; the largest resort here is Siófok, characterized by lively bars and noisy nightlife.

Those in search of a more peaceful atmosphere should head for Balatonvilágos, set atop attractive wooded cliffs, or Balatonberény, which has a nudist beach. Southwest of Balatonberény, the tiny lake known as Kis-Balaton is a protected nature reserve.

A popular destination on the northern shore is the spa town of Balatonfüred, whose mineral springs have been used for curative purposes since Roman times. From here, you can visit the Tihany Peninsula, Hungary's first national park.

At the northwestern tip of the lake, the university town of Keszthely is home to three beaches and the imposing Festetics Palace. Nearby is Hévíz, an old 19th-century spa resort with the world's second-largest thermal lake.

💬 INSIDER TIP
Wine Tasting

Head to the Szépasszony Valley, just west of Eger, to sample the region's wines. These include the famous dry red, Egri Bikavér - otherwise known as Bull's Blood.

⑦
Eger

Eger 🚌🚈 Bajcsy-Zsilinszky utca 9; www.eger.hu

One of Hungary's most popular destinations, Eger is famous for its world-class wines. At the heart of the town, on Eszterházy tér, are the Neo-Classical Cathedral (1830s) and the Lyceum. A highlight of the latter is the observatory, which affords stunning views of the town and surrounding vineyards.

Eger's minaret is a relic of 16th-century Ottoman occupation, while the Baroque Minorite Church on Dobó István tér dates from the 1770s.

Eger Castle was built in the 13th century following the Mongol invasion. The castle complex includes the Bishop's Palace (1470), which houses a museum of historical artifacts.

PRACTICAL
INFORMATION

Here you will find all the essential advice and information you will need before and during your stay in Hungary.

AT A GLANCE

CURRENCY
Forint (HUF)

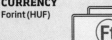

TIME ZONE
CET/CEST. Central European Summer Time runs from the last Sunday in March to the last Sunday in October.

LANGUAGE
Hungarian

ELECTRICITY SUPPLY
Power sockets are of type C and F, fitting two-pronged plugs. The standard voltage is 230V.

EMERGENCY NUMBERS

GENERAL EMERGENCY

112

TAP WATER
Unless otherwise stated, tap water in Hungary is safe to drink.

Getting There

The largest airport in Hungary is Budapest's Ferenc Liszt International Airport. It has multiple connections to cities in the UK and most other major European cities, as well as direct transatlantic flights to New York.

Budapest has direct international rail links to 25 other capital cities, with Keleti Pályaudvar station handling the majority of the international traffic. High-speed trains to Vienna, the main communications hub for Western Europe, depart approximately every three hours and take around 2 hours 25 minutes.

International buses to all European destinations depart from Népliget station in Budapest. Flixbus operates a number of different routes to and from the city.

Personal Security

Hungary is generally a safe country, but it is always a good idea to take sensible precautions against pickpockets. If you have anything stolen, report the crime as soon as possible to the nearest police station. Get a copy of the crime report in order to claim on your insurance.

Health

EU citizens with a European Health Insurance Card (EHIC) are entitled to free emergency medical care in Hungary, but it is also advisable to take out some form of supplementary health insurance. Visitors from outside the EU must arrange their own private medical insurance. For minor ailments, visit a pharmacy (*gyógyszertár* or *patika*). If your nearest store is closed, it should display a list of 24-hour emergency pharmacies.

Passports and Visas

Citizens of the EU, US, Canada, Australia, and New Zealand need only a valid passport to visit Hungary for up to 90 days. EU citizens can also enter with an Identity card. For visa information specific to your home country, consult your nearest Hungarian embassy or check online.

LGBT+ Safety

Budapest has a thriving gay scene, but it is worth noting that extreme right-wing groups have in recent years attacked Gay Pride marches. Same-sex civil partnerships have been legal in Hungary since 2009, although same-sex marriage is banned by the constitution.

Travelers with Specific Needs

Hungary's public transportation systems, museums, and other attractions are gradually being renovated to make them wheelchair-friendly, but people with limited mobility may still encounter accessibility problems. For more detailed information contact the **Hungarian Disabled Association**.
Hungarian Disabled Association
w meosz.hu

Money

Major credit and debit cards are accepted everywhere and contactless payments are becoming common. Minimum amounts are often required for card transactions, however, so carry cash for smaller payments. Currency exchange offices are best avoided.

Cell Phones and Wi-Fi

Visitors traveling to Hungary with EU tariffs can use their devices without being affected by data roaming charges. Visitors from other countries should check their contracts before departure in order to avoid unexpected charges.

Hungary has some of the fastest broadband Internet speeds in the world. Cafés and restaurants usually permit the use of their Wi-Fi on condition that you make a purchase. Wi-Fi is now almost always free in hotels.

Getting Around

The Hungarian national rail network is very efficient, with trains invariably departing and arriving on time. Trains in Hungary are operated by Magyar Államvasutak, known as **MÁV**. Fast InterCity services link the capital with Debrecen, Szeged, Pécs, and Győr, stopping only at major towns and cities. *Gyorsvonat* (fast trains) and *Sebesvonat* (express trains) are slower and make more stops. Regional services, *Személyvonat*, stop at all stations and are very slow. Prices for all trains are relatively cheap. Tickets can be bought from stations or online from MÁV. Note that InterCity services require a prior seat reservation.

The comprehensive national bus network is run by **Volánbusz**, which operates routes to most cities and towns in Hungary. Ticket prices are based on distance traveled, with prices increasing the further you journey.

To rent a car in Hungary you must be aged 21 years or over, and have held a full driver's license for a minimum of a year. An international driver's license also helps. Most of the big, international firms have offices at the airport in Budapest, or you can arrange rental at hotels and travel agencies throughout the country.

Hydrofoil and cruise ship services are available along the Danube between spring and fall, operated by **MAHART Passnave**. Boats run from Budapest to Esztergom, with stops at Szentendre, Visegrád, and Vác.
MÁV
w mavcsoport.hu
MAHART Passnave
w mahartpassnave.hu
Volánbusz
w volanbusz.hu

Visitor Information

Before leaving for Hungary, you can obtain various information leaflets and maps from the **Hungarian National Tourist Office**, which has branches worldwide. Within Hungary, you will find tourist information offices in most large towns. In Budapest, advice on accommodations, sightseeing, and cultural events is given by the offices of **Tourinform Budapest**.
Hungarian National Tourist Office
w hellohungary.com
Tourinform Budapest
w tourinform.hu

CROATIA

Croatia has long been a point of contact between different worlds and cultures. Cohesive states were established in Croatia around 1000 BC by the Illyrians, followed by ancient Greek colonies in the 4th century BC. By the 1st century AD, however, the whole territory had been absorbed into the Roman Empire. The 6th century saw an invasion by the Avars from Central Asia, which was repelled with the help of a Slav tribe known as the Croats. Croatian leaders carved out autonomous states, which became consolidated in the 10th century. In the 11th century, Croatia fell to Hungary, later coming under Venetian rule in 1409 – although Dubrovnik remained a powerful independent city-state. Ottoman invasions in the 16th century led Croatia to join the Austrian Habsburg Empire, and – barring a brief period of Napoleonic rule in the 19th century – it remained under Austrian control until 1918, when Croatia became part of Yugoslavia. Nazi Germany overran Yugoslavia in 1941, installing a brutal fascist government. Resistance came from a movement led by Josip Broz Tito, who in 1945 turned Yugoslavia into a Communist federation of six republics. Croatia eventually declared its independence in 1991, resulting in war with the Serb-dominated Yugoslav army. Croatian independence was recognized in January 1992, but it took until August 1995 for the Croatian army to liberate lands occupied by Serbian separatists. Membership of NATO and the EU have since confirmed Croatia's reintegration into the international community.

CROATIA

1 Zagreb
2 Dubrovnik
3 Split
4 Hvar
5 Korčula
6 Pula
7 Rovinj
8 Zadar
9 Poreč
10 Plitvice Lakes National Park

ZAGREB

 www.infozagreb.hr

Zagreb is the undisputed political, economic, and cultural heart of Croatia, a place that has been at the center of the nation's fortunes since becoming a cathedral city in the 12th century. Brimming with monuments and museums, it is also a relaxing city in which to stroll, take things easy, and enjoy an unhurried cake and coffee.

① Cathedral of the Assumption

🏛 Kaptol ☎ (01) 481 4727 🕐 10am–5pm Mon–Sat, 1–5pm Sun

This twin-towered, Neo-Gothic cathedral is Zagreb's main landmark. The lofty interior contains the tombs of numerous important people from Croatian history, such as Petar Zrinski, Fran Krsto Frankopan, and the Blessed Cardinal Alojzije Stepinac, who was put on trial by the Communist Yugoslav government after World War II. Outside, medieval turrets attest to the stout fortifications that once surrounded the site.

② Dolac Market

Occupying a plateau just above the city's main square is Dolac market, one of Europe's few remaining fruit and vegetable markets that still occupy the very center of a capital city. As well as fresh local produce, visitors can find honeys, preserves, and various other delicatessen products.

③ Tkalčićeva

Occupying the former course of the Medveščak stream, pedestrianized Tkalčićeva is one of Zagreb's most vibrant and visually appealing streets.

It is lined with pastel-painted 18th- and 19th-century houses, most of which now hold restaurants, boutiques, galleries, and – above all – cafés. An umbrella-wielding statue at the southern end honors Marija Jurić Zagorka (1873–1957), renowned journalist and author of historical novels.

④ Upper Town

Zagreb's most evocative quarter is the so-called Upper Town ("Gornji Grad"), which occupies a small hill to the northwest of the city's main square. Filled with Baroque mansions and town houses, it is centered on the medieval church of St. Mark (Crkva svetog Marka), whose brightly tiled roof displays Croatia's coats of arms. Government buildings and cultural institutions line the cobbled streets nearby.

Occupying a particularly handsome mansion is the thought-provoking **Museum of Broken Relationships**, an innovative collection of artifacts relating to break-ups and loss. It began life as a one-off art project in 2004,

← A bustling street in Zagreb's Upper Town, lined by cafés and shops

but struck a chord with the public and became a permanent museum four years later.

The southern rim of the Upper Town is marked by the pedestrianized Strossmayerovo šetalište promenade, which offers superb views of the modern city center below. Overlooking the street is the Lotrščak Tower, home to a small cannon which is fired every day at noon.

Museum of Broken Relationships

🏛 ul Ćirilometodska 2
🕐 9am–10:30pm daily
🌐 brokenships.com

---

⑤

Croatian National Theater

🏛 Trg Republike Hrvatske
🕐 For performances only
🌐 hnk.hr

A sumptuous blend of Neo-Renaissance and Neo-Baroque styles, the Croatian National Theater was built in 1895 by Viennese architects Hermann Helmer and Ferdinand Fellner. In front of it stands *The Well of Life* by 20th-century sculptor Ivan Meštrović. The beautiful Art Nouveau-influenced work consists of a group of bronze nude figures gathered around a circular well.

---

⑥

Archaeological Museum

🏛 Trg Nikole Šubića Zrinskog 19 🕐 10am–6pm Tue–Sat (to 8pm Thur), 10am–1pm Sun 🌐 amz.hr

Housed in the 19th-century Vranyczany-Hafner Palace, this wide-ranging collection embraces everything from prehistory through Greek vases and Egyptology, to medieval sculpture. There are around 400,000 pieces, highlights of which include the Vučedol Dove, an iconic three-legged pot in the shape of a bird that dates to around 2500 BC; and the Zagreb Mummy, an Egyptian mummy wrapped in a shroud that bears a very rare text in ancient Etruscan. Roman tombstones are set in a garden right behind the museum.

💬 INSIDER TIP
Summer in the City

Summer brings out the best in Zagreb's open spaces. The parks and squares host a string of food fairs, while the Upper Town comes to life with outdoor movies and concerts.

⑦

Strossmayer Gallery of Old Masters

🏛 Trg Nikole Šubića Zrinskog 11 🕐 10am–7pm Tue, 10am–4pm Wed-Fri, 10am–1pm Sat & Sun 🌐 info.hazu.hr

Lining the walls of this grand Neo-Renaissance palace are Old-Master heavyweights – Tintoretto, Poussin, Bellini, and Brueghel to name a few. The collection was amassed by 19th-century Croatian bishop Juraj Strossmayer, a major force behind the creation of Zagreb's Academy of Arts and Sciences. Artifacts on display in the gallery include the 11th-century Baška Tablet, one of the oldest existing documents in Croatian culture.

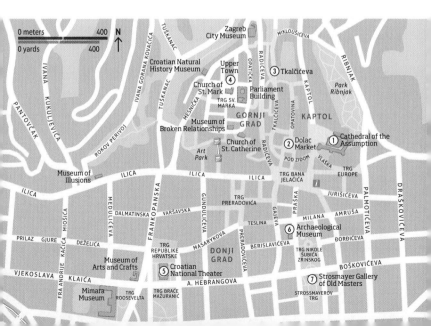

2

DUBROVNIK

 Dubrovnik-Neretva 🚗🚌 ℹ️ Brsalje;
www.visitdubrovnik.hr

With its photogenic alleys overlooked by historic
monuments, the walled city of Dubrovnik is one of
the most magical destinations in the Mediterranean.
The restored Old Town is undoubtedly the main draw,
but you'll also find sophisticated seafood eateries and
a growing number of chic, buzzing bars.

1

Town Walls

🕐 Jun–Jul: 8am–7:30pm
daily; Apr–May & Aug–Sept
8am–6:30pm daily; Oct:
8am–4pm daily; Nov–Mar:
9am–3pm daily 🌐 wallsof
dubrovnik.com

A walk around Dubrovnik's
iconic walls provides stunning
views of the city and an ideal
introduction to its history.
Although begun in the 10th
century, the walls were modified many times, with a major
spurt of re-fortification taking
place in the mid-15th century.
They are 6,363 ft (1,940 m) long,
and in some places reach a
height of 82 ft (25 m). Those
facing inland are up to 20 ft
(6 m) thick and are strengthened by ten semi-circular
bastions. Minčeta, guarding

the northwestern corner, is the
most imposing of the towers.
Designed by Italian architect
Michelozzo Michelozzi in 1461,
this was one of the many parts
of the city featured in the fantasy series *Game of Thrones*.
Visitors walk anticlockwise
round the walls, with the main
access points at Pile Gate and
at the Fort of St. John. Queues
for the wall are long in spring
and summer, and progress is
slow once you get up on to the
parapet. Arrive early if you
want to avoid the crush.

2

Pile Gate

This is the main entrance to
the old fortified center. The
stone bridge leading to the
gate dates from 1537 and
crosses a moat that today

contains a childrens' playpark
and an orchard of citrus fruits.
In a niche above the gate is
Ivan Meštrović's statue of St.
Blaise, the city's patron saint,
who allegedly saved Dubrovnik
from Venetian attack in 972.

3

Big Fountain
of Onofrio

Standing in the square next
to the Pile Gate, this circular
domed structure was built
in 1438–44 by Neapolitan
architect Onofrio della Cava,
who also designed the city's
water supply system. Visitors
to Dubrovnik would wash
in the fountain before pro-
ceeding farther into the city.
It still provides drinking water
to thirsty passersby.

4

Stradun

The wide street that crosses
the Old Town from west to
east was constructed in the
12th century and follows
the line of a channel that
separated the original, early-
medieval settlement from
the mainland. Following the
earthquake of 1667, the stone
houses along the Stradun
were built in uniform style,
producing an architectural
harmony that has been

preserved ever since. Today, the narrow alleyways leading off the Stradun are full of restaurants, cafés, and bars, and the area is a popular place for evening socializing.

Franciscan Monastery

🏛 Placa 2 📞 (020) 321 410 🕐 May-Sep: 9am-6pm daily; Oct-Apr: 9am-2pm daily

Dominating the western end of the Stradun is the large Franciscan Monastery, begun in 1307 but modified many times in later centuries. The tranquil 15th-century cloister leads to the Old Pharmacy (Stara ljekarna), in use since 1317. There is a small museum

---

←

Sunset over the lovely redroofed Old Town of Dubrovnik

here, housing religious works of art and instruments from the pharmaceutical laboratory.

---

⑥

Church of St. Blaise

🏛 Loža 📞 (020) 324 911 🕐 8am-noon & 4:30-7pm daily

St. Blaise was rebuilt in the early decades of the 18th century according to a 17th-century design. On the main altar stands a gold-plated silver statue of the city's patron, St. Blaise. Produced in the 15th century, it depicts the saint holding a model of the city as it looked in the Middle Ages.

---

⑦

Loggia Square

This square, the political and economic heart of Dubrovnik,

marks the eastern end of the Stradun. At its center stands Orlando's column, a popular landmark sculpted by Antonio Ragusino in 1418. On the eastern side of the square is a clock tower holding replicas of two 15th-century hammer-wielding statues that used to strike the bell every hour.

---

⑧ Cathedral and Treasury

🏛 Kneza Damjana Jude 1
📞 (020) 323 459 ⏰ Apr–Oct:
8am–5pm Mon–Sat, 11am–
5pm Sun; Nov–Mar: 8am–
noon & 3-5pm Mon–Sat,
11am–noon & 3-5pm Sun

Despite its medieval origins, the Cathedral was largely rebuilt after the earthquake of 1667. Paintings by Italian and Dalmatian artists decorate the side altars, while an *Assumption* (c. 1552) by Titian dominates the altar. In the Cathedral Treasury (Riznica katedrale) is a fascinating collection of reliquaries and sacred objects.

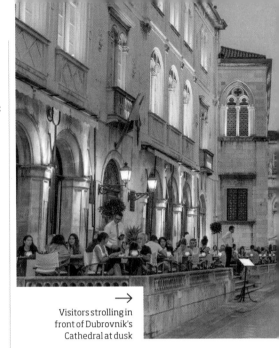

→
Visitors strolling in front of Dubrovnik's Cathedral at dusk

⑨ Dominican Monastery

🏛 Od sv Dominika 4 📞 (020) 321 423 ⏰ 9am–6pm daily (Nov–Apr: to 5pm)

Arranged around a beautiful 15th-century cloister, the monastery is home to the Dominican Museum (Muzej Dominikanskog samostana), one of Dubrovnik's best art collections. Inside are a number of canvases by leading artists of the Dubrovnik Renaissance, notably Nikola Božidarević

SIEGE OF DUBROVNIK

During the Homeland War of 1991–5, the city of Dubrovnik was the target of heavy shelling by the Yugoslav army and Montenegrin irregular forces. The fiercest bombardments took place during the siege of 1991-2, when many historic buildings were damaged. However, swift restoration work soon returned the city to its former self.

and Lovro Dobričević. Hanging above the altar in the monastery church is a large painted crucifix by 14th-century master Paolo Veneziano.

⑩ Rector's Palace

🏛 Pred Dvorom 3 ⏰ Apr–Oct: 9am–6pm daily; Nov–Mar: 9am–4pm daily
🌐 dumus.hr

For centuries, the Rector's Palace was the seat of the Dubrovnik Republic's most important government institutions. It housed both upper and lower chambers of the town council as well as the rector's own living quarters. Constructed on the site of a medieval fortress by 15th-century architect Onofrio della Cava, it has a beautiful entrance porch famous for its delicately carved columns.

The palace now houses the Cultural Historical Museum (Kulturno-povijesni muzej), which relates Dubrovnik history from the 16th century through to the present day. On the ground floor, a former jail and courtroom have been preserved. Coins, medals, ancient weapons, and works of art are on display on the mezzanine floor, while the first floor has Renaissance paintings and portraits of famous personalities from the city's history. During the Dubrovnik Festival, concerts are held in the atmospheric palace courtyard.

⑪ Mount Srđ

Towering above the Old Town to the north is the grey ridge of Mount Srđ. It can be reached by cable car, which whizzes up from a base station just above the city walls in under four minutes. Srđ can also be climbed on foot, in about 90 minutes, via a zig-zagging path known as the "serpentina."

The summit provides awesome views of the city and the coast, especially at sunset, when large crowds assemble to observe the spectacle. Fort Imperial, a Napoleonic-era stronghold near the top, holds a Museum of the Homeland

War (Muzej domovinskog rata), devoted to the Serbian-Montenegrin siege of 1991–2, with maps and photographs on display.

---

 ⑫

Sponza Palace

🏠 Stradun 2 📞 (020) 321 032 🕐 May–Oct: 9am–10pm daily; Nov–Apr: 10am–3pm daily

With a handsome colonnaded porch overlooked by Venetian-Gothic windows, the Sponza Palace is one of Dubrovnik's most graceful buildings. Used at various times as a mint, an armory, and a school, today it is the home of the Dubrovnik archives. It also has a small museum displaying valuable manuscripts, and a memorial room devoted to those who fell in the defense of the city during the siege of 1991–2.

⑬

Lovrijenac Fortress

🏠 Ul od Tabakarije 29
🕐 8am–7:30pm daily

Built on a rock just west of the Old Town, Lovrijenac Fortress guarded the approaches to the city by both sea and land. A triangular, thick-walled fort, it is approached via a steep flight of steps. Above the main entrance is the inscription "Non Bene Pro Toto Libertas Venditur Auro" (Freedom is not to be sold for all the gold in the world), a pithy expression of Dubrovnik's centuries-long resistance to foreign powers. Lovrijenac has frequently been used as one of the outdoor drama venues during the Dubrovnik Festival. It is particularly associated with *Hamlet*, which has been performed here several times over the past 50 years, with well-known faces in the cast. It has also starred as a location in the TV series *Game of Thrones* and *Knightfall*.

→

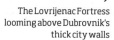
The Lovrijenac Fortress looming above Dubrovnik's thick city walls

3

Split

⌂ Split-Dalmatia
✈🚌🚢🚆 ℹ Peristil;
www.visitsplit.com

The hub of central Dalmatia and Croatia's second-largest city, Split is a boisterous port packed full of Roman and medieval buildings. Split's unique feature is that the city center consists of the remaining parts of the 3rd-century Palace of Roman Emperor Diocletian. The palace walls are largely intact, and the four gates (named the Golden, Silver, Brass, and Iron Gates, and placed at the compass points of the palace) still serve as the main pedestrian entrances to the center.

Entered from the Brass Gate, the former **Palace Basement** (Podrum) provides some idea of the scope of the palace, and now serves as an atmospheric venue for a range of exhibitions. The basement was used as a set for Daenerys' throne room and dragon lock-up in

DIOCLETIAN'S PALACE

After governing the Roman Empire for 20 years, Diocletian retired to his purpose-built palace in Split in 305. After Diocletian's death in 316 the palace fell into disuse, only to be repopulated in 615 by local civilians fleeing Avar invaders. With its Imperial buildings modified and repurposed, it became the center of modern Split.

fantasy series *Game of Thrones*. The palace's interior courtyard now functions as a bustling piazza, while Diocletian's former mausoleum is now the **Cathedral of St. Domnius** (Katedrala svetog Duje), and houses a spectacular collection of original Roman-era friezes and medieval altars. The cathedral's Romanesque bell tower offers expansive views of the city. Located down an

alley opposite the cathedral, a former temple to Jupiter now serves as the **Baptistry of St. John** (Krstionica svetog Ivana). Inside is a baptismal font bearing a relief thought to represent 11th-century Croatian King Zvonimir.

Immediately west of the palace is the medieval part of the city, centered on Narodni trg square and consisting of narrow alleys and intimate piazzas. North of the center, the **Archaeological Museum** (Arheološki muzej) contains a spectacular collection of Roman sarcophagi decorated with exquisitely carved reliefs. Standing at the foot of Marjan hill is the **Meštrović Gallery** (Galerija Meštrović), which contains a compelling collection of sculptures by celebrated Croatian artist Ivan Meštrović.

Split's most popular beach is Bačvice, a broad, shallow bay beloved by local families.

Just 3 miles (5 km) from Split is the ancient city of Salona, which was one of the largest cities in the Roman Adriatic. Today, visitors can explore an

→
Boats moored in the turquoise waters of Hvar Town's pretty harbor

impressive number of ancient temples, churches, and an amphitheater, all set among olive groves and vineyards.

Palace Basement
❂ ⌂ Dioklecijanova ul 1
🕓 9am-5pm daily 🌐 mgst.net

Cathedral of St. Domnius
⌂ Kraj sv Duje 5 🕓 Apr-Oct: 8am-7pm Mon-Sat, 12:30-6pm Sun; Nov-Mar: 8am-5pm daily

Baptistry of St. John
⌂ Ul Kraj Svetog Ivana 2
🕓 9am-7pm daily

Archaeological Museum
❂ ⌂ Zrinsko Frankopanska 25 🕓 Jun-Sep: 9am-2pm & 4-8pm Mon-Sat; Oct-May: 9am-2pm & 4-8pm Mon-Fri, 9am-2pm Sat 🌐 armus.hr

Meštrović Gallery
❂ ⌂ Šetalište Ivana Meštrovića 46 🕓 May-Sep: 9am-7pm Tue-Sun; Oct-Apr: 9am-4pm Tue-Sat, 10am-3pm Sun 🌐 mestrovic.hr

---

 4

Hvar

⌂ Split-Dalmatia 🚌
ℹ www.tzhvar.hr

Renaissance architecture, beaches, and lively cafés make this island one of the jewels of the Adriatic. The main settlement, Hvar Town, has long been popular with artists, yachting folk, and celebrities, and its harborfront is suitably glamorous. The main square (Trg svetog Stjepana) is home to St. Stephen's Cathedral

←
Visitors relaxing in the inner courtyard of Diocletian's palace in Split

(Katedrala sv. Stjepana) and the **Arsenal**, which was built in the late 16th century as a dry dock for Venetian war galleys. A well-restored theater on the first floor dates from 1612 and is one of the oldest in Europe. Steps ascend northwards to the hilltop citadel, which offers superb coastal views.

On the north side of the island, the ancient port of Stari Grad preserves a warren-like center of old stone houses. The main sight here is the **Tvrdalj**, the semi-fortified mansion of 16th-century poet Petar Hektorović. Just east of Stari Grad is Jelsa, a popular base for family beach vacations.

Arsenal
⌂ Trg svetog Stjepana, Hvar Town 🕓 Jun-Sep: 9am-1pm & 5-11pm daily; Oct-May: 11am-noon daily

Tvrdalj
❂ ⌂ Priko, Stari Grad
🕓 May, Jun, & Sep: 10am-1pm daily; Jul & Aug: 10am-1pm & 5-8pm daily

---

 5

Korčula

⌂ Dubrovnik-Neretva 🚌
ℹ www.visitkorcula.eu

Dense forests of Aleppo pine, cypress, and oak characterize this famously green island, a popular vacation spot thanks

to its historic main town and fine sandy beaches. Korčula Town sits on a peninsula surrounded by well-preserved medieval walls. Facing Trg sv Marka, the central piazza, is **St. Mark's Cathedral** (Katedrala sv. Marka) built in pale, honey-colored stone. The main altar holds a Tintoretto painting featuring St. Mark flanked by saints Bartholomew and Jerome. The next-door **Abbey Treasury** (Opatska riznica) contains a wealth of Venetian and Dalmatian art. Opposite, the Town Museum (Gradski muzej) houses archeological finds from ancient Greek to medieval times.

St. Mark's Cathedral
⌂ Trg sv Marka 📞 (020) 715 701 🕓 Hours vary, call ahead

Abbey Treasury
❂ ⌂ Trg sv Marka 📞 (020) 711 049 🕓 Apr-Jun: 10am-2pm Mon-Sat; Jul-Sep: 9am-9pm Mon-Sat; Oct-Mar: 10am-1pm Mon-Sat

---

Did You Know?

According to local legend, Korčula was the birthplace of Marco Polo, the 13th-century Venetian explorer.

↑ A sunset glimpsed through the arched windows of Pula's spectacular Arena

⑥
Pula

📍Istria 🚗🚌🚲🛳
🌐www.pulainfo.hr

A busy port city located at the southern tip of the Istrian peninsula, Pula is the site of a magnificent Roman **Arena**. This huge elliptical amphitheater comprises three tiers of arches and windows, and is one of Croatia's most iconic landmarks. Completed in AD 68, it could accommodate over 20,000 spectators. Now a major tourist attraction, it also serves as the venue for Pula's annual Film Festival and numerous summer concerts. Visitors can climb its stone terraces and visit the underground spaces where wild animals and expectant gladiators once paced. More of Pula's Roman heritage can be seen in the main Forum, where the 1st-century **Temple of Augustus** (Augustov hram)

still has six well-preserved columns topped by beautifully carved capitals. The nearby Arch of the Sergians (Slavoluk Sergijevaca) was erected in the 1st century BC.

The **Archeological Museum of Istria** (Arheološki muzej Istre) houses a vast collection of items from the Neolithic era to the Middle Ages. Of particular interest are pieces from Slavic tombs dating from the 7th to 12th centuries.

Arena

📍Ul Flavijevska ⏰Apr: 8am-8pm daily; May-Sep: 8am-9pm daily (Jul & Aug: to midnight); Oct-Mar: 9am-5pm daily (Oct: to 7pm)

Temple of Augustus

📍Forum ⏰Apr & Oct: 9am-7pm daily; May-Sep: 9am-9pm (Jul & Aug: to 11pm)

Archeological Museum of Istria

📍Carrarina 3 🔒For renovation until 2020 🌐ami-pula.hr

---

⑦
Rovinj

📍Istria 🚌 🌐www.rovinj-tourism.com

Arguably the most chic of the country's northern resorts, Rovinj is a picturesque peninsula town full of winding alleys

and imposing mansions. A significant Italian minority lives here and most signs are bilingual. At the edge of the peninsula is the Cathedral of St. Euphemia, featuring a huge bell tower modeled on that of St. Mark's in Venice (p424). The saint's remains are preserved in a Roman sarcophagus in the apse. The **Town Museum** (Gradski muzej), in the 17th-century Califfi Palace, houses an impressive collection of paintings from the Baroque period to the present day, while the award-winning **Batana Eco-Museum** presents the history of the local batana fishing boat.

Town Museum

♿ 📍Trg maršala Tita 11 ⏰10am-10pm daily 🌐muzej-rovinj.hr

Batana Eco-Museum

♿ 📍Obala Pina Budicina 2 ⏰Hours vary, check website 🌐batana.org

---

⑧
Zadar

📍Zadar 🚗🚌🚲🛳 🌐www.zadar.travel

Offering ancient relics and a vibrant contemporary creative scene, the city of Zadar sprawls across a thumb-shaped peninsula. At its center is the Roman-era Forum, overlooked by the well-preserved Byzantine Rotunda of St. Donat. Further evidence of the city's ancient past can be uncovered at the excellent **Zadar Archeological Museum**, which is stuffed with Roman-era finds, and the **Museum of Ancient Glass**. The latter is housed in the restored Cosmacendi Palace, and displays an impressive array of Roman glassware, from perfume vials to funerary urns.

→

Plitvice Lakes National Park in fall, framed by trees with beautiful burnished leaves

ⓠ HIDDEN GEM
Literary Figure

A young James Joyce worked as an English-language teacher in Pula for six months in 1904-5. Keep an eye out for the statue of the writer outside the Ulix ("Ulysses") café, beside the Arc of the Sergians.

↑ A round vase from the Museum of Ancient Glass, in Zadar

Elsewhere, the Gold and Silver of Zadar museum showcases the city's stunning collection of religious reliquaries and Renaissance paintings. A few steps away is the Cathedral of St. Anastasia, with a richly carved stone interior.

Built into Zadar's quayside is the *Sea Organ* (Morske orgulje), designed by local architect Nikola Bašić. Consisting of pipes of air compressed by seawater, the organ emits a mesmerizing array of sounds that change according to the wind and waves. Nearby is Bašić's *Greeting to the Sun* (Pozdrav suncu), a large disc set in the sidewalk that is formed of 300 light-sensitive plates. Absorbing sunlight by day, the disc emits a hypnotic display of multicolored light patterns at night.

Zadar Archeological Museum

 🏛 Trg opatice Čike 1 🕐 Apr, May, & Oct: 9am-3pm Mon-Sat; Jun-Sep: 9am-9pm daily; Nov-Mar: 9am-2pm Mon-Sat 🌐 amzd.hr

Museum of Ancient Glass

🏛 Poljana Zemaljskog odbora 1 🕐 Jun-Sep: 9am-9pm daily; Oct-May: 9am-4pm Mon-Fri 🌐 mas-zadar.hr

⑨ Poreč

🏛 Istria 🚌🚆 ℹ️ www.myporec.com

The coastal resort of Poreč is home to one of Croatia's most outstanding churches, the walled complex known as the **Euphrasian Basilica** (Eufrazijeva basilica). Built in the mid-6th century, the church is famous for the Byzantine wall mosaics that fill the apse. There are also 6th-century floor mosaics in the baptistry, as well as a museum in the former bishop's residence.

Euphrasian Basilica

 Eufrazijeva 22 🕐 Apr-Oct: 9am-6pm daily (Jul & Aug: to 9pm); Nov-Mar: 9am-4pm daily (to 2pm Sat)

⑩ Plitvice Lakes National Park

🏛 Lika-Senj and Karlovac 🕐 Hours vary, check website 🌐 np-plitvicka-jezera.hr

This national park is the jewel in Croatia's crown. It consists of a string of lakes, linked by waterfalls and surrounded by forested hills. The remarkable landscape was formed over several millennia, with the flow of water across travertine – the soft rock found here – carrying fragments downstream and creating the cataracts that characterize the park today. A network of lakeside paths and boardwalk trails allows visitors to get up close to the turquoise waters, and shuttle buses and lake ferries provide transport around the site. The park is busy in summer, and progress along the trails can be slow. A fall visit can be more rewarding, when leaves surrounding the lakes turn golden; winter also has its attractions, when the frozen landscape lends the park a mystical appeal.

PRACTICAL
INFORMATION

Here you will find all the essential advice and information you will need
before and during your stay in Croatia.

AT A GLANCE

CURRENCY
Croatian Kuna
(HRK)

TIME ZONE
CET/CEST. Central
European Summer
Time runs from the last
Sunday in March to the
last Sunday in October.

LANGUAGE
Croatian

ELECTRICITY SUPPLY
Power sockets are
type F, fitting two-
pronged plugs.
Standard voltage
is 230V.

EMERGENCY NUMBERS

GENERAL EMERGENCY	POLICE
112	**192**

FIRE SERVICE	EMERGENCY AT SEA
193	**9155**

TAP WATER
Unless otherwise
stated, tap water
in Croatia is safe
to drink.

Getting There

Croatia's most important airports are Zagreb,
Zadar, Split, and Dubrovnik. Zagreb is connected
to many European capitals year-round, whereas
flights to other destinations are more seasonal.

There are daily rail services to Zagreb from
several European cities, particularly those in
neighboring countries.

International buses connect Croatia with
bordering countries, as well as Germany and the
Czech Republic. There are almost daily services
from major German cities to Zagreb and coastal
cities, and many Italian cities are also connected
to Zagreb by coach. Additionally, Eurolines and
Flixbus run various services into Croatia.

Blue Line runs regular ferry services between
Ancona (Italy) and Split, as well as seasonal ferries
between Ancona and Hvar. SNAV provides a fast
catamaran service between Ancona and Split,
running from mid-June to late September, while
Venezia Lines links the Northern Adriatic towns
of Poreč, Rovinj, Pula, and Rabac with Venice.

Personal Security

Croatia is generally a safe country, but it is wise
to take precautions against pickpockets. If you
have anything stolen, report the crime to the
nearest police station. Get a copy of the crime
report in order to claim on your insurance.

Health

EU citizens with a European Health Insurance
Card (EHIC) are entitled to free emergency
medical care in Croatia, but it is also advisable
to take out some form of supplementary health
insurance. Visitors from outside the EU must
arrange their own private medical insurance. For
less serious problems, visit a pharmacy *(ljekarna)*,
identified by the green cross above the door.

Passports and Visas

Passports are required for everyone. EU nationals
and citizens of the US, Canada, Australia, and
New Zealand do not need a visa for a stay of up

to 90 days in a 180-day period. For visa information specific to your home country, consult your nearest Croatian embassy or check online.

LGBT+ Safety

Although homosexuality is legal in Croatia it remains somewhat underground; public displays of affection might be met with hostility. LGBT+ venues can mainly be found in Zagreb.

Travelers with Specific Needs

Croatia's old cobbled streets and ancient buildings are ill-equipped for disabled access. Many sights do not have wheelchair access or lifts and only top-end hotels have special facilities. Some transport terminals in big cities are now wheelchair-friendly, but ferries are not. The situation is improving but very slowly, and tourist offices can be over-optimistic about facilities. The **Association of Organizations of Disabled People in Croatia** and **Hsuti** are both sources of useful information.

Association of Organizations of Disabled People in Croatia
w soih.hr
Hsuti
w hsuti.hr

Money

Major credit, debit, and prepaid currency cards are accepted in many shops and restaurants, but not all. Contactless payments are becoming more widely accepted but it is always advisable to carry some cash for smaller purchases. ATMs are widespread in towns and cities; they are less common in rural areas.

Cell Phones and Wi-Fi

Visitors traveling to Croatia with EU tariffs can use their devices without being affected by data roaming charges. Visitors from other countries should check their contracts before departure in order to avoid unexpected charges.

Wi-Fi hotspots are widely available in big cities like Zadar, Dubrovnik, and Zagreb. Cafés and restaurants are usually happy to permit the use of their Wi-Fi on the condition that you make a purchase. Wi-Fi is free in most hotels.

Getting Around

There are two main types of domestic train in Croatia. The first is passenger, or *putnički*, which is generally slow with lots of stops. The second is intercity, or ICN, which is faster and thus more expensive. The entire network is run by **Croatian Railways** and tickets should be purchased at the station before boarding the train; tickets purchased on board might incur a surcharge.

Croatia's buses are a reliable way to get around, but ticket prices are high compared with the rest of Europe. Tickets are normally bought at the bus station before departure, but you can also buy tickets from a newsstand (*tisak*). It is highly recommended to buy well in advance in summer, especially on busy routes out of Dubrovnik, Split, and Zadar. If traveling to the islands by bus, your ticket is valid for the whole journey, including the ferry.

Croatia has some stunning stretches of road so it's worth seeing the country by car. If visiting from outside the EU, you may need to apply for an International Driving Permit – check with your local automobile association before you travel. Croatia's Automobile Club, **HAK**, provides useful information for those traveling by car.

With so many islands, ferries constitute a major part of Croatia's infrastructure. Most ferries and catamarans are run by the state-owned company **Jadrolinija**; timetable and fare information can be found online. Note that some ferries only run in summer.

Croatian Railways
w hzpp.hr
HAK
w hak.hr
Jadrolinija
w jadrolinija.hr

Visitor Information

Tourist information for the whole country is handled by the **Croatian National Tourist Board** (Hrvatska Turistička Zajednica, or HTZ), which has a useful website offering detailed visitor information. In addition, every town and city has an official tourist office that can provide information on local sights, facilities, activities, and accommodations.

Croatian National Tourist Board
w croatia.hr

POLAND

Polish history is a dramatic narrative featuring successive cycles of foreign occupation, resistance, and rebirth. The origins of the Polish nation go back to the 10th century AD, when Slav tribes living in the area of Gniezno united under the Piast dynasty, which ruled Poland with variable fortune until 1370. After this dynasty died out, the Lithuanian Grand Duke Jagiełło took the Polish throne, initiating a long process of consolidation between these nations, culminating in 1569 with the Union of Lublin. The resulting Republic of Two Nations lasted until 1795. After the Jagiellonian dynasty died out in 1572, the Polish authorities introduced elective kings, with the nobility having the right to vote. The 17th century was dominated by wars with Sweden, Russia, and the Ottoman Empire, which considerably weakened the country. In 1795, it was partitioned by Russia, Prussia, and Austria, and was wiped off the map for more than 100 years – Poland did not regain its sovereignty until 1918. The process of rebuilding the nation was still incomplete when the onset of World War II brought a six-year period of German and Soviet occupation. The country suffered great devastation, including huge territorial losses and the murder of virtually its entire Jewish population. After the war, Poland was subjugated by the Soviet Union, eventually regaining its freedom after the 1989 elections. In 1999, Poland became a member of NATO, and in 2004, it joined the EU.

POLAND

① Warsaw
② Kraków
③ Auschwitz-Birkenau Memorial
and Museum

↑ Warsaw's Old Town Market Square, in the early evening

WARSAW

✕ 🅿 🚃 *f* www.warsawtour.pl

Believed to have been founded in the late 13th century, Warsaw became capital of Poland in 1596. The castle and grand Old Town buildings date largely from the Renaissance and Baroque periods, but by the end of World War II, most of the buildings had been reduced to rubble. What you see today is the product of meticulous reconstruction undertaken during the Communist era. Warsaw is rich in museums and sights, and its center has been declared a UNESCO World Heritage Site.

① Old Town Market Square

🏠 Rynek Starego Miasta
Ⓜ Ratusz-Arsenal 🚌 116, 178, 180, 503

Painstakingly restored after World War II, the Old Town Market Square was the center of Warsaw public life until the 19th century, when the focus of the growing modern city moved. The tall, colorful houses that lend the square its unique character were built by wealthy merchants in the 17th century.

The houses on the north-west side form the Museum of Warsaw (Muzeum Warszawy), which offers an engrossing account of the city's history.

In center of the square is a statue of the Warsaw Mermaid, a mythical creature who has been considered the city's protector since the Middle Ages.

St. John's Cathedral

🏠 Świętojańska 8 📞 22-831 02 89 Ⓜ Ratusz-Arsenal 🚌 116, 178, 222, 503 🕐 10am–5pm Mon–Sat, 3–5pm Sun 🚫 During Mass

Completed in the early 15th century, St. John's Cathedral

(katedra św Jana) was originally a parish church, eventually becoming a cathedral in 1798. Several historic events took place here, including the 1764 coronation of Stanisław August Poniatowski, Poland's last king, and the swearing of an oath by the deputies of the *Sejm* (Parliament) to uphold the 1791 Constitution.

After World War II, various 19th-century additions were removed from the facade, and the cathedral was restored to its original Mazovian Gothic style. The interior features religious art, richly carved stalls, and ornate tombs, including those of Gabriel Narutowicz (1865–1922), Poland's first president, assassinated two days after taking office, and Nobel Prize-winning novelist Henryk Sienkiewicz (1846–1916). In a chapel founded by

→ A spectacular stained-glass window in St. John's Cathedral

the Baryczka family hangs a 16th-century crucifix that is credited with several miracles.

Royal Castle

🏛 Plac Zamkowy 4 🚌 116, 178, 180, 503 🕐 Hours vary, check website
🌐 zamek-krolewski.pl

Warsaw's Royal Castle (Zamek Królewski) stands on the site of an original castle built here by the Mazovian dukes in the 14th century. It was transformed between 1598 and 1619 by King Zygmunt III Waza, who asked Italian architects to restyle the castle into a polygon. The king chose this castle as his royal residence in 1596, after the *Sejm* (Parliament) had moved here from Kraków in 1569. Further changes were made in the 18th century, when King Augustus III remodeled the east wing in Baroque style and King Stanisław August Poniatowski added a library.

Completely destroyed by the Germans in World War II, the castle was reconstructed from 1971 to 1988, with public donations of both money and works of art.

The castle's fascinating interiors are the result of the building's dual role as both a royal residence and the seat of parliament. It features Royal Apartments, as well as the Chamber of Deputies and the Senate. Some of the woodwork and stucco is original, as are many of the furnishings and much of the art. Among the most notable paintings on show are 18th-century works by Bellotto and Bacciarelli.

💬 **INSIDER TIP**
Getting Around

The sights in the Old and New Town areas are easily visited on foot, as most of the streets are pedestrianized. Trams are the best transport option for short trips across the center. There is also an extensive bus service, and two metro lines meeting at Świętokrzyska station.

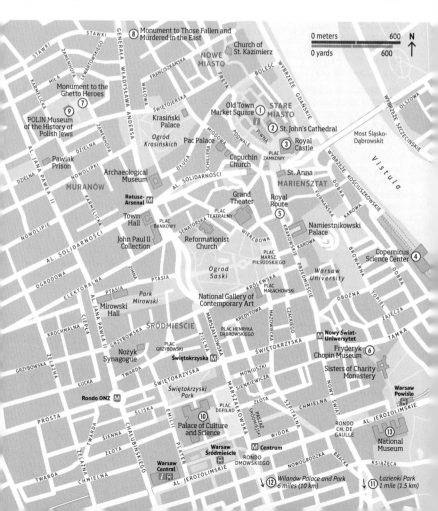

Children enjoying one of the exhibits at the Copernicus Science Center

Fryderyk Chopin Museum

⌂ Ul Okólnik 1
🚌 111, 175, 178, 180, 503
🕐 11am-8pm Tue-Sun
✕ Jan 1, Easter, Corpus Christi, Nov 1, Dec 25
🌐 chopin.museum

Opened in 2010 to mark the 200th anniversary of the birth of one of Poland's most famous sons, the Fryderyk Chopin Museum (Muzeum Fryderyka Chopina) attracts many visitors. The collection takes up four floors of the splendid Gniński-Ostrogski Palace, which was designed by Tylman van Gameren.

The museum houses portraits, letters, and manuscripts, as well as the grand piano at which Chopin composed during the last years of his life. Other exhibits include a gold watch presented to the ten-year-old Fryderyk by an admiring Italian singer and the passport that he used to enter England. The Chopin Society is based here, and regular performances of Chopin's music take place.

Copernicus Science Center

⌂ Wybrzeże Kościusz-kowskie 20 **Ⓜ** Centrum Nauki Kopernik **🚌** 118, 150, 506 **🕐** Hours vary, check website **✕** Mon & public hols **🌐** kopernik.org.pl

One of Poland's most-visited attractions, the Copernicus Science Center (Centrum Nauki Kopernik) opened in 2010. More of a hands-on educational park than a traditional museum, it is filled with games and interactive content and is constantly buzzing with school groups, families, and individuals. There are special areas designated for younger children, as well as sections on biology and technology that keep teenagers and adults entertained. Visitors can also enjoy sweeping views from the roof garden, which is open from May to October. The nearby Copernicus Planetarium shows films on astronomy; a combined ticket is available.

Royal Route

⌂ Krakowskie Przedmieście and Nowy Świat **🚌** 116, 175, 180, 503

The grand Royal Route (Trakt Królewski) is one of Warsaw's most historic and beautiful streets. Starting by Castle Square (Plac Zamkowy), and continuing all the way to the royal palace at Wilanów (p690), this thoroughfare was the path along which Poland's kings would move in procession whenever doing business in the capital.

The route's most interesting section is along the streets of Krakowskie Przedmieście and Nowy Świat. These thoroughfares developed in the late Middle Ages, attracting the city's aristocracy and wealthy merchant class with their rural setting by the banks of the Vistula river. This social elite built grand summer residences and town houses here, while religious orders established lavish churches and monasteries. Many such buildings have been preserved along Krakowskie Przedmieście, including the churches of St. Anna, St. Joseph, and the Church of the Assumption. Warsaw University and the Fine Arts Academy are also located here, while various monuments pay tribute to eminent Poles.

Nowy Świat, meanwhile, has become Warsaw's prime promenading ground thanks to its concentration of chic cafés and smart shops. From there, the route continues along the broad, leafy avenue of Aleje Ujazdowskie to the southern suburbs.

The POLIN Museum of the History of Polish Jews, and *(inset)* one of its exhibits

Monument to the Ghetto Heroes

🏛 Pomnik Bohaterów Getta, Zamenhofa 🚌 111, 180

The Nazis created the Jewish Ghetto in 1940 by driving the Jewish inhabitants of Warsaw and nearby villages into an area in the northwest of the city. It initially housed around 450,000 people, but by 1942, over 300,000 had been transported to death camps, and 100,000 others had died in the ghetto. The Ghetto Uprising of 1943 was an action of heroic defiance against the Nazis by those left, planned not as a bid for liberty, but as an honorable way to die. Built to commemorate this action, the Monument to the Ghetto Heroes stands in the center of the former ghetto. It depicts men, women, and children struggling to flee the burning ghetto, together with a procession of Jews being driven to Nazi death camps.

A Path of Remembrance, lined with a series of granite blocks dedicated to events or heroes of the ghetto, links the memorial to the nearby Bunker Monument and the Umschlagplatz Monument. Engraved with hundreds of names, this marks the place from where many Jews were deported to the death camps, and represents the cattle trucks used for transportation.

---

⑧

Monument to Those Fallen and Murdered in the East

🏛 Ul Muranowska 🚌 116, 178, 503 🚋 18, 35

This stirring monument by Mirosław Biskupski, unveiled in 1995, takes the form of a typical railroad wagon in which Poles were deported into the depths of the Soviet Union. It is filled with a pile of crosses symbolizing the hundreds of thousands of Poles transported east in cattle vans. Many died there of hunger, overwork, or disease.

---

⑨

POLIN Museum of the History of Polish Jews

🏛 Ul Mordechaja Aniele-wicza 6 🚌 111, 180, 227 🕐 10am–6pm Mon, Thu, & Fri, 10am–8pm Wed, Sat, & Sun 🚫 Mon & public hols 🌐 polin.pl

Housed in a breathtaking contemporary building, the country's largest Jewish heritage museum covers

1,000 years of the history of Polish Jews, from the Middle Ages to the present day. Its fascinating displays illustrate how Poland became the center of the Jewish diaspora; the highlight of the collection is the painted ceiling of a 17th-century synagogue that used to stand in Gwozdziec.

Overall, this is a spectacular celebration of Jewish life and culture, although the tone becomes understandably more somber as the exhibition turns to the Holocaust.

EAT

Freta 33

Freta 33 focuses on contemporary European cuisine with a Mediterranean slant, excelling in sophisticated pasta dishes. There's also a well-curated wine list.

📍 Ul Freta 33/35
🌐 freta33.pl

Kafka

A popular lunch spot for its menu of pastas, salads, and soups, Kafka also impresses with colorful, chic design.

📍 Ul Oboźna 3
🌐 kawiarnia-kafka.pl

Palace of Culture and Science

📍 Plac Defilad 1 Ⓜ Centrum
🕐 Viewing Terrace: 10am–8pm daily 🌐 pkin.pl

Possibly the most recognized building in all of Warsaw, this monolithic structure was a "gift" from the Soviet Union to the city's residents, and intended as a monument to "the inventive spirit and social progress." Built in 1952–5 by the Russian architect Lev Rudniev, it was the second-tallest building in Europe at that time, and resembles Moscow's Socialist Realist tower blocks.

This symbol of Soviet domination still provokes extreme reactions among Varsovians, ranging from admiration to demands for its demolition. Since the end of the Soviet era, the building's role has changed: the tower itself now provides office space, and the Congress Hall is a venue for concerts and festivals. It remains a cultural center in other ways, housing the Theater of Dramatic Art, a cinema, puppet theater, technology museum, and a sports complex. It also has a public viewing terrace on the roof, which offers spectacular views across the city.

Łazienki Park

📍 Łazienki Królewskie, Agrykola 1 🚌 108, 116, 138, 166 🕐 Park: daily until dusk; Palace on the Water: mid-Apr–mid-Oct: 10am–6pm Tue–Sun; mid-Oct–mid-Apr: 9am–4pm Tue–Sun
🚫 Public hols 🌐 lazienki-krolewskie.pl

This huge park, studded with monuments, palaces, and temples, dates from the Middle Ages, when it belonged to the Mazovian dukes. By the early 17th century, it was owned by the Polish Crown, and housed a royal menagerie. In 1674, the Grand Crown Marshal Stanisław Herakliusz Lubomirski acquired the park; he altered part of the menagerie and built a hermitage and a bathing pavilion on an island. The pavilion gave the park its name: *łazienki* means "baths."

In the 18th century, the park was owned by King Stanisław August Poniatowski, who had it transformed into a formal garden. A number of buildings were added during this time, and the pavilion was redesigned as a royal summer residence. Known as the Palace on the Water, this is one of the finest examples of Neo-Classical architecture in Poland. It now houses a picture gallery.

The king enjoyed the palace only for a few years: after the Third Partition of Poland, he was forced to abdicate, and left Warsaw on January 7, 1795. The palace was later burned by the Nazis upon their withdrawl from the city during World War II, but was rebuilt by 1965.

Wilanów Palace and Park

📍 S.K Potockiego 10–16
🚌 E2, 116, 164, 180, 317
🕐 Hours vary, check website 🌐 wilanow-palac.pl

Just south of the city, set amid lovely gardens and beautiful formal parkland, stands the palace of Wilanów, one of Poland's most important historical buildings. Although it was a royal residence, the palace was actually designed

The sumptous interiors of the Palace on the Water, in Łazienki Park

→ Wilanów Palace in summer, with its formal gardens in bloom

as a private retreat for King Jan III Sobieski, who valued family life above material splendor. The original property, known as Villa Nova, was purchased in 1677 and within two years had been rebuilt as a mansion, designed by royal architect Augustyn Locci. The facades were adorned with sculptures and murals, while the interiors were decorated by Europe's finest craftsmen.

Enlarged over subsequent years by its many different owners, the palace gained two large wings, a pair of towers, and a first-floor banqueting hall. The north wing comprises 19th-century rooms, formerly used as living quarters and as a gallery. The largest room, the Great Crimson Room, is used as a venue for entertaining VIPs. The south wing includes the Late Baroque Great Dining Room, designed for King August II Mocny, as well as Princess Izabela Lubomirska's apartments, which feature a bathroom dating from 1775.

The most interesting rooms in the main part of the palace are the Neo-Classical Great Hall, with marble detailing and allegorical friezes, and the ornate King's Bedchamber, featuring a 17th-century Turkish bed canopy. There are also several apartments once occupied by King Jan III Sobieski and his wife Marysieńka, which retain many of their original 17th-century features, as well as a fascinating portrait gallery. The grounds outside the palace contain a Chinese Arbour, an orangery, and a former riding school that has been converted to house a poster museum, showcasing a fine collection of graphic art.

---

⑬

National Museum

🏛 Aleje Jerozolimskie 3
🚌 111, 117, 158, 507, 517, 521
🚊 6, 8, 10, 13, 18 🕐 10am–6pm Tue–Sun (to 9pm Fri)
🚫 Public hols 🌐 mnw.art.pl

Originally established in 1862, the National Museum (Muzeum Narodowe) is one of the finest in the country. Collections include ancient Greek, Roman, and Egyptian art, archaeological finds from Faras in present-day Sudan, and a variety of medieval Polish religious works.

In the vast Polish collection are works by Canaletto's nephew Bernardo Bellotto, who settled in Warsaw and painted many fine views of the city, as well as pieces by native Polish artists such as Jan Matejko, who painted Polish historical and political subjects such as *The Battle of Grunwald*. The foreign art collection features Italian, French, Dutch, and Flemish works, including a *Madonna and Child* by Sandro Botticelli.

In an east wing, the **Military Museum** illustrates the history of Polish firearms and armor, with a large outdoor display of tanks, rockets, and aircraft.

Military Museum
🕐 10am–5pm Wed, 10am–4pm Thu–Sun
🌐 muzeumwp.pl

→ A sculpture by Polish artist Zbigniew Pronaszko in the National Museum

❷ KRAKÓW

🗺 Małopolska 🚆🚌 ℹ️ Plac Szczepański 8, 31-011 Kraków; www.visitkrakow.com

For nearly six centuries, Kraków was the capital of Poland and the country's largest city, until the court and parliament moved to Warsaw in 1596. Today, Kraków's greatest attraction arguably lies in the fact that, unlike so many Polish cities, it was scarcely damaged in World War II. In recent years, many buildings have been restored to their former glory.

① Cloth Hall

🗺 Market Square 1/3
🚌 124, 152 🚋 3, 4, 7, 13

The Cloth Hall (Sukiennice) in the middle of Market Square originated in medieval times as a covered market. It was rebuilt after a fire in 1555, replacing an earlier Gothic trade hall from the 1300s, and then remodeled entirely in 1875 with arcades along the exterior that give it a Venetian look. Most of the stalls today sell souvenirs. On the upper floor is a branch of the National Museum in Kraków that displays 19th-century Polish paintings (for which tickets are required), while the lower floor contains a number of cafés – the Noworolski Café is one of the best in Kraków.

② Market Square

🗺 Rynek Główny 🚌 124, 152 🚋 3, 4, 7, 13

Market Square is said to be the largest town square in Europe. In summer, street cafés and restaurants remain open here until the early hours, with flower stalls, street musicians, and artists all adding to the lively atmosphere. Besides the Cloth Hall, two other notable buildings stand in the square: the green-domed church of St. Adalbert and the City Hall Tower, a relic of the original Gothic town hall.

Other structures around the square retain elements from every era in the history of the city. Many are decorated with an emblem that gives the property its name, such as the Palace of the Rams on the square's west side, home of a famous cabaret since 1956. Christopher Palace takes its name from a 14th-century statue of St. Christopher. The house was remodeled in 1682–5 around a beautiful courtyard and is now home to the Museum of Kraków. Beneath the square is Rynek

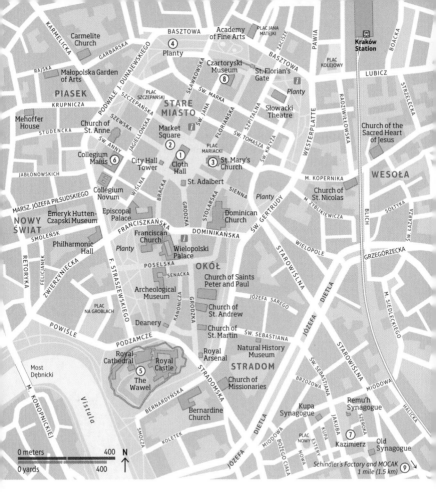

A map of Kraków's Old Town (Stare Miasto) showing numbered sights including Planty, Czartoryski Museum, Market Square, Cloth Hall, St. Mary's Church, The Wawel and Kazimierz.

Underground (Podziemia Rynku), a multimedia museum incorporating medieval artifacts found on the site.

3
St. Mary's Church

🏛 Mariacki Square 5 🚌 124, 152, 304, 424, 502 🚋 1, 3, 18, 24, 52 🕐 11:30am–6pm daily (from 2pm Sun)
🌐 mariacki.com

St. Mary's façade, with its two impressive Gothic towers, is

Market Square in the sunshine, bustling with outdoor cafés

set at an angle on the east side of Market Square. The left-hand tower is topped by a spire added in 1478. It served as the city's watch tower and today a bugle call is still played every hour. The projecting porch between the towers was added in the Baroque period.

The church's greatest treasure is the 39-ft- (12-m-) high altarpiece by Veit Stoss, who lived in Kraków from 1477 to 1496. The outer panels show scenes from the lives of Christ and the Virgin. The middle shutters are opened each day at noon to reveal a huge carved centerpiece, *The Assumption of the Virgin*. There is also a fine crucifix by Veit Stoss, known as the Slacker Crucifix.

4
Planty

Comprised of eight separate gardens, the Planty green belt follows the outline of Kraków's medieval walls, which were demolished in the early 19th century. A circuit through the park of about 3 miles (5 km), starting from the Wawel (*p694*), leads along tree-lined paths and avenues, past fountains and statues. Only a small segment of the city walls survives beside St. Florian's Gate at the north end of the Old Town. The gate was once connected by an underground passage to the nearby well-preserved barbican, built in 1498–9, when Ottoman incursions were a serious threat to the city.

⑤ ⟨🏀⟩ ⟨🥅⟩ ⟨🖥⟩ ⟨🛍⟩

THE WAWEL

🏠 Wawel Hill 🚌 184, 484, 610, 752 🕐 Hours vary, check website 🌐 wawel.krakow.pl

For centuries the symbol of Poland's national, cultural, and spiritual identity, the royal complex of buildings occupying Wawel Hill is revered by Poles.

The Vistulanians were the first to build a citadel on this limestone outcrop in the 9th century, with successive dynasties developing and extending the site. The impressive fortifications encircle a number of buildings, among them the magnificent Renaissance Royal Castle and the Gothic Royal Cathedral. Once the site of coronations and royal burials, the Royal Cathedral is regarded by Poles as a spiritual shrine. The Royal Castle, beside it, was the seat of Poland's royals and remains to this day an enduring symbol of national identity.

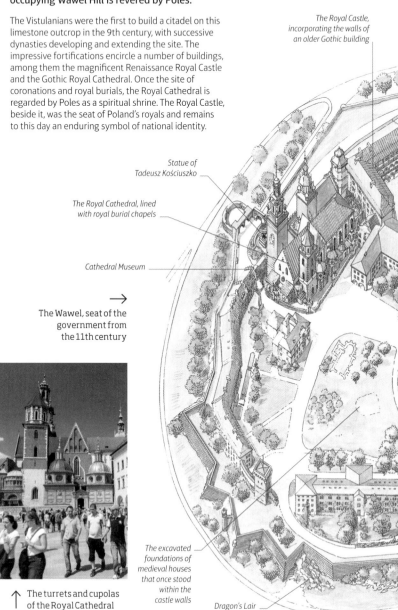

The Royal Castle, incorporating the walls of an older Gothic building

Statue of Tadeusz Kościuszko

The Royal Cathedral, lined with royal burial chapels

Cathedral Museum

→
The Wawel, seat of the government from the 11th century

The excavated foundations of medieval houses that once stood within the castle walls

Dragon's Lair

↑ The turrets and cupolas of the Royal Cathedral

Lost Wawel Exhibition

Fortified walls

Highlights

Royal Castle

▶ One of the most magnificent Renaissance residences in Central Europe, the Wawel Royal Castle was commissioned for Zygmunt I, the penultimate ruler of the Jagiellonian dynasty. Built in 1502-36, the four-winged palace was designed and constructed by the Italian architects Francisco Fiorentino and Bartolommeo Berrecci, and incorporates the 14th-century walls of a Gothic building that once stood on the site. After the royal court was transferred from Kraków to Warsaw in 1609, the palace fell into neglect, deteriorating further under the Swedish occupation of the early 18th century and throughout the era of the Partitions. At the beginning of the 20th century, the castle was returned to the city of Kraków by the occupying Austrian army, and an extensive program of restoration began. Following World War II, the castle was decreed a national museum; today the palace's Italian-inspired interiors have been returned to their former glory, housing vast collections of priceless royal treasures.

Lost Wawel Exhibition

▶ For anyone interested in medieval archaeology, this exhibition is a delight. Various finds from archaeological excavations on the Wawel Hill are exhibited here in a display that charts the development of the Wawel over time. It also includes a virtual image of the Wawel buildings as they existed in the early Middle Ages, and a partially reconstructed pre-Romanesque chapel of saints Felix and Adauctus; built at the turn of the 11th century, it was discovered during research work carried out in 1917. There is also a collection of beautiful glazed ceramic tiles dating from the 16th and 17th centuries, taken from the stoves that were once used to heat the palace.

Royal Cathedral

▽ Wawel Hill's spectacular cathedral, officially called the Cathedral of Saints Stanisław and Wacław, is one of the most important churches in Poland. Originally founded in 1020, the present cathedral is the third to stand on this site - it was completed in 1364 during the reign of Kamierz the Great. The traditional coronation and burial site of Polish monarchs, the cathedral has many fine features. Its series of chapels were constructed between 1517 and 1533 by Florentine architect Bartolommeo Berrecci, while the royal tombs in the cathedral and the Crypt of St. Leonard are a remnant of the 11th-century Cathedral of St. Wacław. They are the final resting place of numerous Polish rulers - among them Jadwiga, Poland's first female monarch - as well as national heroes and poets. The Cathedral Museum houses sacred art and a selection of royal regalia.

Collegium Maius

📍 Jagiellońska 15 🚌 152, 304, 502 🚊 2, 8, 13, 18 🕐 Hours vary, check website 🌐 maius.uj.edu.pl

This is the oldest building of the Jagiellonian University. In the 15th century, a number of houses were amalgamated to create lecture rooms and housing for professors. It was extensively remodeled in the mid-19th century. At the heart of the building is an attractive Gothic cloister. The University Museum moved here after World War II. Visitors can view the 16th-century Libraria and Great Hall, rooms still used by the Senate of the university, and the Treasury. The Copernicus Room is dedicated to the great astronomer, who studied here in 1491–5. Tours are obligatory; book in advance.

Kazimierz

🚌 184, 504 🚊 3, 19, 24

In the late 15th century, Kraków's Jewish quarter was established in the Kazimierz district, east of Wawel Hill. At the outbreak of World War II, there was a community of some 70,000 Jews. The Nazis moved them all to a ghetto across the river, from where

↑ A sun-dappled square within the Collegium Maius, part of the Jagiellonian University

they were eventually deported to concentration camps.

Amazingly, a number of Jewish sites have survived. The restored Old Synagogue now houses the Jewish Museum, while the Remu'h Synagogue (c. 1553) still functions. The latter is named after Rabbi Moses Remu'h, a 16th-century philosopher, whose nearby tomb attracts pilgrims from all over the world. Most of the graves were destroyed by the Nazis, but fragments have been piled up to form a "wailing wall."

Czartoryski Museum

📍 Św. Jana 19 🚌 152, 304, 502 🚊 2, 4, 7, 14, 18, 24 🕐 Closed for refurbishment 🌐 mnk.pl

The core of this museum is the art collection assembled by Princess Isabella Czartoryska in the late 18th century. It contains some magnificent paintings, notably Rembrandt's *Landscape with the Good Samaritan*. There is also a collection of decorative arts from all over Europe and a section on Polish history.

←

The small prayer hall of Remu'h Synagogue, in the Kazimierz district

Did You Know?

After his death in 1974, Schindler was buried in the cemetery on Mount Zion in Jerusalem.

Schindler's Factory and MOCAK

📍 Ul Lipowa 4 🚊 3, 19, 24 🕐 Apr–Oct: 9am–8pm daily (to 4pm Mon, to 2pm first Mon of month); Nov–Mar: 10am–6pm daily (to 2pm Mon) 🌐 mhk.pl

Located in the Zabłocie district, Schindler's Factory is a symbol of humanitarian courage. In 1943, the factory's German owner, Oskar Schindler, saved over 1,000 Jewish people from deportation to the death camps by employing them in his enamel factory and claiming that they were essential to the running of his business.

The factory, now part of the Historical Museum of the City of Kraków, features an exhibit entitled "Kraków under Nazi Occupation 1939–45." Everyday life for Kraków's inhabitants – from the last pre-war summer of 1939 until the arrival of the Red Army in

January 1945 – is illustrated using original documents, recordings, photographs, and installations. The fate of the Jewish population is a major theme, though lives of other citizens are detailed, notably the arrest and murder of prominent members of the city's intellectual and political elite. Poignant exhibits include a wall of photographs of those that Schindler saved.

A section of the building now houses MOCAK (Museum of Contemporary Art in Kraków), which displays the best of Polish contemporary art.

EAT

Wierzynek

Said to be the oldest restaurant in Kraków, Wierzynek takes inspiration from its history of producing lavish feasts for the royal court.

◨ Rynek Główny 15
🌐 wierzynek.pl

***

Szara Gęś

Feast on roast goose and venison at this outstanding - and opulent - eatery in a 14th-century building on the main square.

◨ Rynek Główny 17
🌐 szarages.com

***

Café Camelot

This cosy cafe serves a good choice of main meals and salads, and is known for some of the best apple pie in town.

◨ Świętego Tomasza 15
☎ 12 421 0123

BEYOND KRAKOW

3

Auschwitz-Birkenau Memorial and Museum

◨ Oświęcim 🔲
🕐 Hours vary, check website 🌐 auschwitz.org

Although the name Oświęcim means little to most non-Poles, its German form Auschwitz has become a byword for terror and genocide. It was here near the town of Oświęcim, about 35 miles (55 km) west of Kraków, that the Nazis established their largest complex of concentration and extermination camps. The Auschwitz camp opened in June 1940, and in March 1941 a much larger camp was set up at nearby Birkenau (Brzezinka in Polish). In all, an estimated 1.1 million people were murdered here. The vast majority of them were Jews, but victims also included large numbers of Poles, Soviet POWs, Romani, and political prisoners from all over Europe. The gas chambers, capable of killing thousands daily, were in use from 1942 to January 1945, when the camps were liberated by Soviet troops.

The area has been declared a UNESCO World Heritage Site and the two camps are preserved as the Muzeum Auschwitz-Birkenau – a memorial to its victims and a grim warning to future generations of humankind's capacity for inhumanity. Many structures were hastily destroyed as the Nazis left, in an attempt to hide the evidence of their activities, but the gate, with the chilling words "Arbeit macht frei" ("Work sets you free") above it, still stands. Advance booking of tickets and tours is advised.

The entrance to the ↓ Auschwitz-Birkenau Memorial and Museum

PRACTICAL
INFORMATION

Here you will find all the essential advice and information you will need before and during your stay in Poland.

AT A GLANCE

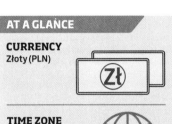

CURRENCY
Złoty (PLN)

TIME ZONE
CET/CEST. Central European Summer Time runs from the last Sunday in March to the last Sunday in October.

LANGUAGE
Polish

ELECTRICITY SUPPLY
Power sockets are types C and E, fitting two-pronged plugs. Standard voltage is 230V.

EMERGENCY NUMBERS

AMBULANCE	FIRE SERVICE
999	**998**

MEDICAL ADVICE	POLICE
94 39	**997**

TAP WATER
Unless otherwise stated, ordinary tap water in Poland is safe to drink.

Getting There

Poland is well connected with the rest of the world. International flights from some 90 cities in 40 countries arrive in Warsaw. The airports at Gdańsk, Katowice, Szczecin, Poznań, Wrocław, Olsztyn, Lublin, Rzeszów, and Kraków also have international flights, linking Poland with much of Western and Eastern Europe.

International train services run between all major European and Polish cities. The journeys by fast train from Warsaw to Prague and Berlin take just eight and seven hours respectively.

Numerous international bus routes connect large cities such as Warsaw and Kraków with other European destinations, and fares can be cheap compared to other modes of transport. The main operators in Poland are FlixBus, Eurolines, and National Express.

Personal Security

Poland is generally a safe country, but it is always a good idea to take sensible precautions against pickpockets. If you have anything stolen, report the crime as soon as possible to the nearest police station. Get a copy of the crime report in order to claim on your insurance.

Health

Citizens of the following countries are entitled to free medical treatment in Poland: EU members, Belarus, Tunisia, Ukraine, Mongolia, China, and the countries of the former Yugoslavia. For visitors from other countries, first aid is provided free of charge at hospitals, but other types of treatment may incur a charge. Nevertheless, all visitors are advised to take out full medical insurance before arriving in Poland. Minor health problems can often be dealt with in a pharmacy (*apteka*), where trained staff can provide advice.

Passports and Visas

Citizens of the US, EU, Australia, New Zealand, and countries of the European Free Trade Association need a valid passport to enter

Poland and can stay for up to 90 days without needing a visa. For visa information specific to your home country, consult your nearest Polish embassy or check online.

LGBT+ Safety

Although Poland has legalized homosexuality, it remains a conservative country in which LGBT+ communities have not always been met with acceptance. There are annual Equality Parades in Warsaw and Kraków, and both cities feature a growing handful of hotels, bars, and clubs that welcome members of the LGBT+ community. Elsewhere, same-sex couples may elicit a negative response from locals and business-owners.

Travelers with Specific Needs

Many main attractions and public buildings have wheelchair access, though it is recommended to call ahead to check accessibility. In Warsaw and Kraków, many trams and buses are wheelchair accessible; the electronic departure board at each stop informs passengers when the next wheelchair-friendly service is due to arrive. Hotels with four or more stars usually have wheelchair-friendly rooms, but these are often in short supply and should be booked well in advance.

Money

Major credit and debit cards are accepted in most shops, businesses, and railroad stations. They can't always be used in bus stations, cafés, and restaurants outside the big cities, however, or at small B&Bs and hostels, so it is a good idea to carry some cash, too. ATMs can be found at most banks, malls, and railroad stations. Cash can also be exchanged at a *kantor* (bureau de change) although rates often vary wildly.

Cell Phones and Wi-Fi

Visitors traveling to Poland with EU tariffs can use their devices without being affected by data roaming charges. Visitors from other countries should check their contracts before departure in order to avoid unexpected charges. Most hotels, cafés, and bars offer free Wi-Fi to customers. There are also free Wi-Fi hotspots in main railroad stations and in city centers.

Getting Around

Express rail lines connect almost all the big cities, and the trains are fast and usually arrive on time. Trains are run by a variety of companies. **PKP InterCity** runs express services and is the best way of traveling between Warsaw, Kraków, and other big cities; the trains have buffet facilities and Wi-Fi. **TLK,** part of the same company, also runs an express service; it is cheaper than InterCity but trains are slightly slower and with older, cramped carriages.

Intercity bus routes in Poland are run by a multitude of different companies. Buses are usually reasonably comfortable and many have additional services such as Wi-Fi. The main bus station in Kraków offers clear timetable information and a range of facilities. However, the situation in Warsaw is more complicated, with many bus operators using individual bus stands located around the Central Railway Station or the Palace of Culture and Science.

The number of intercity highways has increased dramatically in recent years, but much car travel remains on single-lane roads, and driving can be slow. While work to upgrade the road network is being carried out, drivers might be affected by delays. Wherever you drive in Poland, always carry your passport, car insurance, license, green card, and rental contract with you. All the major international car rental companies operate in Warsaw and Kraków.

PKP InterCity and TLK
🅦 intercity.pl

Visitor Information

Most Polish towns and cities have tourist information centers *(informacja turystyczna)*, very often positioned on the main square. They offer free maps and advice on sightseeing and transport options. The **Polish National Tourist Office** maintains branches abroad.

Polish National Tourist Office
🅦 poland.travel

INDEX

Page numbers in **bold** refer to main entries

Index

ACKNOWLEDGMENTS

Dorling Kindersley would like to thank the following people for their contributions to previous editions of the guide: John Ardagh, Rosemary Bailey, David Baird, Josie Barnard, Rosemary Barron, Gretel Beer, Ros Belford, Marc Bennetts, Willem de Blaauw, Kathleen Blankenship Sauret, Susie Boulton, Gerhard Bruschke, Caroline Bugler, Paula Canal, Chloe Carleton, Christopher Catling, Robin Clapp, Anthony Clark, Juliet Clough, Deidre Coffey, Dan Colwell, Marc Dubin, Paul Duncan, Sylvia Earley, Joanna Egert- Romanowska, Olivia Ercoli, Judith Fayard, Jane Foster, Stephanie Ferguson, Lisa Gerard-Sharp, Mike Gerrard, Jane Graham, Andrew Gumbel, Mark Harding, Andy Harris, Vicky Hayward, Zöe Hewetson, Sally Hogset, Adam Hopkins, Lindsay Hunt, Nick Inman, Tim Jepson, Colin Jones, Emma Jones, Marion Kaplan, Ciara Kenny, Alister Kershaw, Piotr Kozlowski, Wojciech Kozlowski, Sarah Lane, Michael Leapman, Philip Lee, Alec Lobrano, Sarah McAlister, Jerzy S. Majewski, Fred Mawer, Lynette Mitchell, Colin Nicholson, Melanie Nicholson-Hartzell, Roger Norum, Tadeusz Olsański, Małgorzata Omilanowska, Agnes Ördög, Robin Osborne, Lyn Parry, Robin Pascoe, Alice Peebles, Tim Perry, Polly Phillimore, Filip Polonski, Paul Richardson, Anthony Roberts, Barnaby Rogerson, Zöe Ross, Doug Sager, Kaj Sandell, Jürgen Scheunemann, Jane Shaw, Barbara Sobeck-Miller, Vladimír Soukup, Solveig Steinhardt, Robert Strauss, Martin Symington, Allan Tillier, Nigel Tisdall, Roger Thomas, Tanya Tsikas, Annika Tuominen, Alison Vagen, Gerard van Vuuren, Roger Williams, Timothy Wright, Scott Alexander Young.

The publisher would like to thank the following for their kind permission to reproduce their photographs:

Key: a-above; b-below/bottom; c-centre; f-far; l-left; r-right; t-top

2-3 Dreamstime.com: Georgios Tsichlis. **4 Alamy Stock Photo:** Tetra Images. **6-7 Dreamstime. com:** Nullplus. **8 Alamy Stock Photo:** Sergey Borisov (cla); eye35 (clb). **Dreamstime.com:** Iryna Vlasenko (cl). **8-9 Alamy Stock Photo:** Novarc Images / Stefano Paterna (b). **10 Alamy Stock Photo:** rudi1976 (ca). **Getty Images:** Taxi / Ascent Xmedia / Milo Zanecchia (clb). **10-1 Dreamstime. com:** Maurizio De Mattei / © Pyramide du Louvre, arch I.M. Pei / Musée du Louvre (b). **11 4Corners:** Luca Da Ros (t). **Alamy Stock Photo:** Janna Danilova (br); Dennis MacDonald (cr). **12 4Corners:** Luigi Vaccarella (t). **Getty Images:** Photographer's Choice / Bruno de Hogues (clb). **12-3 Alamy Stock Photo:** Rodolfo Contreras (b). **13 4Corners:** Maurizio Rellini (t). **Pilsner Urquell/ SABMiller:** (br). **SO36- Sub Opus 36 e.V.:** Prokura Nepp (cr). **16 Getty Images:** Moment / Rich Jones Photography (c). **17 4Corners:** Francesco Carovillano (bl). **Alamy Stock Photo:** Richard Green (tr). **18 Alamy Stock Photo:** eye35.pix (t). **19 AWL Images:** Francesco Riccardo Iacomino (t). **iStockphoto.com:** Nikada (cb). **20 Alamy Stock Photo:** Peter Herbert (t). **21 iStockphoto.com:** E+ / ChrisHepburn (cb); ipag (tl). **22 Dreamstime. com:** Rudi1976 (bl). **iStockphoto.com:** Nikada (t). **23 iStockphoto.com:** E+ / wilpunt (t). **24 Getty**

Images: Photographer's Choice / Mike Hill (br). **iStockphoto.com:** bluejayphoto (tl). **25 Getty Images:** Moment / Lingxiao Xie (tl). **iStockphoto. com:** E+ / izhairguns (br). **26 4Corners:** Massimiliano De Santis (tl). **Dreamstime.com:** Izabela 23 (br). **27 4Corners:** Maurizio Rellini (bl). **iStockphoto.com:** Poike (t). **28 Alamy Stock Photo:** John Bracegirdle (bl); Alan Novelli (t); robertharding / ProCip (cr). **Getty Images:** NurPhoto / Nicolas Economou (crb). **30 123RF. com:** Mareandmare (t). **Alamy Stock Photo:** Philipus (cr); Arie Storm (bl). **Dreamstime.com:** Anyaivanova (crb). **32 Alamy Stock Photo:** Ian Dagnall (tl); Hervé Lenain (tr); Laurence Delderfield (cra). **33 123RF.com:** freeprod (tl). **Alamy Stock Photo:** John Kellerman (tr); Olrat (cla). **34 Alamy Stock Photo:** Mikehoward (crb). **Dreamstime.com:** Luciano Mortula (t). **Getty Images:** Moritz Wolf (cr). **iStockphoto.com:** stefanopolitimarkovina (bl). **36 Alamy Stock Photo:** Sorin Colac (bl); Kirk Fisher (t); Phillip Thomas (crb). **Dreamstime.com:** Evgeniy Fesenko (cr). **38 Alamy Stock Photo:** B.O'Kane (tl). **Dreamstime.com:** Ioan Florin Cnejevici (cla). **38-9 Dreamstime.com:** Minnystock (ca). **iStockphoto. com:** csfotoimages (t). **39 Alamy Stock Photo:** Robertharding / Oliver Wintzen (tr). **40 4Corners:** Claudio Cassaro (t). **Alamy Stock Photo:** MARKA / giulio andreini / exhibition of work by Sigmar Ploke at art museum, Kunsthaus,Zurich © The Estate of Sigmar Polke, Cologne / © DACS 2020 (cr); Stefano Politi Markovina (bl). **Dreamstime. com:** Evgeniy Fesenko (crb). **42 AWL Images:** Sabine Lubenow / Fosters + Partners (cr). **Dreamstime.com:** Abxyz (crb). **iStockphoto.com:** Leonardo Patrizi (t). **Robert Harding Picture Library:** Neale Clark (bl). **44 Alamy Stock Photo:** Thomas Zobl (cla). **Dreamstime.com:** Sorin Colac (tl). **44-5 Alamy Stock Photo:** Robertharding / Frank Fell (ca); Alex Segre (t). **45 Alamy Stock Photo:** Anna Stowe Travel (tr). **46 4Corners:** Gabriele Croppi (tl). **Alamy Stock Photo:** Imagedoc (tr). **46-7 Dreamstime.com:** fotoVoyager (ca). **47 4Corners:** Maurizio Rellini (tl). **Alamy Stock Photo:** Aleksandar Kostadinovski (tr). **48 iStockphoto.com:** E+ / xavierarnau (tl). **48-9 iStockphoto.com:** Ventdusud (b). **49 Dreamstime.com:** Tomas Marek (br). **iStockphoto.com:** E+ / Mlenny (tr); Nikada (cb). **50 Dreamstime.com:** Marcin Jucha (b). **iStockphoto.com:** _ultraforma_ (tr). **51 Alamy Stock Photo:** Sueddeutsche Zeitung Photo / Jose Giribas (tr). **Dreamstime.com:** Dreamer82 (cla). **Getty Images:** Cultura / Nils Hendrik Mueller (cr). **iStockphoto.com:** RossHelen (bl). **52 iStockphoto.com:** E+ / lillisphotography (tl). **52-3 Alamy Stock Photo:** Adrian Sherratt (b). **53 Alamy Stock Photo:** Norman Price (cb). **Dreamstime.com:** Luca Lorenzelli (tr); Tonyv3112. **54 Dreamstime.com:** Perseomedusa (tr). **SuperStock:** Prisma / Raga Jose Fuste (b). **55 Depositphotos Inc:** masterlu (tr). **Dreamstime. com:** Kirill Bobrov (cl); Meinzahn / © Architects R. Ricciotti et R. Carta / Mucem (crb). **56 Van Gogh Museum, Amsterdam (Vincent van Gogh Foundation):** (tr). **56-7 Munchmuseet 2015:** (b). **57 Alamy Stock Photo:** Ian Dagnall / © Succession Picasso / DACS, London 2020 (tr). **Dreamstime.com:** Photogolfer (c). **Rijksmuseum, Amsterdam:** Erik Smits (br). **58 Alamy Stock Photo:** Henk Meijer (t). **iStockphoto.com:** borchee (b). **59 Alamy Stock Photo:** Jürgen Feuerer (tr). **Dreamstime.com:** Vogelsp (cla).

60 **Alamy Stock Photo:** allOver images (cra); dpa picture alliance (tl). **iStockphoto.com:** Alphotographic (b). **61 Alamy Stock Photo:** Boaz Rottem (cr). **Dreamstime.com:** Typhoonski (bl). **Plymouth Gin:** (t). **62 Alamy Stock Photo:** geogphotos (bl). **iStockphoto.com:** danefromspain (b). **63 Alamy Stock Photo:** Petr Svarc (tr). **Getty Images:** AFP / Fabrica Coffrini (br); ullstein bild / Fishman (cl). **64 Alamy Stock Photo:** Wales UK (tr). **Dreamstime.com:** Szymon Kaczmarczyk (b). **65 Alamy Stock Photo:** imageBROKER / Peter Giovannini (cr). **Dreamstime.com:** Michelangelo Oprandi (bl); Unaphoto (cla). **The Viking Ship Museum, Denmark:** (tr). **66 Alamy Stock Photo:** mauritius images GmbH / Udo Bernhart (tr). **iStockphoto. com:** knape (b). **67 Dreamstime.com:** Dimaberkut (crb). **Getty Images:** NurPhoto / Nicolas Liponne (cla). **Lisdoonvarna Festival:** (tr). **68 iStockphoto.com:** MikeMareen (tr). **68-9 iStockphoto.com:** E+ / Maica (b). **69 Alamy Stock Photo:** David Davies (br). **Getty Images:** Lonely Planet Images / David C Tomlinson (clb). **iStockphoto.com:** Olena_Znak (tr). **70-1 Alamy Stock Photo:** dreamer4787 (t). **70 Alamy Stock Photo:** Stefano Politi Markovina (bl). **71 Alamy Stock Photo:** TCD / Prod.DB (cl). **Getty Images:** Moviepix / Silver Screen Collection (b). **72 Alamy Stock Photo:** Jeff Rotman (tr). **Getty Images:** Moment / MassanPH (b); NurPhoto / Artur Widak (cla). **73 4Corners:** Richard Taylor (t). **Getty Images:** Hulton Archive / Hiroyuki Ito (b). **iStockphoto.com:** E+ / gilaxia (cr). **74 Alamy Stock Photo:** Cum Okolo (bl). **Dreamstime.com:** Jackmalipan (t). **75 Alamy Stock Photo:** Prisma by Dukas Presseagentur GmbH / TPX (tr); Jack Sullivan (cla); Riccardo Sala (b). **Museum der Dinge:** Armin Herrmann, 2016 (cr). **76 Dreamstime.com:** Luka Mjeda (cra); Tanaonte (crb). **Getty Images:** AFP / Herbert Neubauerr (cla); Tristan Fewings (cr). **iStockphoto.com:** kamisoka (clb); omersukrugoksu (cl). **77 Alamy Stock Photo:** Fabrizio Malisan (cl). **Dreamstime.com:** Alexlinch (clb); Rudmer Zwerver (tr). **Getty Images:** AFP / Fabrice Coffrini (cr); Anadolu Agency / Burak Akbulut (tl). **iStockphoto.com:** Flavio Vallenari (crb). **78 Alamy Stock Photo:** Funkyfood London - Paul Williams (bc); North Wind Picture Archives (t); Science History Images / Photo Researchers (crb). **79 Alamy Stock Photo:** Falkensteinfoto (br); Glasshouse Images / JT Vintage (tl); North Wind Picture Archives (cla); Hercules Milas (cr). **Dreamstime.com:** Perseomedusa (b). **80-1 iStockphoto.com:** ZU_09 (t). **80 Alamy Stock Photo:** De Luan (bl); North Wind Picture Archives (tl). **Bridgeman Images:** © Giancarlo Costa (cla). **Getty Images:** Universal Images Group / Universal History Archive (crb). **81 Alamy Stock Photo:** Ian Dagnall (tr); Science History Images / Photo Researchers (bl). **82 Dreamstime.com:** Georgios Kollidas (crb). **Getty Images:** Corbis Historical / Michael Nicholson (t). **iStockphoto.com:** sitox (bl). **83 Alamy Stock Photo:** Ian Dagnall (cr); Historical Images Archive (tl); LOC Photo (tr); Trinity Mirror / Mirrorpix (crb). **Bridgeman Images:** (cla). **84 Alamy Stock Photo:** The History Emporium (tl); World History Archive (cb). **84-5 Alamy Stock Photo:** Everett Collection Inc (t). **85 Alamy Stock Photo:** Granger Historical Picture Archive / NYC (tr); Pictorial Press Ltd (bl); John Frost Newspapers (cb). **86 Alamy Stock Photo:** Agencja Forum / Chris Niedenthal / FORUM (crb); Everett Collection Historical / CSU Archives (tl). **Bridgeman Images:** © Gerald Bloncourt (bc). **86-7 Alamy Stock Photo:** Agencja Fotograficzna Caro / Kaiser (t). **87 Dreamstime.com:** Erik De Graaf (cb). **Getty Images:** AFP / Dan Chung (tr); NurPhoto / Jaap Arriens (cra). **88-9 4Corners:** Francesco Carovillano. **90-1 Getty Images:** Moment / Rich Jones Photography. **94-5 4Corners:** Susanne Kremer (t). **96 Alamy Stock Photo:** Chronicle (bc); travelibUK (clb); De Luan (br). **Getty Images:** Hulton Archive / Print Collector (b). **97 Alamy Stock Photo:** Chronicle (bl); Heritage Image Partnership Ltd / London Metropolitan Archives (City of London) (bc); dpa picture alliance archive / Boris Roessler (br). **98 Alamy Stock Photo:** Zoonar GmbH/Andriy Kravchenko (b). **iStockphoto.com:** ZambeziShark (clb). **99 Alamy Stock Photo:** EThamPhoto (tr). **100-1 Alamy Stock Photo:** travellinglight (t). **101 4Corners:** Maurizio Rellini (br). **102 Alamy Stock Photo:** Malcolm Fairman (cla). **102-3 Dreamstime.com:** Andersastphoto (b). **103 123RF.com:** flik47 (clb). **Alamy Stock Photo:** Kumar Sriskandan (tr); travelpix (cl). **104 iStockphoto.com:** stockinasia (t). **104-5 Dreamstime.com:** I Wei Huang (b). **105 Alamy Stock Photo:** Peter Barritt (cb). **106-7 Robert Harding Picture Library:** Markus Lange (b). **107 Alamy Stock Photo:** travelpix (tr). **108 Dreamstime.com:** Dilyana Nikolova (t). **109 4Corners:** Olimpio Fantuz (br). **110 Alamy Stock Photo:** roger tillberg (tl). **110-1 Dreamstime.com:** Juliengrondin (b). **111 iStockphoto.com:** Nikada (tc). **112 Alamy Stock Photo:** Heritage Image Partnership Ltd / Historic England (br). **Getty Images:** Corbis Historical / Fine Art / VCG Wilson (bc). **113 Alamy Stock Photo:** Alan King engraving (bl/SIR WALTER); World History Archive (br/Rudolf Hess). **Getty Images:** Hulton Archive / Culture Club (br). **iStockphoto.com:** espiegle (tr). **SuperStock:** Mauritius (bl). **115 Alamy Stock Photo:** Tony Watson (br). **117 Dreamstime.com:** Marcorubino (cr). **118-9 iStockphoto.com:** Plan-T (b). **120 Alamy Stock Photo:** Steve Vidler (bl). **121 Alamy Stock Photo:** Ian G Dagnall (tr); Prisma by Dukas Presseagentur GmbH / TPX (cra). **122 Dreamstime.com:** Christine Bird (bl). **123 Alamy Stock Photo:** imageBROKER / Moritz Wolf (t). **124 Dreamstime.com:** Ollie Taylor (t). **126-7 Shutterstock:** aroundworld (b). **127 Alamy Stock Photo:** eye35.pix (tl). **128 Alamy Stock Photo:** age fotostock / Sebastian Wasek (tl). **128-9 Alamy Stock Photo:** Ian Dagnall Commercial Collection (b). **129 Dreamstime.com:** Philip Bird (c). **130 Alamy Stock Photo:** Steve Vidler (bl). **131 123RF. com:** pavel dudek (b). **133 Alamy Stock Photo:** Ian Dagnall Commercial Collection / © Blenheim Palace 2019 (cra). **iStockphoto.com:** OlegAlbinsky (t). **134 Getty Images:** Radius Images / JW (b). **135 Alamy Stock Photo:** Ian G Dagnall (tl); Mark Waugh (bc). **136 Getty Images:** Moment / John and Tina Reid (bl). **136-7 AWL Images:** Alan Copson (t). **138 Alamy Stock Photo:** Mike Kipling Photography (t). **140 Dreamstime.com:** Richie Chan (t). **142 Alamy Stock Photo:** eye35 (t). **143 Alamy Stock Photo:** robertharding / Neale Clark (br). **144-5 4Corners:** Susanne Kremer (b). **145 Alamy Stock Photo:** Iain Masterton (tr). **Picfair. com:** Caitlyn Stewart (t). **146 Alamy Stock Photo:** Ian Dagnall (tl). **146-7 iStockphoto.com:** ALBAimagery (b). **147 Alamy Stock Photo:** robertharding / Ann & Steve Toon (tr). **150-1 Alamy Stock Photo:** Richard Green.

154 Getty Images: Moment / Sergiu Cozorici (t); Moment Unreleased / maydays (cra). **156 Alamy Stock Photo:** Greg Balfour Evans (cl). **156-7 © National Gallery of Ireland:** Fennell Photography / Chris Bellew (b). **157 Alamy Stock Photo:** Martin Thomas Photography (tr). **158 Getty Images:** Perspectives / Peter Zoeller (tr). **159 Alamy Stock Photo:** H.S. Photos (br). **Getty Images:** Perspectives / IIC / Axiom (ca). **Office of Public Works, Dublin Castle:** David Davison (tr, cr). **160-1 Getty Images:** Moment Open / David Soanes Photography (t). **161 AWL Images:** Maurizio Rellini (br). **iStockphoto.com:** rimglow (tr). **162 Alamy Stock Photo:** Nazrie Abu Seman (tl). **162-3 Alamy Stock Photo:** Kay Roxby (b). **164 Alamy Stock Photo:** incamerastock / ICP (cl). **165 Getty Images:** Photographer's Choice / Bill Heinsohn (tr). **166 Alamy Stock Photo:** Eye Ubiquitous / Hugh Rooney (bl). **166-7 Dreamstime.com:** Robert Mokronowski (t). **168 Getty Images:** Chris Hill (bl). **169 Dreamstime. com:** Madrugadaverde (t). **170 Alamy Stock Photo:** Stephen Saks Photography (cb). **Dorling Kindersley:** Bunratty Castle, County Clare, Ireland / Joe Cornish (bl). **Dreamstime.com:** Patryk Kosmider (cl). **172 Dreamstime.com:** Pajda83 (clb). **Getty Images:** Moment / Peter Zelei Images (b). **173 Dreamstime.com:** Stefano Valeri (tr). **174 Alamy Stock Photo:** Ian Dagnall (tl). **175 Getty Images:** Chris Hill (b). **178-9 4Corners:** Francesco Carovillano. **182 Dreamstime.com:** Francoisroux (t). **183 Getty Images:** Gallo Images / Ayhan Altun (tr). **184 Dreamstime.com:** Astormfr (bl). **184-5 Alamy Stock Photo:** imageBROKER / Giovanni Guarino (t). **186 Alamy Stock Photo:** Stefano Ravera (tl). **187 Alamy Stock Photo:** Peter Forsberg (b). **188-9 Dreamstime.com:** Maurizio De Mattei / © Pyramide du Louvre, arch I.M. Pei / Musée du Louvre (t). **189 Alamy Stock Photo:** Peter Barritt (tl). **Dreamstime.com:** Maryna Kordiumova (crb/Coronation); Bo Li / © Pyramide du Louvre, arch I.M. Pei / Musée du Louvre (t). **190 Alamy Stock Photo:** Todd Anderson (cr). **Getty Images:** Corbis Historical / Photo Josse / Leemage (bl). **SuperStock:** 4X5 Collection (tl). **191 Alamy Stock Photo:** Peter Horree (br). **RMN:** Photo (C) RMN-Grand Palais (musée du Louvre) / Peter Willi (tl). **192 Alamy Stock Photo:** theendup (t). **193 Dreamstime. com:** Ukrphoto (br). **194 Dreamstime.com:** MrFly (clb). **Getty Images:** Hulton Archive / Roger Viollet (bl). **194-5 Getty Images:** Moment / MathieuRivrin. **196-7 Dreamstime.com:** Evolove (t). **196 Dreamstime.com:** Worakan Thaomor (br). **198-9 Alamy Stock Photo:** UlyssePixel (t). **200 Picfair.com:** Benis Arapovic (clb). **201 Dreamstime.com:** Minacarson (t). **202 Getty Images:** Photolibrary / Julian Elliott Photography (b). **203 CSI:** © E. Luider / EPPDCSI (tr). **204-5 Dreamstime.com:** Dennis Dolkens (b). **205 Alamy Stock Photo:** Elena Korchenko (t). **AWL Images:** Danita Delimont Stock (cla). **Dreamstime.com:** Photofires (cra). **206 123RF.com:** Francesco Bucchi (c). **206-7 Alamy Stock Photo:** Pawel Libera Images (b). **207 Dreamstime.com:** Mathias Pfauwadel (tr). **208 Alamy Stock Photo:** Aurelian Images (bc); Sorin Colac (t). **209 123RF.com:** Luciano Mortula (bl). **211 Alamy Stock Photo:** Marco Cattaneo (cra); Hemis.fr / René Mattes (tr). **212 Alamy Stock Photo:** travellinglight (bl). **212-3 Dreamstime.com:** Olgacov (t). **214-5 123RF.com:** Boris Stroujko (t). **215 Alamy Stock Photo:** ART Collection (clb); Art Collection 2 (bc).

Dreamstime.com: Davide Lo Dico (cl). **216-7 Alamy Stock Photo:** Art Kowalsky (t). **217 Alamy Stock Photo:** Manfred Gottschalk (bl). **219 Alamy Stock Photo:** imageBROKER / Martin Dr.Schulte-Kellinghaus (t). **Dreamstime.com:** Trudywsimmons (cra). **220-1 Alamy Stock Photo:** DanieleC (t). **222 Alamy Stock Photo:** age fotostock / Javier Larrea (br). **223 Alamy Stock Photo:** Peter Horree (br); Jan Wlodarczyk (t). **224 Dreamstime.com:** Rosshelen (tl). **225 Getty Images:** National Geographic Image Collection / Sisse Brimberg (b). **226 AWL Images:** GUY Christian (bl). **226-7 Alamy Stock Photo:** Alpineguide (t). **228 4Corners:** Maurizio Rellini (t). **229 Alamy Stock Photo:** Ian Dagnall (tr). **231 123RF.com:** pavel dudek (t). **232 123RF.com:** pavel dudek (b). **233 4Corners:** Susanne Kremer (tl). **236-7 Alamy Stock Photo:** eye35.pix. **240-1 Dreamstime.com:** Vichaya Kiatyingangsulee (t). **242 Alamy Stock Photo:** Bombaert Patrick. **243 AWL Images:** Jason Langley (cra). **244 Alamy Stock Photo:** Ian Dagnall (cra); John Kellerman (t). **245 Dreamstime.com:** Demerzel21 (bc). **246 Alamy Stock Photo:** Art Kowalsky (b). **246-7 Alamy Stock Photo:** eye35.pix (t). **248-9 Dreamstime.com:** Alexugalek (b). **249 Alamy Stock Photo:** Agenzia Sintes / Fabio Fiorani / Fabio Mazzarella (tr). **250 4Corners:** Günter Gräfenhain (tl). **250-1 Alamy Stock Photo:** Nattee Chalermtiragool (b). **252 Alamy Stock Photo:** Brian Jannsen (t). **254 Dreamstime.com:** Mistervlad (cla). **255 Alamy Stock Photo:** David Kleyn (tr). **256 Dreamstime.com:** Itsanan Sampuntarat (bl). **257 Alamy Stock Photo:** David Kleyn (br). **iStockphoto.com:** querbeet (t). **260-1 AWL Images:** Francesco Riccardo Iacomino. **264 Dreamstime.com:** Olgacov (t). **265 Alamy Stock Photo:** mauritius images GmbH / Rene Mattes (clb). **266 Alamy Stock Photo:** Robert vant Hoenderdaal (bl). **266-7 Museum Het Rembrandthuis:** Mike Bink (t). **268 Robert Harding Picture Library:** Hans Zaglitsch (tl). **269 123RF.com:** Nattee Chalermtiragool (b). **Alamy Stock Photo:** Granger Historical Picture Archive / NYC (tr). **270-1 123RF.com:** macfromlondon (t). **271 123RF.com:** Markus Gann (b). **272-3 Alamy Stock Photo:** Angela Chalmers (b). **273 Alamy Stock Photo:** Iain Masterton (cla). **Picfair.com:** Johannes Tönne (tl). **274 Dreamstime.com:** Jjfarq (t). **274-5 123RF.com:** mediagram (b). **275 Rijksmuseum, Amsterdam:** (cra, cla, bc). **276-7 Dreamstime.com:** Alexander Tolstykh (t). **276 Alamy Stock Photo:** Cyrille Gibot (bl). **278 Alamy Stock Photo:** Sara Winter (cla). **Dreamstime.com:** Oleg Bashkirov (b). **279 Alamy Stock Photo:** Prisma by Dukas Presseagentur GmbH / Van der Meer Rene (tl). **Dreamstime.com:** Colette6 (br). **280 Dreamstime.com:** TasFoto (t). **281 Dreamstime.com:** Vasilis Ververidis (b). **282-3 Dreamstime.com:** VanderWolfImages (t). **282 Dreamstime.com:** Kuan Leong Yong (br). **286-7 iStockphoto.com:** Nikada. **291 Alamy Stock Photo:** Factofoto (t). **292 Alamy Stock Photo:** pocholo (t). **293 Alamy Stock Photo:** Hemis.fr / Alessio Mamo (bl). **294-5 Alamy Stock Photo:** Sean Pavone (b). **295 Alamy Stock Photo:** Tomobis (tr). **AWL Images:** Hemis (cla). **296 Alamy Stock Photo:** age fotostock / Paco Gómez García (t). **296-7 Alamy Stock Photo:** Alex Segre (b). **297 Alamy Stock Photo:** The Archives (br); Prisma Archivo (clb); incamerastock / ICP (cra). **298 Alamy Stock Photo:** Art Kowalsky / Art Kowalsky / Museo Nacional Centro De Arte Reina

Sofia / Brushstroke (1996) By Roy Lichtenstein © Estate Of Roy Lichtenstein / DACS, London 2020 (t). **299 Alamy Stock Photo:** dleiva (bl). **300 Alamy Stock Photo:** Luis Dafos (bl). **301 Robert Harding Picture Library:** Charles Bowman (tr). **302-3 Alamy Stock Photo:** Factofoto (t). **304 Alamy Stock Photo:** Horizon Images / Motion (tl). **304-5 Alamy Stock Photo:** Jerónimo Alba (tr). **305 Alamy Stock Photo:** World History Archive (tr). **306 Dreamstime.com:** Sean Pavone (t). **306-7 iStockphoto.com:** Syldavia (b). **307 Dreamstime. com:** Alfonsodetomas (cra). **308 Getty Images:** Photolibrary / Maremagnum (b). **309 Alamy Stock Photo:** age fotostock / Bruno Almela (cla). **iStockphoto.com:** MarquesPhotography (t). **310-1 Alamy Stock Photo:** Factofoto (t). **312 iStockphoto.com:** Kike_Fernandez (t). **313 iStockphoto.com:** Lux Blue (b). **314-5 Alamy Stock Photo:** Travelscape Images (t). **315 Alamy Stock Photo:** Stefano Politi Markovina (tl). **316-7 Robert Harding Picture Library:** Richard Martin (t). **317 Alamy Stock Photo:** Prisma by Dukas Presseagentur GmbH / Raga Jose Fuste (br). **318 Alamy Stock Photo:** mauritius images GmbH / Jose Fuste Raga (t). **320 iStockphoto.com:** E+ / ferrantraite (tl). **321 Alamy Stock Photo:** Stefano Politi Markovina (b). **322 Alamy Stock Photo:** Michael Abid (bl). **323 Alamy Stock Photo:** robertharding / Neale Clark (cra); Camila Se (tr). **324 Dreamstime.com:** Saiko3p (tl). **325 Dreamstime.com:** Georgios Tsichlis (b). **326 Alamy Stock Photo:** Jan Wlodarczyk (bl). **327 Alamy Stock Photo:** Ken Welsh (b). **329 Alamy Stock Photo:** Endless Travel (cra); Matthias Scholz (t). **Dorling Kindersley:** Max Alexander (br). **330-1 Alamy Stock Photo:** travellinglight (t). **331 Alamy Stock Photo:** Paul Melling (b). **332-3 Alamy Stock Photo:** Cultura Creative (RF) / Marco Simoni (b). **333 Alamy Stock Photo:** Ian Dagnall (tr). **334 Dreamstime.com:** Sorin Colac (t). **336-7 Alamy Stock Photo:** Jürgen Feuerer (t). **337 Dreamstime.com:** Cezary Wojtkowski (cra). **Robert Harding Picture Library:** Lucas Vallecillos (br). **338 Dreamstime.com:** Marcin Jucha (tc). **338-9 Getty Images:** Moment / fhm (b). **339 iStockphoto.com:** stefanopolitimarkovina (tr). **340 Dreamstime.com:** Sean Pavone (b). **342 Dreamstime.com:** Irina Paley (t). **344-5 iStockphoto.com:** SeanPavonePhoto (t). **344 Dreamstime.com:** Raul Garcia Herrera (bl). **345 iStockphoto.com:** sorincolac (br). **348-9 Alamy Stock Photo:** Peter Herbert. **352-3 Getty Images:** Moment Open / PEC Photo (t). **354 Getty Images:** Universal Images Group / Jeff Greenberg (b). **355 Alamy Stock Photo:** StockPhotosArt - Landmarks / Sofia Pereira (br). **356 iStockphoto.com:** LordRunar (bl). **357 Alamy Stock Photo:** RosaIreneBetancourt 14 (tl). **358-9 Dreamstime. com:** Sean Pavone (t). **359 Dreamstime.com:** Vladimir Korostyshevskiy (br). **360 Dreamstime. com:** Leonid Andronov (cl). **361 Dreamstime. com:** Meinzahn (cla). **iStockphoto.com:** luniversa (cr); urf (tl). **362 iStockphoto.com:** gregobagel (bl). **363 Dreamstime.com:** Pierre Jean Durieu (cla); Sean Pavone (t). **364 Dreamstime.com:** Ettore Bordieri (bc). **iStockphoto.com:** SeanPavonePhoto (clb). **SuperStock:** age fotostock / Eduardo Grund (bl). **365 Alamy Stock Photo:** M.Sobreira (br). **366 Alamy Stock Photo:** The Picture Art Collection (bl). **366-7 Picfair.com:** Tiago Sousa (t). **367 Dreamstime.com:** Zts (bl). **368 Dreamstime.com:** Martin Lehmann (t). **369 Alamy Stock Photo:** Cro Magnon (bl).

370 Alamy Stock Photo: Mikehoward 2 (bl). **370-1 Dreamstime.com:** Dan Grytsku (t). **371 Dreamstime.com:** Anamomarques (br). **374-5 iStockphoto.com:** ipag. **378 iStockphoto.com:** Moment / Alexander Spatari (cra). **379 Alamy Stock Photo:** adam eastland (cra). **380 iStockphoto. com:** TatyanaGl (bl). **381 iStockphoto.com:** DigitalVision Vectors / ZU_09 (tc); E+ / georgeclerk (cla). **Robert Harding Picture Library:** Neale Clark (cra). **382-3 123RF.com:** manjik (b). **383 Alamy Stock Photo:** Dennis Hallinan (cl); Mikel Bilbao Gorostiaga- Travels / *Sfera con sfera, 1989-1990/ bronze, ø 400 cm/Città del Vaticano/ Musei Vaticani/ Cortile della Pigna* by Arnaldo Pomodoro (tl). **Dreamstime.com:** Alexey Belyaev (tr). **384 Getty Images:** Universal Images Group (br). **384 Getty Images:** Moment / joe daniel price (br). **385 AWL Images:** Maurizio Rellini (t). **386 500px:** Gabi Rusu (t). **Dreamstime.com:** Scaliger (b). **387 Alamy Stock Photo:** IanDagnall Computing (tr). **388 iStockphoto.com:** lillisphotography (cl). **388-9 123RF.com:** Iakov Kalinin (b). **389 Dreamstime.com:** Noppasin Wongchum (t). **390 Alamy Stock Photo:** age fotostock / Historical Views (bl); UlyssePixel (t). **391 Getty Images:** Stefano Montesi - Corbis (bl). **392-3 Dreamstime. com:** Alexander Tolstykh (t). **392 Dreamstime. com:** Sergii Koval (bc). **394 iStockphoto.com:** Romaoslo (cra). **394-5 Alamy Stock Photo:** Ken Welsh (b). **396-7 Dreamstime.com:** Martin Molcan (t). **398 Alamy Stock Photo:** Gunter Kirsch (b). **399 Dreamstime.com:** M. Rohana (tr). **400 Alamy Stock Photo:** Fabrizio Troiani (t). **401 Dreamstime.com:** Anna Pakutina (cra). **402-3 Dreamstime.com:** Photogolfer (b). **404-5 iStockphoto.com:** E+ / borchee (t). **404 Alamy Stock Photo:** funkyfood London - Paul Williams (cr). **405 Alamy Stock Photo:** John Kellerman (tc). **406 Alamy Stock Photo:** Kirk Fisher (t). **407 Dreamstime.com:** Veronika Galkina (b). **408-9 iStockphoto.com:** Eileen_10 (b). **409 Getty Images:** AFP / Alberto Pizzoli (tl); Mondadori Portfolio (cra); Corbis Historical / Fine Art / VCG Wilson (cla); Hulton Fine Art Collection / Mondadori Portfolio / Archivio Quattrone (c); Corbis Historical / Summerfield Press (br). **410 Dreamstime.com:** Jenifoto406 (t); Zummolo2014 (bl). **411 Alamy Stock Photo:** Art Kowalsky (bl). **412 123RF.com:** jakobbradlgruber (b). **413 Dreamstime.com:** Luciano Mortula (t). **SuperStock:** imageBROKER / Barbara Boensch (br). **414 iStockphoto.com:** Faabi (b). **415 Alamy Stock Photo:** World History Archive (crb). **SuperStock:** age fotostock / Vdovin (b). **416-7 Dreamstime.com:** Andrey Omelyanchuk (t). **416 123RF.com:** Giuseppe Anello (cl). **418 Dreamstime.com:** Minnystock (t). **418-9 Dreamstime.com:** Marco Saracco (t). **419 Alamy Stock Photo:** Wire.Dog (tr). **420 Dreamstime. com:** Rudi1976 (tl). **421 iStockphoto.com:** bluejayphoto (b). **423 Dreamstime.com:** Minnystock (t). **425 Alamy Stock Photo:** Prisma Archivo (cra/Engraving). **Dreamstime.com:** Emicristea (cra); Denis Lazarenko (br); William Perry (tr). **Getty Images:** De Agostini Picture Library (ca); Universal Images Group / PHAS (tl). **426 Getty Images:** LightRocket / Frank Bienewald (t). **427 Getty Images:** Mondadori Portfolio (br). **429 Dreamstime.com:** Andrey Omelyanchuk (t, cra). **430 Dreamstime.com:** Eliane Haykal (tr). **430-1 SuperStock:** AGF / a gf photo / Smith Mark Edward (b). **431 SuperStock:** age fotostock / Marco Brivio (cl).

432 Dreamstime.com: Giuseppemasci (bl).
433 Dreamstime.com: Stefano Armaroli (t). 434
iStockphoto.com: ArtMarie (t). 435 Dreamstime.
com: Alfiofer (cra); Alvaro German Vilela (bl).
436 Dreamstime.com: Minnystock (t). 437
Dreamstime.com: Dzianis Rabtsevich (bl).
438 Alamy Stock Photo: REDA &CO srl / Riccardo
Lombardo (tl). 438-9 Dreamstime.com:
Michelangelo Oprandi (b). 439 Dreamstime.com:
Alberto Masnovo (tr). 442-3 iStockphoto.com: E+
/ ChrisHepburn. 446 iStockphoto.com:
tanukiphoto (t). 447 iStockphoto.com: Czgur (t).
448 Alamy Stock Photo: Jan Wlodarczyk (clb).
448-9 Alamy Stock Photo: sanga park (b). 449
Alamy Stock Photo: Florilegius (ca); James Davis
Photography (tr); Sergio Monti (cla). Getty
Images: Hulton Archive / Print Collector / Ann
Ronan Pictures (tc). 450-1 Dreamstime.com:
Georgios Tsichlis (b). 451 Alamy Stock Photo:
Konstantinos Tsakalidis (tr). Dreamstime.com:
Alvaro German Vilela (cb). 452-3 Alamy Stock
Photo: Peter Eastland (t). 453 Alamy Stock
Photo: Peter Eastland (bl). 454-5 Alamy Stock
Photo: MB_Photo (t). 454 123RF.com: saiko3p
(cr). 455 Alamy Stock Photo: Hemis.fr / Franck
Guiziou (bc). 456-7 Dreamstime.com: Stanislav
Moroz (b). 457 Alamy Stock Photo: Granger
Historical Picture Archive / NYC (tr). 458 Alamy
Stock Photo: Jan Wlodarczyk (bl). 459 Alamy
Stock Photo: Michele Falzone (cra); Jan
Wlodarczyk (t). 460-1 Alamy Stock Photo: Alex
Archontakis (b). 461 Alamy Stock Photo: Stefano
Paterna (tl). 462 Alamy Stock Photo: Peter
Eastland (cra). iStockphoto.com:
FilmColoratStudio (t). 463 AWL Images: Neil
Farrin (tr). 464 4Corners: Johanna Huber (tl).
464-5 Alamy Stock Photo: Jan Wlodarczyk (b).
466 Dreamstime.com: Milan Gonda (t). 467
Alamy Stock Photo: Violeta Meletis (br). 468
iStockphoto.com: majaiva (t). 470 Dreamstime.
com: Ionut David (t). 473 Alamy Stock Photo:
Roy Conchie (t). 474 Alamy Stock Photo: Jan
Wlodarczyk (t). 478-9 iStockphoto.com: Nikada.
482 Dreamstime.com: Ixuskmitl (t). 483 Alamy
Stock Photo: Eddy Galeotti (tr). 484 Alamy
Stock Photo: Iain Masterton (b). 485 123RF.com:
iloveotto (br). Alamy Stock Photo: John
Kellerman (tl). 486-7 Dreamstime.com:
Minnystock (b). 487 Getty Images: Corbis
Documentary / Ron Watts (tl). 489 Dreamstime.
com: Alessandro Flore (br); Jaroslav Moravcik (cr).
Festival of Lights: Frank Hermann (tr). 490
Alamy Stock Photo: Eden Breitz (b). 490-1
Alamy Stock Photo: Stephen Spraggon (t).
491 Dreamstime.com: Bumbleedee (cra).
492 Depositphotos Inc: konrad.kerker (b).
493 Alamy Stock Photo: Iain Masterton / Karl
Schmidt-Rottluff © DACS 2020 (tl). 494 4Corners:
Reinhard Schmid (t). 495 Alamy Stock Photo:
Pictorial Press Ltd (tr). 496-7 Alamy Stock Photo:
Kenneth Hunter (t). 497 Alamy Stock Photo:
dpa picture alliance (ca); Philip Game (crb).
Dreamstime.com: Mistervlad (tr). 498
iStockphoto.com: Nikada (b). 499 4Corners:
Reinhard Schmid (t). 500 Dreamstime.com: Dirk
E Ellmer (tc). 500-1 Alamy Stock Photo: Novarc
Images / Hans P. Szyszka (b). 501 iStockphoto.
com: bluejayphoto (t). 502-3 iStockphoto.com:
MissPassionPhotography (b). 503 Alamy Stock
Photo: travelstock44.de / Juergen Held (t). 504-5
Alamy Stock Photo: Michael Abid (t). 507 Alamy
Stock Photo: Peter Schickert (cra). iStockphoto.
com: gregobagel (t). 508 Alamy Stock Photo: Ian

G Dagnall (b). 509 Alamy Stock Photo:
mauritius images GmbH / Steve Vidler (tr);
Zoonar GmbH / Wolfilser (bl). 510 Alamy Stock
Photo: Steve Vidler (tl). 510-1 123RF.com: preve
beatrice (b). 512 Getty Images: Joerg Koch (b).
513 iStockphoto.com: bluejayphoto. 514
iStockphoto.com: JWackenhut (cla); marima-
design (t). 515 Alamy Stock Photo: Westend61
GmbH / Werner Dieterich (b). 516-7 Alamy Stock
Photo: Ian Dagnall (b). 517 iStockphoto.com:
SerrNovik (tr). 518 AWL Images: Matteo Colombo
(t). 518-9 4Corners: Christian Bäck (b). 520
Dreamstime.com: Noppasin Wongchum (t).
522-3 4Corners: Francesco Carovillano (t). 524
Alamy Stock Photo: Victor Lacken (tl). 525
iStockphoto.com: jotily (b). 528-9 Dreamstime.
com: Rudi1976. 532 Dreamstime.com: Yup265
(t). 534-5 Alamy Stock Photo: John Kellerman (t).
535 Alamy Stock Photo: Boelter (clb); Tasfoto
(crb); Hercules Milas / © Successió Miró / ADAGP,
Paris and DACS London, 2020 (br). 537 123RF.
com: tupungato (t). Hofburg & Schönbrunn
Palace: Schloss Schönbrunn Kultur- und
Betriebsges.m.b.H. / Lois Lammerhuber (ca).
Reuters: Dominic Ebenbichler (crb). 538 Alamy
Stock Photo: Hercules Milas (t). 539 Alamy
Stock Photo: John Kellerman (b). KHM-
Museumsverband: (cr). 540 Alamy Stock Photo:
MARKA / maurizio grimaldi (t). 541 Alamy Stock
Photo: Karl Jena (b). Dreamstime.com:
Ginasanders (tr). 542-3 Dreamstime.com:
Vichaya Kiatyingangsulee (t). 543 Getty Images:
ASAblanca / Josef Polleross (br). 544 iStockphoto.
com: bluejayphoto (b). 545 Dreamstime.com:
Saiko3p (tr); TasFoto (tl). 546 Dreamstime.com:
Joaquin Ossorio Castillo (tl). 546-7 Dreamstime.
com: Minnystock (b). 550-1 iStockphoto.com: E+
/ wilpunt. 554 Dreamstime.com: Elena Duvernay
(tl). 554-5 Dreamstime.com: Prasit Rodphan (b).
556 Dreamstime.com: Xantana (t). 557
4Corners: Luca Da Ros (b). 558-9 Alamy Stock
Photo: Ian Dagnall (b). 559 Getty Images:
Westend61 (tr). 560-1 Dreamstime.com: Sorin
Colac (t). 560 Swiss National Museum, Zurich /
Schweizerisches Nationalmuseum: (bl). 561
Alamy Stock Photo: Glyn Thomas (tr). 562 Alamy
Stock Photo: Eva Bocek (b). Dreamstime.com:
Victorflowerfly (cl). 563 123RF.com: rudi1976 (tl).
564 Dreamstime.com: Lianem (tr). 564-5 Alamy
Stock Photo: imageBROKER / Iris Kürschner (b).
568-9 iStockphoto.com: bluejayphoto.
572-3 Dreamstime.com: Rudi1976 (t). 574
Dreamstime.com: Hans Christiansson (b).
575 Nationalmuseum, Stockholm: Melker
Dahlstrand (tr). 576 Alamy Stock Photo: Majority
World CIC / Suchit Nanda (tl). 577 Alamy Stock
Photo: Kathleen Smith (b). 578 123RF.com:
Stefan Holm (clb). Dreamstime.com: Rolf52 (b).
578-9 Alamy Stock Photo: Folio Images / Werner
Nystrand (t). 580 Dreamstime.com: Olgacov (b).
581 Alamy Stock Photo: Meritzo (tl). 582 Getty
Images: Corbis Documentary / James L. Amos (tl).
582-3 Alamy Stock Photo: Rolf_52 (b). 583
iStockphoto.com: 4FR (tr). 586-7 Getty Images:
Photographer's Choice / Mike Hill. 590-1
Dreamstime.com: Nanisimova (b). 592 Alamy
Stock Photo: Grethe Ulgjell (tc). 592-3 123RF.
com: Andrey Omelyanchuk (t). 594 Alamy Stock
Photo: Hemis.fr / Bertrand Gardel (bl, tr). 595
Alamy Stock Photo: Heritage Image Partnership
Ltd / Werner Forman Archive / Thjodminjasafn,
Reykjavik, Iceland (National Museum) (cra); North
Wind Picture Archives (t). Getty Images: De

Penguin
Random
House

Main Contributors Elspeth Beidas,
Jonathan Bousfield, Teresa Fisher,
Rebecca Hallett, Mike MacEacheran,
Lynnette McCurdy Bastida, Amy Brown,
Nina Hathway, Vivien Stone, Kristina Woolnough,
Edward Aves, Ros Belford, Caroline Bishop,
Ben Ffrancon Davies, Sally Davies, Marc di Duca,
Marc Dubin, Nick Edwards, Mary-Ann Gallagher,
Robin Gauldie, Darragh Geraghty, Mike Gerrard,
Taraneh Ghajar Jerven, Matthew Hancock,
Philip Lee, Darren Longley, Matt Norman,
Doug Sager, Paul Sullivan, Mandy Tomlin,
Craig Turp, Christian Williams

Senior Editor Ankita Awasthi Tröger

Senior Designer Tania Da Silva Gomes

Project Editor Elspeth Beidas

Project Art Editors Dan Bailey,
William Robinson

Designers Jordan Lambley, Stuti Tiwari Bhatia,
Bharti Karakoti, Kanika Kalra, Simran Lakhania,
Ankita Sharma, Chhaya Sajwan,
Bhagyashree Nayak, Hansa Babra,
Priyanka Thakur

Factcheckers Caroline Bishop,
Jonathan Bousfield, Marc Dubin, Teresa Fisher,
Rebecca Hallett, Krisztian Hildebrand, Carol King,
Mike MacEacharan, Lynnette McCurdy Bastida,
Sean Sheehan, Joana Taborda,
Gerard van Vunren, Lisa Voormeij

Managing Editor Hollie Teague

Art Director Maxine Pedliham

Publishing Director Georgina Dee

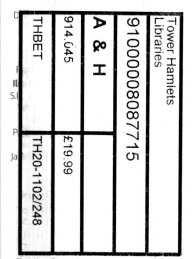

**The information in this
DK Eyewitness Travel Guide is checked regularly.**
Every effort has been made to ensure that this book
is as up-to-date as possible at the time of going to
press. Some details, however, such as telephone
numbers, opening hours, prices, gallery hanging
arrangements and travel information, are liable to
change. The publishers cannot accept responsibility
for any consequences arising from the use of this
book, nor for any material on third party websites,
and cannot guarantee that any website address
in this book will be a suitable source of travel
information. We value the views and suggestions
of our readers very highly. Please write to: Publisher,
DK Eyewitness Travel Guides, Dorling Kindersley,
80 Strand, London, WC2R 0RL, UK, or email:
travelguides@dk.com

First edition 2001

Published in Great Britain by Dorling Kindersley Limited,
80 Strand, London, WC2R 0RL

Published in the United States by DK Publishing,
1450 Broadway, Suite 801, New York, NY 10018

Copyright © 2001, 2020 Dorling Kindersley Limited
A Penguin Random House Company
19 20 21 22 10 9 8 7 6 5 4 3 2 1

All rights reserved.

A CIP catalog record for this book
is available from the British Library.

A catalog record for this book is available
from the Library of Congress.

ISSN: 1542 1554
ISBN: 978 0 2414 0861 2

Printed and bound in China.

www.dk.com